THE PENGUIN Good

HUON HOOKE discovered wine while working as a raw and slightly astringent cadet reporter on *The Murrumbidgee Irrigator* in the New South Wales Riverina. He followed the flow south to Albury where he matured somewhat (with the help of local Rutherglen tokay) and then across to the Barossa where he further ripened, studying wine marketing in the warm climate of Roseworthy College. He spent a while mellowing in the cellars of Best's and Yellowglen where he worked vintage, finally reaching marketability when he arrived in Sydney in 1982 to work in wine retailing. A fiercely independent freelancer, he has supported himself solely from writing, lecturing, judging and educating for fifteen years. Currently, he writes a weekly column in the *Sydney Morning Herald* and *Good Weekend*, and monthly in *Gourmet Traveller*, and contributes to various publications, including *Decanter* and two overseas wine guides apart from this one. He judges in about ten shows a year and runs wine courses in Sydney where he lives. He chairs the judging of Australia's Wine List of the Year Awards (see inside) and occasionally finds time to relax and enjoy a glass of the product while watching the cricket. He published a biography, *Max Schubert Winemaker*, in 1994, *Words on Wine* in 1997, and *The Penguin Wine Cellar Book* in 1999.

RALPH KYTE-POWELL was introduced to wine as a boy by a father who sipped table wines long before such things became fashionable. He joined his dad at wine tastings and on vineyard trips, and cellared his first bottle of wine in his bedroom cupboard as a teenager in the late sixties. On leaving school he studied law at Melbourne University until the first-year exams exposed just how much time he'd spent studying, and how much he'd spent drinking wine. He was tossed out of university, of course, and the world of wine beckoned. Since then he's worked for some of Australia's leading wine merchants at both wholesale and retail level. He's worked in wineries at vintage both in Australia and France, managed a wine store, worked as a sommelier and a restaurant manager, lectured on wine, been part-owner and licensee of a successful small hotel, and judged at regional wine shows. He started writing about wine in 1993 in response to a request from Geoff Slattery, a friend who was starting up the *Melbourne Weekly* magazine. Since then he's written extensively on the subject in various magazines and newspapers, and had a regular radio spot. Currently he writes weekly columns in the *Age* and *Sunday Life!*, contributes to other magazines, and is a judge of Australia's Wine List of the Year Awards. He enjoys cooking too, attempting ridiculously complex dishes with mixed success. And, of course, he still enjoys a good bottle of wine.

1999 | 2000

THE PENGUIN

Good Australian Wine *guide*

10th
ANNIVERSARY
EDITION

HUON HOOKE & RALPH KYTE-POWELL

PENGUIN BOOKS

Penguin Books Australia Ltd
487 Maroondah Highway, PO Box 257
Ringwood, Victoria 3134, Australia
Penguin Books Ltd
Harmondsworth, Middlesex, England
Penguin Putnam Inc.
375 Hudson Street, New York, New York 10014, USA
Penguin Books Canada Limited
10 Alcorn Avenue, Toronto, Ontario, Canada M4V 3B2
Penguin Books (NZ) Ltd
Cnr Rosedale and Airborne Roads, Albany, Auckland, New Zealand
Penguin Books (South Africa) (Pty) Ltd
5 Watkins Street, Denver Ext 4, 2094, South Africa
Penguin Books India (P) Ltd
11, Community Centre, Panchsheel Park, New Delhi 110 017, India

First published by Penguin Books Australia Ltd 1999

10 9 8 7 6 5 4 3 2 1

Front cover photograph by IPL Image Group
Back cover photograph of Huon Hooke (left) and
Ralph Kyte-Powell (right) at Walter's Wine Bar
Southgate, Melbourne, by Rick de Carteret
Cover design by Tony Palmer, Penguin Design Studio
Typeset in Adobe Garamond by Midland Typesetters
Maryborough, Victoria
Printed and bound in Australia by Australian Print Group
Maryborough, Victoria

ISBN 0 14 028773 6
ISSN 1038-6467

www.penguin.com.au

Contents

ACKNOWLEDGEMENTS

The authors wish to thank all those people in the wine industry who helped make this book possible. Instead of listing them and risking omissions, thanks to all – including the dedicated folk at Penguin Books who worked on this book, particularly Helen Pace.

Introduction

The boom in demand for Australian wine continues. In the ten years of *The Penguin Good Australian Wine Guide* we've seen it grow in ways that Mark Shield and Phillip Meyer couldn't have imagined when they put together the first *Guide* in 1989. Back then we produced 485 000 tonnes of wine grapes; this year the figure exceeded 1 000 000 tonnes, a record for the industry, and all forecasts indicate that those figures will continue to rise to fuel an industry that shows no signs of losing its momentum. Export is the key, although domestic consumers do their bit too, god bless 'em.

On the export front the emphasis is still on value-for-money wines, but the Australian industry has skilfully avoided being lumped into the ranks of generic wines, where people buy on price alone and don't give two hoots where the product comes from. Australian wine is being bought because it's Australian. In London restaurants the locals go to the Aussie section just as they would the French or Italian; it means something to them, it has its own unique profile.

That distinctive export profile of Australian wine as big-fruited, friendly and larger-than-life is being reinforced by foreign commentators and wine trade figures. A lot of these opinion-makers are looking more and more for the biggest of wines, a sort of caricature Australian style, as the norm. With red wines they go into amazing raptures about the brawniest, strongest, ripest and oakiest. The subtle, refined, classiest wines are criticised for not being in the Australian style.

This has two outcomes for domestic consumers. First, it pushes up prices across the board, initially at the higher-priced end, as foreign markets clamour for the latest and biggest. Second, it encourages local winemakers to strive to make the ripest, most alcoholic, oakiest reds imaginable. These body-slammers certainly attract attention in a tasting line-up, but can you actually drink a few glasses of them with good food? They have their place, but Australian wine these days should be about regionality and variety, rather than a standardised product. A delicate Tassie pinot is just as valid as a profound meal-in-a-bottle Barossa shiraz.

Speaking of prices for big reds, the collector market for these and some of the latest big-name whites has shown no sign of falling off. Speculators buy wines like Grange and Hill of Grace with nary a thought of ever drinking them. We've seen stacks of Grange warehoused as a sort of liquid superannuation fund, in the hope that future curio collectors will part with big bucks to have them, not to drink, but to show off, caress, and put back in the cupboard.

These big reds are usually strongly oak-influenced and their style begs the question of whether consumers really like all that timber in their wines. Many winemakers obviously think so, and many wine drinkers, perhaps educated to like the taste of oak more than the taste of fruit, would seem to agree. At the same time we've noticed a lessening of overt oak character in a lot of chardonnays in favour of more fruit, often enhanced by more complex barrel-ferment and lees influences. Bravo.

Chardonnay remains a favourite on both export and domestic fronts. Vineyard plantings over recent years to meet anticipated demand have resulted in a record crop this year. Where once there wasn't enough chardonnay to go around, now we're starting to see an oversupply. The result has been chardonnay in wine casks, unthinkable only a few short years ago. Other new products this year included a rash of new brands and concept wines, many in catchy presentations and some in hideously hued bottles designed to capture the attention of Generations X, Y and Z.

All this enthusiasm for Australian wine has led to continued planting of vineyards, and a growth in interest from European wine producers in Australia as a future investment. A handful of producers, most notably the Chapoutiers from the Rhone in France, have already commenced operations, and the last year has seen some surprising visitors sniffing around in our vineyards.

Despite all these healthy signs in the industry generally, some of our boutique producers are working very hard for little return. They compete with hundreds of others for a tiny share of the market. It's probably not too bad if your vineyard is a lifestyle exercise or if it's worked as a cash-crop farm, but not so easy if it's purely a wine business. Speculative get-rich-quick schemes based on vineyard investment are starting to multiply too, and our advice is beware. In the next few years we may well see vineyards being sold off at discounted prices or abandoned, sometimes without even producing a crop.

As wine prices have generally increased in the domestic market, the bigger wine companies have consolidated their position as the safest buys in all price categories. Their real stronghold is in the $8–$15 area, which is the domain of about a dozen companies out of perhaps a thousand wineries in the country. Unable to compete due to economies of scale, the smaller producers have to work hard to get people to spend more for their 'handmade' products. The best of them are superb, lots are very good, but there are many wines of questionable value and some are simply awful. Shop carefully among the plethora of small vineyard labels and you'll be amply rewarded.

The GST is just around the corner and various parts of the, wine industry are lobbying hard to get the best deal. Don't hold your breath for a price drop though. Sales tax on wine is currently at 41 per cent. If you thought this would be replaced by a GST of 10 per cent, think again. The powers that be have thought up the cutely named WET (Wine Equalisation Tax) which will more than make up the difference. There's almost certain to be an increase in the tax take. Watch for further developments.

Wine Australia 1998 in Melbourne came and went. It was a great success, attracting about 28 000 visitors and following the Sydney '96 event in fine style. Consumers relished the opportunity to taste, compare, discuss and learn with some of the country's biggest wine names. As in Sydney it was all done in a well-behaved, good-humoured manner. Melbourne is host again in 2000 and organisers are predicting that everything will be bigger and better.

The past year also saw the usual to-ings and fro-ings of wine industry personnel. Perhaps most notable was the departure to Wirra Wirra in McLaren Vale of Dr Tony Jordan, who took the ground-breaking Domaine Chandon enterprise from its inception to its present eminent position. Another high-profile departure was Dominique Portet from Taltarni, who retired due to health con-siderations. Philip Dowell left Coldstream Hills for the US and is being replaced by Paul Lapsley, late of Houghton's.

Sadly, two industry personnel left us forever during the year, and the world of Australian wine isn't the same without them. Our friend, colleague and co-author of the *Guide* from its beginnings, Mark Shield, died in October 1998. (A tribute to Mark follows.) Also lost to us in January 1999 was Colin Richardson, wine educator, Fine Wine Manager for Remy Australie and well-known wine judge, a fine gentleman and a great and generous friend to all in the wine industry. We miss them both very much.

The general quality of wines in consideration for this year's *Guide* emphasised the high technical standards of Australian wine. It also confirmed just how good our big wine companies are at making excellent wine across a variety of price points. Faulty wines were very rare from the major producers. It's a shame that the same can't be said for many of our small wineries. Although some of Australia's greatest wines come from small wineries, they are also responsible for an inordinate proportion of the very worst. Corked wines were still a nuisance, despite a sustained PR onslaught from some in the Portuguese cork industry to try to convince us that we don't know what we're talking about, there's no such problem – but if there is, it's not their fault.

This year's selection has been the subject of long hours of tasting, discussion and debate between the authors. We think we've come up with a balanced selection of wines, nearly all of which are distributed nationally. Those that aren't available everywhere are usually to be found at cellar door or by mail order with a little bit of sleuthing, and keep in mind that some selections sell out fast. As usual, the prices quoted are calculated on normal retail mark-ups of about 40 per cent on cost. Occasionally prices may go up without warning, but on the other hand very competitive discounting can lead to big savings over quoted prices on some wines. Remember, it pays to shop around for the best price.

Farewell Mark Shield

It is our melancholy duty to record the death of our friend and colleague, Mark Shield, who helped found this book and who was a co-author for its first nine editions. Mark fell ill soon after completing his work on last year's *Guide* and died in Melbourne from the effects of leukaemia and meningitis on 4 October, 1998. He was fifty-one.

The huge crowd that gathered in Melbourne for his funeral was appropriate testimony to the high regard in which he was held by his peers, and to the valuable contribution he made to popularising wine and making it accessible to ordinary people. In an industry that often seems to go out of its way to glamorise wine and make it appear prestigious and elitist, Mark was notable for being down-to-earth and unpretentious.

In his columns for the *Sunday Age*, the *Qantas Club* magazine, the *Australian Wine Industry Journal* and various regional newspapers, including the *Launceston Examiner*, Mark demystified wine and took pleasure in steering people towards good bottles. Instead of being remote and exclusive the way the wine business often is, he invited people in. His style was witty, pithy, clipped and unstarched. He delighted in pricking the pomposity of others, and he was scrupulously honest and non-partisan. Some of the stuffed-shirt types in the wine business took his seemingly casual attitude as a negative, failing to see the real Mark Shield.

Mark was a large, bearded, carrot-haired larrikin, a happy drinker whose ample girth proudly advertised his love of wine and food. He was a one-off, an original character with a unique view of the wine world, and that made him a valuable commentator. He always wrote for the public, never the industry or wine trade, and his talent as a communicator, in both the spoken and written word, enabled him to tap into an entirely new audience. It disgusted him that so much wine writing was, if not exactly sycophantic, then at least too mild and uncritical. While others grovellingly referred to Penfolds Yattarna as the White Grange, Mark called it the White Bin 389. He often lamented that wine journalists lacked 'The Write Stuff' and unlike his hero Chuck Yeager, seldom pushed the boundaries of the envelope.

Over the years, the *Guide* was the vehicle for many memorable Shield quips. He described one chardonnay as 'like an elephant in a tutu'. He said 'Adam Wynn is to chardonnay as Chopin was to the prelude'. A wine that promised more on the nose than it delivered on the palate was always 'like going home and finding your bank manager in bed with your innamorata'. One wine he recommended was 'likely to sell faster than an Exocet missile at a Beirut bazaar'. He claimed to have been the first to use the name Dolly Parton to describe a style of full-bodied, buxom chardonnay popular in the eighties.

He was truly a multimedia wine personality, often appearing on television and radio. Until a short time before his death he did regular wine spots with Angela Catterns on ABC Radio. He was masterful with the quick one-liner, and could deliver it just as easily on-air as off. But he was most at home with his family in the house he dubbed the Richmond Rat Shack or propped up on Mahogany Ridge, his nickname for the front bar at his local watering hole, the All Nations Hotel in Richmond. Mark, who liked to cook (pies – especially game or steak and kidney pies – were his speciality) also did several guest stints in the kitchen there. Indeed, he was a dedicated pub-goer, and being an unreconstructed kind of bloke, he loved unreconstructed pubs such as the All Nations and, before it was renovated, the Spreadeagle. He was always railing against 'born-again pubs' in his columns and pub guide books.

When asked 'What's your favourite wine?' Mark always replied 'The next one'. He never kept a cellar and always said that there was no need to store wine: its value was in the drinking. And anyway, a good wine is like a bus: if you wait, another one will come along in a minute. When wine coolers were briefly fashionable in the late eighties, he wrote 'Lips that touch coolers will never touch mine'. Later, when Chirac started bombing Mururoa and Mark boycotted all things French, he modified this to 'Lips that touch French Champagne will never touch mine'.

ike the proverbial rat with a gold tooth, this humble publi-
has sharpened its image over the years. Each year it contains
duction that covers the main events, trends and changes of
year, plus several brief chapters on wine-related topics. Two
: one of wine terms, the other of tasting terms, appear at
's end, along with a directory of wineries that have been
n the *Guide* over the years. For the fourth time we include
from the annual Australia's Wine List of the Year Awards,
oth Ralph and Huon judge. Finally, most wines include
mmendation linked to which is an index, so you can look
you're planning to eat and seek out an appropriate bottle
ny it.
enguin Good Australian Wine Guide has been on the
s regularly for the last three or four years, and sales con-
with each edition. We hope you – like many others –
style of the book accessible, the opinions fearless, and
olourful, sometimes witty, occasionally irreverent.
the record, here are the ten winners of the Penguin
ear Award:

Mildara Coonawarra Cabernet Sauvignon 1988
Peter Lehmann Clancy's 1988
Wolf Blass Classic Shiraz 1988
Domaine Chandon Brut 1990–91
Chateau Reynella Basket Pressed Cabernet
Merlot 1992
Henschke Abbott's Prayer 1993
McWilliams Barwang Cabernet Sauvignon 1994
Petaluma Chardonnay 1996
Lindemans Bin 65 Chardonnay 1998
Wolf Blass Gold Label Riesling 1999

Mark's nickname was Dry Bucket because he never spat wine
out, even when judging. He had a very good palate and was a regular
at the Barossa Show, but just how he retained his concentration and
judgement was a mystery to his peers. Ironically, it was only
explained in a short article for a retailer's newsletter published after
Mark died. He wrote 'I can't taste properly if I spit: I need the
sensation on the back of my throat to get a handle on the wine'.

Mark's columns were entertaining and often skirted around the
central theme of wine or some other form of alcohol. They often
contained references to jazz music – about which he was passionate
and knowledgeable – his pets, family and other interests, such as
Formula One car-racing, aeroplanes and especially old war birds. His
columns were peopled by mysterious ladies such as The Bantam and
Miss Tishy. The column titles alone tell you a lot about him: there
was 'Noble Rot' in the *Age* 'Epicure' for many years and later 'Barfly's Brief', 'Rough Marc' in *Wine & Spirit* magazine, and 'Miser's
Cellar' in the *Examiner*. Mark delighted in being seen as a renegade,
an iconoclast, even an outsider – the bad boy of wine writing.

Mark was well trained for writing about wine and drink. Before
embarking on his writing career in the early eighties, Mark worked
in bottle shops, in marketing for wine companies (notably Taltarni),
and as a sales rep for wine and spirits firms such as Burns Philp. He
was associated with the wine business for twenty-five years, the last
fifteen of them as a freelance writer. He wrote or co-authored at
least sixteen books and wrote for virtually every wine or liquor publication in this country at some time or other, and many newspapers.

His 'Rough Marc' column in *Wine & Spirit* magazine in the
latter half of the eighties was arguably his finest work, a mixture of
humour, irreverence, stuffed-shirt deflation and criticism that was as
entertaining as it was informative. He occasionally wrote for rival
magazines under the nom de plume Dirk Buckler, 'buckler' being
an alternative word for 'shield'. Mark also made his name writing
for 'Epicure' in the *Age* in the eighties; wine, beer and spirits columns
for *Good Weekend*; the reborn Melbourne *Herald Sun* in the early
nineties; and for the latter part of his career, the *Sunday Age*. His
two-volume video, *Discovering Australian Wine with Mark Shield*, is
the most watchable wine video ever produced in Australia.

Architect and former publican Ted Fraser, one of Mark's best friends, called him 'a complete socialist; he almost used to look for people to help'. This is true: Mark was a very caring person who was always more concerned for other people's welfare than his own, which he neglected. Indeed, says Fraser, his nickname was The Bank of Richmond, because he was always helping his mates out of financial bother. A measure of his generosity was the amount of work he did for charity, including a stint behind the kettles at Carlton & United Breweries, brewing a steam beer that was sold for charity through the *Age*'s columns.

Mark is survived by his wife Alison, teenage sons Alistair and Guy, and a daughter by his first marriage, Kirsten. He also leaves a gaping hole in the fields of wine writing and broadcasting which won't easily be filled.

Ten Years of *The Good Australian Wine Guide*

With this issue we celebrate the tenth *Australian Wine Guide*. And what a tim the millennium, the year of the Sydr It's time to break out the bubbly and

Permit us a little reflection. Th wine guide. Its sales figures, aside fr Penguin happy, indicate the form Mark Shield and the folks at Peng but how and where did it all beg

When the head honchos at wine and drinks writer Mark S said words to this effect: 'We know what's good to drink a

The rest is history. Shi nian Phillip Meyer, a lecture his co-author, and away th 1990 and was an immediat duced a slim companion p *Wine Book*.

By the time of the ways, and Meyer left t Now the *Guide* had a main capital cities, and tragic and untimely bourne scribe Ralpl tasting bench.

cation
an intr
the past
glossaries
the book
featured i
the results
in which
a food rec
up the foo
to accompa

The I
bestseller lis
tinue to rise
will find the
the writing c
Just for
Wine of the `

1990–91
1991–92
1992–93
1993–94
1994–95

1995–96
1996–97
1997–98
1998–99
1999–2000

The Rating System

The rating system used in this guide is designed to give you an immediate assessment of a wine's attributes, as they will affect your purchasing decision. The symbols provide at-a-glance information, and the written descriptions go into greater depth. Other wine guides are full of numbers, but this one places importance on the written word.

The authors assess quality and value; provide an estimate of cellaring potential and optimum drinking age; and give notes on source, grape variety, organic cultivation where applicable, decanting, and alcohol content. We list previous outstanding vintages where we think they're relevant.

We assess quality using a cut-down show-judging system, marking out of a possible 10. Wine show judges score out of 20 points – three for nose, seven for colour, 10 for palate – but any wine scoring less than 10 is obviously faulty, so our five-glass range (with half-glass increments) indicates only the top 10 points. When equated to the show system, three glasses is roughly equivalent to a bronze medal, and five glasses, our highest award, equals a high gold medal or trophy-standard wine.

Value is arrived at primarily by balancing absolute quality against price. But we do take some account of those intangible attributes that make a wine more desirable, such as rarity, great reputation, glamour, outstanding cellarability, and so on. We take such things into account because they are part of the value equation for most consumers.

If a wine scores more for quality than for value, it does not mean the wine is overpriced. As explained below, any wine scoring three stars for value is fairly priced. Hence, a wine scoring five glasses and five stars is extraordinary value for money. Very few wines manage this feat. And, of course, good and bad value for money can be found at $50 just as it can at $5.

If there are more stars than glasses, you are looking at unusually good value. We urge readers not to become star-struck: a three-glass three-star wine is still a good drink.

Where we had any doubt about the soundness of a wine, a second bottle was always sampled.

Quality

ⵣⵣⵣⵣⵣ   The acme of style, a fabulous, faultless wine that Australia should be proud of.

ⵣⵣⵣⵣⵜ   A marvellous wine that is so close to the top it almost doesn't matter.

ⵣⵣⵣⵣ   An exciting wine that has plenty of style and dash. You should be proud to serve this.

ⵣⵣⵣⵜ   Solid quality with a modicum of style; very good drinking.

ⵣⵣⵣ   Decent, drinkable wine that is a cut above everyday quaffing. You can happily serve this to family and friends.

ⵣⵣⵜ   Sound, respectable wines, but the earth won't move.

ⵣⵣ   Just okay, but in quality terms, starting to look a little wobbly.

(Lower scores have not been included.)

Value

★★★★★   You should feel guilty for paying so little: this is great value for money.

★★★★ᵗ   Don't tell too many people because the wine will start selling and the maker will put the price up.

★★★★   If you complain about paying this much for a wine, you've got a death adder in your pocket.

★★★ ɣ   Still excellent value, but the maker is also making money.

★★★   Fair is fair, this is a win–win exchange for buyer and maker.

★★ ɣ   They are starting to see you coming, but it's not a total rip-off.

★★   This wine will appeal to label drinkers and those who want to impress the bank manager.

★ ɣ   You know what they say about fools and their money . . .

★   Makes the used-car industry look saintly.

Grapes

Grape varieties are listed in dominant order; percentages are cited when available.

Region

Where the source of the grapes is known, the region is stated. If there is more than one region, they are listed in dominant order. Many large commercial blends have so many source regions that they are not stated.

Cellar

Any wine can of course be drunk immediately, but for maximum pleasure we recommend an optimum drinking time, assuming correct cellaring conditions. We have been deliberately conservative, believing it's better to drink a wine when it's a little too young than to risk waiting until it's too old.

An upright bottle ▌ indicates that the wine is ready for drinking now. It may also be possible to cellar it for the period shown. Where the bottle is lying on its side ▬ the wine is not ready for drinking now and should be cellared for the period shown.

◖ Drink now: there will be no improvement achieved by cellaring.

◖ 3   Drink now or during the next three years.

●━ 3–7   Cellar for three years at least before drinking; can be cellared for up to seven years.

●━ 10+   Cellar for 10 years or more; it will be at its best in 10 years.

Alcohol by Volume

Australian labelling laws require that alcohol content be shown on all wine labels. It's expressed as a percentage of alcohol by volume, e.g. 12.0% A/V means that 12 per cent of the wine is pure alcohol.

Recommended Retail Price

Prices were arrived at either by calculating from the trade wholesale using a standard full bottle shop mark-up, or by using a maker-nominated recommended retail price. In essence, however, there is no such thing as RRP because retailers use different margins. The prices in this book are indicative of those in Sydney and Melbourne, but they will still vary from shop to shop and city to city. They should only be used as a guide. Cellar-door prices have been quoted when the wines are not available in the retail trade.

♥ Organic

The wine has passed the tests required to label it as 'organically grown and made'.

▌ Decant

The wine will be improved by decanting.

⑤ Special

The wine is likely to be 'on special', so it will be possible to pay less than the recommended retail price. Shop around.

Mark's nickname was Dry Bucket because he never spat wine out, even when judging. He had a very good palate and was a regular at the Barossa Show, but just how he retained his concentration and judgement was a mystery to his peers. Ironically, it was only explained in a short article for a retailer's newsletter published after Mark died. He wrote 'I can't taste properly if I spit: I need the sensation on the back of my throat to get a handle on the wine'.

Mark's columns were entertaining and often skirted around the central theme of wine or some other form of alcohol. They often contained references to jazz music – about which he was passionate and knowledgeable – his pets, family and other interests, such as Formula One car-racing, aeroplanes and especially old war birds. His columns were peopled by mysterious ladies such as The Bantam and Miss Tishy. The column titles alone tell you a lot about him: there was 'Noble Rot' in the *Age* 'Epicure' for many years and later 'Barfly's Brief', 'Rough Marc' in *Wine & Spirit* magazine, and 'Miser's Cellar' in the *Examiner*. Mark delighted in being seen as a renegade, an iconoclast, even an outsider – the bad boy of wine writing.

Mark was well trained for writing about wine and drink. Before embarking on his writing career in the early eighties, Mark worked in bottle shops, in marketing for wine companies (notably Taltarni), and as a sales rep for wine and spirits firms such as Burns Philp. He was associated with the wine business for twenty-five years, the last fifteen of them as a freelance writer. He wrote or co-authored at least sixteen books and wrote for virtually every wine or liquor publication in this country at some time or other, and many newspapers.

His 'Rough Marc' column in *Wine & Spirit* magazine in the latter half of the eighties was arguably his finest work, a mixture of humour, irreverence, stuffed-shirt deflation and criticism that was as entertaining as it was informative. He occasionally wrote for rival magazines under the nom de plume Dirk Buckler, 'buckler' being an alternative word for 'shield'. Mark also made his name writing for 'Epicure' in the *Age* in the eighties; wine, beer and spirits columns for *Good Weekend*; the reborn Melbourne *Herald Sun* in the early nineties; and for the latter part of his career, the *Sunday Age*. His two-volume video, *Discovering Australian Wine with Mark Shield*, is the most watchable wine video ever produced in Australia.

Architect and former publican Ted Fraser, one of Mark's best friends, called him 'a complete socialist; he almost used to look for people to help'. This is true: Mark was a very caring person who was always more concerned for other people's welfare than his own, which he neglected. Indeed, says Fraser, his nickname was The Bank of Richmond, because he was always helping his mates out of financial bother. A measure of his generosity was the amount of work he did for charity, including a stint behind the kettles at Carlton & United Breweries, brewing a steam beer that was sold for charity through the *Age*'s columns.

Mark is survived by his wife Alison, teenage sons Alistair and Guy, and a daughter by his first marriage, Kirsten. He also leaves a gaping hole in the fields of wine writing and broadcasting which won't easily be filled.

Ten Years of *The Penguin Good Australian Wine Guide*

With this issue we celebrate the tenth edition of *The Penguin Good Australian Wine Guide*. And what a time to be doing it: the end of the millennium, the year of the Sydney Olympic Games, ra ra ra. It's time to break out the bubbly and shake it all about.

Permit us a little reflection. This is Australia's most successful wine guide. Its sales figures, aside from keeping the bean counters at Penguin happy, indicate the formula is a winner. It's a tribute to Mark Shield and the folks at Penguin that the format works so well, but how and where did it all begin?

When the head honchos at Penguin Australia called Melbourne wine and drinks writer Mark Shield into their offices in 1989, they said words to this effect: 'We want a book on wine. We want to know what's good to drink and what's good value'. End of brief.

The rest is history. Shield enlisted the help of fellow Melburnian Phillip Meyer, a lecturer in wine at William Angliss College, as his co-author, and away they went. The first edition appeared in 1990 and was an immediate success. In 1992 Shield and Meyer produced a slim companion paperback called *The No Nonsense Australian Wine Book*.

By the time of the fifth edition in 1994, there was a parting of ways, and Meyer left to be replaced by Sydneysider Huon Hooke. Now the *Guide* had a well-known author in each of Australia's two main capital cities, and its sales received a shot in the arm. With the tragic and untimely passing of Mark Shield in 1998, fellow Melbourne scribe Ralph Kyte-Powell was hired to take his place at the tasting bench.

Like the proverbial rat with a gold tooth, this humble publication has sharpened its image over the years. Each year it contains an introduction that covers the main events, trends and changes of the past year, plus several brief chapters on wine-related topics. Two glossaries: one of wine terms, the other of tasting terms, appear at the book's end, along with a directory of wineries that have been featured in the *Guide* over the years. For the fourth time we include the results from the annual Australia's Wine List of the Year Awards, in which both Ralph and Huon judge. Finally, most wines include a food recommendation linked to which is an index, so you can look up the food you're planning to eat and seek out an appropriate bottle to accompany it.

The Penguin Good Australian Wine Guide has been on the bestseller lists regularly for the last three or four years, and sales continue to rise with each edition. We hope you – like many others – will find the style of the book accessible, the opinions fearless, and the writing colourful, sometimes witty, occasionally irreverent.

Just for the record, here are the ten winners of the Penguin Wine of the Year Award:

1990–91	Mildara Coonawarra Cabernet Sauvignon 1988
1991–92	Peter Lehmann Clancy's 1988
1992–93	Wolf Blass Classic Shiraz 1988
1993–94	Domaine Chandon Brut 1990–91
1994–95	Chateau Reynella Basket Pressed Cabernet Merlot 1992
1995–96	Henschke Abbott's Prayer 1993
1996–97	McWilliams Barwang Cabernet Sauvignon 1994
1997–98	Petaluma Chardonnay 1996
1998–99	Lindemans Bin 65 Chardonnay 1998
1999–2000	Wolf Blass Gold Label Riesling 1999

The Rating System

The rating system used in this guide is designed to give you an immediate assessment of a wine's attributes, as they will affect your purchasing decision. The symbols provide at-a-glance information, and the written descriptions go into greater depth. Other wine guides are full of numbers, but this one places importance on the written word.

The authors assess quality and value; provide an estimate of cellaring potential and optimum drinking age; and give notes on source, grape variety, organic cultivation where applicable, decanting, and alcohol content. We list previous outstanding vintages where we think they're relevant.

We assess quality using a cut-down show-judging system, marking out of a possible 10. Wine show judges score out of 20 points – three for nose, seven for colour, 10 for palate – but any wine scoring less than 10 is obviously faulty, so our five-glass range (with half-glass increments) indicates only the top 10 points. When equated to the show system, three glasses is roughly equivalent to a bronze medal, and five glasses, our highest award, equals a high gold medal or trophy-standard wine.

Value is arrived at primarily by balancing absolute quality against price. But we do take some account of those intangible attributes that make a wine more desirable, such as rarity, great reputation, glamour, outstanding cellarability, and so on. We take such things into account because they are part of the value equation for most consumers.

If a wine scores more for quality than for value, it does not mean the wine is overpriced. As explained below, any wine scoring three stars for value is fairly priced. Hence, a wine scoring five glasses and five stars is extraordinary value for money. Very few wines manage this feat. And, of course, good and bad value for money can be found at $50 just as it can at $5.

If there are more stars than glasses, you are looking at unusually good value. We urge readers not to become star-struck: a three-glass three-star wine is still a good drink.

Where we had any doubt about the soundness of a wine, a second bottle was always sampled.

Quality

♟♟♟♟♟	The acme of style, a fabulous, faultless wine that Australia should be proud of.
♟♟♟♟?	A marvellous wine that is so close to the top it almost doesn't matter.
♟♟♟♟	An exciting wine that has plenty of style and dash. You should be proud to serve this.
♟♟♟?	Solid quality with a modicum of style; very good drinking.
♟♟♟	Decent, drinkable wine that is a cut above everyday quaffing. You can happily serve this to family and friends.
♟♟?	Sound, respectable wines, but the earth won't move.
♟♟	Just okay, but in quality terms, starting to look a little wobbly.

(Lower scores have not been included.)

Value

★★★★★	You should feel guilty for paying so little: this is great value for money.
★★★★╞	Don't tell too many people because the wine will start selling and the maker will put the price up.
★★★★	If you complain about paying this much for a wine, you've got a death adder in your pocket.

★★★ʳ   Still excellent value, but the maker is also making money.

★★★   Fair is fair, this is a win–win exchange for buyer and maker.

★★ʳ   They are starting to see you coming, but it's not a total rip-off.

★★   This wine will appeal to label drinkers and those who want to impress the bank manager.

★ʳ   You know what they say about fools and their money . . .

★   Makes the used-car industry look saintly.

Grapes

Grape varieties are listed in dominant order; percentages are cited when available.

Region

Where the source of the grapes is known, the region is stated. If there is more than one region, they are listed in dominant order. Many large commercial blends have so many source regions that they are not stated.

Cellar

Any wine can of course be drunk immediately, but for maximum pleasure we recommend an optimum drinking time, assuming correct cellaring conditions. We have been deliberately conservative, believing it's better to drink a wine when it's a little too young than to risk waiting until it's too old.

An upright bottle ▮ indicates that the wine is ready for drinking now. It may also be possible to cellar it for the period shown. Where the bottle is lying on its side ▬ the wine is not ready for drinking now and should be cellared for the period shown.

◊ Drink now: there will be no improvement achieved by cellaring.

◊ 3 Drink now or during the next three years.

▬ 3–7 Cellar for three years at least before drinking; can be cellared for up to seven years.

▬ 10+ Cellar for 10 years or more; it will be at its best in 10 years.

Alcohol by Volume

Australian labelling laws require that alcohol content be shown on all wine labels. It's expressed as a percentage of alcohol by volume, e.g. 12.0% A/V means that 12 per cent of the wine is pure alcohol.

Recommended Retail Price

Prices were arrived at either by calculating from the trade wholesale using a standard full bottle shop mark-up, or by using a maker-nominated recommended retail price. In essence, however, there is no such thing as RRP because retailers use different margins. The prices in this book are indicative of those in Sydney and Melbourne, but they will still vary from shop to shop and city to city. They should only be used as a guide. Cellar-door prices have been quoted when the wines are not available in the retail trade.

⊕ Organic

The wine has passed the tests required to label it as 'organically grown and made'.

⌁ Decant

The wine will be improved by decanting.

⑤ Special

The wine is likely to be 'on special', so it will be possible to pay less than the recommended retail price. Shop around.

Best Wines

One of the hardest tasks allotted us in preparing this guide is that of choosing the winners. There are so many worthy wines in contention that the 'short list' in all categories is far from short. Add to this the fact that so many excellent wines have very limited availability, and the difficulties are compounded. It seems that despite an ever-increasing level of production, demand for the best wines often exceeds supply. So we're glad to report that this year's Penguin Wine of the Year Award goes to a wine that's widely available, and at a price that shouldn't break the bank. It's also gratifying to be able to select a riesling, a variety that's starting to regain some of the recognition it had before the chardonnay revolution.

Riesling also popped up as our Best White Wine with a classic from a maker with riesling credentials second to none. Great Antipodean chardonnay wasn't forgotten, but it wasn't the Australians who made off with our Best Chardonnay Award. Instead the Kiwis, with a super-fine entrant, won the award ahead of an all-star line-up of the best from Oz.

The red selection was exciting, due in no small part to some very good 1997 vintage wines that have appeared over the last year. This is particularly true of the cooler regions with the result that there are more good pinot noirs available now than ever before. Excellent shiraz and cabernet also abound from vineyards everywhere. In fact the Best Red Wine Award went to a blend of the two varieties, a modern translation of a time-honored Australian combination.

Enough preamble, on to the Awards. And the winners are . . .

Penguin Wine of the Year

Wolf Blass Gold Label Riesling 1999

Every way you look at it, a blinder of a wine. An outstanding quality riesling, made in reasonably large quantity and widely distributed. It's a blend of the two best riesling regions – Clare Valley and Eden Valley – and it sells for a song: as low as $12.99 on discount. From all angles this had to be the wine of the year, and what a boost for the Riesling Revival! (See page 340.)

Best Red Wine & Best Red Blend/Other Variety

Majella The Malleea 1997

Brian Lynn's Majella brand showcases the cream of the grapes from his model Coonawarra vineyard. The Malleea, a cabernet shiraz, is his flagship, a thoroughly delectable drop of red. (See page 116.)

Best White Wine & Best Riesling

Henschke Julius Eden Valley 1998

The purity of Eden Valley riesling meets two of the finest craftsmen and women of wine in Australia today: Stephen and Prue Henschke, who are famous for their reds. But hey – what about their whites! (See page 254.)

Best Sparkling Wine

Pirie 1995

We approached this debut sparkling from Andrew Pirie's Pipers Brook with some scepticism, but it definitely doesn't suffer from debutante blues. It's a stunner! Tremendous depth and complexity, with the tightness and finesse only Tassie can give. (See page 366.)

Best Fortified Wine

Stanton and Killeen Vintage Port 1993
Chris Killeen is a VP enthusiast – well, somebody has to be! He carries the flame for this dinosaur style in Rutherglen, making a true traditional style with no corner-cutting or kowtowing to drink-now trends. (See page 388.)

Picks of the Bunch

BEST CABERNET SAUVIGNON
Rymill 1996
This lovely drop of authentic Coonawarra cab epitomises the philosophy of Rymill winemaker John Innes: red wine shouldn't be over-oaked or otherwise contrived in deference to the show system. (See page 154.)

BEST PINOT NOIR
Bannockburn 1997
Gary Farr is one of the leaders of the pinot revolution, and his style is as idiosyncratic as his wines. A more fastidious, handmade approach would be hard to find. His '97 is an outstanding vintage. (See page 36.)

BEST SHIRAZ
Craiglee 1997
Pat Carmody is an understated gent who avoids razzamatazz and just concentrates on making good wine. The '97 is a fabulous shiraz – one of his very best – and a refreshing alternative to the more commonplace blockbusters. (See page 62.)

BEST CHARDONNAY
Te Mata Estate Elston 1998
Intensity with subtlety and finesse – that's what Elston is all about. Considering it's a benchmark New World chardonnay, has a track record and ages beautifully, the price is more than reasonable. (See page 327.)

BEST SAUVIGNON BLANC
Riddoch 1998
This is Katnook's second-string sauvignon, significantly cheaper than the Katnook Estate model, which is truly amazing considering its superb quality. (See page 310.)

BEST SEMILLON
Nepenthe Lenswood 1998
This Adelaide Hills winery is one of the sensational new entries in the wine market in the last two years. Everything they've done is show-stopping. This is about as perfect an each-way style as we've seen. Drink now or cellar for a few years. (See page 290.)

BEST SWEET WINE
Brown Brothers Noble Riesling 1996
Browns were the first in this country to (intentionally) make a botrytis wine, back in 1962 – the first Noble Riesling. It's richer and lusher than ever these days, and fresher too, since they're releasing it younger. Bravo! (See page 214.)

BEST WHITE BLEND/OTHER VARIETY
Heggies Viognier 1998
No company has worked harder to perfect the viognier grape in Australia than Yalumba, home of Heggies, and the '98 is their best yet. Truly a hedonistic drop. (See page 253.)

Bargains

BEST BARGAIN RED
Ryecroft Cabernet Shiraz 1998
Good-value cheaper reds are very thin on the ground. There's some real rubbish in cheaper bottled reds now, reflecting the shortage of red grapes in recent vintages. This is a beauty. At $11–$13 you simply won't find better value. (See page 154.)

BEST BARGAIN WHITE
Peter Lehmann Eden Valley Riesling 1998
Riesling is generally under-priced, none more so than Lehmann's.
Think of what wines are food-friendly, ageworthy, delicious whether
young, old or middling, and then look at the price of this! (See
page 301.)

BEST BARGAIN BUBBLY
Brown Brothers Moscato 1998
Trust Browns to pioneer this erstwhile Piedmontese style: they've
been first with so many grapes and styles. It's a great summer drink
and deserves to be in everyone's fridge. (See page 349.)

BEST BARGAIN FORTIFIED
Lindemans Macquarie Tawny Port
There are some real bargains in port, which only goes to prove what
we've always said: the least fashionable wines are the best value. This
is one of the great buys. It beats plenty of much dearer ports for
flavour. (See page 380.)

Best New Producer

Turramurra Estate, of the Mornington Peninsula, Victoria
David and Paula Leslie are very serious about quality; they've done
their homework and have produced head-turning wines from the
word go. David quit his career as a pathologist to study wine science
full time at Wagga, giving him a solid technical background to go
with his boundless passion. With just three vintages released so far,
they have fielded a bevy of stunning chardonnays; the pinot noirs
and sauvignon blancs only marginally less impressive, and the cabernet and shiraz are already making bids for the honour of the best
of these marginal varieties on the peninsula.

Australia's Wine List of the Year Awards, 1999

Looking for somewhere to dine out that has a good wine list and won't break the bank? Then check the following list. Here are about 200 dining establishments of various sizes, styles and cuisines all over Australia whose wine list has reached a level of quality the judges deem worthy of recommending. A panel of twelve first-phase judges, headed by Huon Hooke, assesses nearly 400 wine lists every year on several criteria.

Of most importance is the *quality* of the wines. *Price* and *value for money* are also fundamental. (Establishments with higher overheads, due to high-rent location, quality of glassware, napery, and so on, are expected to have higher mark-ups.) So is *balance*. By balance we mean there should be a good choice of wines from a variety of regions, grape varieties, makers and styles, with older vintages worth extra points. (To be recommended, a wine list must give vintage dates, which we regard as a vital part of a wine's identity.) The wine selection should *suit the food* on offer (fish restaurants should have appropriate wines; not too many heavy reds), and the choice and value of *wines offered by the glass* should be given more than scant attention. Another consideration is the *design and layout* of the list. This is especially vital for large lists, but any wine list will be easier to navigate and less threatening for the diner if it's laid out in a logical, sensible and attractive way.

So what are the changes in the wine lists this year? First, the good news. Changes, of course, don't happen quickly or dramatically in the wine lists of a nation's restaurants. In the six years in which the awards have been running, we can say that prices have become more reasonable, and that there are fewer establishments charging the outrageous mark-ups we saw in 1994, a legacy of the profligate eighties. There are more really outstanding wine lists, because more restaurateurs have got serious about raising standards. It gets harder every year to pick a national winner. The lift in wine-list quality is only to be expected, and mirrors the improvement in every aspect of the wine, food and hospitality industries.

The rise of by-the-glass wine has meant it's now the norm rather than the exception. Again, it parallels wider developments, such as the desire to drink less but drink better, random driver breath-testing, and so on. Also, it reflects the booming interest in wine: diners are more interested in tasting a selection of wines with a meal instead of just one or two, and in suiting the wine to the food. They want variety, and they're hungry for new tastes. By-the-glass wine allows them to mix and match, to 'graze' on wine.

Riesling is making a re-entry in wine lists, especially – and appropriately – in seafood restaurants. Riesling is a great food wine and deserves a better reception at the dining table than it's had for the past decade or so. Likewise pinot noir and rosé: Australians, who until the nineties seemed to believe every red wine should be dark and hairy-chested, have discovered the glories of subtler, lighter reds. For instance, we now acknowledge that pinot is better with duck, quail, pigeon and many other middleweight meat dishes than, say, a gutsy shiraz or cabernet.

Another change is being seen in remote country restaurants. They seldom have great lists because of two main factors: the difficulty of wine supply, and the lack of a strong flow of free-spending, hard-core wine enthusiasts. But this year there are several impressive country wine lists from such places as Portland, Echuca and Mildura. This is an encouraging sign that the fine wining and dining experience we take for granted in the major cities is spreading into the bush.

And now the bad news. Unforgivable spelling and factual mistakes still occur with irritating frequency on all but the best wine lists. There are still some enormous, cumbersome lists, as well as those with an impressively large selection which – when you look closely – are cluttered with tired old wines that have been kept far too long and are probably well over the hill. There are many instances of enormous young reds being offered to diners immediately on release, before they're even semi-mature. As well, there are many wine lists dominated by the currently fashionable overripe, over-oaked, over-alcoholic, tannic, immature young reds. As with all fashions, this one will pass. And finally, there's a disturbing trend to offer wines from fashionable makers, voguish grape varieties or chic regions that don't justify their premium prices. Fashion is not sufficient reason to stock a poor-value or inferior wine.

Happily, the quibbles are minor compared with the pleasure we have in bringing you this list of eateries with fine wine lists. You can be sure of a decent bottle at a fair price at any of these establishments.

National Winner

Syracuse Restaurant & Wine Bar, Vic. ♥♥♥

Hall of Fame National Winners
(previous national winners maintaining three-glass ratings)

Forty One, NSW (1998) ♥♥♥

France-Soir, Vic. (1997) ♥♥♥

Walter's Wine Bar, Vic. (1996) ♥♥♥

Dear Friends Garden Restaurant, WA (1995) ♥♥♥

Cicada, NSW (1994) ♥♥♥

Hall of Fame Category & State Winners
(three-time winners of their state or category)

The Grape Food & Wine Bar (Qld) ♥♥♥

Universal Wine Bar (SA) ♥♥♥

State & Territory Winners

ACT	Juniperberry Restaurant ♥♥♥
NSW	Ampersand Restaurant & Bar ♥♥♥
NT	Hanuman Thai & Nonya Restaurant ♥
Qld	Walter's Wine Bar & Restaurant ♥♥♥

SA	Chloe's Restaurant ♟♟♟
Tas.	Franklin Manor ♟♟
Vic.	Syracuse Restaurant & Wine Bar ♟♟♟
WA	Friends Restaurant ♟♟♟

Category Winners

| BEST RESTAURANT | Syracuse Restaurant & Wine Bar, Vic. ♟♟♟ |

| BEST SMALL WINE LIST | la mensa, NSW ♟♟ |

| BEST CLUB RESTAURANT | Avondale Golf Club, NSW ♟♟ |

| BEST PUB RESTAURANT | Ozone Hotel, Vic. ♟♟♟ |

| BEST CAFÉ/ BRASSERIE/ TRATTORIA | Universal Wine Bar, SA ♟♟♟ |

| BEST COUNTRY/ REGIONAL RESTAURANT | Stefano's Restaurant, Mildura Grand Hotel, Vic. ♟♟♟ |

VERY HIGHLY RECOMMENDED ♟♟♟
Adams of North Riding Restaurant, Vic.; Ampersand Restaurant & Bar, NSW; Banc, NSW; B-Coz Restaurant, Vic.; Belmondo, NSW; Blake's Restaurant, SA; Buon Ricordo, NSW; Caffe Della Piazza, ACT; Charcoal Grill on the Hill, Vic.; Chloe's Restaurant, SA; Cicada, NSW; Circa, The Prince, Vic.; Claudine's Restaurant, NSW; Darling Mills, NSW; Dear Friends Garden Restaurant, WA; Dogs Bar, Vic.; Donovans, Vic.; Downs Club, Qld; Duck Restaurant & Wine Bar, Vic.; Est Est Est, Vic.; Forty One Restaurant, NSW; France-Soir Restaurant, Vic.; Friends Restaurant, WA; Grape Food & Wine Bar, The, Qld; Jacques Reymond Restaurant, Vic.;

Jardines Restaurant, NSW; Juniperberry Restaurant, ACT; La Grillade Restaurant, NSW; Langton's Restaurant & Wine Bar, Vic.; Le Restaurant, Vic.; Luxe, Vic.; Marchetti's Latin Restaurant, Vic.; Mask of China, Vic.; Melbourne Wine Room, The, Vic.; Merrony's, NSW; Morans Restaurant, NSW; One Fitzroy Street, Vic.; Ozone Hotel, Vic.; Pier Restaurant, NSW; Stefano's Restaurant, Mildura Grand Hotel, Vic.; Stephenies, WA; Syracuse Restaurant & Wine Bar, Vic.; Universal Wine Bar, SA; Walter's Wine Bar, Vic.; Walter's Wine Bar & Restaurant, Qld; Watermark Restaurant, NSW.

HIGHLY RECOMMENDED ♟♟

44 King Street, WA; Alexanders Restaurant, Tas.; Altos, WA; Arun Thai Restaurant, NSW; Atlantic Restaurant, ACT; Avondale Golf Club, NSW; Bar Corvina, Vic.; Barry's Restaurant, Guest House & Cottages, NSW; Bayswater Brasserie, NSW; Becco, Vic.; Bella Luna, Vic.; Bistro Deux, NSW; Bistro Moncur, NSW; Blakes Restaurant, Vic.; Blue Elephant, Vic.; Café Latte, Vic.; Caterina's Cucina E Bar, Vic.; Chesser Cellar, The, SA; Chine on Paramount, Vic.; Cibo Ristorante Pasticciera, SA; Cicciolina, Vic.; Court Wine Bar & Cellar Restaurant, WA; Courtney's Brasserie, NSW; Darley's Restaurant, NSW; Dining Room, The, NSW; Durham's Restaurant, SA; Edward's Waterfront, Vic.; Elbow Room Restaurant, Tas.; Eleonores Restaurant, Vic.; Enzo Restaurant, Vic.; European, The, Vic.; Fairmont Restaurant, NSW; Fortuna Village Restaurant, Vic.; Franklin Manor, Tas.; Galileo, NSW; Gekko Restaurant, NSW; George's Restaurant, NSW; Grand Mercure Hotel Bowral Heritage Park, NSW; Grossi Florentino, Vic.; Grossi Florentino 'The Grill', Vic.; Hotel Australia, Vic.; Indiana Teahouse, WA; International, NSW; Isthmus of Kra, Vic.; Jamesons Restaurant, Qld; Jonah's, NSW; Kok (Shirk) Restaurant, NSW; La Fontaine Restaurant, Qld; Lake House, Vic.; La Madrague Restaurant, Vic.; la mensa, NSW; Linden Tree Restaurant, Vic.; Logues Eating House, NSW; Lynch's Wintergarden Restaurant, Vic.; Marchetti's Tuscan Grill, Vic.; Marco Polo East West Cuisine, Qld; Martini Restaurant, NSW; Melbourne Supper Club, Vic.; Mezzalira Restaurant, ACT; Old George & Dragon Restaurant, NSW; One One Seven Restaurant, NSW; Pavilion on the Park, NSW; Point, The, Vic.; Quay Restaurant, NSW; Richmond Hill Café & Larder, Vic.; Salt Restaurant,

NSW; Saucier Restaurant, Vic.; Scusa Mi Ristorante & Bar, Vic.; Stag, The, Vic.; Stokehouse, The (upstairs), Vic.; Tetsuya's Restaurant, NSW; Toofeys, Vic.; Witch's Cauldron Restaurant, WA.

RECOMMENDED 🍷

Adams at La Trobe University Club, Vic.; Aix Bistro Café, Qld; Alex's Ristorante Italiano, NSW; Alley Blue Kitchen & Bar, Vic.; Antibar, NSW; Antics Restaurant, NSW; Arc Bistro, Qld; Archie's on the Park, NSW; Artis Restaurant, Qld; Avenue on Chifley, NSW; Bay View Restaurant, NSW; Beach House, Qld; Berry Café and Wine Centre, Vic.; Bistro Inferno, Vic.; Boardroom Restaurant, NT; Boat House by the Lake, ACT; Boltz Café, SA; Bonne Femme, NSW; Borsato Ristorante Italiano, Vic.; Bravo Wine Bar and Bistro, Qld; Brooklyn Hotel, NSW; Cafe Provincial, Vic.; Caffe Bizzarri, Vic.; Caffe Cento Venti, Vic.; Casino Grill, SA; Catalina Restaurant, Qld; Chad's Indigo Bistro Bar, Qld; Chairman and Yip, ACT; Champagne Brasserie, Qld; Charters Towers, Qld; Churchers Restaurant & Wine Bar, Vic.; Cin Cin, WA; Clancy's, Vic.; Club Grill, NSW; Clubhouse Restaurant, Qld; Continental Hotel Sorrento, Vic.; Corn Exchange Restaurant, NSW; Cosi Bar Ristorante, Vic.; Credo Restaurant, NSW; Criterion Restaurant, NSW; Daniel's Steak & Seafood Restaurant, NSW; East Empress Restaurant, Vic.; Epoca Caffe Bar Restaurant, Vic.; Europa Café, Vic.; Fireplace, Qld; Flinders Licensed Seafood Restaurant, Qld; Gertie's, Qld; Grand National Restaurant, NSW; Grotto, The, WA; Hagger's Restaurant, Vic.; Half Moon, Vic.; Hanuman Thai & Nonya Restaurant, NT; Harbourside Restaurant, NSW; Hardy's Restaurant, SA; Harrys Bistro & Café, Vic.; Harveys Restaurant, Vic.; Heritage Court Restaurant, NSW; Highlander Restaurant, Tas.; Hills Lodge Boutique Hotel, NSW; Isis Brasserie, Qld; Isis Restaurant, Vic.; Jaspers, NSW; Jordon's International Seafood Restaurant, NSW; Kingsleys Steakhouse, NSW; Kingston Hotel, Vic.; L'Incontro Italian Restaurant, NSW; Lygon Street Restaurant, Qld; Lyrebird Restaurant, Qld; Macrossans, Qld; Madison Motor Inn, NSW; Manse Restaurant, SA; Marine Café, Vic.; Marylands Country House, Vic.; Mecca Restaurant, Vic.; Mercer's Restaurant, Vic.; Metropolitan Hotel, Vic.; Mezzaluna Restaurant, NSW; Michael's Riverside Restaurant, Qld; Mietta's Queenscliff Hotel, Vic.; Milsons Restaurant, NSW; Mixing

Pot Restaurant, NSW; Morgans Restaurant, NSW; Nataraj Restaurant, Vic.; National Golf Club, Vic.; Near East Restaurant, Vic.; Neptune Palace, NSW; Niche Dining House, NSW; Orso Bayside Restaurant, NSW; Oscar W's Wharfside Redgum Grill & Deckbar, Vic.; Owensville, Vic.; Peacock Gardens Restaurant, NSW; Peninsula Country Golf Club, Vic.; Peppers Delgany Portsea, Vic.; Portsea Hotel, Vic.; Potters Cottage Restaurant, Vic.; Punch Lane Wine Bar Restaurant, Vic.; RACV Club, Vic.; Ravesi's on Bondi Beach, NSW; Rawsons Restaurant, NSW; Reifs Restaurant & Bar, Vic.; Ricky Ricardos, Qld; Ristorante Fellini, Qld; Sails Beach Café, Qld; Shakahari Vegetarian Restaurant, Vic.; Shark Fin House, Vic.; Siggi's at the Heritage on the Botanic Gardens, Qld; Silo Bakery, ACT; Sorrento Golf Club, Vic.; St Mounts Guesthouse & The Pines Restaurant, NSW; Stella, Vic.; Stokehouse, The (downstairs), Vic.; Sweetwater Café, Vic.; Tory's Seafood Restaurant, NSW; Union Hotel Dining Room, NSW; Villa D'Este Restaurant, WA; Volare Restaurant, Qld; Waterfront Seafood & Grill Sushi & Oyster Bay, Vic.; Wattle Hill Restaurant, NSW; Windows on the Bay, Vic.; Yarra Glen Grand Bistro, Vic.; Yarra Glen Grand Dining Room, Vic.; Zacks on Bent Street, NSW.

Red Wines

Abercorn Mudgee Shiraz

Abercorn is an 8.5-hectare vineyard on Cassilis Road, Mudgee, which is run by ex-journo Tim Stevens. The wines are made under contract elsewhere. The best way to get them is through a mailing list.

CURRENT RELEASE 1997 The use of French oak shows in this wine. It has a dry, savoury, nutty aroma, and there are spice and dried bay-leaf inflexions. There's a lot of oak-matured character in the wine, and it's a serious food style. The palate has gripping tannins, and the finish leaves you wanting food with it. Try it with pork chops and mustard.

Quality	ŶŶŶŶ
Value	★★★ʳ
Grapes	shiraz
Region	Mudgee, NSW
Cellar	▮ 8
Alc./Vol.	13.5%
RRP	$21.50 (cellar door)

Alkoomi Blackbutt

Blackbutts are handsome eucalyptus trees found in the area of the Alkoomi vineyard. The name is reserved for Alkoomi's premier red wine.

CURRENT RELEASE 1996 This is a refined red with an elegant, reserved nose of black plum and cedary oak. The palate is tight and sinewy, not overtly ripe-fruity but with understated dark berry flavour, a good measure of French oak and fine tannins. Definitely needs time to blossom. Serve it with roast leg of lamb.

Quality	ŶŶŶŶʔ
Value	★★★ʳ
Grapes	cabernet sauvignon; malbec; merlot; cabernet franc
Region	Great Southern, WA
Cellar	➡ 2–10
Alc./Vol.	13.5%
RRP	$51.80

All Saints Cabernet Sauvignon

Quality	▼▼▼▼
Value	★★★⸀
Grapes	cabernet sauvignon
Region	Rutherglen, Vic.
Cellar	▮ 4
Alc./Vol.	13.5%
RRP	$18.00

All Saints reds, under the tutelage of Brown Brothers, have improved in recent years. They are now modern wines, yet they retain a bit of Rutherglen generosity.
CURRENT RELEASE 1997 A mark of recent All Saints' reds is notable American oak input. The fruit usually stands up to it though, as in this cabernet. The nose has cassis and blackberry aromas dressed up in charry vanillin oak. In the mouth it has tasty dark fruit character and balanced tannins, once again with a good slug of sweet oak. Good with chipolata sausages.

All Saints Heritage Red

Quality	▼▼▼⸀
Value	★★★⸀
Grapes	cabernet franc;
	cabernet sauvignon;
	malbec
Region	North East Vic.
Cellar	▮ 2
Alc./Vol.	13.5%
RRP	$11.00 (cellar door)

This is All Saints' quaffer, a red for everyday drinking. Despite having a large cabernet franc component (a most un-traditional thing in north-east Victoria), this always has a rather traditional personality.
CURRENT RELEASE 1998 The nose has sweet blackberry fruit aromas with a rustic earthy touch that adds character. The palate is straightforward with ripe fruity flavour, some toasty notes and very dry, grainy tannins at the end. Thankfully it isn't swamped by American oak, like some other reds in the All Saints family. Good with a pizza.

All Saints Shiraz

Quality	▼▼▼⸀
Value	★★★
Grapes	shiraz
Region	North East Vic.
Cellar	▬ 1–5
Alc./Vol.	14.0%
RRP	$18.00

Shiraz has always been significant in Victoria's north-east due to its versatility. It could make good port when the market for table wine dries up.
CURRENT RELEASE 1997 Recent vintages of All Saints Shiraz have flirted with American oak influence; now the '97 vintage has succumbed totally to that flash Yank's obvious charms. The result: a wine that shows pronounced chocolate-sweet vanillin oak on nose and palate, with some sweet fruit hiding in the middle of all the tall timber. Dry oaky tannins mark the finish. Needs time to evolve. Try it with a chargrilled rump steak.

Allandale Mudgee Cabernet Sauvignon

Though based in the Hunter, Allandale's range of wines is broadened by fruit sourced in the cool Hilltops region and the warmer Mudgee vineyards. Maker Bill Sneddon. CURRENT RELEASE 1997   Mudgee makes big characterful red wines and this is one of them. Delicate it ain't, but if you like earthy, blackberry jammy wines of rather rustic personality it may be for you. It has big warm flavour, and dry tannins finish things off well. It should be good with a navarin of lamb.

Quality	♆♆♆♆
Value	★★★
Grapes	cabernet sauvignon
Region	Mudgee, NSW
Cellar	♦ 4
Alc./Vol.	14.5%
RRP	$23.85

Andrew Garrett Cabernet Merlot

The Andrew Garrett name is now a Mildara brand. Andrew Garrett the man is pursuing other wine interests. This label can still be pretty good value. CURRENT RELEASE 1997   Blackcurrant and blackberry with an overlay of earthy interest mark the nose here. The palate is medium-bodied, with smooth berry flavour and a restrained touch of sweet oak. Balanced tannins make a pleasant finale. Try it with a beef casserole.

Quality	♆♆♆♆
Value	★★★★
Grapes	cabernet sauvignon; merlot
Region	McLaren Vale & Padthaway, SA
Cellar	♦ 3
Alc./Vol.	13.0%
RRP	$14.00 Ⓢ

Angove's Classic Reserve Cabernet Sauvignon

Angove's has been run by the same family for four generations. In recent times they've been concentrating a bit more than they used to on wines of table-wine quality. CURRENT RELEASE 1997   Classic Reserve is a very grand name for a very simple wine. The light nose has cassis syrup aromas – pleasant, fruity and clean. The palate is no powerhouse, but the flavour is softly fruity with balanced drying tannins at the end. A happy companion to pasta with bolognese sauce.

Quality	♆♆♆
Value	★★★
Grapes	cabernet sauvignon
Region	Murray Valley, SA
Cellar	♦ 1
Alc./Vol.	13.0%
RRP	$10.00 Ⓢ

Angove's Classic Reserve Shiraz

Quality	♀♀♀
Value	★★★
Grapes	shiraz
Region	Murray Valley, SA
Cellar	🍾 1
Alc./Vol.	12.5%
RRP	$10.00 Ⓢ

To call this Angove's budget label 'Classic Reserve' might be playing loose with the language; they aren't wines for cerebral analysis and discussion. Nevertheless, this is a presentable range of easy-drinkers.

CURRENT RELEASE 1997   An appealing purplish colour makes an attractive introduction to this simple young red. The nose has plummy aromas suggesting some carbonic maceration influence, and a touch of earthiness adds a savoury note. In the mouth it's light and gentle with soft tannins. Undemanding drinking on a budget. Try it with charcuterie.

Annie's Lane Contour Shiraz

Quality	♀♀♀♀♀
Value	★★★★
Grapes	shiraz
Region	Clare Valley, SA
Cellar	🍾 3–8
Alc./Vol.	13.5%
RRP	$34.00

From a 30-year-old contour-planted vineyard in Watervale, this is the shiraz David O'Leary makes when he's really trying. It reflects a trend towards the use of French rather than American oak in Clare shiraz.

CURRENT RELEASE 1996   Outstanding colour and strength of character are Clare-Watervale hallmarks. It has a classically proportioned regional nose of intense reduced blackberryish fruit, sweet oak, minerals and a hint of bitter chocolate. The palate is seamless, with intense black-fruit flavour and long, ripe, pleasantly mouth-puckering tannins. Drink it with chargrilled porterhouse.

Annie's Lane Shiraz

Quality	♀♀♀♀
Value	★★★★
Grapes	shiraz
Region	Clare Valley, SA
Cellar	🍾 5
Alc./Vol.	14.0%
RRP	$16.00

Winemaker David O'Leary has a way with shiraz that saw some fine wines made during his time at BRL Hardy. Recent years have seen him do the same for Mildara Blass's Clare Valley enterprise.

CURRENT RELEASE 1997   Archetypal Clare shiraz here. Purplish crimson colour of good density. The nose has intense blackberry fruit aromas with some minerally interest, and balanced oak. The palate follows suit with penetrating, dry fruit flavour, mocha oak and dry tannins. Good value. Pan-fried calf's liver will accompany it well.

Arlewood Reserve Cabernet

Arlewood's Margaret River cabernet vines are now over ten years old and the wines seem to be improving as the vineyard matures. Winemaking is done at Chateau Xanadu.
CURRENT RELEASE 1997 This looks to be the best Arlewood cabernet so far. The nose has leafy blackcurrant aromas with a fruit-cakey merlot component. High-quality oak makes an impression too. The palate has cassis and oak flavours with great structure and a hefty backbone of very firm tannins. Needs time. Try it with a roast leg of lamb.

Quality	♈♈♈♈
Value	★★★★
Grapes	cabernet sauvignon; merlot; cabernet franc
Region	Margaret River, WA
Cellar	☛ 2–8
Alc./Vol.	13.5%
RRP	$27.50

Arrowfield Show Reserve Cabernet Sauvignon

Arrowfield are Hunter-Valley-based, but that doesn't stop them from sourcing grapes from other regions. Maker Don Buchanan.
CURRENT RELEASE 1997 This is a densely constructed red with slightly jammy plum, earth, mocha and oxidative touches on the nose. In the mouth it's big-flavoured and ripe with dark fruit. Charry barrel-ferment characters add dimension, and the long, ripe tannins are well balanced.

Quality	♈♈♈♈
Value	★★★★
Grapes	cabernet sauvignon
Region	McLaren Vale, SA; King Valley, Vic.
Cellar	▮ 3
Alc./Vol.	13.9%
RRP	$21.00

Arthur's Creek Cabernet Sauvignon

Arthur's Creek has been a twenty-year labour of love for Melbourne QC, S.E.K. Hulme. So much so that he took a long time to actually release any for sale, and then only the best after appropriate bottle-age. Often more than one bottle-aged vintage is available.
CURRENT RELEASE 1994 A densely fruited nose of blackcurrant and blackberry fruit has some leafy and minty touches. The palate has concentrated berry flavour and the texture is dense. Ripe firm tannins finish things off. Still has a way to go.

Quality	♈♈♈♈♈
Value	★★★★
Grapes	cabernet sauvignon
Region	Yarra Valley, Vic.
Cellar	▮ 4
Alc./Vol.	14.0%
RRP	$34.95 ▮

Ashton Hills Reserve Pinot Noir

Quality	ΤΤΤΤ?
Value	★★★
Grapes	pinot noir
Region	Adelaide Hills, SA
Cellar	➥ 1–4
Alc./Vol.	13.7%
RRP	$40.00

Winemakers in other South Australian regions hold pinot noir in low regard, but the boys and girls in the Adelaide Hills love it. Ashton Hills is made by Stephen George, who is also responsible for the formidable Wendouree reds from Clare.

CURRENT RELEASE 1997   Some pinot noirs are exotically rich, and others are delicate. This leans toward the former camp with an intense gamy-sweet nose of sexy liqueur cherry fruit and spicy oak. The palate is rich in ripe fruit, but a rather hard, slightly stemmy, finish detracts a little at the moment. Time in bottle might provide the solution. Try it with braised duck.

Ashwood Grove Cabernet Petit Verdot Malbec

Quality	ΤΤΤΤ
Value	★★★★
Grapes	cabernet sauvignon; petit verdot; malbec
Region	Murray Valley, Vic.
Cellar	❷ 3
Alc./Vol.	13.5%
RRP	$15.80

Most of the big new names along the Murray Valley are progressing from the everyday quaffing market to something more serious. In turn, they're giving these irrigated vineyards a more elevated status in the wine world. The Ashwood Grove black label range is an example.

CURRENT RELEASE 1997   A lot of character here with a deep colour and a warmly inviting nose of ripe blackberry, clean earth and spicy, cedary oak. The palate is generous with more black-fruit flavour, a chunky texture and finely woven dry tannins. PS: Petit verdot is a minor red variety in Bordeaux. Try this wine with raan.

Austins Barrabool Shiraz

Quality	ΤΤΤΤ
Value	★★★
Grapes	shiraz
Region	Geelong, Vic.
Cellar	➥ 1–4
Alc./Vol.	14.0%
RRP	$45.00

The Barrabool Hills, near Geelong, were thick with vineyards last century, but when the destructive vine parasite phylloxera arrived, an industry was ruined. A few small vineyards like Austins have been planted in recent years to resurrect the industry.

CURRENT RELEASE 1997   On the nose, pepper, plum and red-cherry fruit aromas vie for attention with some raw American oak, which dominates at the moment. The tightly constructed palate has similar reduced-fruit and oak flavours. The flavour is long and finishes with grippy, dry tannins.

AusVetia Shiraz

This oddly named wine is a joint venture between Penley Estate's Kym Tolley and a Swiss connection (Helvetia, get it?). The regional and varietal mix, winemaking methods and barrel-ferment in new American oak, all point towards a Grange imitation.

CURRENT RELEASE 1995   Our first bottle was corked, which would have been a drat if you'd paid $65 for it! It's a serious Grange knock-off, and a very suave effort. Toasty oak, barbecued-meat and earthy shiraz aromas come through on the nose, and it's full-bodied without being hefty. The flavours are smooth, mellow, chocolatey and savoury – more than simple fruit – and the structure is elegant and dry with persistent tannins. Serve it with aged Swiss gruyère.

Quality	▼▼▼▼?
Value	★★★⊦
Grapes	shiraz 95%; cabernet sauvignon 5%
Region	Barossa Valley & McLaren Vale, SA 95%; Coonawarra, SA 5%
Cellar	▮ 12+
Alc./Vol.	14.0%
RRP	$65.00 ▮

Badger's Brook Pinot Noir

This is the second label of a new producer in the Yarra Valley called Storm Ridge. Their cellar-door sales outlet is located on the Maroondah Highway, Coldstream, just past Domaine Chandon. Maker Michael Warren.

CURRENT RELEASE 1998   This is a light-bodied pinot of considerable charm and quite good value for money. The colour is a light but vivid purple–red, and the nose has some simple cherry fruit characters and restrained oak. The palate has a sweet Cherry Ripe flavour and it will gain complexity with a year or two in bottle. There's some firmness on the finish with a hint of stalky green-ness, but this is nicely countered by fruit-sweetness. It would go well with tuna.

Quality	▼▼▼▼
Value	★★★★
Grapes	pinot noir
Region	Yarra Valley, Vic.
Cellar	▮ 3
Alc./Vol.	12.8%
RRP	$20.00 (cellar door)

Baileys 1920s Block Shiraz

Quality	♟♟♟♟
Value	★★★⅂
Grapes	shiraz
Region	Glenrowan, Vic.
Cellar	➧ 5–25
Alc./Vol.	14.0%
RRP	$26.00 ▮

The Baileys wines come from Kelly country at Glenrowan, and were once described as red with a touch of Ned. This is joyfully a traditional-style Baileys red, although the winemakers are now Mildara.

CURRENT RELEASE 1997 This is a bawling, stroppy infant. It needs to be put to bed and forgotten about for a while. The colour is deep and dark, and there's a lot of fresh oak on the nose together with concentrated red berry fruits and dry spices. The palate is quite raw and astringent with acid/tannin aggression and gutsy flavour. It could turn out very well, but its future is in the lap of the gods. Cellar, then serve with aged cheddar.

Baileys Shiraz

Quality	♟♟♟
Value	★★★
Grapes	shiraz
Region	Glenrowan, Vic.
Cellar	▮ 10+
Alc./Vol.	13.5%
RRP	$18.00 ⑤

Baileys is a traditional winery renowned for heroic gutsy reds, but you'll need to pay an extra $10 for the 1920s Block Shiraz to get that sort of wine these days. It's part of the Mildara Blass company.

CURRENT RELEASE 1997 This is a rather peculiar style. It has a coconutty oak aroma and some porty overtones, with a suspicion of oxidation. There are cooked fruit and dry spice aromas, with nutmeg predominating. The palate is lean, dry and savoury, and the acid is slightly prominent. It needs more fruit to balance. Serve it with a hearty stew.

Balgownie Cabernet Sauvignon

Quality	♟♟♟♟
Value	★★★★
Grapes	cabernet sauvignon
Region	Bendigo, Vic.
Cellar	➧ 2–10
Alc./Vol.	14.0%
RRP	$22.00

Balgownie was bought by Mildara Blass from original proprietor Stuart Anderson about fifteen years ago. Now they've sold it, although they'll continue to distribute the wine.

CURRENT RELEASE 1997 In warm years the Balgownie reds are big, firm wines worth plenty of time in the bottle. Here the nose has blackberry aromas, olive and earth. In the mouth it has dense flavour of good persistence with a firm, grippy finish. Worth ageing, then serve it with roasted vegetables and baked gnocchi.

Balgownie Shiraz

Despite Balgownie's recent sale, the winemaking team will remain the same. Good news indeed, since recent Balgownie reds have been excellent. Maker Lindsay Ross.

CURRENT RELEASE 1997 This is a big brute of a central Victorian shiraz. It has a powerful chocolatey blackberry nose without regional mintiness. The palate is very full-flavoured and warm with dark berries, richness, good length and firm, grainy tannins. Needs cellar time, then serve it with braised oxtail.

Quality	YYYY
Value	★★★★
Grapes	shiraz
Region	Bendigo, Vic.
Cellar	2–7
Alc./Vol.	13.5%
RRP	$22.00

Balnaves Cabernet Sauvignon

The Balnaves winery and cellar-door sales buildings are highly original edifices built of BHP Colorbond (corrugated iron). Both have won awards. Maker Peter Bissell.

CURRENT RELEASE 1996 A really delicious Coonawarra which drinks nicely already. The nose is slightly minty, with undercurrents of toasty oak and ripe berries. It's smooth and ripe-tasting, with savoury flavours and gentle tannins. What Len Evans used to call an each-way style (drink now or cellar). Goes well with pink lamb chops.

Quality	YYYY½
Value	★★★★
Grapes	cabernet sauvignon
Region	Coonawarra, SA
Cellar	12+
Alc./Vol.	12.5%
RRP	$28.00

Balnaves The Blend

The Balnaves family has been around the district for many years. The Balnaves department store in Penola is run by distant relatives of the owner of the winery, Doug Balnaves. This 'Bordeaux blend' is a new label.

CURRENT RELEASE 1996 Compared to the cabernet, this has less colour and is a tad lighter, with leafy, peppermint characters. There are chocolate and vanilla tastes on the palate, and the oak is lording it over the somewhat herbaceous fruit. It has fine, tight structure. Good to drink with veal scaloppine.

Quality	YYYY
Value	★★★★
Grapes	merlot 45%; cabernet sauvignon 35%; cabernet franc 20%
Region	Coonawarra, SA
Cellar	6
Alc./Vol.	13.5%
RRP	$19.00

Bannockburn Pinot Noir

Quality	♟♟♟♟♟
Value	★★★★
Grapes	pinot noir
Region	Geelong, Vic.
Cellar	�ం 1–6+
Alc./Vol.	13.5%
RRP	$45.00

PENGUIN
BEST
PINOT
NOIR

Bannockburn's vineyard was devastated by a hailstorm in November 1997, which destroyed the 1998 crop. But all was not lost. Industry friends from all over Australia came to winemaker Gary Farr's rescue with parcels of their best chardonnay, shiraz and pinot noir. Farr will make three varietal blends from them to tide him over the lean times.

CURRENT RELEASE 1997   This looks to be one of the best Bannockburns to date – a fascinating wine, lush and complex with a great future ahead of it. The nose and palate are richly endowed with plum and stewed cherry notes, gamy richness, undergrowthy touches, and savoury smoky sweetness. It's silky-smooth in the mouth with a restrained underpinning of fine tannins. The aftertaste is savoury and lingering. One glass of this will never be enough. A great wine for pink-roasted pigeons.

Bannockburn Shiraz

Quality	♟♟♟♟♟
Value	★★★★ʏ
Grapes	shiraz
Region	Geelong, Vic.
Cellar	▮ 5+
Alc./Vol.	13.5%
RRP	$36.00

In the last decade Bannockburn shiraz has veered dramatically away from Australian tradition towards an uncompromisingly French style. Complexity and elegance are the keynotes, and it's won a lot of admirers, including the authors.

CURRENT RELEASE 1997 A seductive wine with almost pinot-like softness and elaborate character. The nose is aromatic with warm spice, cherry, black pepper and gamy scents. The palate is exotically lush and deep, smooth and long. It has good acidity, and fine tannins back things up. Linger over it: more facets open up as you drink it. Serve with roast fillet of beef and a reduction sauce.

Barossa Valley Estate Ebenezer Cabernet Merlot

With a big field of professional grapegrowers as share-holders, this company has access to some excellent fruit. Maker Natasha Mooney.

CURRENT RELEASE 1997 This is a lovely drop of red, although it doesn't have a lot of varietal character. It has a deep colour, and a bouquet of toasty coconut, raspberry, spice, almond and earth aromas. It's deep, dense and chunky in the mouth, and the flavour spectrum owes a lot to oak. It has good weight and length and should take some cellaring well. Try with T-bone steak.

Quality	♟♟♟♟♟
Value	★★★
Grapes	cabernet sauvignon; merlot
Region	Barossa Valley, SA
Cellar	🍶 10
Alc./Vol.	14.0%
RRP	$26.50 Ⓢ 🍶

Barossa Valley Estate Ebenezer Shiraz

The Ebenezer region is in the north of the Barossa Valley, where some of the most powerful concentrated reds of the Barossa originate.

CURRENT RELEASE 1996 This is a powerful wine with plenty of everything. The colour is a youthful purple–red, and the nose is very intense with charred American oak, plum, cherry, herbs and a hint of spice. The flavour is huge: dense, powerful and quite astringent. It needs time. The palate has some mint and massive sweet fruit as well. It should turn into a cracker. Cellar, then serve with chargrilled kangaroo.

Quality	♟♟♟♟♟
Value	★★★★
Grapes	shiraz
Region	Barossa Valley, SA
Cellar	➥ 2–12+
Alc./Vol.	14.0%
RRP	$26.50 Ⓢ 🍶

Barossa Valley Estate 'Spires' Shiraz Cabernet

This winery, a part-share of which has returned to the BRL Hardy fold, is building a flash new winery in the Barossa proper, in Marananga.

CURRENT RELEASE 1998 Youthful colour with a lot of purple. Good blackberry, blackcurrant cabernet aromas, ripe and even a trifle jammy. The palate has a suspicion of sweetness, and there's a trace of bitterness on the finish. Plenty of flavour, and quite good value. Food: beef rissoles.

Quality	♟♟♟
Value	★★★★
Grapes	shiraz; cabernet sauvignon
Region	Barossa Valley, SA
Cellar	🍶 4
Alc./Vol.	13.5%
RRP	$11.20 Ⓢ

Barrington Estate Pencil Pine Red

Quality	♥♥♥♡
Value	★★★
Grapes	shiraz; cabernet sauvignon; pinot noir; merlot
Region	not stated
Cellar	♦ 4
Alc./Vol.	13.0%
RRP	$18.00

This is the second label of the people who produce Yarraman Road in the Upper Hunter Valley. Winemaker is an Englishman, Dan Crane.

CURRENT RELEASE 1998   Although no region is stated on the label, this has some Hunter character. It has full purple–red colour, a shy aroma with some gamy shiraz overtones, and a whiff of lactic character. The palate has pleasantly fresh cherry, berry fruit with a lick of tannin and quite respectable structure. Drink now with san choy bow.

Basedow Shiraz

Quality	♥♥♥♥
Value	★★★★
Grapes	shiraz
Region	Barossa Valley, SA
Cellar	♦ 7
Alc./Vol.	14.0%
RRP	$20.50 ⑤

This winery has been through more marriages than Liz Taylor, but now seems to be happily bedded down with Terry Hill's Hill International.

CURRENT RELEASE 1997   This is a nice little red with lots of exotic nuances. It has a stewy, jammy nose, with sweet berries and crushed leaves vying for attention in the mouth. It's medium-weight, and has some tightness in its structure. Soft tannins are easy on the gums. Serve with aged cheddar.

Bass Phillip Premium Pinot Noir

Quality	♥♥♥♥♥
Value	★★★★
Grapes	pinot noir
Region	South Gippsland, Vic.
Cellar	⬤ 1–6
Alc./Vol.	12.8%
RRP	$75.00 ▮

At Bass Phillip you won't find a flash cellar-door operation, nor will you find a high-tech winery full of whiz-bang gadgetry. Here the basics – the earth, the vine, the place – are allowed to express themselves in the most natural way. The wines that result are often breathtakingly impressive, but unfortunately very hard to find.

CURRENT RELEASE 1998   Tasted as a barrel sample, this encapsulates the Bass Phillip pinot style. The nose has little direct fruitiness; instead it's a super-complex melange of exotic scents. There's spice, earth, undergrowth, chocolate and dark plum. The palate follows in a similar warm, complex vein, with super-rich opulence of flavour, great depth and a long rich aftertaste. Try it with kangaroo pie.

Best's Great Western Cabernet Sauvignon

Buying Best's wines these days is like donating to charity: because of frost, Best's harvested less than half its normal crop at Great Western in each of the last three vintages. CURRENT RELEASE 1996 The colour is deep and blackish; the nose is definitive cabernet with aromas of squashed blackcurrants, rose petals and crushed leaves. It's lean and very cool-climate, with a trace of hollowness in the mid-palate, but it's very elegant with fruit-sweetness and attractive flavour. Drink with rare beef.

Quality	¶¶¶¶
Value	★★★
Grapes	cabernet sauvignon 85%; merlot 15%
Region	Great Western, Vic.
Cellar	∎ 6
Alc./Vol.	14.5%
RRP	$26.25 ∎

Best's Great Western Pinot Noir

The Thomsons of Best's have had pinot noir in their vineyard for over a century, but have only lately started to bottle some as a varietal. Maker Viv Thomson. CURRENT RELEASE 1998 This is a decent red wine but in common with its predecessors, it just lacks the distinctive charm and varietal character of the pinot grape. The colour is good and deep, and it smells of vanillin oak and simple grassy/cherry fruit. There's plenty of body and flavour, with some tannin lending astringency to the finish, and a hint of bitterness that should soften. Try it with lamb chops.

Quality	¶¶¶¶
Value	★★★
Grapes	pinot noir
Region	Great Western, Vic.
Cellar	∎ 5+
Alc./Vol.	13.5%
RRP	$23.00

Best's Victoria Cabernet Sauvignon

This is the junior Best's cabernet. It's cheaper than the Great Western because the grapes come from the Murray River area to the north, where production costs are lower. CURRENT RELEASE 1997 This is good value. It has some interesting flavours: cherry, wet straw, plum and smoke. It's light- to middle-weight, with a typical cabernet leanness and some tannin astringency to close. Best with food: try Lebanese yeeros.

Quality	¶¶¶
Value	★★★
Grapes	cabernet sauvignon; cabernet franc
Region	Sunraysia, Vic.
Cellar	∎ 4
Alc./Vol.	13.5%
RRP	$15.50 Ⓢ

Bindi Block Five Pinot Noir

Quality	🍷🍷🍷🍷🍷
Value	★★★★
Grapes	pinot noir
Region	Macedon Ranges, Vic.
Cellar	1–5+
Alc./Vol.	13.0%
RRP	$43.00 (cellar door)

Block Five is a new section of the tiny Bindi vineyard. Its soil differs slightly from the rest of the vineyard, producing a wine of extreme depth and character. Makers Michael Dhillon and Stuart Anderson.

CURRENT RELEASE 1997 The vines yielded just one tonne per acre and it shows in the power of this superb wine. It has deep colour and full body for a pinot. The bouquet has marvellous gamy, dark cherry, mixed spice, earth and sap complexities. The palate has tremendous depth, richness and structure. Backbone and fruit-sweetness aplenty. Drinks well now with quail, but will be even better in one or two years.

Bindi Original Vineyard Pinot Noir

Quality	🍷🍷🍷🍷🍷
Value	★★★★
Grapes	pinot noir
Region	Macedon Ranges, Vic.
Cellar	6+
Alc./Vol.	13.0%
RRP	$30.00 (cellar door)

The Dhillons of Bindi are hell-bent on making great wine. The yield for this pinot was 1.3 tonnes per acre, which is typical for Bindi but less than most *grand cru* Burgundies.

Previous outstanding vintages: '93, '94, '96

CURRENT RELEASE 1997 A more refined, less powerful wine than the Block Five, but no less superb. Marvellous dark cherry, ripe pinot aromas which follow through to a deliciously deep, complex palate. It has fully ripe fruit flavours, no stalkiness, and unusually good extract for an Australian pinot. Great to drink with spit-roasted quails.

Blackjack Shiraz

Quality	🍷🍷🍷🍷½
Value	★★★★
Grapes	shiraz
Region	Bendigo, Vic.
Cellar	1–12+
Alc./Vol.	13.2%
RRP	$22.00 (cellar door)

Blackjack is at Harcourt, near Bendigo. The area used to be known as an orchard district but is increasingly into grapes. Makers Ian McKenzie and Ken Pollock.

CURRENT RELEASE 1997 A big-fruited Bendigo red of impressive depth and stature. It just needs time to build some complexity. Vibrant ripe berry jam and slightly tarry aromas, shiraz spice and a hint of gunpowder from oak. Gains a twist of mint with airing. Very sweet and fruit-driven. Would suit venison stew.

Blass Adelaide Hills Cabernet Merlot

The grapes were grown in vineyards at Kuitpo and Woodside. The Blass people know all the buzzwords: this one is 'basket-pressed'. Maker Caroline Dunn.

CURRENT RELEASE 1997 Peppermint Pattie the second? This is an elegant wine, as you'd expect from the Hills. It has an aromatic, minty, perfumed nose and there's a spiciness to the quite intense palate. Smart stuff indeed, to serve with veal schnitzel.

Quality	▼▼▼▼?
Value	★★★★
Grapes	cabernet sauvignon; merlot
Region	Adelaide Hills, SA
Cellar	▌ 10+
Alc./Vol.	12.5%
RRP	$18.00

Blass Barossa Valley Shiraz

Did someone cry Wolf? This is another new label from the Mildara Blass people, and they've done away with half of the legend.

CURRENT RELEASE 1996 The nose is attractively floral and aromatic, with sweet berries and oaky notes. There's a swatch of acid/tannin/oak astringency and it could do with a little cellaring time. A stylish red, and not as oaky as the Vineyard Selection. Try it with braised lamb shanks.

Quality	▼▼▼▼?
Value	★★★★
Grapes	shiraz
Region	Barossa Valley, SA
Cellar	▌ 10
Alc./Vol.	12.5%
RRP	$18.00

Blass Vineyard Selection Cabernet Sauvignon

The labels of this new series of Blass wines are full of buzz phrases. This one says 'low-yielding vineyard'. It's an individual vineyard selection from the Bethany area.

CURRENT RELEASE 1996 'No wood, no good' was the Blass motto of yore. This smells primarily of singed barrels. Coconut and vanilla give way to coffee grounds, and there are red berries deeply buried within. Hard to see the wine ever overcoming the wood assault, but time will tell. Try blackened hamburgers.

Quality	▼▼▼▼
Value	★★★
Grapes	cabernet sauvignon
Region	Barossa Valley, SA
Cellar	➤ 2–10+
Alc./Vol.	13.0%
RRP	$30.00 ▐

Blass Vineyard Selection Shiraz

Quality	ŶŶŶŶ?
Value	★★★ŕ
Grapes	shiraz
Region	Eden Valley, SA
Cellar	➡ 2–12+
Alc./Vol.	12.5%
RRP	$30.00 ▮

The new-look packaging dispenses with Wolf Blass's first name. The labels are slicko, and the new red winemaker Caroline Dunn gets her name on the label.

CURRENT RELEASE 1996 Some debut! This is a power-packed shiraz, stacked with oak but also masses of berry and spice flavours. All it needs is time, and your patience. It's a bit tough and woody at present, so leave it for a year or so. Then serve with beef casserole.

The Blend Shiraz

Quality	ŶŶŶŶŶ
Value	★★★
Grapes	shiraz
Region	Hunter Valley, NSW; Barossa Valley, Coonawarra & McLaren Vale, SA; South-west Coastal Plain, WA
Cellar	▮ 10+
Alc./Vol.	13.8%
RRP	$50.00 ▮

Judith Kennedy, managing director of Boutique Wines Australia, persuaded five small wineries across Australia to provide a parcel of premium wine for her first vintage of The Blend. The aim is to promote the interests of small wineries. Contributors were Saddlers Creek (Hunter), Charles Cimicky (Barossa), Leconfield (Coonawarra), Hamilton (McLaren Vale) and Killerby (WA).

CURRENT RELEASE 1997 This unlikely blend is a big success. It's voluptuously rich and chunky; ripe and lush; a delicious synthesis of peppery cooler-grown and sweeter plum/prune, blackberry warm-area flavours. The latter predominate. It's elegant and more-ish, and goes well with steak and kidney pie.

Bloodwood Cabernet Sauvignon

Quality	ŶŶŶ
Value	★★ŕ
Grapes	cabernet sauvignon
Region	Orange, NSW
Cellar	▮ 3
Alc./Vol.	12.8%
RRP	$22.00 (cellar door)

Stephen and Rhonda Doyle's Bloodwood was the first vineyard in the Orange district. They sell grapes to other makers including Jon Reynolds, who makes their wine at his Yarraman, Hunter Valley, winery.

CURRENT RELEASE 1996 There's trouble at the mill 'ere: the grapes didn't get properly ripe. It smells of mint, camphor, tomato and crushed leaves. The bodyweight is medium to light, and there's an acerbic acid/tannin astringency bringing up the rear. It needs to be served with food: try racks of pink lamb.

Boston Bay Cabernet Sauvignon

Boston Bay is an isolated vineyard near Port Lincoln on South Australia's Eyre Peninsula. Maker David O'Leary. CURRENT RELEASE 1997 A good vintage for cabernet at Boston Bay without the weedy characters present in cooler years. On the nose there are blackcurrant, cherry and chocolate aromas, ahead of a medium-bodied palate with dry blackcurrant flavour, good length, balanced oak input and moderate tannins. Try it with moussaka.

Quality	ΨΨΨΨ
Value	★★★
Grapes	cabernet sauvignon
Region	Port Lincoln, SA
Cellar	↓ 3
Alc./Vol.	13.6%
RRP	$22.95

Brands Stentiford's Reserve Old Vines Shiraz

Captain Stentiford planted the Brands' original vineyard. He was an original 'blockie' in John Riddoch's Coonawarra Fruit Colony in the late nineteenth century. *Previous outstanding vintages: '86, '88, '90, '91* CURRENT RELEASE 1995 New name, new label, new style too. This had 20 months in new French oak and it shows. It's a lean style as befits the vintage, with lots of toasty oak to smell and savoury barrel-maturation complexities. Good wine, but lacks a little in power and doesn't speak of Coonawarra. Try it with casseroled kid.

Quality	ΨΨΨΨ
Value	★★★
Grapes	shiraz
Region	Coonawarra, SA
Cellar	➥ 2–7+
Alc./Vol.	13.5%
RRP	$38.00 ↓

Brangayne of Orange The Tristan

The Hoskins family of Brangayne are off to a very impressive start. They exhibit a flair for label design as well as wine production, although the nuts and bolts of winemaking are seen to by contractor Simon Gilbert. CURRENT RELEASE 1997 In keeping with all the Brangayne wines, this is a smart opening act. It's ripe, rich and spicy. It shows plenty of quality oak, and the palate has length and grip. The astringency says leave it alone for a couple of years, and it should reward with a lovely glass of red. Try it with roast beef.

Quality	ΨΨΨΨየ
Value	★★★★
Grapes	cabernet sauvignon; shiraz; merlot
Region	Orange, NSW
Cellar	➥ 2–8+
Alc./Vol.	13.5%
RRP	$20.00 (mailing list)

Bremerton Old Adam Shiraz

Quality	♥♥♥♥
Value	★★★
Grapes	shiraz
Region	Langhorne Creek, SA
Cellar	➥ 2–10+
Alc./Vol.	13.5%
RRP	$32.00 ▮

The Bremerton winery, cellar-door sales and the Wilson family's home are encircled by a one-metre levee bank to protect them from the famous Bremer River floods. Maker Rebecca Wilson.

CURRENT RELEASE 1996   This red is full of hellfire and brimstone: with a name like Old Adam it must have been there at Creation. There's a strong toasted oak aroma and a suggestion of volatile acidity which doesn't mar it. The palate is laden with dark berry flavours and it leaves some astringency that puts the tastebuds on edge. Serve with shepherd's pie.

Bremerton 'YV' Shiraz

Quality	♥♥♥♥
Value	★★★★
Grapes	shiraz
Region	Langhorne Creek, SA
Cellar	▮ 5+
Alc./Vol.	13.7%
RRP	$18.00 Ⓢ

The YV stands for young vines, which seems rather quirky given the (arguably excessive) reverence accorded to old vines these days. Vine youth didn't worry the quality here. They were four to seven years old.

CURRENT RELEASE 1997   A very attractive young shiraz. It has stacks of cherry fruit, cedary, toasty perfumes from good oak, and smooth drinkability. There is a tightness of structure and medium-bodied elegance that appeals. Serve it with roast lamb.

Bridgewater Mill Millstone Shiraz

Quality	♥♥♥♥⸱
Value	★★★⸱
Grapes	shiraz
Region	McLaren Vale, Langhorne Creek & Adelaide Hills, SA
Cellar	▮ 10+
Alc./Vol.	13.5%
RRP	$24.60

This wine has in the past seemed rather raw and unfinished, but like Sergeant Pepper, it's getting better all the time. Maker Brian Croser and team.

CURRENT RELEASE 1996   A more elegant style of Millstone. It has excellent power and concentration, but also good vinosity. The aromas are of black pepper with a gamy softness and some edgy, almost metallic, nuances. There are sweet berries and vanilla mouth flavours. Try it with rare barbecued rump steak.

Brookland Valley Merlot

Merlot is grown all over Australia but there's little consistency of style. At Brookland Valley, BRL Hardy's Margaret River outpost, it makes an aromatic style, which often has notable oak influence.

CURRENT RELEASE 1996 This is a fragrant wine, likeable but not memorable. The nose has sweet berry aromas with a hint of leafiness within a framework of spicy-sweet oak. In the mouth it's medium-bodied. The flavours start with pleasant plummy fruit, but bacon-scented oak takes over halfway. Tannins are in harmony.

Quality	♥♥♥♥
Value	★★★
Grapes	merlot
Region	Margaret River, WA
Cellar	▮ 4
Alc./Vol.	13.8%
RRP	$33.00

Brown Brothers Everton

Everton is a place not far from the Brown establishment at Milawa. It's just a brand name nowadays, although the company once made a wine from a vineyard there. This wine is a fruit-salad mixture.

CURRENT RELEASE 1996 This is a lightweight easy-drinking style of red. The colour is medium–deep and that sets the tone. It's rather oak-dominated, and the bouquet has ethereal oaky, almost spirity, elements that appear to be oak-derived. It's light and soft in the mouth and drinks well young, with chicken satays.

Quality	♥♥♥
Value	★★★
Grapes	cabernet sauvignon; merlot; shiraz; malbec; cabernet franc
Region	North East Vic.
Cellar	▮ 3
Alc./Vol.	13.0%
RRP	$13.50 ⑤

Brown Brothers King Valley Barbera

Browns have invested quite heavily in this northern Italian grape: they've planted quite a spread of it at their high-altitude Banksdale vineyard.

CURRENT RELEASE 1996 A very attractive red, but it doesn't taste exotic or evoke anything of Italy. Mulberry and cranberry are suggested in the aromas, as well as flowers and herbs. It's fruit-dominant, unlike some earlier attempts, and is smooth and flavoursome in the mouth with fresh acid to close. It's light- to medium-weight, so try it with spit-roasted quails.

Quality	♥♥♥♥
Value	★★★★
Grapes	barbera
Region	King Valley, Vic.
Cellar	▮ 4
Alc./Vol.	14.0%
RRP	$15.15 ⑤

Brown Brothers Victoria Cabernet Sauvignon

Quality	ŶŶŶŶ̧
Value	★★★★̧
Grapes	cabernet sauvignon
Region	various, Vic.
Cellar	▮ 5+
Alc./Vol.	14.0%
RRP	$19.20 Ⓢ

This is marketed under the Victoria label, which means the grapes come from various places in north-east Victoria, not just Milawa or the King Valley. Maker Terry Barnett and team.

CURRENT RELEASE 1997 Quite the best cabernet from Browns in many years, this is a delicious drink-now cabernet of good flavour and interest. There are sweet berry aromas with a twist of mint, and the oak is in harmony. The tidy, well-structured palate has just the right amount of soft tannin to balance it, and it slips down easily. Very more-ish with crown roast of hare.

Brown Brothers Victoria Shiraz

Quality	ŶŶ̧
Value	★★̧
Grapes	shiraz
Region	various, Vic.
Cellar	▮ 3
Alc./Vol.	13.5%
RRP	$19.20 Ⓢ

We never see a bad wine under Browns' Victoria range, but they're often a trifle bland. This is a blend from various areas, probably based on the Sunraysia.

CURRENT RELEASE 1996 The aroma is dominated by toasty oak. The colour shows a bit of age; it's medium ruby with a faint purple tint. The nose is an exercise in charred oak, smelling like singed coconut. It's a simple, basic red and will appeal to lumber lovers. Try it with heavily charred barbecue sausages.

Buller 'Sails' Cabernet Shiraz Merlot

Quality	ŶŶ̧
Value	★★̧
Grapes	cabernet sauvignon;
	shiraz; merlot
Region	Murray Valley, Vic.
Cellar	▮ 3+
Alc./Vol.	13.5%
RRP	$16.00 Ⓢ

This is Buller's entry in the snappy packaging stakes, or what the Southcorp people would call 'concept' wine. Maker Richard Buller Jnr.

CURRENT RELEASE 1997 The dominant aromas here are green, stalky, sappy smells, reminiscent of absinthe. The palate is lean, green and shows some apparently unripe fruit characters, but there are no winemaking faults. Take it to a barbecue.

Buller Shiraz Mondeuse

Andy Buller is one of the committed winemakers of Rutherglen. He's made port in Portugal, where they live and breathe fortified wines.

CURRENT RELEASE 1996 Here's one for those addicted to whoppers: huge colour, colossal fruit and tannin astringency to go with its 15.9 per cent alcohol. There are creosote and gumleaf/mint aromas, and it has enormous extract and tannin grip. Needs to be aged, but for how long – and how it will turn out – is anyone's guess. Try it with jugged hare.

Quality	¶¶¶¶
Value	★★★½
Grapes	shiraz; mondeuse
Region	Rutherglen, Vic.
Cellar	➡ 5+
Alc./Vol.	15.9%
RRP	$25.40

Buller Victoria Classic Shiraz Grenache

Shiraz-grenache blends have become very popular in recent times. It seems that often a little grenache softens a blend and renders it drinkable earlier. Maker Richard Buller.

CURRENT RELEASE 1998 This is a light wine in every regard – the colour is light, the aroma is light, the oak is lightly applied. There are plum, cherry and vanilla notes, and the flavour is basic with no frills. Quite good at the price. Serve it with shish kebabs.

Quality	¶¶¶
Value	★★★
Grapes	shiraz; grenache
Region	Sunraysia, Vic.
Cellar	2
Alc./Vol.	14.5%
RRP	$11.80 (S)

Campbells Bobbie Burns Shiraz

Recent years have seen Campbells repositioning themselves in the market with some very smart packaging, upgraded wines, and revised (upwards) pricing.

CURRENT RELEASE 1997 Bobbie Burns has long been one of Rutherglen's best reds, and its position has been reinforced recently by handy wines like this. It has a potent nose full of warm fruit characters like plum jam and licorice strap, and there's a bit of peppery zip as well. The palate is satisfying with mellow mid-palate fruit, a chewy texture and firm tannins. Roast beef would be perfect here.

Quality	¶¶¶¶½
Value	★★★★
Grapes	shiraz
Region	Rutherglen, Vic.
Cellar	➡ 1–6
Alc./Vol.	14.3%
RRP	$21.00

Candlebark Hill Cabernet Merlot

Quality	♡♡♡♡
Value	★★★
Grapes	cabernet sauvignon; merlot
Region	Macedon, Vic.
Cellar	➡ 1–4
Alc./Vol.	14.0%
RRP	$29.00

New names are cropping up all the time. This vineyard is at Kyneton in Central Victoria, a district that can be distinctly cool.

CURRENT RELEASE 1997   Coconut and vanilla aromas from a hefty measure of American oak lead the charge here. Look deeper and you'll find some floral perfumes and a nucleus of tight, concentrated blackcurranty fruit. The palate follows suit with oak to the fore and black fruit at the core. Acidity is good, and tannins are well balanced.

Canobolas-Smith Alchemy

Quality	♡♡♡♡♡
Value	★★★★
Grapes	cabernet sauvignon; cabernet franc; shiraz
Region	Orange, NSW
Cellar	➡ 2–10+
Alc./Vol.	15.3%
RRP	$22.00 (cellar door)

The name Alchemy refers to the skill, part science and part art, which is used to blend a complete wine from several components, in this case cabernet sauvignon, cabernet franc and shiraz. Base metals into gold and all that. Maker Murray Smith.

CURRENT RELEASE 1996   This is a big bruiser with a serious alcohol reading. It's very big and concentrated, and the colour is a vividly youthful purple–red. It smells of dark berries, peppermint and chocolate, with a hint of jamminess, and it's deep, dense and fleshy in the mouth. A full-on style that takes no prisoners. Try it with beef wellington.

Cape Horn Cabernet Sauvignon

Quality	♡♡♡
Value	★★★
Grapes	cabernet sauvignon
Region	Murray Valley, Vic.
Cellar	▮ 2
Alc./Vol.	12.0%
RRP	$18.00

This old vineyard was re-established in 1994 by Sue and Ian Harrison. The Cape Horn in question isn't down in the roaring forties: it's a feature on the Murray River near Echuca.

CURRENT RELEASE 1997   This has tight blackcurrant and leafy aromas with a camphor-like touch. The palate lacks a bit of depth, but it does have same tangy minty black-fruit flavour ahead of a dry grip of tannin on the finish. Grill some little lamb cutlets to have with it.

Cape Mentelle Shiraz

Cape Mentelle is a benchmark for the more elegant type of Aussie shiraz, so the oddball '96 vintage was quite a surprise for us. Happily the 1997 edition is back to top form.

CURRENT RELEASE 1997 The nose is a very complex mix of delectable black-cherry fruit, some earthy undergrowthy character and zippy peppery spice. The palate is intense, with fleshy cherry-berry flavour and savoury spice. Balanced, drying tannins support everything admirably. A more-ish red to drink now, but well worth a bit of age. A great match for lyonnaise sausages with braised lentils.

Quality	🍷🍷🍷🍷🍷
Value	★★★★½
Grapes	shiraz
Region	Margaret River, WA
Cellar	6
Alc./Vol.	14.5%
RRP	$27.00

Cape Mentelle Trinders Vineyard Cabernet Merlot

Trinders Cabernet Merlot is regarded as Cape Mentelle's most approachable red in its youth, but there's no need to hurry – it also has the pedigree to age well.

CURRENT RELEASE 1997 This is a more voluptuous Trinders than the '96. Succulent aromas of dark berries, blood plum and high-class spicy-sweet oak meet the nose. The smoothly seductive palate has lovely balance of fruit-sweet flavour and fine-grained tannins. Works well with roast beef and Yorkshire pudding.

Quality	🍷🍷🍷🍷½
Value	★★★★
Grapes	cabernet sauvignon; merlot
Region	Margaret River, WA
Cellar	5
Alc./Vol.	14.1%
RRP	$24.70

Cape Mentelle Zinfandel

'Zin' is a Californian favourite that is rare in Australia. Cape Mentelle's version is our best, a wild and woolly wine that's impossible to ignore.

CURRENT RELEASE 1997 As usual, this is a souped-up hot rod of a red wine. Potent aromas of blackberries, oriental spices and spiky leaves charge the nose. The palate is fruit-dominated and decadently rich, with dark berry and chocolatey flavours, a wild chewy texture and big grippy tannins. Improves with decanting and stands up well to Chinese glazed beef spare ribs.

Quality	🍷🍷🍷🍷½
Value	★★★★½
Grapes	zinfandel
Region	Margaret River, WA
Cellar	10
Alc./Vol.	15.5%
RRP	$30.00

Cassegrain White Pinot Chardonnay

Quality	♥♥♥↓
Value	★★★↓
Grapes	pinot noir; chardonnay
Region	Hastings Valley, NSW
Cellar	▮ 1
Alc./Vol.	13.8%
RRP	$15.00

Is a pale-pink wine, made from both red and white grapes, a red or a white? Authors of wine books are often beset by such difficult questions. We decided this was a red . . . well, at least it's heading in that direction.
CURRENT RELEASE 1998   This has an attractive pink blush, which is bright and lively. On the nose it has light strawberry aromas. The palate is attractively soft but dry in the agreeable European style. A pleasant warm-weather wine to serve chilled with a spread of cold meats and seafood.

Castle Rock Pinot Noir

Quality	♥♥♥♥
Value	★★★★↓
Grapes	pinot noir
Region	Great Southern, WA
Cellar	▮ 3
Alc./Vol.	13.0%
RRP	$23.00

The Great Southern region of Western Australia is evolving as the state's number one pinot noir region. In common with other specialist pinot districts, standards are frustratingly inconsistent.
CURRENT RELEASE 1998   A fresh pinot which shows whole berry influence on the nose, with 'pretty' raspberry and red-cherry aromas. There's also a leafy touch. The palate is soft and cherry-flavoured with everything in nice balance for early drinking. It finishes dry and slightly firm. A good match for a charcuterie selection.

Chain of Ponds Amadeus Cabernet Sauvignon

Quality	♥♥♥♥♥
Value	★★★★
Grapes	cabernet sauvignon
Region	Adelaide Hills, SA
Cellar	➥ 3–8
Alc./Vol.	14.0%
RRP	$29.00

Caj and Genny Amadio, proprietors of Chain of Ponds, are substantial suppliers of Adelaide Hills grapes to other makers. Some fruit is reserved for this range of high-quality wines under their own label.
CURRENT RELEASE 1997   Cabernet in the Adelaide Hills performs best in warmer years like '97. This is a serious red, which should develop real elegance with age. The nose is perfumed and intense, with classical blackcurrant, clean-earth and leafy touches against a background of cedary oak. The flavours follow the nose with succulent cassis-like fruit; very structured and firm with a tight backbone of ripe tannins. Serve with braised veal shanks.

Chain of Ponds Ledge Shiraz

Chain of Ponds wines go from strength to strength, and now that the Americans have discovered them there'll be less to go around. Grab 'em while you can.

CURRENT RELEASE 1997 This is a very impressive shiraz with great potential. The deep, dense colour suggests great extract and muscle; the nose confirms it with super-concentrated blackberry fruit and tangy spice. In the mouth it's full-bodied, with reduced dark berry flavour, a charry touch and big grippy tannins. Give it cellar time, then drink it with game pie.

Quality	🍷🍷🍷🍷🍷
Value	★★★★
Grapes	shiraz
Region	Adelaide Hills, SA
Cellar	▬ 3–10
Alc./Vol.	14.0%
RRP	$31.00

Chapel Hill Cabernet Sauvignon

The Chapel Hill winery is sited beside an old stone chapel, which forms the tasting area for visitors. The rolling Southern Vales hills surround it – a great place to visit. Maker Pam Dunsford.

CURRENT RELEASE 1997 The nose is sweet and appealing with black fruits and more restrained oak treatment than Chapel Hill cabernets of yore. The palate has soft berry fruit with satisfying long flavour and a signature of fine-grained tannins. Has the structure to age well. Serve with pink lamb cutlets.

Quality	🍷🍷🍷🍷
Value	★★★★
Grapes	cabernet sauvignon
Region	McLaren Vale &
	Coonawarra, SA
Cellar	▬ 1–8
Alc./Vol.	13.5%
RRP	$26.30

Chapel Hill Shiraz

Chapel Hill winemaker Pam Dunsford thinks a lot about wine and constantly works to improve her reds. They get better all the time.

CURRENT RELEASE 1997 Attractively purple-tinged in the glass, this is a complete young shiraz which will only get better the longer you keep your hands off it. The nose has blackberry aromas with a dab of perfumed sweetness, and a savoury touch too. The oak is well handled and it doesn't dominate. The palate is long, complex and easy to drink with a signature of fine, ripe tannins. Try it with a rib roast of beef.

Quality	🍷🍷🍷🍷🍷
Value	★★★★
Grapes	shiraz
Region	McLaren Vale, SA
Cellar	▮ 8
Alc./Vol.	14.0%
RRP	$29.60

Chapel Hill The Vicar

Quality	♟♟♟♟♟
Value	★★★★
Grapes	cabernet sauvignon; shiraz
Region	McLaren Vale, SA
Cellar	➟ 1–10
Alc./Vol.	13.5%
RRP	$29.60

For her top red, Pam Dunsford looks to tradition with a cabernet-shiraz blend. The name is appropriate, since Chapel Hill is based in an old church.

CURRENT RELEASE 1996 This is a powerful young regional red with a nose of intense black fruits, sweet and savoury spice, mocha and vanillin oak. The palate has direct blackberry fruit of great intensity with an oaky background and firm, dry tannins.

Charles Melton Nine Popes

Quality	♟♟♟♟♟
Value	★★★★
Grapes	grenache; shiraz; mourvèdre
Region	Barossa Valley, SA
Cellar	⬙ 5
Alc./Vol.	14.5%
RRP	$33.00

Charlie Melton recognised the value of all those wizened old Barossa grenache and mourvèdre (aka mataro) vines ahead of the pack. Using them as his raw material, along with old vine shiraz, he crafts his answer to the French Chateauneuf-du-Pape.

CURRENT RELEASE 1997 Nine Popes is a tightly packed red wine that seems to become more refined with each vintage. This edition is still powerful, yet its warm bouquet of integrated dark cherry fruit, mocha, earth and toasty oak has subtlety too. In the mouth it's seamless in texture with fleshy cherry/berry fruit and savoury notes, sweet oak and grainy soft tannins. Despite its obvious ageworthiness, it drinks well right now.

Charles Melton Rose of Virginia

Quality	♟♟♟♟♟
Value	★★★★★
Grapes	grenache
Region	Barossa Valley, SA
Cellar	⬙ 1
Alc./Vol.	12.0%
RRP	$15.00

Although it's a very fruity style, this rosé is always a step further down the road to real solid red wine than the frivolous pink efforts of many wineries. Maker Graham 'Charlie' Melton.

CURRENT RELEASE 1999 Suspend any prejudices you may have against rosé, and look at this one with alfresco food and a warm afternoon in mind. Bright in colour – a rather deep hot pink with a magenta touch – it has an essency nose of flowers, raspberry and pink musk-sticks. The palate is super-juicy with fresh raspberry flavour, a dab of sweetness and a clean finish. Serve it out-of-doors in summer, well chilled with big platters of Provençale-style cold meats and vegetables.

Charles Melton Shiraz

Old vines impart special depth and richness to this flavoursome Barossa red. It successfully straddles the line between traditional and modern winemaking.

CURRENT RELEASE 1997   An unusual Charlie Melton Shiraz, at the moment less voluptuous than usual and simpler in structure. The nose has high-toned aromas of cherries, berries, spice and dusty vanillin oak. The palate has ripe berry, coffee and oak flavours, medium–full body and dry tannins. It's okay, but the usual fruit character is somewhat muted. Age may be the answer. Serve it with braised lamb shanks.

Quality	????
Value	★★★
Grapes	shiraz
Region	Barossa Valley, SA
Cellar	☛ 1–4+
Alc./Vol.	14.0%
RRP	$33.00

Charles Sturt Limited Release Cabernet Sauvignon

Winemaking at Charles Sturt University fulfils a dual role. Not only is it a commercial proposition, it also teaches students wine industry skills.

CURRENT RELEASE 1996   This is clean-tasting, copybook cabernet with a pure varietal personality – as one would expect from such an august institution. Juicy blackcurrant fruit aromas, leafy austerity and cedary oak make for an attractive nose. That succulent blackcurrant quality is there in the mouth too, and fine-grained, long tannins support it well. Roast lamb will do well.

Quality	?????
Value	★★★★
Grapes	cabernet sauvignon
Region	Coonawarra, SA; King Valley, Vic.; Wagga Wagga, NSW
Cellar	☛ 2–5
Alc./Vol.	13.5%
RRP	$22.00

Chateau Tahbilk Cabernet Sauvignon

The more things change . . . Tahbilk reds have a timelessness of style that makes them history in a bottle. Our fathers, and maybe our grandfathers if they felt the inclination, could have enjoyed Chateau Tahbilk wines just like this one. Makes you kinda humble, don't it?

CURRENT RELEASE 1996   Right in the Tahbilk groove. Mature blackberry, spice, earth and savoury touches on the nose; strong black fruit, good depth and tight dry tannins in the mouth. Large old oak is used, which has a benign influence that is out of step with much modern thinking. Try it with Scotch fillet of beef roasted as a piece.

Quality	????
Value	★★★★
Grapes	cabernet sauvignon; cabernet franc
Region	Goulburn Valley, Vic.
Cellar	☛ 2–8+
Alc./Vol.	13.0%
RRP	$18.00

Chateau Tahbilk Shiraz

Quality	ΥΥΥ?
Value	★★★
Grapes	shiraz
Region	Goulburn Valley, Vic.
Cellar	➥ 2–6+
Alc./Vol.	12.5%
RRP	$16.00

Tahbilk shiraz doesn't seem to excite as it once did, but then there's a lot of competition. Like the Tahbilk cabernet sauvignon it's still a very traditional recipe: if it ain't broke why fix it?

CURRENT RELEASE 1996   Tight black fruit meets the nose with that sort of dissolved mineral aroma that marks many of the most traditional Aussie reds. There's also some spice and the gentle influence of old casks. The palate has a hint of berry sweetness with a firm, tannic finish.

Chatsfield Shiraz

Quality	ΥΥΥΥ
Value	★★★★
Grapes	shiraz
Region	Mount Barker, WA
Cellar	↓ 5+
Alc./Vol.	14.5%
RRP	$22.00

In common with a growing number of quality-oriented smallish producers in the Great Southern region of Western Australia, Chatsfield is gaining real notoriety for good shiraz in the elegant style.

CURRENT RELEASE 1997   Very regional in style with a complex nose of pepper, plum, sweet spice and a floral touch. The middleweight palate has intense spicy dark cherry flavour of real intensity and length. Good acidity and fine tannins support things well. A well-balanced red to enjoy with roast duck and sour cherries.

Ciavarella Cabernet Sauvignon

Quality	ΥΥΥΥ
Value	★★★★★
Grapes	cabernet sauvignon
Region	King Valley, Vic.
Cellar	↓ 3
Alc./Vol.	13.2%
RRP	$13.00

The Ciavarellas' vineyard was established in 1978 at Oxley in the King Valley. Until fairly recently they sold their grapes to other makers, but now they make wine themselves.

CURRENT RELEASE 1997   A discovery at a low price, this flavoursome red has a potent mix of aromas like black plum, currants, earth and savoury oak. The medium-bodied palate has soft berry flavour, some cedary oak and fine-grained tannins. Drinks well right now with a lip-smacking character that keeps you coming back for more. Sip this with braised kid.

Clarendon Hills Cabernet Sauvignon

The slopes around Clarendon are almost in the Adelaide Hills. These higher hillside vineyards are said to give wines of greater finesse than their neighbours in McLaren Vale proper.

CURRENT RELEASE 1997 This is a big super-ripe cabernet with lots of concentrated black-fruit aroma and flavour of almost liqueur-like intensity. Surprisingly there's also a leafy touch in there. In the mouth there's a lot of extracted fruit and a warm alcoholic note. It finishes very dry with a formidable wall of firm tannins. An interesting red that needs time in bottle, although we can't quite tell you how long. Then you should try it with a rib roast of beef.

Quality	♥♥♥♥
Value	★★★
Grapes	cabernet sauvignon
Region	McLaren Vale, SA
Cellar	⬤ 3–10+?
Alc./Vol.	14.0%
RRP	$98.70

Clarendon Hills Kangarilla Vineyard Old Vines Grenache

A handful of American wine commentators have been going into fits of excitement over the Clarendon Hills reds recently. Wines of huge impact are their bag, and Clarendon Hills delivers the goods. As a result, prices have gone over the top. Maker Roman Bratasiuk.

CURRENT RELEASE 1997 If you've been turned off grenache by the lollyish confections of some makers, try this. It's grenache with attitude: a big rustic wine with tons of character and extract. Nose and palate have intense raspberry and loganberry fruit with some smoky and gamy complexity. The flavour is framed by solid, firm tannins. A hefty wine of strong individual character. Try it with chargrilled ox rump.

Quality	♥♥♥♥
Value	★★★
Grapes	grenache
Region	McLaren Vale, SA
Cellar	⬤ 2–8+
Alc./Vol.	14.5%
RRP	$65.80

Clarendon Hills Liandra Shiraz

Quality	????
Value	★★ʰ
Grapes	shiraz
Region	McLaren Vale, SA
Cellar	▮ 8
Alc./Vol.	14.5%
RRP	$106.95

The Clarendon Hills range comprises a variety of wines, each sourced from a different plot of old vines, mostly in the hill vineyards on the fringe of the McLaren Vale area. Maker Roman Bratasiuk.

CURRENT RELEASE 1997 This is a more conventional, 'safer' sort of shiraz from Clarendon Hills. It has intense blackberry on the nose with subtle vanillin oak. The palate is rich and dense in ripe fruit, full-flavoured and well balanced. A smooth mouthful, which will only get better. An excellent companion to roast beef.

Clarendon Hills Piggott Range Vineyard Shiraz

Quality	????
Value	★★ʰ
Grapes	shiraz
Region	McLaren Vale, SA
Cellar	➥ 1–10
Alc./Vol.	14.5%
RRP	$123.40

Clarendon Hills wines are at the pointy end of wine pricing, asking (and getting) big dollars for their various vintages. Relative value is a question for the consumer to decide. The wines have suitably overt personalities that are impossible to ignore.

CURRENT RELEASE 1997 Clarendon Hills reds tend to polarise tasters, such is their uncompromising style. This shiraz won't be to everyone's taste, but if you like French-inspired wines of great complexity, save up and buy a bottle. The nose has potent plum, spice, smoke and marzipan aromas. In the mouth it has some gamy flavours, and it's savoury and complex like mature parmigiano. The finish has dry tannins and a long aftertaste.

Clonakilla Shiraz

Quality	?????
Value	★★★★★
Grapes	shiraz; viognier (5%)
Region	Canberra, ACT
Cellar	➥ 2–6+
Alc./Vol.	14.0%
RRP	$36.00

In the space of a few short years Clonakilla Shiraz has given the Canberra district its first great wine. Makers Dr John Kirk and son Tim.

CURRENT RELEASE 1998 A very complex and interesting wine. The nose is uncannily like reds from the northern Rhone in France. It has exotic spice, pepper and gamy overtones to dark cherry fruit on the nose. The palate is silken in texture with wild, gamy shiraz flavours, good length and a lick of cedary oak at the end. Balanced fine-grained tannins complete the picture. Needs time. Serve with roasted pigeons.

Cockfighter's Ghost Pinot Noir

Cockfighter's Ghost's base is in the Hunter Valley, but they source this pinot from Western Australia where it's made by the famous John Wade.

CURRENT RELEASE 1997 This has very aromatic modern pinot noir aromas – complex and hard to describe. There's plum, spice and hints of gaminess, bracken and stems. The palate is medium-bodied with stewed plum and spice flavours, and a dry, smoky finish.

Quality	▼▼▼▼
Value	★★★★
Grapes	pinot noir
Region	Pemberton & Great Southern, WA
Cellar	🍾 3
Alc./Vol.	14.0%
RRP	$20.95

Cofield Merlot

Merlot is a newcomer to Victoria's north-east and what its future is there, is anyone's guess. Max Cofield's version is promising; pity about his plain-Jane light-blue labels!

CURRENT RELEASE 1997 Merlot ought to be smooth and inviting, and this one is right on the ball. The nose has blackberry and dark cherry aromas, and oak takes a back seat. In the mouth it has ripe flavour, softness and mild tannins. Another easy-drinking Cofield red.

Quality	▼▼▼▼▼
Value	★★★★★
Grapes	merlot
Region	Rutherglen, Vic.
Cellar	🍾 3
Alc./Vol.	13.7%
RRP	$17.50

Cofield Shiraz

Rutherglen is undergoing the quietest of revolutions, and it all has to do with red table wines rather than the staple fortifieds. These reds are still generously proportioned, but they aren't the jammy, port-like drops of old.

CURRENT RELEASE 1997 A generously flavoured young wine which points a direction for Rutherglen reds to take. The nose is big and ripe with dark berry fruit and warm spices. In the mouth it has good body with seductive softness and moderate tannins to finish. Drinks well young, but it should keep well short- to medium term. A hearty beef casserole would suit it well.

Quality	▼▼▼▼
Value	★★★★⟡
Grapes	shiraz
Region	Rutherglen, Vic.
Cellar	🍾 4
Alc./Vol.	13.5%
RRP	$17.50

Coldstream Hills Briarston

Quality	♟♟♟♟
Value	★★★⸱
Grapes	cabernet sauvignon; merlot; malbec; cabernet franc
Region	Yarra Valley, Vic.
Cellar	▮ 4
Alc./Vol.	13.0%
RRP	$21.95

Briarston is the name of a new Coldstream Hills vineyard in the Yarra Valley. It gives its name to this red, which used to be labelled Cabernet Merlot.

CURRENT RELEASE 1997 This wine offers plum and berry fruit, herbal and leafy touches and measured oak influence. In the mouth it has medium body with a soft middle palate and moderate, dry tannins at the end. Try it with herbed roast veal.

Coldstream Hills Merlot

Quality	♟♟♟♟⸱
Value	★★★★
Grapes	merlot
Region	Yarra Valley, Vic.
Cellar	▮ 4
Alc./Vol.	13.5%
RRP	$26.00 ▮

Some pundits have predicted that merlot is going to be the next big thing in Australia, as it is in a few other countries. We're still waiting. Perhaps Coldstream Hills is going to lead the way with this new addition to the range.

CURRENT RELEASE 1997 Well-defined merlot fruit is a feature here. It improves with decanting, and has those typical plum-pudding, earthy and leafy aromas coupled with a good measure of charry oak. The palate is dense in plump dark fruit with a gamy touch, and a signature of balanced, soft tannins. A good match for pot-roasted topside with winter vegetables.

Coldstream Hills Pinot Noir

Quality	♟♟♟♟
Value	★★★⸱
Grapes	pinot noir
Region	Yarra Valley, Vic.
Cellar	▮ 3
Alc./Vol.	13.5%
RRP	$26.00

At Coldstream Hills they use all the Burgundian tricks to build character into their pinots. The result usually has exemplary varietal personality and good complexity.

CURRENT RELEASE 1998 In early life the 1998 Coldstream has a bit more pinot mystery than the last couple of vintages. It smells of plummy fruit with some of those smoky, meaty and undergrowthy touches that make pinot-philes shiver with excitement. In the mouth there are plums, earth and game; a soft, plump mid-palate; and long, mellow tannins. Great with grilled marinated quail on polenta.

Coldstream Hills Reserve Cabernet Sauvignon

In the best vintages, James Halliday reserves a quantity of his best cabernet for release under this label. To prove how serious he is about it, none is produced in lesser years like 1996.

CURRENT RELEASE 1997 This isn't a blockbuster cabernet; it's quite a subdued drop really. The nose has pleasant cool-climate cabernet aromas – cassis, leafiness – and the hallmark spicy French oak. The palate has fine blackcurrant and leafy flavours, tangy acidity and dry fine-grained tannins. Everything's well balanced, but the fruit is hiding at the moment. Give it time to open up, then serve it with roast lamb.

Quality	♥♥♥♥
Value	★★★
Grapes	cabernet sauvignon
Region	Yarra Valley, Vic.
Cellar	➥ 2–6+
Alc./Vol.	13.5%
RRP	$45.00

Coldstream Hills Reserve Pinot Noir

Coldstream Hills' best parcels of pinot find their way into the Reserve. The wines often need time for a heavy dose of very good French oak to integrate.

CURRENT RELEASE 1997 The '97 vintage was a very good, low-yielding Yarra Valley vintage just made for pinot noir. This Reserve wine doesn't disappoint. Deeply coloured, it's still a bit closed up underneath a spicy overlay of charry oak. Look deeper and you'll find all those exquisite black-cherry and blood-plum aromas, along with earthy, foresty smells. Not a pinot for early consumption; this should develop into something quite profound with bottle-age.

Quality	♥♥♥♥♥
Value	★★★★
Grapes	pinot noir
Region	Yarra Valley, Vic.
Cellar	➥ 1–5
Alc./Vol.	$13.5%
RRP	$42.00

CURRENT RELEASE 1998 Coldstream Hills' pinots need time to develop, as do a lot of top pinot noirs. It's a pity so many are gulped down before they have a chance to build in bottle. At the moment this is a tight, closed wine with a good measure of charry, bacon-smoky oak. In the middle there's intense, spicy black-cherry fruit with a seductive overlay of foresty complexity. This really must be kept to realise its potential. Serve with some pot-roasted pigeons.

Quality	♥♥♥♥♥
Value	★★★★
Grapes	pinot noir
Region	Yarra Valley, Vic.
Cellar	➥ 1–5
Alc./Vol.	14.0%
RRP	$45.00

Coriole Redstone

Quality	🍷🍷🍷🍷
Value	★★★★
Grapes	shiraz; cabernet sauvignon; grenache; merlot
Region	McLaren Vale, SA
Cellar	🍷 3
Alc./Vol.	13.5%
RRP	$18.00

Red ironstone abounds in the Coriole vineyard, hence the name. This stone was used to build some of the first buildings at Coriole nearly 140 years ago.

CURRENT RELEASE 1997 This is an agreeable Southern Vales red with good regional personality. The nose has earthiness, a hint of leather, and blackberry fruit. In the mouth it's a pleasantly earthy middleweight with a straightforward dry flavour, soft tannins and a gentle berry aftertaste. Easy drinking with a wild mushroom risotto.

Cowra Estate Cabernet Sauvignon Shiraz

Quality	🍷🍷🍷🍷
Value	★★★★
Grapes	cabernet sauvignon; shiraz
Region	Cowra, NSW
Cellar	🍷 3
Alc./Vol.	13.0%
RRP	$12.00

The vineyards of Cowra, in the New South Wales Central Ranges, are a reliable source of good-value wines. John Geber's Cowra Estate is a significant player.

CURRENT RELEASE 1997 A basic cab blend with aromas of redcurrant, earth and dusty oak. The palate is pleasant: a light- to medium-weight with some savoury notes to add dimension to a nucleus of simple sweet fruit. Dry tannins impart grip to the finish. Try it with doner kebab.

Crabtree Watervale Cabernet Sauvignon

Quality	🍷🍷🍷🍷
Value	★★★★
Grapes	cabernet sauvignon; shiraz
Region	Clare Valley, SA
Cellar	➾ 1–5
Alc./Vol.	12.0%
RRP	$18.00

Robert Crabtree has heard about the way businesses are worried about the Y2K bug. It hasn't phased him though. He says that if it arrives in his vineyard, just give him the name of the appropriate chemical and he'll spray it out of existence. In the meantime we have time to enjoy his pre-Y2K reds.

CURRENT RELEASE 1996 This has herbal and black-fruit aromas with juicy appeal and subdued oak. The palate is tangy and youthful with rich dry fruit character and fine tannins. It will be better with age. Try it with tagliatelle with cheese, olives, garlic and virgin olive oil.

Crabtree Watervale Shiraz Cabernet Sauvignon

Compared with the brawny drops made by some of his neighbours, Robert Crabtree's reds are at the lighter, finer end of the Clare spectrum.

CURRENT RELEASE 1996   This is very fresh and lively for a Clare red. The nose has tangy, minty aromas with berry and cassis undertones and just a hint of dusty oak. The palate is medium-bodied with berry and crushed-leaf flavours. Zippy acidity and a moderate level of alcohol give an impression of lightness, but it's not wimpy. Tannins are soft and balanced. A good red for chicken schnitzels.

Quality	?????
Value	★★★★
Grapes	shiraz; cabernet sauvignon
Region	Clare Valley, SA
Cellar	← 1–4
Alc./Vol.	12.5%
RRP	$18.00

Craiglee Cabernet Sauvignon

Although Craiglee is, strictly speaking, in the Macedon region of Victoria, its wines are quite different. They're riper and more consistent, reflecting a warmer, lower-altitude site. The skill of winemaker Pat Carmody helps too.

CURRENT RELEASE 1997   Typically bright deep colour and a complex nose reflect the Craiglee style. It has a bouquet of blackcurrant pastille with hints of briar and earth. In the mouth it has intense black fruit with a gamy touch and subtle oak flavour. The finish is warm with alcohol, and the tannins are very gripping. Needs time. Serve with chargrilled meats.

Quality	?????
Value	★★★★
Grapes	cabernet sauvignon
Region	Sunbury, Vic.
Cellar	← 2–6
Alc./Vol.	15.0%
RRP	$23.00

Craiglee Shiraz

Quality	♟♟♟♟♟
Value	★★★★★
Grapes	shiraz
Region	Sunbury, Vic.
Cellar	➥ 1–10+
Alc./Vol.	14.5%
RRP	$30.00

PENGUIN BEST SHIRAZ

This oasis – just fifteen minutes past Melbourne Airport – takes you back to the heady days of Victorian wine last century. A must-visit winery if you're in that neck of the woods. Maker Pat Carmody.

CURRENT RELEASE 1997 **This is a bigger, richer Craiglee than the '96, reflecting the warm vintage. The nose still has the peppery, spicy edge that marks the style, but the dense black-cherry fruit aroma is more opulent and concentrated. The palate has deep dark cherry and plum flavour with a seasoning of spice and understated oak influence. It's smooth and silky, with great length and presence. Tannins are ripe and balanced. A wonderful match for braised duck risotto.**

Cranswick Estate Cocoparra Vineyard Shiraz

Quality	♟♟♟♟
Value	★★★★
Grapes	shiraz
Region	Riverina, NSW
Cellar	▮ 3
Alc./Vol.	14.0%
RRP	$18.00 ⑤

The Riverina is certainly dry country if you turn the Murrumbidgee water off, as every vineyard relies on irrigation for its existence. In this case, Cranswick use regulated deficit irrigation to control the amount of water and therefore the intensity of character in the grapes. It seems to work well.

CURRENT RELEASE 1996 Plenty of straightforward character here with good concentration. It has a syrupy blackberry nose with some spicy oak input. In the mouth it's a tasty middleweight; juicy dark fruit flavour leads the way and vanillin oak supports it, but the flavour is rather short. Good with chargrilled porterhouse steak.

Cranswick Estate Vignette Cabernet Merlot

Cranswick is becoming a big player on the Riverina wine scene, with ambitious plans for future expansion of both export and domestic markets. Winemaker Ian Hongell's enthusiasm was a great asset, but he's moved elsewhere.
CURRENT RELEASE 1997 A respectable young red that offers more interest than many in this price range. The nose has ripe black-fruit aromas with a hint of mint, some sweet oak and a faintly tarry touch. The palate is a bit unyielding, but it does have a core of blackcurrant fruit in the middle and an interesting chewy texture. The finish is slightly hard. Try it with a garlic bruschetta steak sandwich.

Quality	▼▼▼℩
Value	★★★⊦
Grapes	cabernet sauvignon; merlot
Region	Riverina, NSW
Cellar	▮ 2
Alc./Vol.	12.5%
RRP	$12.00 Ⓢ

Cranswick Estate Vignette Shiraz

The Riverina is a big source of Australia's vin ordinaire, but the wines aren't quite as ordinaire as they used to be. Here's a case in point.
CURRENT RELEASE 1997 This has good depth of youthful purplish colour. The nose has notable raw vanillin oak smells, as well as some reduced, tarry, blackberry fruit aromas. The palate isn't as powerful as the nose might suggest, but it's adequately endowed with dry berry flavour dressed with a touch of chippy oak. Dry tannins finish things off. A good barbecue red.

Quality	▼▼▼
Value	★★★
Grapes	shiraz
Region	Riverina, NSW
Cellar	▮ 2
Alc./Vol.	13.0%
RRP	$12.00 Ⓢ

Crawford River Cabernet Merlot

The Crawford River vineyard is near Portland in southern Victoria. As you would expect in a place so cool, the cabernet-based reds can be touch and go in cold years, but very good in the warm ones. Maker John Thomson.
CURRENT RELEASE 1997 The '97 vintage was the sort of sunny vintage that Crawford River reds need. This has intense fruit aromas with a purity and succulence reminiscent of tart/sweet blackcurrants. A herbal edge and balanced sweet oak add interest. In the mouth it's alive with a tangy core of blackcurrant fruit ahead of some grippy tannins. The aftertaste is long and fragrant. Try it with pink baby lamb cutlets.

Quality	▼▼▼▼℩
Value	★★★★
Grapes	cabernet sauvignon; merlot; cabernet franc
Region	Portland, Vic.
Cellar	⊸ 2–6
Alc./Vol.	12.5%
RRP	$23.00

Crofters Cabernet Merlot

Quality	ΤΤΤΤΤ
Value	★★★★
Grapes	cabernet sauvignon; merlot
Region	Frankland River & Mount Barker, WA
Cellar	➛ 2–8
Alc./Vol.	14.0%
RRP	$23.00

In the space of a few short years this understated label from Houghton has become one to look out for. It shows how good Great Southern cabernet blends can be, and it keeps getting better.

CURRENT RELEASE 1997 Cassis liqueur and juicy blackberry aromas interwoven with finely poised French oak give this intense young red a very seductive nose. In the mouth the flavour is deep and concentrated, with true finesse and length. Classy oak balances things beautifully, and fine ripe tannins carry the long finish perfectly. A bit closed at the moment; it needs time to blossom. Good with racks of lamb.

D'Arenberg D'Arry's Original

Quality	ΤΤΤΤ𝑡
Value	★★★★★
Grapes	shiraz; grenache
Region	McLaren Vale, SA
Cellar	▮ 7+
Alc./Vol.	14.5%
RRP	$18.10

This has long been D'Arry Osborn's signature wine, and now his son Chester is making it his too. Made from shiraz and grenache in roughly equal proportions, it's a link with the McLaren Vale reds of yesteryear. Living history.

CURRENT RELEASE 1997 A good example of the D'Arenberg style. Sweet berry and plum aromas stop just short of being jammy, and earthy, composty touches add plenty of interest. The palate is ripe with red berries and savoury flavours ahead of ripe dry tannins. Serve it with braised lamb shanks.

D'Arenberg The Footbolt Shiraz

Quality	ΤΤΤΤ𝑡
Value	★★★★𝑡
Grapes	shiraz
Region	McLaren Vale, SA
Cellar	▮ 7+
Alc./Vol.	14.0%
RRP	$18.10

D'Arenberg reds are very traditional styles. Sometimes this means they stray a bit too far on to the earthy, rustic side of things. When it doesn't, this Old Vine Shiraz is a friendly old thing to have around.

CURRENT RELEASE 1997 This has that honest warmth that's so satisfying in good D'Arenberg red wines. The nose has earthy blackberry and raspberry aromas with a savoury touch of spice. The palate is powerful and earthy with real depth of flavour, smooth texture and firm dry tannins. A good red for steak and kidney pudding.

D'Arenberg Twenty-Eight Road Mourvèdre

Unblended mourvèdre is a rarity: usually it can't stand hanging around without its pals, grenache and shiraz. But coaxed out of the shadows it can be a fascinating savoury drop.

CURRENT RELEASE 1997   This is a rather four-square, rustic red of real power. The bouquet has blackberry, dissolved minerals, earth and old oak. In the mouth it has a gamy touch to the dark berry fruit, and the chewy, grainy texture of mourvèdre is very appealing. Firm, ripe tannins finish things off perfectly. A good wine for cotechino and lentils.

Quality	ŸŸŸŸ?
Value	★★★★★
Grapes	mourvèdre
Region	McLaren Vale, SA
Cellar	⬤ 1–10
Alc./Vol.	14.0%
RRP	$21.30

Dalfarras Cabernet Sauvignon

This is unusually old for a current-release red, but then it would probably have been formidable any younger. It's tough enough at eight years of age!

CURRENT RELEASE 1991   This is very oaky and very astringent. There are charred-wood and vanilla aromas and the palate is hard, grippy and oaky-tasting. There's a suspicion of greenness in the wine. Better with food than solo, so serve it with a hearty casserole.

Quality	ŸŸŸ?
Value	★★★
Grapes	cabernet sauvignon
Region	Coonawarra, SA; Goulburn Valley, Vic.
Cellar	▮ 5
Alc./Vol.	13.0%
RRP	$21.30 ▮

Dalwhinnie Moonambel Cabernet

The relationship of the Jones family of Dalwhinnie and Don Lewis of Mitchelton, who makes the wines, has been an outstanding success if the wines are anything to go by.

Previous outstanding vintages: '80, '84, '86, '88, '90, '93, '94, '95

CURRENT RELEASE 1997   This is a big bruiser! Don't buy unless you intend to cellar it for at least five years, preferably longer. It will reward 10 years, and last for 20. Dense, dark colour; closed on the nose and rather oaky now, but has the fruit to balance. Mouth-numbing tannic grip. Awesome power and concentration. A wine for the patient! When mature, serve with aged cheeses.

Quality	ŸŸŸŸŸ
Value	★★★★
Grapes	cabernet sauvignon
Region	Pyrenees, Vic.
Cellar	⬤ 5–20+
Alc./Vol.	14.0%
RRP	$43.00 ▮

Dalwhinnie Moonambel Shiraz

Quality	❦❦❦❦❦
Value	★★★★
Grapes	shiraz
Region	Pyrenees, Vic.
Cellar	� 5–20+
Alc./Vol.	14.0%
RRP	$48.00 ▊

This wine is emerging as one of the great Australian shirazes, built in a seriously structured style and capable of long-term maturation. Maker Don Lewis. Grower David Jones.

Previous outstanding vintages: '80, '85, '88, '90, '91, '92, '94, '95

CURRENT RELEASE 1997   Here's a wine to be reckoned with! It's very big and solidly built, demanding cellaring. The aromas are of sweet licorice, blackberry, cranberry and a hint of regional mint; the palate has immense depth and power. It's astringent at present, and it would be a waste to open a bottle now. Cellar it, then serve with aged cheddar.

Darling Park Merlot

Quality	❦❦❦❦
Value	★★★
Grapes	merlot
Region	Mornington Peninsula, Vic.
Cellar	▮ 4
Alc./Vol.	13.0%
RRP	$25.00

Darling Park's label is baroque in the extreme, and depicts some sort of bacchanalian revelry.

CURRENT RELEASE 1998   This is an elegant, soft, fruity style of merlot which drinks well young. The colour is deep purple–red; the nose has blackberry and mulberry fruit aromas together with a gunpowder character from oak. The palate is well balanced and stylish, although it has no great persistence. Drink now with stir-fried beef and rice noodles.

Darling Park Pinot Noir

Quality	❦❦❦❦
Value	★★★★
Grapes	pinot noir
Region	Mornington Peninsula, Vic.
Cellar	▮ 3
Alc./Vol.	12.8%
RRP	$18.00 (cellar door)

Darling Park was established at Red Hill by John Sargeant in 1986. There are 2.7 hectares of vines. Contract winemaker Kevin McCarthy.

CURRENT RELEASE 1998   This is a pretty pinot, fruit-driven and full of youthful appeal. The colour is purple–red, and the aromas are simple cherry, grassy and fruit-driven. The palate is quite firm with some green tannins, which give it a kind of toughness on the finish. Would be better with food. Try oven-roasted squab.

David Traeger Shiraz

David Traeger used to be a winemaker at Mitchelton and still practises his art in the district. The grapes for this wine come from the Nagambie Lakes area.
CURRENT RELEASE 1996 This is an unusual wine with liberal toasty American oak showing on the nose and a rather acidic palate. For that reason it really needs to be paired with food. The nose displays spicy, cool-grown fruit as well as oak, and it's quite vibrant. The palate has a touch of astringency, and the flavours are bright and fresh. It needs time. If drinking now, have it with lamb and barley casserole.

Quality	????
Value	★★★
Grapes	shiraz
Region	Goulburn Valley, Vic.
Cellar	5
Alc./Vol.	12.5%
RRP	$21.65

Deakin Estate Cabernet Sauvignon

History doesn't record whether Prime Minister Alfred Deakin was a wine drinker, but never mind, this is very good value-for-money stuff.
CURRENT RELEASE 1998 A clean, simple, fruity wine which offers exactly what we'd want at the price. The colour is full purple–red; the aromas are sweet and suggest cherry brandy and strawberry jam. There's a lollyish overtone. The palate is light- to medium-bodied, soft and round, simple in flavour, but quite adequate. Have it with a Four 'n Twenty pie.

Quality	???
Value	★★★★
Grapes	cabernet sauvignon
Region	Murray Valley, Vic.
Cellar	2
Alc./Vol.	14.0%
RRP	$9.50 Ⓢ

Deakin Estate Merlot

When some greedy merlot makers are charging huge prices ($50 to $100+) for a single bottle, wines like this look even better value than they would otherwise. Maker Mark 'Noisy' Zeppel.
CURRENT RELEASE 1998 Medium–light purple–red colour; simple cherry/berry, fruit-driven aromas; pleasant, light, soft palate with the accent on fresh fruit. There's a hint of jamminess that's perfectly within bounds, and tannin is minimal. This wine will give joy to many. Goes with veal scaloppine.

Quality	???
Value	★★★★
Grapes	merlot
Region	Murray Valley, Vic.
Cellar	2
Alc./Vol.	13.5%
RRP	$9.50 Ⓢ

Deakin Estate Shiraz

Quality	♥♥♥◗
Value	★★★★◗
Grapes	shiraz
Region	Murray Valley, Vic.
Cellar	◗ 3
Alc./Vol.	14.5%
RRP	$9.50 Ⓢ

Deakin Estate is part of the Wingara Wine Group, which also owns Katnook in Coonawarra. Maker Mark Zeppel.
CURRENT RELEASE 1998   A good-value cheapie. The colour is full purple–red, and it has a sweet, blackcurrant fruit nose with little if any oak discernible. The palate is ripe, and there are grassy flavours. It has a lean, narrow structure, and it falls away slightly on the finish. It concludes with some astringency. Try shepherd's pie.

Devil's Lair Margaret River

Quality	♥♥♥♥
Value	★★★◗
Grapes	cabernet sauvignon; merlot; cabernet franc
Region	Margaret River, WA
Cellar	➡ 1–10+
Alc./Vol.	14.0%
RRP	$37.00

Devil's Lair is now part of the Southcorp Group, and with extra planting activity the vineyard now totals 40 hectares. Maker Janice McDonald.
CURRENT RELEASE 1996   This is a lighter, more elegant style of Margaret River cabernet, and different from the customary, richer Willyabrup style from further north. The colour is an excellent deep red–purple, and the aromas are very fresh, raw, youthful and blackcurranty. There are crushed-leaf and oak elements as well. It has elegance and youthful cassisy cabernet character, but it perhaps lacks the weight of traditional Margaret River cabernet, being medium-bodied at best. It needs a year or two before drinking. Good with steak tartare.

Diamond Valley Close Planted Pinot Noir

Quality	♥♥♥♥◗
Value	★★★
Grapes	pinot noir
Region	Yarra Valley, Vic.
Cellar	➡ 2–5+
Alc./Vol.	12.9%
RRP	$49.35

A part of the Diamond Valley vineyard is modelled according to the viticultural techniques of Burgundy, with vines planted very close together. This is said to give great intensity and character. It seems to work, although whether it's superior to the Estate White Label Pinot Noir is a moot point.
CURRENT RELEASE 1997   Serious pinot noir here. The bouquet is potent with a complex melange of dark foresty smells, dark cherries, clay and wood smoke. In the mouth it's still a bit reserved; in the manner of many pinots, it needs time to build flavour. There's a good measure of smoky, plummy fruit, but it falls away a bit at the end. Try it with saddle of hare.

Diamond Valley Vineyards Blue Label Pinot Noir

Diamond Valley's David Lance was one of the first people in the Yarra Valley to produce topnotch pinot noir. His Blue Label wines are made from grapes bought from other growers, all in the Yarra Valley.

CURRENT RELEASE 1998 This is a pleasant, lighter style of Yarra pinot. The nose has meaty, slightly animal, pinot noir characters, and the palate is lean and straightforward without a great deal of concentration. It's quite attractive to enjoy now or to keep for the short term. Drinks very well with beef carpaccio.

Quality	▼▼▼▼
Value	★★★★
Grapes	pinot noir
Region	Yarra Valley, Vic.
Cellar	▮ 3
Alc./Vol.	13.0%
RRP	$19.70

Dowie Doole Merlot

Hooley dooley – what a great name for a wine. This brand is a meeting of minds between architect Drew Dowie and ex-banker Norm Doole. Maker Brian Light (contract).

CURRENT RELEASE 1998 Only one problem: it's far too young! The colour is vivid purple; the nose is inky and undeveloped; the palate shows some youthful acid and plenty of guts, but is still in the process of becoming WINE! There are some leafy nuances, but it has plenty of substance. Cellar, then serve with lamb satays.

Quality	▼▼▼▼
Value	★★★
Grapes	merlot
Region	McLaren Vale, SA
Cellar	➛ 1–6+
Alc./Vol.	13.0%
RRP	$19.50

Drayton's Vineyard Reserve Merlot

A Hunter merlot? Why not, if you can make one as good as this – and from an ordinary vintage as well. It's Draytons' first merlot. Maker Trevor Drayton.

CURRENT RELEASE 1997 Excellent plum and cherry aromas with a hint of gunpowder. The fruit is the main event, and any oak is well in the background. Very impressive concentration, with grip and authority. Succulent ripe fruit flavours. Food: steak and kidney pie.

Quality	▼▼▼▼▼
Value	★★★★
Grapes	merlot
Region	Hunter Valley, NSW
Cellar	▮ 5
Alc./Vol.	12.5%
RRP	$23.00

Drayton's Vineyard Reserve Pokolbin Shiraz

Quality	♟♟♟♟
Value	★★★
Grapes	shiraz
Region	Hunter Valley, NSW
Cellar	▮ 5
Alc./Vol.	12.5%
RRP	$23.00 ▮

This is from Drayton Family Wines, the original and main Drayton producer. There are several Drayton outfits in the Hunter these days. Maker Trevor Drayton.

CURRENT RELEASE 1997 The '97 Hunter reds have a lot of earthy regional character, as this does. The colour is medium red, and it smells of leather and earth, with soft mellow fruit. It's an elegant wine, with plenty of grip and the acid is noticeable. Best with a meal: try it with osso bucco.

Dromana Estate Reserve Pinot Noir

Quality	♟♟♟♟♟
Value	★★★★
Grapes	pinot noir
Region	Mornington Peninsula, Vic.
Cellar	▮ 5+
Alc./Vol.	13.0%
RRP	$45.00

Garry Crittenden of Dromana Estate only bottles Reserve wines in vintages when it's warranted, which is the way it should be with all producers, but regrettably isn't.

CURRENT RELEASE 1997 A fine wine indeed, this shows uncommonly good fruit concentration. The colour is beginning to develop, and so is the bouquet – with intriguing, complex, Burgundy-like foresty, earthy, sappy and gamy nuances. Deep, rich and autumnal, it has a notable but well-balanced tannin grip, although RK-P has reservations about some bitterness he found in the wine. Goes great guns with duck cassoulet.

Dromana Estate Shiraz

Quality	♟♟♟♟
Value	★★★
Grapes	shiraz
Region	Mornington Peninsula, Vic.
Cellar	▮ 5
Alc./Vol.	13.9%
RRP	$30.00

Garry Crittenden has 5 hectares at Dromana, but also buys grapes for his other brands, Schinus and the Garry Crittenden 'I' range.

CURRENT RELEASE 1997 This is only the second vintage of Dromana shiraz, and a very creditable attempt it is. The nose is complex with Rhone-like spices and some vegetal highlights. The palate is medium-bodied, soft and gentle, with oak playing a purely supportive role. It's savoury on the palate and has its charms, although there's a little greenness in the wine. It would go well with rabbit casserole.

Elderton Cabernet Sauvignon

Elderton's cabernet sauvignon vineyard, at the northern end of the Barossa Valley, is over fifty years old. Mature vines are a prerequisite for the best wines.

CURRENT RELEASE 1997 The nose has blackberry aromas wrapped in sweet vanillin oak. In the mouth there's mocha richness and fruit flavour of lush texture, with more of Elderton's trademark toasty oak. Acidity is good, and there's a firm foundation of grippy tannins. Needs time. Try it with a thick T-bone.

Quality	♟♟♟♟
Value	★★★★
Grapes	cabernet sauvignon
Region	Barossa Valley, SA
Cellar	➡ 1–6+
Alc./Vol.	14.0%
RRP	$22.00

Elderton Command Shiraz

Once the epitome of the super-oaky butch Barossa red, Command has been going to finishing school over the last couple of vintages. It's still big and solid, but do we detect some refinement creeping in?

CURRENT RELEASE 1995 Charry oak still plays an important part in this latest edition of Elderton's flagship, but the plum and blackberry fruit stands up to it quite well. There is real concentration on the palate, which is dense, warm and long-finishing. Oaky flavour and austere tannins emphasise the need for age. Needs a powerful dish like oxtail braised in red wine.

Quality	♟♟♟♟♟
Value	★★★★
Grapes	shiraz
Region	Barossa Valley, SA
Cellar	➡ 2–8+
Alc./Vol.	14.0%
RRP	$70.00

Elderton CSM

The Elderton reds are no blushing violets: usually they have pronounced oak influence and a good whack of alcohol with some ripe fruit in there somewhere.

CURRENT RELEASE 1996 This is a full-on style with a powerful, ripe nose of deep chocolatey smells, rich dark fruit and sweet oak. In the mouth you'll find big Barossa flavour of the blackberry and charry oak type, with a good measure of grainy tannin at the end. Try it with a brawny beef hotpot.

Quality	♟♟♟♟
Value	★★★
Grapes	cabernet sauvignon; shiraz; merlot
Region	Barossa Valley, SA
Cellar	▮ 6
Alc./Vol.	14.0%
RRP	$33.50

Elderton Tantalus Red

Quality	????
Value	★★★★
Grapes	shiraz; cabernet sauvignon
Region	Barossa Valley, SA
Cellar	▲ 3
Alc./Vol.	13.0%
RRP	$12.95

Tantalus was a figure in Greek mythology. He was punished by the gods by being kept hungry and thirsty for eternity, while being tantalised by fruit and water that was just out of reach.

CURRENT RELEASE 1998 Elderton's usual powerful style takes a holiday in this well priced, appetising young red. It has a fruit-dominant, loganberry sort of nose with some sweet spice and a whisper of oak. In the mouth there's berry flavour of medium intensity with ripe tannins on a dry finish.

Element Cabernet Shiraz

Quality	????
Value	★★★★ℓ
Grapes	cabernet sauvignon; shiraz; grenache
Region	Swan Valley, WA
Cellar	▲ 3
Alc./Vol.	13.3%
RRP	$12.95

From Western Australia's Sandalford, this product is designed with younger wine drinkers in mind.

CURRENT RELEASE 1998 Young and direct, this is a nicely fashioned red with plenty of sweet berry fruit on the nose. The palate is medium-bodied and fruit-driven with easy tannins. Not a wine to fuss about – just glug it down. Serve with pasta with tomato and parmigiano.

Emerald Estate Shiraz

Quality	???ℓ
Value	★★★
Grapes	shiraz
Region	Clare Valley, SA
Cellar	▲ 3
Alc./Vol.	$13.5%
RRP	$18.00

Emerald Estate is at Stanley Flat in the Clare Valley, a relatively new name in an old area. Tim Adams, of the bone-crushing handshake, calls the shots as far as wine-making is concerned.

CURRENT RELEASE 1997 Good density of dark colour augurs well here. The nose is a warm amalgam of ripe berry fruit with some sweet caramelly oak. It's smooth on the palate due to succulent berry-fruit character. Balanced oak input and moderate dry tannins make it an easy-drinker. Good with herbed minute steaks.

Evans and Tate Gnangara Shiraz

Over twenty years ago Gnangara arrived as a rather prestigious, new-wave Swan Valley wine, at a time when most West Australian reds were regarded very dismissively. Now there's more competition, and today's lighter-styled Gnangara no longer occupies the high ground.
CURRENT RELEASE 1997   Light in colour and density. The nose is light too, an uncomplicated mix of earthy scents, berry and undergrowthy notes. The palate follows suit with shallow fruit character, simple structure and a rather hard finish.

Quality	♥♥♥
Value	★★⟨
Grapes	shiraz
Region	various, WA
Cellar	▮ 2
Alc./Vol.	13.0%
RRP	$14.95

Evans and Tate Margaret River Shiraz

Evans and Tate successfully made the transition from the hot Swan Valley to more moderate Margaret River climes. Now they are expanding into previously untried inland parts of the Margaret River district under the direction of skilled winemaker Brian Fletcher. Watch this space.
CURRENT RELEASE 1996   Dense and deeply coloured, this has very good, modern shiraz personality. The nose has concentrated black-cherry fruit, a touch of pepper and some cedar-sweet oak. A mouthful reveals clean, fleshy, dark berry flavour, attractive fruit sweetness, good oak and long, fine tannins.

Quality	♥♥♥♥⟨
Value	★★★⟨
Grapes	shiraz
Region	Margaret River, WA
Cellar	➤ 2–7
Alc./Vol.	13.5%
RRP	$40.00

Eyton on Yarra NDC Cabernet Sauvignon

N.D.C. are the initials of Eyton's late founder Newell David Cowan. The appellation is reserved for the top wines of the estate. Maker Matt Aldridge.
CURRENT RELEASE 1997   A cool customer from a warm vintage, this is a Yarra cabernet of complexity and interest. Blackberry and mulberry aromas with some spice and minty touches, and sweet oak, fill the nose. In the mouth it's quite spicy and slightly gamy, with round mouth-feel, good length and fine tannins. A good wine for slow-roasted leg of lamb.

Quality	♥♥♥♥⟨
Value	★★★
Grapes	cabernet sauvignon
Region	Yarra Valley, Vic.
Cellar	➤ 1–5
Alc./Vol.	12.7%
RRP	$40.00

Eyton Pinot Noir

Quality 🍷🍷🍷🍷
Value ★★★
Grapes pinot noir
Region Yarra Valley, Vic.
Cellar 3
Alc./Vol. 12.5%
RRP $22.00

The ambitious Eyton-on-Yarra enterprise seems to have stabilised after an erratic early period. New winemaker Matt Aldridge, from Killerby in Western Australia, is settling in nicely.

CURRENT RELEASE 1997 Pinot noir works well in the Yarra Valley, and '97 was a good year for it. This has good colour, and an attractive varietal nose of sweet blood-plum and autumnal forest-floor aromas. In the mouth there's supple pinot flavour, mellow with soft red fruits – but some stemmy bitterness intrudes on the finish at the moment. Age may be the remedy. Try this with coq au vin.

Felton Road Block 3 Pinot Noir

Quality 🍷🍷🍷🍷🍷
Value ★★★★
Grapes pinot noir
Region Central Otago, NZ
Cellar 6+
Alc./Vol. 13.5%
RRP $56.75

Aussie pinot-philes will be disturbed to see the word Bannockburn stamped on the cork! In fact it's the nearest town to the vineyard. In just two vintages, Felton has lobbed right into the New Zealand pinot elite. Maker Blair Walter.

CURRENT RELEASE 1998 This is the deluxe edition from Felton Road, and it shows more oak and a hint more stalk character than the family model. It has a dark and serious shade of red–purple, and a less evolved bouquet of meaty, gamy, earthy characters mixed with berries, stalks and hints of oak. There's tremendous fruit-sweetness on the mid-palate, and it's beautifully intense and elegant. The structure is tight and fine, and the finish has a flick of tannin. Peking duck here.

Felton Road Pinot Noir

When Burgundy guru Anthony Hanson was asked by Decanter magazine which new-world pinot impressed him most, he answered Felton Road. We can see what he was on about.

Previous outstanding vintages: '97

CURRENT RELEASE 1998 A delicious pinot showing none of the greenness that besets some from this chilly region. Full purple–red hue; smooth ripe cherry, lightly meaty bouquet with a hint of fine oak, and already some complexity. It flows smooth and seamless across the tongue, and the gamy fruit characters hold your interest till the end of the bottle. Serve with veal sweetbreads.

Quality	▼▼▼▼(
Value	★★★ꜝ
Grapes	pinot noir
Region	Central Otago, NZ
Cellar	▮ 4
Alc./Vol.	13.5%
RRP	$46.00

Fermoy Estate Cabernet Sauvignon

Fermoy is one of the quiet achievers of the area. The wines are made in a somewhat alternative style to the typical Margaret River wines, by winemaker Michael Kelly.

CURRENT RELEASE 1997 This wine emphasises secondary complexities rather than simple fruit characters. The colour is medium purple–red, and the nose has light but attractive leafy, berry aromas with some dusty cool-area herbaceousness. It develops undergrowth and straw/autumnal nuances with breathing. It shows some youthful astringency from green fruit, and finishes with marked bitterness. We wouldn't like to guess its future. Try it with braised beef cheeks.

Quality	▼▼▼(
Value	★★ꜝ
Grapes	cabernet sauvignon
Region	Margaret River, WA
Cellar	➡ 2–10+
Alc./Vol.	13.5%
RRP	$23.80

Fiddlers Creek Cabernet Shiraz

The name refers to a violinist who entertained the miners during the goldmining days in the Avoca district in the 1860s. Maker Kim Hart.

CURRENT RELEASE 1997 The colour is somewhat light, and the nose reveals some herbaceous cabernet fruit as well as raspberry aromas. A light-bodied red with some slightly green flavours and a lick of firm tannin to close. A decent quaffing red. Goes with meat loaf.

Quality	▼▼▼
Value	★★★ꜝ
Grapes	cabernet sauvignon; shiraz
Region	not stated
Cellar	▮ 2
Alc./Vol.	12.5%
RRP	$12.00 Ⓢ

Fire Gully Pinot Noir

Quality	♥♥♥♥
Value	★★★⋆
Grapes	pinot noir
Region	Margaret River, WA
Cellar	🍾 2
Alc./Vol.	13.5%
RRP	$20.50

The new Fire Gully label features Taoist symbols for 'fire' and 'valley', and looks very smart. Winemaker is Mike Peterkin of Pierro.

CURRENT RELEASE 1998   A delicious pinot with the right sort of food. It's light in every regard: pale ruby–purple in hue; fragrant strawberry/cherry in scent; and beautifully ethereal, light-bodied and fruity on the tongue. It has very soft, light tannins, and it could easily be chilled in warmer weather. Seductive stuff, and great with salmon and leek risotto.

Flanagan's Ridge Cabernet Merlot

Quality	♥♥♥⋆
Value	★★★⋆
Grapes	cabernet sauvignon; merlot
Region	Wrattonbully, SA
Cellar	➦ 1–6+
Alc./Vol.	12.5%
RRP	$16.00

Mildara was first to use the new name Wrattonbully on a wine, with this new brand. It originally read 'Koppamurra', but it was lawyers at 50 paces, and fancy footwork followed.

CURRENT RELEASE 1996   This is good! They always said Koppamurra/Wrattonbully would produce excellent reds. It has good colour, a typical cabernet nose of berries, crushed leaves and oak, and the tannins are a tad rough at this juncture. Give it a year and it should soften further. It drinks well with pink roast lamb.

Flanagan's Ridge Wrattonbully Shiraz

Quality	♥♥♥♥⋆
Value	★★★★★
Grapes	shiraz; cabernet sauvignon
Region	Wrattonbully, SA
Cellar	🍾 6+
Alc./Vol.	12.5%
RRP	$16.00 🍾

Wrattonbully has been hailed as the new Coonawarra. The soil is just as good, the climate is almost identical, and the price of land is much, much cheaper.

CURRENT RELEASE 1996   This is a wine of contrasts. The aromas are of spices, berries and crushed leaves, plus a hint of Ribena; it's reminiscent of cabernet. The sweet oak adds coffee and vanilla highlights. There's a heap of flavour on the sweetly attractive middle palate, as well as smooth tannins. It has length and elegance. There's just a hint of greenness, which adds a trace of hardness to the finish. It drinks well with lamb shanks.

The Fleurieu Shiraz

Four wineries clubbed together to produce this regional wine as a fund-raiser for the McLaren Vale and Fleurieu Visitor Centre: BRL Hardy, Brian Light, Haselgrove and Woodstock.

Previous outstanding vintages: '94

CURRENT RELEASE 1995 This is a beautiful big red, and all the more so because they didn't hit it with too much oak (probably by accident: they were saving money!). Fruit holds centre-stage. It's a dense, fleshy, full-bodied and quite tannic red, which tastes of fruit-cake and berries with typical regional earthiness. It really fills the mouth. A humdinger. Try it with rump steak.

Quality	♟♟♟♟♟
Value	★★★★★
Grapes	shiraz
Region	McLaren Vale, SA
Cellar	🍶 15
Alc./Vol.	13.5%
RRP	$27.55 🍷

Fox River Pinot Noir

For a 'second label' or sous-marque, Fox River is certainly not second-rate wine. This is Exhibit A. It comes from the Goundrey bunker.

CURRENT RELEASE 1998 Sweet, properly ripe, floral pinot fruit is the hallmark. It's clean and fruit-accented, with a seductively slinky pinot texture and wild berry flavour. The oak is subtle. A fine wine to have with tuna carpaccio.

Quality	♟♟♟♟
Value	★★★★
Grapes	pinot noir
Region	Great Southern, WA
Cellar	🍶 3
Alc./Vol.	13.0%
RRP	$18.40

Frankland Estate Olmo's Reward

Olmo's Reward is not a racehorse but the name given to a Bordeaux blend, in recognition of American viticulturist Harold Olmo, who was instrumental in vines being first planted in south-west Western Australia.

CURRENT RELEASE 1995 This is a heavily structured red which emphasises savoury, secondary characters rather than primary fruit. The colour is medium–full red–purple, and it has a lot of viscosity in the glass. The bouquet is subdued and possibly slightly oxidised, but quite complex. It's big and tannic; the palate is strongly structured with a firm grip. It would cellar well, and needs strong food. Try it with rib of beef.

Quality	♟♟♟♟
Value	★★★⊩
Grapes	cabernet franc; merlot; cabernet sauvignon; malbec; petit verdot
Region	Great Southern, WA
Cellar	⊷ 2–6+
Alc./Vol.	14.0%
RRP	$29.50 🍷

Galah Wine Cabernet Sauvignon

Quality	♟♟♟♟
Value	★★★★
Grapes	cabernet sauvignon
Region	Clare Valley, SA
Cellar	➡ 2–6
Alc./Vol.	14.5%
RRP	$20.00 (mailing list) 🍾

Galah wines are well-kept secrets, sold only via a mailing list, and never mentioning the source of the fruit they're made from. Since maker Stephen George consults to the famous Wendouree estate at Clare, you don't have to be a genius to work out where some of it is sourced.

CURRENT RELEASE 1997 This is a potent, old-fashioned red which tastes as though it has dissolved minerals in it. It has a complex bouquet of spicy blackcurrant fruit with earthy, tarry, pebbley notes, a hint of mint and subtle oak. The palate is slightly rustic, powered by essency blackberry fruit with mouth-drying grippy tannins to finish things off. Try it with cotechino and lentils.

Galah Wine Shiraz

Quality	♟♟♟♟♟
Value	★★★★
Grapes	shiraz
Region	Clare Valley, SA
Cellar	➡ 2–10
Alc./Vol.	14.0%
RRP	$20.00 (mailing list) 🍾

Stephen George's links with Wendouree are readily apparent in the type of shiraz he makes under his Galah Wine label.

CURRENT RELEASE 1997 A shiraz made in a timeless style that could be called modern traditional – the time-honoured goodies are there with none of the draw-backs. The nose is reserved yet complex, with dark cherry fruit in the middle surrounded by licorice, spice, clean-earth and meaty touches. Oak is restrained. The palate is very concentrated and solid with black-cherry/minerally fruit, a cedary touch, firm, tight structure and ripe dry tannins. Try it with an aged porterhouse.

Garden Gully Grenache

The two owners of Garden Gully should know a bit about the Great Western district, having both worked in the area for many years. A sparkling red heads the range and the table wines are typically full-flavoured.

CURRENT RELEASE 1997 This grenache has sweetish red-berry fruit aromas along with some peppery spice and gamy touches. The palate has ripe fruit and spice, and good depth of berry flavour which sits in nice balance with rather soft tannins. A red of easy drink-ability which would accompany hearty dishes, like steak and kidney pie, well.

Quality	♟♟♟♟
Value	★★★★
Grapes	grenache
Region	Great Western, Vic.
Cellar	🍷 3
Alc./Vol.	14.5%
RRP	$18.00

Garry Crittenden 'I' Barbera

Garry Crittenden's recycling bin is always full of Italian wine bottles: it's his passion, so it's not surprising that he leads the way with Australian wines made from Italian grape varieties.

CURRENT RELEASE 1997 Tired of conventional wine fare? Jaded by a diet of Aussie red? Help is at hand, courtesy of Garry Crittenden. This is a super young wine with an intriguing Italianate bouquet which is savoury and more-ish. It has cherry, dried plum and earthy aromas, and ripe concentration on the tightly structured palate. Lively acidity leaves a fresh, appetising impression. Try it with saltimbocca alla romana.

Quality	♟♟♟♟♟
Value	★★★★★
Grapes	barbera
Region	King Valley, Vic.
Cellar	🍷 2
Alc./Vol.	13.5%
RRP	$20.00

Garry Crittenden 'I' Dolcetto

Dolcetto is the early-ripening red grape of Piedmont in northern Italy. It gives the local wine fraternity something to guzzle while they're waiting for their formidable nebbiolos to mature. Here, in Garry Crittenden's hands, it makes a similarly gulpable young red, which is all too easy to drink.

CURRENT RELEASE 1998 Another typically varietal 'I' red with a nose of cherry, spice and minerals. The palate is tight and lively with intense, but not sweet, cherry and licorice flavour, medium body and a very dry firm finish. Goes well with pappardelle and chicken livers.

Quality	♟♟♟♟♟
Value	★★★★
Grapes	dolcetto
Region	King Valley & Great Western, Vic.
Cellar	🍷 2
Alc./Vol.	13.5%
RRP	$20.00

Garry Crittenden 'I' Nebbiolo

Quality ΨΨΨΨ
Value ★★★★
Grapes nebbiolo
Region King Valley, Vic.
Cellar 1–6+
Alc./Vol. 14.0%
RRP $20.00

In its northern Italian home nebbiolo is famous for its strong personality and longevity. Garry Crittenden's versions paint the same picture in the Antipodes.

CURRENT RELEASE 1997 Don't let nebbiolo's pale colour deceive you: it's potent, serious red wine. Here the bouquet is powerful with a nose of tar, mocha, dark fruit and spice. The palate is dry and unyielding with a densely textured savoury core, brisk acidity, and a very solid wall of tannins at the end. Age will do it no harm at all. Serve it with something suitably robust – maybe lamb shanks braised in red wine.

Garry Crittenden 'I' Sangiovese

Quality ΨΨΨΨ
Value ★★★★
Grapes sangiovese
Region King Valley, Vic.
Cellar 3
Alc./Vol. 13.0%
RRP $20.00

Garry Crittenden's 'I' range of Italian varietals get a more authentically Italian feel with every vintage. Sangiovese is the chianti red grape. It takes a little assimilation to get the hang of what these grapes are all about, but persevere and you'll be richly rewarded.

CURRENT RELEASE 1998 This has copybook sangiovese varietal aromas of dark cherry, earth, nuts and tobacco . . . all very mysterious really. In the mouth it's dry, savoury and chewy with a grippy finish. Initially the fruit flavour is subdued, but it lingers more-ishly. A bottle once opened disappears with amazing speed. Needs the right food to be at its best. Drink it with baked cannelloni.

Geoff Merrill Cabernet Merlot

This is a multi-regional blend, reflecting the links Geoff Merrill has with other areas, in particular with Alister Purbrick of Chateau Tahbilk.

CURRENT RELEASE 1996   The Geoff Merrill reds have gained a bit in alcohol in recent years, but that hasn't necessarily meant a corresponding increase in apparent body for this cabernet blend. It's a leaner style, with redcurrant, vanilla and leafy aromas. In the mouth it has light medium-weight, a touch of mint, some coconutty oak and a dry finish. Try it with a cheesy pizza.

Quality	♟♟♟?
Value	★★★
Grapes	cabernet sauvignon; merlot; cabernet franc
Region	McLaren Vale & Coonawarra, SA; Goulburn Valley, Vic.
Cellar	▮ 3
Alc./Vol.	13.0%
RRP	$16.00

CURRENT RELEASE 1997   An internationally styled red with attractive berry and subdued sweet oak notes on the nose. The palate is round, soft and well balanced with a slightly rustic touch to it. A good match for roast lamb, slow-roasted like Mum used to.

Quality	♟♟♟♟
Value	★★★⭒
Grapes	cabernet sauvignon; merlot; cabernet franc
Region	McLaren Vale & Coonawarra, SA; Goulburn Valley, Vic.
Cellar	▮ 5
Alc./Vol.	13.0%
RRP	$19.75

Geoff Merrill Shiraz

Recent vintages of Geoff Merrill wines have seen them take on a riper, more generous personality, which fits regional style well.

CURRENT RELEASE 1997   A well made commercial style of shiraz that should be a crowd-pleaser. It has clean sweet berry, plum, and vanillin oak aromas and flavours. The palate is medium-weight, smooth and balanced. It's a good match for grilled lamb steaks.

Quality	♟♟♟♟
Value	★★★⭒
Grapes	shiraz
Region	McLaren Vale, SA; Goulburn Valley, Vic.
Cellar	▮ 4
Alc./Vol.	13.5%
RRP	$19.75

Giaconda Cabernet

Quality	ΨΨΨΨ℩
Value	★★★⋆
Grapes	cabernet sauvignon; cabernet franc; merlot
Region	Beechworth, Vic.
Cellar	▮ 4
Alc./Vol.	13.0%
RRP	$40.00

Rick Kinzbrunner's pinot noir and chardonnay get the accolades. So much so that a lot of people probably don't realise that there's a third Giaconda wine, a cabernet blend. This is the quiet achiever of the stable and it can be very good.

CURRENT RELEASE 1996   The nose has cassis, plum and cedary aromas in classical style. The middleweight palate offers a combination of supple black-fruit flavours and subtle, fragrant wood. It's not a blockbuster, relying on finesse and good underlying structure rather than sheer power. It should develop well medium-term and will be a good companion to pink-roasted racks of lamb.

Giaconda Pinot Noir

Quality	ΨΨΨΨΨ
Value	★★★⋆
Grapes	pinot noir
Region	Beechworth, Vic.
Cellar	▮ 4+
Alc./Vol.	13.5%
RRP	$55.00

Rick Kinzbrunner's Giaconda wines have a cult following which makes them as rare as hens' teeth. If you're lucky enough to get your hands on some, you're in for a treat.

CURRENT RELEASE 1997   This has a fascinating, fragrant bouquet and flavour, where fruit character melds into exotic, multi-faceted complexity. Gamy richness, succulence, foresty smells, intense plummy fruit – it's all there. The flavour is marvellously persistent; the mouthfeel is velvety and intense, yet by no means heavy. An excellent Giaconda pinot.

Gilberts Mount Barker Shiraz

Quality	ΨΨΨΨ
Value	★★★⋆
Grapes	shiraz
Region	Mount Barker, WA
Cellar	▮ 5
Alc./Vol.	14.5%
RRP	$25.00

Mount Barker shiraz is cast in a lighter, more elegant mould than traditional Aussie shiraz. Those who like their reds to be big, hairy-knuckled brutes should look elsewhere.

CURRENT RELEASE 1997   The Great Southern style of typically cool-climate shiraz is well illustrated in Gilberts' latest. The nose has dark cherry character and a fair smack of smoky, peppery spice. There are also some savoury/leafy tones; but it's far from unripe, with plenty of spicy-sweet cherry fruit mid-palate and a fine signature of ripe, soft tannins.

Goundrey Reserve Cabernet Sauvignon

Although wine was grown in a small way in the Mount Barker region in the second half of the nineteenth century, its potential was first officially recognised in 1955. The first commercial vineyard was established in 1966, and today it's a big business.

CURRENT RELEASE 1996 This is a rich wine featuring an admirably smooth marriage between deep fruit character of medium ripeness and toasty oak. The nose and palate have cassis, briar, leaf and earthy/gamy touches with a lick of savoury wood. The flavour is satisfying and long, with lively acidity and fine tannins.

Quality	▼▼▼▼
Value	★★★★
Grapes	cabernet sauvignon
Region	Lower Great Southern, WA
Cellar	5
Alc./Vol.	13.0%
RRP	$28.95

Goundrey Reserve Shiraz

The Great Southern region of Western Australia produces very good shiraz, a fact sometimes overlooked by shiraz fans in the eastern states. Goundrey can be one of the best.

CURRENT RELEASE 1997 A very spicy, modern shiraz. The nose has strong pepper, blackberry and black-cherry aromas, and well-handled cedary oak. The palate is savoury and a bit severe at the moment, with dry, spicy, cool-climate shiraz flavours of good intensity. Fine tannins finish things off well. Serve it with a rare fillet steak.

Quality	▼▼▼▼
Value	★★★
Grapes	shiraz
Region	Lower Great Southern, WA
Cellar	1–5+
Alc./Vol.	14.0%
RRP	$25.95

Gramp's Cabernet Merlot

In 1847 Johann Gramp planted his first vineyard in the Barossa. The enterprise he founded grew into Orlando, but the Gramp name lives on as an Orlando brand.

CURRENT RELEASE 1996 A straightforward cabernet without great complexity, this has a bouquet of plum and balanced oak. The palate is rather simple. Direct berry flavour, some spicy oak and medium tannins are the formula, and while there's not much wrong with it, real excitement is on hold. Try it with hamburgers.

Quality	▼▼▼
Value	★★★
Grapes	cabernet sauvignon; merlot
Region	various, SA
Cellar	2
Alc./Vol.	13.5%
RRP	$16.50

Grant Burge Cameron Vale Cabernet Sauvignon

Quality	ᵀᵀᵀᵖ
Value	★★★ᵏ
Grapes	cabernet sauvignon
Region	Barossa Valley, SA
Cellar	▮ 3
Alc./Vol.	14.0%
RRP	$19.75

The Grant Burge red style is all about generosity of flavour. This makes the wines good each-way bets: easy to drink young and ageworthy too.

CURRENT RELEASE 1997 This doesn't have quite the impact of other reds in the Grant Burge stable. There's a sweet blackberry and cassis nose, and a straightforward palate of moderate richness with balanced oak and fine tannins. It's good, but it's not a thriller. Try it with a mixed grill.

Grant Burge Filsell Shiraz

Quality	ᵀᵀᵀᵀ
Value	★★★★
Grapes	shiraz
Region	Barossa Valley, SA
Cellar	▮ 5
Alc./Vol.	14.0%
RRP	$22.20

Grant Burge's Filsell vineyard is an 80-year-old block near Lyndoch in the Barossa, one of several named plots owned by Grant and Helen Burge.

CURRENT RELEASE 1997 Very Barossa Shiraz in the ripe, American-oaked vein. The nose has sweet vanilla and coconut touches to the fore, but ripe blackberry and spice aromas are hidden in there too. It tastes smooth and mouth-filling, with a big dollop of fruit-sweet plummy flavour in the middle of that dose of timber. A good red for a steak and kidney pie.

Grant Burge The Holy Trinity

Quality	ᵀᵀᵀᵀ
Value	★★★ᵏ
Grapes	grenache; shiraz; mourvèdre
Region	Barossa Valley, SA
Cellar	▮ 3+
Alc./Vol.	14.0%
RRP	$29.70

Called The Holy Trinity for all sorts of convoluted reasons, some of which are detailed on the back of the custom-designed bottle. Needless to say it's a blend of three grape varieties, all native to the Rhone in France, but the wine speaks with a definite Aussie accent.

CURRENT RELEASE 1996 A good wine with some blackberry and raspberry intensity, but less oak aroma and flavour might have made it even better. Not that it's over-oaked, but these Rhone blends are essentially savoury wines that are better standing mainly on their fruit. The palate has a pleasant softness and ripeness, and moderate tannins make it an easy proposition in its youth. Serve it with beef olives.

Greenock Creek Cabernet Sauvignon

At Greenock Creek they believe in taking advantage of all that Barossa sunshine to create red wines of massive proportions. Delicate they ain't, but if you like body-slammers they might be for you.

CURRENT RELEASE 1996 This isn't quite as big as some Greenock Creek wines, but it's not Beaujolais either! The nose has slightly reductive jammy fruit with some olive aromas and almost a touch of creosote. The palate is tight and ungiving with black-fruit flavours and lean astringent tannins. Could work with spaghetti with parmigiano, garlic and virgin olive oil.

Quality	ŸŸŸ℔
Value	★★★ｋ
Grapes	cabernet sauvignon
Region	Barossa Valley, SA
Cellar	➥ 1–5
Alc./Vol.	13.9%
RRP	$25.00

Green Point Pinot Noir

These table wines from Domaine Chandon don't command the same attention as the fizzy ones, but they are steadily improving. Maker Wayne Donaldson.

CURRENT RELEASE 1998 This is an easy wine to gulp down for its cherry-like fruit, but there's also some delicate complexity to keep things interesting. Autumn-garden aromas and some subtle savoury spice add interest, and although it's not a big wine it finishes soft and long. A good match for mirin marinated quail, boned and cooked on the grill.

Quality	ŸŸŸŸ
Value	★★★★
Grapes	pinot noir
Region	Yarra Valley, Vic.
Cellar	▮ 3
Alc./Vol.	14.0%
RRP	$22.00

The Green Vineyards Shiraz

This operation was a hobby that grew like Topsy. It produces cool-climate wines from a variety of sources in southern Victoria. Maker Sergio Carlei.

CURRENT RELEASE 1996 This is at the leaner end of the shiraz scale, a wine to make big Barossa red lovers wince, but it's well made and interesting. The nose has white pepper, cherry and gentle oak aromas. The palate doesn't have the power we usually associate with Heathcote wines, and it's just a whisker short, but it does have pleasantly spicy berry flavours and soft tannins. Worth trying with a spicy antipasto of mixed meats.

Quality	ŸŸŸ℔
Value	★★★
Grapes	shiraz
Region	Heathcote, Vic.
Cellar	▮ 2
Alc./Vol.	13.0%
RRP	$27.00

Gulf Station Cabernet Sauvignon

Quality	♀♀♀↑
Value	★★★
Grapes	cabernet sauvignon
Region	Yarra Valley, Vic.
Cellar	▮ 3
Alc./Vol.	13.0%
RRP	$16.00

This De Bortoli label maintains a quite separate identity. Gulf Station is actually a 150-year-old homestead and property near Yarra Glen. Its link with these wines is tenuous to say the least.

CURRENT RELEASE 1997   This has an intense cassis and herbaceous nose with fruit dominating some slightly raw oak. In the mouth it's medium-bodied with simple flavours of black fruit and dry oak. Tannins are moderate. A cabernet that doesn't need much ageing. Serve it with grilled bratwurst.

Haan Prestige Merlot

Quality	♀♀♀♀
Value	★★★
Grapes	merlot 87%;
	cabernet sauvignon
	13%
Region	Barossa Valley, SA
Cellar	▮ 6+
Alc./Vol.	14.2%
RRP	$35.00 ▮

The vineyard is in the Siegersdorf locality of the Barossa, also known as Dorrien. The wine was aged in a mix of new French and older barrels, some shaved.

CURRENT RELEASE 1996   There are cedary, toasty and almost rancio characters from oak and abundant wood maturation. The palate has a great deal of sweetness from very ripe grapes plus vanillin oak. There are some dark chocolate flavours too. A popular style; teams well with roasted, liver-stuffed quails.

Hamilton Gumpers Block Shiraz

Quality	♀♀♀↑
Value	★★★
Grapes	shiraz
Region	McLaren Vale, SA
Cellar	▮ 8
Alc./Vol.	13.3%
RRP	$20.00 Ⓢ

The number of wines appearing under the Hamilton label in recent times seems to have snowballed. The wines rarely hit the heights they used to and we wonder if the resources are being stretched a little.

CURRENT RELEASE 1997   This is a very youthful wine with simplistic grassy, herbal fruit aromas, and a toasty oak embellishment that sits slightly apart from the wine. The palate is dry, slightly austere and lacks a little charm, although it has no faults either. It has the structure to handle a robust beef casserole.

Hamilton Hut Block Cabernet

Richard Hamilton's wine company is gearing up for major expansions. He's not alone: every second winery in Australia has been seduced by the boom.

CURRENT RELEASE 1997 There's a greenish stalky aroma together with blackcurrant and sundry berries. The tannins are firm and border on tough, while the palate is medium-bodied and quite elegant, with a long follow-through. It could do justice to a T-bone steak.

Quality	🍷🍷🍷🍷
Value	★★★½
Grapes	cabernet sauvignon
Region	McLaren Vale, SA
Cellar	1–7+
Alc./Vol.	13.5%
RRP	$21.65 (S)

Hamilton The Hills Pinot Noir

The (Richard) Hamilton group is a rapidly growing concern, with well-made wines covering pretty well all the bases.

CURRENT RELEASE 1998 The colour is deep and purplish, suggesting it's been carefully protected from the air during winemaking. The nose is simple but pleasant cherry/strawberry with a hint of sap. The oak is well in the background. It's a clean, straightforward wine that won't move the earth. Serve with beef carpaccio, capers, shaved parmesan and olive oil.

Quality	🍷🍷🍷½
Value	★★★
Grapes	pinot noir
Region	Adelaide Hills, SA
Cellar	3
Alc./Vol.	12.0%
RRP	$24.60

Hanging Rock Heathcote Shiraz

This is consistently John Ellis's best table wine. The fruit is sourced from the Heathcote area, which is much warmer than Macedon and therefore more reliable for ripening shiraz.

CURRENT RELEASE 1997 What a lovely big lump of a wine. It's very deep, ripe and friendly. The colour is a dense purple–red, and the bouquet provides almond, plum and spice aromas with well-integrated toasty oak and a hint of hung game. There are lashings of fruit on the tongue and it really satisfies. Drink with blanquette de veau.

Quality	🍷🍷🍷🍷🍷
Value	★★★½
Grapes	shiraz
Region	Heathcote, Vic.
Cellar	12+
Alc./Vol.	13.5%
RRP	$42.40

Hanging Rock Winery 'Rock' Shiraz Grenache Pinot Noir

Quality	▼▼▼⁄
Value	★★★⁄
Grapes	shiraz; grenache; pinot noir
Region	not stated
Cellar	▮ 2
Alc./Vol.	12.0%
RRP	$13.60

This is John Ellis's cheap and cheerful blended wine from all over the place. It has no pretensions to greatness but is all about value.

CURRENT RELEASE 1998 It has a vibrant, light purple–red colour, and the sweet strawberry aroma of pinot noir comes through clearly on the nose. It's fresh and clean, and has plenty of charm. Don't expect a full-bodied red: this is light-bodied, reflecting the grenache and pinot noir content. The finish is nevertheless quite firm and tight with some attractive tannin drying the aftertaste. Good with pressed tongue.

Happs Merlot

Quality	▼▼▼
Value	★★⁄
Grapes	merlot
Region	Margaret River, WA
Cellar	▮ 4
Alc./Vol.	14.0%
RRP	$33.00 ▮

Erl Happ is a potter turned winemaker. He's very intense about his viticulture, putting a lot of effort into his trellising and canopy systems.

CURRENT RELEASE 1997 This is a big, brawny merlot with plenty of guts and a serious, tannic structure. But there's a meaty character that detracts from the bouquet and provides a bitterness on the finish. A pity, because the fruit is undoubtedly first class. Try it with game pie.

Hardys Eileen Hardy Shiraz

Quality	▼▼▼▼▼
Value	★★★⁄
Grapes	shiraz
Region	McLaren Vale & Padthaway, SA
Cellar	➟ 5–15+
Alc./Vol.	14.5%
RRP	$65.00 ▮

If you equate bigness with quality, you'll love this. It would be vinfanticide to drink it within six years. Maker Stephen Pannell.

Previous outstanding vintages: '70, '71, '75, '76, '79, '81, '82, '86, '87, '88, '90, '91, '93, '94, '95

CURRENT RELEASE 1996 Ugh! This is a case of the ol' iron fist in a velvet glove. It's very raw and concentrated and needs time. The colour is almost black, and it smells of plums and skins and iron tonic. It's too raw and astringent to drink, and the swatches of tannin have the one redeeming feature of being balanced by masses of fruit flavour. It will be superb when mature. Cellar, then drink it with strong food, such as aged hard cheeses.

Hardys Tintara Grenache

Tintara is an old brand name that Hardys recently revived. It dates back to the days of pioneer McLaren Vale winemaker Dr A.C. Kelly. The grapes are from old, dry-grown vines, open-fermented, basket-pressed and aged in French oak.

Previous outstanding vintages: '96

CURRENT RELEASE 1997 This is a wine of character; it has a certain old-world charm. There are charred-oak and meaty aromas that give way to mixed-spice and pepper scents with airing. It has lively, intense flavour, a lean profile and a tight tannin finish. One of the more serious grenaches on the market. Great with game pie.

Quality	▼▼▼▼▼
Value	★★★★
Grapes	grenache
Region	McLaren Vale, SA
Cellar	▮ 10
Alc./Vol.	14.5%
RRP	$25.00 ▮

Hardys Tintara Shiraz

What a wonderful job the BRL Hardy people have done in resurrecting the old etched-glass Tintara inscription and putting it on a thoroughly stylish, shapely bottle. Maker Steve Pannell.

Previous outstanding vintages: '95

CURRENT RELEASE 1996 A dense, chunky wine with deep colour, flavours of coffee, charred oak, vanillin and ripe plum. The palate has loads of tannin, fruit-sweetness and extract. It's a profound, lush red that's lovely now, but that will be at its best in six to eight years. It's as good as some wines twice its price. Serve with rare steak.

Quality	▼▼▼▼▼
Value	★★★★★
Grapes	shiraz
Region	McLaren Vale, SA
Cellar	▬ 2–20
Alc./Vol.	14.5%
RRP	$27.00 ▮

CURRENT RELEASE 1997 This is comfort food. Old-fashioned blackberry style with very ripe fruit and quite a lot of wood. There are cedar and rancio-like oak-aged characters. Ultra-ripe sweet fruit on the tongue does mortal combat with mouth-puckering tannins. A fabulous wine, only slightly less majestic than the Eileen and half the price. Cellar, then serve with marinated buffalo fillet.

Quality	▼▼▼▼▼
Value	★★★★★
Grapes	shiraz
Region	McLaren Vale, SA
Cellar	▬ 3–15+
Alc./Vol.	14.5%
RRP	$28.50 ▮

Haselgrove Grenache

Quality 🍷🍷🍷½
Value ★★★
Grapes grenache
Region McLaren Vale, SA
Cellar 🍾 3
Alc./Vol. 15.0%
RRP $16.00 (S)

Grenache has become a strong niche item in the drink-now wine market. It's rarely wood-aged, and is very soft and low in tannin but big on sweet ripe flavours; therefore it can be sold young. Maker Nick Haselgrove.

CURRENT RELEASE 1998 This has the typical very sweet ripe-fruit aromas and high alcohol commonly seen in this grape variety. There are some slightly feral, meaty characters, and jammy, hot-area, ultra-ripe fruit aromas. The palate has good sweet ripe flavours and finishes with some astringency from tannin and alcohol, which is on the high side and which gives a rather hot finish. It lacks a bit of finesse, but goes well with devilled kidneys.

Haselgrove H Reserve Shiraz

Quality 🍷🍷🍷🍷½
Value ★★★½
Grapes shiraz
Region McLaren Vale, SA
Cellar 🍾 12+
Alc./Vol. 14.0%
RRP $37.00 🍾

The black label with the big H is the reserve bottling of this increasingly impressive winery.

Previous outstanding vintages: '96

CURRENT RELEASE 1997 This is an exuberant, over-the-top shiraz packed with jammy, overripe fruit and oak vanilla. It's floral and almost spirity to smell, with more than a passing resemblance to vintage port. A sumptuous wine with plenty of tannin giving a dry, savoury finish. Drink it with parmesan cheese.

Haselgrove Merlot

Quality 🍷🍷🍷🍷
Value ★★★★
Grapes merlot
Region McLaren Vale, SA
Cellar 🍾 1–5+
Alc./Vol. 13.5%
RRP $19.00 (S)

Winemaker Nick Haselgrove is a member of a famous McLaren Vale family. His antecedents include Colin (of Chateau Reynella) and Ronald (of Mildara), both legends in their lifetimes.

CURRENT RELEASE 1998 This McLaren Vale merlot is a tad immature, but what potential! Dense purple hue, raw blackberry and coconut aromas, richly concentrated, stacks of fruit. Just needs time, and then should turn out a beauty. Try it with a thick, juicy rump steak.

Heathcote Winery Mail Coach Shiraz

They're making 'em big down at Heathcote! Could Heathcote be the new McLaren Vale? Maker Mark Kelly.

CURRENT RELEASE 1997 Drought-year concentration shows in this stroppy, raw, aggro infant. The aromas remind of gumleaf and iron tonic. The acid and tannin levels result in a burst of astringency, and it's not ready to drink by a long shot. Cellar, then have it with steak and kidney pie.

Quality	▽▽▽▽
Value	★★★ʳ
Grapes	shiraz
Region	Heathcote, Vic.
Cellar	➟ 3–10+
Alc./Vol.	13.9%
RRP	$21.30

Heathcote Winery Seventh Horse Shiraz

This is the cheapest of Heathcote's reds; nevertheless the '97 managed a trophy at the Adelaide Show. Winemaker Mark Kelly says he dare not change it too much!
Previous outstanding vintages: '97

CURRENT RELEASE 1998 Warning: this was tasted as a barrel sample, and not the finished wine. The sample we saw showed great promise, with a blackish density of colour, an oaky caramel–vanilla aroma and lots of extract and concentration on the palate. It's very raw and unready, but all the early signs are good.

Quality	▽▽▽▽
Value	★★★★
Grapes	shiraz; cabernet sauvignon
Region	Padthaway, SA 60%; Heathcote, Vic. 40%
Cellar	➟ 2–6+
Alc./Vol.	14.0%
RRP	$14.80

Heggies Merlot

Mr Heggie was the previous owner of the land on which Yalumba planted this vineyard. The various wines have been in search of a style for years, but they are on the improve nowadays. Maker Simon Adams.

CURRENT RELEASE 1995 It's older than most reds on the market, but the oak still dominates. It smells of toasted wood and singed coconuts. It tastes better than it smells, and is rich and well concentrated, with plenty of grainy, rustic tannin. The finish is very dry. Serve with a hearty casserole.

Quality	▽▽▽▽
Value	★★★
Grapes	merlot
Region	Eden Valley, SA
Cellar	▮ 5+
Alc./Vol.	12.5%
RRP	$23.00 ▮

Heggies Pinot Noir

Quality	ＹＹＹＹＹ
Value	★★★★★
Grapes	pinot noir
Region	Eden Valley, SA
Cellar	▮ 5+
Alc./Vol.	13.5%
RRP	$23.00 ▮

Those who judge books by their covers will be impressed by the heavyweight bottle – it weighs a tonne! Don't drop it on your toe. Maker Simon Adams.

CURRENT RELEASE 1997   Big bottle, big wine. This is very complex and, dare we use that overworked description, Burgundian? It has a distinct raisined fruit character together with undergrowth, stalk, jam and assertive oak nuances. The taste is smooth, complex and layered; rich and balanced. Very impressive stuff. Improves with breathing, and goes well with roast pigeon in demiglaze.

Henschke Cyril Henschke

Quality	ＹＹＹＹＹ
Value	★★★ｒ
Grapes	cabernet sauvignon 70%; merlot 16%; cabernet franc 14%
Region	Eden Valley, SA
Cellar	▮ 10+
Alc./Vol.	13.5%
RRP	$76.00 ▮

Cyril Henschke was a remarkable chap. He had the foresight to single out the Hill of Grace vineyard and not only to bottle it separately from 1958 onwards, but also to call the wine simply Hill of Grace, thereby anticipating today's marketing by 40 years.

Previous outstanding vintages: '86, '87, '88, '90, '91, '92, '93, '94

CURRENT RELEASE 1995   Serious cabernet! The nose has lots of wood, but also blackberry and plum fruit, and the result is a very complex bouquet with earth and mint and berries. A rich, fleshy wine in the mouth, it has marvellous length and balance. Enjoy with seared lamb fillet.

Henschke Hill of Grace

No thanks to a rare hailstorm, there's very little of the '93 vintage of Australia's second-most-famous wine. We mention it for the record. Hill of Grace's 40th vintage was celebrated in 1998.

Previous outstanding vintages: '82, '84, '86, '88, '90, '91, '92

CURRENT RELEASE 1993 The reduced yields can be seen in the incredible concentration of this vintage. The cooler ripening conditions are apparent in the pepper/spice aromas. The colour is dense and dark, and it smells of maraschino cherry, spices, oak and pepper. It's a vibrant and surprisingly youthful wine, which promises to age slowly. A freak wine with fathomless depth and immense persistence. Cellar! Then have with cheese.

Quality	🍷🍷🍷🍷🍷
Value	★★★
Grapes	shiraz
Region	Eden Valley, SA
Cellar	4–20+
Alc./Vol.	13.5%
RRP	$150.00

CURRENT RELEASE 1994 This is a fabulous wine! It fully justifies the reputation. A more typical Hill of Grace than the '93, perhaps, with a winning combination of elegance and power. Nutty oak and berry/cherry fruit are slightly unintegrated, and it should be cellared. It's very alive in the mouth, and shows fresh acidity. It has great body and length, and should develop into an outstanding Hill of Grace. Then serve with roast beef.

Quality	🍷🍷🍷🍷🍷
Value	★★★½
Grapes	shiraz
Region	Eden Valley, SA
Cellar	5–20+
Alc./Vol.	14.0%
RRP	$165.00

Henschke Mount Edelstone

The name of the hill means Noble Stone. We're not sure about the rocks, but the wine is noble enough. With Hill of Grace, this is one of the great Henschke vineyards, overseen by viticulturist Prue Henschke and husband/winemaker Stephen.

Previous outstanding vintages: '78, '80, '84, '86, '88, '90, '91, '92, '93, '94

CURRENT RELEASE 1996 This is just a babe in arms, so lively is its youthful astringency. It needs time. You also have to like gumleaf/mint/eucalyptus characters, which this vintage has in abundance. It's flavour-packed, spicy and firm, and should age beautifully. Food: rare kangaroo fillet.

Quality	🍷🍷🍷🍷
Value	★★★
Grapes	shiraz
Region	Eden Valley, SA
Cellar	3–15+
Alc./Vol.	13.5%
RRP	$54.00

Hewitson l'Oizeau Shiraz

Quality	☖☖☖☖
Value	★★★
Grapes	shiraz
Region	Fleurieu Peninsula, SA
Cellar	🍷 10+
Alc./Vol.	13.5%
RRP	$37.00 🍷

Dean Hewitson burst onto the wine market in 1998 with a small cluster of impeccably made wines, produced from grapes sourced from various districts.

CURRENT RELEASE 1996 This is an impressive first effort. The colour is a vivid, youthful shade of purple–red. It smells of vanilla, plum and anise. In the mouth it has rich, sweet, smooth flavour with generous fruit, good extract and a soft tannin finish. It's a mere babe, and needs time to grow up. Then serve with osso bucco.

Highbank Basket Pressed Coonawarra

Quality	☖☖☖☖
Value	★★★
Grapes	cabernet sauvignon 65%; merlot 23%; cabernet franc 12%
Region	Coonawarra, SA
Cellar	➥ 2–12+
Alc./Vol.	13.5%
RRP	$38.50 🍷 ✌

This is probably the only organically grown vineyard in Coonawarra. The grower is Dennis Vice. The wines are made with the assistance of Trevor Mast, of Mount Langi Ghiran.

CURRENT RELEASE 1997 This is really a quite delicious red wine with great complexity, and it opens up with breathing. The colour is a full purple–red with blackish tints, and the nose has sweet mulberry, slightly medicinal ripe-fruit aromas with touches of blackcurrant and tobacco. In the mouth it's powerful with some astringent tannins and a little austerity, which suggests it will benefit from time. Very good intensity and weight, with a lingering aftertaste. Goes better with food than without. Cellar, then drink with hard cheeses.

Highwood Shiraz

Quality	☖☖☖
Value	★★★★
Grapes	shiraz
Region	Barossa Valley & McLaren Vale, SA
Cellar	🍷 5
Alc./Vol.	14.5%
RRP	$11.90 Ⓢ

This is one of the many brands of winemaker and entrepreneur, Rob Dundon. He continues to impress with a remarkable range of inexpensive wines.

CURRENT RELEASE 1998 This vibrant young Barossa/McLaren Vale blend is deep purple, smelling of charred oak, vanilla and ripe plums. It has deep, sweet blackberry-like fruit on the tongue, and firm tannin to close. Drinks well now, but has the stuffing to cellar. Try it with Irish stew.

Hillstowe Buxton's Merlot Cabernet

Hillstowe have recently built themselves a winery in downtown Hahndorf, the town that every visitor to South Australia visits. Cunning move!
CURRENT RELEASE 1996 You have to like the meaty, gamy smell of this wine, and if you can accept that, you'll probably find it's a very good wine to drink. Call it feral or whatever, the wine has an animal overtone. The tannins are furry and it has a kind of rustic charm. Try it with jugged hare.

Quality	♈♈♈
Value	★★★
Grapes	merlot 55%; cabernet sauvignon 45%
Region	McLaren Vale, SA
Cellar	▮ 5
Alc./Vol.	14.0%
RRP	$21.30 ⑤ ▮

Hillstowe Mary's Hundred Shiraz

Mary Laurie lays claim to being the first female vigneron in South Australia. Hillstowe is run by fifth-generation Lauries today.
CURRENT RELEASE 1997 This is very youthful wine for its age, and it needs time. The nose has charred wood smells and grapey aromas with hints of aniseed and cherry pip. The palate is slightly lean and perhaps lacks flesh. There's a lot of drying tannin on the finish, and oak vanillin crops up again on the aftertaste. It's slightly unintegrated, and will probably benefit from time in the cellar. Lay it down, then try with aged cheddar.

Quality	♈♈♈♈
Value	★★★
Grapes	shiraz
Region	McLaren Vale, SA
Cellar	━ 2–8+
Alc./Vol.	14.0%
RRP	$40.00 ▮

Hillstowe Udy's Mill Pinot Noir

The Udys were a sawmilling family of an earlier time. The site of their mill is within stone's throw of the vines. Viticulturist Chris Laurie.
CURRENT RELEASE 1997 A fragrant, light-bodied, charming pinot noir. The colour is medium–light purple–red; the nose is perfumed with strawberry/cherry and vegetal fruit aromas, plus some classy, spicy oak. There's a trace of tannin toughness on the tongue, and it's best served with food. Try spit-roasted quails.

Quality	♈♈♈♈
Value	★★★
Grapes	pinot noir
Region	Adelaide Hills, SA
Cellar	▮ 4
Alc./Vol.	13.0%
RRP	$30.00

Hollick Cabernet Sauvignon Merlot

Quality	♈♈♈♈
Value	★★★↑
Grapes	cabernet sauvignon; merlot
Region	Coonawarra, SA
Cellar	▲ 4
Alc./Vol.	13.0%
RRP	$22.20

Ian Hollick's Coonawarra reds are made in a generally lighter style than some of his neighbours' wines. They are invariably well made and pleasant to sip.
CURRENT RELEASE 1997   The nose has tangy blackcurrant aromas with some leafy touches and understated oak treatment. The palate is medium-bodied with blackberry flavour, a savoury note and tangy acidity. Moderate tannins make this red pleasant to drink in its youth. Serve it with herbed veal chops.

Hollick Shiraz Malbec Cabernet

Quality	♈♈♈♈
Value	★★★
Grapes	shiraz; malbec; cabernet sauvignon
Region	Coonawarra, SA
Cellar	▲ 2
Alc./Vol.	13.0%
RRP	$17.25

This is at the bottom of the Hollick range. It's designed to be a simple, undemanding red for early drinking.
CURRENT RELEASE 1997   No great complexity in this fresh young wine. It's a lighter style with a nose of simple red cherry and berry fruit unencumbered by any obvious oak. The palate is similarly straightforward with direct fruitiness and moderate tannins. A good companion to unfussy pasta dishes.

Homes Cabernet Merlot

Quality	♈♈♈♈
Value	★★★★
Grapes	cabernet sauvignon; merlot
Region	Langhorne Creek, SA
Cellar	▲ 5+
Alc./Vol.	14.0%
RRP	$19.00 Ⓢ

Ian and Sue Home's new crop of wines have abstract artworks on the labels. You mightn't love them but you won't be able to ignore them!
CURRENT RELEASE 1997   This tastes like a typical rich, chocolatey Langhorne Creek cabernet. There's an unusual smoky, oily character on the nose, but it builds attractive chocolate and coffee flavours in the mouth. There's plenty of flesh and texture to its weighty, chunky style. The finish is savoury and long. Try it with aged fillet of beef.

Houghton Jack Mann

We wonder what the famous Jack Mann, legendary winemaker of over 50 vintages at Houghton, would have thought of this. He didn't like oak flavour in his wines. **CURRENT RELEASE 1995** This is very, very oaky. It's a big brute of a wine that will no doubt live for ages, so maybe we'll eat our words. But we'll be in our wheelchairs and well and truly off the grog by the time it's mature. Concentrated in every way, it has dense colour, great intensity of piercing flavour, masses of tight-grained tannin and considerable length. Cellar, then serve with cheese.

Quality	♛♛♛♛
Value	★★✦
Grapes	cabernet sauvignon; shiraz; malbec
Region	Frankland River, WA
Cellar	➙ 5–15+
Alc./Vol.	14.0%
RRP	$50.00 🍶

Hungerford Hill Hilltops Cabernet Sauvignon

The grapes for this wine come from vineyards at Young, New South Wales, which is the centre of the region now known as the Hilltops. Maker Ian Walsh.

CURRENT RELEASE 1996 This is an impressive youngster which needs a bit of time. It's powerful and concentrated. The colour is a deep red–purple with dark reflections; the nose reveals leafy, blackcurrant cabernet aromas with some rose petals. It really comes into its own with breathing. It's quite tannic and has excellent depth of flavour, superb cabernet structure and elegance. It needs time, and has the potential to turn into a ripper. Best cellared, then serve with rare roast lamb.

Quality	♛♛♛♛♛
Value	★★★★★
Grapes	cabernet sauvignon
Region	Hilltops, NSW
Cellar	➙ 1–12+
Alc./Vol.	13.5%
RRP	$18.00 Ⓢ

CURRENT RELEASE 1997 This needs time. It's closed and tight to taste, with a certain austerity. The nose offers fragrant vanilla oak and some hints of berry, and there's an acid/tannin astringency in the mouth. It's firm and grippy, but seems to have good potential. Cellar, then have with venison.

Quality	♛♛♛♛
Value	★★★★
Grapes	cabernet sauvignon
Region	Hilltops, NSW
Cellar	➙ 2–8+
Alc./Vol.	13.5%
RRP	$19.00 Ⓢ

Hungerford Hill Tumbarumba Pinot Noir

Quality	♟♟♟♟
Value	★★★▸
Grapes	pinot noir
Region	Tumbarumba, NSW
Cellar	➘ 1–5+
Alc./Vol.	13.0%
RRP	$23.30 ⑤

The Hungerford Hill brand is a mouse that roared. It started off in the Hunter, expanded to Coonawarra and joined the Southcorp fold. Now it's distinguished by being a New-South-Wales-only brand with regional wines from all round the state. Maker Ian Walsh.
Previous outstanding vintages: '97
CURRENT RELEASE 1998 This is just a baby and it demands your patience. It's rather oaky and tannic at present, but has the goods. The colour is very deep; the aromas are a bit 'dry-red-ish' meaning it lacks pinot charm. Oaky vanilla, spicy, crushed-leaf and plum aromas are apparent, and it's solid and chunky to taste. Cellar, then have with roast pheasant.

Ingoldby Cabernet Sauvignon

Quality	♟♟♟♟
Value	★★★▸
Grapes	cabernet sauvignon
Region	McLaren Vale, SA
Cellar	♟ 3
Alc./Vol.	13.5%
RRP	$15.00 ⑤

The Ingoldby name has been famous around McLaren Vale for a long time. Now it's a Mildara Blass outpost and the wines are more modern than they once were, but they still have typical Southern Vales generosity of flavour.
CURRENT RELEASE 1997 This isn't a refined, cutting-edge red, but it does have plenty of honest regional cabernet character. The nose and palate have blackberry, mint and vanillin oak in harmonious balance. It's a satisfying drop in the mouth with good depth of flavour and balanced tannins. Serve it with lasagne.

Ivanhoe Wines Shiraz

Quality	♟♟♟
Value	★★★
Grapes	shiraz
Region	Hunter Valley, NSW
Cellar	♟ 5
Alc./Vol.	12.9%
RRP	$19.90

Ivanhoe Wines was established in 1996 and is ensconced in Marrowbone Road, Pokolbin, in the Lower Hunter Valley. It's run by Stephen and Tracy Drayton. Their vineyards extend to 25 hectares.
CURRENT RELEASE 1997 This wine shows some of the excess acidity of the '97 Hunter vintage. The colour is medium deep purple–red, and it has an unusual gamy, spicy nose with a vanillin oak aspect. The palate is medium-bodied, lean and tight, and a little hard on the finish. Aromatic oak carries the day. It would go with steak and kidney pie.

James Busby Barossa Valley Shiraz

The James Busby brand is owned by Liquorland, Australia's biggest retail liquor chain. James Busby of course was one of the founding fathers of the Australian wine industry. CURRENT RELEASE 1996 Busby brought shiraz vines to Australia, and he would have approved of this use of the variety. The nose has sweet jammy, blackberry aromas and a hint of herbs. The palate has sweet ripe fruit on entry, and good depth of flavour for the price, although it's rather short on the finish and carries a fair deal of astringency. It would go well with lamb satay.

Quality	♥♥♥
Value	★★★¥
Grapes	shiraz
Region	Barossa Valley, SA
Cellar	▮ 4+
Alc./Vol.	13.4%
RRP	$12.00

Jim Barry The Armagh

This blockbuster Clare shiraz has been a price pacesetter since it was first released. You have to cellar it to get your money's worth. In contrast to the wine, the label is a masterpiece of restraint. Maker Mark Barry.
Previous outstanding vintages: '90, '91, '92, '93, '95
CURRENT RELEASE 1996 A typical Armagh whopper! It has a dense purplish colour, an intense eucalyptus/mint nose with aromatic oak, licorice and plum. Some would describe it as over the top, as the palate is massive and carries a firm tannin handshake. It needs a lot of cellar time and will always be minty. A Grange pretender that should repay long cellaring. Serve with spicy Italian sausages.

Quality	♥♥♥♥¥
Value	★★¥
Grapes	shiraz
Region	Clare Valley, SA
Cellar	➤ 3–15+
Alc./Vol.	14.0%
RRP	$120.00 ▮

Jimmy Watson's Cabernet Shiraz

The wine was allegedly inspired by Allan Watson, Jimmy's son and owner of the eponymous Melbourne wine bar. No doubt the fame of the JW Trophy was also a factor. It's made by Mildara Blass.
CURRENT RELEASE 1997 This is a very different cuppa tea from the wines that typically win the Jimmy Watson Trophy. It's lightly oaked and soft, with medium weight and ready drinkability. The aromas are of plum skin and cherry pip. In the mouth it's soft and easy to drink with vanilla and coffee joining the berry flavours. Try it with grilled pork chops.

Quality	♥♥♥¥
Value	★★★¥
Grapes	cabernet sauvignon; shiraz
Region	Barossa Valley & Padthaway, SA
Cellar	▮ 4
Alc./Vol.	12.5%
RRP	$15.60 ⑤

Jingalla Great Southern Red

Quality 🍷🍷🍷½
Value ★★★½
Grapes cabernet sauvignon; others
Region Great Southern, WA
Cellar 4
Alc./Vol. 11.75%
RRP $15.00 (cellar door)

Jingalla is a family-owned business run by the Coads and the Clarkes. There are 8 hectares of vineyards, and the wines are contract-made at Goundrey.

CURRENT RELEASE 1997 This is a very attractive wine, with some lifted aromatics reminiscent of rose and raspberry. The colour is not deep: it's a medium–light red–purple, and the nose has some spicy oak but also the aforesaid perfumes. In the mouth it's light- to medium-weight with appealing flavour, again recalling rose petals and berries, and there's a suggestion of merlot. It's a very attractive wine, medium-bodied at the most, smooth, supple and lithe. It would go well with veal sweetbreads.

Jingalla Reserve Shiraz

Quality 🍷🍷🍷½
Value ★★★
Grapes shiraz
Region Great Southern, WA
Cellar 5
Alc./Vol. 12.0%
RRP $23.00

Jingalla is situated at the entrance to the Porongurup Range National Park, which is a very pretty part of the world.

CURRENT RELEASE 1996 This wine is a cool-climate style of shiraz with some vegetal characters. It has a medium purple–red colour, and the aromas are of roses, spices, crushed leaves and black pepper. The palate is lean and medium-bodied at best. It betrays its cool-climate origins. A very attractive lighter-bodied wine, which goes with lighter foods such as veal saltimbocca.

Joseph Cabernet Sauvignon Merlot

Quality 🍷🍷🍷🍷½
Value ★★★½
Grapes cabernet sauvignon 90%; merlot 10%
Region McLaren Vale & Coonawarra, SA
Cellar 2–12+
Alc./Vol. 14.5%
RRP $39.50

The fine print says 'moda amarone', a reference to the northern-Italian method of partially air-drying the harvested grapes before crushing. This increases the sugar by shrivelling the berries, concentrating the flavours. Maker Joe Grilli.

Previous outstanding vintages: '90, '91, '93, '94, '95, '96

CURRENT RELEASE 1997 Big extraction here. The colour is dark and there are oaky vanilla aromas galore. There are firm, almost bitter, tannic extractives on the tongue. A heavily worked wine that has great potential and needs a fair bit of time. Should go well with barbecued kangaroo.

Kangarilla Road Shiraz

Kangarilla Road is a mid-sized McLaren Vale operation which started life as Cambrai. Former proprietor Graham Stevens was a keen experimenter who bequeathed new owner, Kevin O'Brien, McLaren Vale's only plantings of zinfandel.

CURRENT RELEASE 1997   The colour is dark red, and the nose has a Cherry Ripe sort of dark-chocolate-sweetfruit thing as well as some raspberry and a hint of spice. The palate has attractive berry flavour and restrained oak balanced by firm, though not aggressive, tannins.

Quality	♥♥♥♥
Value	★★★★
Grapes	shiraz
Region	McLaren Vale, SA
Cellar	🍷 4+
Alc./Vol.	13.3%
RRP	$17.75

Karl Seppelt Langhorne Creek Shiraz

Langhorne Creek is a region that has seen enormous growth in vineyard planting area in the last few years. Its name was promoted widely by one Wolfgang Blass, who relied on its grapes for many of his better red wines. CURRENT RELEASE 1996   This is a typical Langhorne Creek wine with a strong gumleaf/mint aroma. The colour is full purple–red, and it has a pungent Dencorub or menthol aroma which is rather aggressive and somewhat confronting. The palate has grippy astringency and is quite rustic. Some may find it a bit on the rough side. It would go best with food: try a hearty beef stew.

Quality	♥♥♥
Value	★★★
Grapes	shiraz
Region	Langhorne Creek, SA
Cellar	🍷 5
Alc./Vol.	13.5%
RRP	$19.00

Karl Seppelt Springton Cabernet Sauvignon

Karl was once at the helm of the then family-owned Seppelt wine company, but when Adsteam bought it, he took to the hills to do his own thing. The wines are made at Petaluma under contract.

CURRENT RELEASE 1996   A real find! This is a delicious red. The colour is deep and youthful; the nose has spicy, dusty cabernet aromas and some earthy, oaky complexities. The fruit is to the fore and it's lush, sweet and ripe. The wood is high quality and there's superb density, flesh and texture in the mouth. A seamless cabernet which will also keep. Food: pink roast lamb.

Quality	♥♥♥♥♥
Value	★★★★
Grapes	cabernet sauvignon
Region	Eden Valley, SA
Cellar	🍷 10+
Alc./Vol.	13.0%
RRP	$19.00

Katnook Estate Cabernet Sauvignon

Quality	♥♥♥♥♥
Value	★★★★
Grapes	cabernet sauvignon
Region	Coonawarra, SA
Cellar	➧ 2–10
Alc./Vol.	13.5%
RRP	$45.00

Coonawarra make some special wines, but visitors looking for picturesque vineyard country will be disappointed. It's a very flat strip of vineyard in a very flat landscape. CURRENT RELEASE 1997 Totally immature, but you can see the potential in this baby. The colour is deep and the nose has great concentration. There are superintense aromas of cassis, warm dark earth, bitter chocolate, thorny leaves and bacon-scented smoky oak. The palate is tight and chewy with great depth and fine-grained drying tannins. Leave it alone for a few years then try it with Scotch fillet of beef.

Katnook Estate Merlot

Quality	♥♥♥♥
Value	★★★
Grapes	merlot
Region	Coonawarra, SA
Cellar	↓ 4
Alc./Vol.	14.0%
RRP	$45.00

The 1987 vintage was the first Katnook Merlot released. Back then, maker Wayne Stehbens made an early-picked fruit-driven style. Things have since got more serious, with very ripe grapes and 30 per cent new French oak. CURRENT RELEASE 1997 This has a good measure of the fruity smoothness that people look for in merlot. The nose has spiced plum varietal fruit with an interesting leafy, undergrowthy touch and a dab of savoury charry oak. The palate has spice and berry flavours, and a tight texture. It finishes with fine tannins. A good wine without doubt, but it lacks a bit of majesty.

Katnook Estate Odyssey Cabernet Sauvignon

Quality	♥♥♥♥♥
Value	★★★
Grapes	cabernet sauvignon
Region	Coonawarra, SA
Cellar	➧ 1–10+
Alc./Vol.	14.0%
RRP	$80.00

The first Odyssey, from the 1991 vintage, was released in 1996 to commemorate the centenary of the first vintage on the property. Maker Wayne Stehbens pulls out all stops for this one. CURRENT RELEASE 1994 A super-dense appearance gives an early indication of the level of extract here. The nose has blackcurrant liqueur, clean earth, mocha and spicy wood in great concentration. There's plenty of new oak, but there's plenty of fruit too. In the mouth that intense black-fruit flavour has a slight earthy, cedary touch. The palate is absolutely seamless: a long, smooth progression through to integrated, fine-grained tannins.

Kay's Amery Cabernet Sauvignon

McLaren Vale cabernet can be a squeaky-clean modern style or it can be an old-fashioned drop that tastes of the earth whence it came. The latter is gaining renewed acceptance among people looking for wines with a bit of individual character. Amery fits the bill.

CURRENT RELEASE 1997 This is like a time capsule of what McLaren Vale cabs used to be like – spruced up a bit of course, but all the old personality is there. The bouquet has earthy notes, hints of berry jam and old leather. It tastes of dark berries and has dry, grippy tannins at the end. A tear of nostalgia can fall from your eye if you have too much.

Quality	♥♥♥♥
Value	★★★⯪
Grapes	cabernet sauvignon
Region	McLaren Vale, SA
Cellar	♦ 5
Alc./Vol.	13.8%
RRP	$21.00

Kay's Amery Shiraz

Amery reds have long been true to traditional style, although they're a bit fresher now than they once were. Maker Colin Kay.

CURRENT RELEASE 1997 True Southern Vales aromas mark the nose here. It's earthy, with slightly jammy blackberry and spice. In the mouth it's hearty and easy to like, with a good measure of attractive raspberry and blackberry fruit, a grainy, chewy texture and ripe, drying tannins.

Quality	♥♥♥♥
Value	★★★⯪
Grapes	shiraz
Region	McLaren Vale, SA
Cellar	➥ 1–5
Alc./Vol.	13.4%
RRP	$21.00

Kilikanoon Cabernet Sauvignon

'Kilika' is an Aboriginal word meaning 'scrub'; 'noon' is English for lunch, hence 'lunch in the scrub', so the label says. The significance escapes us.

CURRENT RELEASE 1997 This is a fairly simple Clare cabernet. The nose has mint, blackcurrant, mulberry and spicy oak aromas. The palate is tight and blackcurranty with dry but soft tannins. Try with Swedish meatballs.

Quality	♥♥♥⯪
Value	★★★
Grapes	cabernet sauvignon
Region	Clare Valley, SA
Cellar	➥ 1–3
Alc./Vol.	14.0%
RRP	$19.00

Kingston Estate Cabernet Sauvignon

Quality	♈♈♈♈
Value	★★★★ᖾ
Grapes	cabernet sauvignon
Region	Murray Valley, SA
Cellar	▮ 2
Alc./Vol.	13.0%
RRP	$12.00 Ⓢ

Kingston Estate is one of a handful of highly motivated producers in Australia's Riverland areas who are serious about lifting their quality profile. These days they are able to source grapes of a quality unheard of not that long ago. It shows in a range of great-value table wines.
CURRENT RELEASE 1998   You could be mistaken for thinking this cabernet carries a much bigger price tag. It has quite stylish dark plum and blackberry on the nose, leading to a middleweight palate of surprising intensity. There's also a dab of oak to add dimension. Ripe tannins complete the picture.

Kingston Estate Merlot

Quality	♈♈♈♈
Value	★★★★
Grapes	merlot
Region	Murray Valley, SA
Cellar	▮ 1
Alc./Vol.	13.5%
RRP	$14.00 Ⓢ

Merlot is still in no-man's-land in Australia. Maybe it's because most people really don't know what it ought to taste like. Don't expect enlightenment to come out of this bottle.
CURRENT RELEASE 1998   An attractively fruity table wine from South Australia's Riverland. There's a bit of leafiness to the cherry aroma and a whiff of spice too. The palate has similar elements and is soft in structure, fresh, fault-free and undemanding. Drink it young with light luncheon fare.

Knappstein Cabernet Merlot

Quality	♈♈♈♈
Value	★★★
Grapes	cabernet sauvignon; merlot
Region	Clare Valley, SA
Cellar	⭲ 2–6+
Alc./Vol.	13.5%
RRP	$21.00

There's a timelessness about the old villages and wineries of the Clare Valley: it's like an historic oasis on the road to the outback. The old stone brewery that is the Knappstein winery fits the feel of things perfectly.
CURRENT RELEASE 1997   There's some blackberry fruit on the nose and a touch of menthol, with oak playing a quiet supporting role. The palate is straightforward with black-fruit flavour in the middle, more of that leafy mintiness, and rather hard tannins. Needs time to harmonise. Past experience tells us that it will. Serve it with sweet little lamb cutlets.

Knappstein Enterprise Cabernet Sauvignon

The Enterprise wines are the top of the tree from Knappstein. They're big bruisers: heavy on muscle, light on subtlety. Maker Andrew Hardy.

CURRENT RELEASE 1996 Is more better? Andrew Hardy certainly believes so; this has more of everything, with its super-dense colour, and powerfully concentrated nose of stewed blackberries, mint and dusty French oak. The power really unfolds on the palate with potent berry flavour and dry oaky tannins. Cellar for years, then drink it with a rib of beef or a brontosaurus steak.

Quality	🍷🍷🍷🍷½
Value	★★★½
Grapes	cabernet sauvignon
Region	Clare Valley, SA
Cellar	4–10+
Alc./Vol.	14.0%
RRP	$28.00

Knappstein Shiraz

Petaluma's takeover and the arrival of Andrew Hardy as winemaker haven't changed the Knappstein wines much. The reds still capture true Clare regionality.

CURRENT RELEASE 1997 A traditionally constructed shiraz driven by ripe fruit, not oak. The nose has blackberry, spice and an undergrowthy touch. The palate is medium in body and smooth, with a nice dollop of sweet ripe shiraz fruit in the middle ahead of a drying tannin finish. Racks of lamb will do well.

Quality	🍷🍷🍷🍷
Value	★★★½
Grapes	shiraz
Region	Clare Valley, SA
Cellar	5
Alc./Vol.	14.0%
RRP	$21.00

Krondorf Pioneers Rest Shiraz Cabernet

It's hard to keep track of the plethora of different Mildara Blass brands in the marketplace. Pioneers Rest is another that appeared recently.

CURRENT RELEASE 1997 This has good colour – quite deep for an inexpensive young wine. The nose has dark plum, a hint of licorice and a dab of charry oak. This popular formula is repeated on the palate – similar charry, chunky flavours in a medium-bodied style with some slight firmness at the end. Try it with pizza.

Quality	🍷🍷🍷½
Value	★★★½
Grapes	shiraz; cabernet sauvignon
Region	Barossa Valley, SA
Cellar	4
Alc./Vol.	13.0%
RRP	$12.00

Lachlan Ridge Merlot

Quality	♥♥♥
Value	★★★★
Grapes	merlot
Region	not stated
Cellar	▌ 3
Alc./Vol.	13.0%
RRP	$8.99

Judging by the name, this must be Cowra fruit, but the label doesn't bother you with too much information. It's a Liquorland house wine.

CURRENT RELEASE 1998 It's an attractive, light-bodied, drink-now red, which is dangerously easy to quaff. Floral, leafy, mulberry and cassis aromas are slightly herbaceous and quite inviting. The emphasis is on smoothness and drinkability. The crushed-leaf, capsicum aromas are not exactly premium, but it's a good drink with a hamburger.

Lark Hill Cabernet Merlot

Quality	♥♥♥
Value	★★★
Grapes	cabernet sauvignon 65%; merlot 30%; cabernet franc 5%
Region	Canberra District, NSW
Cellar	➾ 3–13
Alc./Vol.	13.0%
RRP	$24.00 (cellar door)

Lark Hill is one of the pioneers of the Canberra District, the vineyard being established in 1978 at Bungendore. Maker Sue Carpenter.

CURRENT RELEASE 1997 For a cool-climate wine this is amazingly big and extractive. The colour is very dark purple–red and the nose is oaky, slightly porty, and somewhat extracted. The palate is likewise heavily extracted and tannic, with unexpected weight and density. There's a touch of bitterness on the finish, and it needs several years before broaching. Cellar, then serve with steak and kidney pie.

Lark Hill Pinot Noir

Quality	♥♥♥♥
Value	★★★★
Grapes	pinot noir
Region	Canberra District, NSW
Cellar	▌ 5
Alc./Vol.	13.5%
RRP	$24.00 (cellar door)

The region here is Canberra District, but like most of this area's vineyards, Lark Hill is outside the ACT boundary – in New South Wales. Maker Sue Carpenter. *Previous outstanding vintages: '96, '97*

CURRENT RELEASE 1998 Like all good wine, this tends to grow on you. It has good depth of colour, and the nose is toasty, sappy, undergrowthy and a touch 'wild'. The sappy stalk characters are also on the palate but are nicely balanced with soft, sweet cherry, gamy and earthy subtleties. A complex pinot that goes great guns with barbecued duck. It'll be even better in 2000.

Leconfield Shiraz

This company has produced some crackerjack shiraz from Coonawarra over the years, but the grape variety is notorious for the cyclical nature of its quality in Coonawarra.

CURRENT RELEASE 1997 This is a rather meagre, light-bodied wine which seems to show unripe fruit characters. The colour is light purple–red, and the nose has stalky, crushed-leaf and peppercorn aromas. There's some aromatic oak and a spicy, meaty shiraz aroma too. The palate is lean, dry and a trifle austere. It needs food, and could go well with veal.

Quality	???
Value	★★★
Grapes	shiraz
Region	Coonawarra, SA
Cellar	7
Alc./Vol.	13.0%
RRP	$25.00 Ⓢ

Leeuwin Prelude Cabernet Merlot

The Leeuwin Estate cabernet style is distinctive and confronting: there's a seeming contradiction of green, possibly unripe, flavours with a powerful, tannic palate structure, no doubt the result of extended skin maceration after fermentation. Maker Bob Cartwright.

CURRENT RELEASE 1996 A biggie, naturally, but the colour is showing a tint of age and the dry, savoury style hints at a long time spent in wood. It develops crushed-leaf green fruit aromas with airing, and the tannins are somewhat harsh and astringent. Will it ever soften? Cellar, then try it with beef casserole.

Quality	????
Value	★★★
Grapes	cabernet sauvignon 77%; merlot 23%
Region	Margaret River, WA
Cellar	3–8
Alc./Vol.	14.0%
RRP	$29.50

Lenswood Vineyards Pinot Noir

Tim Knappstein has been hot on the trail of the pinot noir holy grail these last few years. In an earlier life, he ran the winery that still carries his name in Clare.
Previous outstanding vintages: '90, '91, '94, '95, '96
CURRENT RELEASE 1997 The Knappstein style is big and concentrated with quite a large helping of oak. The '97 is no exception: if anything the oak is slightly heavy-handed. The colour is dark purple–red; the nose shows vanilla and cedary oak perfumes that breathe to reveal maraschino cherry. It has good body and length, with spice and cherry/plum flavours. Serve it with clay-baked guinea fowl.

Quality	?????
Value	★★★★
Grapes	pinot noir
Region	Adelaide Hills, SA
Cellar	5
Alc./Vol.	13.8%
RRP	$40.00

Lenton Brae Cabernet Merlot

Quality	♟♟♟↑
Value	★★★
Grapes	cabernet sauvignon; merlot; shiraz
Region	Margaret River, WA 85%; Ferguson Valley, WA 15%
Cellar	1–5+
Alc./Vol.	13.5%
RRP	$19.00

The Lenton Brae winery is owned by an architect, which is no surprise as it's a very thoughtful design. The building material is stabilised rammed earth, a Margaret River speciality.

CURRENT RELEASE 1998   This is a bit young to leave its mother; the aromas and flavours are somewhat raw and immature. The nose has fresh oak vanilla and ripe red berry aromas. It's a little light-on, but the flavours are attractive and will be more so in another year. Drink it with kassler.

Lenton Brae Margaret River

Quality	♟♟♟♟♟
Value	★★★★
Grapes	cabernet sauvignon 90%; merlot 10%
Region	Margaret River, WA
Cellar	1–10+
Alc./Vol.	14.5%
RRP	$28.00

From the '97 vintage, the 'Cabernet Sauvignon' has been dropped and the wine is simply called Margaret River. It's a growing trend. The grapes are estate-grown and hand-picked. Maker Edward Tomlinson.

CURRENT RELEASE 1996   An excellent cabernet that shows why Margaret River is famous for this style. The aromas are dusty, earthy and woodsy with hints of linseed oil and roasted nuts. It's deep and concentrated on the palate, and has a savoury, strongly wood-matured flavour, concluding with a dry tannin finish. It suits aged cheeses.

Quality	♟♟♟♟↑
Value	★★★★
Grapes	cabernet sauvignon; merlot; petit verdot
Region	Margaret River, WA
Cellar	2–10+
Alc./Vol.	14.0%
RRP	$29.50

CURRENT RELEASE 1997   This is a smart Bordeaux-style red. The bouquet recalls old furniture, walnuts, rose petals and cassis. There's a lot of oak, cleverly integrated with high-quality fruit. It has good intensity and a very dry finish. A good food wine: try with boeuf bordelaise.

Leo Buring Clare Valley Shiraz

This is a new one from Leo Buring, who are more famous for their white wines, especially their sensational Clare rieslings.
CURRENT RELEASE 1997 Quite a woody youngster with powerful toasty American oak aromas together with ripe, plummy, shiraz fruit. Demands a little time to come together properly. The palate has excellent depth, is quite chunky, and has lots of vanilla, coffee-like flavour with some blackberry and dusty overtones. Try it with kangaroo steak.

Quality	ΨΨΨΨ
Value	★★★r
Grapes	shiraz
Region	Clare Valley, SA
Cellar	▮ 10
Alc./Vol.	13.5%
RRP	$27.00 Ⓢ

Lillydale Vineyards Cabernet Merlot

This 13-hectare vineyard in the Seville district of the Yarra was established in 1976 by Alex and Judith White, who sold it to McWilliams. Maker Max McWilliam.
CURRENT RELEASE 1997 This is a charmer, which drinks well young. The nose is all sweet berries and blackcurrants, with fine fruit–oak balance. It's medium- to full-bodied and has some flesh and richness. It's very smooth and should improve in the short term. Try it with veal cutlets.

Quality	ΨΨΨΨ
Value	★★★r
Grapes	cabernet sauvignon; merlot
Region	Yarra Valley, Vic.
Cellar	▮ 6
Alc./Vol.	13.0%
RRP	$18.90 Ⓢ

Lindemans Bin 45 Cabernet Sauvignon

Bin numbers hark back to the days when cellar-hands used to stack bottles by hand in brick compartments in tunnels, where they matured before sale. The compartment was known as a bin, and often gave its number to the wine it held.
CURRENT RELEASE 1998 This is light, fruity and simple, but exactly what's required at the price. It smells of Ribena or blackcurrant cordial, with a hint of peppermint. It's fairly basic and lightly structured, but it's hard to complain at the price. The quality is good. Goes with stir-fried pork.

Quality	ΨΨΨ
Value	★★★r
Grapes	cabernet sauvignon
Region	not stated
Cellar	▮ 2
Alc./Vol.	13.0%
RRP	$10.00 Ⓢ

Lindemans Bin 50 Shiraz

Quality	♥♥♥
Value	★★★
Grapes	shiraz
Region	not stated
Cellar	▮ 2
Alc./Vol.	13.5%
RRP	$10.50 Ⓢ

The Bin 65 Chardonnay's tearaway success has spawned a large family of Bin wines with the same label. Perhaps Lindemans need to practise birth control.

CURRENT RELEASE 1998   The colour is promising: deep and dark. There are earthy, meaty and grapey aromas of warm-area shiraz, and it's light and simple in the mouth. A presentable wine with no pretence to greatness; you get what you pay for. Drinks well with spaghetti and meatballs.

Lindemans Hunter Valley Shiraz

Quality	♥♥♥♥
Value	★★★★
Grapes	shiraz
Region	Hunter Valley, NSW
Cellar	▮ 15+
Alc./Vol.	12.5%
RRP	$21.00 Ⓢ ▮

This used to be labelled Hunter River Burgundy. The bin number remains: this one's Bin 9003. That's to differentiate it from other bottlings from the same year. Maker Patrick Auld.

Previous outstanding vintages: '83, '86, '87, '91

CURRENT RELEASE 1995   The Hunter has more vintage variation than most areas, but '95 sees this classic right back on form. It has a medium brick-red hue and a mellow bouquet of earthy, toasty, dusty matured-fruit characters. It's already losing its primary fruit, which is typical of Hunter reds of this age. The palate has coffee, sweet developed fruit flavours and liberal tannins. The finish is dry and savoury, and it promises to age well. Already drinks well, with beef casserole.

Lindemans Limestone Coast Shiraz

Quality	♥♥♥
Value	★★★★
Grapes	shiraz
Region	Padthaway & Robe, SA
Cellar	▮ 4
Alc./Vol.	13.5%
RRP	$11.00 Ⓢ

The Limestone Coast is a new zone which takes in Coonawarra, Padthaway, Wrattonbully and the coastal areas of south-east South Australia, including Robe and Mount Benson.

CURRENT RELEASE 1998   This is a fresh, raw youngster which has good depth of flavour and character for the price. The nose shows it to be a tad immature, with aromas of berries, plums and light spices which carry through to the palate. It has good length and grip, although it's a trifle simplistic. Goes well with burgers.

Lindemans Padthaway Cabernet Merlot

These days Lindemans is one of the most successful brand names in Australian wine. Interestingly for students of marketing, it works right across the price categories.

CURRENT RELEASE 1997 Essence of blackcurrants! Fruit is very much what this style is all about, and it delivers in spadefuls. The nose shows blackberry and blackcurrant aromas; it's smooth in the mouth and easy to drink, with gentle tannins and impeccable balance. Hard to fault at the price. Serve it with a washed-rind cheese, like Milawa Gold.

Quality	♥♥♥♥?
Value	★★★★★
Grapes	cabernet sauvignon; merlot
Region	Padthaway, SA
Cellar	🍷 8+
Alc./Vol.	13.5%
RRP	$19.20 ⑤

Lindemans Padthaway Pinot Noir

It's a quirk of the wine biz that very few pinots under $20 are worth bothering with, but HH reckons this is outstanding value. Phillip John and the lads at Lindemans have laboured hard to fathom pinot, and they're making progress.

Previous outstanding vintages: '97

CURRENT RELEASE 1998 This needs some air to build its bouquet, but the fleshy depth of palate flavour sets it apart. An excellent bouquet of ripe fruit, cherry and ethereal perfumes plus a whiff of oak eventually float from the glass. The colour is deep, and the palate has weight and density. Good with casseroled rabbit.

Quality	♥♥♥♥?
Value	★★★★★
Grapes	pinot noir
Region	Padthaway, SA
Cellar	🍷 5+
Alc./Vol.	13.5%
RRP	$17.00 ⑤

Lindemans Pyrus

This is one of Lindemans' so-called Coonawarra red trio, the others being Limestone Ridge and St George. Maker Greg Clayfield and team.

Previous outstanding vintages: '85, '86, '88, '90, '91

CURRENT RELEASE 1995 From a less-successful year this has beaten the odds and come up trumps. It tastes smooth and ripe and complete. It has the usual Lindemans forest of new oak, and really needs time to mellow out a little. There are earthy, gamy and chocolatey aromas, and it's a very elegant mouthful of wine. An improver! Serve it with standing rib roast of beef.

Quality	♥♥♥♥♥
Value	★★★★
Grapes	cabernet sauvignon; merlot; cabernet franc; malbec
Region	Coonawarra, SA
Cellar	➡ 2–10+
Alc./Vol.	13.0%
RRP	$35.00 🍷

Lindemans Steven Vineyard Shiraz

Quality	♟♟♟♟
Value	★★★★
Grapes	shiraz
Region	Hunter Valley, NSW
Cellar	▲ 20
Alc./Vol.	13.0%
RRP	$28.00 ▮

This is not just a vineyard selection, it's Lindemans' best Hunter red wine of the year. The bin number is 9225, if you wanted to know.

CURRENT RELEASE 1996 This is an outstanding Hunter red. Typically forward colour and bouquet: earthy, leathery Hunter regional nose with a hint of coffee. The palate is savoury with lashings of tannin to go with lip-smacking fruit. Has tight structure and a dry finish. It will cellar well, and is a classic in the making. Goes well with venison.

Lowe Hunter Valley Merlot

Quality	♟♟♟
Value	★★★
Grapes	merlot
Region	Hunter Valley, NSW
Cellar	▲ 5
Alc./Vol.	13.0%
RRP	$24.60 (mailing list)

David Lowe and Jane Wilson make their wines at Hunter winery Oakvale while they're building their own at Mudgee. They take grapes from Orange and the Hunter as well as from the family vineyard at Mudgee.

CURRENT RELEASE 1998 This seems rather young and unready to be bottled and on sale, but then we know the cash-flow pressures on small winemakers. It has a vivid purple colour and a slightly raw fruit nose, but the palate is surprisingly soft and easygoing. It has good flavour and structure and should repay some cellar time. Drink with gourmet sausages and mash.

Maglieri Cabernet Sauvignon

Quality	♟♟♟♟
Value	★★★★
Grapes	cabernet sauvignon
Region	McLaren Vale, SA
Cellar	➥ 1–5
Alc./Vol.	13.5%
RRP	$18.00

The Maglieris popularised the local lambrusco style of sweet, spritzy red. It's hard to believe reds like this cabernet come from the same producers.

CURRENT RELEASE 1997 This is a friendly red that's a bit closed up at the moment. Ripe blackberry, dusty oak and a slightly leafy, savoury earthiness mark the nose. The palate is ripe enough, with medium body and dry tannins that add a slightly astringent touch to the finish, but it will open up more in a year or so. Serve this with a beef casserole.

Maglieri Merlot

Merlot doesn't jump to mind when thoughts of McLaren Vale reds surface. However, the variety has promise in the district; it's soft richness can dovetail sweetly into the earthy regional character.

CURRENT RELEASE 1997   Lots of sweet charm on the nose here. Blackcurrant and raspberry-like fruit, a hint of plum pudding and some sweet oak lead to a flavoursome palate. It's medium-bodied with a generous, fruity middle, soft leafiness and moderate tannins. May be at its best young with coq au vin de McLaren Vale.

Quality	♟♟♟♟
Value	★★★★
Grapes	merlot
Region	McLaren Vale, SA
Cellar	🍷 3
Alc./Vol.	13.0%
RRP	$22.00

Maglieri Shiraz

For a long time Maglieri have been using McLaren Vale grapes to make lambrusco, a semi-sparkling sweet red. We think there are better uses for such fruit, as this shiraz shows.

CURRENT RELEASE 1997   A good dark colour introduces this well-made, flavoursome red. The nose has typical spiced blackberry fruit with some well-handled American oak to add dimension. The palate is loaded with fruit-sweet berry flavour and a toasty lick of oak behind it. Tannins are dry and balanced, and it finishes long and aromatic. Try it with Chinese soy-braised beef.

Quality	♟♟♟♟♟
Value	★★★★★
Grapes	shiraz
Region	McLaren Vale, SA
Cellar	🍷 5
Alc./Vol.	14.0%
RRP	$22.00

Maglieri Steve Maglieri Shiraz

It wasn't that long ago that most wineries would have found it unthinkable to have a shiraz as their super-prestige wine. Now they're everywhere.

CURRENT RELEASE 1997   Deep, dense blackish colour suggests power and body. The bouquet is full-on, with jammy blackberry, licorice, dark chocolate and oak. The palate is dense and heavy with fruit extract. Tannins are of suitably hefty proportions. Age is mandatory for this bruiser, then serve it with a charry rib roast of beef.

Quality	♟♟♟♟♟
Value	★★★★
Grapes	shiraz
Region	McLaren Vale, SA
Cellar	⊸ 2–10
Alc./Vol.	14.0%
RRP	$36.00

Magpie Estate The Malcolm

Quality	♛♛♛♛♛
Value	★★
Grapes	shiraz
Region	Barossa Valley, SA
Cellar	▮ 15
Alc./Vol.	16.0%
RRP	$95.00

There are many extraordinary things about this wine, including the price. It was made to prescription by Rolf Binder of Veritas. It scored 99+ from American Robert Parker. No doubt the alcohol content and the word 'unfiltered' got him in.

CURRENT RELEASE 1996   Strictly hand-to-hand combat. If you like overripe, over-wooded, over-alcoholic reds, this is your tea bag. Dense purple–red colour; vanilla-milkshake, caramel aromas from overdone heavy-toast American oak. The taste is massive, sumptuous, fleshy, terrifically concentrated and richly fruit-cakey, with a grippy tannin finish. But is it wine?

Main Ridge Half Acre Pinot Noir

Quality	♛♛♛♛♛
Value	★★★★
Grapes	pinot noir
Region	Mornington Peninsula, Vic.
Cellar	▮ 4
Alc./Vol.	13.5%
RRP	$38.00

Twenty-five years ago Nat and Rosalie White pioneered commercial viticulture on the Mornington Peninsula. They've suffered the vicissitudes of a marginal climate with characteristic good humour, and made nice wine along the way.

CURRENT RELEASE 1997   Nat White's latest thing is the use of a proportion of wild vineyard yeasts in his wines. This is the first pinot thus made. The colour is deep, and the nose has sweet strawberry, wet-earth and compost aromas. The long palate has good intensity of red-fruit flavour, which is rich and fine-textured. Soft tannins round it off well. A great match for Cantonese roast duck.

Majella Cabernet

Majella has been a significant grapegrower in Coona-warra for many years. Owner Brian Lynn has only moved into wine production in the last few. Maker Bruce Gregory.

CURRENT RELEASE 1997   Very Coonawarra cabernet. Super-dense in colour, this has that real intensity of cedar and blackcurrant on the nose with a floral note and lots of dusty, spicy oak. The palate follows suit: it's very concentrated yet not too big, with a firm backbone of tannins. This shows plenty of oak influence, but the fruit stands up to it and will emerge more as the wine softens with age. Try it with roasted racks of lamb.

Quality	ＰＰＰＰＰ
Value	★★★ｒ
Grapes	cabernet sauvignon
Region	Coonawarra, SA
Cellar	➡ 2–10
Alc./Vol.	13.0%
RRP	$34.50

Majella Shiraz

Majella's grapes have long enjoyed a big reputation around Coonawarra. Rumour has it that the Majella shiraz has been a component of the much-lauded Wynns Michael Shiraz.

CURRENT RELEASE 1997   Just as the Majella Cabernet is archetypally varietal, so is the shiraz. This has a very deep, immature colour with a lush nose full of intense blackberry, cassis, spice and pepper. In the mouth it's super-intense and very long-flavoured. Oak is there too, but it's so well handled that you hardly notice it along-side that deep fruit character. This will live long; wait a while and serve it with rare roast fillet of beef.

Quality	ＰＰＰＰＰ
Value	★★★★ｒ
Grapes	shiraz
Region	Coonawarra, SA
Cellar	➡ 2–10
Alc./Vol.	13.5%
RRP	$30.00

Majella The Malleea

Quality	♟♟♟♟♟
Value	★★★★★
Grapes	cabernet sauvignon; shiraz
Region	Coonawarra, SA
Cellar	➸ 2–12
Alc./Vol.	13.2%
RRP	$58.00

PENGUIN BEST RED WINE AND BEST RED BLEND

The pick of the Majella crop finds its way into The Malleea. The blend of cabernet and shiraz is very traditional Coonawarra, but the wine is modern in style.

CURRENT RELEASE 1997 **The '96 Malleea starred in these pages last year and we're pleased to announce it was no flash in the pan – the '97 is a ripper too! The colour is super-dense, impenetrable actually, and the nose has concentrated black-fruit, spicy oak and bitter chocolate aromas. In the mouth it's a tightly constructed, long-flavoured youngster with everything in the right place; it just needs time to lose the awkwardness of youth. Cellaring is essential, then serve it with a loin of lamb.**

Maritime Estate Pinot Noir

Quality	♟♟♟♟
Value	★★★⯪
Grapes	pinot noir
Region	Mornington Peninsula, Vic.
Cellar	♟ 2
Alc./Vol.	13.4%
RRP	$22.00

Mornington Peninsula pinot noir is very responsive to vintage variation. Happily, both '97 and '98 were good years after a disastrous '96. Makers Kathleen Quealy and Kevin McCarthy.

CURRENT RELEASE 1997   A nose of sweet cherry with a whisper of oak makes a pleasant introduction to this young pinot. It's well made but not especially complex, with simple, ripe, strawberryish pinot fruit and good tannin structure. A pleasant Peninsula pinot from young vines. Future releases should be even better.

Maxwell Ellen Street Shiraz

Quality	♟♟♟♟
Value	★★★★
Grapes	shiraz
Region	McLaren Vale, SA
Cellar	♟ 4
Alc./Vol.	14.0%
RRP	$22.50

Maxwell's is one of those small-to-middling wineries that adds great interest to any visit to the McLaren Vale region. They also make mead from honey to sustain any passing Vikings.

CURRENT RELEASE 1997   The attractive characters that make McLaren Vale reds such friendly critters are here in good measure. It's a rich, soft red with lush blackberry fruit, measured cedary oak and a touch of regional earthiness. Easy tannins and good acidity give definition. Goes well with braised steak and kidney.

Maxwell Reserve Merlot

Merlot is popping up all over the country, although the vastly different styles it's made into are sure to cause confusion among consumers. It's grown just about everywhere, and McLaren Vale has been producing a couple of especially good examples – like this one. Maker Mark Maxwell.

CURRENT RELEASE 1997 This is a big merlot which showcases the softness of the variety well. The nose has rich plummy fruit with a nice lick of oak. In the mouth there's plump berry and dark plum flavour of good depth, ahead of soft fine tannins. A generous mouthful of wine that goes well with fillet steak.

Quality	🍷🍷🍷🍷½
Value	★★★★
Grapes	merlot
Region	McLaren Vale, SA
Cellar	5
Alc./Vol.	14.0%
RRP	$28.75

McLarens on the Lake Cabernet Shiraz

McLarens on the Lake is a tourist-oriented venture of Andrew Garrett's at McLaren Vale. The reasonably priced reds make no claim to regional origins, but they can be pretty good value.

CURRENT RELEASE 1998 Plummy fruit on the nose has some undergrowth and spice nuances, which seem more shiraz- than cabernet-influenced. In the mouth it has undemanding blackberry flavour of medium body and slightly bitter tannins at the end. Good with veal alla pizzaiola.

Quality	🍷🍷🍷
Value	★★★
Grapes	cabernet sauvignon; shiraz
Region	South East Australia
Cellar	2
Alc./Vol.	13.0%
RRP	$12.00 ($)

McWilliams Barwang Cabernet Sauvignon

The Hilltops region gives New South Wales a promising entrant in the cooler-climate stakes. The Barwang reds can be very good indeed. Maker Jim Brayne.

CURRENT RELEASE 1997 Dense and deep in colour, this has intense blackcurrant fruit on the nose which gives a mouth-watering fragrance. There's some vanillin oak too, but it doesn't overwhelm. The palate isn't big, but it's concentrated and elegant, with dry grippy tannins to finish off. A lip-smacking good red to try with roast lamb.

Quality	🍷🍷🍷🍷🍷
Value	★★★★★
Grapes	cabernet sauvignon
Region	Hilltops, NSW
Cellar	1–5+
Alc./Vol.	13.5%
RRP	$20.00

McWilliams Barwang Shiraz

Quality	♥♥♥♥
Value	★★★★★
Grapes	shiraz
Region	Hilltops, NSW
Cellar	▮ 5
Alc./Vol.	13.5%
RRP	$20.00

This vineyard pioneered viticulture in the Young/Hill-tops region of New South Wales nearly twenty-five years ago. Since its acquisition by McWilliams in 1989, it has been expanded considerably.

CURRENT RELEASE 1997 A well-made modern-style shiraz from a vintage that obviously suited the Hilltops district. It has a succulent nose of cherry, plum and spice, which is enhanced by a dusting of vanillin oak. The palate has supple cherry flavour with balanced ripe tannins. Try it with pot-roasted nut of veal.

McWilliams Hanwood Cabernet Sauvignon

Quality	♥♥♥
Value	★★★
Grapes	cabernet sauvignon
Region	Riverina, NSW
Cellar	▮ 1
Alc./Vol.	13.0%
RRP	$11.00 ⑤

McWilliams has done a lot of work to improve Riverina wines over the years. The latest from winemaker Jim Brayne is a rating system to grade different vineyards according to quality of grapes produced.

CURRENT RELEASE 1998 Hanwood cabernet is an everyday red to drink young – not a wine for deep analysis. It's a light- to medium-bodied wine, with straight-forward blackcurrant and berry aroma and flavour, dressed with a dash of coconutty oak. Friendly, soft tannins round things off nicely. Try it with some meaty pork sausages.

McWilliams Mount Pleasant Philip

Quality	♥♥♥♥
Value	★★★★
Grapes	shiraz
Region	Hunter Valley, NSW
Cellar	▮ 3
Alc./Vol.	11.5%
RRP	$14.00

Mount Pleasant wines keep you in contact with tried-and-true tradition. They remain Hunter wines as they used to be, but without all the faults.

CURRENT RELEASE 1994 A dark brick-red wine that's history in a glass. There's old-fashioned Hunter fruit on the nose – ripe berry with leathery, earthy touches. The palate follows with similar savoury flavour and an authentic regional feel, thanks to lightish medium body, good length and typically soft tannins. The mellowness of maturity is an added bonus. Try it with braised steak and onions.

Merricks Estate Pinot Noir

Merricks Estate is run by affable Melbourne solicitor George Kefford and family. Their vineyard was established over twenty years ago, which makes them old hands among the Mornington Peninsula wine fraternity. Maker Alex White.

CURRENT RELEASE 1997 A direct, uncomplicated pinot with an aromatic bouquet of cherry and plum, which suggests the influence of some whole bunches in the ferment. This simple fruitiness continues in the mouth. The palate is medium-bodied and soft on the finish. Not very complex, but easy to drink in warm weather with some cold meats and salad.

Quality	♟♟♟♟
Value	★★★
Grapes	pinot noir
Region	Mornington Peninsula, Vic.
Cellar	▮ 3
Alc./Vol.	13.0%
RRP	$29.60

Miranda High Country Dark Horse Merlot Malbec

Miranda is an energetic company that now puts out so many different wines it's hard to follow them all. The High Country range comes from Miranda's north-east Victorian outpost.

CURRENT RELEASE 1997 It's rare to see these two varieties blended together. Here they've produced a red of medium density with a light berry and vanilla nose, which has a tweak of minty freshness. The palate has light berry flavour with a touch of charry oak. Soft tannins make it easy to drink with pasta.

Quality	♟♟♟♟
Value	★★★★
Grapes	merlot; malbec
Region	King Valley & Ovens Valley, Vic.
Cellar	▮ 2
Alc./Vol.	13.5%
RRP	$12.00

Miranda White Shiraz

The label designers are having a field day at Miranda with new gimmicks appearing all the time. This pink wine comes in a frosted bottle with a see-through panel revealing in ghostly relief the shadow of a drover on horseback. What theatre!

CURRENT RELEASE 1998 A pale rose-pink drop with a crisp redcurrant aroma and a fruity, soft, yet surprisingly dry, palate. It's low in alcohol, which makes it a good summer-weight rosé you can slurp down without risking a thumping headache. Try with cold soy chicken.

Quality	♟♟♟
Value	★★★★
Grapes	shiraz
Region	Riverina, NSW
Cellar	▮ 1
Alc./Vol.	10.5%
RRP	$11.00

Mitchell Peppertree Shiraz

Quality	♟♟♟♟𝅭
Value	★★★★
Grapes	shiraz
Region	Clare Valley, SA
Cellar	🍷 6
Alc./Vol.	13.5%
RRP	$24.50

Andrew and Jane Mitchell's shiraz is in a more modern style than some of the Clare Valley traditionalists which makes it much more approachable in its youth. It keeps well too.

CURRENT RELEASE 1997   This is a stylish shiraz which has good intensity of dark berry and plum fruit on the nose along with some spicy complexity and well-measured spicy-sweet oak. In the mouth it's smooth and long-flavoured with intensity and depth, but it's not overpowering. Tannins are ripe and fine. Try it alongside roast fillet of beef.

Mitchelton Goulburn Valley Shiraz

Quality	♟♟♟♟
Value	★★★⭑
Grapes	shiraz; grenache; mourvèdre
Region	Goulburn Valley, Vic.
Cellar	🍷 2
Alc./Vol.	13.0%
RRP	$15.95

Mitchelton winemaker Don Lewis has been remodelling some of his wines in recent years with less obvious oak influence. Along the way his fascination with Rhone varieties has grown, which is probably why this shiraz has 15 per cent grenache and mourvèdre in it.

CURRENT RELEASE 1996   This is a savoury red in the modern cafe style. Spicy blackberry and raspberry fruit aromas lead the way on the nose; in the mouth similar berry flavours meet harmoniously with just a dusting of vanillin oak. It's medium in body and soft in tannins. A likeable wine to accompany pasta with pumpkin, thyme and parmigiano.

Monichino Cabernet Sauvignon

Quality	♟♟♟♟
Value	★★★★⭑
Grapes	cabernet sauvignon
Region	Goulburn Valley, Vic.
Cellar	⟷ 1–4
Alc./Vol.	13.5%
RRP	$14.00 (mailing list)

The Monichino winery is a bit out of the way at Katunga, north of Shepparton. This puts it in the warm top half of Victoria, but the wines can have a freshness that belies their origins.

CURRENT RELEASE 1997   This is an attractively complete red wine of straightforward personality. The nose and palate have blackberry fruit character with well-measured charry oak. The palate is a bit closed at the moment, but good underlying fruit flavour, smoothness and balanced tannins carry the day. Should improve short term. Serve it with braised veal with polenta.

Montana Reserve Pinot Noir

New Zealand pinot noirs have been causing a bit of a flap in Australia with some voices suggesting they beat the Australian article hands down. As always, there are good and bad whichever side of the Tasman you're on. CURRENT RELEASE 1997 Correct pinot colour: brick red and not too dense. The nose has plummy fruit with some leafy/forest-floor complexities and a hint of stemminess. The palate is fruit-sweet with plummy fruit, which makes it an easy-drinker. The finish is slightly stemmy with a hint of bitterness. Drink it with weisswurst.

Quality	▼▼▼▼
Value	★★★
Grapes	pinot noir
Region	Marlborough, NZ
Cellar	🍶 3
Alc./Vol.	13.5%
RRP	$26.00

Montrose Sangiovese

Italian grape varieties have been grown by Montrose at Mudgee for a couple of decades, a legacy of the original Italian ownership of the vineyard, and their Italian winemaker. They didn't set the world on fire back then, but the upsurge in interest in these grapes over the last few years has led Montrose to market them again as individual varietals.
CURRENT RELEASE 1997 Multiculturalism in wine. Some of these Australian–Italian reds are truly exciting, offering a tasty alternative to the everyday home-grown style. The distinctive earthy cherry aromas of sangiovese are there on the nose, and the palate is dry, savoury and long with typical grippy tannins. Good with roast pork spruced up with rosemary and garlic.

Quality	▼▼▼▼▼
Value	★★★★
Grapes	sangiovese
Region	Mudgee, NSW
Cellar	🍶 3
Alc./Vol.	13.0%
RRP	$22.00

Moondah Brook Cabernet Sauvignon

Quality 🍷🍷🍷🍷
Value ★★★★½
Grapes cabernet sauvignon
Region various, WA
Cellar 🍾 3
Alc./Vol. 13.0%
RRP $17.00 Ⓢ

Although Moondah Brook is located in a very warm region at GinGin, north of Perth, in recent years a good proportion of the fruit has come from the cooler south. The result has been a steady increase in wine quality. Value is exemplary across the board.
CURRENT RELEASE 1997 The fruit makes a big statement in this crowd-pleasing style. On the nose it has juicy blackberry aromas with oak taking a back seat. The palate is soft and round with attractive black-fruit flavour and a whisper of toasty oak. Soft tannins complete the picture. A very friendly red. Try it with a cheese platter and a few friends.

Moondah Brook Maritime Dry Red

Quality 🍷🍷🍷½
Value ★★★
Grapes cabernet sauvignon; shiraz
Region Swan Valley, other WA
Cellar 🍾 1
Alc./Vol. 12.5%
RRP $10.00

A non-vintage red like this is an oddity in Australia these days. Even the most lowly labels now bear a year.
CURRENT RELEASE *non-vintage* No frills here – just a simple red with dark berry aromas and a minty touch on the nose, ahead of a soft, berry-flavoured palate. Tannins don't intrude much on a slightly short finish. A red for everyday drinking with foods like pasta.

Moondah Brook Shiraz

Quality 🍷🍷🍷🍷
Value ★★★★½
Grapes shiraz
Region various, WA
Cellar 🍾 4
Alc./Vol. 13.5%
RRP $17.00

At Moondah Brook they have a flair for producing generously flavoured wines at just the right price. Shiraz is a consistent star of the range.
CURRENT RELEASE 1997 This is right on the money. It smells of blackberry and plum with clean earth and some spice. In the mouth there's plenty of honest ripe flavour – juicy blackberry again with some dark chocolatey richness. The tannins provide some pleasing grip at the back of the palate. Good with some grilled fresh mild chorizo sausages and mashed potato.

Moorilla Estate Pinot Noir

Moorilla Estate, a pioneer of Tasmanian viticulture, seems to be over a troubled period and heading in the right direction. Maker Alain Rousseau.

CURRENT RELEASE 1998   Tasmanian winemakers put great store in pinot noir, but quality varies considerably. Moorilla's standard pinot has a raspberry-scented, pleasantly fruity, light nose. The palate has cherry-like flavour, fruity and soft in the middle with some firmness behind it. Try it with a brace of quail.

Quality	🍷🍷🍷🍷
Value	★★★↓
Grapes	pinot noir
Region	Tamar Valley, Tas.
Cellar	🍷 2
Alc./Vol.	12.5%
RRP	$28.00

Moorilla Estate Reserve Pinot Noir

Pinot noir succeeds in Tasmania where other red varieties fail. It's not always as good as the Taswegians claim, but it does show promise for the future.

CURRENT RELEASE 1998   We'll say from the outset that HH loved this wine, but that RK-P was less enthusiastic. Although this is the Reserve label, and one would expect it to be a big step up from the standard edition, the '98 doesn't offer that much more. It has a bit more complexity and depth, but it's still a lightish pinot with juicy cherry character, a herbal touch, and a hint of gaminess. It finishes soft and fragrant. Has interesting synergy with Tassie ocean trout.

Quality	🍷🍷🍷🍷
Value	★★★
Grapes	pinot noir
Region	Derwent Valley, Tas.
Cellar	🍷 2
Alc./Vol.	12.5%
RRP	$49.00

Moorooduc Estate Pinot Noir Wild Yeast

Wild yeast is the latest buzzword among serious pinot growers. Natural vineyard yeasts spontaneously start fermentations in much of Europe but it's a radical thing here. Richard McIntyre at Moorooduc is a convert.

CURRENT RELEASE 1997   Moorooduc's pinots are usually quite delicate expressions of a given vintage. The year 1997 was big on the Mornington Peninsula, but the Moorooduc has a cool personality that thaws as you get acquainted. The nose has fine strawberry and gamy aromas with a slightly stemmy regional edge. In the mouth there's a core of juicy ripe fruit, more gamy tones and some grip at the end. Needs age to build mellow complexity. Good with grilled marinated quail.

Quality	🍷🍷🍷🍷
Value	★★★↓
Grapes	pinot noir
Region	Mornington Peninsula, Vic.
Cellar	🍷 5
Alc./Vol.	13.5%
RRP	$49.00

Moss Wood Cabernet Sauvignon

Quality 🍷🍷🍷🍷🍷
Value ★★★★
Grapes cabernet sauvignon
Region Margaret River, WA
Cellar 2–10+
Alc./Vol. 14.0%
RRP $70.00

Moss Wood is one of the leading producers of Margaret River cabernet, making wines of great finesse which have achieved a cult following among discerning wine lovers. They are also popular with wine investors.

CURRENT RELEASE 1996 Harmony is the word here. The nose has intense sweet cassis aromas and lovely chocolatey richness dressed in cedary oak. The palate is ripe and lush with concentrated blackcurrant flavour, which has a slightly austere edge to it. Classy oak and fine ripe tannins are in perfect balance, even at this tender age. Everything dovetails into everything else to make a complete red wine that will only get better. Try it with roast fillet of beef.

Moss Wood Special Reserve Cabernet Sauvignon

Quality 🍷🍷🍷🍷🍷
Value ★★★★
Grapes cabernet sauvignon
Region Margaret River, WA
Cellar 10+
Alc./Vol. 13.5%
RRP $85.00

This mightily impressive Moss Wood Special Reserve is as rare as hen's teeth. Trust us and grab a bottle if you ever see one. You'll thank us for the experience.

CURRENT RELEASE 1994 This is special. The colour is deep and the bouquet is complex with rich cassis fruit at the core, soft leafiness, a touch of violet, and a good measure of cedary oak. In the mouth it shows great depth and lovely balance. The palate repeats the lush blackcurrant and beautifully integrated sweet oak theme in a seamless progression through to ripe, fine-grained tannins. Roast butterflied leg of lamb would suit.

Mount Avoca Shiraz

Quality 🍷🍷🍷🍷½
Value ★★★★
Grapes shiraz
Region Pyrenees, Vic.
Cellar 4
Alc./Vol. 13.5%
RRP $18.00

Like most Pyrenees red wines, Mount Avoca's are robust, flavoursome, and worthy of age. But unlike some, they're not too tough to drink young.

CURRENT RELEASE 1997 This has good deep colour, and the nose has ripe blackberry and spice aromas which are tight and intense. The palate has supple berry flavour of good concentration with fine, ripe tannins in excellent balance. Oak plays a subdued supporting role. A round, complete red which can be enjoyed now or cellared medium term. Try it with roast beef.

Mount Ida Shiraz

Mount Ida was established by well-known artist Leonard French in 1978. Now it's part of the Mildara Blass empire.

CURRENT RELEASE 1997 Heathcote has established itself as a source of good shiraz in a relatively short time with wines constructed like this. It's a dense purplish–red colour, and it has concentrated aromas reminiscent of syrupy plum, blackberry, and bakery spices. The nose shows less vanillin oak than the '96 at the same stage, and the wine is better balanced overall. Oak is more apparent on the palate where it joins intense, long, dark berry flavour, tangy acidity and grippy, ripe tannins. The palate needs bottle age to open up. Try it with a char-grilled rare porterhouse steak.

Quality	￥￥￥￥₹
Value	★★★★
Grapes	shiraz
Region	Heathcote, Vic.
Cellar	➟ 2–7
Alc./Vol.	12.5%
RRP	$30.00

Mount Langi Ghiran Joanna Cabernet Sauvignon

Trevor Mast has spread his wings from his Victorian base, and now he sources grapes from various South Australian vineyards to make a non-estate-grown range of Langi Ghiran wines. This cabernet comes from Joanna, north of Coonawarra.

CURRENT RELEASE 1997 A new Langi Ghiran which fits the winery's quality profile well. The nose is chock-full of cassis, spice, mint and chocolatey richness with balanced spicy oak. It's an appealing mouthful too, rich in black fruits with a mouth-filling dense texture and long, fine tannins. Should age well medium term. A good wine to serve with a veal tourte.

Quality	￥￥￥￥₹
Value	★★★★
Grapes	cabernet sauvignon
Region	Limestone Coast, SA
Cellar	▮ 5
Alc./Vol.	13.0%
RRP	$29.50

Mount Langi Ghiran Langi Shiraz

Quality	?????
Value	★★★★r
Grapes	shiraz
Region	Grampians, Vic.
Cellar	◊ 8
Alc./Vol.	13.0%
RRP	$50.00

Trevor Mast's Langi Shiraz is one of the most complete, stylish examples in the country. Unfortunately there's never enough to go around.

CURRENT RELEASE 1997   Purplish–red in colour, this has a fragrant nose of great distinction with ripe black cherry, plum, peppery spice and an almost floral touch. Oak influence is very subdued. In the mouth it's intense but not at all heavy, with smooth berry flavour, lively spice, fine tannins and a long finish. Beautifully put together. Try it with braised duck.

Mount Mary Pinot Noir

Quality	?????
Value	★★★★
Grapes	pinot noir
Region	Yarra Valley, Vic.
Cellar	◊ 5
Alc./Vol.	13.5%
RRP	$60.00 (mailing list)

Great wine doesn't need to be a blockbuster. At Mount Mary, pinot noir makes a lyrical, elegant statement that's at odds with some of the raw pinots we see these days. Alas, there isn't much of it about.

CURRENT RELEASE 1996   Paler in colour than some modern pinots, this has a lovely perfumed bouquet of raspberry and wild strawberry, with beautifully integrated oak providing a subtle seasoning. The palate is delectable and refined, satin-textured, and oh so long. Moderate subtle tannins carry a lingering, fragrant signature. A delight. Try it with magret of duck.

Mount Mary Quintet Cabernets

Quality	?????
Value	★★★★r
Grapes	cabernet sauvignon; cabernet franc; merlot; malbec; petit verdot
Region	Yarra Valley, Vic.
Cellar	◊ 5+
Alc./Vol.	12.5%
RRP	$60.00 (mailing list) ◊

Mount Mary reds vie with Penfolds Grange and Henschke Hill of Grace in the collector/investment stakes. This means a lot of it is bought to be hoarded, shown off and traded rather than consumed, which is a pity.

CURRENT RELEASE 1996   This Mount Mary came with a newsletter from proprietor Dr John Middleton pointing out that there was a worthwhile place for lesser vintages of his excellent reds. We agree: this '96 came from a less-than-perfect year but is an admirable effort. The nose has delicate cabernet fruit in the finely perfumed blackcurrany vein, robed in very subtle oak. The palate is elegant and soft with a long finish and fine tannins. Try it with roast veal.

Mountadam Pinot Noir

Adam Wynn and his late father David started messing around with pinot noir at Mountadam long before most of today's pinot experts had heard of it.

CURRENT RELEASE 1997 An admirable follow-up to an admirable '96 vintage. This has plums, earth, undergrowth and tobacco aromas on the complex yet reserved nose. The palate is more outgoing with a rich fruit-sweet flavour that is intense and long, and has a good underlying structure of ripe tannins. A winner served with Cantonese roast duck.

Quality	?????
Value	★★★⋆
Grapes	pinot noir
Region	Eden Valley, SA
Cellar	🍷 5
Alc./Vol.	14.0%
RRP	$42.75

CURRENT RELEASE 1998 The nose is sweetly fruity with raspberry and boiled-sweets aromas showing some whole berry influence. There's also a touch of undergrowth about it. In the mouth it's well endowed with earthy, plummy fruit flavour. It has smooth texture and a dry, slightly stemmy finish. Will be better in a year or so. Try it with veal cutlets.

Quality	????
Value	★★★⋆
Grapes	pinot noir
Region	Eden Valley, SA
Cellar	➖ 1–4
Alc./Vol.	14.0%
RRP	$42.75

Murrindindi Cabernets

The rolling hills of Murrindindi are a picturesque place in which to grow grapes. Some years are wet and chilly though, and the wines can suffer as a result. Happily the Cuthbertson family only release the red when it's up to scratch: if it doesn't meet their standards, they sell it off.

CURRENT RELEASE 1995 This has a fine cool-grown cabernet nose without any greenness. The bouquet has cassis, chocolate, leaf and cedary oak aromas. The flavours follow the nose perfectly with real finesse. The palate is tightly structured and subtly flavoured. Should keep well medium term. Serve with veal escalopes rolled around fontina cheese.

Quality	?????
Value	★★★★⋆
Grapes	cabernet sauvignon; cabernet franc; merlot
Region	Murrindindi, Vic.
Cellar	🍷 5
Alc./Vol.	13.0%
RRP	$23.00

Nepenthe Lenswood Pinot Noir

Quality	ҐҐҐ҇
Value	★★★⯎
Grapes	pinot noir
Region	Adelaide Hills, SA
Cellar	▮ 4
Alc./Vol.	14.0%
RRP	$28.00

Winemaker Peter Leske kept the wine writers entertained last vintage with regular mailings of his daily diary entries. Very illuminating, but he can't spell Baumé. (Typical pedantic writer's comment. Ed.)

CURRENT RELEASE 1998   A joyful sort of wine which is full of cheer. It has a medium–light colour, but that means little with pinot. The fruit-led aroma is of cherry and strawberry, and the fruit intensity follows onto the palate where it's sweet and ripe with a brandied-cherry quality and some alcohol warmth. Excellent body, length and ripeness. High-quality fruit and subtly managed oak. Great with prawn ravioli.

Nepenthe The Fugue

Quality	ҐҐҐҐҐ
Value	★★★★
Grapes	cabernet sauvignon; merlot
Region	Adelaide Hills, SA
Cellar	⬤ 2–7+
Alc./Vol.	14.0%
RRP	$28.00 ▮

That's fugue, not fug. One's a mental state the morning after; the other's a piece of music. Considering the first vines were planted in 1994, this is a hell of an achievement. Maker Peter Leske.

CURRENT RELEASE 1997   This is a wine to put down. It's closed, and the fruit is subdued; oak and extractive characters dominate. It's tight and tough with lashings of tannin. The finish is dry and austere and it's quite unready to drink. It opens up beautifully after a day's breathing. Cellar, then have with aged gruyère cheese.

Normans Cabernet Sauvignon

Quality	ҐҐҐҐ
Value	★★★★
Grapes	cabernet sauvignon
Region	South Eastern Australia
Cellar	⬤ 1–5+
Alc./Vol.	13.0%
RRP	$17.00 Ⓢ

This company was founded by one Jesse Norman – not a singer, but a wine man. It has a winery at Clarendon on the Adelaide Hills–McLaren Vale border, and one in the Riverland.

CURRENT RELEASE 1998   It's obvious that good-quality grapes went into this wine, but the winemakers don't seem to have done enough with them. It's a vivid purple–red, and there are raw, rather unfinished grapey aromas of sour cherry and plum skin. It's a fruit bomb – not complex, but could surprise with an extra year or so in storage. Try it with pork spare ribs.

Normans Cabernet Sauvignon Cabernet Franc

It's unwieldy to put all that on a label, but the way our labelling laws are, that's the way it has to be. 'Cabernets' is not a recognised term.

CURRENT RELEASE 1996 Put this on your aching joints instead of liniment! It has an overriding aroma of eucalyptus – a feature of the Langhorne Creek area. In the mouth it has a tonne of flavour, and is soft and fleshy with good extract and smoothness. Peppermint Pattie eat your heart out. Try it with lamb and mint sauce.

Quality	♟♟♟♟
Value	★★★
Grapes	cabernet sauvignon; cabernet franc
Region	Langhorne Creek, SA
Cellar	♦ 7+
Alc./Vol.	12.5%
RRP	$24.50 Ⓢ

Normans Chais Clarendon Cabernet Sauvignon

Normans is a public company listed on the Stock Exchange, so you can buy shares in the wine biz if you so desire. Maker Roger Harbord.

CURRENT RELEASE 1996 This is a serious cabernet with excellent depth, weight and structure. The colour is a very dark purple–red, and the nose has concentrated ripe fruit aromas with oak in fine balance. The palate has depth, weight and length, and there's some astringency on the finish that will contribute to its ageing potential, which is undoubtedly good. Goes very well with venison.

Quality	♟♟♟♟♟
Value	★★★★
Grapes	cabernet sauvignon
Region	McLaren Vale, SA
Cellar	♦ 10+
Alc./Vol.	12.5%
RRP	$35.40 Ⓢ

Normans Chais Clarendon Shiraz

Chais is a French word for 'winery'. You have your chateau and behind it your *chais*, but as far as we're aware there's no French connection at Normans. (Nor is there a chateau!)

CURRENT RELEASE 1996 This is Normans' top-shelf label and it seldom disappoints. The colour is dark red–purple, and the nose has youthful charred-oak and plum aromas. It's a very big, ripe, solid wine with a firmly tannic palate loaded with oak, and is designed to be cellared. A blockbuster, loaded with potential. Cellar it, then serve with aged gruyère.

Quality	♟♟♟♟♟
Value	★★★
Grapes	shiraz
Region	McLaren Vale, SA
Cellar	➡ 2–12+
Alc./Vol.	13.5%
RRP	$40.00 Ⓢ ▌

Normans Coonawarra Cabernet Sauvignon

Quality	♟♟♟♟
Value	★★ᴖ
Grapes	cabernet sauvignon
Region	Coonawarra, SA
Cellar	▮ 5
Alc./Vol.	12.5%
RRP	$24.50 Ⓢ

This is one of the new range of regional varietals that Normans put out in 1999. Maker Roger Harbord.

CURRENT RELEASE 1997   The colour is a little on the light side but it has good purple–red tints. The aroma is slightly simple and raspberry-cordial-like, and there's a hint of greenness. It's a fruit-driven light- to medium-bodied wine that has no faults – it just lacks a little depth and complexity. There are some minty and floral aromas, which build with airing. Try it with egg and bacon pie.

Normans Foundation Shiraz Cabernet

Quality	♟♟♟
Value	★★★
Grapes	shiraz; cabernet sauvignon
Region	not stated
Cellar	▮ 1
Alc./Vol.	12.5%
RRP	$13.40 Ⓢ

The Raelene Boyle Cancer Foundation gets $2 of the price of every bottle sold.

CURRENT RELEASE 1997   This is a very soft, mature, ready-drinking red wine. The colour looks quite aged with a developed brick-red hue. The nose has both jammy and dusty oak overtones, and little development. It's light-bodied, soft and basic, with a plain herbal flavour and forward development. Drink up. Goes well with spaghetti bolognese.

Normans Merlot

Quality	♟♟♟♟
Value	★★★ᴖ
Grapes	merlot
Region	various, SA
Cellar	▮ 3
Alc./Vol.	13.5%
RRP	$17.00 Ⓢ

What is a merlot supposed to taste like? Well, here's yet another interpretation. It sings its own song, but it's a good drink.

CURRENT RELEASE 1998   The nose opens low-key and remains shy. The palate has moderate weight and presence, some density and grip, but is rather nondescript. It's a good, inexpensive claret style to drink now. Try it with meatballs.

Normans Shiraz

The former Family Reserve series of Normans has been repackaged with a diagonally positioned rectangular label. Simplicity is the key. Maker Roger Harbord.

CURRENT RELEASE 1998   This basic dry red has a vivid purplish colour that shows its youth. The aromas are spicy, peppery and meaty, and express the shiraz grape well. The palate is lean and slightly hollow, but has a good grip on the finish. It's an elegant, lighter-bodied red to quaff with Wiener schnitzel.

Quality	♏♏♏
Value	★★★
Grapes	shiraz
Region	various, SA
Cellar	▯ 3
Alc./Vol.	13.5%
RRP	$17.00 Ⓢ

Oakridge Cabernet Sauvignon Merlot

Oakridge is now a big operation with plenty of share-holders and visitors trooping out to the Yarra Valley to visit. A new winery and ambitious production targets will ensure that we hear the name a lot more.

CURRENT RELEASE 1997   This doesn't have the concentration of some of its predecessors, maybe because the Reserve labels get the pick of the crop. Nevertheless it's a pleasant drink with good blackcurrant-like cabernet characters and a little leafy/stemmy austerity. Oak treatment is kept restrained throughout.

Quality	♏♏♏
Value	★★★
Grapes	cabernet sauvignon; merlot
Region	Yarra Valley, Vic.
Cellar	▯ 3
Alc./Vol.	13.3%
RRP	$20.00

Old Station Shiraz

This vineyard was planted beside the railway station at Watervale in 1926. The vineyard's still there; the railway isn't.

CURRENT RELEASE 1997   This is a rustic wine with old-fashioned blackberry-jam aromas on the nose along with a touch of aldehyde. In the mouth it's full-bodied with earthy flavour, some rough edges and dry tannins. A bit of a time capsule really; a lot of Aussie red used to be like this. Try it with a hearty steak and onion pie.

Quality	♏♏♏
Value	★★★▸
Grapes	shiraz
Region	Clare Valley, SA
Cellar	▯ 4
Alc./Vol.	13.9%
RRP	$20.85

Orlando Jacaranda Ridge Cabernet Sauvignon

Quality	♟♟♟♟
Value	★★★
Grapes	cabernet sauvignon
Region	Coonawarra, SA
Cellar	▮ 5+
Alc./Vol.	13.5%
RRP	$50.00

Jacaranda Ridge is a flagship red for Orlando based on special grapes and given some bottle-age before sale. In common with other such flagship wines, oak has always played a large part in its make-up. The fruit is there too, but one wonders what it would be like without all that timber.

CURRENT RELEASE 1994   Nearly three years in new oak shows in this wine. The nose has a large measure of vanillin wood, but blackcurrant syrup aromas in the midst of it make a statement on behalf of the fruit. In the mouth it's a big, grainy-textured wine with dark-fruit notes, lots of oaky flavour and drying tannins on the finish. Try it with a thick T-bone steak.

Orlando Jacob's Creek Shiraz Cabernet Sauvignon

Quality	♟♟♟
Value	★★★
Grapes	shiraz; cabernet sauvignon
Region	not stated, SA
Cellar	▮ 1
Alc./Vol.	13.0%
RRP	$9.00

Jacob's Creek has launched millions of Britons on a love affair with Australian wine. You see it on the table in English television shows, in shops, in out-of-the-way places – everywhere.

CURRENT RELEASE 1997   This is exactly in the Jacob's Creek style – a pleasant young red with clean fruity redcurrant aromas, straightforward berry flavour and soft tannins. Serve it with lasagne.

Orlando St Hugo Cabernet Sauvignon

Quality	♟♟♟♟♟
Value	★★★★
Grapes	cabernet sauvignon
Region	Coonawarra, SA
Cellar	▮ 8
Alc./Vol.	13.5%
RRP	$34.00

Orlando make a handful of more expensive reds than St Hugo. The most obvious difference has usually been the level of oak influence: in St Hugo it's much more moderately handled and easier to cope with.

CURRENT RELEASE 1996   This was a very good vintage in Coonawarra, and the result is the best St Hugo for years. It's a very dense wine with an attractive, concentrated nose of ripe blackcurrant, blackberry and dark chocolate. In the mouth it has black-fruit sweetness and perfectly balanced oak. The texture is seamless and smooth with well-weighted tannins on a long finish. Good with a barbecue of marinated lamb fillets.

Osborns Pinot Noir

The Mornington Peninsula has a plethora of small vineyards like Osborns. This estate is at Merricks North, at the warmer end of the Peninsula.

CURRENT RELEASE 1997 This was a drought vintage that produced deeper-coloured, bigger Mornington pinots than usual. Osborns has a promising, spicy, intense red-berry nose, which is ripe and sweet with some complex smoky, undergrowthy aromas. In the mouth it has a velvety fruit character which is long and warmly satisfying. Mild tannins support things well. A surprisingly good pinot from relatively young vines. Try it with roast duck.

Quality	?????
Value	★★★★
Grapes	pinot noir
Region	Mornington Peninsula, Vic.
Cellar	2
Alc./Vol.	14.0%
RRP	$25.00

Palliser Estate Pinot Noir

Palliser has 85 hectares of vines at Martinborough, which takes it somewhat out of the boutique league. Maker Allan Johnson.

Previous outstanding vintages: '96

CURRENT RELEASE 1997 Pinot on steroids! This has exceptional depth of colour, aroma and flavour. The fruit is fully ripe and well concentrated, and is backed by good oak. There's plenty of smooth tannin and great extract. It's fleshy and lingering on the tongue. Superb now, but also seems to have a great future. Serve with roast pigeon breast.

Quality	?????
Value	★★★★★
Grapes	pinot noir
Region	Martinborough, NZ
Cellar	5+
Alc./Vol.	14.0%
RRP	$32.00

Paracombe Cabernet Franc

This is the small (12 hectares) Adelaide Hills vineyard of Paul Drogemuller. The wines are made under contract elsewhere.

CURRENT RELEASE 1997 Unusual to see this as a straight varietal. It's an attractive, lighter-bodied red and recalls the cabernet francs of the Loire Valley. There are leafy and plum-like fruit characters overlain by gunpowdery oak. It's aromatic and medium-bodied with some grainy tannins. The alcohol comes as a surprise: don't expect a big red. It would team well with pan-fried veal.

Quality	????
Value	★★★
Grapes	cabernet franc
Region	Adelaide Hills, SA
Cellar	3
Alc./Vol.	14.5%
RRP	$21.00 (V)

Paracombe Shiraz Cabernet

Quality	♥♥♥
Value	★★★
Grapes	shiraz; cabernet sauvignon
Region	Adelaide Hills, SA
Cellar	▮ 4
Alc./Vol.	13.5%
RRP	$21.00 ♥

The grapes were grown organically in the Adelaide Hills. The wine is mainly shiraz with just a garnish of cabernet sauvignon.

CURRENT RELEASE 1995 This wine has a slightly rough barrel odour about it. It's possible that it was aged in older wood. There are toasty, earthy, mushroom-like aromas, and it improves on the palate where there's good flavour and elegance. There's a certain savouriness to the palate flavours and it's well balanced for early drinking. Goes well with roast squab.

Paringa Estate Pinot Noir

Quality	♥♥♥♥♥
Value	★★★★⯪
Grapes	pinot noir
Region	Mornington Peninsula, Vic.
Cellar	➤ 1–5
Alc./Vol.	13.8%
RRP	$40.00

Paringa pinot noir is a tour de force, which can polarise opinion. The blockbuster '97 even got your mild-mannered authors arguing. HH is besotted; RK-P is not so sure. They got out the boxing gloves before tasting the '98 edition.

CURRENT RELEASE 1998 Less emphatic than the '97 vintage but still hard to ignore. The colour is ruby of medium depth, and the dark roast-coffee scents of highly charred French oak lead the nose. There's also sweet black-cherry fruit, a hint of beetroot, and mulchy complexity. The palate is powerful – deep, rich and complex with good length and ripe, dry tannins. Ideally needs cellaring to blossom. Try it with Peking duck.

Passing Clouds Angel Blend

Quality	♥♥♥
Value	★★★
Grapes	cabernet sauvignon; cabernet franc; merlot
Region	Bendigo, Vic.
Cellar	➤ 3–10+
Alc./Vol.	13.0%
RRP	$30.00

Collectors of extraordinary wine labels should grab this one. It's baroque in the extreme. Maker Graeme Leith.

CURRENT RELEASE 1996 A typical Bendigo-district gum-leafy blockbuster. The wine has camphor, earth, and eucalypt aromas, and the palate is very big, aggressive, astringent and really quite fierce at this stage. It needs time! There's plenty of flavour, plenty of guts; what it lacks in subtlety it makes up for in spirit. Cellar, and then serve with Skippy burgers.

Passing Clouds Graeme's Blend

Those who read lifestyle magazines will recognise the smiling, bearded face of winemaker Graeme Leith from some of the Tourism Victoria advertisements.

CURRENT RELEASE 1996 This is an aggressive young red that needs to be either cellared or served with strong food. The aroma is strong on peppermint and garden mint. There's also a thread of black pepper. The palate is very intense with high acid and some astringency, giving it an austere, slightly forbidding taste. Cellar this and then serve with jugged hare.

Quality	🍷🍷🍷
Value	★★★
Grapes	shiraz; cabernet sauvignon
Region	Bendigo, Vic.
Cellar	2–10+
Alc./Vol.	13.0%
RRP	$23.00

Passing Clouds Shiraz

This is a parched stretch of central Victoria where the clouds, if there are any, scud past at high altitude without pausing to rain on the vines. Maker Graeme Leith.

CURRENT RELEASE 1996 This seems to have a case of the cool-year jitters. The colour is medium red; the aroma has Ribena and methoxypyrazine (asparagus-like) unripe notes with hints of tomato sauce. Lean and somewhat short to taste. Try it with a burger and tomato sauce.

Quality	🍷🍷½
Value	★★
Grapes	shiraz
Region	Bendigo, Vic.
Cellar	4
Alc./Vol.	13.5%
RRP	$23.00

Paul Osicka Shiraz

This well-established producer is at Graytown, not far from the Goulburn Valley's Tahbilk and Mitchelton, but somehow it's found itself in the Bendigo region.

CURRENT RELEASE 1997 Typically for the maker, this is a big, ballsy, generously proportioned shiraz. It's fruit-driven, and the aromas are herbal, minty and plummy with some spicy undercurrents. There's well concentrated flavour and the finish is quite astringent. Cellar, then serve with standing rib roast of beef.

Quality	🍷🍷🍷🍷
Value	★★★★
Grapes	shiraz
Region	Bendigo, Vic.
Cellar	2–12+
Alc./Vol.	13.9%
RRP	$23.00

Pauletts Andreas Shiraz

Quality	♟♟♟♟♟
Value	★★★★
Grapes	shiraz
Region	Clare Valley, SA
Cellar	➥ 3–15+
Alc./Vol.	14.0%
RRP	$42.00

The land now owned by the Pauletts was bought in 1866 by one Andreas Weiman, whose descendants owned it continuously for 114 years. Winemaker Neil Paulett uses open slate fermenters and a basket press.

CURRENT RELEASE 1996   What a lovely drop of red! It's a big, firm, authoritative wine which is slightly closed at present, but which has the makings of a brilliant bottle. Rich and well structured, it's chock-a-block with dark berry, toast and vanilla flavours that linger on and on. Cellar, then serve with venison.

Pauletts Cabernet Merlot

Quality	♟♟♟♟♟
Value	★★★★★
Grapes	cabernet sauvignon; merlot
Region	Clare Valley, SA
Cellar	♟ 5
Alc./Vol.	14.0%
RRP	$18.30

The Clare Valley is a lovely place to visit for its wine, but it's also very scenic in its own right. The Polish Hill River region around Pauletts' winery is particularly lovely.

CURRENT RELEASE 1997   Good Clare cabernet blends (like this) add a chewy textural component to the intense flavours the district imparts. They don't just go with good food: they *are* good food. This has a nose of ripe black-fruit aromas and a sort of thorny-leaved savouriness that adds real interest. The palate is rich in black-berryish fruit flavour with measured ripe, dry tannins. Good with lamb shanks braised in red wine.

Pauletts Shiraz

Quality	♟♟♟♟
Value	★★★★
Grapes	shiraz
Region	Clare Valley, SA
Cellar	♟ 6
Alc./Vol.	14.0%
RRP	$18.30

Pauletts' vineyard is less than twenty years old, but the wines have the assured style of a much longer-established place.

CURRENT RELEASE 1997   The oak seems a little more pronounced in this wine than in the cabernet, but the driving force is still deep dark fruit character. The nose has black plum, berry and vanilla aromas with some rich dark chocolate touches. The palate is medium-bodied with solid fruit in the middle and balanced wood. Dry tannins frame everything nicely. A good match for a lamb pie.

Pegasus Bay Maestro

The problem with growing the Bordeaux varieties in a region as cold as the Christchurch district is getting them to ripen fully. Green flavours are common. No such problem with this.

CURRENT RELEASE 1995   The wine is showing a little development in its brick-red shade, but it has good depth of colour. The nose has some development and lots of complexity: chocolate, fruitcake, preserved fruits, prunes and vanilla. The palate is smooth and mellow and has sweet fruit in the middle with drying tannins towards the finish. There are raisin, prune and jam-like flavours as well. It's an absolutely delicious drink, and shows none of the greenness typical of New Zealand reds. Drink it with veal parmigiana.

Quality	🍷🍷🍷🍷🍷
Value	★★★★
Grapes	cabernet sauvignon; cabernet franc; merlot
Region	Canterbury, NZ
Cellar	🍾 5
Alc./Vol.	13.0%
RRP	$30.00 (cellar door)

Pegasus Bay Pinot Noir

The Donaldson family vineyard, winery and restaurant is located just outside Christchurch, where founder Professor Ivan Donaldson is a neurologist.

Previous outstanding vintages: '96

CURRENT RELEASE 1997   Another lovely pinot from this chilly part of Kiwiland. The colour is medium–deep red–purple, and it smells of maraschino cherries, sweetly ripe with some sappy undertones. It has plenty of guts and concentration, fruit-sweetness and a lingering finish. A satisfying pinot that could cellar well. Try it with Portuguese thrice-braised duck.

Quality	🍷🍷🍷🍷🍷
Value	★★★★
Grapes	pinot noir
Region	Canterbury, NZ
Cellar	🍾 5+
Alc./Vol.	13.0%
RRP	$39.50

Penfolds Bin 407 Cabernet Sauvignon

Quality	▼▼▼▼▼
Value	★★★★★
Grapes	cabernet sauvignon
Region	Coonawarra, Bordertown, Padthaway, McLaren Vale & Barossa Valley, SA
Cellar	⊷ 2–12+
Alc./Vol.	13.5%
RRP	$26.00 Ⓢ 📶

This is a Penfolds wine first, and a cabernet a distant second. In other words, it's a house style. It was created in 1990 to fill the gap vacated by the upwardly mobile Bin 707.

Previous outstanding vintages: '90, '91, '92, '93, '94

CURRENT RELEASE 1996   Scorched-wood   aromas open the batting, and it needs time for the fruit to recover. Toasted vanilla oak marks it as a Penfolds wine, and there are coffee grounds and red-berry tastes in the mouth. The profile is lean and tight, very cabernet in structure, and it should reward in a few years. Great potential. Serve with venison.

Penfolds Bin 707 Cabernet Sauvignon

Quality	▼▼▼▼▼
Value	★★★
Grapes	cabernet sauvignon
Region	Coonawarra, Barossa Valley, Padthaway & McLaren Vale, SA
Cellar	⊷ 5–20+
Alc./Vol.	13.5%
RRP	$90.00+ 📶

The price is heading north at a rapid rate of knots, hauled along by the relentless wake of Grange. The wine seems to get bigger every year, too. It's one of the most reliable cellaring reds in the land. There was no '95 vintage.

Previous outstanding vintages: '64, '76, '80, '83, '84, '86, '87, '90, '91, '92, '93, '94

CURRENT RELEASE 1996   This is a massive wine with a colour that stains the glass purple. It's enormously concentrated in every way. Because of aggressive tannin and the dominance of charred American oak, it must be cellared for some years. It smells of singed coconuts, and the palate is monstrous, with very grippy tannin. It's virtually undrinkable now. Cellar, then serve with reggiano cheese.

Penfolds Coonawarra Bin 128

For a company that's big on shiraz, Bin 128 has often seemed like an afterthought, without the usual Penfolds grunt. Not so in '96. Maker John Duval and team.
Previous outstanding vintages: '71, '78, '80, '82, '86, '88, '90, '91, '93, '94
CURRENT RELEASE 1996 An utterly magical Bin 128. This has all you could want, and then some. Profound purple–red colour, and rich dark-chocolatey, ripe aromas with raspberry and cherry touches. Full-bodied and lushly fruited in the mouth, it has blackberry concentration, ponderous power and density, and a deft balance between fruity and more complex flavours. Masterful. Drink it with Heidi gruyère.

Quality	🍷🍷🍷🍷🍷
Value	★★★★★
Grapes	shiraz
Region	Coonawarra, SA
Cellar	15
Alc./Vol.	13.5%
RRP	$20.00

Penfolds Grange

Grange is one of the most predictable wines of the year: there's never a bad vintage or even a lesser vintage of Grange these days. Blending across many regions and vineyards helps ensure consistency of style. Maker John Duval and team.
Previous outstanding vintages: '52, '53, '55, '62, '63, '66, '71, '76, '83, '86, '88, '90, '91, '93
CURRENT RELEASE 1994 At only five years old this is already terrifically enjoyable, but it would be a sin to open a $300 bottle just yet. The colour is dark red–purple with black reflections. It has a very complex bouquet with anise, leather, undergrowth, singed meat aromas, and a great deal of oak, which is already starting to integrate beautifully. It's full-bodied in the mouth and very powerful with lashings of tannin, but the sweetness of the fruit and oak peeps through the tremendous structure. The aftertaste is mouth-puckering and grippy, and the flavours of barbecued meats, undergrowth and berries continue for a long time. A terrific wine, which fully supports the reputation. Serve it with confit of duck.

Quality	🍷🍷🍷🍷🍷
Value	★★
Grapes	shiraz
Region	various, including Barossa Valley, McLaren Vale, Clare Valley, Padthaway & Coonawarra, SA
Cellar	5–25+
Alc./Vol.	13.5%
RRP	$250–$300

Penfolds Kalimna Bin 28

Quality	♟♟♟♟
Value	★★★
Grapes	shiraz
Region	Barossa Valley & other, SA
Cellar	▬ 8+
Alc./Vol.	13.5%
RRP	$20.00 Ⓢ

This is a Barossa-based shiraz with a distinguished lineage. It used to be based on the Kalimna vineyard in the north of the Barossa, a vineyard Max Schubert used to say was Penfolds' best.
Previous outstanding vintages: '82, '83, '86, '87, '88, '90, '91, '92, '93, '94
CURRENT RELEASE 1996 A commendable shiraz, although shaded by the Bin 128 every time we've tasted them together. The nose displays cherry, plum and stewed-fruit aromas with background oak. It's smooth and medium-bodied in the mouth with gentle tannins, and it already drinks very well. Try it with lamb shanks.

Penfolds Koonunga Hill Shiraz Cabernet

Quality	♟♟♟♟
Value	★★★★
Grapes	shiraz; cabernet sauvignon
Region	not stated
Cellar	▬ 5
Alc./Vol.	13.5%
RRP	$12.00 Ⓢ

According to market researcher A.C. Nielsen, this is the third-biggest-selling red wine under $12 in Australia.
CURRENT RELEASE 1997 Not only is it only one of the biggest-selling red wines, it's also one of the best value-for-money. The colour is nice and dark; the aromas are of ripe berries and meaty characters reflecting wood maturation and age development. The palate is lean and somewhat austere with a distinct tannin finish. The mellow fruit flavours are sweet, soft and smooth on the palate. Try it with a lamb yeeros.

Penfolds Old Vine Grenache Mourvèdre Shiraz

Quality	♟♟♟♟
Value	★★★★
Grapes	grenache; mourvèdre; shiraz
Region	Barossa Valley, SA
Cellar	▬ 6+
Alc./Vol.	13.0%
RRP	$21.50 ▯

This wine surfs on the Rhone-blend wave that was started – in this country at least – by Charles Melton Nine Popes. As usual, Penfolds didn't rush in with a me-too product but thoughtfully released a quality red, right on the money.
Previous outstanding vintages: '92, '94
CURRENT RELEASE 1996 Rustic and earthy are words that spring to mind. It has a commendable degree of matured complexity. It tastes savoury, cedary and earthy rather then grapey, and finishes with drying tannins. It's mellow and drinks beautifully now, with saddle of hare.

Penfolds Rawson's Retreat

The main grape variety is shiraz but there's also a fair amount of ruby cabernet, a hybrid bred for giving cabernet-like wines in hot climates.
CURRENT RELEASE 1998 This is a light-bodied, simple quaffing dry red, which offers good value for money. The colour is full purple–red; the aroma of cherry skins and plum pips has a delicate background of wood. The palate is fairly light-bodied and fruity with reasonable flavour depth, finished by a lick of tannin. It's the goods at the right price. Try it with meatballs.

Quality	♥♥♥
Value	★★★⊦
Grapes	shiraz; ruby cabernet; cabernet sauvignon
Region	not stated
Cellar	╽ 2
Alc./Vol.	13.5%
RRP	$9.00 Ⓢ

Penfolds St Henri Shiraz Cabernet

Within Penfolds' repertoire this has always been an eccentric style, aged in old 2000-litre casks rather than small oak. Maker John Duval and team.
Previous outstanding vintages: '80, '82, '83, '85, '86, '90, '91, '93, '94
CURRENT RELEASE 1995 A lovely old-fashioned mouthful of red – a nostalgic blast from the past. Nice deep colour; big ripe earthy, almost ferruginous, bouquet starting to show some development. The palate is solid and robust, with plenty of drying tannin. Not a wine of finesse, but honest and rustic. Food: aged hard cheeses.

Quality	♥♥♥♥
Value	★★★
Grapes	shiraz; cabernet sauvignon
Region	various, SA
Cellar	╽ 10
Alc./Vol.	13.5%
RRP	$42.50 ▮

Penley Estate Cabernet Sauvignon

This boy knows how to make cabernet! The '93 vintage won the Penguin Best Red Wine award. Maker is Kym 'Drizabone' Tolley.
Previous outstanding vintages: '90, '91, '93, '94
CURRENT RELEASE 1996 Cancel all incoming calls! This is party time. Wonderful flavour and power; dusty, brazil-nutty, concentrated aromas; superb sweet fruit and drying tannin in the mouth. A humdinger of a wine, laden with complex flavour and mouth-coating tannin. Seamless and sophisticated. Serve with rare rump steak and bearnaise.

Quality	♥♥♥♥♥
Value	★★★★
Grapes	cabernet sauvignon
Region	Coonawarra, SA
Cellar	╽ 12+
Alc./Vol.	13.0%
RRP	$50.00 ▮

Penley Estate Shiraz Cabernet

Quality	???????
Value	★★★★✦
Grapes	shiraz; cabernet sauvignon
Region	Coonawarra, McLaren Vale & Barossa Valley, SA
Cellar	▮ 6+
Alc./Vol.	13.0%
RRP	$27.00 ▮

Kym Tolley has 98 hectares of vines at his Coonawarra property, but still chooses to buy grapes in for some of his wines, such as this one. Cab-shiraz blends are a tried-and-true Aussie formula.

CURRENT RELEASE 1996   This is a generous red with plenty of everything. It has a sweet-oak, slightly jammy ripe-fruit aroma, and the vanilla/berry flavours run through the palate. Soft, broad, rich and chocolatey, it fills the mouth with a warmth of ripe fruit, oak and tannin. It has potential for ageing too. Serve with a rich casserole.

Penley Phoenix Cabernet Sauvignon

Quality	???
Value	★★✦
Grapes	cabernet sauvignon
Region	Coonawarra, SA
Cellar	▮ 3
Alc./Vol.	14.0%
RRP	$20.50

Why Phoenix? It's nothing to do with rising from the ashes. The Phoenix Winemaking and Distilling Company was the Tolley family's first winery in Adelaide in the nineteenth century. Maker Kym Tolley.

CURRENT RELEASE 1997   This is a slightly green-tasting cabernet. The colour is of moderate intensity, and the aroma recalls cassis and crushed leaves. The taste is lean and somewhat astringent. It's not a very friendly style. Best with food: try lamb kebabs.

Petaluma Coonawarra

Quality	?????
Value	★★★★
Grapes	cabernet sauvignon 60%; merlot 40%
Region	Coonawarra, SA
Cellar	➡ 3–12+
Alc./Vol.	13.7%
RRP	$49.00 ▮

Brian Croser has joined the anti-filtration brigade, so make sure you strain the wine through your whiskers. (In subtle lettering on the front label is the word 'unfiltered'.) It should endear the wine to Robert Parker.

Previous outstanding vintages: '79, '82, '88, '90, '91, '92, '93, '94, '96

CURRENT RELEASE 1997   A very fine wine even by Petaluma standards. The smallest yields ever in the Evans vineyard have rendered a vividly purple-coloured, powerfully blackcurrant-flavoured wine of superb balance. There are hints of cabernet cassis and crushed leaves, subtle oak and a fine thread of tannin. Deep, lively, intense and delicious. Cellar, then serve with cheddar.

Peter Lehmann Cabernet Sauvignon

Lehmann's winery is now a major operation, crushing over 10 000 tonnes of grapes and successfully listed on the stock exchange. Maker Andrew Wigan and team.
Previous outstanding vintages: '94, '96
CURRENT RELEASE 1997 Attractive mulberry, blackberry aromas are countered by some stalkiness, and the wine has plenty of body and astringency. There are some herbal varietal cabernet notes. It has potential, but needs time to mellow and develop complexity. Serve with marinated buffalo fillet.

Quality	♟♟♟♟
Value	★★★★
Grapes	cabernet sauvignon
Region	Barossa Valley, SA
Cellar	▮ 10
Alc./Vol.	14.0%
RRP	$20.50 ⑤ ▮

Peter Lehmann Shiraz

Nice wine, but a magnum sold for $200 at the Barossa Festival auction, a good reason to avoid glamour auctions and large-format bottles. Maker Andrew Wigan.
Previous outstanding vintages: '92, '93, '94, '96
CURRENT RELEASE 1997 The price is slowly rising, and so's the amount of oak. There are cherry, strawberry-like aromas with vanilla-bean American oak, and it gives the impression of separate fruit-plus-oak style at time of release, although it surely will integrate in time. Firm oak tannins give a savoury impression and dry aftertaste. Serve with rissoles.

Quality	♟♟♟♟
Value	★★★★
Grapes	shiraz
Region	Barossa Valley, SA
Cellar	➡ 1–9+
Alc./Vol.	14.5%
RRP	$19.50 ▮

Pewsey Vale Cabernet Sauvignon

This vineyard, in the Eden Valley region, has always impressed with riesling, but less so with cabernet. Maker Brian Walsh and team.
CURRENT RELEASE 1996 A typical straightforward, ready-drinking, undemanding red from Pewsey. The nose has slightly green, herbal aromas with some red-berry fruit; the palate is narrow in structure and lacks a little flesh and fruit-sweetness, but it's a perfectly respectable drink-now red at the price. Try a rabbit casserole.

Quality	♟♟♟
Value	★★★★
Grapes	cabernet sauvignon
Region	Eden Valley, SA
Cellar	▮ 5
Alc./Vol.	12.5%
RRP	$14.75 ⑤

Pfeiffer Cabernet Sauvignon

Quality	▼▼▼▼⸺
Value	★★★★
Grapes	cabernet sauvignon
Region	Rutherglen, Vic.
Cellar	⬯ 2–12+
Alc./Vol.	14.0%
RRP	$19.20 ⬩

Chris Pfeiffer is locking his horns in wine politics these days. He's president of the Victorian Wine Industry Association.

CURRENT RELEASE 1997 A very impressive Rutherglen cabernet, which has more varietal character than most. Smoky, toasty, vanilla oak-driven bouquet, then crushed-leaf and blackberry flavours of great depth and persistence. It's already quite complex. Try it with aged cheddar.

Pike's Premio Sangiovese

Quality	▼▼▼▼⸺
Value	★★★★
Grapes	sangiovese
Region	Clare Valley, SA
Cellar	⬩ 7
Alc./Vol.	13.5%
RRP	$21.30

Most Australian attempts at this Tuscan grape have been disappointingly light, but this one has real stuffing. Maker Neil Pike.

CURRENT RELEASE 1997 An excellent first effort, with more than a hint of chianti. The colour is deep, and it smells of dried herbs and cherry with licorice overtones and background oak. It has excellent depth of flavour, plenty of extract and a very tasty, savoury finish. It would team well with osso bucco.

Pipers Brook Vineyard Pellion Pinot Noir

Quality	▼▼▼▼
Value	★★★
Grapes	pinot noir
Region	Pipers Brook, Tas.
Cellar	⬩ 4+
Alc./Vol.	12.8%
RRP	$28.70

Pipers Brook winemaker Andrew Pirie has been grappling with this tricky variety for many years, and the '98 is arguably his best yet.

CURRENT RELEASE 1998 This is a very pretty wine. It has cordial-like strawberry, cherry fruit aromas with some grassy overtones, and a hint of aspirin. The palate is light- to medium-bodied, smooth and clean, with pristine pinot fruit flavour and gentle tannins on a light structure. It drinks well with Tasmanian salmon.

Pirramimma Petit Verdot

This is the third wine the Johnston family of Pirramimma has released from this rare grape, which is
mostly used as a lesser blending variety in Bordeaux.
CURRENT RELEASE 1996 This is a pretty decent drop
of red, but it's not easy to ascertain what the grape tastes
like – there's so much coconut/vanilla flavour from
American oak getting in the way. The nose offers
unusual floral, essency, almost citrus-like aromas and a
heap of vanilla. It's quite big, dry and tannic in the
mouth, which is characteristic of petit verdot. It needs
food, so try it with boeuf bordelaise.

Quality	▼▼▼▼
Value	★★★ь
Grapes	petit verdot
Region	McLaren Vale, SA
Cellar	⬥ 2–7+
Alc./Vol.	13.0%
RRP	$21.50 ▮

Pirramimma Stocks Hill Shiraz

Hearty cuisine and McLaren Vale red wine go hand in
hand. The Johnstons of Pirramimma make typical
regional reds of good character.
CURRENT RELEASE 1997 A well-balanced young red
with satisfying flavour, which won't break the bank. The
nose has raspberry and blackberry aromas with some
earthy regional notes and a dab of spice. In the mouth
it's medium-bodied with ripe fruit and spice flavours,
ahead of some firm tannic grip. Oak is restrained
throughout. Serve with Irish stew.

Quality	▼▼▼▼
Value	★★★★ь
Grapes	shiraz
Region	McLaren Vale, SA
Cellar	▮ 5
Alc./Vol.	13.5%
RRP	$16.45

Plantagenet Cabernet Sauvignon

The winery was established in 1974, making it one of
the senior enterprises in the region. Owner Tony Smith.
*Previous outstanding vintages: '81, '83, '85, '86, '90, '91,
'94*
CURRENT RELEASE 1996 This is always an elegant
style of cabernet, and so far the '96 needs time to allow
the oak to integrate properly. The colour is medium
ruby, and there are perfumed, essency aromas of dark
chocolate and blackcurrant. Caramel and vanilla also
feature. The profile is lean and tight. Cellar, then serve
with pink lamb.

Quality	▼▼▼▼
Value	★★★
Grapes	cabernet sauvignon
Region	Great Southern, WA
Cellar	⬥ 2–12
Alc./Vol.	14.5%
RRP	$28.50 ▮

Plunkett Shiraz

Quality	ϾϾϾϿ
Value	★★★
Grapes	shiraz
Region	Strathbogie Ranges, Vic.
Cellar	▮ 6
Alc./Vol.	13.0%
RRP	$22.30

The Plunkett vineyard seems to hover on the edge as far as ripening shiraz is concerned. Even in a warm dry year like '97, its cool-climate origins are evident.

CURRENT RELEASE 1997 An elegant shiraz. The colour isn't terribly deep, and the bouquet has lighter fruit aromas with some cherry perfumes allied with gunsmoke and cedar. There's some acid showing in the mouth, and this makes it taste lean. A light- to medium-weight red that's best with food. Try Peking duck.

Port Phillip Estate Reserve Pinot Noir

Quality	ϾϾϾϾϾ
Value	★★★★
Grapes	pinot noir
Region	Mornington Peninsula, Vic.
Cellar	▮ 4+
Alc./Vol.	14.0%
RRP	$32.00

This won the Penguin Best Pinot Noir award three years ago with the '95 vintage, but things have progressed since then. Winemaker is still Lindsay McCall of Paringa Estate; grapes are grown by Diana and Jeffrey Sher.
Previous outstanding vintages: '95
CURRENT RELEASE 1997 A superb pinot in the full-on, foresty style. Less oaky than McCall's own Paringa wine, but no less impressive, this is a very complex drink. It has a deep colour, sumptuous undergrowth, sappy, sousbois characters with cherry buried deep within. It has a core of sweet fruit, and there's a lot of stalk influence. Superb with stuffed duck braised in white wine and stock.

Quality	ϾϾϾϾϿ
Value	★★★★ᴋ
Grapes	pinot noir
Region	Mornington Peninsula, Vic.
Cellar	▮ 5+
Alc./Vol.	13.5%
RRP	$35.00

CURRENT RELEASE 1998 Yet another lip-smacking '98 Peninsula pinot. The wine is very sweet to smell and taste, with candied cherry and sappy aromas, and it's as smooth as silk in the mouth. There's also a lick of nice cedary oak. It's light- to medium-bodied, with very gentle tannins. Masterful stuff. Enjoy this with veal sweetbreads.

Port Phillip Estate Reserve Shiraz

Shiraz is a marginal grape on the peninsula, but it's the warm, low-yield years like '97 that pull it through. Maker Lindsay McCall (contract).

CURRENT RELEASE 1997 This rare wine has a vivid purple colour, a cool-climate nose of dry spices (pepper, cloves), cedary oak, and lashings of fruit and oak flavours in the mouth. Remarkable structure and grip, and there's more than a whisper of the Rhone about it. Try it with kangaroo with pepperberries.

Quality	♥♥♥♥？
Value	★★★⋆
Grapes	shiraz
Region	Mornington Peninsula, Vic.
Cellar	↑ 5+
Alc./Vol.	14.4%
RRP	$32.00 ▮

Preece Cabernet Sauvignon

The Preece labels are models of style and economy. This one is a little round disk. Makers Don Lewis and Alan George.

CURRENT RELEASE 1997 The deep, dark colour is promising and the wine does not disappoint. The aromas are of crushed leaves and squashed berries with some tarry oaky inflexions. It has more guts than expected on the palate: it's slightly inky with some heavy extraction and grabby tannins. Not an elegant red, but it does have flavour. Food: steak and kidney pie.

Quality	♥♥♥
Value	★★★
Grapes	cabernet sauvignon
Region	Goulburn Valley & King Valley, Vic.
Cellar	↑ 5
Alc./Vol.	13.5%
RRP	$16.00 Ⓢ

Preece Merlot

Mitchelton stole a march on Seppelt when they named a wine after their first (consultant) winemaker, Colin Preece. Colin Preece worked all his life at Seppelt's Great Western winery, helping out at Mitchelton in his retirement.

CURRENT RELEASE 1997 The colour's a medium–light red–purple and there are scents of vanilla, coconut and cranberry. The oak is slightly dominant at this stage, and there's a little astringency, which should soften over a year. Needs food if drunk now. Should team well with roast duck.

Quality	♥♥♥？
Value	★★★⋆
Grapes	merlot
Region	various, Vic.
Cellar	↑ 4
Alc./Vol.	14.0%
RRP	$17.00 Ⓢ

Punters Corner Cabernet Sauvignon

Quality	♟♟♟♟
Value	★★★★
Grapes	cabernet sauvignon
Region	Coonawarra, SA
Cellar	▮ 6
Alc./Vol.	13.5%
RRP	$26.00

This vineyard's name brings to mind the punters who descend each year for the Coonawarra Cup. RK-P remembers it as great fun, but only vaguely through the haze caused by unlimited local red wine, consumed in 38-degree heat.

CURRENT RELEASE 1997   A ripe, inky Coonawarra cabernet with a tangy, clean nose of mint and blackcurrant. Oak is subtle, and the palate has more of that blackcurranty fruit, good texture and moderate tannins. It's a richly flavoured red with lots of straightforward appeal. Try it with veal cutlets.

The Red Essentials O'Dea's Vineyard Cabernet

Quality	♟♟♟♟
Value	★★★
Grapes	cabernet sauvignon
Region	Coonawarra, SA
Cellar	▮ 5
Alc./Vol.	13.0%
RRP	$19.00 ⑤

It's all very Oirish. O'Dea's vineyard grew the grapes and Dave O'Leary made the wine. The 'Essentials' brands (there's also a riesling trio, The Clare Essentials), are an interesting twist in branding by the brand masters, Mildara.

CURRENT RELEASE 1997   Oak and acid are the notable features of this wine. It has a good full colour and the oak/fruit combination gives charred-meat and burnt-wood aromas. The high acid lends the palate a certain leanness to go with the cassis and raspberry flavours. It's slightly short and astringent to close. Food: pasta with a mushroom sauce.

The Red Essentials Wrattonbully Shiraz

Quality	♟♟♟♟♟
Value	★★★★★
Grapes	shiraz
Region	Wrattonbully, SA
Cellar	▮ 8+
Alc./Vol.	13.5%
RRP	$19.00 ⑤

This is an individual vineyard wine from Schultz's vineyard, and the winemaker is David O'Leary. It's yet another example of what a great red region Wrattonbully is turning out to be.

CURRENT RELEASE 1997   This is a beautiful wine and a real surprise package. The bouquet showcases herbal, spicy, white pepper, Rhone-like, cool-area aromatics. The palate is tightly structured and elegant, with excellent flavour. It's fleshy and well endowed with sweet berry flavour. All in all an impressive wine to serve with rare roast beef.

Red Hill Estate Pinot Noir

The property is named after Red Hill, a town on the higher part of the Mornington Peninsula, which in turn gets its name from its rich red volcanic soils. Rich soils tend to promote vigorous vine growth, however, which can be a problem. Maker Jenny Bright.

CURRENT RELEASE 1998   This was a stand-out vintage in the area, and this superb wine is the result. It has an intense scent of cherry and strawberry – very full and properly ripe with no greenness. The oak is in the background, allowing full expression to the grape. There's rather pronounced acid on the finish, but it's a beautiful wine and looks to have a future. Serve with porcini mushroom risotto and truffle oil.

Quality	♟♟♟♟
Value	★★★★
Grapes	pinot noir
Region	Mornington Peninsula, Vic.
Cellar	♦ 4
Alc./Vol.	12.9%
RRP	$28.00

Reynolds Orange Merlot

Orange is a happening place. The area under vineyards is exploding and we predict it will soon be like the Adelaide Hills – every major wine company will want a slice of the action.

CURRENT RELEASE 1998   The colour is very impressive: deep and dense. The first impression is of lashings of oak and herbaceous fruit. It has a tomato ketchup character together with blackberry jam flavours. Earthy, ripe berry tastes plus a hint of gaminess fill the palate, which has an angular profile. Try it with roast duck.

Quality	♟♟♟♟
Value	★★★♦
Grapes	merlot
Region	Orange, NSW
Cellar	♦ 5
Alc./Vol.	13.0%
RRP	$24.00 (cellar door)

Riddoch Coonawarra Shiraz

The big surprise with Katnook's Jimmy Watson Trophy win in 1998 was the fact that much of the fruit came from very young vines. The same vines provided this wine. Maker Wayne Stehbens.

CURRENT RELEASE 1997   Son of Jimmy! This is the pup of Katnook's Watson winner and a smart wine it is, with rich meaty, gamy and toasty aromas of spicy berry and plum fruit and sweet oak. It has good concentration and a warmth of alcohol (14 per cent) on the finish. Outstanding value for money, as it discounts at $15. Serve with lamb's fry and bacon.

Quality	♟♟♟♟
Value	★★★★★
Grapes	shiraz
Region	Coonawarra, SA
Cellar	♦ 12+
Alc./Vol.	14.0%
RRP	$18.00 Ⓢ

Robertson's Well Cabernet Sauvignon

Quality	♥♥♥⬗
Value	★★★
Grapes	cabernet sauvignon
Region	Coonawarra, SA
Cellar	⬥ 2–5+
Alc./Vol.	13.0%
RRP	$21.00 ⑤ 🍾

This is a Coonawarra from the Mildara Blass stable. The name celebrates an early landowner in the Coonawarra district. Maker Gavin Hogg.

CURRENT RELEASE 1996   This is a wine that demands a bit of patience. It's overwhelmingly oaky at present. The palate has good depth of flavour, but the wine is dominated by the charry taste of heavy-toast oak. It's hard to see the charm in the wine underneath all that wood. Cellar, then serve with well-charred hamburgers.

Robertson's Well Shiraz

Quality	♥♥♥♥♥
Value	★★★★★
Grapes	shiraz
Region	Coonawarra, SA
Cellar	🍾 10+
Alc./Vol.	12.5%
RRP	$21.00 ⑤ 🍾

This is one of the best shirazes we've seen out of Coonawarra in 1997. We predict that moving David O'Leary to the Coonawarra winery will turn out to be a sage move for the Mildara camp.

CURRENT RELEASE 1997   This is an excellent wine whichever way you look at it. The colour is a deep purple–red with blackish reflections. It has a dry earthy, undergrowth bouquet with dried spice components. Sweeter berry aromas come through with airing. On the palate, it's elegant and savoury – a very, very stylish medium- to full-bodied wine. Delicious already, but will improve. It finishes with mouth-puckering tannins, so would handle strong flavours such as standing rib roast of beef.

Rochford Premier Pinot Noir

Quality	♥♥♥♥♥
Value	★★★★
Grapes	pinot noir
Region	Macedon Ranges, Vic.
Cellar	🍾 6
Alc./Vol.	13.0%
RRP	$32.80

This property has recently changed hands and is now operated by Helmut Konecsny and Yvonne Lodico-Konecsny. They have seven hectares of vines in the Macedon region.

Previous outstanding vintages: '91, '92, '94

CURRENT RELEASE 1997   Typical of the vineyard style, this shows concentrated colour, aroma and fruit flavour, but with better-than-usual ripeness. Attractive strawberry, cherry aromas are clean and pure pinot; the oak is secondary, and the medium-weight palate has good flavour and structure, with just a little stalkiness to close. Serve it with guinea fowl.

Rosemount Balmoral Syrah

This wine takes its name from the 1852 homestead of the Oatley family, founders of Rosemount Estate. The grapes come from very low-yielding, ancient vines at McLaren Vale. Maker Philip Shaw and team.

Previous outstanding vintages: '91, '92, '94, '95

CURRENT RELEASE 1996 This is a monster of a wine, and totally typical of this very consistent style. The colour is dark purple–red; the bouquet has charred oak, vanilla, caramel and cedar overtones. In the mouth it's exceptionally powerful, chunky, chewy and rich. It's very full-bodied with a lot of extract, generous coffee, chocolate flavours, and smooth but abundant tannins. Because of the high level of oak used, it really needs to be cellared. Then serve it with chargrilled rump steak.

Quality	🍷🍷🍷🍷🍷
Value	★★★½
Grapes	shiraz
Region	McLaren Vale, SA
Cellar	➡ 2–12+
Alc./Vol.	14.0%
RRP	$65.70

Rosemount Mountain Blue Shiraz Cabernet

This wine has single-handedly focused the spotlight on Mudgee lately. It's one of the more outstanding reds to come out of the region. The grapes come from mature vineyards and the yields are very low.

Previous outstanding vintages: '94, '95

CURRENT RELEASE 1996 This wine runs the full gamut of spices: cinnamon, cloves and a hint of mint as well. It's quite oaky in its youth, but has the flavour to balance. It's full-bodied and really fills the mouth with a great wealth of complex flavours. The fruit-sweetness on the middle palate is especially appealing in such a full-throttle red wine. Goes well with rare roast beef.

Quality	🍷🍷🍷🍷🍷
Value	★★★½
Grapes	shiraz; cabernet sauvignon
Region	Mudgee, NSW
Cellar	➡ 2–12+
Alc./Vol.	14.0%
RRP	$55.00

Rosemount Pinot Noir

Rosemount are the masters of many grape varieties and regions, but pinot noir has proved more difficult for them than most.

CURRENT RELEASE 1997 This is a slightly stewy kind of pinot which has some stern tannins and a touch of austerity on the palate. It could be faulted as a slightly 'dry reddish' style that lacks pinot charm. It does, however, have plenty of flavour and structure.

Quality	🍷🍷🍷
Value	★★★
Grapes	pinot noir
Region	not stated
Cellar	4
Alc./Vol.	13.0%
RRP	$16.40 (S)

Rosemount Shiraz

Quality	🍷🍷🍷🍷
Value	★★★★★
Grapes	shiraz
Region	mainly McLaren Vale, SA
Cellar	6
Alc./Vol.	13.5%
RRP	$15.80 (S)

The diamond label shiraz is a perennial favourite of just about everybody, especially the American *Wine Spectator* magazine, which drools over it year after year. Maker Philip Shaw, Charles Whish and team.

Previous outstanding vintages: all of them

CURRENT RELEASE 1998 A very concentrated wine, so thick you could almost stand a spoon in it. Vanilla, dark chocolate and caramel flavours hint at strong use of American oak, while the palate shows traces of herbs and spices. Nevertheless, a straightforward wine which could improve with age. Great with blanquette de veau.

Rosemount Shiraz Cabernet

Quality	🍷🍷🍷½
Value	★★★★½
Grapes	shiraz; cabernet sauvignon
Region	not stated
Cellar	3
Alc./Vol.	13.5%
RRP	$12.80 (S)

Rosemount celebrated the company's 25th anniversary in the 1998 vintage. This wine won a trophy and two gold medals in its year of vintage. It's a good wine, but we wonder at the merit of giving awards to wines in their unfinished state.

CURRENT RELEASE 1998 It's hard to see this winning a trophy, but it's excellent value for money. The colour is a lighter shade of purple–red, and the nose has light and fairly simple cherry and herbal aromas without noticeable impact from oak. The palate is light-bodied and pleasantly fruity. It has good basic structure and a gentle grip on the finish. The intensity and appeal are higher than expected for a wine that sells widely at $10. Try it with well-herbed hamburgers.

Rosemount Show Reserve Cabernet Sauvignon

Very early, Rosemount made the decision to source grapes from the regions where they do best, hence they bought land in Coonawarra for cabernet. Smart move.
Previous outstanding vintages: '87, '88, '90, '91, '92, '93, '94

CURRENT RELEASE 1996 A typical cool southern-end Coonawarra style: leafy, tobaccoey with some pepper, spice and vegetation. The colour is a promising blackish tint, and the palate shows blackcurrant cabernet fruit after breathing. Fairly herbaceous, but an elegant, easy to drink style. Goes with lamb fillet and pesto.

Quality	🍷🍷🍷🍷
Value	★★★
Grapes	cabernet sauvignon
Region	Coonawarra, SA
Cellar	10+
Alc./Vol.	13.5%
RRP	$27.00 (S)

Rosemount Show Reserve Shiraz

This one has earned its stripes – and its handle (Show Reserve, that is). It has four big gold discs plastered across its chest. Maker Philip Shaw and crew.

CURRENT RELEASE 1996 This will eventually be an excellent, maybe even great, glass of red, but it's too oaky to get near it at present. It's full-bodied, rich and the fruit's undoubtedly well concentrated, so we're confident it will find its balance. Powerful, bolshie, assertive stuff, concluding with abundant tannin. Cellar, then have with rump steak.

Quality	🍷🍷🍷🍷½
Value	★★★½
Grapes	shiraz
Region	McLaren Vale, SA
Cellar	2–8+
Alc./Vol.	14.5%
RRP	$28.00 (S)

Rouge Homme Pinot Noir

This marque was minted by the Redman (how's your French?) family many moons ago. It was bought in 1965 by Lindemans and thence to the Southcorp behemoth. Maker Paul Gordon.

CURRENT RELEASE 1997 This is one of the better-value pinots around. The nose is smoky, gamy and quite complex and shows some oak. It's smooth and light- to medium-bodied with the same meaty, gamy characters that run smoothly on the palate, concluding with some tannin grip. It has plenty of pinot character and tastes like the genuine article. Try it with quail.

Quality	🍷🍷🍷🍷
Value	★★★★½
Grapes	pinot noir
Region	Coonawarra, SA
Cellar	5
Alc./Vol.	13.0%
RRP	$17.85 (S)

Rouge Homme Shiraz Cabernet

Quality	♟♟♟
Value	★★★↑
Grapes	shiraz; cabernet sauvignon
Region	Coonawarra, SA
Cellar	▮ 4
Alc./Vol.	13.5%
RRP	$14.60 ⑤

In Coonawarra they seem able to dial up the tonnes-per-hectare and accurately grow grapes appropriate to the price of the wine. This is basic-level Coonawarra.

CURRENT RELEASE 1997   This wine is clean and well turned out, but it won't challenge the tastebuds. The aromas are floral, raspberryish and crushed-leafy, and it's light- to middleweight in the mouth with modest tannins. A good ready-drinking red with balance and drinkability. Try it with pork sausages and garlic mash.

Ryecroft Cabernet Shiraz

Quality	♟♟♟♟
Value	★★★★★
Grapes	cabernet sauvignon; shiraz
Region	various, SA
Cellar	▮ 5+
Alc./Vol.	13.5%
RRP	$13.00 ⑤

Ryecroft used to be a McLaren Vale brand, but now that Rosemount owns it, the wines are blended from various regions. Maker Charles Whish.

CURRENT RELEASE 1998   **Great stuff! This is an outstanding, inexpensive red with depth of flavour and interest way above its price level. The colour is deep purple–red, and the nose has meaty, spicy aromas with some oak. It's rich in the mouth and has really nice, ripe, sweet fruit flavour. Remarkably concentrated, its depth of spiciness and tannin structure really satisfies. The finish lingers long. All in all a very generous glass of wine for just $11–$13. Drink with grilled lamb chops.**

PENGUIN BEST BARGAIN RED

Rymill Cabernet Sauvignon

Quality	♟♟♟♟♟
Value	★★★★★
Grapes	cabernet sauvignon
Region	Coonawarra, SA
Cellar	➥ 2–12+
Alc./Vol.	13.0%
RRP	$21.00 ▮

Peter Rymill's showpiece winery at the northern end of Coonawarra is one of the sights to see in the district. The wines, made by John Innes, are underrated.

CURRENT RELEASE 1996   **Here's a big powerful cabernet which doesn't rely on oak for its intensity. The nose is wonderfully gamy and complex with a leafy herbaceous edge, and dense red-berry ripe fruit characters. The palate is quite powerful, with gripping tannins that pucker the mouth and a claret-like structure. It's very young; needs time and will live for just about ever. Great with hard cheeses.**

PENGUIN BEST CABERNET SAUVIGNON

Saddler's Creek Bluegrass Cabernet Sauvignon

The Hunter revival has spawned many new names. Saddler's Creek is one of them, a forward-looking operation with a range of flavoursome wines.

CURRENT RELEASE 1997 A modern, rather 'un-Hunter' sort of red which has lots of vanilla–caramel oak-derived aromas surrounding some underplayed sweet fruit. The palate has a mouth-coating texture with dry, fine tannins and a slightly oxidative hint on the finish. Try it with osso bucco alla Milanese.

Quality	♟♟♟♟
Value	★★★
Grapes	cabernet sauvignon
Region	Hunter Valley, NSW
Cellar	♟ 2
Alc./Vol.	13.6%
RRP	$22.50

Salisbury Cabernet Sauvignon

The Murray Valley provides vast quantities of table wine for Australia's everyday drinking. It's a competitive market, and the quality has been steadily improving. Even the labelling is better these days: Salisbury's looks almost aristocratic.

CURRENT RELEASE 1998 This is a typically simple Riverland red driven by plummy fruit and earthy aromas on the nose, and soft berry fruit in the mouth. It's light and pleasant with gentle tannins to make for easy-drinking. It's made very much for current consumption, so don't keep it for too long or you'll be disappointed.

Quality	♟♟♟
Value	★★★★
Grapes	cabernet sauvignon
Region	Murray Valley, Vic.
Cellar	♟ 1
Alc./Vol.	12.0%
RRP	$10.00 Ⓢ

Salisbury Grenache

The irrigated lands around Mildura are a big source of vin ordinaire and these days they're having a go at vin not-so-ordinaire. Salisbury Estate's wines usually fit into the former category.

CURRENT RELEASE 1998 The colour is the pale-ish crimson of grenache, and the nose has the typical sweet raspberry varietal aromas. The palate is grapey and uncomplicated with a dry finish. Despite quite high alcohol, this remains a simple light red with no perceptible oak which could (and perhaps should) be chilled to enhance its fresh fruitiness. Summer picnics will suit this style, but watch that 13.5 per cent alcohol on a warm day.

Quality	♟♟♟
Value	★★★
Grapes	grenache
Region	Murray Valley, Vic.
Cellar	♟ 1
Alc./Vol.	13.5%
RRP	$10.00 Ⓢ

Saltram Classic Shiraz

Quality 🍷🍷🍷🍷½
Value ★★★★★
Grapes shiraz
Region Barossa Valley, SA
Cellar 3
Alc./Vol. 13.5%
RRP $11.00 ($)

The famous Saltram winery – one of the Barossa's oldest – recently celebrated its 140th anniversary, not long after owners Mildara Blass decided to stop making wine there. Such are the machinations of big businesses and their bean counters.

CURRENT RELEASE 1997 Great value in a straightforward, crowd-pleasing red wine with more interest than many. Jammy blackberry drives the nose with some interesting tarry, savoury notes. Similar berry flavour fills the mouth, finishing with dry, slightly firm, tannins. An attractive companion to grilled spring lamb cutlets.

Saltram Mamre Brook Cabernet Sauvignon

Quality 🍷🍷🍷🍷½
Value ★★★★
Grapes cabernet sauvignon
Region Barossa Valley, SA
Cellar 2–7
Alc./Vol. 13.5%
RRP $20.00

The Saltram Mamre Brook range goes from strength to strength. They're just the sort of generously flavoured wines that Australians love, and the prices are very fair for the quality. Maker Nigel Dolan.

Previous outstanding vintages: '96

CURRENT RELEASE 1997 This is a dense, dark wine with black-fruit aromas and a good measure of toasty coconut and spicy American oak. The wood doesn't overwhelm the ripe fruit though, which tracks down the palate with powerful sweet berry flavour. Tannins are firm, but in balance. A satisfying red worth laying down for a few years. Serve with roast beef.

Saltram Mamre Brook Shiraz

Quality 🍷🍷🍷🍷½
Value ★★★★½
Grapes shiraz
Region Barossa Valley, SA
Cellar 1–5
Alc./Vol. 14.0%
RRP $20.50

Mamre Brook was once Saltram's expensive prestige label. These days it's a good-quality mid-priced brand worth looking out for. Maker Nigel Dolan.

Previous outstanding vintages: '96

CURRENT RELEASE 1997 The '96 Mamre Brook Shiraz showed a lot more oak than this edition, but it's still there. This year the fruit makes more of a statement with cherry, mint and peppery tones to go with the perfumed wood. It's a rich wine with good structure and firm tannins. Worth keeping.

Sandhurst Ridge Shiraz

Bendigo and shiraz go together like . . . well, Bendigo and shiraz really. The symbiotic relationship has created a new regional style for Australia. Sandhurst Ridge is a promising new name from nearby Marong.
CURRENT RELEASE 1997   This has deep colour and a tight regional nose of mint, dark cherry and a seasoning of vanillin oak. Black fruit fills the palate; it's intense and fine-textured, with snappy acidity and fine drying tannins. An appealing red to drink with herbed roasted vegetables.

Quality	ŸŸŸŸ↑
Value	★★★↑
Grapes	shiraz
Region	Bendigo, Vic.
Cellar	➡ 1–5
Alc./Vol.	13.0%
RRP	$27.00

Scarpantoni Block 3 Shiraz

A flurry of excitement greets each new red from Scarpantoni's plot and, like many big-flavoured reds these days, they sell out quickly. Hurry along if you want any.
CURRENT RELEASE 1997   Concentration is the word here, from its deep colour, through the potent bouquet and on to the deeply flavoured palate. Dark plum, sweet blackberry and dusty-sweet vanillin oak are the main characters. It's full-bodied and ripe with balanced tannins. Try with Middle Eastern lamb stew and couscous.

Quality	ŸŸŸŸ↑
Value	★★★★★
Grapes	shiraz
Region	McLaren Vale, SA
Cellar	➡ 2–6
Alc./Vol.	14.0%
RRP	$17.00

Scarpantoni Cabernet Sauvignon

It hasn't taken long for Scarpantoni's red wines to climb from relative obscurity to desirability. These days they sell quickly.
CURRENT RELEASE 1997   This isn't exactly a trendy style. It's out of the McLaren Vale mainstream, like something from yesteryear, with its jammy, porty blackberry nose and extractive qualities. The palate is big in flavour and deeply textured, with little overt oak character. Tannins are agreeably dry. Pot-roasted topside would be good here.

Quality	ŸŸŸŸ
Value	★★★★
Grapes	cabernet sauvignon
Region	McLaren Vale, SA
Cellar	▮ 3
Alc./Vol.	13.5%
RRP	$17.00

Schinus Merlot

Quality	ΤΤΤΤ
Value	★★★★⋆
Grapes	merlot
Region	Goulburn Valley, Vic.; McLaren Vale, SA
Cellar	🍷 2
Alc./Vol.	13.0%
RRP	$15.00

The Schinus wines are made to offer fresh, early drinking without too much fuss. In this they succeed well. Despite being made on the Mornington Peninsula, they rely heavily on fruit from other regions. Maker Garry Crittenden.

CURRENT RELEASE 1998 This is a fruit-dominant style with a sweet fresh nose of juicy plum and red berry. The palate is pleasantly fruity with soft, light texture and gentle tannins. An ideal warm-weather red wine, which could even be slightly chilled on hot days. Good with cold meats and salad.

Scotchmans Hill Pinot Noir

Quality	ΤΤΤΤ
Value	★★★
Grapes	pinot noir
Region	Geelong, Vic.
Cellar	🍷 2
Alc./Vol.	13.3%
RRP	$26.50

Scotchmans Hill did a lot to popularise pinot noir as a cafe and restaurant wine. Their success, and that of the more serious pinots of Bannockburn, makes us wonder why more people don't plant pinot noir in the Geelong region.

CURRENT RELEASE 1998 This is right in the easy-drinking Scotchmans style. Strawberryish varietal character gives attractive fruit aromas and sweetness. The soft, smooth middle palate will make a lot of friends, and a dry finish keeps it appetising with food. Be adventurous and drink it with a tuna steak.

Seaview Edwards and Chaffey Cabernet Sauvignon

Quality	ΤΤΤΤ⋆
Value	★★★★
Grapes	cabernet sauvignon
Region	McLaren Vale, SA
Cellar	➡ 2–8+
Alc./Vol.	13.5%
RRP	$31.50

The top of the Seaview tree, Edwards and Chaffey cabernet is meant to be cellared to realise its full potential, although sometimes it has youthful drinkability as well.

CURRENT RELEASE 1997 A deeply coloured young red, this has an unevolved nose which has plenty of raw fruit and oak characters. Blueberry, black fruit, dark chocolate and vanilla aromas lead on to a substantial palate of good depth and length with a rich middle and very firm tannins underneath. A good match for a char-grilled porterhouse.

Seaview Edwards and Chaffey Shiraz

This is Seaview's Premium collection from their McLaren Vale vineyards. The smart black label is one to look for, as the quality is outstanding across a range that includes a bubbly, a chardonnay and two stout reds.
CURRENT RELEASE 1996 Dense and youthfully purple, this powerful red is still far from evolved. The bouquet has intense chocolatey blackberry aromas that stand up well to a big dose of spicy oak. In the mouth it's strongly flavoured with fruit-sweet berries and toasty oak. The palate is profound and long-flavoured with abundant clean acidity and harmonious, fine-grained tannins. Despite its obvious ageworthiness, its inherent balance means it drinks well right now with a charred rump steak.

Quality	♟♟♟♟♟
Value	★★★★
Grapes	shiraz
Region	McLaren Vale, SA
Cellar	▮ 8
Alc./Vol.	14.3%
RRP	$32.00

Seaview Grenache Shiraz

The perennially good value Seaview range has expanded recently with the addition of grenache to the mix. Not that long ago winemakers were wondering what to do with it. Ain't fashion a funny thing?
CURRENT RELEASE 1997 Berry and earthy aromas meet the nose along with hints of mint and vanilla. The aromas are savoury and so is the palate, which has medium body and tight, but not intimidating, tannin structure. A safe bet with grilled loin lamb chops.

Quality	♟♟♟♟
Value	★★★★
Grapes	grenache; shiraz
Region	McLaren Vale, SA
Cellar	▮ 3
Alc./Vol.	13.5%
RRP	$12.00

Seaview Shiraz

Seaview are firmly entrenched as a source of some of Australia's best value red wines. After many years as multi-regional blends, they have now returned to their McLaren Vale roots.
CURRENT RELEASE 1997 Blackberry jam, spice and a whiff of dusty oak follow the usual Seaview formula on the nose. The palate repeats those flavours with attractive smoothness and slightly astringent tannic structure. It's essentially a current-drinker, but it might also be worth a bit of time in the cellar. Serve with roast veal.

Quality	♟♟♟♟
Value	★★★★
Grapes	shiraz
Region	McLaren Vale, SA
Cellar	▮ 3
Alc./Vol.	13.5%
RRP	$13.95

Seppelt Chalambar Shiraz

Quality	♟♟♟♟♟
Value	★★★★★
Grapes	shiraz
Region	various, Vic.
Cellar	▮ 7
Alc./Vol.	13.5%
RRP	$19.50

Chalambar is a name with a lot of history. In fact, one of the authors remembers an early sixties vintage Chalambar as the first bottle of wine he ever 'cellared' in his bedroom cupboard (as a naughty teenager, believe it or not). The last few Chalambars have regained some of the prestige originally attached to the name.

CURRENT RELEASE 1997 A warm and welcoming wine with a touch of class that makes it great value. The colour is deep and the nose has dark cherry and berry fruit aromas, along with some warm sweet spice and dusty oak. It's a complete mouthful with lovely smoothness, plummy depth, textural interest, and ripe, fine-grained tannins. A good companion for braised steak and kidney with parsley dumplings.

Seppelt Great Western Shiraz

Quality	♟♟♟♟♟
Value	★★★
Grapes	shiraz
Region	Great Western, Vic.
Cellar	⟼ 1–7+
Alc./Vol.	13.5%
RRP	$36.50

Seppelt Great Western Shiraz has long been recognised as an Australian classic, although various Seppelt management teams failed to realise it over the years, and the wine became an occasional oddity. Happily the current regime recognises what a wealth there is in those very old Great Western shiraz vines, and they have acted accordingly.

CURRENT RELEASE 1995 Subtlety is the keynote here. It's not the most emphatic of reds, yet it keeps you coming back for more. The nose has spice, seasoned leather, berry and chocolate aromas of real finesse. In the mouth it's dry, understated and long-flavoured with a tight underpinning of grippy tannins. Works well with a lamb casserole.

Seppelt Moyston Cabernet Shiraz

Back in the early sixties this was a prestigious label, but as demand increased something had to give: either the price went up or the quality came down. Seppelts took the latter course, and today it's a keenly priced everyday red.

CURRENT RELEASE 1997 A straightforward crowd-pleaser of a red, which is fault-free and easy to like. On the nose there are berry and earthy notes along with a hint of licorice. The palate is light and pleasantly fruity, with an agreeable soft finish. A good red for an office party buffet when cost is a consideration.

Quality	♟♟♟♟
Value	★★★★
Grapes	cabernet sauvignon; shiraz
Region	various, south-east Australia
Cellar	🍾 1
Alc./Vol.	13.0%
RRP	$8.00

Seppelt Sunday Creek Pinot Noir

Most quality pinot noir commands a pretty healthy price tag. Can good pinot be reasonably priced? Try Sunday Creek and see for yourself.

CURRENT RELEASE 1998 This is a delight and oh-so-easy to drink. The colour is deep, and it smells of intensely aromatic sappy/juicy cherry fruit, skilfully dusted with subtle French oak. The palate is ripe with cherries, and the texture is sweetly silky. Soft tannins support things well, and the aftertaste is aromatic and long. Try it with a mixed platter of Chinese roast duck, char siew and crispy pork.

Quality	♟♟♟♟♟
Value	★★★★★
Grapes	pinot noir
Region	various, Vic.
Cellar	🍾 4
Alc./Vol.	13.5%
RRP	$19.00

Seppelt Terrain Cabernet Sauvignon

Who says big businesses have no heart? The Southcorp crowd sometimes do take pity on us cash-strapped wine consumers by providing a stunning bargain or two. This is one of them.

CURRENT RELEASE 1997 Good purplish–red colour promises much here – and it delivers. The nose has a level of succulent blackcurranty varietal aroma which is surprising in such a modestly priced drop. That fruit character tracks down the palate with good depth and richness, nicely balanced by moderate, ripe tannins. Try it with grilled marinated lamb steaks.

Quality	♟♟♟♟♟
Value	★★★★★
Grapes	cabernet sauvignon
Region	various, SA
Cellar	🍾 3
Alc./Vol.	13.5%
RRP	$10.00 Ⓢ

Seppelt Terrain Series Shiraz

Quality	™™™
Value	★★★★★
Grapes	shiraz
Region	various, SA
Cellar	▮ 3
Alc./Vol.	13.5%
RRP	$10.00 ⑤

Another Southcorp bargain – maybe not in quite the same league as the Seppelt Terrain Cabernet Sauvignon, but not bad at all. Often discounted, these are wines to buy by the case.

CURRENT RELEASE 1997   Deep colour is an early indicator of quality here, and the nose has sweet jammy shiraz fruit aplenty. Blackberry and spice flavours fill the palate in a smoothly textured, intense package. It's not subtle, but it has warm flavour. Lends itself well to something like a daube of beef.

Sevenhill Shiraz

Quality	™™™
Value	★★★⚹
Grapes	shiraz
Region	Clare Valley, SA
Cellar	➡ 1–6
Alc./Vol.	14.2%
RRP	$23.00 ▮

The Jesuits of Sevenhill make a lot more than sacramental wine. Their old vineyard is the source of shiraz grapes that make red wines of great character.

CURRENT RELEASE 1997   A strong argument for the benefits of decanting young reds: with a bit of aeration this wine improves out of sight. Fragrant sweet berry aromas develop, and the palate opens up to reveal good concentration of black cherry and berry fruit. The finish is rather hard at the moment – slightly bitter in fact – but time may sort things out for the better.

Seville Estate Shiraz

Quality	™™™™⚹
Value	★★★
Grapes	shiraz
Region	Yarra Valley, Vic.
Cellar	➡ 2–8
Alc./Vol.	14.0%
RRP	$45.00

Seville Estate has been a standard-bearer for the cause of Yarra Valley shiraz for many years. Surprisingly not many Yarra vineyards have followed in their footsteps.

CURRENT RELEASE 1997   Cool-grown Victorian shiraz has its admirers and its knockers. Both sides have a point, and the style usually relates to climate. If it's been a warm year, go for it; if it's been chilly and wet, cross the road and avoid it. The year 1997 was warm, and this is a tasty young drop full of spice and interest. The nose has white pepper aromas, cherry fruit and a hint of lead-pencils oak. The palate is medium in body with good concentration of dry fruity taste and heaps of spice. Grippy tannins mark the finish. Cellar and serve with peppery, marinated grilled chicken.

Shottesbrooke Cabernet Sauvignon Merlot Malbec

Shottesbrooke proprietor Nick Holmes was once winemaker at Ryecroft, one of the old names of McLaren Vale wine. On his own spread he produces more elegant wines than most.

CURRENT RELEASE 1997 A very stylish young cabernet blend with a rather European accent, which is at odds with the McLaren Vale norm. The nose has plummy fruit, some dark berries and a herbal note. In the mouth it's subtly aromatic with a fleshy texture and loads of earthy, gamy fruit. Some lifted oak characters enhance things well, and tannins are dry and fine. Good with a roasted free-range chicken.

Quality	🍷🍷🍷🍷🍷
Value	★★★★½
Grapes	cabernet sauvignon; merlot; malbec
Region	McLaren Vale, SA
Cellar	5
Alc./Vol.	14.0%
RRP	$22.20

Skillogalee Shiraz

Thank heaven for Clare reds: they offer plenty of what most drinkers of Australian wines want – ripe flavour, good body and real personality. Maker Dave Palmer.

CURRENT RELEASE 1997 This has a lot of minty aroma, which shades pleasant berry nuances a little at the moment. The minty touch is there on the palate too, but it also has some sweet berry flavour and a fleshy, round texture that suggests good levels of ripeness. Balanced, dry tannins dovetail nicely. Grill a fillet steak to serve with this.

Quality	🍷🍷🍷🍷
Value	★★★
Grapes	shiraz
Region	Clare Valley, SA
Cellar	3
Alc./Vol.	13.5%
RRP	$27.00

Skillogalee The Cabernets

Founded nearly thirty years ago, Skillogalee, near Sevenhill in the Clare Valley, makes red wines very much in the regional style.

CURRENT RELEASE 1997 This takes minty/menthol characters right to the edge. Light berry aromas are in there along with some vanillin oak, but the mint dominates at the moment. The palate is clean and fresh-tasting, but rather short with a firm finish.

Quality	🍷🍷🍷½
Value	★★★
Grapes	cabernet sauvignon; cabernet franc; malbec
Region	Clare Valley, SA
Cellar	4
Alc./Vol.	13.5%
RRP	$27.00

Spray Farm Pinot Noir

Quality ŸŸŸŸ
Value ★★★½
Grapes pinot noir
Region Geelong, Vic.
Cellar 1
Alc./Vol. 13.5%
RRP $17.50

These wines are made at Scotchmans Hill on the Bel4larine Peninsula from grapes grown on the nearby Spray Farm property. They are generally a bit lighter than the Scotchmans' wines.

CURRENT RELEASE 1998 Light pinots elicit yawns from the best of us, but when that lightness of being is partnered by good pinot varietal character, it's different. This fits the bill. Strawberry aromas and a gamy, earthy touch mark the nose. In the mouth it's light and soft with similar flavours and a soft finish.

St Hallett Cabernet Merlot

Quality ŸŸŸŸ
Value ★★★½
Grapes cabernet sauvignon; merlot
Region Barossa Valley, SA
Cellar 3
Alc./Vol. 13.5%
RRP $18.95

In recent years the St Hallett reds have impressed with their reliability rather than their brilliance. This cabernet blend shows what we mean. Maker Stuart Blackwell.

CURRENT RELEASE 1997 This is a nice, undemanding red that's very easy to enjoy. The nose has ample mellow fruit of the blackberry-ish sort, and the palate is similarly ripe and smooth with soft tannins. A good prospect for current drinking, and it ought to keep well for a few years. A great steak and chips red.

St Hallett Old Block Shiraz

Quality ŸŸŸŸ
Value ★★½
Grapes shiraz
Region Barossa Valley, SA
Cellar 5+
Alc./Vol. 13.5%
RRP $45.20

Old Block was one of the pioneering old-vine Barossa shiraz wines at a time when such grapes were badly undervalued. Many others have followed in its footsteps.

CURRENT RELEASE 1996 The Old Block ain't what she used to be, or perhaps our memories are playing tricks on us. The nose has cherry and blackberry fruit tones with a dressing of vanilla and caramel-like oak. In the mouth it's medium in body with fine tannins to finish. There's nothing wrong with this wine, but it lacks a bit of the stuffing it once had.

St Leonards Wahgunyah Shiraz

St Leonards has had more starts than that well-known nag. It's now owned by Peter Brown, one of the Browns of Milawa.

CURRENT RELEASE 1996   This shiraz greets you with a promising deep colour. The nose has a jammy berry aroma and lots of sweet oak which combine to give a slightly porty nose. There's rich fruit on the palate, but heavy-handed oak treatment and woody tannins dominate at the moment. Serve it with lasagne.

Quality	♟♟♟⁄
Value	★★★
Grapes	shiraz
Region	Rutherglen, Vic.
Cellar	☜ 2–6
Alc./Vol.	14.5%
RRP	$35.00

Stanley Bros Black Sheep

This lightly constructed malbec – merlot blend is the black sheep in a family of substantial Barossa reds. Maker Lindsay Stanley.

CURRENT RELEASE 1998   Although this isn't a power-packed wine, it does show some Barossa sunshine in its flavours. The nose has raspberry and blackberry fruit aromas and an overlay of coconutty oak. In the mouth it's not a very elaborate drink; the simple fruit and oak flavours backed by dry tannins won't provoke much discussion around the dining table. Serve with lamb chops.

Quality	♟♟♟⁄
Value	★★★
Grapes	malbec; merlot
Region	Barossa Valley, SA
Cellar	▮ 2
Alc./Vol.	12.5%
RRP	$15.50

Stanton and Killeen Jack's Block Shiraz

Red table wine from Rutherglen has always had its supporters, although the traditional porty style was about as fashionable as button-up boots in the wine community at large. These days makers like Stanton and Killeen are rewriting the book, with reds of real character and style.

CURRENT RELEASE 1997   A revelation of what's possible with Rutherglen dry reds. The nose has sumptuous dark berry aromas with sweet spice and chocolatey, charry barrel influence. The palate is deliciously deep and velvet-rich with a cedary touch and fine balanced tannins. Try it with lamb shanks braised in red wine.

Quality	♟♟♟♟♟
Value	★★★★★
Grapes	shiraz
Region	Rutherglen, Vic.
Cellar	▮ 10+
Alc./Vol.	14.7%
RRP	$21.70

Stonier's Cabernet

Quality	🍷🍷🍷🍷
Value	★★★½
Grapes	cabernet sauvignon; cabernet franc; merlot
Region	Mornington Peninsula, Vic.
Cellar	5
Alc./Vol.	13.5%
RRP	$19.70

Cabernet has a sorry history on the Mornington Peninsula, often providing weedy, mean wines that send you looking for something else to drink. But in a hot vintage, and in the hands of a very good winemaker, it's a different story. Maker Tod Dexter.

CURRENT RELEASE 1997 Peninsula cabernet rarely gets as ripe as it did in 1997. At Stonier's, they've fashioned it into a wine of distinction. The nose has leafy, sweet cassis and blackberry aromas. The palate has real concentration of juicy black-fruit flavour, surprising body and finely balanced tannins. Should cellar well in the medium term. Roast fillet of beef will accompany this well.

Stonier's Reserve Pinot Noir

Quality	🍷🍷🍷🍷🍷
Value	★★★½
Grapes	pinot noir
Region	Mornington Peninsula, Vic.
Cellar	4+
Alc./Vol.	13.5%
RRP	$40.00

There's a lot of pinot noir on the Mornington Peninsula, but not all makers regularly come up with the goods in quality terms. Stonier's do so consistently.

CURRENT RELEASE 1997 A great Mornington vintage although quantities were down by a lot. When Stonier's Reserve first came on the market the fruit was rather closed up and French oak dominated; but given time to settle down, it has changed for the better. That typically fragrant plum and strawberry aroma has come to the fore, and hints of mysterious foresty smells have started to evolve. The palate has richness and smoothness with good depth and a long fruit-sweet finish. Serve it with sautéed veal kidneys.

Storm Ridge Pinot Noir

This is a second label from Michael Warren of the new Badger's Brook estate in the Yarra Valley. The Storm Ridge name is reserved for non-estate wines.

CURRENT RELEASE 1998 Good pinot noir rarely comes cheap(ish). When it does, the authors of this book dip their lids in salute; there should be more of it. Storm Ridge is just such a wine, a fresh young drop with very correct varietal aroma and flavour. Stewed cherry and strawberry fruit of real succulence make it very easy to drink, and some spice and leafy undergrowth add serious interest. Light but still intense, it's meant to be gulped down in its youth with a minimum of fuss. Try it with roast free-range chicken.

Quality	♥♥♥♥?
Value	★★★★★
Grapes	pinot noir
Region	Mornington Peninsula & Yarra Valley, Vic.
Cellar	▮ 2
Alc./Vol.	13.2%
RRP	$17.00

Stumpy Gully Cabernet Sauvignon

The small property of Frank and Wendy Zantvoort is at Moorooduc at the warmer end of the Mornington Peninsula. If cabernet is going to do well anywhere on the Peninsula, it should be here.

CURRENT RELEASE 1997 Just when you've spent lots of breath telling Mornington Peninsula vignerons how silly they are persisting with cabernet, along comes a vintage like 1997 to confound you. At Stumpy Gully, the warm year has given very small quantities of a wine with a very dense, dark colour. It has a classic varietal nose of cassis and currant leaf with a warm whiff of licorice. The palate has intense black-fruit flavour, a tight structure, and fine tannins. Try with herbed roast veal.

Quality	♥♥♥♥
Value	★★★⊦
Grapes	cabernet sauvignon
Region	Mornington Peninsula, Vic.
Cellar	▮ 5
Alc./Vol.	13.0%
RRP	$20.00

Summerfield Cabernet Sauvignon

Quality	♥♥♥♥♥
Value	★★★★
Grapes	cabernet sauvignon
Region	Pyrenees, Vic.
Cellar	➡ 1–7
Alc./Vol.	14.5%
RRP	$25.00

Ian Summerfield quietly goes about his business of making some of the Pyrenees region's best reds. The wines are in a fruit-dominant style that pleases a lot of people.

CURRENT RELEASE 1997   Very dense and deep purple in colour, this has a powerful nose of dark berries, sweet spice, spearmint and mulchy complexity. Smoky oak is there, but it doesn't dominate. The palate is medium-bodied and tasty, full of dark berry flavour with balanced oak and dry tannins on the finish. Serve with some grilled lamb leg steaks.

Summerfield Shiraz

Quality	♥♥♥♥♥
Value	★★★★★
Grapes	shiraz
Region	Pyrenees, Vic.
Cellar	▮ 10
Alc./Vol.	14.5%
RRP	$25.00

The Summerfield vineyard in the Pyrenees specialises in red wines with a smooth richness that makes them more attractive in youth than some of their Central Victorian neighbours. They age well too.

CURRENT RELEASE 1997   This is a deliciously forward young red with lashings of ripe fruit, great complexity and depth. The colour is dense and purple-tinged. Aromas and flavours of plum pudding, spice, blackberry and mint provide a lot of interest. There's almost a liqueur-like fruit character – it's so rich and concentrated. Tannins are finely balanced, oak plays a secondary role, and the aftertaste is long. Pyrenees shiraz at its best, which is certain to grow even more elaborate character with age. Try it with glazed beef spare ribs.

Taltarni Cabernet Sauvignon

It will be interesting to see if the style of this wine changes now that both Dominique Portet and his side-kick Greg Gallagher, who steered the ship till now, have departed.

Previous outstanding vintages: '79, '88, '90, '91, '94

CURRENT RELEASE 1996 There's a touch of Ribena here, which reflects the cool '96 season. The nose suggests mulberry, tobacco and earth, and it's already starting to show development. The flavours are lean and savoury, with drying tannin and perhaps lacking a little fruit intensity. A good, but not outstanding, Taltarni cab. Try it with braised lamb shanks.

Quality	￼ ￼ ￼ ￼
Value	★★★
Grapes	cabernet sauvignon; merlot; cabernet franc
Region	Pyrenees, Vic.
Cellar	￼ 6
Alc./Vol.	12.8%
RRP	$27.25

Taltarni Merlot

There are distinct cabernet overtones to this wine; no wonder merlot is included in the cabernet 'family' of grapevines. It's also Taltarni's flagship, if price is a guide.

CURRENT RELEASE 1996 We can't recall being more impressed by a Taltarni merlot. This is the goods. It's a delicious drop of red, smelling of mulberry and cassis, some blackcurrant again on the tongue, but no greenness. It's fleshy, full-bodied and has hidden depths. The structure is excellent with persuasive, but not sadistic, tannins. The finish is long and really satisfies. A champ with cassoulet.

Quality	￼ ￼ ￼ ￼
Value	★★★
Grapes	merlot
Region	Pyrenees, Vic.
Cellar	￼ 8+
Alc./Vol.	13.2%
RRP	$31.75

Taltarni Merlot Cabernet

This year's crop of Taltarni reds is impressive. We find they're showing more fruit than usual, which is a plus. Maker Greg Gallagher and team.

CURRENT RELEASE 1997 It's spent 18 months in French oak but still the fruit comes through with bells ringing and flags flying. The colour is deep purple–red, and it smells very cab–merlot-ish: mulberry and cherry, bordering on plum. The trademark Taltarni tannin is there, giving it a big, forceful finish, but the flavour concentration balances the grip. It's a lovely mouthful of red that should age well.

Quality	￼ ￼ ￼ ￼ ￼
Value	★★★★★
Grapes	merlot; cabernet sauvignon
Region	Pyrenees, Vic.
Cellar	￼ 8+
Alc./Vol.	13.7%
RRP	$17.50

Taltarni Shiraz

Quality	♟♟♟
Value	★★☆
Grapes	shiraz
Region	Pyrenees, Vic.
Cellar	▮ 5
Alc./Vol.	13.7%
RRP	$27.75 ▮

Taltarni's guiding light, Dominique Portet, resigned early in 1999. Long-standing chief winemaker Greg Gallagher has also resigned to follow other directions.

CURRENT RELEASE 1997   This wine lacks the power and stuffing one usually finds in red wines from the Pyrenees district, especially in 1997. The colour is a medium purple–red; the nose is fairly light with plum and cherry aromas and a herbal overtone, with relatively low-key oak. It's medium-bodied at best and fairly straightforward. Drinks well young and could be teamed with pink lamb chops.

Talunga Shiraz

Quality	♟♟♟
Value	★★☆
Grapes	shiraz
Region	Adelaide Hills, SA
Cellar	▮ 4
Alc./Vol.	14.0%
RRP	$21.00

The vineyard is at Gumeracha in the oh-so-fashionable Adelaide Hills, and is managed by Vince Scaffidi.

CURRENT RELEASE 1997   A very pretty wine, which is to say light and aromatic but lacking a little in substance. The aromas are floral and raspberryish, with some simple oak embellishment. It's light- to medium-bodied, with a lean profile and straightforward but pleasant flavours. Food: spaghetti bolognese.

Tamburlaine The Chapel Reserve Red

Quality	♟♟♟☿
Value	★★☆
Grapes	shiraz
Region	Hunter Valley, NSW
Cellar	▮ 5+
Alc./Vol.	13.0%
RRP	$27.30

Tamburlaine is on McDonald's Road, Pokolbin. It's owned by a syndicate who are becoming increasingly focused in Orange. They have an interest in a vineyard there and are building a winery. Maker Mark Davidson.

CURRENT RELEASE 1998   Perfumed, charry oak dominates the wine and there's prominent acid on the palate. This highlights the cherry, currant fruit flavours. It has plenty of wood astringency, which makes it taste slightly hollow. Try it with lamb kebabs.

Tapestry Cabernet Sauvignon

Tapestry is a brand owned by Brian Light of Merrivale Winery, McLaren Vale. Light previously made a name for himself as winemaker at Normans.
CURRENT RELEASE 1996 This is a complex, exotic, interesting wine in the best sense of the word. There are attractive composted vegetable and sweet berry aromas. The palate has loads of lush, plump sweet fruit, good intensity and depth. It has a lively palate with softness and drinkability. Goes well with beef stirfry.

Quality	♥♥♥♥
Value	★★★⊁
Grapes	cabernet sauvignon
Region	McLaren Vale, SA
Cellar	◊ 6+
Alc./Vol.	12.5%
RRP	$21.30

Tarrawarra Pinot Noir

Tarrawarra is the name of an abbey which is within sight of the vineyard, and which was there long before the winery. Maker Clare Halloran.
CURRENT RELEASE 1997 Tarrawarra is always one of the bigger pinots, and the '97 is no exception. From a drought year, it's a very concentrated wine, with strong gamy, meaty and undergrowth aromas, and some cherry fruit notes peeking through. The palate has good tannin and extract, is well structured, and possesses depth and power. The undergrowth and cherry/meaty complexities come through strongly in the mouth as well, and the finish is tremendously long. Should cellar well. Try it with Peking duck.

Quality	♥♥♥♥♥
Value	★★★★
Grapes	pinot noir
Region	Yarrra Valley, Vic.
Cellar	◊ 7
Alc./Vol.	12.5%
RRP	$40.00

Tatachilla Cabernet Sauvignon

The original Tatachilla winery was established in 1901. It's been through many ups and downs in the interim, to emerge in the nineties in its most successful guise ever.
CURRENT RELEASE 1997 Yet another burster of a red from Tatachilla, who it seems can do no wrong with red wines. Very deep, youthful colour; excellent weight and structure in the mouth; lashings of ripe sweet fruit, liberal toasty oak and smooth savoury tannins, all in happy harmony. A serious red with a future. Try it with roast lamb.

Quality	♥♥♥♥⏓
Value	★★★★
Grapes	cabernet sauvignon
Region	McLaren Vale, SA
Cellar	◊ 10+
Alc./Vol.	14.0%
RRP	$24.50 ▮

Tatachilla Clarendon Vineyard Merlot

Quality	ΨΨΨΨΨ
Value	★★★★★
Grapes	merlot
Region	McLaren Vale, SA
Cellar	▮ 5+
Alc./Vol.	14.0%
RRP	$30.00 ▮

This did very well in the Sydney International Wine Competition, beating all the heavier-bodied reds and everything else for the best wine of the show.

CURRENT RELEASE 1997 This is one of the best merlots on the market, and alongside some other wannabes, relatively affordable. It's bulging with ripe plum, berry, undergrowth and spicy oak aromas, all well integrated. It's smooth, fleshy, nicely rounded and has lovely balance. Delicious! Try it with roast guinea fowl.

Tatachilla Padthaway Cabernet Sauvignon

Quality	ΨΨΨΨ
Value	★★★★
Grapes	cabernet sauvignon
Region	Padthaway, SA
Cellar	▮ 10
Alc./Vol.	13.5%
RRP	$20.00

The Tatachilla people are always coming up with something new and surprising. Managing Director Keith Smith was previously boss at Wolf Blass and Kaiser Stuhl, and knows how to run a wine company.

CURRENT RELEASE 1997 A winning combination of toasty sweet oak and sweet berry fruit is the key to this one. Oak is used to maximum effect, and there's nicely concentrated, fleshy berry flavour on the tongue. It's lively, intense and balanced, and will reward cellaring. It drinks well with pan-roasted lamb backstraps.

Tatachilla Partners Cabernet Sauvignon Shiraz

Quality	ΨΨΨ
Value	★★★★
Grapes	cabernet sauvignon; shiraz
Region	various, SA
Cellar	▮ 4+
Alc./Vol.	14.0%
RRP	$14.00 Ⓢ

This winery used to be known as the Southern Vales Co-operative; prior to that it was owned from about 1901–1961 by Penfolds. Maker Michael Fragos.

CURRENT RELEASE 1998 This is a simple, fruity young red without apparent oak character. The colour is a deep purple–red; the aroma is youthful, with rather raw but fresh young cherry aromas and a hint of cough medicine. The palate is again fruit-driven and has good depth of flavour, finishing with well-balanced tannin. It's soft enough to drink right now, and would go well with vitello tonnato.

Taylors Shiraz

The winemaking team has undergone a reshuffle at Taylors, with the exit of Andrew Tolley and the arrival of Neil Jericho.

CURRENT RELEASE 1997 A change of style here: it's high in alcohol and shows overripe characters. There are heady, sweet, jammy, rather confectionery-like aromas of alcohol and ultra-ripe grapes. The palate is simplistic and rather stolid, with heaps of clean fruit flavour but not a lot of charm. It needs time to mellow out. Then serve with beef stroganoff.

Quality	🍷🍷🍷½
Value	★★★½
Grapes	shiraz
Region	Clare Valley, SA
Cellar	🍾 8
Alc./Vol.	14.5%
RRP	$16.50 (S)

Te Mata Estate Bullnose Syrah

This was made from only the fifth crop off new vines. Only one-third new oak is used, to allow the fruit to shine through. We need hardly add that great New Zealand shiraz is almost as rare as a Kiwi on the wing.

Previous outstanding vintages: '96

CURRENT RELEASE 1997 This is an extraordinary shiraz! It's practically impossible to buy, but we think it's worth recording. It's wonderfully elegant and the ripeness of the fruit is miraculous. The colour is dark purple–red; the bouquet exudes black pepper, mixed spice and gamy complexities. The taste is fruit-sweet, deep and seamless. A very sexy shiraz that avoids the usual cold-climate traps for this grape. Enjoy alongside cassoulet.

Quality	🍷🍷🍷🍷🍷
Value	★★★★★
Grapes	syrah (shiraz)
Region	Hawkes Bay, NZ
Cellar	🍾 10+
Alc./Vol.	13.0%
RRP	$30.00 (cellar door)

Te Mata Estate Coleraine Cabernet Merlot

Quality 🍷🍷🍷🍷½
Value ★★★
Grapes cabernet sauvignon; cabernet franc; merlot
Region Hawkes Bay, NZ
Cellar 10+
Alc./Vol. 13.5%
RRP $65.00

John Buck's Te Mata Estate has two main vineyards in addition to contracted growers. He grows 800 tonnes of grapes – more than he needs. His own crush is 450 tonnes a year from which he produces 30 000 cases of wine.

Previous outstanding vintages: '89, '91, '94, '95

CURRENT RELEASE 1996 This is one of the greatest reds of New Zealand and a good vintage. The colour is very deep, and the nose is fabulous. Irresistible aromas of blackcurrant, mulberry and cranberry fruit entwined with perfumed, cedary oak waft from the glass. In the mouth it has great intensity and power, coupled with excellent structure, which bodes well for its future. Serve with New Zealand venison.

Quality 🍷🍷🍷🍷🍷
Value ★★★½
Grapes cabernet sauvignon; cabernet franc; merlot
Region Hawkes Bay, NZ
Cellar 12+
Alc./Vol. 13.0%
RRP $65.00

CURRENT RELEASE 1997 This is a delicious red. The colour is vivid purple, and it has a vibrant aroma of sweet blackberry and cassis, showing concentrated 'essence of cabernet' and hints of honey and vanilla. Fruit is the main event, with a background of quality oak. The tannins are in balance and the fruit is properly ripe. Great with rare fillet steak.

Temple Bruer Cabernet Merlot

Quality 🍷🍷🍷½
Value ★★★
Grapes cabernet sauvignon 54%; merlot 33%; cabernet franc 13%
Region Langhorne Creek, SA
Cellar 1–10+
Alc./Vol. 13.5%
RRP $15.80

In addition to having a 24-hectare vineyard at Milang, the Bruers have a large commercial grapevine nursery.

CURRENT RELEASE 1996 This wine is dominated by a pungent minty herbaceousness. It does have palate flavour, but it's rather tight and tough with assertive tannins. The gumleaf/eucalyptus flavours permeate the wine. It needs time, then serve with buffalo steaks.

Temple Bruer Cornucopia Grenache

David Bruer used to be a chemistry lecturer at Roseworthy Agricultural College. He taught one of the authors (HH).

CURRENT RELEASE 1997 This is a very unusual wine with sappy, porty, sweet jammy fruit aromas, coupled with quite high acidity on the palate. The two attributes are a puzzling combination. There's a lot of mint in the flavour spectrum and slight bitterness on the finish. It improves with air. Try it with well-herbed rissoles.

Quality	🍷🍷🍷
Value	★★★
Grapes	grenache
Region	McLaren Vale & Clare Valley, SA
Cellar	🍾 2
Alc./Vol.	14.0%
RRP	$13.80 (♥)

Temple Bruer Shiraz Malbec

The Bruer family of Temple Bruer pride themselves on running an organic vineyard in the Langhorne Creek region. This wine is made from 100 per cent estate-grown grapes.

CURRENT RELEASE 1996 A seriously good red wine – the best we've seen from Temple Bruer for some time. The colour is very deep purple–red with blackish tints, and the nose is strongly marked by oak, although the wine is still young and needs time. The palate is quite concentrated with excellent density of flavour, marvellous depth of fruit, and oak starting to integrate. The finish is very long and satisfying. Flavours of violets and blackberries permeate the wine. It needs time. Cellar, then serve with rare roast beef.

Quality	🍷🍷🍷🍷½
Value	★★★★½
Grapes	shiraz 74%; malbec 26%
Region	Langhorne Creek, SA
Cellar	🍾 2–10+
Alc./Vol.	14.2%
RRP	$15.80 🍾 (♥)

T'Gallant Juno Pinot Noir

Quality	🍷🍷🍷🍷½
Value	★★★½
Grapes	pinot noir
Region	Mornington Peninsula, Vic.
Cellar	[bottle] 3
Alc./Vol.	13.6%
RRP	$43.00

T'Gallant's new range of super-premiums are named after heavenly bodies. The fruit for this pinot came off the Lyncroft vineyard. Makers Kevin McCarthy and Kath Quealy.

CURRENT RELEASE 1997 This is a lovely, elegant and very complex pinot. The colour is mid-purple–red and the nose shows undergrowth, sappy/floral and berry aromas, with a suggestion of stalks from whole-bunch fermentation. It's light- to medium-bodied, soft and easy on the gums. It drinks well now and has a good range of pinot flavours. Great with marinated quail.

Torbreck Runrig

Quality	🍷🍷🍷🍷🍷
Value	★★★★
Grapes	shiraz; viognier
Region	Barossa Valley, SA
Cellar	[bottle lying down] 5–15+
Alc./Vol.	14.5%
RRP	$41.00 (cellar door) [barrel]

The idea of blending a little white wine (especially viognier) with shiraz originated in Côte Rotie, France. Peter Lehmann did it at Saltram several decades ago – but not with viognier.

CURRENT RELEASE 1996 Torbreck is an exciting new addition to the Barossa, and here's why. The colour of this power-packed red is inky black, and the flavour is plush and extravagant. The nose displays cedary, toasty, floral and minty aromas – very ripe and concentrated. It's massive and quite heavily extracted, and it demands patience. The luscious fruit and big structure will guarantee rewards with time. Cellar, then serve with venison.

Torbreck The Steading

Quality	🍷🍷🍷🍷½
Value	★★★★
Grapes	grenache; mataro; shiraz
Region	Barossa Valley, SA
Cellar	[bottle] 12+
Alc./Vol.	14.5%
RRP	$23.00 (cellar door) [barrel]

This new Barossa winery is operated by Dave Powell, who formerly worked at Rockford. Similar philosophies apply and the result is red wines of great character, concentration and depth.

CURRENT RELEASE 1997 This is the drink-now Torbreck (joke!). It's softer and more approachable than the Runrig. The nose is shy but laden with earth, berry, cherry and licorice/anise nuances. There's excellent fruit depth on the palate, and the blackberry, spicy fruit-sweetness is nicely balanced by smooth but assertive tannin. Delicious stuff! Try it with braised lamb shanks.

Trentham Estate Shiraz

Trentham Estate produces 30 000 cases of wine a year, not so small for a family operation drawing its grapes from its own vines. Maker Tony Murphy; viticulturist Pat Murphy.

CURRENT RELEASE 1997   A big, rich, rather unpolished shiraz. What it lacks in elegance it makes up for in guts. Plum, vanilla and toasty oak aromas are underlined by herbal and spice nuances. There's some astringency on the finish, and it would be best served with food. Try osso bucco.

Quality	♀♀♀⅃
Value	★★★★
Grapes	shiraz
Region	Murray Valley, NSW
Cellar	🍷 5+
Alc./Vol.	14.0%
RRP	$17.00 Ⓢ

Trio Station 3 Steps Cabernet Sauvignon

Trio Station 3 Steps is the cheaper label of the Vincorp group, a publicly listed company that owns Virgin Hills and that intends to be a mover and shaker in the wine industry. Maker Mark Sheppard.

CURRENT RELEASE 1998   This is good value and pleasant current drinking. The bouquet has earthy, coffee and mulberry aromas with a stalky overtone. It has adequate palate flavour, and is straightforward and medium- to light-bodied. It's much better value than the Reserve label, which is double the price. Serve with hamburgers.

Quality	♀♀♀
Value	★★★⅃
Grapes	cabernet sauvignon
Region	various, Vic.
Cellar	🍷 3
Alc./Vol.	12.5%
RRP	$14.00 Ⓢ

Trio Station 3 Steps Shiraz Cabernet

Considering its provenance and price, this is amazingly good. The shiraz is from first-crop vines at Mildura; the cabernet from Central Victoria. The brand is new and comes from Vincorp at Kyneton, where the winemaker is Mark Sheppard.

CURRENT RELEASE 1998   A lovely spicy youngster with a delicious blend of blackcurranty cabernet and peppery/spicy shiraz aromas. It's elegant, somewhat Rhone-like, and has a lot of panache. A good first effort. Try it with spicy meatballs baked in a tomato sauce.

Quality	♀♀♀♀⅃
Value	★★★★★
Grapes	shiraz; cabernet sauvignon
Region	Murray Valley & Central Victoria, Vic.
Cellar	🍷 4
Alc./Vol.	13.0%
RRP	$13.00

Tuck's Ridge Altera Pinot Noir

Quality	♟♟♟♟
Value	★★★⸜
Grapes	pinot noir
Region	Mornington Peninsula, Vic.
Cellar	▮ 2
Alc./Vol.	13.0%
RRP	$18.00

This is a new label for a less expensive, lighter-bodied, less serious pinot than the standard Tuck's Ridge issue. Winemaker Daniel Greene.

CURRENT RELEASE 1998 A very pretty little wine – and that's not a put-down. It's exactly what we expected: a light purple–red hue, and exuberant young pinot aromas of ripe cherry, which carry through to the light-bodied palate. There's negligible oak or tannin grip. It's a very slurpable lighter pinot to have with seared tuna.

Tuck's Ridge Pinot Noir

Quality	♟♟♟♟
Value	★★★
Grapes	pinot noir
Region	Mornington Peninsula, Vic.
Cellar	▮ 4
Alc./Vol.	13.4%
RRP	$23.60

Tuck's Ridge, established in 1988, is a 26-hectare vine4yard at Red Hill South on the Mornington Peninsula. Maker Daniel Greene.

CURRENT RELEASE 1998 This is one of the better Tuck's Ridge pinots, but perhaps not quite up to the excellent '97. The nose has vanilla and cherry aromas, slightly straightforward; the palate is lean and has quite firm structure. There are herbal flavours, and it has reasonable length. It would go well with duck à l'orange.

Tunnel Hill Pinot Noir

Quality	♟♟♟
Value	★★⸜
Grapes	pinot noir
Region	Yarra Valley, Vic.
Cellar	▮ 3
Alc./Vol.	13.0%
RRP	$21.30 Ⓢ

The second label of Tarrawarra Estate is named after a disused railway tunnel on the property. Some good quaffing pinots have come out under this label in the past. Maker Clare Halloran.

Previous outstanding vintages: '94, '97

CURRENT RELEASE 1998 A basic pinot at a price that's somewhat more than basic. There are green herb overtones to the sappy, strawberry-like fruit, and it seems rather skinny on the palate. It finishes dry with a touch of austerity. Better with a meal: try serving it with mushroom risotto.

Turkey Flat Butchers Block

A block is usually a section of vineyard, but this refers to a genuine butcher's block. The old cellar-door sales building used to be a butchery. This is a new release. Peter Schulz could have called this MSG but for negative connotations!

CURRENT RELEASE 1997   A fabulous first-up release: very aromatic sweet berry nose, spicy and peppery with the most spice coming from the mourvèdre. Soft, gentle tannins, lovely to drink already and beautifully balanced. Try it with barbecued roo.

Quality	♟♟♟♟♟
Value	★★★★★
Grapes	mourvèdre; shiraz; grenache
Region	Barossa Valley, SA
Cellar	▬ 6+
Alc./Vol.	14.5%
RRP	$27.90

Turkey Flat Cabernet Sauvignon

Turkey Flat wines are made under the care of Colin Glaetzer at Barossa Vintners, the new contract wine-making enterprise in which viticulturist Peter Schulz is a partner.

CURRENT RELEASE 1997   This is not especially caber-net-like, but it's a darned good Barossa red wine. Rich plum, cherry aromas; smooth ripe palate flavours as plush as a deep-pile carpet. Chunky yet elegant, it's a user-friendly drop of red. Serve with boeuf à la mode.

Quality	♟♟♟♟♟
Value	★★★⊦
Grapes	cabernet sauvignon
Region	Barossa Valley, SA
Cellar	▬ 10+
Alc./Vol.	14.2%
RRP	$34.50 ▮

Turkey Flat Shiraz

None of the Turkey Flat reds see any new oak, according to principal Peter Schulz. The grapes are mainly from very old vines, well over a century old.

CURRENT RELEASE 1997   Despite the moratorium on new oak, this has a dominant vanilla aroma which pre-sumably just needs a little patience to integrate further. Its whopping 14.7 per cent alcohol doesn't show; indeed, the profile is on the lean side, and it has a savoury finish with plenty of drying tannin. Cellar, then have with braised lamb shanks.

Quality	♟♟♟♟
Value	★★★
Grapes	shiraz
Region	Barossa Valley, SA
Cellar	➤ 2–10
Alc./Vol.	14.7%
RRP	$40.00 ▮

Turramurra Estate Cabernet

Quality	♟♟♟♟♟
Value	★★★⊦
Grapes	cabernet sauvignon
Region	Mornington Peninsula, Vic.
Cellar	➽ 1–5
Alc./Vol.	13.9%
RRP	$33.00

Turramurra Estate is a small new Mornington Peninsula vineyard. Like many others, owners David and Paula Leslie grow some cabernet sauvignon despite its checkered history in the region. In hot years like 1997 it comes into its own.

CURRENT RELEASE 1997   The best Mornington cabernet from '97? Could be. This is a solid, structured red wine that shows the possibilities of cabernet down there when everything goes well. The nose has blackberry, leather and olive aromas touched by classy oak. The palate has ripe, long flavour with a firm structure of ripe tannins. A classy wine that goes well with roast lamb.

Tyrrell's Long Flat Red

Quality	♟♟♟
Value	★★★★
Grapes	shiraz; cabernet sauvignon; malbec
Region	not stated
Cellar	▮ 3
Alc./Vol.	13.0%
RRP	$9.00 ⑤

Tyrrell's first released Long Flat Red in 1966. They have a vineyard named Long Flat in the Hunter, but the wine has for some time been a blend of various areas.

CURRENT RELEASE 1998   This is a good-value quaffing dry red that won't break the bank. It bottoms out at $5.99. The nose is grapey with cherry-like scents; the palate flavour is clean with good intensity, light body, attractive fruit and easy-drinking balance. Great with bangers and mash.

Tyrrell's Rufus Stone Heathcote Shiraz

Quality	♟♟♟♟?
Value	★★★★
Grapes	shiraz
Region	Heathcote, Vic.
Cellar	➽ 2–10
Alc./Vol.	14.0%
RRP	$25.00 ⑤ ▮

Tyrrell's recognised the value of the Heathcote region some years ago and developed a large vineyard there. The grapes are handled by Murray Tyrrell's son-in-law, John Ellis, at Hanging Rock.

CURRENT RELEASE 1997   A dense-coloured, heavily concentrated wine which needs plenty of time to mellow. Oak gives vanilla, caramel notes to the nose and dominates the spicy fruit at this stage. It's a big, rich, chocolatey wine, but it's more elegant than its McLaren Vale cousin. Goes well with rare roast sirloin.

Tyrrell's Rufus Stone McLaren Vale Shiraz

This is about as far-fetched as a modern concept wine can get. Sir Walter, a Tyrrell ancestor, was suspected of having shot William Rufus, the King of England, with a stray arrow. The place is marked today by the 'Rufus stone'. The grapes came from Johnston's Pirramimma. CURRENT RELEASE 1997 This is a voluptuous red in typical McLaren Vale style. The colour is dark and dense, the nose is spicy, vanillin, ripe and plummy, and the taste is plump and fruit-sweet. A gorgeous, fleshy, fun wine. Serve it with saddle of hare.

Quality	🍷🍷🍷🍷🍷
Value	★★★★⯪
Grapes	shiraz
Region	McLaren Vale, SA
Cellar	� 1–8+
Alc./Vol.	14.0%
RRP	$25.00 Ⓢ

Vavasour Pinot Noir

This winery in the Awatere Valley, adjacent to Marlborough's more famous Wairau Valley, has 13 hectares of vines and produces 25 000 cases. Maker Glenn Thomas. CURRENT RELEASE 1997 A typically dark-coloured, full and fruity Kiwi pinot which just needs time to mature. Dark cherry and cedary oak aromas greet the nose, and it's sweet and fleshy in the mouth. There's no stalkiness, and it tastes nice and ripe. A serious addition to the swelling ranks of fine Kiwi pinot. It goes with sautéed chicken livers.

Quality	🍷🍷🍷🍷⯪
Value	★★★★
Grapes	pinot noir
Region	Marlborough, NZ
Cellar	🍶 5+
Alc./Vol.	13.5%
RRP	$24.50

Veritas Bull's Blood Shiraz Mourvèdre Pressings

The Binder family came from Hungary, hence the traditional Hungarian description of Bull's Blood for this thunderous pressings wine. Maker Rolf Binder. CURRENT RELEASE 1996 The colour is an impenetrable black, which is a warning of things to come. This is a big black beauty, crammed with spice (cloves, pepper), licorice and dark berry flavours. It has a very dry, tannic finish, but it's skin tannin – if anything, the oak is downplayed. A yummy big softie. Serve with goulash.

Quality	🍷🍷🍷🍷🍷
Value	★★★★★
Grapes	shiraz; mourvèdre
Region	Barossa Valley, SA
Cellar	🍶 15
Alc./Vol.	13.5%
RRP	$26.00 (cellar door) 🍶

Virgin Hills

Quality	▼▼▼▼
Value	★★★
Grapes	cabernet sauvignon; shiraz; malbec; merlot
Region	Macedon Ranges, Vic.
Cellar	▮ 8
Alc./Vol.	12.0%
RRP	$40.00

This wine has been an Australian icon. A well-known Australian wine writer selected Virgin Hills as his 'desert island wine'. It has certainly had a patchy history, part of the reason being a cold and marginal climate. It recently changed hands and is now part of Vincorp.
Previous outstanding vintages: '74, '75, '76, '80, '82, '85, '88, '90, '91, '92, '94
CURRENT RELEASE 1995 This is much better than the '96 but still one of the lighter vintages of Virgin Hills. The aromas are of blackcurrant and crushed vine leaves. It's fresh and lively and very elegant, and we suspect this style of wine is generally overlooked in this era of fashionable blockbusters. A good wine to serve with duck.

Quality	▼▼
Value	★★
Grapes	cabernet sauvignon 66%; shiraz 18%; malbec 11%; merlot 5%
Region	Macedon Ranges, Vic.
Cellar	▮ 5
Alc./Vol.	12.0%
RRP	$40.00

CURRENT RELEASE 1996 It has to be said that this is a low-point for such an esteemed marque. The '96 is an ordinary wine for the money, and very lightweight. It's green and unripe-tasting, and the palate is positively thin. It was a cool, sun-bereft season in southern Victoria, and this had dire effects on cool-climate reds other than pinot. One to avoid. Footnote: this vintage was later recalled by the winery because of a stability problem.

Quality	▼▼▼▼▼
Value	★★★★
Grapes	cabernet sauvignon; shiraz; merlot; malbec
Region	Macedon, Vic.
Cellar	━ 2–15+
Alc./Vol.	11.3%
RRP	$40.00 ▮

CURRENT RELEASE 1997 Is this the best Virgin Hills ever? Quite possibly, although we're old enough to remember the '76 when it was a babe. This is quite simply a stunner. Deep colour, sweet blackberry, blackcurrant and spice aromas, showing riper fruit and a shade more oak than usual. In the mouth, it has great intensity and power, without sacrificing its usual elegance. Finishes with length and grip. Outstanding! (And there's no price increase!) Serve with venison.

Warrenmang Estate Shiraz

Warrenmang isn't only a vineyard and winery: owners Luigi and Athalie Bazzani also offer stylish accommodation among the vines and a restaurant that's worth staying for.

CURRENT RELEASE 1997 A dense, murky dark colour hints at the power within this hefty red. The nose is potent with pepper, black cherry, vanillin wood and a choc-mint regional touch. In the mouth it's intense, with big wild fruit in the middle, toasty oak, the warmth of 15.5% alcohol, and serious slabs of tannin. Not a wine for wimps. Try it with a roast rib of beef.

Quality	♟♟♟♟♟
Value	★★★★
Grapes	shiraz
Region	Pyrenees, Vic.
Cellar	➡ 3–10
Alc./Vol.	15.5%
RRP	$30.00

Warrenmang Grand Pyrenees

The Warrenmang reds are traditionally big bruisers that take no prisoners. Grand Pyrenees is the cabernet blend, which is sometimes less powerful than the Estate Shiraz, but only by a whisker.

CURRENT RELEASE 1997 The colour is deep and dense in typical Warrenmang fashion. The nose is an interesting study in contrasts – sweet mulberry fruit of ripe richness leads the way, and hints of dried herbs lend a slightly Italianate savour. Spicy oak brings up the rear. The flavour is dense with juicy black-fruit flavour and balanced dry tannins. Roast a leg of lamb for this one.

Quality	♟♟♟♟♟
Value	★★★ᵏ
Grapes	cabernet sauvignon; cabernet franc; merlot; shiraz
Region	Pyrenees, Vic.
Cellar	➡ 2–10+
Alc./Vol.	14.5%
RRP	$33.50

Water Wheel Cabernet Sauvignon

Peter Cumming is an easy-going, friendly sort of bloke, and his wines exhibit the same admirable traits. Value for money is always exceptional.

CURRENT RELEASE 1997 Water Wheel cabernets are often a bit more generous in their youth than many Bendigo district reds. Here we have aromas of blackberry and plum with a dressing of vanillin oak. The palate has attractive fruit-sweetness and depth, underpinned by dry tannins, and finishes long. Try it with roast beef and Yorkshire pud.

Quality	♟♟♟♟
Value	★★★★ᵏ
Grapes	cabernet sauvignon
Region	Bendigo, Vic.
Cellar	▮ 5
Alc./Vol.	14.5%
RRP	$18.00

Water Wheel Shiraz

Quality	♟♟♟♟
Value	★★★★
Grapes	shiraz
Region	Bendigo, Vic.
Cellar	▮ 6
Alc./Vol.	14.5%
RRP	$18.00

Water Wheel's shiraz is a perennial bargain. Incidentally, they don't only grow grapes at Water Wheel, they also produce the fattest, juiciest, tastiest cherries imaginable. **CURRENT RELEASE 1997** Perhaps reflecting a hotter than normal 1997, this dark wine has slightly jammy blackberry fruit on the nose, which smells a little like port. The palate follows in powerful fashion: very ripe and full-bodied with berry and vanillin oak flavours. It finishes long, with tight tannins and noticeable alcoholic warmth. A good match for beef olives.

Wayne Thomas Shiraz

Quality	♟♟♟♟
Value	★★★⊁
Grapes	shiraz
Region	McLaren Vale, SA
Cellar	▮ 5
Alc./Vol.	13.5%
RRP	$18.90

Wayne Thomas used to own Fern Hill vineyard, and before that he worked at Saltram and Ryecroft. He brings a lot of experience to this new label. **CURRENT RELEASE 1997** There's a rustic, old-fashioned personality to this wine. Blackberry and plum fruit partner gamy, wild, savoury touches on the nose. In the mouth the theme continues, with savoury earthy flavour and a smooth middle palate. Fine, soft tannins make it easy to drink. Choose something rich and gamy to partner this red.

Whisson Lake Carey Gully Pinot Noir

Quality	♟♟♟♟⊍
Value	★★★⊁
Grapes	pinot noir
Region	Adelaide Hills, SA
Cellar	▮ 2
Alc./Vol.	13.7%
RRP	$33.00

This hails from the Piccadilly Valley area. The Adelaide Hills is emerging as an interesting source of pinot. Maker Roman Bratasiuk (contract). **CURRENT RELEASE 1995** A bottle-aged pinot of structure and character. It goes beyond the simple cherry fruit of most Aussie pinots and seems to reflect a Burgundian ideal. The colour is an aged medium brick red; the bouquet has meaty, licorice and prune aromas with some volatility and interesting feral overtones. It's lean and quite tannic, with raisiny aged flavours and a hint of 'crushed-ant' volatility. A complex, satisfying drink. Should go with coq au vin.

Willow Creek Pinot Noir

Peter Harris's Willow Creek estate is expanding with a new winery and new visitor facilities. The staples are the usual Mornington Peninsula trio of chardonnay, pinot noir and cabernet sauvignon.

CURRENT RELEASE 1997 The colour is a correct pinot brick red. There's no mistaking the variety on the perfumed nose either: cherry, leaf, earth and boiled-beetroot aromas give it some real complexity. Similar flavours run through the palate, which has succulent fruit, good acidity and slightly stemmy tannins on a long finish.

Quality	????
Value	★★★★
Grapes	pinot noir
Region	Mornington Peninsula, Vic.
Cellar	4
Alc./Vol.	13.5%
RRP	$27.00

The Willows Cabernet Sauvignon

The Scholz family have a 35-hectare vineyard at Light Pass. Winemaker is Peter, who honed his skills at Peter Lehmann.

CURRENT RELEASE 1996 A tightly-bound cabernet which is out of the Barossa mainstream. While it perhaps lacks the usual generosity of flavour, it has solid structure and a firm finish. There are tomato and cassis aromas with more than a hint of herbaceousness. Try it with a meat pie and sauce.

Quality	???
Value	★★★
Grapes	cabernet sauvignon
Region	Barossa Valley, SA
Cellar	6
Alc./Vol.	13.5%
RRP	$20.50

The Willows Shiraz

Peter Scholz has quit working full time for Peter Lehmann to concentrate on building up his own brand. He'll continue to work vintage at PL's and make his own wines there. Lehmann's also take his excess grapes.

CURRENT RELEASE 1996 We've heard of Dolly Parton chardonnays, but is there such a thing as a Dolly Parton shiraz? Buxom, cuddly, friendly and not too complicated. This is well stacked with sweet, ripe, plummy Barossa fruit and vanillin US oak, and it slips down smoothly. A lovely drink that could improve with age. Suits spinach-stuffed veal shoulder.

Quality	????
Value	★★★★
Grapes	shiraz
Region	Barossa Valley, SA
Cellar	7+
Alc./Vol.	14.0%
RRP	$20.50 Ⓢ

Wirra Wirra Original Blend Grenache Shiraz

Quality	♥♥♥♥
Value	★★★★
Grapes	grenache; shiraz
Region	McLaren Vale, SA
Cellar	🍾 5+
Alc./Vol.	15.0%
RRP	$22.00

Grenache and shiraz was the 'original blend' of many a McLaren Vale winery before cabernet et al. arrived. We might imagine that this is what those wines of the olden days were like, but in fact it's much better.
CURRENT RELEASE 1997   This is a warmly welcoming old-fashioned red with loads of character and none of your fancy modern tricks. The nose has soft berry, earth and pepper aromas with a touch of vanilla bean. Oak very much takes a back seat. The palate is rich and mouth-filling with dense, savoury fruit, a gamy thread and dry tannins. The warmth of 15 per cent alcohol doesn't seem out of place in a wine like this. Serve it with a game pie.

Wirra Wirra RSW Shiraz

Quality	♥♥♥♥
Value	★★★★
Grapes	shiraz
Region	McLaren Vale, SA
Cellar	➡ 2–10
Alc./Vol.	14.0%
RRP	$35.00

Since it was restored from ruins in the sixties, the Wirra Wirra winery's red wines have got progressively better. Now their flagship wines, RSW Shiraz and The Angelus Cabernet Sauvignon, are among McLaren Vale's very best.
CURRENT RELEASE 1996   A very impressive shiraz of grand proportions, which uses a good measure of French oak rather than the more common Yankee stuff. The nose is power-packed, full of blackberry fruit, tea-leaves, dark chocolate and toasty cedary oak. In the mouth it has great depth of ripe blackberry and spice shiraz flavour, chunky texture and clean acidity. Fine, dry tannins balance things sweetly.

Wolf Blass Black Label Cabernet Shiraz

Quality	♥♥♥
Value	★★
Grapes	cabernet sauvignon; shiraz
Region	Langhorne Creek, McLaren Vale & Eden Valley, SA
Cellar	➡ 2–8
Alc./Vol.	13.5%
RRP	$95.00

Black Label is the epitome of the oaky Wolf Blass style. Consumers are starting to look for more fruit-driven wines, and this red is starting to taste a bit passé.
CURRENT RELEASE 1995   At the price this has to be very questionable value. The nose shows the legacy of three years in new oak – it smells of coconut-vanillin oak and little else. Yes, there's a touch of dark fruit there, but it's basically a one-dimensional red wine. The palate is big, thick and oaky with dry woody tannins. Would stand up to an aged buffalo steak.

Wolf Blass Grey Label Cabernet Sauvignon Shiraz

This used to be a favoured red of the 'suits' in the days when expense-account lunches weren't as austere as they are today.

CURRENT RELEASE 1996 This style seems to have been evolving in recent years with a reduction in the American oak input of the past. Notable caramelly oak is still there behind the berry aromas of the nose, but in less emphatic guise. The palate has cherry and blackcurrant fruit with an oaky spine and reasonable length, but it lacks the complexity and drinkability of some of the competition. Try it with Szechuan black pepper beef.

Quality	♥♥♥♥
Value	★★★
Grapes	cabernet sauvignon; shiraz
Region	Langhorne Creek, SA
Cellar	🍷 5
Alc./Vol.	13.5%
RRP	$30.00

Wood Park Shiraz Cabernet Sauvignon

Wood Park wines are a real find for us this year. After tasting the chardonnay we keenly looked forward to the red. We weren't disappointed. Maker John Stokes.

CURRENT RELEASE 1997 Deep purplish in colour, this has a ripe and attractive bouquet with intense dark berry fruit and stylish oak treatment. In the mouth it's complete and harmoniously balanced. Blackberry flavour, a hint of tea-leaf, and perfectly integrated oak and tannins combine seamlessly across the middleweight palate. Very good. Try this with a venison casserole.

Quality	♥♥♥♥♥
Value	★★★★⟡
Grapes	shiraz; cabernet sauvignon
Region	King Valley, Vic.
Cellar	🍷 4
Alc./Vol.	13.5%
RRP	$24.00

Woodstock Cabernet Sauvignon

Scott Collett of Woodstock is a red wine man with a reputation based on a consistent, flavoursome line of McLaren Vale shirazes and cabernets.

CURRENT RELEASE 1997 The Woodstock style of cabernet is smooth and generously flavoured, without any rough edges. This is right up to speed, with a ripe blackberry nose which has balanced sweet/savoury oak and a slightly minty edge. The palate tracks the nose with more of that plump fruit character, good depth and attractively dry tannins. A good companion for a rare porterhouse steak.

Quality	♥♥♥♥
Value	★★★★
Grapes	cabernet sauvignon
Region	McLaren Vale, SA
Cellar	🍷 6+
Alc./Vol.	13.7%
RRP	$19.70

Woodstock Grenache

Quality 🍷🍷🍷🍷
Value ★★★★½
Grapes grenache
Region McLaren Vale, SA
Cellar 3
Alc./Vol. 14.0%
RRP $14.50

The old McLaren Vale mainstay makes good wine in the hands of Scott Collett at Woodstock. There isn't any of the jammy, confectionery character found in some grenache.

CURRENT RELEASE 1997 Good depth and density of colour augur well here. The nose follows with concentrated complex aromas of dark cherries and berries, chocolate, spice and undergrowth. Those aromas track down the palate, which has considerable alcoholic warmth and power. Tannins are typically soft. Good with spiced Italian sausages.

Woodstock Shiraz

Quality 🍷🍷🍷🍷
Value ★★★★
Grapes shiraz
Region McLaren Vale, SA
Cellar 5+
Alc./Vol. 13.5%
RRP $18.10

Bold, hearty red wines are Woodstock's stock-in-trade. Both shiraz and cabernet are made in a satisfying robust style.

CURRENT RELEASE 1997 A powerfully flavoured regional shiraz with ripe blackberry and cherry fruit in the middle of beaut composty, earthy character, and dusty oak. The palate follows suit with ripe fruit, savoury interest, and mellow texture. Slightly astringent tannins don't intrude too much for current enjoyment. Try it with kofta kebabs.

Woodstock The Stocks Shiraz

Quality 🍷🍷🍷🍷½
Value ★★★★
Grapes shiraz
Region McLaren Vale, SA
Cellar 10
Alc./Vol. 14.0%
RRP $29.60

The Stocks is made from very old shiraz vines and aged in new American oak. It was first made in the '91 vintage. Maker Scott Collett.

CURRENT RELEASE 1996 Toasty-sweet oak leads the way on the nose here, with ripe berries and chocolatey richness underneath. The palate is fruit-packed and ripe, but it's not too overdone. Similarly, vanillin oak is apparent but not overwhelming, and the dry tannins are in good balance. An almost elegant super-shiraz for McLaren Vale.

Wyndham Estate Cabernet Sauvignon Shiraz Ruby Cabernet

Wyndham Estate makes an unashamedly commercial range of wines that avoids regional style considerations in favour of anonymous consistency.

CURRENT RELEASE 1998   For many years Wyndham seem to have been toying with residual sweetness in their reds, and this is no exception. Both nose and palate are fruity-sweet with plum, blackberry and spice. The palate has a slightly cloying character ahead of soft furry tannins.

Quality	♟♟♟
Value	★★丬
Grapes	cabernet sauvignon; shiraz; ruby cabernet
Region	not stated
Cellar	▮ 2
Alc./Vol.	11.5%
RRP	$7.95 Ⓢ

Wynns Cabernet Sauvignon

Wynns is one of Australia's best-known cabernets. It also has great credentials for the cellar. Some of these Coonawarra wines from the fifties still hold up well.

CURRENT RELEASE 1996   Deep-purple and dense, this has benchmark cabernet character, leafy blackcurrant and cassis liqueur, berries, spice, and clean cabernet earthiness. It also has some mocha and sweet oak barrel influences, but they enhance rather than dominate. Despite obvious ageworthiness, it drinks well right now. Super with pink-roasted racks of lamb.

Quality	♟♟♟♟♟
Value	★★★★★
Grapes	cabernet sauvignon
Region	Coonawarra, SA
Cellar	▮ 10+
Alc./Vol.	13.0%
RRP	$22.00 Ⓢ

CURRENT RELEASE 1997   Rather closed at the moment, this still has hallmark Wynns' cabernet style. The nose has tart blackcurrant, a hint of olive and a touch of spicy, nutty oak. The palate follows the nose in character: it's medium-bodied and tight with good length and fine dry tannins on the finish. Give it time, then serve it with roast lamb.

Quality	♟♟♟♟丬
Value	★★★★★
Grapes	cabernet sauvignon
Region	Coonawarra, SA
Cellar	➡ 2–10+
Alc./Vol.	13.5%
RRP	$23.00

Wynns John Riddoch Cabernet Sauvignon

Quality	�
Value	★★★⋆
Grapes	cabernet sauvignon
Region	Coonawarra, SA
Cellar	⬤➤ 1–10+
Alc./Vol.	13.0%
RRP	$79.50

This is Wynns' top Coonawarra cabernet. It's become a bit of a collector's item in the manner of these things, and it's priced accordingly. Value is in the eye of the beholder.

CURRENT RELEASE 1996   Lovely essency cassis aroma with a touch of spearmint and beautifully handled savoury oak makes an impressive introduction to this deep-coloured wine. The palate is refined and civilised, with intense mid-palate flavour and fine-grained ripe tannins. A classic Coonawarra cabernet in the making; all it needs is time. Good with a lamb and kidney pie.

Wynns Shiraz

Quality	♟♟♟♟♟
Value	★★★★⋆
Grapes	shiraz
Region	Coonawarra, SA
Cellar	⬤ 5+
Alc./Vol.	13.0%
RRP	$16.50 ⑤

Though no longer the fantastically low-priced bargain it was a few years ago, Wynns Shiraz is still great value. Variations in style due to vintage conditions are part and parcel of the style, but it's never less than very good.

CURRENT RELEASE 1997   A blackish purple colour introduces one of the best Wynns Coonawarra shirazes in memory. On the nose, spice, black cherry and berry fruit dominate, with a dab of sweet oak in the background. The palate is rich in dark-fruit flavour, with good length and well-measured tannins. Excellent with spicy Middle Eastern lamb kebabs.

Xanadu Cabernet Reserve

Quality	♟♟♟♟
Value	★★★
Grapes	cabernet sauvignon
Region	Margaret River, WA
Cellar	⬤➤ 2–10+
Alc./Vol.	13.5%
RRP	$57.00 ◾

Seems like they're dropping the word chateau off the name – and not before time. This is sometimes one of the stand-out cabs from the region. Maker Jurg Muggli. *Previous outstanding vintages: '91, '95*

CURRENT RELEASE 1996   This is a distinctive style. It combines mulched leaf and other vegetal aromas with a firm tannin grip. Paradoxically, there are sweet jammy aromas as well, and the wine has tonnes of structure. It should cellar well, and then serve with beef wellington.

Xanadu Cabernet Sauvignon

This is a take-no-prisoners style (see the Chateau Xanadu Cabernet Reserve). The wines are expensive and definitely not early-drinkers.

CURRENT RELEASE 1997 The trademark Xanadu astringency is here in full voice. It definitely needs time – and this isn't even the Reserve! Raspberry, vanilla and playdough aromas are simply raw and undeveloped. It's one-dimensional at present. There's a whopper tannic grip and a slight hollowness in the mid-palate. One for those with faith to cellar.

Quality	♥♥♥
Value	★★★
Grapes	cabernet sauvignon
Region	Margaret River, WA
Cellar	➡ 2–8+
Alc./Vol.	13.5%
RRP	$33.00 ▮

Xanadu Secession Cabernet Shiraz

This is a new line for Xanadu, a partner for the popular Secession semillon sauvignon blanc.

CURRENT RELEASE 1998 This is a good drink-now red with a spicy, peppery, shiraz-dominated nose. The palate is fruit-driven and mild, with modest concentration and very little oak character. It has reasonable immediate palate flavour, but without excitement. It would go very well with a spicy meat hotpot.

Quality	♥♥♥⬤
Value	★★★
Grapes	cabernet sauvignon; shiraz
Region	Margaret River, WA
Cellar	▮ 4+
Alc./Vol.	13.5%
RRP	$20.50

Yalumba Bush Vine Grenache

Grenache is everybody's darling these days, even those weary old vines that used to be fodder for Barossa fortified wines. Yalumba uses some of them for this plump style.

CURRENT RELEASE 1997 Typical love-'em-or-hate-'em grenache characters rule here. The nose has sweet raspberry aromas with some gamy, meaty touches. The palate is big, juicy and soft with raspberry fruit. Fine tannins give some structure. Barbecue some lamb chops to go with this one.

Quality	♥♥♥⬤
Value	★★★
Grapes	grenache
Region	Barossa Valley, SA
Cellar	▮ 2
Alc./Vol.	15.0%
RRP	$14.95

Yalumba Oxford Landing Cabernet Sauvignon & Shiraz

Quality	♟♟♟
Value	★★★
Grapes	cabernet sauvignon; shiraz
Region	Murray Valley, SA
Cellar	▮ 1
Alc./Vol.	13.0%
RRP	$8.50

Oxford Landing is Yalumba's fightin' brand, made in vast quantities and designed to tussle with Jacob's Creek and the rest for a slice of the under-$10 market. Like its rivals, it's also a successful export commodity.

CURRENT RELEASE 1998 This is a trim little commercial number that doesn't disappoint in its price range. It has pleasant leafy berry aroma and flavour, lightish medium body and easy drinkability. No great complexity, but no problems either. Serve with pizza.

Yalumba Oxford Landing Limited Release Merlot

Quality	♟♟♟♟
Value	★★★★
Grapes	merlot
Region	Murray Valley, SA
Cellar	▮ 2
Alc./Vol.	13.0%
RRP	$9.95

Having both 'Oxford Landing' and 'Limited Release' on a label seems an oxymoron, but why can't a big Riverland vineyard have a little bit of something special?

CURRENT RELEASE 1998 This is a little step up from the standard Oxford Landing label, and it shares the same virtues of easy drinking and a very reasonable price. It's a berry-flavoured drop with a touch of earthiness, clean and soft with easy balance. A good match for pasta with ragu.

Yalumba Reserve Clare Valley Cabernet Sauvignon

Quality	♟♟♟♟
Value	★★★★
Grapes	cabernet sauvignon
Region	Clare Valley, SA
Cellar	▮ 5
Alc./Vol.	14.0%
RRP	$22.95 ▮

A special bottling of cabernet from the Waninga Vineyard, west of Sevenhill in the Clare Valley. The vineyard was planted in 1973.

CURRENT RELEASE 1996 This is a big-flavoured red with rich, spicy dark plum and sweet currant aromas, along with the distinctive ferruginous note that comes from good Clare ground. In the mouth it's dense with rich and potent spicy fruit, balanced oak and dry tannins. Try it with braised beef spare ribs.

Yalumba Signature Cabernet Sauvignon Shiraz

An oldie but a goodie, which started off in 1962 as a special bottling of the Galway Vintage Claret. It maintains an enviable reputation for consistency.

CURRENT RELEASE 1995 A bit of a time capsule of a wine, which isn't to say that it's too old-fashioned to enjoy greatly today. The nose has maturing dry blackberry fruit aromas, some briary touches, and dusty, spicy oak. The palate is medium-bodied with ripe berry fruit and long, fine-grained tannins. It's a satisfying mouthful with a certain timeless quality about it. Try it with braised steak and parsley dumplings.

Quality	▼▼▼▼⸍
Value	★★★★⸍
Grapes	cabernet sauvignon; shiraz
Region	Barossa Valley, SA
Cellar	▮ 5
Alc./Vol.	13.5%
RRP	$32.95

Yalumba The Menzies Cabernet Sauvignon

Bob Menzies' liking for a particular Yalumba Barossa red of forty years ago inspired this label. The wine in the bottle comes from an entirely different source, but it does have a historic feel about it.

CURRENT RELEASE 1996 This is a traditional dry red style with slightly developed blackberry fruit on the nose and a hint of cedar. The palate is medium-bodied with smooth, traditionally flavoured berry fruit, finishing in rather astringent dry tannin. Will probably live for a long time – mellowing, but not changing too much. Serve with roast leg of lamb and baked vegetables.

Quality	▼▼▼▼
Value	★★★⸍
Grapes	cabernet sauvignon
Region	Coonawarra, SA
Cellar	▮ 5
Alc./Vol.	14.0%
RRP	$22.95

Yalumba The Octavius

This could well be christened 'Oaktavius': it's a formidably oaked red. If you like the flavour of wood go for it, if you like fruit in your wines look elsewhere.

CURRENT RELEASE 1995 In true Octavian fashion, this wine is loaded with charry, vanillin, coconutty oak to the exception of all other aromas and flavours. A tour de force of the cooper's art certainly, but isn't wine more than that? This tempts a couple of questions. Will it lose that overt oakiness with age? If so, will we live long enough to see it happen?

Quality	▼▼▼⸍
Value	★★
Grapes	shiraz
Region	Barossa Valley, SA
Cellar	⬤ 5–15?
Alc./Vol.	14.0%
RRP	$56.00

Yarra Burn Bastard Hill Pinot Noir

Quality	♟♟♟♟ʔ
Value	★★★★
Grapes	pinot noir
Region	Yarra Valley, Vic.
Cellar	▬ 1–6
Alc./Vol.	13.5%
RRP	$44.95

Some winemakers think pinot noir is a bit of a bastard, and the plethora of ordinary wines are testament to the fact that they find it hard to cope with. Appropriately enough, this bastard of a grape variety is right at home on the Bastard Hill at Yarra Burn.

CURRENT RELEASE 1997 Wow! This pinot has real impact, just the thing to convince even a Barossa shiraz drinker that pinot has some merit. The nose is a complex and powerful mix of plum, mulch, earth and vanilla bean – rich, gamy and tantalising. In the mouth it has mouth-filling depth and weight with real length and a structure of grippy drying tannins. Delicacy is on hold at the moment, but see what happens with bottle-age. A good wine for pad-see-uw (a rich dish of Thai rice noodles with beef and Chinese broccoli).

Yarra Ridge Reserve Cabernet Sauvignon

Quality	♟♟♟♟ʔ
Value	★★★ʕ
Grapes	cabernet sauvignon
Region	Yarra Valley, Vic.
Cellar	▬ 2–7
Alc./Vol.	13.0%
RRP	$38.00

The Yarra Valley is a surprisingly versatile region, capable of making good wine from a broader range of varieties than many other districts. Cabernet is a staple.

CURRENT RELEASE 1997 This has that murky density and purplish colour that often indicates a gutsy young red wine of potential – and it is. The nose has tight cassis, fruitcake, dry earth and dusty, charry oak aromas. The palate has medium intensity, but it's a bit closed. Tannins are firm but fine. Give it cellar time, then serve it with roast leg of lamb.

Yarra Ridge Reserve Shiraz

Quality	♟♟♟♟ʔ
Value	★★★ʕ
Grapes	shiraz
Region	Yarra Valley, Vic.
Cellar	▬ 1–6+
Alc./Vol.	13.0%
RRP	$38.00

Shiraz works well in the Yarra Valley in warmer years. The torrid '97 vintage was the culmination of just such a season. Maker Rob Dolan.

CURRENT RELEASE 1997 Modern cool-climate shiraz has an exciting spiciness that is rather addictive. Here we have a bouquet and palate of lively peppery spice and dark cherry fruitiness. Skillfully handled oak adds another element. The palate is densely flavoured but not overblown, and tannins are ripe and fine-grained.

Yarra Valley Hills Warranwood Cabernet Sauvignon

Yarra Valley Hills wines are made from three vineyards in different sites in the Yarra Valley region. Warranwood is at the eastern end of the region.

CURRENT RELEASE 1997 The nose is an interesting mix of ripe fruit characters and slightly green elements. Black fruit and spice are at its core, but herbal and tobacco aromas are there too. A notable measure of bacon-scented charry oak backs things up. The medium-bodied palate follows suit with a stemmy undertone and rather lean astringent tannins. Try it with smoked lamb racks.

Quality	♟♟♟♟
Value	★★★
Grapes	cabernet sauvignon
Region	Yarra Valley, Vic.
Cellar	▮ 3
Alc./Vol.	12.5%
RRP	$24.50

Yering Station ED Pinot Noir Rosé

Who drinks rosé these days? Very few people. In Europe it's different, particularly in warmer parts with climates more like Australia's. Maybe we've had too many poor cloying confections in the past to be bothered. At Yering Station they're trying to change things.

CURRENT RELEASE 1998 A rosé worth looking for with alfresco summer dining in mind, but not out of place in cooler weather either. Attractively salmon pink, this has unmistakeable pinot aromas of the strawberry sort. Earthy and nutty touches add dimension. The palate follows suit with soft red-berry flavour, which is dry and persistent. A good wine for picnics or antipasto of cold meats and sausages.

Quality	♟♟♟♟
Value	★★★
Grapes	pinot noir
Region	Yarra Valley, Vic.
Cellar	▮ 2
Alc./Vol.	11.0%
RRP	$18.50

Yering Station Pinot Noir

This is Yering Station's standard pinot noir. These days there's also a Reserve that gets the Rolls-Royce treatment. The more modest drop is designed to be a gulpable wine in its youth.

CURRENT RELEASE 1998 The colour has medium density, and the nose has a direct fruity aroma, reminiscent of strawberries and red cherries and spice. In the mouth there's juicy cherry-like flavour of medium body. It has pleasant intensity and juicy drinkability. It doesn't have the over-stemmy traits that mark some young Victorian pinots, and tannins are mild. Try it with baked ham.

Quality	♟♟♟♟♟
Value	★★★★
Grapes	pinot noir
Region	Yarra Valley, Vic.
Cellar	▮ 3
Alc./Vol.	13.5%
RRP	$21.50

Yering Station Reserve Pinot Noir

Quality	♟♟♟♟♟
Value	★★★★
Grapes	pinot noir
Region	Yarra Valley, Vic.
Cellar	▲ 5+
Alc./Vol.	13.0%
RRP	$42.00

Yering Station Reserve wines follow the trend for bottling top wines in big heavy bottles. Be careful not to drop one on your toe! This pinot noir won two trophies at the recent Southern Victorian Wine Show.

CURRENT RELEASE 1997   Pinot noir with real impact. The nose is decadently rich and dense with essency black-cherry fruit, dried herbs and chocolatey barrel-ferment characters. The palate has fleshy fruit-sweet dark cherry flavour, spicy oak, real length, and ripe, dry tannins. The mouth-feel is velvety, and it will no doubt be better with age. Right now it matches roast fillet of beef very well.

Yering Station Reserve Shiraz

Quality	♟♟♟♟♟
Value	★★★★
Grapes	shiraz
Region	Yarra Valley, Vic.
Cellar	➡ 1–5
Alc./Vol.	13.5%
RRP	$42.00

Yarra Valley shiraz differs greatly from the Australian traditional style, and even more so when it's made in an unashamedly French manner. Maker Tom Carson.

CURRENT RELEASE 1997   Complexity and finesse. The bouquet has an almost pinot-like richness of fruit. Aromas of dark cherry, game, almond and mellow spice meet the nose. The palate is long and silky-textured with cherry and plum flavours that are intense but not heavy. There's balanced oak, and it finishes with slightly astringent but fine tannins.

Zema Estate Family Selection Cabernet Sauvignon

Quality	♟♟♟♟♟
Value	★★★★
Grapes	cabernet sauvignon
Region	Coonawarra, SA
Cellar	▲ 15
Alc./Vol.	13.5%
RRP	$42.65

Coonawarra had a very good year in '96, and this is a limited release of 8500 numbered bottles. Maker Matt Zema.

CURRENT RELEASE 1996   This is a serious wine with delicious flavour and heaps of style. It's very much a claret-style red. The colour is deep purple–red, and the nose is concentrated blackcurrants – a classic cabernet aroma. The palate has excellent weight, beautifully handled oak and a delicious flavour of well-integrated blackberry fruit and cedary oak. The finish is big, full and firm, and the flavour has great style and length. A special-occasion wine to serve with rare roast beef.

White Wines

Abbey Vale Chardonnay

It's hard to believe that thirty years ago there were no Margaret River wines at all. These days the region has worked its way into the minds of all Australian wine lovers as one of the best.

CURRENT RELEASE 1998 The Margaret River region can give chardonnay a particular juiciness that's quite distinctive. Abbey Vale has succulent melon, apple and peach aromas and flavours. There's only a whisper of oak to back things up; the fruit stands almost alone. It finishes clean and crisp. Not very complex, but agreeable with a plate of chilli calamari.

Quality	♟♟♟♟
Value	★★★
Grapes	chardonnay
Region	Margaret River, WA
Cellar	🍷 2
Alc./Vol.	13.8%
RRP	$20.75

Abbey Vale Verdelho

They love verdelho in the West, and many are the folk who espouse it as the coming thing. It often has a sweet fruit-juicy quality that should endear it to those poor souls who balk at chardonnay.

CURRENT RELEASE 1998 Wow, the varietal character fairly leaps out of the glass here: a tropical, passionfruity aroma of appealing freshness. The palate has fruit salad flavours with a very light herbaceousness that adds a crisp tang to the juicy fruit. It finishes crisp and lively. Try it with a seafood platter.

Quality	♟♟♟♟
Value	★★★
Grapes	verdelho
Region	Margaret River, WA
Cellar	🍷 1
Alc./Vol.	13.5%
RRP	$20.75

Adina Pinot Grigio

Quality	♈♈♈⛢
Value	★★★
Grapes	pinot grigio
Region	Hunter Valley, NSW
Cellar	🍷 2
Alc./Vol.	12.5%
RRP	$18.00

Pinot Grigio is a rare commodity in the Hunter Valley. In some much cooler areas, people put great store in its future.

CURRENT RELEASE 1998 This has a direct, vinous nose that adds nutty aromas to citrus fruit. It doesn't have great impact in the mouth, but the savoury flavour is attractively dry with a slightly Italianate earthiness. Something to consider if you're looking for a change, and a good companion to pasta with seafood.

Alkoomi Frankland River Riesling

Quality	♈♈♈♈♈
Value	★★★★★
Grapes	riesling
Region	Great Southern, WA
Cellar	🍷 6+
Alc./Vol.	11.0%
RRP	$17.00

Move over Clare and Eden Valley: riesling has found a great new home in the south of Western Australia. Alkoomi is one of a growing number of expert producers.

CURRENT RELEASE 1998 In common with many of the Great Southern rieslings this is a delight, but it's a bit shy and retiring in its youth. If experience is anything to go by, it will blossom into greatness with time. At the moment it's a pale, intense wine with fine, delicate varietal character. The nose and palate have fragrant lime and aromatic spice touches, and the palate is long and tingly fresh. Simple grilled fish would be perfect.

Alkoomi Sauvignon Blanc

Quality	♈♈♈♈⛢
Value	★★★★⛢
Grapes	sauvignon blanc
Region	Frankland River, WA
Cellar	🍷 2
Alc./Vol.	12.0%
RRP	$19.00

A downturn in the price of wool in the 1960s led Merv and Judy Lange to explore the possibility of planting grapes on their property. Their Alkoomi vineyard was established in 1971, and has now grown to over 45 hectares.

CURRENT RELEASE 1998 The climate in this part of southern Western Australia seems to suit sauvignon blanc well. This is a thrilling young wine with zippy passionfruit and green-leafy aromas. The palate has tropical fruit softness with a grassy edge, and a mouth-watering balance of fruit and acidity. Drink young with goat's cheese croutons and rocket leaves.

Allandale Chardonnay

A succession of generous chardonnays has made Allandale a Hunter winery worth looking out for. They are at the big-flavoured end of the spectrum.

CURRENT RELEASE 1998 This is a richly endowed young chardonnay, which still has finesse. The nose has succulent peachy fruit in perfect balance with restrained sweet oak. In the mouth it has an unctuous texture with stone-fruit flavour, measured wood influence, and a long satisfying aftertaste. Deliciously drinkable with pot-roasted chicken with chestnuts.

Quality	🍷🍷🍷🍷🍷
Value	★★★★½
Grapes	chardonnay
Region	Hunter Valley, NSW
Cellar	🍾 2
Alc./Vol.	13.0%
RRP	$18.00

Allinda Chardonnay

One of the smaller Yarra Valley vineyards. Allinda winemaker Al Fencaros gained valuable local experience working for De Bortoli in the Yarra Valley.

CURRENT RELEASE 1998 This chardonnay has been worked to the max. The winemaker has employed all the tricks of the trade to build complexity into it. The result is a good wine, but one in which fruit character is somewhat obscured by all the trimmings. The nose and palate have melted-butter richness, bacon-bone oak touches, some roasted nuts and an unctuous creamy character. If you like tons of complex flavour, this is for you. Try it with chicken in a creamy white wine sauce.

Quality	🍷🍷🍷🍷
Value	★★★½
Grapes	chardonnay
Region	Yarra Valley, Vic.
Cellar	🍾 2
Alc./Vol.	12.6%
RRP	$19.00

All Saints Late Harvest Semillon

Most people don't look to the Rutherglen region as a source of high-quality sweet whites, but the folks at All Saints are doing an admirable job with sweet semillon. In some years it can be botrytis-influenced, in others not, but it should never be ignored.

CURRENT RELEASE 1997 No botrytis here, but this is still a luscious sweetie of freshness and interest. It has a sweet bouquet reminiscent of barley sugar, peach and citrus. The palate is juicy and smooth with peachy sweetness, long flavour and a clean finish. Delicious with poached peaches.

Quality	🍷🍷🍷🍷
Value	★★★★
Grapes	semillon
Region	Rutherglen, Vic.
Cellar	🍾 2
Alc./Vol.	10.0%
RRP	$17.00

Amberley Semillon Sauvignon Blanc

Quality	♥♥♥♥
Value	★★★↾
Grapes	semillon; sauvignon blanc
Region	Margaret River, WA
Cellar	↓ 3
Alc./Vol.	12.5%
RRP	$18.95

At Margaret River this ubiquitous blend is often given more complex winemaking treatment than it receives elsewhere. The result is 'serious' white wine. Amberley is one of the best.

CURRENT RELEASE 1998 This is a fine style which opens with interesting interplay between the grape varieties and the wood input. The nose has grassy sauvignon and tasty lemon-scented semillon aromas with a subtle touch of nutty lees and toasty oak. The palate is soft and fragrant in the middle, while firm acidity gives a tight dry finish. An easy-to-like style which needs food to show its best. Try it with a seafood claypot dish.

Andrew Garrett Chardonnay

Quality	♥♥♥♥
Value	★★★★
Grapes	chardonnay
Region	McLaren Vale & Padthaway, SA
Cellar	↓ 2
Alc./Vol.	13.0%
RRP	$13.50 Ⓢ

These days this is a Mildara Blass brand that offers good quality at a reasonable price, while never scaling the heights.

CURRENT RELEASE 1998 The nose has peach and melon varietal aromas with some vanilla and creamy notes from barrel treatment. The oak is held more in check than it was last vintage. Satisfying peachy fruit character comes through in the mouth as well as some oaky notes. It's smooth and the finish has a dry tang.

Angove's Classic Reserve Chardonnay

Quality	♥♥♥↾
Value	★★★↾
Grapes	chardonnay
Region	Riverland, SA
Cellar	↓ 1
Alc./Vol.	13.5%
RRP	$12.00 Ⓢ

Thomas Carlyon Angove pioneered winemaking in the Renmark area nearly ninety years ago. Today, the fourth generation of Angoves presides over a vast enterprise.

CURRENT RELEASE 1998 This is a developed commercial style with a golden colour and a honeyed nose. It exhibits rich fruit character in the peach/tropical fruit style, and the palate is full and round. Soft acidity and a keen price make for easy drinking, but don't keep it for long. Try it with chicken schnitzel.

Angove's Sarnia Farm Chardonnay

Sarnia Farm was one of the first vineyards planted by Dr William Angove over 100 years ago. That original Sarnia Farm is now gone, but the name lives on in this range from Angove's new set-up at Padthaway.

CURRENT RELEASE 1997 This is a good commercial style, which has an attractive melon aroma nicely touched by butter and cashew. In the mouth it's easy to drink, with smooth texture, peachy flavour and a dry finish. Will suit little fried octopuses well.

Quality	▼▼▼▼
Value	★★★★
Grapes	chardonnay
Region	Padthaway, SA
Cellar	🍾 1
Alc./Vol.	13.0%
RRP	$16.50 Ⓢ

Annie's Lane Riesling

The old Quelltaler name is gone, but its spirit lives on in the old cellars at Watervale and the vineyards that surround it. Annie's Lane wines are produced there by Mildara Blass. Maker David O'Leary.

CURRENT RELEASE 1998 Clare Valley riesling at its best – and check the price. The nose has penetrating lime sherbet aromas with classical floral touches, pungent spice and talc. The palate is crisp, intense and long; it's dry with lime flavours and spice, which lead to a crisp, zippy finish. Good now but worth keeping too. Great served with pan-fried whiting fillets.

Quality	▼▼▼▼▼
Value	★★★★★
Grapes	riesling
Region	Clare Valley, SA
Cellar	🍾 5+
Alc./Vol.	11.5%
RRP	$14.50

CURRENT RELEASE 1999 A pale, bright young riesling with more precocious appeal than many. The nose is fruity and sweet with aromas of flowers and spiced stewed apple. In the mouth it has succulent fruit mid-palate with a fragrant dry aftertaste. Will be better with time in bottle.

Quality	▼▼▼▼▼
Value	★★★★★
Grapes	riesling
Region	Clare Valley, SA
Cellar	🍾 5
Alc./Vol.	11.0%
RRP	$14.50

Annie's Lane Semillon

Quality	▼▼▼▼
Value	★★★★
Grapes	semillon
Region	Clare Valley, SA
Cellar	▮ 5
Alc./Vol.	13.5%
RRP	$14.50

Quelltaler semillon introduced a lot of people to oak-influenced whites back in the days BC (before chardonnay). Today the wine bears the Annie's Lane moniker and it shows very little wood influence.

CURRENT RELEASE 1998   In the Quelltaler semillons of old the timber could be a bit overdone, but not any more. Annie's Lane is dominated by lemon-scented, herbal fruit of pure varietal character; any barrel influence barely shows. It's an appetising, straightforward semillon with a firm, dry backbone. Should age well. Serve it with pan-fried flathead fillets.

Arrowfield Hunter Valley Unoaked Chardonnay

Quality	▼▼▼
Value	★★★
Grapes	chardonnay
Region	Upper Hunter Valley, NSW
Cellar	▮ 1
Alc./Vol.	12.9%
RRP	$18.10

Arrowfield winemaker Don Buchanan is a brave man. Why? He likes to fly ultralights, those spindly little wing-and-a-prayer aircraft that look like they're powered by rubber bands.

CURRENT RELEASE 1998   For an unwooded wine this has quite good fruit richness, albeit in a light, undemanding style. The aromas are reminiscent of succulent stone fruit, and the palate is a gentle concoction of nectarine-like fruit and herbal notes. It's a smooth, dry-finishing drop that will please a lot of people.

Ashton Hills Chardonnay

Quality	▼▼▼▼
Value	★★★★
Grapes	chardonnay
Region	Adelaide Hills, SA
Cellar	▮ 5
Alc./Vol.	14.0%
RRP	$29.70

The original vines at Ashton Hills replaced brussels sprouts in the front paddock. Much as we all love this much-maligned vegie, we think the decision was the right one.

CURRENT RELEASE 1997   A bright yellow–gold chardonnay with a restrained, complex bouquet that charms you from the word go. Subtle nectarine fruit, yeast lees and buttery, nutty oak are all in gentle harmony. The palate is long and rich, but not heavy. Fine fruit flavours and mealy touches are dressed in balanced toasty oak and tangy acidity.

Ashton Hills Riesling

The new vineyards of the Adelaide Hills were planted while poor old riesling was in the doldrums. As a result there isn't much up there. You're far more likely to encounter sauvignon blanc or chardonnay, but riesling does perform beautifully on those cool slopes.

CURRENT RELEASE 1998   An exotic young wine with a load of spicy fruit character that makes it vaguely reminiscent of European riesling. As well as pungent spice, the nose has hints of apple, lychee and zesty lime. In the mouth it's still spicy with a dry flavour, a smooth texture and a crisp finish. Serve with Vietnamese rice paper rolls.

Quality	ΨΨΨΨ?
Value	★★★⊦
Grapes	riesling
Region	Adelaide Hills, SA
Cellar	♦ 4
Alc./Vol.	13.0%
RRP	$21.60

Ashwood Grove Chardonnay

Murray Valley chardonnays are often precocious little darlings that cry for attention at a very young age. Ashwood Grove is no exception.

CURRENT RELEASE 1998   This is a very ripe young wine with an obvious nose of fig syrup and peach. A hint of nutty lees influence adds interest. The palate is soft, round and buttery-rich, with light acidity on a dry finish. Designed to be drunk young and well chilled. Try it with cold chicken.

Quality	ΨΨΨ
Value	★★★⊦
Grapes	chardonnay
Region	Murray Valley, Vic.
Cellar	♦ 1
Alc./Vol.	13.5%
RRP	$12.50

Ashwood Grove Sauvignon Blanc

Sauvignon blanc is a love–hate sort of grape that excites some people enormously and turns others off like nothing else.

CURRENT RELEASE 1998   Here we have a simple young sauvignon with grassy, herbal aromas and an initial whiff of sulfur, which blows off quickly. The palate is dry and herbaceous, but really rather neutral, lacking the zip that sauvignon has when it's grown in cooler climes. Very reasonably priced, though. Try it with a Thai salad.

Quality	ΨΨΨ
Value	★★★
Grapes	sauvignon blanc
Region	Murray Valley, Vic.
Cellar	♦ 1
Alc./Vol.	12.5%
RRP	$12.50

Austins Barrabool Chardonnay

Quality	�♣♣♣
Value	★★★
Grapes	chardonnay
Region	Geelong, Vic.
Cellar	3
Alc./Vol.	13.0%
RRP	$27.00

One wonders why there aren't more vineyards in the Geelong district. Austins is right in the area that gained fame for its wine last century, but they don't have many vine-growing neighbours. This is made by John Ellis at Hanging Rock.

CURRENT RELEASE 1997   A succulent young chardonnay with sweet citrus and Passiona-like aromas combined with a subtle wheatmeal note. The flavours follow suit, soft and juicy on the mid-palate with a tight structure of acidity. Should match shellfish well.

Babich Marlborough Sauvignon Blanc

Quality	♣♣♀
Value	★★★
Grapes	sauvignon blanc
Region	Marlborough, NZ
Cellar	2
Alc./Vol.	13.5%
RRP	$14.00

Babich is located in the Henderson area near Auckland but, like so many others, now gets a lot of its fruit from down south. Maker Neil Culley.

CURRENT RELEASE 1998   This needed time to settle down. It had a sulfurous nose and what might be referred to kindly as old-fashioned French character. It had light fruit and some hardness on the finish. May come good in time, and note the price: there aren't many as cheap as this any more.

Ballingal Estate Premium Semillon

Quality	♣♣♣♀
Value	★★★★✦
Grapes	semillon
Region	Riverina, NSW
Cellar	1
Alc./Vol.	13.0%
RRP	$15.00 Ⓢ

This has three gold medals to its credit, but it's remarkably developed for a '98. Ballingal Estate is one of the brands of Tony Sergi's fast-growing Riverina Wines. Maker Sam Trimbole.

CURRENT RELEASE 1998   Best drink this quickly: it seems to be ageing as fast as an express train. The colour is deep yellow, and the toasty/straw aromas show a lot of development. It's rich and soft on the tongue with a little sweetness, and the acid level seems quite modest. Serve with lemon chicken.

Balnaves Chardonnay

The Balnaves wines have turned a corner since ex-Wynns deputy winemaker Peter Bissell was employed. Doug Balnaves' grapes are getting the attention they deserve. **CURRENT RELEASE 1997** This is a truly lovely chardonnay, redolent of honey and butterscotch, with hints of fig and pineapple. The oak is nicely integrated. A fine chardonnay with delicacy and restraint, but with the hallmark viscosity, richness and length of the grape variety. Great with grilled lobster.

Quality	♀♀♀♀♀
Value	★★★★★
Grapes	chardonnay
Region	Coonawarra, SA
Cellar	▮ 4
Alc./Vol.	13.5%
RRP	$18.00 (cellar door)

Bannockburn Chardonnay

This lovely wine is made according to the traditions of Burgundy. That makes it relatively expensive, but it's very reasonable compared with French equivalents (and better than many).
CURRENT RELEASE 1997 This latest vintage cements Bannockburn Chardonnay's reputation even more. It's a delight to sip over time as even more complexities reveal themselves. How to describe it? Nuts, sweet butter, stone fruit, vanilla cream – the list goes on. In the mouth it's seamless, fragrant and fine with a lovely, long aftertaste. Don't chill it much, and serve it with fish quenelles and crayfish sauce.

Quality	♀♀♀♀♀
Value	★★★★★
Grapes	chardonnay
Region	Geelong, Vic.
Cellar	▮ 5+
Alc./Vol.	14.0%
RRP	$44.50

Barossa Valley Estate Moculta Semillon

Moculta is the second label of Barossa Valley Estate and usually represents superb value for money. This wine won a gold medal at the Melbourne Wine Show, which is pretty good for a $13 dry white.
CURRENT RELEASE 1998 This is a very delicate style of unwooded semillon, with some austerity. The nose has lemony, minerally aromas, and the palate has lightly herbal and again lemony flavours of good intensity and excellent length. It should age well, but it already drinks nicely with cold seafood salad.

Quality	♀♀♀♀
Value	★★★★★
Grapes	semillon
Region	Barossa Valley, SA
Cellar	▮ 4+
Alc./Vol.	13.0%
RRP	$13.50 ⑤

Barossa Valley Estate Spires Semillon Chardonnay

Quality	♟♟♟
Value	★★★★
Grapes	semillon;
	chardonnay
Region	Barossa Valley, SA
Cellar	▮ 3
Alc./Vol.	13.0%
RRP	$9.00 Ⓢ

The many spired Lutheran churches in the Barossa are supposed to have inspired (sorry) this new series of wines.

CURRENT RELEASE 1998　Plenty of flavour but no subtlety – but then what do you want for $9? The aromas are green and herbal, with some hints of peach. It's a big mouthful of straightforward herbal sem-chard flavour with no apparent oak, and happily it finishes dry. Should go a treat with salmon and dill quiche.

Barrington Estate Semillon

Quality	♟♟♟♟
Value	★★★
Grapes	semillon
Region	Hunter Valley,
	NSW
Cellar	➡ 2–6+
Alc./Vol.	9.8%
RRP	$18.00 Ⓢ

This is the second label of the people from Yarraman Road. Principal is Gary Blom, who owns arguably the world's biggest movie screen – the Imax Theatre in Sydney.

CURRENT RELEASE 1998　This is taking traditional, low-alcohol, dry Hunter semillon to the extreme. Whether it's a ridiculous extreme is up to you. It has a nose of dry grass and straw. The mouth flavours are predominantly lemon and straw, very lean and tart in the acid department. A chablis style that's best cellared. To drink it now would require food: try raw oysters.

Basedow Semillon

Quality	♟♟♟
Value	★★★
Grapes	semillon
Region	Barossa Valley, SA
Cellar	▮ 2
Alc./Vol.	13.0%
RRP	$13.00 Ⓢ

This wine used to be labelled Basedow White Burgundy, but it's now known as Semillon White Burgundy. In the past it won masses of gold medals and trophies. These days it tends to be regarded as a bit too woody.

CURRENT RELEASE 1997　Go get those tweezers! This is a very big, heavily wooded white that tests one's tolerance for oak flavour. The nose is very powerful and dominated by toasty, coconutty oak. In the mouth it's full-bodied and broad, somewhat inelegant, and the finish is all oak. Try it with smoked chicken.

Best's Great Western Chardonnay

The labels of this old Victorian winery are a good example of how a traditional design can be subtly modified over the years into something tastefully modern.
Previous outstanding vintages: '88, '90, '95, '96
CURRENT RELEASE 1997 An intriguing wine which was very shy at first, but which really came good with airing. Be patient! The restrained aroma reminds of fresh fruit salad, and it has zesty acidity and delicate, but focused, palate flavour. Oak is tidily tucked into the background. It's all about finesse, and is ageing slowly. Try it with prosciutto melone.

Quality	♆♆♆♆
Value	★★★★
Grapes	chardonnay
Region	Great Western, Vic.
Cellar	▲ 6+
Alc./Vol.	14.0%
RRP	$26.00

Best's Great Western Riesling

Best's has vineyards and wineries at both Lake Boga, in the Sunraysia, and Great Western. They're a major contrast in climates. Maker Viv Thomson.
CURRENT RELEASE 1998 This has a trace of residual sweetness, which may polarise drinkers. It's restrained and slow-ageing, with a light yellow hue and a powder-puff, essency riesling nose. There are orange and grapefruit flavours. The finish is firm. A prawn cocktail would be in order.

Quality	♆♆♆
Value	★★★
Grapes	riesling
Region	Great Western, Vic.
Cellar	▲ 5
Alc./Vol.	12.0%
RRP	$16.00

Best's Victoria Chenin Blanc

The label tells us this was made from grapes grown on the limestone-based soils of the St Andrews vineyard, which is in the Swan Hill area of northern Victoria.
CURRENT RELEASE 1998 The colour is pale yellow, and everything about this wine is understated. The bouquet shows estery green-apple aromas, typical of the chenin grape. It's light and well balanced on the tongue, finishing drier than most chenins. A clean, well made, straightforward dry white. Try it with waldorf salad.

Quality	♆♆♆
Value	★★★⟩
Grapes	chenin blanc
Region	Sunraysia, Vic.
Cellar	▲ 2
Alc./Vol.	12.5%
RRP	$12.80 ⑤

Bethany Chardonnay

Quality	♟♟♟
Value	★★★
Grapes	chardonnay
Region	Barossa Valley, SA
Cellar	▮ 1
Alc./Vol.	13.5%
RRP	$17.00

The village of Bethany is the site of the original Barossa Valley settlement. The winery owners are the Schrapel family, brothers Geoffrey and Robert being present-generation winemakers.

CURRENT RELEASE 1997 A typical fast-developing, broadly structured Barossa-style chardonnay. It has deep yellow colour and a slightly squashy aroma. The palate is big and a trifle clumsy. It lacks finesse, but it's big on flavour. Drink it soon as it's ageing fast. Suits stuffed roast chicken.

Bindi Chardonnay

Quality	♟♟♟♟♟
Value	★★★★⊁
Grapes	chardonnay
Region	Macedon Ranges, Vic.
Cellar	▮ 7+
Alc./Vol.	13.5%
RRP	$30.00 (cellar door)

Michael Dhillon, a young winemaker whose family owns Bindi, spent months in Burgundy studying winemaking and viticulture in an effort to come to grips with the elusive pinot noir and chardonnay.

Previous outstanding vintages: '91, '94, '95, '96

CURRENT RELEASE 1997 The yield was 0.8 tonnes per acre and you can see the concentration in the wine. It's the best Bindi chardonnay yet: a wonderfully power-packed yet elegant wine, smelling of honey, oatmeal, toasted nuts and grapefruit. A creamy malolactic character builds with airing. A multi-faceted wine of great charm and depth. Serve with grilled lobster.

Bindi Quartz Chardonnay

Quality	♟♟♟♟♟
Value	★★★⊁
Grapes	chardonnay
Region	Macedon Ranges, Vic.
Cellar	▮ 4
Alc./Vol.	13.5%
RRP	$40.00 (cellar door)

This is a selection from a specific piece of vineyard on quartz-based soil. The grapes ripened, paradoxically, with a higher sugar level *and* higher acid, and more intense flavour. Only 70 dozen were bottled.

CURRENT RELEASE 1995 Chablis comes to Macedon! This is a very tight, flinty, minerally chardonnay with high-acid austerity. There's a waft of sulfur to begin with, which doesn't mar it. It's tightly wound and delicate, is ageing slowly, and should live long. Drink it with oysters.

Blass Adelaide Hills Chardonnay

The grapes came from Kuitpo and Forreston. If there's a buzzword the Mildara Blass people haven't used on a label, we'd like to know about it. This one's subtitled 'lees contacted'. See the glossary for demystification.
CURRENT RELEASE 1998 Everyone's doing an Adelaide Hills chardonnay, but this one's a bit weak: it's just too light and short. The colour is light yellow, and it has shy, creamy, melon-like aromas. In this case, the lees contact failed to fill out the deficient palate. Still, a delicate clean wine, which doesn't offend. Serve with prosciutto melone.

Quality	♟♟♟
Value	★★★
Grapes	chardonnay
Region	Adelaide Hills, SA
Cellar	♦ 2
Alc./Vol.	13.5%
RRP	$18.00

Blass Clare & Eden Valleys Riesling

The new Blass label is full of the latest buzzwords. It says the wines display 'distinctive varietal and regional flavours' – we wonder how a 50–50 blend can be regional? Maker Wendy Stuckey.
Previous outstanding vintages: '96, '97
CURRENT RELEASE 1998 A triple trophy winner at the Sydney Show, and we can see why. It's built in the full-on, up-front Blass style we've come to know. Rich stone-fruit aromas and exaggerated fruit all round. Soft and weighty, with a smooth dry finish. Impressive stuff, but not for riesling purists. Food: Vietnamese salad.

Quality	♟♟♟♟♟
Value	★★★★
Grapes	riesling
Region	Clare Valley & Eden Valley, SA
Cellar	♦ 5+
Alc./Vol.	11.0%
RRP	$18.00 ⑤

Brands Laira Riesling

This is a nicely mature riesling from a region not well known for that variety. It shows what benefits a short time in the cellar can work with good riesling.
CURRENT RELEASE 1996 Delicious stuff! The colour is deep yellow and the bouquet reminds of buttered toast, while the palate flavours add citrus and minerally, flinty nuances. It retains its delicacy, and is soft and restrained. Good now, with fish in beurre blanc.

Quality	♟♟♟♟♟
Value	★★★★★
Grapes	riesling
Region	Coonawarra, SA
Cellar	♦ 4+
Alc./Vol.	11.5%
RRP	$14.00 ⑤

Brangayne of Orange Chardonnay

Quality	?️?️?️?️
Value	★★★★
Grapes	chardonnay
Region	Orange, NSW
Cellar	↓ 3
Alc./Vol.	13.0%
RRP	$16.50

Full marks for elegant packaging here. They must be opera buffs: Brangayne was a character in Wagner's *Tristan und Isolde*. Maker Simon Gilbert (contract).

CURRENT RELEASE 1998 A fruit-driven chardonnay with real cool-climate subtlety. The colour is pale yellow, and it has typical chardonnay aromas of cashew nut, grapefruit and honeydew melon. It's clean, fresh and sprightly, with good fruit weight and little obvious oak character. Restraint and finesse. Drink it with pasta with eggplant.

Brangayne of Orange Sauvignon Blanc

Quality	?️?️?️
Value	★★★⯪
Grapes	sauvignon blanc
Region	Orange, NSW
Cellar	↓ 1
Alc./Vol.	12.5%
RRP	$16.50

This grape variety likes cool climates and should do well at Orange, where there seems to be a new vineyard every time we look around. This 26-hectare planting is owned by the Hoskins family. Maker Simon Gilbert (contract).

CURRENT RELEASE 1998 The label is colourful and entertaining. The wine is straightforward, with crushed stalk and leaf aromas. It's broad and soft on the tongue, and has a grip on the finish. It misses the usual sauvignon blanc zing, but could go well with caesar salad.

Briar Ridge Chairman's Selection Chardonnay

Quality	?️?️?️?️⯪
Value	★★★★
Grapes	chardonnay
Region	Hunter Valley, NSW
Cellar	↓ 2
Alc./Vol.	12.5%
RRP	$21.30

Read all about it. This wine carried off several trophies at the New South Wales Small Winemakers Show at Forbes. Yes, folks: Forbes, NSW, has its own wine competition.

CURRENT RELEASE 1997 This is a lovely subtle, lighter-bodied wine, with tropical fruit and buttery characters on the nose, and very good chardonnay varietal character. Soft and balanced on the palate, it's deliciously drinkable and ready to go. Try it with roast chicken.

Briar Ridge Early Harvest Semillon

All the Briar Ridge semillons are in fact early-harvested. This is how the classic, delicate, age-worthy, low-alcohol Hunter Valley semillon style is produced. Maker Neil McGuigan.

CURRENT RELEASE 1998 This is a great each-way semillon: you can drink it now with seafood or cellar it until it becomes richer and more interesting. The colour is pale; the nose is fine with lemon and lightly herbal aromas. It's delicate, restrained and shy in flavour, with some creamy lanolin tones and a tart but soft finish. Serve it with any pan-fried white-fleshed fish.

Quality	ТТТТ
Value	★★★★
Grapes	semillon
Region	Hunter Valley, NSW
Cellar	↓ 8
Alc./Vol.	10.7%
RRP	$18.90

Briar Ridge Hand Picked Chardonnay

This is the standard arrow in the Briar Ridge chardonnay quiver. Hand-picked grapes are something of a rarity these days, with mechanical harvesters doing most of the work.

CURRENT RELEASE 1998 Sensitive oak handling is a feature of this delicate, tight, finely structured wine. You'll find cashew nut and butter overtones and subtle oak, although some toastiness from bottle-age is starting to creep in. It's a restrained style, and it should keep well. Try it with whitebait fritters.

Quality	ТТТТ̧
Value	★★★★
Grapes	chardonnay
Region	Hunter Valley, NSW
Cellar	↓ 3+
Alc./Vol.	12.8%
RRP	$18.90

Briar Ridge Neil McGuigan Signature Chardonnay

This new label replaces the Chairman's Selection chardonnay. The grapes were picked from low-yielding vines (2–3 tonnes per acre), and all of the wine sees new oak.

CURRENT RELEASE 1998 This is typical of the Neil McGuigan new-style Briar Ridge whites. The nose is delicate and retiring; the palate is again restrained, but has excellent character, penetration and persistence. It has a little more oak flavour than Briar Ridge's regular model, and a lot more complexity. There are also peachy flavours. The wine successfully combines richness and finesse. Serve with veal sweetbreads.

Quality	ТТТТТ
Value	★★★★↑
Grapes	chardonnay
Region	Hunter Valley, NSW
Cellar	↓ 4+
Alc./Vol.	13.2%
RRP	$21.30

Briar Ridge Stockhausen Semillon

Quality	🍷🍷🍷🍷
Value	★★★★
Grapes	semillon
Region	Hunter Valley, NSW
Cellar	➥ 3–10+
Alc./Vol.	11.0%
RRP	$21.30

Neil McGuigan is doing great things with the Briar Ridge whites. The year 1998 was a top vintage in the Hunter. Karl Stockhausen consults to the winery.

CURRENT RELEASE 1998   This is an even more acidic wine than the Early Harvest model. It's built for long-term cellaring. There's less of the herbal character and more of the lemon/citrus notes to smell. The palate is searingly acidic and bone dry, very delicate and tautly structured. It needs a lot of time. If you drink it now, serve with raw oysters.

Briar Ridge Verdelho

Quality	🍷🍷🍷🍷
Value	★★★⯪
Grapes	verdelho
Region	Hunter Valley, NSW
Cellar	🍷 5
Alc./Vol.	14.0%
RRP	$19.00

The year 1998 was a dream vintage, the likes of which the Hunter doesn't see too often. The grapes got fully ripe and the vintage wasn't rained on. Maker Neil McGuigan.

CURRENT RELEASE 1998   Despite the high alcohol, this was a restrained style of verdelho at the time of tasting. It has the crisp acidity typical of this maker's whites, and looks as though it will age gracefully. The colour is medium–light; the delicate aromas are of banana and citrus fruits. It's dry in the mouth and has a lean, taut structure. It's designed to go with food. Try it with any white-fleshed fish.

Brokenwood Harlequin

Quality	🍷🍷🍷🍷
Value	★★★★
Grapes	chardonnay; verdelho; sauvignon blanc
Region	various
Cellar	🍷 4
Alc./Vol.	13.0%
RRP	$16.00

This is Brokenwood's new entry in the burgeoning business of brand-launching. It's a blend of regions and grape varieties. The operatic figure of Harlequin represents fun and good times, which is how the sybarites of Brokenwood dream of living!

CURRENT RELEASE 1998   This hits all the right cues. It's light but flavoursome, intense but not heavy, lively but not tart, dry but not austere. It has good flavour and style, with the chardonnay richness showing through. Clean peach and nectarine fruit flavours are very appealing. Serve with most entrées.

Brokenwood Semillon

Brokenwood is one of the serious players in the semillon field. They make a wine that is delicious as a bouncy youngster, but that ages gently into a classic. Maker Iain Riggs.

Previous outstanding vintages: '83, '85, '86, '91, '92, '94, '95, '96, '97

CURRENT RELEASE 1998 Benchmark young Hunter semillon from a top vintage. It has a brilliant young colour and a delicate lemon/straw youthful aroma. It's crisp and alive on the tongue. Vibrant lemon zest flavour, plenty of fruit and not austere as some vintages can be. A great each-way wine. Drink now with a mixed seafood platter, or cellar.

Quality	ΨΨΨΨΨ
Value	★★★★★
Grapes	semillon
Region	Hunter Valley, NSW
Cellar	10
Alc./Vol.	11.0%
RRP	$19.70 Ⓢ

CURRENT RELEASE 1999 This is too young to evaluate properly. It's all banana, doughy/yeasty fresh-fermentation aromas. In the mouth it's austere and acidic. The flavours are straw-like at this time, and it has model delicacy, light body and freshness. It should turn into a beauty with a few months in bottle, and age for years afterwards.

Quality	ΨΨΨΨ
Value	★★★★
Grapes	semillon
Region	Hunter Valley, NSW
Cellar	1–8+
Alc./Vol.	11.0%
RRP	$19.70 Ⓢ

Brookland Valley Sauvignon Blanc

Brookland Valley was established by the Jones family in 1984. Now it's one of BRL Hardy's expanding portfolio of vineyards.

CURRENT RELEASE 1998 No mistaking the variety here – archetypal tropical fruit salad and gooseberry/herbaceous aromas surge from the glass. The palate has similar elements and a zing of tingly acidity keeps it clean as a whistle. Try it with stir-fried shellfish and green vegetables.

Quality	ΨΨΨΨ
Value	★★★★
Grapes	sauvignon blanc
Region	Margaret River, WA
Cellar	1
Alc./Vol.	13.0%
RRP	$23.00

Brown Brothers Noble Riesling

Quality	♛♛♛♛♛
Value	★★★★
Grapes	riesling
Region	Milawa, Vic.
Cellar	▲ 3
Alc./Vol.	10.0%
RRP	$21.00 (375 ml)

PENGUIN BEST SWEET WINE

This has the longest pedigree of any Australian botrytis wine. It goes back to 1962.
Previous outstanding vintages: '92, '94
CURRENT RELEASE 1996 This is an intoxicating sticky in every sense of the word! Some bottle-age shows in its dark amber colour and bouquet of preserved citrus and lightly burnt toast. It's rich, sweet and unctuous in the mouth, showing a lot of botrytis and beneficial bottle-development. The marmalade, resin, vanilla and toast flavours are complex and seductive. Great with classic tarte tatin.

Brown Brothers Riesling

Quality	♛♛♛
Value	★★★
Grapes	riesling
Region	King Valley, Vic.
Cellar	▲ 3
Alc./Vol.	12.5%
RRP	$14.70

The King Valley has quickly become one of the biggest and fastest-growing wine regions in Victoria. Brown Brothers can claim much of the credit for fostering it.
CURRENT RELEASE 1998 An odd, geranium-like aroma is the stand-out feature of this very herbal-scented riesling. It's a lightweight riesling, which could use more intensity on the palate. There's a suspicion of traminer in the powder-puff scent it leaves in the glass. Try it with pasta and pesto.

Brown Brothers Verdelho

Quality	♛♛♛
Value	★★★
Grapes	verdelho
Region	North East Vic.
Cellar	▲ 2
Alc./Vol.	14.0%
RRP	$16.80 ⑤

There aren't many grape varieties the Brown brethren haven't tried their hand at over the years. Verdelho isn't closely linked with their region, but they make a fair fist of it. Maker Roland Wahlquist and team.
CURRENT RELEASE 1998 There's a touch of richness and a hint of spice, which are features of most good verdelhos. The colour is light yellow, and the nose has fresh hay and gentle spice inflexions. It's medium-bodied and dry in the mouth, with balanced acidity and a clean finish. It could go well with yabby salad.

Brown Brothers Victoria Chardonnay

This is simply the best chardonnay we've seen from Brown Brothers in ages. The 'Victoria' range often gives the impression of plodding adequacy, but along with the cabernet, the chardonnay this year offers stand-out value. Maker Terry Barnett and team.

CURRENT RELEASE 1998   This is a subtle, fruit-driven chardonnay of excellent flavour and balance. It's lightly wooded, and smells of citrus fruits, peach, vanilla and toast with a garland of herbs. It has big, but not broad, flavour that lingers long on the aftertaste. The only thing it needs is a little more complexity – a minor quibble. Try it with agedashi tofu.

Quality	♥♥♥♥♥
Value	★★★★★
Grapes	chardonnay
Region	North East Vic.
Cellar	▮ 3
Alc./Vol.	14.0%
RRP	$17.60 ⑤

Browns of Padthaway Riesling

The Browns have been contract grapegrowers for many years. Is it a coincidence that their wines tend to be light and the reds rather vegetal, suggesting generous yields?

CURRENT RELEASE 1998   This is one of the Browns' best wines, a well-flavoured, tightly structured, minerally riesling. It has slatey, floral aromas with a hint of earth, and a dry and quite intense palate. It goes well with Pekinese shallot pancake.

Quality	♥♥♥¼
Value	★★★★
Grapes	riesling
Region	Padthaway, SA
Cellar	▮ 4
Alc./Vol.	12.0%
RRP	$14.10 ⑤

Buller Victoria Classic Chenin Blanc Colombard

Most of the Buller clan hang out at Rutherglen, but their cheaper table wines are produced in a separate winery at Beverford, near Swan Hill on the Murray River. Maker Richard Buller Jr.

CURRENT RELEASE 1998   This is a light-bodied, clean, crisp dry white offering good value at the price. There's a whiff of sulfur, which will go in time, and some earthy and powder-puff fruit aromas. It's fresh, lively and dry on the finish. An adaptable food wine. Try it with cold cooked prawns.

Quality	♥♥♥
Value	★★★
Grapes	chenin blanc; colombard
Region	Murray Valley, Vic.
Cellar	▮ 2
Alc./Vol.	13.5%
RRP	$11.30 ⑤

Buller Victoria Classic Spatlese Lexia

Quality	♟♟♟⸮
Value	★★★⸸
Grapes	muscat gordo blanco
Region	Sunraysia, Vic.
Cellar	▮ 1
Alc./Vol.	8.5%
RRP	$11.30 Ⓢ

Both Best's and Buller's have secondary wineries at Lake Boga near Swan Hill but neither mention it on their label. Instead they put their more desirable addresses: Bullers at Rutherglen, and Best's at Great Western. It's misleading, but the labelling laws permit it.

CURRENT RELEASE 1998 This is a high-fidelity sweet, late-picked muscat style. The colour is pale, and the aromas are of lychee, rose petals and a hint of ginger. It's simple and grapey-sweet to taste – very true to variety – with low-alcohol lightness and a clean, fresh finish. A good aperitif style.

Cape Horn Chardonnay

Quality	♟♟♟⸮
Value	★★★★
Grapes	chardonnay
Region	Murray Valley, Vic.
Cellar	▮ 1
Alc./Vol.	14.0%
RRP	$18.00

An old vineyard resurrected on a bend on the Murray River near Echuca. A century ago it provided wine to those involved in the bustling river trade. Maker John Ellis.

CURRENT RELEASE 1998 A simple young chardonnay with a fruity nose of peachy varietal aroma and well-handled background oak. In the mouth it has juicy fruit mid-palate, attractive softness and subtle barrel influence. A slight firmness at the end gives structure to the palate. A no-fuss wine for a meal of yabbies.

Cape Mentelle Chardonnay

Quality	♟♟♟♟♟
Value	★★★★
Grapes	chardonnay
Region	Margaret River, WA
Cellar	▮ 5
Alc./Vol.	14.1%
RRP	$30.50

Cape Mentelle is one of Australia's leading mid-sized wineries, achieving top quality with both reds and whites. The chardonnay epitomises the complex house style that's evolved over the last decade.

CURRENT RELEASE 1997 The bouquet is complex and fine. Lovely subtle touches of butterscotch, nuts and cream are submerged in elegant nectarine and melon-like fruit aromas. The palate is long and silky with a citrus tang, melony richness, and all those intangible complexities that make really fine chardonnay. Try Moreton Bay bug tails with tagliatelle to accompany this.

Cape Mentelle Semillon Sauvignon Blanc

There are lots of these blends in Margaret River and they're cropping up everywhere else as well. Cape Mentelle remains one of the best.

CURRENT RELEASE 1998 Tropical fruit, a hint of blackcurrant and citrus tones drive the nose, with a complex dab of nutty, creamy, lees aroma. In the mouth it has real depth with persistent fruit salad/citrus flavour. A clean, dry finish keeps things fresh.

Quality	?????
Value	★★★ｒ
Grapes	semillon; sauvignon blanc
Region	Margaret River, WA
Cellar	2
Alc./Vol.	13.5%
RRP	$21.00

Capel Vale CV Unwooded Chardonnay

In twenty years Capel Vale has grown to be a significant player in the Western Australian wine scene. The broad range of wines makes use of various vineyard sources throughout the south-west of the state.

CURRENT RELEASE 1998 The juicy tropical fruit that's so much a part of WA chardonnay is here aplenty. The nose has melon and passionfruit aromas, and the palate follows suit, adding a slightly herbal note. The finish is crisp and refreshing. A soft white with more personality than many oak-free chardonnays.

Quality	????
Value	★★★★
Grapes	chardonnay
Region	various, South West WA
Cellar	3
Alc./Vol.	13.0%
RRP	$15.95

Capel Vale Verdelho

From an original base at Capel, on Geographe Bay north of Margaret River, Capel Vale's vineyard sources have expanded to include some in more southerly climes.

CURRENT RELEASE 1998 A pale-coloured white with the typically grapey verdelho aromas, a hint of apricot and some high-toned notes on the nose. The palate has juicy, grapey flavour, which almost suggests sweetness, and a whisper of oak adds texture and depth rather than a flavour element. Try it with mee goreng.

Quality	????
Value	★★★
Grapes	verdelho
Region	Pemberton, WA
Cellar	2
Alc./Vol.	13.8%
RRP	$15.95

Carramar Estate Oak Fermented Semillon

Quality	▼▼▼?
Value	★★★
Grapes	semillon
Region	Riverina, NSW
Cellar	▮ 2
Alc./Vol.	13.0%
RRP	$12.00

Another of the revitalised crop of semillons that the Riverina folk are working hard to promote. Carramar Estate is also known as Casella Wines.

CURRENT RELEASE 1998   Slightly raw oak leads the way here, but lemony fruit stands up to it quite well. The palate has more varietal lemon-scented flavour, and more oak. There's an unctuous mouth-feel, perhaps due to some residual sugar in combination with 13 per cent alcohol. A good match for snapper and lemon butter.

Cassegrain Verdelho

Quality	▼▼▼▼
Value	★★★⯪
Grapes	verdelho
Region	Hastings Valley, NSW
Cellar	▮ 2
Alc./Vol.	13.0%
RRP	$15.95

At Cassegrain on the north coast of New South Wales they battle a subtropical climate with mixed success. The whites are often the pick of the wines.

CURRENT RELEASE 1998   A soft, gently fruity white that will please a lot of people, this has soft melon fruit aromas with a pleasant floral touch. The palate is medium-bodied and has a fruity sherbet tang to it. It might improve with a little bottle-age. A crab mousse would go well with it at the moment.

Castle Rock Chardonnay

Quality	▼▼▼▼?
Value	★★★★★
Grapes	chardonnay
Region	Great Southern, WA
Cellar	▮ 4
Alc./Vol.	13.5%
RRP	$20.00

Cool-climate chardonnay, WA style. This vineyard is down south in the Porongurup Ranges near Albany.

CURRENT RELEASE 1997   The nose is very stylish, with well integrated fruit and very subtle oak elements. Cool-climate white peach fruit dominates at the moment, and complex nutty, vanilla cream and toasty touches mark a fine long palate. It finishes elegantly with a firm backbone of acidity. Very enjoyable with poached yabbies.

Castle Rock Riesling

Castle Rock Rieslings age extremely well. They start life rather restrained, then build into something special with time.

CURRENT RELEASE 1998 In youth this has floral perfume, a touch of spice, and some lime aromas. The palate is dry and subtly aromatic with a fine texture and a tight minerally structure. If you've never cellared white wines, start with these. When young, this will suit the freshest shellfish; when older, try it with pan-fried trout.

Quality	♟♟♟♟♟
Value	★★★★★
Grapes	riesling
Region	Great Southern, WA
Cellar	➥ 1–8+
Alc./Vol.	12.0%
RRP	$16.45

Chain of Ponds Riesling

A lyrical name for one of the Adelaide Hills' up-and-coming concerns. The owners, the Amadio family, grow a range of different grape varieties – both white and red – and enjoy success across the board.

CURRENT RELEASE 1998 Adelaide Hills riesling has a particular spicy intensity, and this is no exception. The nose is very aromatic, with some lemon essence aromas and a hint of bakery spice. In the mouth the tight citrus flavour is rather austere, but there's good weight and texture ahead of a tangy finish. It's a rather contained wine waiting to blossom fully with bottle-age. Keep it for a couple of years then serve it with a crab salad.

Quality	♟♟♟♟♟
Value	★★★★
Grapes	riesling
Region	Adelaide Hills, SA
Cellar	➥ 1–8+
Alc./Vol.	12.0%
RRP	$15.60

Chapel Hill Unwooded Chardonnay

Unwooded chardonnay is often a pretty lacklustre tipple, but the Chapel Hill wines are a cut above most of the competition. They have good depth and they age surprisingly well. Maker Pam Dunsford.

CURRENT RELEASE 1998 This has the sort of mellow, direct fruitiness that all unoaked chardonnays ought to have. Peach, melon, lemon and herbs mark the nose, which has attractive delicacy. The palate has soft, full flavour and the smooth dry finish has a pleasant fruity tang. Serve with scampi and black beans.

Quality	♟♟♟♟
Value	★★★✦
Grapes	chardonnay
Region	not stated
Cellar	▮ 4
Alc./Vol.	13.0%
RRP	$16.45

Chapel Hill Verdelho

Quality	▼▼▼▼
Value	★★★★
Grapes	verdelho
Region	McLaren Vale, SA
Cellar	▮ 2
Alc./Vol.	13.0%
RRP	$18.10

Verdelho is being touted by some as the next big thing. It does make appealing, juicy white wine, so maybe they're right, whoever 'they' are.

CURRENT RELEASE 1998   Chapel Hill winemaker Pam Dunsford's speciality is unwooded white wine, particularly chardonnay. Her verdelho sums up the variety with precision: fruit salad aromas with a slight herbaceous tang, softly fruity flavour on a dry palate, and a succulent crisp finish. Easy to like. Try it with a Thai chicken salad.

Chateau Leamon Riesling

Quality	▼▼▼▼
Value	★★★★
Grapes	riesling
Region	Bendigo, Vic.
Cellar	▮ 3
Alc./Vol.	12.0%
RRP	$14.15

There isn't a great deal of riesling in Central Victoria, since most of the new vineyards were planted at a time when it was hardly the flavour of the month. The few that do exist can sometimes be very good.

CURRENT RELEASE 1998   This has lively varietal character with a nose of florals, dusty spices and citrus. In the mouth it's delicate, with an almost ethereal lime flavour, a whiff of spice and a tangy, fragrant finish. Try it with sashimi.

Chateau Tahbilk Marsanne

Quality	▼▼▼▮
Value	★★★
Grapes	marsanne
Region	Goulburn Valley, Vic.
Cellar	▮ 6+
Alc./Vol.	13.0%
RRP	$13.25

Chateau Tahbilk should be an essential stop on any exploration of Victoria's vineyards. Few Australian wineries impart such a sense of living history. Maker Alister Purbrick.

CURRENT RELEASE 1998   The modern Tahbilk marsannes are fresher and fruitier than the much-talked-about classics of yesteryear were in their youth. They should still retain the legendary longevity. This latest edition has a honeyed floral nose, which is quite delicate. The palate is soft and dry with a hint of grapefruit and a chalky, dry, finish. Works well with a seafood risotto.

Chatsfield Chardonnay

You hear a lot about the German, Swiss and French vignerons' contributions to the history of Australian wine. What we forget is that most of the people involved have in fact been Anglo-Celtic types. Continuing the tradition is Irish-born Ken Lynch at Chatsfield.

CURRENT RELEASE 1997   Chardonnay from the south of Western Australia has a certain tropical fruit character that makes it delicious. Chatsfield has juicy peach, melon and pineapple aromas, with some complexity coming from buttery malolactic influence. The palate is creamy and nutty, full in body, and clean with good length. Will probably be best drunk young while it retains all that succulent fruit. Serve it with prosciutto melone.

Quality	♛♛♛♛♙
Value	★★★★
Grapes	chardonnay
Region	Great Southern, WA
Cellar	▮ 2
Alc./Vol.	13.5%
RRP	$23.35

Chatsfield Gewürztraminer

Many years before the chardonnay revolution, gewürztraminer was regarded by some as the new-wave white grape for Australia. It proved a bit of a fizzer, eventually ending as fodder for many semi-sweet traminer–riesling blends. A handful of serious varietal wines continue to be made, though.

CURRENT RELEASE 1998   A complex nose with an impressive varietal bouquet of musk sticks, florals and lime. In the mouth a measure of residual sugar gives it dimension, and it tastes of sweet citrus. Acidity is clean and fresh – a surprise for a gewürz. Serve it well chilled with sticky rice parcels.

Quality	♛♛♛♛♙
Value	★★★★★
Grapes	gewürztraminer
Region	Great Southern, WA
Cellar	▮ 2
Alc./Vol.	14.0%
RRP	$21.05

Chatsfield Riesling

Great Southern riesling is rarely less than excellent. Chatsfield makes one of the best.

CURRENT RELEASE 1998   This has a perfumed, lifted nose of spice, flowers and citrus. The palate is dry and quite austere at the moment, with a tangy zip and an underlying minerally strength. In common with most rieslings from this region, it's ungiving at present, and it needs time to reveal itself.

Quality	♛♛♛♛♙
Value	★★★★↟
Grapes	riesling
Region	Great Southern, WA
Cellar	➡ 1–5+
Alc./Vol.	12.3%
RRP	$21.05

Chestnut Grove Verdelho

Quality	♟♟♟♟
Value	★★★
Grapes	verdelho
Region	Pemberton, WA
Cellar	▲ 2
Alc./Vol.	13.0%
RRP	$17.00

Verdelho has been a popular variety in the West for many years. It's interesting that many newer plantings like Chestnut Grove have also tried it out, rather than just sticking to the more fashionable varieties.

CURRENT RELEASE 1998 This has typical fruit salad verdelho aromas with some grassy leafiness too. The middle palate is grapey and light, but a tad short. Quite tart acidity dries the finish. A refreshing warm-weather white to drink chilled with shellfish.

The Clare Essentials Carlsfield Riesling

Quality	♟♟♟♟♟
Value	★★★★★
Grapes	Riesling
Region	Clare Valley, SA
Cellar	▲ 6+
Alc./Vol.	11.5%
RRP	$15.40 Ⓢ

Hats off to Mildara for sticking its neck out and launching a cluster of new Clare rieslings under individual vineyard labels. The original three (from the '97 vintage) has shrunk to the two best in '98, and they are well worth tracking down.

CURRENT RELEASE 1998 This is a delicate riesling with a fine flowery nose and great subtlety all round. The palate is intense and tightly focused, with lean, tart lime-juice flavours and a dry, but smooth, finish. It will reward cellaring. Good now with pan-fried whiting.

The Clare Essentials Polish Hill River Riesling

Quality	♟♟♟♟
Value	★★★★
Grapes	riesling
Region	Clare Valley, SA
Cellar	▲ 5
Alc./Vol.	11.5%
RRP	$15.40 Ⓢ

Happily, Mildara has restored the original name to the historic Quelltaler winery, although it uses the Annie's Lane, Clare Essentials and other brand names on the wines made there.

CURRENT RELEASE 1998 This is a more delicate wine than the Carlsfield and looks subdued and shy – frail, even – in its youth. There are suggestions of quince and vanilla, and the acidity is quite elevated. Cellar it or serve now with food. Try a delicate crab roulade.

Clonakilla Viognier

Viognier is a mysteriously aromatic variety that hails from France's Rhone Valley. At Clonakilla, near Canberra, the Kirks grow viognier principally to blend with their shiraz to make a fragrant red according to north Rhone practice. A trickle of it is bottled on its own from time to time.

CURRENT RELEASE 1998 Let's face it, viognier is weird. It's amazing floral, spicy character is immediately recognisable, but you're always left wondering whether you really like it or not. Clonakilla is right in style. The nose has musk stick, mandarin and floral aromas, and the palate is warm and rather broad with a distinctive floral flavour and aftertaste. The finish is rather hard. Could be good with soft cheeses.

Quality	🍷🍷🍷🍷
Value	★★★½
Grapes	viognier
Region	Canberra, ACT
Cellar	1
Alc./Vol.	13.5%
RRP	$16.00 (375 ml) (cellar door)

Cloudy Bay Chardonnay

Apparently Cloudy Bay Chardonnay is the favourite tipple of ex-Python and latter-day Phileas Fogg, Michael Palin. He shows impeccable taste.

CURRENT RELEASE 1997 Cloudy Bay is always a luscious sort of chardonnay with a luxurious juiciness. On first acquaintance it seems less complex than many of its competitors, probably due to its overt fruitiness. This edition has the usual tropical fruit, peach and grapefruit characters, but underneath them is a more subtle, creamy, honeyed personality trimmed with subtle toasty oak. It's a style that's probably best young and lively. Try it with quick-fried calamari.

Quality	🍷🍷🍷🍷½
Value	★★★★
Grapes	chardonnay
Region	Marlborough, NZ
Cellar	2
Alc./Vol.	14.3%
RRP	$31.25

Cloudy Bay Sauvignon Blanc

Quality	♟♟♟♟♟
Value	★★★★★
Grapes	sauvignon blanc
Region	Marlborough, NZ
Cellar	▮ 3
Alc./Vol.	13.5%
RRP	$21.00

The sauvignon blanc grape enjoys such a rare symbiotic relationship with this vineyard at Marlborough that Cloudy Bay is now a world benchmark for the variety. **CURRENT RELEASE 1998** Few world-class wines are as consistent as Cloudy Bay. Here we have archetypal varietal character, which in 1998 seems a wee bit riper than usual. The nose has intense passionfruit and restrained tomato leaf aromas; the palate has similar flavours, which have an almost essency intensity. The finish is long and tangy. Try it with crudités and tomato mayonnaise.

Cockfighter's Ghost Chardonnay

Quality	♟♟♟♟
Value	★★★
Grapes	chardonnay
Region	Hunter Valley, NSW
Cellar	▮ 3
Alc./Vol.	12.7%
RRP	$17.75

Poor old Cockfighter was a horse who drowned in quicksand in the Wollombi Brook next to this vineyard. His ghost is said to still haunt these parts. **CURRENT RELEASE 1998** This is more restrained than many Hunter chardonnays, adding some regional herbal notes to aromas of stone fruit and subtle oak. The palate is soft and gentle with nectarine flavours leading the way, and a dry, clean finish. A good partner for risotto with sweet potato and thyme.

Cockfighter's Ghost Semillon

Quality	♟♟♟♟
Value	★★★⯪
Grapes	semillon
Region	Hunter Valley, NSW
Cellar	➥ 1–5+
Alc./Vol.	10.6%
RRP	$16.50

Sydney merchant banker David Clarke owns this Hunter Valley vineyard along with its neighbour, Poole's Rock. Maker Neil McGuigan. **CURRENT RELEASE 1998** This is a typically understated young Hunter semillon, which will probably age well. The nose has lemon, dry grass and chalk aromas with a touch of sulfur. In combination this gives a rather European feel. The palate has a soft middle of medium depth, despite the low alcohol, ahead of dry austerity on the finish. Try it with a shellfish salad.

Coldstream Hills Chardonnay

This standard Coldstream Hills Chardonnay is deliberately made in a different style to the Reserve; that is, without malolactic fermentation and with a different regime of oak treatment. Makers James Halliday and Paul Lapsley.

CURRENT RELEASE 1998   A 'standard' label that deserves attention for its above-standard quality. The nose has melon, peach, malt and custardy aromas, which lead in nicely to a harmonious palate. It's tasty and smooth with complex melon and peach fruit character, subdued nutty oak, and a long clean signature at the end. Serve it with a warm scallop salad.

Quality	？？？？？
Value	★★★
Grapes	chardonnay
Region	Yarra Valley, Vic.
Cellar	3
Alc./Vol.	13.5%
RRP	$23.00 Ⓢ

Coldstream Hills Reserve Chardonnay

This is the chardonnay James Halliday makes in hommage to Burgundy. He pulls out all stops in the quest for complexity and longevity.

CURRENT RELEASE 1998   Older vintages of this top-of-the-range white have aged very well. In fact, it needs time more than most chardonnays. This vintage is no exception. At the moment the oak influence is pronounced, with sweet and spicy, smoked-bacon-scented French oak leading the way over nectarine, peach and buttery aromas. The creamy fruit is there in the mouth, but firm structure, tangy acidity and a strong underpinning of classy oak grab the limelight. Give it a couple of years, then enjoy it with blanquette of veal.

Quality	？？？？？
Value	★★★★
Grapes	chardonnay
Region	Yarra Valley, Vic.
Cellar	1–5
Alc./Vol.	14.0%
RRP	$41.50

Constable and Hershon Limited Reserve Chardonnay

Quality	♥♥♥♥
Value	★★★
Grapes	chardonnay
Region	Hunter Valley, NSW
Cellar	▮ 4
Alc./Vol.	12.5%
RRP	$25.00

Even teetotallers (perish the thought!) should visit this Hunter vineyard to stroll its lovely formal gardens. Maker Neil McGuigan.

CURRENT RELEASE 1997   A rather angular sort of chardonnay. Maybe it will be more giving as it ages. The nose has stone-fruit and melted butter aromas with a dab of slightly resinous sweet oak. The palate has oak dominating peachy fruit, which gives a slightly hollow impression mid-palate. Crisp acidity keeps the flavour fresh and lively. Try it with teppan yaki seafood.

Coolangatta Estate Alexander Berry Chardonnay

Quality	♥♥♥♥
Value	★★★
Grapes	chardonnay
Region	South Coast, NSW
Cellar	▮ 3
Alc./Vol.	13.3%
RRP	$17.00

The Alex on the label was the founder of the township of Berry, hub of the Shoalhaven district. History abounds here: it's a place with a past. Made at Tyrrell's for the Bishop family of the Coolangatta Estate resort.

CURRENT RELEASE 1998   True to form, this is a straightforward, fruity style, which treads lightly in the wood department. It smells of cashew nuts and toast, with a hint of resin from the wood. There's peachy fruit and some sweetness on the palate, and the resiny wood character shows again. It has plenty of flavour and will please many. Serve with scallop gratin.

Coriole Lalla Rookh Semillon

Quality	♥♥♥♥
Value	★★★★
Grapes	semillon
Region	McLaren Vale, SA
Cellar	▮ 3
Alc./Vol.	13.0%
RRP	$15.50

McLaren Vale semillon is a bigger, riper beast than its Hunter Valley cousin. When it's given a bit of oak fermentation and lees contact it makes a very flavoursome mouthful.

CURRENT RELEASE 1998   This has a pale appearance which gives little clue to a quite powerful personality. The nose has lemon, pastry and herbal aromas with a hint of spice and some nutty lees influence. In the mouth it has real depth and chewy texture. Lemon/herb flavours finish dry and tangy. A good white to accompany a chicken risotto.

Crabtree Watervale Riesling

Crabtree's vineyard was planted by one Adolph Glaetzer in 1932. The riesling is on shaley loam over limestone, the classic soil type for this variety in Watervale.

CURRENT RELEASE 1998 This sums up what makes great Clare Valley riesling. It's delightfully fine and delicate, yet it has real backbone. A floral perfume leads the way with a spring-like lime juice touch and minerally aspects. The palate is tight with pristine juicy lime flavour, a hint of spice and a firm, tangy finish. Needs time. Serve with whiting meunière.

Quality	?????
Value	★★★★★
Grapes	riesling
Region	Clare Valley, SA
Cellar	8
Alc./Vol.	11.5%
RRP	$14.00

Craiglee Chardonnay

Craiglee means red wine to most people, but winemaker Pat Carmody has quietly developed an individual chardonnay style at this historic site.

CURRENT RELEASE 1998 Pat Carmody doesn't encourage the malolactic process in his chardonnay, which usually results in a more elegant, lean-boned style than the Australian norm. The '98 is at odds with that; it's still brightly-coloured and fresh, with nectarine, citrus and subtle French oak aromas, but the palate is much richer and weightier than most Craiglees. It has deep stone-fruit flavour, fruit and alcohol sweetness, nutty touches and balanced acidity. The aftertaste is long. Good with pan-fried snapper.

Quality	?????
Value	★★★★
Grapes	chardonnay
Region	Sunbury, Vic.
Cellar	5
Alc./Vol.	15.0%
RRP	$23.00

Cranswick Estate Autumn Gold Botrytis Semillon

Another of the multitude of botrytised sweeties from the Riverina. They're really serious about this style, with generally very good results.

CURRENT RELEASE 1996 Still luscious but less so than the very good '94. The nose has honeyed peach and marmalade aromas dressed up in spicy oak, with the typical touch of volatility that often marks this style. The palate is sweet and intense. Concentrated acidity balances the sweetness. Try it with blue cheese.

Quality	????
Value	★★★⊦
Grapes	semillon
Region	Riverina, NSW
Cellar	3
Alc./Vol.	11.0%
RRP	$23.00 (375 ml)

Cranswick Estate Barrel Fermented Semillon

Quality	????
Value	★★★⯪
Grapes	semillon
Region	Riverina, NSW
Cellar	▮ 2
Alc./Vol.	12.5%
RRP	$16.00

Riverina semillon is best known for the luscious botrytised sweet whites it produces. Most production actually goes into dry white wine, a type the Riverina makers are trying to push along with products like this.

CURRENT RELEASE 1997   This has attractively subtle varietal aromas of lemon and herbs – fresh and appetising. A sensibly restrained touch of oak adds substance, and in the mouth it has good intensity and a fine long aftertaste. On the label, television chef Peter Howard says it's a good match for blue swimmer crab salad drizzled with a lime mayo dressing. Sounds okay to us too.

Crawford River Riesling

Quality	?????
Value	★★★★★
Grapes	riesling
Region	Portland, Vic.
Cellar	▮ 6
Alc./Vol.	12.5%
RRP	$22.20

Portland, on the Victorian south-west coast, has a handful of isolated vineyards nearby. The biggest is Seppelt at Drumborg, but Crawford River can sometimes be the best.

CURRENT RELEASE 1998   This is a delightful cool-climate riesling that sings with pure varietal character. The nose has exquisite passionfruit aromas with a zesty citrus tang. The palate follows suit wonderfully, and although dry, it has thrilling, juicy fruit-sweetness. A backbone of zippy acidity counterpoints all that and should make for long life. Try it with steamed fish with ginger and spring onion.

Crofters Chardonnay

Quality	????
Value	★★★⯪
Grapes	chardonnay
Region	Mount Barker & Harvey, WA
Cellar	▮ 2
Alc./Vol.	13.0%
RRP	$16.00

BRL Hardy's Houghton outpost in Western Australia is making a mark with Crofters red wines. The whites haven't hit the same heights yet.

CURRENT RELEASE 1998   A lot of work has gone into this wine to create a complex mouthful. It works well enough, but there are a couple of rough edges. The nose and palate have dried fig and peach characters with some regional fruit salad and leafy notes. Dusty oak makes its contribution as well, but a whiff of volatility detracts somewhat from the overall feel of the wine.

Cullen Chardonnay

Matriarch Di Cullen, the pioneering winemaker at Cullen and mum of present winemaker Vanya, was honoured with an AO (Order of Australia medal) in June 1999 for her service to the Margaret River wine industry. *Previous outstanding vintages: '91, '92, '93, '94, '95, '96* CURRENT RELEASE 1998   Not long in the bottle when we tasted it, this looked quite oaky but undoubtedly had the concentration to perform with a year or more's cellaring. It smells of cedar, nectarine, grapefruit and toasted nuts, and is powerfully structured. There's a clean acid cut, which adds an appealing tanginess. Very long finish, too. Cellar, then serve with lobster.

Quality	▼▼▼▼▼
Value	★★★★
Grapes	chardonnay
Region	Margaret River, WA
Cellar	➥ 1–7
Alc./Vol.	13.5%
RRP	$47.50

Cullen Sauvignon Blanc Semillon

Few sauvignon blanc–semillon blends in Australia have the impact of this one. Made in a complex style that's reminiscent of good dry white Bordeaux, it presents a fascinating alternative to chardonnay in the full-bodied white stakes.
CURRENT RELEASE 1998   The nose has the sort of subtle complexity that has you returning to your glass again and again. It has hay, citrus and herbal notes with nutty, leesy overtones. It tastes clean and tight with a very long palate of intense vinous flavour. Oak is there to add structure and textural qualities rather than flavour, and the finish is chalky, dry and refined. A classy white to serve with meaty fish, like swordfish.

Quality	▼▼▼▼▼
Value	★★★⯪
Grapes	sauvignon blanc; semillon; chardonnay
Region	Margaret River, WA
Cellar	▮ 5
Alc./Vol.	13.5%
RRP	$29.00

Dalfarras Marsanne

Quality	♟♟♟
Value	★★★
Grapes	marsanne
Region	Goulburn Valley, Vic.
Cellar	↓ 2
Alc./Vol.	13.0%
RRP	$15.60

Emanating as it does from the Chateau Tahbilk cellars, a Dalfarras marsanne is no surprise. This one is wooded, unlike the Tahbilk wine. Maker Alister Purbrick.

CURRENT RELEASE 1997 A wine with character. There's plenty of wood to sniff, together with developed apricot kernel and overripe fig marsanne characters, and a sort of petroleum overtone. The palate has adequate flavour with some oak astringency to close. The aftertaste is oddly unsatisfying. Try it with egg and bacon pie.

Dalfarras Sauvignon Blanc

Quality	♟♟♟
Value	★★★
Grapes	sauvignon blanc
Region	McLaren Vale, SA; Goulburn Valley, Vic.
Cellar	↓ 1
Alc./Vol.	12.5%
RRP	$15.60

The Purbricks of Dalfarras and Chateau Tahbilk have a business relationship with Geoff Merrill, hence some of the Dalfarras grapes emanate from McLaren Vale. Maker Alister Purbrick.

CURRENT RELEASE 1998 The aromas are different: there's an intriguing hint of crushed rose petals, together with spicy and sweaty aromas more typical of the grape. It opens slightly sweet on the tongue, then the acid comes in to provide balance. The flavour is light-bodied and a tad thin. It should work with a terrine of roasted red peppers.

Deakin Estate Sauvignon Blanc

Quality	♟♟♟
Value	★★★★
Grapes	sauvignon blanc
Region	Murray Valley, Vic.
Cellar	↓ 1
Alc./Vol.	12.5%
RRP	$10.65 Ⓢ

Alfred Deakin initiated the agricultural development of north-west Victoria in the 1890s. Without him the irrigation scheme mightn't have started when it did.

CURRENT RELEASE 1998 This seems to have some of the harsh, green, stalky characters of early-picked grapes, which people in hot areas do in an effort to get varietal character. The palate is broad and smooth, and while it lacks good sauvignon blanc 'cut', it's quite a good drink at the price. Food: stuffed capsicum.

De Bortoli Noble One Botrytis Semillon

This is the benchmark for big, bouncy, boots-and-all botrytis semillon in this country. It was first made in 1982 when Darren De Bortoli came home to make the wine as a fresh Roseworthy graduate.

Previous outstanding vintages: '82, '87, '90, '93, '94, '95
CURRENT RELEASE 1996   Oak makes a big statement in this wine: it has always been a feature, and it drives the complexity of the wine. The colour is dark amber; the bouquet is developing with smoky, toasty wood, some volatility, and rich marmalade, toffee, vanilla characters. A multi-faceted style that keeps you wanting more. Great with crème brûlée.

Quality	♥♥♥♥♥
Value	★★★★
Grapes	semillon
Region	Riverina, NSW
Cellar	🍶 3
Alc./Vol.	11.5%
RRP	$25.60 (375 ml)

De Bortoli Windy Peak Chardonnay

Windy Peak is one of the subsidiary labels of De Bortoli's Yarra Valley winery. The grapes are sourced from various regions of Victoria. Maker: Steve Webber and team.

CURRENT RELEASE 1998   An excellent commercial wine: soft and rounded in structure, and very easy to drink. Slightly dusty, cedary nose with peach and spice undercurrents. The palate is very soft with a touch of subliminal sweetness, good richness, and lightly handled charry oak. Good flavour for the price. It should appeal to masses of people, and goes well with antipasto.

Quality	♥♥♥♥
Value	★★★★★
Grapes	chardonnay
Region	various, Vic.
Cellar	🍶 2
Alc./Vol.	13.5%
RRP	$13.90 ⑤

De Bortoli Windy Peak Rhine Riesling

Name-wise, this wine's in a time warp. Riesling is the true name of the grape. This has won two silver medals, and we agree with that assessment. Maker Steve Webber.
CURRENT RELEASE 1997   Subdued smoky, tea-leafy aromas are entwined with minerally scents. It's a delicate, soft, gentle riesling. It finishes fruity, but dry. Excellent flavour and style for the price. Serve it alongside snapper quenelles.

Quality	♥♥♥♥
Value	★★★★★
Grapes	riesling
Region	various, Vic.
Cellar	🍶 4
Alc./Vol.	13.0%
RRP	$13.90 ⑤

Devil's Lair Chardonnay

Quality	♟♟♟♟♟
Value	★★★★
Grapes	chardonnay
Region	Margaret River, WA
Cellar	▮ 6
Alc./Vol.	13.5%
RRP	$38.50

Southcorp is planning big things for this brand. Major new vineyards, winery extensions ... could it be they plan to take on Leeuwin Estate as the chardonnay kings? Maker Janice McDonald.

CURRENT RELEASE 1997 This is a real humdinger, but it takes a while to come out of its shell. It opens with lots of oak, and builds butterscotch, honey, vanilla and tropical fruit flavours. A complex, tautly structured, serious wine with a firm dry finish and good length. A real classic. Don't over-chill it, and serve with char-grilled crayfish.

Devil's Lair Fifth Leg

Quality	♟♟♟
Value	★★
Grapes	sauvignon blanc; chardonnay; semillon
Region	Margaret River, WA
Cellar	▮ 1
Alc./Vol.	13.5%
RRP	$22.00

This seems to be pitched at the Trendy Young Things market, what with its highly designed package, its zany back label and rather over-baked price. Now part of the Southcorp stable.

CURRENT RELEASE 1998 Cosmetic aromas, lollyish and slightly green, but clean. It's very lightweight, flimsy even. The herbaceous, confectionery-like sauvignon blanc flavour is fairly dry, but rather weak and short for the money. Serve with a niçoise salad.

Diamond Valley Blue Label Chardonnay

Quality	♟♟♟♟
Value	★★★★
Grapes	chardonnay
Region	Yarra Valley, Vic.
Cellar	▮ 3
Alc./Vol.	13.5%
RRP	$21.00

This is Diamond Valley's second-string label, intended for earlier drinking than the white-label estate wine. Maker David Lance.

CURRENT RELEASE 1998 For a second label this is a beaut – a smoothly stylish wine driven by tangy peachy fruit with some appealing nutty touches. There's also a bit of French-accented complexity. It finishes clean, long and interesting. Serve it with scallops.

Diamond Valley Blue Label Sauvignon Blanc

Sauvignon blanc doesn't immediately spring to mind when you think of the Yarra Valley, but there are some pretty competent examples in the region.
CURRENT RELEASE 1998 This sauvignon blanc is a picture of restraint. The usual overt herbaceous qualities are tempered somewhat; the nose still has grassiness, but there are also pleasant notes of citrus and flowering herbs. The palate has a bit more depth than most, and is clean and dry-finishing. Just the thing for a fresh asparagus quiche.

Quality	♟♟♟♟
Value	★★★★
Grapes	sauvignon blanc
Region	Yarra Valley, Vic.
Cellar	♦ 2
Alc./Vol.	12.5%
RRP	$16.35

Doonkuna Chardonnay

Doonkuna is now owned by Barry Moran. Lady Jan Murray sold it a couple of years ago following the death of her husband Sir Brian Murray. Winemaker now is Malcolm Burdett.
CURRENT RELEASE 1996 A typical cool-climate style, with delicate, restrained fruit and quite strong malolactic characters. The palate has real delicacy and good structure. There are complex toasted-nut and buttery malolactic complexities as well. Should go well with a warm scallop salad.

Quality	♟♟♟♟♟
Value	★★★★
Grapes	chardonnay
Region	Canberra District, NSW
Cellar	♦ 4
Alc./Vol.	13.0%
RRP	$20.00

Dowie Doole Chenin Blanc

This is a newie from McLaren Vale grapegrowers, Drew Dowie and Norm Doole. Dowie is an architect and Doole is behind the Boar's Rock contract winemaking operation.
CURRENT RELEASE 1998 Good chenin is a rare breed, although McLaren Vale has several nice ones. This wine's honeyed, grassy and floral aromas are of more than passing interest. Finely structured and smooth with crisp acidity. Take it to a vegetarian restaurant.

Quality	♟♟♟♟
Value	★★★★
Grapes	chenin blanc
Region	McLaren Vale, SA
Cellar	♦ 3
Alc./Vol.	12.5%
RRP	$15.00

Drayton's Vineyard Reserve Chardonnay

Quality	ŸŸ?
Value	★★⊁
Grapes	chardonnay
Region	Hunter Valley, NSW
Cellar	▮ 1
Alc./Vol.	12.0%
RRP	$20.00

This comes from the estate of Drayton Family Wines at Pokolbin. Winemaker is Roseworthy gold medallist Trevor Drayton, and '98 was an outstanding year.

CURRENT RELEASE 1998 The colour is mid-yellow and fairly forward; the bouquet is dominated by resiny aromas that may be a blend of oak and rapid bottle-aged characters. There's a hint of Friar's Balsam, for those with long memories. The acid stands out a little, and it could use a little more fruit depth. Serve with whitebait fritters.

Drayton's Vineyard Reserve Semillon

Quality	ŸŸŸ?
Value	★★★
Grapes	semillon
Region	Hunter Valley, NSW
Cellar	▮ 5
Alc./Vol.	11.5%
RRP	$20.00

Drayton's is a very old Hunter Valley company that's proud of being family-owned, and proud of the fact that all their grapes come from their own vineyards. Maker Trevor Drayton.

CURRENT RELEASE 1998 This is a very dry, classic Hunter semillon which drinks well now with seafood and fish, but which really needs to be cellared to bring out its best. The nose is light and simple with herbal and lemony aromas, and in the mouth the lemony flavours reappear. It has good finesse, liveliness and intensity, but it's just a little straightforward at this early stage. Food: snapper tails.

Dromana Estate Reserve Chardonnay

Quality	ŸŸŸ?
Value	★★⊁
Grapes	chardonnay
Region	Mornington Peninsula, Vic.
Cellar	▮ 3+
Alc./Vol.	13.5%
RRP	$45.00

There's nothing bashful about the prices down there on the Mornington Peninsula, but the production costs are very high and 1997 was a year of sub-economic low yields.

CURRENT RELEASE 1997 A typically delicate regional style with some butterscotch and bacon-bone smoky complexities. The palate has restrained melon-like fruit and needs lighter foods. Try it with crudités and aioli.

Eaglehawk Riesling

Eaglehawk was one of a number of different names given at various times to the old Quelltaler enterprise at Clare by Mildara Blass. It's all academic now, as the parent company has closed it down as a working winery as part of a comprehensive rationalisation. We lament its passing.
CURRENT RELEASE 1999   Good varietal character here on the nose – floral, musky and spicy. The palate lets things down a tad. It's tasty and dry with good varietal flavour, but it falls away a bit, lacking the final intensity of the best. Priced competitively and good value though. Try it with fresh spring rolls.

Quality	???
Value	★★★★
Grapes	riesling
Region	not stated
Cellar	2
Alc./Vol.	11.0%
RRP	$12.00 $

Eden Ridge Sauvignon Blanc

The Wynns of Mountadam have been at the forefront of many new directions in Australian wine. Eden Ridge was one of them, a label reserved for wines made from organically grown grapes with minimal preservatives.
CURRENT RELEASE 1997   Very varietal aromas here, and it's fresher and better made than a lot of organic wines. The nose has asparagus, honey, and herbaceous notes, which aren't as severe as in some cool-grown sauvignons. The palate follows suit, with soft mid-palate fruit balanced by drying acidity. Thai asparagus stirfry would be good here.

Quality	???
Value	★★★
Grapes	sauvignon blanc
Region	Eden Valley, SA
Cellar	1
Alc./Vol.	12.5%
RRP	$21.40 ⓥ

Elderton Golden Semillon

Although Elderton are Barossa-based, this botrytised sweet wine is sourced from the Griffith district in the Riverina. Many growers in other parts of the country are doing the same, such is the Riverina's reputation for these sweet whites.
CURRENT RELEASE 1997   A deep, old golden wine with an intense bouquet of sweet stone fruit, tea leaf and marmalade. The palate has liqueurish sweetness with candied citrus peel and sweet tea. It finishes with crisp acidity, and the aftertaste is long and sweet. Try this with some gorgonzola.

Quality	????
Value	★★★★
Grapes	semillon
Region	Riverina, NSW
Cellar	1
Alc./Vol.	11.0%
RRP	$17.25 (375 ml)

Element Chardonnay

Quality	YYYY
Value	★★★★★
Grapes	chardonnay
Region	various, WA
Cellar	▲ 2
Alc./Vol.	12.7%
RRP	$12.95

'Born of earth, wind, fire and water, Element is the essence of nature.' So goes the motto for this product. No comment from the authors.

CURRENT RELEASE 1997 This is a surprise packet at a very reasonable price. It's a well-made young wine with melon, spice and minerals on the nose, and subtle hints of oak. The palate is fruit-driven, crisp and tasty with attractive melon flavour and a little sweetness. A good match for a gourmet chicken club sandwich.

Elgee Park Baillieu Myer Family Reserve Chardonnay

Quality	YYYYY
Value	★★★★
Grapes	chardonnay
Region	Mornington Peninsula, Vic.
Cellar	▲ 4
Alc./Vol.	14.0%
RRP	$24.50

Although small-scale viticulture had been attempted before on the Mornington Peninsula, Baillieu Myer pioneered the present industry when he established his Elgee Park in 1972. Now there are scores of vineyards down there. Maker Tod Dexter.

CURRENT RELEASE 1997 There's some of the magic winemaker Tod Dexter brings to the Stonier's chardonnays in this Elgee Park effort. From a warm drought year, it has a big nose: complex with nutty, butterscotch touches to the rich peachy fruit. In the mouth it's full-bodied with smooth texture. Ripe stone fruit and mealy flavours feature ahead of a long, toasty finish. Would suit southern rock lobster famously.

Evans and Tate Gnangara Chardonnay

Quality	YYYY
Value	★★★★
Grapes	chardonnay
Region	various, WA
Cellar	▲ 1
Alc./Vol.	13.0%
RRP	$17.40

Evans and Tate's progressive relocation from the Swan Valley to Margaret River over recent years was prompted by the quality limitations of the former site. Maker Brian Fletcher.

CURRENT RELEASE 1998 A simple Western Australian chardonnay with the fruit salad overtones of unoaked material. It has a tropical aroma with a grassy tang; the flavour is reminiscent of tropical fruit and melon, with some herbaceous qualities and a crisp end. Try it with a Thai prawn salad.

Eyton Chardonnay

Eyton is one of several must-visit spots in the beautiful Yarra Valley. It's a showplace winery with a tower, and it has a professionally run restaurant that makes excellent use of the local produce and wines.

CURRENT RELEASE 1998   A distinctly cool-climate chardonnay with a slight shaded fruit character that gives a certain leafiness. Some melony fruit is there, and a caramel touch reflects malolactic influence. Very tart acidity underpins it all. Serve it with shellfish.

Quality	▼▼▼▼
Value	★★★
Grapes	chardonnay
Region	Yarra Valley, Vic.
Cellar	▮ 2
Alc./Vol.	13.0%
RRP	$22.00

Eyton Dalry Road Chardonnay

Eyton on Yarra is a grand place with one of the tidiest wineries around. Everything is so spick and span that it would shame most Aussie winemakers.

CURRENT RELEASE 1998   Oak barely makes an appearance in this fruit-dominant young chardonnay. The nose has attractive melon fruit and a dab of pastry-like lees aroma to add interest. In the mouth it's soft and smoothly textured, with long peachy flavour and a crisp ending. Good with a picnic of cold chicken.

Quality	▼▼▼▼
Value	★★★★
Grapes	chardonnay
Region	Yarra Valley, Vic.
Cellar	▮ 2
Alc./Vol.	13.0%
RRP	$17.20

Fairhall Downs Chardonnay

This is another new winery in the burgeoning Marlborough district of New Zealand.

CURRENT RELEASE 1997   Lovely complex Burgundian style which promises to repay cellaring. It has a pale colour and restrained fruit – of a grapefruit/melon persuasion – and is lightly oaked. There are butterscotch and malt flavours as well, and the profile is leanish and elegant, but tight and long on the finish. Exotic and impressive. Try it with sautéed Balmain bug tails.

Quality	▼▼▼▼▼
Value	★★★★⋆
Grapes	chardonnay
Region	Marlborough, NZ
Cellar	▮ 5
Alc./Vol.	14.0%
RRP	$20.50

Fairhall Downs Sauvignon Blanc

Quality	♥♥♥?
Value	★★★
Grapes	sauvignon blanc
Region	Marlborough, NZ
Cellar	▮ 1
Alc./Vol.	13.0%
RRP	$19.70

The puff tells us this won a gold medal in the Liquorland Top 100, a competitive tasting conducted in New Zealand.

CURRENT RELEASE 1998 Passionfruit juice! That's it: if you like your wine to taste like passionfruit juice, go for it. That aroma suggests vigorous vines and shaded bunches. It's a light but lively wine, fresh and clean; however, it's a trifle watery and lacks a bit of intensity. Drink up soon, with New Zealand green-lip mussels.

Felton Road Dry Riesling

Quality	♥♥♥
Value	★★★
Grapes	riesling
Region	Central Otago, NZ
Cellar	➙ 1–5+
Alc./Vol.	12.0%
RRP	$26.30

This upstart vineyard in Central Otago came out of the blue to produce a great 1996 pinot noir. They are still working on the riesling.

CURRENT RELEASE 1998 The colour is pale, and there's a whiff of acetone to open the act. It's light-bodied and shy, a blushing debutante, and the acid is ferocious on the finish. Cellar it, or drink it with something oily to mop up that acid. Try buttered scallops.

Fermoy Estate Semillon

Quality	♥♥♥?
Value	★★★
Grapes	semillon
Region	Margaret River, WA
Cellar	▮ 3
Alc./Vol.	13.5%
RRP	$19.35

This Margaret River wine has 14 per cent sauvignon blanc blended into the semillon. It's been subjected to barrel-fermentation and wood-ageing during which the lees were stirred. A very complex style.

CURRENT RELEASE 1998 Heavily charred oak dominates the nose of this youngster. Oak renders the palate slightly thick and broad, and it lacks the delicacy you might expect from semillon. As the wine breathes it reveals more crushed-leaf, capsicum-like Margaret River semillon fruit aromas. The palate is quite intense and flavoursome, and the style will have its devotees. Good with chargrilled vegetables.

Fiddlers Creek Sauvignon Blanc

This is a fighting varietal brand for Blue Pyrenees Estate. It's based on fruit from various regions that remain a mystery. Maker Kim Hart.

CURRENT RELEASE 1998   This is a puzzling wine. It doesn't have a great deal of varietal character, but there's a lot to it. The flavour is generous, and the finish is nice and long with a slight grip and a trace of hardness, which doesn't faze us. Goes well with vegetable terrine.

Quality	￥￥￥
Value	★★★★
Grapes	sauvignon blanc
Region	not stated
Cellar	￠ 1
Alc./Vol.	12.5%
RRP	$12.00 ⑤

Fiddlers Creek Semillon

This has come up a peg or three since last year's review. Typical of semillon: rather than tiring, it just keeps powering along. Maker Kim Hart.

CURRENT RELEASE 1997   Still a youngster at two years old, this is a pale lemon in shade. It has delicate aromas of straw and lemon, with the merest beginnings of toasty development. It's similarly delicate and light-bodied to taste, with a classically dry finish that's nevertheless soft and smooth. Good drinking with antipasto.

Quality	￥￥￥￥
Value	★★★★★
Grapes	semillon
Region	Pyrenees, Vic.
Cellar	￠ 5+
Alc./Vol.	13.5%
RRP	$12.00 ⑤

Fire Gully Semillon Sauvignon Blanc

This is the second label of Pierro, the grapes coming from Marg and Ellis Butcher's vineyard in Margaret River. Maker Mike Peterkin.

CURRENT RELEASE 1998   Oak is the main event here. It's anything but the simple grassy style you might expect. The colour is medium yellow; the nose reveals toasty, cedary oak of a superior grade. In the mouth it's light and soft, with a dry finish. If anything, it lacks a little zip. A good partner for smoked chicken salad.

Quality	￥￥￥
Value	★★★
Grapes	semillon; sauvignon blanc
Region	Margaret River, WA
Cellar	￠ 2
Alc./Vol.	12.5%
RRP	$20.50

The First Hunter Valley Semillon

Quality	♥♥♥
Value	★★★
Grapes	semillon
Region	Hunter Valley, NSW
Cellar	🍷 3+
Alc./Vol.	10.5%
RRP	$15.00

This is a blend of grapes from Drayton's, McWilliams and Tyrrell's. It's called The First because it's marketed young – a few weeks after vintage – as the first wine of the Hunter vintage.

Previous outstanding vintages: '98

CURRENT RELEASE 1999 This is a very raw, estery, youthful white wine, which still needs a little time to come together fully. By the time you read this it should be drinking perfectly! The aroma is dominated by peppermint, almost toothpaste-like, fruit esters. In the mouth it's light-bodied, lean and dry with high acidity. It has tight, delicate fruit, and an almost austere finish. It would benefit from time, but could be drunk young with fish. Try grilled garfish.

Flinders Bay Semillon Sauvignon Blanc

Quality	♥♥♥♥
Value	★★★
Grapes	semillon; sauvignon blanc
Region	Margaret River, WA
Cellar	🍷 1
Alc./Vol.	13.3%
RRP	$17.25

This brand was begun by former Sydney retailer Bill Ireland and vigneron Alastair Gillespie. It has a great humpback whale on the label. This wine comes from vines at Witchcliffe and Karridale.

CURRENT RELEASE 1998 The colour is rather forward – a full yellow – and there are dusty, herbaceous aromas. The palate holds plenty of soft, full flavour and a rounded profile. The flavour is better than the aroma. It would team well with fried whitebait.

Forrest Estate Riesling

Quality	♥♥♥
Value	★★★
Grapes	riesling
Region	Marlborough, NZ
Cellar	🍷 4
Alc./Vol.	12.5%
RRP	$16.40

Riesling doesn't have a huge following in New Zealand, but the climate's right for some fine aromatic styles.

CURRENT RELEASE 1998 Aromas of lemon essence abound, and the wine is light and shy. It carries quite a deal of sweetness and is verging on a late-picked style. It's clean and well made. Try it with pan-fried scallops.

Forrest Estate Sauvignon Blanc

John Forrest is keen to invest this wine with more character than the common-or-garden-variety sauvignon blancs in his region. To that end he barrel-ferments and malos parts of the blend.

CURRENT RELEASE 1998 There's a minty aspect to the nose, which no doubt comes from the oak. It lacks the trademark varietal fruit pungency of Marlborough, but has decent flavour and quality, with good balance and softness on the palate. Food: Bluff oysters.

Quality	♥♥♥♪
Value	★★★
Grapes	sauvignon blanc
Region	Marlborough, NZ
Cellar	▪ 2
Alc./Vol.	13.0%
RRP	$19.70

Fox River Chardonnay

This is the little brother of the Goundrey Reserve, and the botrytis theme is played even more strongly here.
Previous outstanding vintages: '97
CURRENT RELEASE 1998 This shows some age in its full yellow colour and there are dried apricot and fig jam aromas. The palate gives an impression of sweetness and is a little flat; it tastes like botrytis visited the vineyard. If it's possible for a white wine to be jammy, this is! Try it with grilled figs and prosciutto.

Quality	♥♥♥
Value	★★ゃ
Grapes	chardonnay
Region	Great Southern, WA
Cellar	▪ 1
Alc./Vol.	13.0%
RRP	$18.40

Fox River Classic White

Fox River, not to be confused with Fox Creek, is a second-label of Goundrey Wines. The winemaker these days is Keith Bown.
CURRENT RELEASE 1997 This smells very sweaty – a telltale sign of shaded bunches in vigorous vineyards, and probably young vines. In keeping with the nose, it tastes light and simple and slightly sweet. It has no glaring faults, but neither does it challenge the senses. Try it with steamed fish.

Quality	♥♥♪
Value	★★ゃ
Grapes	chenin blanc;
	semillon
Region	Great Southern, WA
Cellar	▪ 1
Alc./Vol.	12.5%
RRP	$14.10

Fox River Sauvignon Blanc

Quality	♟♟♟
Value	★★★
Grapes	sauvignon blanc
Region	Great Southern, WA
Cellar	♦ 1
Alc./Vol.	12.0%
RRP	$14.10

The label actually reads: 'Fox River Sauvignon Blanc – for the moment'. What does that mean – it might turn into something else in a few minutes?

CURRENT RELEASE 1998   This a workmanlike effort which won't make the earth move, but neither should it disappoint. The aromas are of parsley and green stalks. The same flavours appear on the palate, and it's rather one-dimensional. Try it with pressed tongue and parsley.

Garry Crittenden 'I' Arneis

Quality	♟♟♟♟
Value	★★★★
Grapes	arneis
Region	Mornington Peninsula, Vic.
Cellar	♦ 2
Alc./Vol.	13.5%
RRP	$22.00

This is one for fans of the obscure. Arneis is a little-known, almost extinct, Italian white grape grown in tiny pockets north of Alba in Piedmont. If anyone was going to fool around with arneis in Australia, it had to be Garry Crittenden. Few understand Italian grape varieties as he does.

CURRENT RELEASE 1999   This first Aussie arneis is a very attractive young wine. It's subtle and well mannered with gentle stone-fruit aromas and a hint of almond syrup on the nose. The palate is light, dry, flinty and nutty with a clean finish. An interesting, easy-drinking white to have with grilled fish.

Geoff Merrill Reserve Chardonnay

Quality	♟♟♟♟
Value	★★★
Grapes	chardonnay
Region	Coonawarra, SA; Goulburn Valley, Vic.
Cellar	♦ 1
Alc./Vol.	12.5%
RRP	$27.00

The Reserve label wines are kept back by Geoff Merrill for release with bottle-age. Whether they have benefited from the experience is open to debate.

CURRENT RELEASE 1993   From its deep golden colour to its vanilla, buttered-toast and dried citrus peel nose, this wine seems very mature. The palate is dried out with old white wine flavours and solid structure. Better with food. Try it with a bouillabaisse.

Geoff Weaver Chardonnay

Geoff Weaver used to be boss of winemaking at Hardys, so he knows a thing or two about the business. These days all his skill is channelled into these wines from his own Adelaide Hills plot.

CURRENT RELEASE 1997 The Adelaide Hills region produces some of Australia's best chardonnay. Geoff Weaver's version continues to be one of the stars. This has lovely, restrained harmony on the nose with no one character standing out above the others. There's nectarine fruit aroma, nutty nuances, and beautifully integrated spicy oak. The palate is silky and soft, deceptively drinkable, but still reserved. Like most Weaver chardonnays it needs age to be at its best. Try it with bug tails.

Quality	🍷🍷🍷🍷🍷
Value	★★★★★
Grapes	chardonnay
Region	Adelaide Hills, SA
Cellar	5
Alc./Vol.	14.0%
RRP	$34.50

Geoff Weaver Sauvignon Blanc

Geoff Weaver's wines are graced with one of the loveliest labels in Australian wine, complete with an original Weaver painting.

CURRENT RELEASE 1998 Adelaide Hills sauvignon blanc may be Australia's best. Geoff Weaver's is right in the regional style with pristine varietal aromas: like green leaves, capsicum and ripe green fruits. The palate is intense but still light and drinkable, with clean, tangy flavour and zippy acidity. A good match for prawns with tomato salsa.

Quality	🍷🍷🍷🍷½
Value	★★★★
Grapes	sauvignon blanc
Region	Adelaide Hills, SA
Cellar	2
Alc./Vol.	13.0%
RRP	$21.40

Giaconda Chardonnay

Quality	❦❦❦❦❦
Value	★★★★★
Grapes	chardonnay
Region	Beechworth, Vic.
Cellar	➻ 1–6+
Alc./Vol.	13.5%
RRP	$65.00

Giaconda wine is as rare as hen's teeth, but you occasionally see it on a wine list, and if you're super-lucky you might encounter one under the counter at a bottle shop. Australian chardonnay doesn't come any better than this.

CURRENT RELEASE 1997 Giaconda is an essay in power and subtlety at the same time. The bouquet is very complex, with a lot of secondary winemaker-induced touches that add nutty, toasty, creamy interest to a core of elegantly subdued melony fruit. The restrained palate is multi-layered and as much about texture as flavour. It's seamless and fine with creamy richness and a long aftertaste that seems to go on forever. Try it cool, not chilled, with blanquette of veal.

Glenguin Chardonnay

Quality	❦❦❦❦
Value	★★★★
Grapes	chardonnay
Region	Hunter Valley, NSW
Cellar	➻ 1–4
Alc./Vol.	13.0%
RRP	$21.00

The Tedders at Glenguin set out to make Hunter chardonnay in a more elegant style. Robin Tedder likes the wine to be food-friendly and subtle.

CURRENT RELEASE 1997 This is an understated wine that could be missed in a line-up of big fat chardonnays. It has a reserved personality, with Hunter regional touches of straw, honey and citrus added to the peach, mineral and nutty chardonnay characters. It's long, restrained and dry. Easy to like with whiting meunière.

Glenguin Semillon

Quality	❦❦❦❦?
Value	★★★★
Grapes	chardonnay
Region	Hunter Valley, NSW
Cellar	➻ 2–8
Alc./Vol.	10.4%
RRP	$18.50

Glenguin boss, Lord Robin Tedder, is a real peer of the realm whose title relates to Glenguin in Scotland, the home of Glengoyne malt whisky. It seems his entry into the world of booze was somehow preordained.

CURRENT RELEASE 1998 This is a bright young wine with a tingle of gas and a classic Hunter semillon nose of lemon, hand cream and dried grass. The palate is lemony and lean with tart acidity and a citrus aftertaste. A zippy wine that ought to be cellared to realise its potential. Serve it with a meaty fish, like skate.

Golden Grove Estate Chardonnay

This is one of the more high-profile Queensland win ries, run by the Costanzo family at Ballandean. Maker Sam Costanzo.
CURRENT RELEASE 1998   This is the pick of Golden Grove's wines, a very creditable fruit-accented chardonnay of good freshness. It's pale-yellow-coloured, smelling of peach and nectarine, and a light toasted-nut oak overtone. It has some spice flavours on the palate, which is rich and weighty but without great length. Goes well with roasted, stuffed chicken.

Quality	♟♟♟♟
Value	★★★★★
Grapes	chardonnay
Region	Granite Belt, Qld
Cellar	↓ 2
Alc./Vol.	12.5%
RRP	$14.00 (cellar door)

Goldwater Roseland Chardonnay

Barry Goldwater was an American presidential candidate who wanted to nuke North Vietnam. Needless to say this winery is NOT named after him.
CURRENT RELEASE 1997   This is no shrinking violet. It's a big intense wine that fairly jumps out of the glass. The nose has succulent stone-fruit and tropical aromas with a trimming of spicy oak. In the mouth it has very full, juicy fruit flavour with a rather alcoholic feel. A larger-than-life chardonnay, intriguing to drink. Serve it with Chinese chicken and almonds.

Quality	♟♟♟♟♟
Value	★★★★
Grapes	chardonnay
Region	Marlborough, NZ
Cellar	↓ 2
Alc./Vol.	13.5%
RRP	$24.00

Gramp's Botrytis Semillon

Techniques of growing and making botrytised sweet white wine have been mastered by Australian winemakers in a very short time. The wines usually don't have quite the finesse of similarly made European wines, but look at the relative prices.
CURRENT RELEASE 1997   Great value in a sweet white that doesn't overwhelm the senses with sugariness. The nose is lush with peach, apricot and citrus aromas. The palate is tangy-sweet and light for this style of wine. It's fine but still luscious, with a counterpoint of tangy acidity and a subtle apricot aftertaste.

Quality	♟♟♟♟♟
Value	★★★★★
Grapes	semillon
Region	Riverina, NSW
Cellar	↓ 2
Alc./Vol.	11.0%
RRP	$16.50 (375 ml)

Gramp's Chardonnay

Quality	♟♟♟♟
Value	★★★★
Grapes	chardonnay
Region	Barossa Valley, SA
Cellar	🍷 2
Alc./Vol.	13.5%
RRP	$16.50

Johann Gramp left Bavaria for South Australia in 1837. Ten years later he planted the Barossa's first vineyard, which grew into Orlando. It's good to see the name surviving on this brand from the Orlando-Wyndham group.

CURRENT RELEASE 1998 This is an easy to like young chardonnay with a fresh straw colour and attractive stone-fruit aromas with a herbal note. The nose is enhanced by balanced sweet oak and a yeasty touch. The palate has rich peachy flavour, very ripe and satisfying, with a pleasant oak-accented aftertaste. Try it with sweet corn fritters with salsa.

Grant Burge Summers Chardonnay

Quality	♟♟♟♟
Value	★★★★⊢
Grapes	chardonnay
Region	Barossa Valley, SA
Cellar	🍷 3
Alc./Vol.	13.5%
RRP	$16.45

Grant Burge is Barossa born and bred, so it's not surprising that he is able to source very good grapes from various places in the Valley. The wines exemplify the full-flavoured Barossa style.

CURRENT RELEASE 1998 This is a great value-for-money chardonnay, better than some more expensive wines. It has a complex nose of rich, sweet, stone-fruit aromas with a balanced dressing of toasty oak. The palate is a smooth combination of peachy fruit nicely balanced by spicy oak. A pleasant zip of acidity keeps it fresh. Baked snapper recommends itself.

Grant Burge Thorn Riesling

Quality	♟♟♟♟♟
Value	★★★★⊢
Grapes	riesling
Region	Eden Valley, SA
Cellar	🍷 5+
Alc./Vol.	12.0%
RRP	$14.80

With so much Barossa blood coursing through his veins, it's natural that Grant Burge would make a good riesling from up in them thar Barossa hills.

CURRENT RELEASE 1998 In '98 Grant Burge's Thorn Riesling is more delicate than usual. The colour is pale and green-tinged, and the nose has floral lemon blossom aromas. In the mouth there's clean limey flavour with some spicy richness against a firm structure of acidity. Will undoubtedly grow in richness with bottle-age. Serve with pan-fried whiting fillets.

Grant Burge Zerk Semillon

Zerk sounds like the name of a visitor from the planet Zarquon, but actually it's the name of a vineyard. Barossa semillon is a different thing to the more delicate Hunter Valley style, and Grant Burge's version is typically big and flavoursome.

CURRENT RELEASE 1998   Very Barossa semillon on the nose: lemon essence, lanolin and a bit of spicy oak. In the mouth it's concentrated and rich with broad, almost tropical, fruit, a dose of sweet oak and a clean finish. Would go well with a Sunday roast chicken.

Quality	♥♥♥♥
Value	★★★★
Grapes	semillon
Region	Barossa Valley, SA
Cellar	🍾 3
Alc./Vol.	13.0%
RRP	$14.80

Green Point Chardonnay

Green Point is the original homestead at Domaine Chandon. It gives its name to estate-grown chardonnay and pinot noir table wines, which complement the excellent range of sparkling wines produced there. Maker Wayne Donaldson.

CURRENT RELEASE 1998   With this wine, Domaine Chandon enters the big league as a producer of chardonnay table wine. It's a French-accented wine with very complex stone fruit, nutty yeasty lees and vanilla cream on the nose and palate. It's mouth-filling, yet subtle, smooth, long and beautifully balanced. Hang the expense – buy a lobster for this.

Quality	♥♥♥♥♥
Value	★★★★★
Grapes	chardonnay
Region	Yarra Valley, Vic.
Cellar	🍾 4
Alc./Vol.	14.0%
RRP	$22.30

The Green Vineyards Chardonnay

The Green Vineyards' chardonnay is made in a deliberately non-interventionist way by Sergio Carlei. Vintage is important, since in cooler years these cool-grown wines can be a bit too green (no pun intended).

CURRENT RELEASE 1997   This is a lovely wine that encapsulates many of the things that make people rave about cool-grown Australian chardonnay. The nose has subtle stone-fruit and citrus aromas with a hint of nettle and some vanilla cream. In the mouth it has great harmony, with a seamless fruit/lees/oak mix that's in perfect balance with good acidity and a clean, crisp finish. Try it with ocean trout cutlets.

Quality	♥♥♥♥♥
Value	★★★★★
Grapes	chardonnay
Region	Yarra Valley, Vic.
Cellar	🍾 4
Alc./Vol.	13.0%
RRP	$27.00

Gulf Station Semillon Sauvignon Blanc

Quality	♛♛♛♜
Value	★★★★
Grapes	semillon; sauvignon blanc
Region	Yarra Valley, Vic.
Cellar	🍷 2
Alc./Vol.	12.0%
RRP	$16.00

De Bortoli have made some successful wines in warmer years with Yarra Valley semillon. In Gulf Station they blend it with sauvignon blanc into a well-priced dry white. Makers Steve Webber and team.

CURRENT RELEASE 1998   This is a pleasant light wine which doesn't make too many demands. The nose has light citrus aromas with a hint of grassiness. The palate has more depth than the nose suggests. It tastes clean and lemony with a herbal edge; it finishes crisp and dry.

Hamilton Ayliffe's Orchard Sauvignon Blanc

Quality	♛♛♜
Value	★★★
Grapes	sauvignon blanc
Region	McLaren Vale, SA
Cellar	🍷 1
Alc./Vol.	13.5%
RRP	$11.00 ⑤

We wonder what fruit they grew in Ayliffe's orchard? Melons, asparagus and herbs, if this wine is any guide! CURRENT RELEASE 1998   This is light and somewhat sweaty in its herby, honeydew melon fruit, while the flavours turn thick and cloying on the palate. But it's a perfectly decent sauvignon blanc at this low price. There are tea-leafy nuances, and the tannins give it a rather tough finish. Best with food: try whitebait fritters.

Hamilton The Hills Chardonnay

Quality	♛♛♛♛
Value	★★★
Grapes	chardonnay
Region	Adelaide Hills, SA
Cellar	🍷 4
Alc./Vol.	13.0%
RRP	$22.00

When South Australians refer to The Hills, it's understood they're talking about the Adelaide Hills, a very trendy area for arty–crafty boutiques, picnic races, pet alpacas and vineyards.

CURRENT RELEASE 1998   Everyone's just gotta have an Adelaide Hills chardonnay now, and this is a good debut. There are cashew nut, melon and gooseberry aromas, and it's a subtle, fruit-driven style. It has some backbone, and the finish carries crisp acid. Try it with whiting quenelles.

Hamilton The Slate Quarry Riesling

The Hamilton mob has contracted a severe case of the D'Arenbergs. Branding is rife, with creeks, quarries, orchards and other landmarks suddenly assuming major importance.

CURRENT RELEASE 1998 Lightweight, almost flimsy, riesling, which nevertheless shows a delicacy and restraint that's rarely seen in this grape in McLaren Vale. Racy citrus/lemon aromas; dry and somewhat austere on the palate. Could reward some time in the cellar. Goes well with oysters.

Quality	▼▼▼⁄
Value	★★★★
Grapes	riesling
Region	McLaren Vale, SA
Cellar	▮ 5
Alc./Vol.	11.3%
RRP	$11.00 Ⓢ

Hamilton's Bluff Canowindra Grossi Chardonnay

This is a new producer at Canowindra, near Cowra. Canowindra Grossi is the name of a rare fish fossil found in the area in 1956. There's now a fish museum there. Maker Andrew Margan (contract).

CURRENT RELEASE 1998 It would go well with fish, too, but not the 360-million-year-old type. This is a light-coloured, fruit-driven style which smells of melon and cut-grass herbaceousness. It's lean and tight on the tongue with lemony acidity, good balance, and a clean, refreshing finish.

Quality	▼▼▼⁄
Value	★★★★
Grapes	chardonnay
Region	Cowra, NSW
Cellar	▮ 2
Alc./Vol.	12.5%
RRP	$14.00 (cellar door)

Hamilton's Bluff Chairman's Reserve Chardonnay

Hamilton's Bluff hit the big time immediately, with its chardonnay selected for Qantas international first class. The chairman in this case is architect John Andrews. The wine is contract-made by Andrew Margan.

CURRENT RELEASE 1998 This starts off with lots of promise. The nose is expressive and offers rich butter-scotch, stone-fruit aromas, but when you taste, there's a belt of acid that tends to unbalance the palate. It tastes lean and bracing and a tad austere. Needs a little bottle-age or food – or both. Try buttery pan-fried flounder.

Quality	▼▼▼⁄
Value	★★★
Grapes	chardonnay
Region	Canowindra, NSW
Cellar	➥ 1–5
Alc./Vol.	13.0%
RRP	$19.00 (cellar door)

Hardys Adelaide Hills Sauvignon Blanc

Quality	♛♛♛
Value	★★★
Grapes	sauvignon blanc
Region	Adelaide Hills, SA
Cellar	▮ 1
Alc./Vol.	11.5%
RRP	$19.00 Ⓢ

They're all doin' it . . . buying grapes from little pocket-hanky-sized vineyards in the Adelaide Hills, that is. This comes from near Hahndorf.

CURRENT RELEASE 1998 This is a pretty wine – beguiling to sniff, but the palate flavour is fairly light. It smells of passionfruit juice and green herbs. The taste is light, simple and clean, but ultimately it doesn't make the earth move. Good drinking with fresh oysters.

Harewood Estate Chardonnay

Quality	♛♛♛♛?
Value	★★★⊦
Grapes	chardonnay
Region	Great Southern, WA
Cellar	▮ 4
Alc./Vol.	14.0%
RRP	$30.00

Keith and Margie Graham run this small, 8-hectare vineyard at Denmark. John Wade, who makes the wine, says Denmark grows some of the best grapes in Western Australia. The grapes are hand-picked.

Previous outstanding vintages: '96

CURRENT RELEASE 1997 This is a very polished wine. You can detect the hand of a pro (Wadey). The butterscotch-like malolactic character is somewhat assertive, but there are complex mealy and peachy characters, too. It's a rich wine, densely packed with flavour. It fills the mouth and lingers long on the aftertaste. An impressive wine that goes well with a scallop and leek gratin.

Haselgrove 'H' Botrytis Sauvignon Semillon

Quality	♛♛♛♛
Value	★★★★
Grapes	sauvignon blanc; semillon
Region	McLaren Vale, SA
Cellar	▮ 3
Alc./Vol.	10.0%
RRP	$18.00 (375 ml)

The grapes were harvested at the end of May, which is late indeed down in McLaren Vale. Maker Nick Haselgrove.

CURRENT RELEASE 1998 This is a sticky with a difference – the difference being the sauvignon blanc fruit and the intriguing pear-juice flavour in this medium–sweet wine. There are ripe honeydew melon characters too, and the finish has a stewed-pear quality. Only lightly botrytised, we suspect, but a lovely lighter style. Try it with baked apple or pear.

Haselgrove 'H' Chardonnay

This is the first white wine we've seen from the newly named Wrattonbully region, formerly known as Koppamurra. Haselgrove's partner, Alambie Wines, developed one of the biggest vineyards there. Maker Nick Haselgrove.

CURRENT RELEASE 1998 This is a much finer, more restrained and more appealing chardonnay than the previous vintage. That's the cooler-grown Wrattonbully fruit at work, we suspect. The nose has restrained grapefruit/citrus and apricot aromas, with oak well in the background. Good intensity and a compact structure. Fine lemon and vanilla in the mouth, with a winning balance of richness and finesse, and a very long carry. Should repay a year's keeping. Try it with grilled scampi.

Quality	♟♟♟♟♟
Value	★★★★★
Grapes	chardonnay
Region	Wrattonbully, SA 79%; McLaren Vale, SA 21%
Cellar	↓ 5
Alc./Vol.	13.5%
RRP	$20.50

Haselgrove Sauvignon Blanc

This is part of Haselgrove's 'picture series' whose labels depict a brightly coloured vineyard scene. McLaren Vale is one of the more reliable sources of sauvignon blanc.

CURRENT RELEASE 1998 A light, easy-drinking, typical mid-priced sauvignon blanc. It has an aroma of fresh herbs and estery fermentation odours. The finish is soft and pulls up short. It's a clean, adequate wine, which would suit caesar salad.

Quality	♟♟♟
Value	★★★
Grapes	sauvignon blanc
Region	McLaren Vale, SA
Cellar	↓ 1
Alc./Vol.	12.5%
RRP	$15.25 ⑤

Hay Shed Hill Sauvignon Blanc

Funny name for a winery, but it's a winery with a difference: there's a lot of interesting iron sculpture around the cellar-door sales. It used to be called Sussex Vale. Maker Peter Stanlake.

CURRENT RELEASE 1998 The prices in Margaret River are a worry. There's not much for the mums and dads any more. This is a touch volcanic to begin. The palate is better, with some richness and weight, enlivened by fresh acidity. There's a suggestion of wood, and while it doesn't have a lot of varietal character, it has flavour. Food: asparagus quiche.

Quality	♟♟♟↑
Value	★★↑
Grapes	sauvignon blanc
Region	Margaret River, WA
Cellar	↓ 2
Alc./Vol.	12.0%
RRP	$22.00

Hay Shed Hill Semillon

Quality 🍷🍷½
Value ★★½
Grapes semillon
Region Margaret River, WA
Cellar 1
Alc./Vol. 13.0%
RRP $22.80

It's curious that even ordinary Margaret River semillon is more expensive than the best from the Hunter. Do the grapes cost more to grow there?

CURRENT RELEASE 1998 This is a barrel-fermented style which doesn't trumpet its oak. The colour is pale, and there are capsicum and nettle aromas. There's a fair deal of sweetness, which tends to mask any fruit flavour. It has no technical faults, but the fruit seems to have gone walkabout. Serve it with avocado and tossed green salad.

Heathcote Winery Viognier

Quality 🍷🍷🍷🍷🍷
Value ★★★½
Grapes viognier
Region Heathcote, Vic.
Cellar 3
Alc./Vol. 13.9%
RRP $32.80

Viognier (pronounced vee-ohn-yay) is one of the new buzz varieties. It comes from the northern Rhone Valley in France where it makes a great dry white called Condrieu. Maker Mark Kelly.

CURRENT RELEASE 1998 A subtle but distinctive wine that captures the essence of the viognier grape. It smells doughy from fermentation esters, and also of spice, musk and a little pineapple. The palate is full with dry, tight structure, and it has a slight grip on the finish. It was fermented in older French barriques, and the oak doesn't show. A top effort. Try it with pasta with clams.

Heggies Botrytis Riesling

Quality 🍷🍷🍷🍷
Value ★★★★
Grapes riesling
Region Eden Valley, SA
Cellar 3+
Alc./Vol. 10.0%
RRP $16.00 (375 ml) (S)

Riesling rarely achieves the high Baumés you see in semillon. Hence botrytis riesling is normally a more delicate, less sweet, wine.

Previous outstanding vintages: '94, '96, '97

CURRENT RELEASE 1998 This really hides its light under a bushel. It's a medium yellow shade and has a lovely fragrant, delicate aroma of citrus, honey and creamy/yeasty esters. The palate is all about subtlety: it doesn't impress with brute force. Restrained, citrusy and fine. It could reward short-term cellaring. Be careful if serving it with sweet foods. Try an unsweetened fruit salad.

Heggies Chardonnay

This is a single-vineyard wine, made by Simon Adams at Yalumba. Heggies sits up at 520–560 metres in the Eden Valley region.

CURRENT RELEASE 1997   There's a lot of malolactic character here, which borders on the overbearing. It has a slightly rancid-butter aroma, and there are oaky aromas too. Fruit comes to the rescue in the mouth, with finer peach and citrus flavours. The mouth-feel is good, and it promises to show more complexity and integration with time. Goes with sautéed scallops.

Quality	♟♟♟♟
Value	★★★
Grapes	chardonnay
Region	Eden Valley, SA
Cellar	🍷 6
Alc./Vol.	13.5%
RRP	$23.00

Heggies Riesling

The style of this wine has changed in recent times: it used to be a very early-picked, austere, low-alcohol number released with some bottle-age. We prefer this style.

CURRENT RELEASE 1998   A very refined riesling. The colour is pale yellow, and the nose offers delicate lemon zest, sherbety aromas. There's a little CO_2, and it's just a baby. Clean and fragrant, it has finesse aplenty. Serve it with crab.

Quality	♟♟♟♟♟
Value	★★★★★
Grapes	riesling
Region	Eden Valley, SA
Cellar	🍷 7+
Alc./Vol.	12.5%
RRP	$16.40 Ⓢ

Heggies Viognier

The folks at Yalumba are getting good at this difficult northern Rhone Valley grape. The trick is very low yields and very ripe grapes. Maker Simon Adams.

Previous outstanding vintages: '93, '96

CURRENT RELEASE 1998   Generous but unsubtle – a wine for those who love full-frontal whites. The nose has exuberant tropical fruit and spice aromas; in the mouth peach and other stone-fruits suggest themselves. There's a hint of fresh oak too. A big, broad, opulent wine with lots of viscosity and excitingly distinctive flavour. Great alongside chicken and a spicy Thai dressing.

Quality	♟♟♟♟♟
Value	★★★★
Grapes	viognier
Region	Eden Valley, SA
Cellar	🍷 3
Alc./Vol.	13.5%
RRP	$23.00 Ⓢ

PENGUIN BEST WHITE BLEND/ OTHER VARIETY

Henschke Green's Hill Riesling

Quality	ѠѠѠѠѠ
Value	★★★★★
Grapes	riesling
Region	Adelaide Hills, SA
Cellar	🍷 7+
Alc./Vol.	13.4%
RRP	$21.30

The Adelaide Hills should be producing a bevy of great rieslings, but few people are trying. It may be a reflection on the state of the market. But they are worth seeking. CURRENT RELEASE 1998 A truly wonderful riesling from a top vintage. It has a purity of fruit and seamlessness to delight the senses. Doughy, floral, creamy aromas lead into a refined, delicate, yet intense, palate. It manages to combine richness with finesse, softness, and dryness without austerity. Succulent stuff! Try it with asparagus and parmesan gratin.

Henschke Joseph Hill Gewürztraminer

Quality	ѠѠѠѠѠ
Value	★★★★⯪
Grapes	gewürztraminer
Region	Eden Valley, SA
Cellar	🍷 4+
Alc./Vol.	13.5%
RRP	$21.30

It's such a shame traminer is not more highly sought-after in Australia: the best are truly superb wines, and this is one. Take it to a Chinese, Vietnamese or Thai restaurant, and see how well it goes with the fare. CURRENT RELEASE 1998 Intense bath-powder gewürz aromas leap from the glass. A rich, ripe, pungent style that finishes dry and avoids the phenolic grip of many of its peers. Full-bodied and lingering, with impeccable balance. Goes well with lightly spiced Thai chicken.

Henschke Julius Eden Valley Riesling

Quality	ѠѠѠѠѠ
Value	★★★★★
Grapes	riesling
Region	Eden Valley, SA
Cellar	🍷 10
Alc./Vol.	13.5%
RRP	$19.70

This makes an interesting contrast with the Green's Hill wine, the slightly fuller, softer style of this wine traceable to a lower altitude and slightly warmer climate. *Previous outstanding vintages: '90, '92, '93, '95, '97* **CURRENT RELEASE 1998 A superb wine loaded with floral, stone-fruit and lightly bready aromas. It's light yellow–green in shade. The flavour flows soft and seamless across the palate, and concludes with a dry, but not severe, finish. Try it with sushi.**

PENGUIN BEST WHITE WINE AND BEST RIESLING

Henschke Sauvignon Blanc Semillon

The Henschke duo of viticulturist Prue and winemaker Stephen maintain a high quality level in whatever grape or wine style they tackle.
CURRENT RELEASE 1998 An excellent style, which treads the fine line of optimum grape ripeness. The alcohol has been toned down, and the ripe, straw–hay, citrusy and herby flavours avoid hard-edged greenness. It has generous, distinctive flavour and fine balance. Drinks well with a vegetable terrine.

Quality	♟♟♟♟
Value	★★★★
Grapes	sauvignon blanc 83%; semillon 17%
Region	Eden Valley, SA
Cellar	🍶 3
Alc./Vol.	13.5%
RRP	$19.70

Hesperos Sauvignon Blanc

This boutique Margaret River brand is vinified by Jurg Muggli at Chateau Xanadu, and much of it is exported to Switzerland and Germany.
CURRENT RELEASE 1998 It's difficult to see the grape beneath the wood! The nose and palate are dominated by toasty, smoky oak, and the finish carries a load of astringency from the oak as well. Not really varietal, it will appeal strictly to lovers of oaky white wines. Try it with chargrilled chicken.

Quality	♟♟♟
Value	★★★
Grapes	sauvignon blanc
Region	Margaret River, WA
Cellar	🍶 3
Alc./Vol.	13.5%
RRP	$20.50

Highland Heritage Estate Mountain Flame

This is a wine book, but what's wrong with the odd raspberry liqueur? Especially as it's made from 'berries grown on the estate', and 'cool-climate raspberries are as superior as cool-climate grapes'.
CURRENT RELEASE *non-vintage* This is delicious stuff. The raspberry aromas come through in quadraphonic. It has a flushed, hot-pink colour, and while it smells like raspberry cordial and tastes fairly one-dimensional, it has oodles of charm. It's very sweet, and would be great over ice-cream or well chilled as a digestif.

Quality	♟♟♟?
Value	★★★
Grapes	raspberries
Region	Orange, NSW
Cellar	🍶
Alc./Vol.	14.5%
RRP	$21.00 (500 ml)

Highland Heritage Mount Canobolas Chardonnay

Quality	♥♥♥♥
Value	★★★⋆
Grapes	chardonnay
Region	Orange, NSW
Cellar	▮
Alc./Vol.	13.5%
RRP	$24.60

Phew – what a mouthful of a title! This comes from a vineyard located just outside the city of Orange, off the Mitchell Highway. It's not really on Mount Canobolas at all. Makers John Hordern and Rex D'Aquino.

CURRENT RELEASE 1996 The wine is very developed, but still drinks well. It has a deep yellow colour, and the blend of toasted oak and bottle-age gives the bouquet a rubbery overtone. Toasted bread is also evident. Rich, buttery, layered and dry on the finish, it's fully mature and should be drunk forthwith. Serve it with a creamy brie.

Hill Smith Estate Airstrip Block Chardonnay

Quality	♥♥♥♥⸮
Value	★★★★⋆
Grapes	chardonnay
Region	Eden Valley, SA
Cellar	▮ 4
Alc./Vol.	14.0%
RRP	$18.00 Ⓢ

The Hill Smith Estate was developed by Yalumba in the 1970s to produce cool-climate grapes for finer table wines than the Barossa floor. Maker Louisa Rose.

CURRENT RELEASE 1998 One of the better wines we've seen under this label, it's a delicate, yet intensely flavoured, refined style. The fruit flavours are of melon and lemon/citrus, and it has charm and subtlety. Wood has been employed sparingly. Alcohol adds a semblance of sweetness. Try it with Thai ma hor.

Hillstowe Buxton Sauvignon Blanc

Quality	♥♥♥♥⸮
Value	★★★★⋆
Grapes	sauvignon blanc
Region	Adelaide Hills &
	McLaren Vale, SA
Cellar	▮ 2
Alc./Vol.	13.0%
RRP	$16.70 Ⓢ

Whence cometh the name Buxton? Well, Buxton Forbes Laurie was the founder of the family tradition of wine-growing, five generations ago. Now Chris and his son Hamish Laurie do the yakka.

CURRENT RELEASE 1998 This has become a finer drop since they introduced Adelaide Hills to the blend. It's medium yellow in shade, and smells of properly ripe grapes, stone fruits and freshly shelled nuts. It's rich and smooth in the mouth with an apricot kernel flavour. The finish is long and tight with hints of lychee and spices. Try it with dim sum.

Hillstowe Udy's Mill Chardonnay

This is a stunning-looking vineyard at Lenswood, managed by Dr Christie Laurie and his son Hamish. The wine won a trophy at the 1999 Top 100.
CURRENT RELEASE 1997 A delicate cool-area wine with some bacon and spicy aromas over fine, melon-like fruit. The palate is light-bodied and borders on the austere, with a fresh, clean acid finish. Subtlety is its strong suit – no single element stands out. Goes well with snapper quenelles.

Quality	▼▼▼▼?
Value	★★★☆
Grapes	chardonnay
Region	Adelaide Hills, SA
Cellar	▮ 4
Alc./Vol.	13.5%
RRP	$29.00

Homes Chardonnay

Ian Home was the guy who started Yellowglen. He saw an opportunity when Mildara came along, and sold to them. He has several other wine interests, including Massoni. This is part of a new series with artworks on the labels.
CURRENT RELEASE 1998 This is a wine of character. The colour is pale yellow and it smells of baked apples, cooked fruits, butterscotch and other nice things. Oak vanilla peeps through too. The palate is dry and finishes with a little austerity. Best with food: try it with antipasto.

Quality	▼▼▼▼
Value	★★★☆
Grapes	chardonnay
Region	Mornington Peninsula, Vic.
Cellar	▮ 4
Alc./Vol.	13.5%
RRP	$19.00 ⑤

Hungerford Hill Cowra Chardonnay

The original Hungerford Hill was an adventurous project with a resort, winery, shops and restaurants in central Pokolbin. It's still there under fragmented ownership, and has nothing to do with this brand any more. The label makes a point of being bizarre.
CURRENT RELEASE 1998 Definitely one of the better-value chardonnays we've seen from Cowra. Citrus peel and cashew nut aromas mingle with dusty oak in the bouquet, while the tight palate flavours are firm and persistent. The finish is intense and dried off by some assertive oak. It would team well with smoked chicken.

Quality	▼▼▼▼
Value	★★★★★
Grapes	chardonnay
Region	Cowra, NSW
Cellar	▮ 3
Alc./Vol.	13.5%
RRP	$14.00 ⑤

Hungerford Hill Semillon

Quality	♟♟♟♟
Value	★★★★
Grapes	semillon
Region	Hilltops & Cowra, NSW
Cellar	🍶 6+
Alc./Vol.	12.5%
RRP	$16.00 Ⓢ

Hungerford Hill do a good line in inscrutable labels. This one's a blend of Hilltops and Cowra grapes, Hilltops being the new name of the Young district in southern NSW.

CURRENT RELEASE 1998   Dusty, green herbal aromas with a trace of free sulfur. This is a very clean, well made, intensely flavoured semillon with a crisp, dry finish. There's a trace of tartness due to high acid, which will help it age. Good wine for cellaring! Food: fresh oysters.

Hungerford Hill Tumbarumba Chardonnay

Quality	♟♟♟♟
Value	★★★
Grapes	chardonnay
Region	Tumbarumba, NSW
Cellar	🍶 4
Alc./Vol.	13.5%
RRP	$22.00 Ⓢ

Don't hold your breath for the 1999 Tumbarumba wines – there won't be any, at least not from this company. A crippling frost was the culprit.

CURRENT RELEASE 1996   This is developing some curious bottle characters. The colour is still medium-light yellow and it smells slightly funky, with oaky, earthy, smoky and background citrus aromas. The lemon/grapefruit citrusy nuances come through in the mouth as well, where it has good weight and persistence. Goes with pan-fried brook trout.

Hunter's Chardonnay

Quality	♟♟♟♟♟
Value	★★★★★
Grapes	chardonnay
Region	Marlborough, NZ
Cellar	🍶 5+
Alc./Vol.	13.0%
RRP	$22.00

Hunter's was established in 1983 and has 45 hectares under vines. It incorporates a wine bar, restaurant and art gallery. They also make wine . . .

CURRENT RELEASE 1996   This chardonnay is unusual in being released with bottle-age, which in this case is a bonus. It's still fresh. There are rich, enticing peach and butterscotch aromas with yeasty stirred-lees complexities. Despite the richness and depth of flavour you can taste its high acidity, which adds to the appeal. Great with crayfish.

Hunter's Gewürztraminer

Gewürztraminer (or just traminer) is an underrated grape in Australia. It's sometimes disparaged as 'training wheels' for the wine drinker. In fact good traminer can provide great pleasure.

CURRENT RELEASE 1998 Because of the warm, ripe year this is less pungent than usual. The nose is spicy but not over the top. It has big, almost chunky, flavour. The structure is broad and rich with some phenolics (tannins) assisting the mouth-feel. Try it with a cold duck and lychee salad.

Quality	🍷🍷🍷🍷
Value	★★★★
Grapes	gewürztraminer
Region	Marlborough, NZ
Cellar	🍾 5
Alc./Vol.	13.5%
RRP	$17.00

Hunter's Riesling

Hunter's pride themselves on making the driest riesling in New Zealand. This is not difficult: most have a little sweetness to counter the sharp acidity.

CURRENT RELEASE 1998 Yes, it's dry indeed. And because the vintage was dry, there's no sign of botrytis, another common feature of New Zealand riesling. It has impressively pungent lime juice and tropical fruit aromas. The palate flavour is intense; it has delicacy and finishes dry, with a slight grip. It needs food and goes well with spicy Thai prawns.

Quality	🍷🍷🍷🍷½
Value	★★★★½
Grapes	riesling
Region	Marlborough, NZ
Cellar	🍾 8
Alc./Vol.	12.5%
RRP	$17.00

Hunter's Winemaker's Reserve Sauvignon Blanc

The winemaker in question is Gary Duke. He was last sighted in Australia when he was 2IC to John Ellis at Hanging Rock.

CURRENT RELEASE 1998 This is a selection of the best fruit of the vintage, but not wood-aged. It has a herbal, gooseberry fruit aroma and a more intense, lively, fresh and zesty palate than the standard Hunter's sauvignon blanc. The finish is very long. Excellent wine: try it with crab cakes.

Quality	🍷🍷🍷🍷½
Value	★★★★
Grapes	sauvignon blanc
Region	Marlborough, NZ
Cellar	🍾 3
Alc./Vol.	13.0%
RRP	$23.00

Ingoldby Chardonnay

Quality	♆♆♆♆
Value	★★★★⊦
Grapes	chardonnay
Region	McLaren Vale, SA
Cellar	⬥ 2
Alc./Vol.	13.0%
RRP	$14.00

McLaren Vale is traditionally red country, but the ever-adaptable chardonnay has readily found a home there. Ingoldby is a name with long regional associations that is now a Mildara Blass subsidiary.

CURRENT RELEASE 1998   This is a juicy young chardonnay with attractive syrupy fig and peach aromas. There's also a touch of coconut from the oak. The palate follows suit with rich flavour: it's full and harmoniously put together with balanced oak influence. A good companion to chicken and white wine casserole.

Ironwood Estate Riesling

Quality	♆♆♆♆♆
Value	★★★★★
Grapes	riesling
Region	Great Southern, WA
Cellar	⬥ 8+
Alc./Vol.	12.0%
RRP	$14.00

This is a new outfit at Porongurup, owned by Eugene and Mary Harma. It's a partner in the new Porongurup Winery Pty Ltd. The vines were planted in 1996, and 1999 is their maiden vintage. The '96 is from purchased Porongurup fruit.

CURRENT RELEASE 1996   What a stunning debut! This is a classic Aussie riesling: lime and toast aromas beginning to show some development; light-bodied, delicate but also soft in the mouth. It's dry but not austere, and has minerally palate flavours, lovely balance and drinkability. A good food style, so team it with oysters.

Ivanhoe Late Picked Gewürztraminer

Quality	♆♆♆♆
Value	★★★
Grapes	gewürztraminer
Region	Hunter Valley, NSW
Cellar	⬥ 3
Alc./Vol.	10.6%
RRP	$18.20 (375 ml)

Stephen Drayton, son of Reg and Pam Drayton, recently went his own way from the family company and started the Ivanhoe label, based on his Ivanhoe vineyard in the Pokolbin area.

CURRENT RELEASE 1998   Slinky packaging here, and a pretty slick wine. It's quite sweet – about auslese level – and has plenty of traminer spice on nose and palate. Clean and grapey, and would go well with sautéed chicken livers.

James Busby Sauvignon Blanc

What gives Liquorland the right to use a famous wine man's name on its own-brand wines? Well, it's a case of first in, first served.

CURRENT RELEASE 1997 This won't send the taste-buds into a frenzy, but neither will it break the bank. The colour shows some aged development, and the nose is herbal and squash-like. It tastes like the fruit was skin-contacted. The palate is broad, rich and developed, and concludes with a trace of hardness. It needs food, such as toad-in-the-hole.

Quality	🍷🍷
Value	★★★
Grapes	sauvignon blanc
Region	Barossa Valley, SA
Cellar	🍷 1
Alc./Vol.	12.1%
RRP	$11.99

Jane Brook Sauvignon Blanc

The Swan Valley doesn't spring to mind as a great region for sauvignon blanc. Wisely, Jane Brook have sourced some of their fruit from a cooler area.

CURRENT RELEASE 1998 This is a crisp, lightweight white to drink young. It smells of freshly sliced capsicum, and the flavour is similarly crisp and green-edged. It's delicate and very lively on the tongue, and it finishes with a slight grip. Good with asparagus and beurre blanc.

Quality	🍷🍷🍷
Value	★★★
Grapes	sauvignon blanc
Region	Pemberton & Swan Valley, WA
Cellar	🍷 1
Alc./Vol.	12.0%
RRP	$15.50

Jane Brook Wood Aged Chenin Blanc

The Atkinsons of Jane Brook are active marketers: they do major cellar-door sales, enjoy a lively export trade, and were one of the first to offer wine on-line.

CURRENT RELEASE 1998 The oak input is mercifully light. The colour is pale yellow, and there's the merest suggestion of oak, while the aroma has an unexpected hint of muscat. It has a rose-petal fragrance and is light, dry and straightforward in the mouth. Try it with stir-fried vegetables.

Quality	🍷🍷
Value	★★☆
Grapes	chenin blanc
Region	Swan Valley, WA
Cellar	🍷 1
Alc./Vol.	13.2%
RRP	$16.50

Jim Barry Watervale Riesling

Quality	▽▽▽▽
Value	★★★★⊦
Grapes	riesling
Region	Clare Valley, SA
Cellar	⬧ 7+
Alc./Vol.	12.5%
RRP	$14.00 Ⓢ

The Barry family purchased the Florita vineyard, formerly owned by Leo Buring/Lindemans and the source of many great Buring rieslings, in 1986. They now put the Florita name on their label. Maker Mark Barry.

CURRENT RELEASE 1998 True to form, this is a classic steely, dry style. The aromas are of dry grass–hay and straw; the taste is lean and minerally, almost austere. It doesn't have a lot of floral aromatics, but it has cellaring potential. Good with pan-fried scallops.

Jingalla Late Harvest Riesling

Quality	▽▽▽
Value	★★★⊦
Grapes	riesling
Region	Great Southern, WA
Cellar	⬧ 3
Alc./Vol.	13.0%
RRP	$12.00 (cellar door)

The deep south of Western Australia is well suited to riesling, especially the later-picked styles, as botrytis is a frequent visitor to the vineyards.

CURRENT RELEASE 1998 This is one of those no-man's-land styles: it's not sweet enough for a dessert wine, but premium riesling drinkers might find it too sweet. It's light-bodied, with moderate sweetness and a trace of botrytis. The colour is a quite developed yellow, and the bouquet is toasty and marmalade/citrusy. It has riesling varietal character. Try it with buttery scallops.

Jingalla Premium Riesling

Quality	▽▽▽
Value	★★★
Grapes	riesling
Region	Great Southern, WA
Cellar	⬧ 2
Alc./Vol.	13.0%
RRP	$20.30

This won a silver medal at the Perth Show. The Jingalla labels are stylish and different; they draw attention to the wine's link with the soil.

CURRENT RELEASE 1998 This is showing some forward development and possibly a hint of botrytis influence. It has a full yellow colour, and the nose is toasty, honeyed and rich. The mouth-feel is chewy and a tad phenolic, and it finishes dry. It's smooth and broad and doesn't have traditional riesling structure. Could go well with crumbed lamb's brains.

Jingalla Wood-aged Verdelho

The Coads from Jingalla have joined forces with the
Lynches from Chatsfield and others to build a new contract winemaking facility at Porongurup. Its first vintage
was 1999.

CURRENT RELEASE 1998   This is a very forward wine,
no doubt thanks to the oak influence. The colour is full-
blown yellow; the bouquet is rich, broad and already
developed, and offers some spice, honey and peach
aromas. It's dry, soft and generous in the mouth, and
should go with pan-fried sardines.

Quality	♥♥♥⦶
Value	★★⦑
Grapes	verdelho
Region	Great Southern, WA
Cellar	🍷 1
Alc./Vol.	13.5%
RRP	$24.50

Karri Grove Estate Verdelho

The south west of Western Australia still has impressive
stands of jarrah, red gum and karri trees, hence the
name.

CURRENT RELEASE 1999   This fresh young verdelho
sums up the appeal of this variety grown in southern
Western Australia. Appealing juicy fruit leads the way.
A tropical fruit salad of aromas surges from the glass,
sweetly seductive. The palate has succulent melon
flavour, which is straightforward and gulpable. The
finish is clean and dry. Try it with a tropically inclined
seafood platter.

Quality	♥♥♥♥
Value	★★★★
Grapes	verdelho
Region	Great Southern, WA
Cellar	🍷 1
Alc./Vol.	13.5%
RRP	$17.75

Katnook Estate Chardonnay

Katnook chardonnay is an unusual critter, a Coonawarra
chardonnay that rubs shoulders on bottle-shop shelves
with Australia's best. Does it belong in such august
company? We think yes. Maker Wayne Stehbens.

CURRENT RELEASE 1997   This is a tight young chardonnay that needs time to evolve. The nose has peachy
fruit and cashew richness framed in spicy oak. The palate
is restrained, long and elegant, with tangy citrus and
stone-fruit flavours and a dry lick of oak. There's a
certain austerity about it at the moment, which will
mellow with age. Good with salmon.

Quality	♥♥♥♥⦶
Value	★★★⦑
Grapes	chardonnay
Region	Coonawarra, SA
Cellar	🍷 5
Alc./Vol.	13.5%
RRP	$30.00

Katnook Estate Riesling

Quality	♟♟♟♟♟
Value	★★★★★
Grapes	riesling
Region	Coonawarra, SA
Cellar	▮ 5+
Alc./Vol.	13.0%
RRP	$16.45

Although riesling isn't Coonawarra's most famous product, it can be very fine. Only a handful persevere with it these days.

CURRENT RELEASE 1998 This green-tinged young white has the sort of nose that stops you in your tracks. It's simply exquisite – a delicious melange of flowers, passionfruit and citrus. In the mouth it's pretty classy too, with spice, tangy lime and green apple flavours. The signature lively acidity is there, which should ensure long life. Serve it with steamed coral trout with ginger, spring onion and coriander.

Katnook Estate Sauvignon Blanc

Quality	♟♟♟♟♟
Value	★★★⯪
Grapes	sauvignon blanc
Region	Coonawarra, SA
Cellar	▮ 3
Alc./Vol.	15.0%
RRP	$26.30

Katnook have never been backward in charging big bucks for their sauvignon blanc. It's one of the country's best, though. Recent vintages have had more depth and complexity than previously. Maker Wayne Stehbens.

CURRENT RELEASE 1998 Strong sauvignon elements of green leaf, gooseberry and citrus on the nose reach a degree of richness and concentration that is rare in the breed. The palate has tropical fruit flavour allied with surprising depth and weight, with a long clean finish. A good match for little goat's cheese and tomato pastries with a rocket salad.

Kim Crawford Marlborough Sauvignon Blanc

Quality	♟♟♟♟♟
Value	★★★★⯪
Grapes	sauvignon blanc
Region	Marlborough, NZ
Cellar	▮ 2
Alc./Vol.	13.0%
RRP	$18.50

Australia (and the world) is being flooded with New Zealand sauvignon blanc. Not all of it is of the highest standard, but the good 'uns capture the absolute essence of the variety like no one else.

CURRENT RELEASE 1998 Marlborough sauvignon at its best. A pale straw-coloured wine with some depth. The nose is herbaceous, and it also has richer melon and fleshy green fruit aromas. The palate has appealing full-ness, with tropical fruit and gooseberry flavours leading to acidity on the finish, which is clean and tangy, but not harsh. Try it with green-lip mussels.

Knappstein Riesling

The Knappstein name has been linked with riesling from Clare for decades. Under Andrew Hardy's tutelage, the tradition continues.

CURRENT RELEASE 1998 The very essence of Australian regional style, this has a classic Clare Valley riesling nose of zesty lime, floral talc and cinnamon–spice. In the mouth it has good body and intensity with a lively citrus flavour, tangy acidity and a long signature. Stands up well to vegetable pakoras.

Quality	♟♟♟♟♟
Value	★★★★⯪
Grapes	riesling
Region	Clare Valley, SA
Cellar	➨ 1–5+
Alc./Vol.	12.5%
RRP	$17.50

Kulkunbulla Nullarbor Chardonnay

It's amazing how many Australians don't know what Nullarbor means. Give you a clue: it's not Aboriginal and it has something to do with this being an unwooded style.

CURRENT RELEASE 1998 This is a light-bodied but remarkably unctuous wine considering the light alcohol strength. The fig-like aroma shows some early development, and while the palate lacks structure and is slightly mawkish, it has good immediate flavour of peach and apricot. Don't chill it for too long, then serve it with vegetable terrines.

Quality	♟♟♟
Value	★★⯪
Grapes	chardonnay
Region	Hunter Valley, NSW
Cellar	▮ 1
Alc./Vol.	12.0%
RRP	$17.70

Kulkunbulla Semillon

Kulkunbulla is a syndicate of investors who bought a section of the old Brokenback vineyard on Broke Road, Polkolbin. The major bits of Brokenback are owned by Tyrrell's and Rothbury.

CURRENT RELEASE 1998 This is a very delicate, low-alcohol classic Hunter Valley style of semillon, made without wood. The aromas are of fresh lemon juice and dry grass, typical Hunter semillon, with a whiff of free sulfur. The palate is delicate and perhaps slightly low in the acid department, but seems destined to cellar well. Try it with sushi.

Quality	♟♟♟⯪
Value	★★⯪
Grapes	semillon
Region	Hunter Valley, NSW
Cellar	▮ 6+
Alc./Vol.	10.5%
RRP	$21.60

Kulkunbulla The Brokenback

Quality	♈♈♈♈⸗
Value	★★★⸗
Grapes	chardonnay
Region	Hunter Valley, NSW
Cellar	⬥ 4
Alc./Vol.	12.5%
RRP	$33.45

Kulkunbulla is headed by Gavin Lennard and its first vintage was 1997. Maker David Lowe (contract).

CURRENT RELEASE 1998   A delicious chardonnay of finesse and style. Smoky and toasty oak characters are apparent in the aroma together with some sur-lie and melon fruit. The oak needs a few months to better integrate. The fruit is refined and restrained – not the opulent Hunter genre at all. The wine has plenty of 'legs' in the glass and viscosity on the palate, and one glass leads to another. Try it with crab cakes.

Lamonts Frankland River Riesling

Quality	♈♈♈♈
Value	★★★★
Grapes	riesling
Region	Frankland River, WA
Cellar	⬥ 4+
Alc./Vol.	12.8%
RRP	$14.00 (cellar door)

Lamonts is in the hot Swan Valley, but winemaker Mark Warren sensibly sources riesling grapes from the Frankland River area in the cooler south-west of Western Australia.

CURRENT RELEASE 1997   Age has conferred a deep yellow colour and toasty bottle-matured complexity on this riesling. There are minerally characters as well. It retains its lightness, is dry and finely balanced, and drinks very nicely now, with oysters mornay.

Quality	♈♈♈⸗
Value	★★★⸗
Grapes	riesling
Region	Frankland River, WA
Cellar	⬥ 3
Alc./Vol.	13.0%
RRP	$14.00 (cellar door)

CURRENT RELEASE 1998   This is a broad, flavoursome style with some sweetness on the palate. It has a dusty, straw-like aroma that perhaps lacks some floral high notes. It's full and broad and quite commercial in its appeal. Team it with a scallop and mango feuilleté.

Lark Hill Semillon Sauvignon Blanc

The Canberra region has put on a growth spurt lately, what with BRL Hardy and others planting mega-vineyards. Maker Sue Carpenter.

CURRENT RELEASE 1997 This is getting on in years for an SSB, but seems to be ageing slowly. It continues to drink well and retain freshness. Fragrant floral and asparagus-like aromas; softer, richer palate than usual for this style – it makes an impact. There's plenty of acid and a little astringency on the long finish. Try it with chicken and grapes in verjuice.

Quality	ㅇㅇㅇ
Value	★★★
Grapes	semillon; sauvignon blanc
Region	Canberra Region, NSW
Cellar	1
Alc./Vol.	12.0%
RRP	$17.00 (cellar door)

Leasingham Bin 7 Riesling

Leasingham has been through a renaissance in recent times, thanks in no small part to chief winemaker Richard Rowe. He recently quit and joined a new Clare district venture called Kirribilly.

CURRENT RELEASE 1998 This is one of the most consistent, value rieslings of the area. It has a pristine lime-juice aroma with a garnish of green herbs. In the mouth, it has a very juicy feel with a little sweetness well balanced by acid, giving it a frisky freshness. Light, lively, delicious. Serve with Pekinese wontons.

Quality	ㅇㅇㅇㅇ
Value	★★★★★
Grapes	riesling
Region	Clare Valley, SA
Cellar	5
Alc./Vol.	12.0%
RRP	$15.00 $

Leasingham Classic Clare Riesling

Leasingham is one of the great producers of Clare riesling with a long and distinguished past. The Classic is usually released with some bottle-age, so you may have to wait a while for the '98.

CURRENT RELEASE 1998 This is a great riesling! It's blessed with a stunning depth of fruit and seems destined for a long life. The aromas are of wild flowers and dry straw, and the palate flavours are fluent and seamless. The purity of fruit is very exciting. Serve it with King George whiting.

Quality	ㅇㅇㅇㅇㅇ
Value	★★★★★
Grapes	riesling
Region	Clare Valley, SA
Cellar	10
Alc./Vol.	12.5%
RRP	$22.00 $

Leconfield Chardonnay

Quality	♟♟♟
Value	★★★
Grapes	chardonnay
Region	Coonawarra, SA
Cellar	▮ 5
Alc./Vol.	13.5%
RRP	$18.00 Ⓢ

Ralph Fowler has left for greener pastures not too far from Coonawarra at Mount Benson. He will be a loss for the burgeoning Hamilton group.

CURRENT RELEASE 1998 There's plenty of colour – it's medium–full yellow – but the wine is delicate, fruit-driven and fresh. It's very lightly oaked, and smells of raw cashew nuts and honeydew melon. The weight is light to medium, and it's just a little simplistic. Could be better at one to two years old. Yabbies would be good here.

Leconfield Old Vines Riesling

Quality	♟♟♟♟
Value	★★★★
Grapes	riesling
Region	Coonawarra, SA
Cellar	▮ 5
Alc./Vol.	11.5%
RRP	$17.70

Are 'old vines' a marketing aid for riesling now? Well, why not? – assuming they produce a superior wine to the rest of the vineyard.

CURRENT RELEASE 1998 This is a rich, soft style without very intense varietal character. The aromas are of straw and dry grass, and there's a powder-puff, essency character on the palate. It's starting to build toastiness. The palate is very soft, and while it lacks a little riesling cut, it has richness. A very good companion to pan-fried flounder.

Leeuwin Estate Art Series Chardonnay

The '95 won last year's Penguin Best White Wine and Best Chardonnay awards. The '96 is right on target, and the painting on the label, by John Perceval, is one of the best ever. An Aussie icon, and despite all temptation, the price was only raised by 10 per cent. We give it five stars for value as an extended index finger to Petaluma and Penfolds.

Previous outstanding vintages: '80, '81, '82, '83, '85, '87, '89, '90, '92, '93, '95

CURRENT RELEASE 1996 A thrilling, ultra-distinctive Aussie chardonnay! It's a powerhouse of concentration, and they get away with an amazing amount of oak because the fruit is so powerful – it just soaks it all up. The colour is medium–deep yellow, and it smells of roasted nuts, vanilla and honey with an almond/marzipan edge. Like a cigar-chomping banker, it's big, rich and showy – but in this case, it's more than just front. It really delivers, with an almost endless follow-through. Drink with lobster thermidor.

Quality	♥♥♥♥♥
Value	★★★★★
Grapes	chardonnay
Region	Margaret River, WA
Cellar	6
Alc./Vol.	14.5%
RRP	$74.00

Leeuwin Estate Art Series Sauvignon Blanc

A $30 sauvignon blanc? It had to happen first in Margaret River! At least the wine is A1. It's hard to quibble about price when the wine is truly excellent. Maker Bob Cartwright.

CURRENT RELEASE 1998 This is beautiful sauvignon blanc! Typically pale in shade, it has a lifted, aromatic nose showing passionfruit, gooseberry, honey and tropical fruits. It's quite complex, and there's an extra layer provided by a suggestion of wood. The palate is quite delicate and is superbly flavoured, with a long, warm, dry aftertaste. Great with warm goat's cheese tartlets.

Quality	♥♥♥♥♥
Value	★★★★
Grapes	sauvignon blanc
Region	Margaret River, WA
Cellar	3
Alc./Vol.	13.5%
RRP	$30.00

Leeuwin Prelude Chardonnay

Quality	🍷🍷🍷🍷
Value	★★★½
Grapes	chardonnay
Region	Margaret River, WA
Cellar	🍾 4
Alc./Vol.	13.5%
RRP	$29.50

As the name suggests, this is released earlier than the Art Series (two years, in fact) and has a lot less wood influence. Interesting they drop the word 'Estate' from the Prelude wines: does this mean some of the grapes are bought in?

CURRENT RELEASE 1998 This is a very pretty wine with a pungent passionfruit/grapefruit character, which is unusual and distinctive; it's slightly reminiscent of sauvignon blanc. Oak makes a minor contribution. There are cashew and caramel nuances, and it's all about immediate palate, not persistence. Try sautéed marron tails.

Lenswood Vineyards Chardonnay

Quality	🍷🍷🍷🍷🍷
Value	★★★★½
Grapes	chardonnay
Region	Adelaide Hills, SA
Cellar	🍾 4+
Alc./Vol.	14.0%
RRP	$33.00

Tim Knappstein sold his name along with his winery when he moved from Clare to the Adelaide Hills. Hence this wine doesn't carry his name, except the initials TK.

Previous outstanding vintages: '96

CURRENT RELEASE 1997 Yet more evidence that the Adelaide Hills is where it's all happening with chardonnay. This is a beautiful wine, full of creamy, buttery, peach and tangy citrus flavours. Hints of cashew nuts too, but nothing sticks out: in other words, it's nicely balanced. The acidity seems quite high, lending a welcome friskiness to the palate. Great with crayfish.

Lenswood Vineyards Sauvignon Blanc

Quality	🍷🍷🍷🍷🍷
Value	★★★★½
Grapes	sauvignon blanc
Region	Adelaide Hills, SA
Cellar	🍾 3
Alc./Vol.	13.0%
RRP	$23.80

The Knappsteins have 22 hectares planted at Lenswood, which has been officially registered as a sub-region of the Adelaide Hills. The largest share is sauvignon blanc, which is well suited to the site.

Previous outstanding vintages: '97

CURRENT RELEASE 1998 A very refined style of sauvignon, which has tropical fruit, gooseberry and estery aromas as distinct from the less desirable capsicum and asparagus. It's subtle, rather than pungent, the flavours flowing softly along the tongue with graceful harmony and persistence. Delicious with fresh oysters.

Lenswood Vineyards Semillon

Tim and Annie Knappstein make their wines at Nepenthe. The district has very few actual working wineries because of environment protection laws.

CURRENT RELEASE 1997   Now we're cooking with gas! This is a big improvement on the excessively pungent early attempts. It's lightly herbal and tastes ripe, as opposed to green and jungle-y. It's fine, soft, fruity and rounded, although the creamy barrel-ferment and lemon/citrus flavours are intense. It's a seamless, gentle wine. It would partner green salad, tomato and bocconcini very nicely.

Quality	♟♟♟♟♟
Value	★★★★⯪
Grapes	semillon
Region	Adelaide Hills, SA
Cellar	▮ 6
Alc./Vol.	13.0%
RRP	$23.80

Lenton Brae Chardonnay

Hello – here's another impressive Margaret River chardonnay that's making a statement. The winery is run by Bruce Tomlinson, outspoken ringleader of the Independent Wineries Association. Maker Ed Tomlinson.

CURRENT RELEASE 1998   Typical of the region, this is a big, strong wine. Caramel and butterscotch dominate the bouquet, and citrusy fruit is evident beneath the strong barrel, lees and malolactic flavours. It could use a few more months in the bottle to harmonise fully, but it's already an excellent drink. Serve with sautéed Western Australian marron.

Quality	♟♟♟♟⯪
Value	★★★★
Grapes	chardonnay
Region	Margaret River, WA
Cellar	▮ 4+
Alc./Vol.	13.5%
RRP	$24.00

Lenton Brae Semillon Sauvignon Blanc

Quality	♛♛♛♛
Value	★★★★
Grapes	semillon; sauvignon blanc
Region	Margaret River, WA
Cellar	🍾 2
Alc./Vol.	14.0%
RRP	$17.00

This shotgun marriage of two sympathetic grape varieties plays especially nice tunes at Margaret River. Maker Ed Tomlinson.

CURRENT RELEASE 1998   The concentrated fruit typical of the district is evident here. Low yields are the key. It has fragrant gooseberry/grassy varietal aromas and builds a honey note in the mouth. There's a strong impression of sweetness, which may be partly due to alcohol and concentrated fruit. Quite rich and full in the mouth. Yum with dressed bocconcini, tomato and basil.

Leo Buring Clare Valley Riesling

Quality	♛♛♛♛
Value	★★★★★
Grapes	riesling
Region	Clare Valley, SA
Cellar	🍾 5+
Alc./Vol.	11.5%
RRP	$12.00 Ⓢ

This is one of the best value-for-money whites in the country, generally retailing at $10. Riesling itself is desirably unfashionable: that makes for a good quality–price equation. Maker Geoff Henriks.

CURRENT RELEASE 1998   A fine, delicate, easy-drinking style which will repay moderate cellaring. The aromas are delicately flowery and estery; the taste is youthful and fairly straightforward, but it also has satisfying fullness and richness. Tops when served with any kind of shellfish.

Leo Buring Clare Valley Semillon

Quality	♛♛♛♛♛
Value	★★★★★
Grapes	semillon
Region	Clare Valley, SA
Cellar	🍾 5+
Alc./Vol.	12.0%
RRP	$11.60 Ⓢ

The number of superb semillons coming out of Clare is on the increase. This is one, and it's also keenly priced. Maker Geoff Henriks and team.

CURRENT RELEASE 1998   An understated style which is adaptable with food. The colour is a glowing light yellow–green; the nose displays delicate lemon fruit. It's refined and dry, without being austere: a great food style. Seamless and beautifully poised, it's easy to drink more than one glass and would cellar well. Try with antipasto.

Leo Buring Leonay Eden Valley Riesling

Since the 1950s, Leo Buring has been the standard-bearer for Australian riesling. Today, there are two Leonays released with some bottle-age: one from Water-vale, the other from Eden Valley. Maker Geoff Henriks. CURRENT RELEASE 1994 Time has allowed a delight-ful toasty, citrus/floral bouquet of great allure to develop. There's a hint of earthiness, and it's very complex. The palate retains its finesse and will continue to do so with further age. It finishes dry, but not austere. Great with spanner crab omelette.

Quality	♥♥♥♥◗
Value	★★★★◗
Grapes	riesling
Region	Eden Valley, SA
Cellar	▮ 6+
Alc./Vol.	12.5%
RRP	$23.00 Ⓢ

CURRENT RELEASE 1995 Not as fine as the best vintages of this marque, the '95 has some earthy hints amid the toastiness and there are stone-fruit and lime nuances. Bottle-age has filled it out and given the wine much of its character. The palate has lemony flavours and a herbal aftertaste. It could go very well with pasta and pipis.

Quality	♥♥♥♥
Value	★★★◗
Grapes	riesling
Region	Eden Valley, SA
Cellar	▮ 5
Alc./Vol.	11.5%
RRP	$28.00 Ⓢ

Lillydale Vineyards Sauvignon Blanc

The name of the town at the entrance to the Yarra Valley is Lilydale, with one 'l'. This vineyard was given two, to short-circuit any controversy. It's owned by McWilliams these days.
CURRENT RELEASE 1998 This is a good honest sau-vignon that smells and tastes as it should. This, unfor-tunately, is rare for Australian SB. Delicate gooseberry aroma with a high note of green capsicum. The palate has an appealing blend of riper and greener varietal fla-vours, good balance and a crisp, tangy finish. Goes great guns with raw oysters.

Quality	♥♥♥♥
Value	★★★★
Grapes	sauvignon blanc
Region	Yarra Valley, Vic.
Cellar	▮ 2
Alc./Vol.	12.5%
RRP	$18.00 Ⓢ

Lillypilly Semillon

Quality	♟♟♟
Value	★★★⟅
Grapes	semillon
Region	Riverina, NSW
Cellar	▮ 2
Alc./Vol.	13.2%
RRP	$14.30 Ⓢ

The winemaker, Robbie Fiumara, duxed the wine science course at Charles Sturt Uni – née Riverina College. He beavers away producing remarkably good wines in an unfashionable area.

CURRENT RELEASE 1998 A very unusual semillon, but a perfectly good wine. The aromas remind of candied fruits, with plenty of sweet-smelling esters. There's a trace of sweetness on the palate, and this is countered by fresh acid. It's a straightforward wine with good weight and texture. Food: scallops with lime juice and soy sauce.

Lindemans Bin 65 Chardonnay

Quality	♟♟♟
Value	★★★★
Grapes	chardonnay
Region	various
Cellar	▮ 2
Alc./Vol.	13.0%
RRP	$9.70 Ⓢ

The '98 was last year's Penguin Wine of the Year, and this wine continues to be a benchmark for large-volume (circa 1.5 million dozen), affordable, quaffing white wine. Maker Phillip John and team.

CURRENT RELEASE 1999 This style is typified by clean, ripe fruit and remarkable softness on the palate. While not especially varietal – there's an unusual spicy, oily character – it has good intensity and balance. It doesn't stand out like the '98 did at this age, but it maintains the impeccable drinkability of the marque. Try it with a prawn cocktail.

Lindemans Hunter Valley Reserve Chardonnay

Quality	♟♟♟
Value	★★⟅
Grapes	chardonnay
Region	Hunter Valley, NSW
Cellar	▮ 1
Alc./Vol.	12.5%
RRP	$22.00

This is the *numero uno* from Lindemans Ben Ean winery. Its bin number is Bin 8880, which helps you identify it from other wines made in the same vintage.

CURRENT RELEASE 1996 An extra year of bottle-age has conferred a deep yellow colour, and the bottle-age character combines with strong oak to give a dominant toasty, sawdusty bouquet. The profile is lean and narrow and the wood flavour continues throughout. For lumber lovers. Try it with chargrilled prawns.

Lindemans Hunter Valley Semillon

This is Bin 9255. The final 55 signifies the first-released semillon of the vintage, which distinguishes it from others when more than one has been made. Maker Pat Auld.

Previous outstanding vintages: '65, '68, '70, '79, '80, '86, '87, '91, '93, '94, '95

CURRENT RELEASE 1996   A restrained, shy style which needs to be coaxed out of the shell. The aromas are straw, grassy green herbs and lemon sherbet, with a dusty overtone. The palate has zesty acid and captivating fruit, but seems a trifle short. It should repay some cellaring. Suits crab timbales if you drink it now.

Quality	♟♟♟♟
Value	★★★r
Grapes	semillon
Region	Hunter Valley, NSW
Cellar	🍷 6+
Alc./Vol.	11.0%
RRP	$18.90 Ⓢ

Lindemans Limestone Coast Chardonnay

The Limestone Coast is a new viticultural zone that covers the south-east of South Australia. It takes in Coonawarra, Padthaway, Wrattonbully and the new coastal areas of Robe and Mt Benson.

CURRENT RELEASE 1998   They grow a lot of softwood timber plantations down that way, and the wine is like the revenge of the forests: it's dominated by burnt-wood characters. Caramel/toast singed-oak aromas pervade both nose and palate. The big finish is quite astringent, with alcohol warmth and wood again playing a lead role. Hard to see how this will develop, but you could drink it now with charred barbecue pork sausages.

Quality	♟♟♟
Value	★★★
Grapes	chardonnay
Region	Limestone Coast, SA
Cellar	🍷 2
Alc./Vol.	13.5%
RRP	$11.30 Ⓢ

Lindemans Padthaway Chardonnay

Quality	♟♟♟♟
Value	★★★★
Grapes	chardonnay
Region	Padthaway, SA
Cellar	🍷 3
Alc./Vol.	13.5%
RRP	$15.00 Ⓢ

We seem to remark every year that the oak is being used more and more sparingly. It's one of the best-value chardonnays on the market. Maker Greg Clayfield and team.
Previous outstanding vintages: '96, '97
CURRENT RELEASE 1998   Clean, inviting aromas of pineapple, iced pastries and other confections greet the nose. In the mouth it's fine and fruit-driven with delicacy and restrained oak. Trim, taut and terrific. History shows they also age well, gaining richness and weight, so if that's how you like 'em, stash it away for a couple of years. Right now it goes with braised calamari.

Lowe Unwooded Semillon

Quality	♟♟♟♟
Value	★★★⯪
Grapes	semillon
Region	Hunter Valley, NSW
Cellar	🍷 7+
Alc./Vol.	11.0%
RRP	$17.55

Labelling semillon 'unwooded' is a novel idea – most semillon *is* unwooded. Perhaps they're hoping to hitch a less-trendy grape to the relentless unwooded chardonnay juggernaut. From 70-year-old vines on sandy flats at Rothvale.
CURRENT RELEASE 1998   Good wine! The classic Hunter semillon aroma of Sunlight soap is there – a sort of lemony, waxy character which is very appealing. It's classically dry, and there are straw overtones too. It avoids the green/herbaceous notes you can find in some regions. There's a little grip to the finish and it would team well with pan-fried mullet with garlic and parsley.

Madfish Premium Dry White

Quality	♟♟♟♟
Value	★★★
Grapes	chardonnay; semillon; sauvignon blanc
Region	Great Southern, WA
Cellar	🍷 2
Alc./Vol.	13.5%
RRP	$18.90

The Madfish wines (now without the Bay in the name) are the second string of the illustrious Howard Park. The Aboriginal design on the label is an impressive work of art.
CURRENT RELEASE 1998   Clean as a whistle and easy to like, Madfish white has peach and melon aromas with a hint of green pea and herbaceousness. The palate has soft, succulent fruit balanced by quite tart acidity. A good wine for some grilled fish, mad or otherwise.

Maglieri Chardonnay

This McLaren Vale winery is the newest edition to the Mildara Blass portfolio (at the time of publication). Long-term winemaker John Loxton remains at the helm. CURRENT RELEASE 1998 Work has gone into improving the chardonnay at Maglieri, if this is anything to go by. It's easy to drink with attractive stone-fruit and lime aromas, and a little praline-like complexity. Dusty oak sits in the background, and it tastes smooth and long. Try it with quick-fried calamari and Chinese vegetables.

Quality	TTTT
Value	★★★★⭑
Grapes	chardonnay
Region	McLaren Vale, SA
Cellar	🍷 2
Alc./Vol.	13.5%
RRP	$ 14.00

Maglieri Semillon

Semillon of good quality can be found in a number of South Australian regions these days. This one comes from McLaren Vale. Maker John Loxton. CURRENT RELEASE 1998 There's an almost chardonnay-like feel to this semillon due to its reserved varietal character, subtle nutty barrel influence and smoothness. Aromas and flavours suggest citrus, and it has a nice tang at the end. Try it with garlic prawns.

Quality	TTTT
Value	★★★
Grapes	semillon
Region	McLaren Vale, SA
Cellar	🍷 2
Alc./Vol.	12.5%
RRP	$15.00

Main Ridge Chardonnay

In the hands of makers like Nat White at Main Ridge, Mornington Peninsula chardonnay becomes a very fine wine capable of ageing well. CURRENT RELEASE 1998 The complex style of Main Ridge chardonnay finds great expression in this latest effort. The nose has restrained, fragrant stone-fruit, muesli and nutty aromas. The palate has a nutty, rather French, character with subtle fruit, perfectly integrated oak, a touch of caramel and a long, chalky-dry finish. A rather lovely chardonnay to linger over with something like salmon.

Quality	TTTTT
Value	★★★★
Grapes	chardonnay
Region	Mornington Peninsula, Vic.
Cellar	⬤ 1–5
Alc./Vol.	13.0%
RRP	$38.00

Maritime Estate Pinot Grigio

Quality	ΨΨΨΨ
Value	★★★⸜
Grapes	pinot grigio
Region	Mornington Peninsula, Vic.
Cellar	⭃ 2
Alc./Vol.	13.9%
RRP	$18.00

On the Mornington Peninsula pinot grigio (or pinot gris, depending on your sympathies) has a lot of supporters. Whether or not it will win the hearts and minds of consumers is a moot point. Makers Kathleen Quealy and Kevin McCarthy.

CURRENT RELEASE 1998 An exotic wine with the savoury 'foreign' varietal character of pinot grigio that might attract the A.B.C. (anything but chardonnay) drinkers. The nose has hazelnutty touches and a whiff of tropical fruit. The flavour follows the line of the nose with a hint of spice as well. It's smooth, typically unctuous, and dry. Try it with garlic prawns.

Martindale Hall Riesling

Quality	ΨΨΨΨ
Value	★★★★
Grapes	riesling
Region	Clare Valley, SA
Cellar	⭃ 4
Alc./Vol.	12.0%
RRP	$21.00

Such a tewwibly awistocwatic name for a Clare Valley wiesling, wot? Actually Martindale Hall is a lovely old mansion in the district. This is one of Andrew Garrett's new labels.

CURRENT RELEASE 1998 Delicate florals and a touch of lime juice cordial meet the nose here. The palate is pungent and full with clean lime flavours, a steely backbone underneath, and a dry, tingly finish. Clare riesling without the austerity of some. Drinks well young: try it with crab cakes.

Martindale Hall Sauvignon Blanc

Quality	ΨΨΨΨ
Value	★★★★
Grapes	sauvignon blanc
Region	Clare Valley, SA
Cellar	⭃ 2
Alc./Vol.	13.0%
RRP	$21.00

Andrew Garrett's Martindale Hall wines are packaged in gimmicky bottles that are hard to take seriously, but these are serious wines with sharp varietal definition.

CURRENT RELEASE 1998 Very tight herbaceous aromas lead the way here, but there's also a touch of fruit salad and passionfruit about it. In the mouth there's juicy fruit flavour which is kept lively and sharp by crisp, tangy acidity. A good match for calamari with coriander and Thai flavourings.

McLarens on the Lake Colombard Semillon Chardonnay

McLarens on the Lake is a tourist-oriented winery complex set up by Andrew Garrett at McLaren Vale. This low-priced range makes no claim to regionality.
CURRENT RELEASE 1998   This is a very simple white which won't exactly thrill you to pieces. The nose is grapey with some citrus fragrance, and the palate is lightish with a herbal touch to that grape and citrus flavour. It finishes crisp. A fish-and-chips wine.

Quality	♀♀♀
Value	★★★
Grapes	colombard; semillon; chardonnay
Region	not stated
Cellar	▮ 1
Alc./Vol.	11.5%
RRP	$12.40

McWilliams Barwang Chardonnay

Barwang is perhaps better known for its well-balanced flavoursome reds than its chardonnay, which is a lighter alternative to the full-blown Aussie style. Maker Jim Brayne.
CURRENT RELEASE 1997   A rather shy chardonnay with direct peachy varietal aromas and a hint of nuttiness. The palate is clean and subtle, without great power but pleasant enough in the more elegant mould. It finishes soft and clean. No complaints here, but it would be nice to see a bit more complexity and oomph. Try it with a salad of smoked eel.

Quality	♀♀♀♀
Value	★★★
Grapes	chardonnay
Region	Hilltops, NSW
Cellar	▮ 2
Alc./Vol.	13.5%
RRP	$16.00

McWilliams Hanwood Chardonnay

Hanwood Chardonnay is a reasonably priced wine that illustrates what's possible with the economies of scale available in the Riverina. Maker Jim Brayne.
CURRENT RELEASE 1998   Fruit dominates here, as it should in a wine intended for unfussed early consumption. It has melon, peach, and a hint of fruit salad on the nose, and direct, soft fruit in the mouth. Quite high alcohol gives it smoothness, and a mere whisper of oak gives it a nutty seasoning. Try it with yaki soba.

Quality	♀♀♀♀
Value	★★★★⊦
Grapes	chardonnay
Region	Riverina, NSW
Cellar	▮ 1
Alc./Vol.	14.0%
RRP	$10.50 Ⓢ

McWilliams Hanwood Verdelho

Quality	♥♥♥♪
Value	★★★⊦
Grapes	verdelho
Region	Riverina, NSW
Cellar	▮ 1
Alc./Vol.	13.5%
RRP	$10.00 ⑤

Verdelho is a grape of the Portuguese island of Madeira where it makes fantastic fortified wine, capable of long cask-ageing. In Australia it's usually made into simple fruity whites like this.

CURRENT RELEASE 1998   This is a pale quaffer with a typically varietal nose that's soft and grapey. There's a hint of melon on the soft palate, and a whisper of residual sweetness emphasises that juicy freshness. The finish is dry.

McWilliams Mount Pleasant Elizabeth

Quality	♥♥♥♥♪
Value	★★★★★
Grapes	semillon
Region	Hunter Valley, NSW
Cellar	▮ 5
Alc./Vol.	10.5%
RRP	$15.00 ⑤

An Australian classic that often has the scribes in raptures. It might be the Hunter's best-known wine, and it gives a glimpse of how much these whites need age to fulfil their promise.

CURRENT RELEASE 1994   Like the authors, this wine is still fresh despite its age. It has an absolutely classical bouquet of lemon, honey and herbs. The palate is very dry and only just starting to build that delicious buttered-toast complexity of maturity. It signs off clean and dry. Will improve further in bottle. Drinks well with prawn cutlets.

Merricks Estate Chardonnay

Quality	♥♥♥♥
Value	★★★
Grapes	chardonnay
Region	Mornington Peninsula, Vic.
Cellar	➥ 1–3
Alc./Vol.	13.5%
RRP	$29.60

One of the longest-established Mornington Peninsula vineyards, Merricks Estate may be best known for one of the district's few shiraz reds. Chardonnay works well here too.

CURRENT RELEASE 1998   Oak dominates this young white at the moment. Stone-fruit and grapefruit aromas and a touch of buttery richness are in there as well, and they may further emerge with some time in bottle. The palate is strongly oak-influenced with subdued citrus flavours and a long toasty aftertaste. Try with soft cheeses.

Milburn Park Chardonnay

Large quantities of this type of early-developing, ripe, oak-influenced white wine emerge from the big Murray Valley wineries every year. They are a staple of thousands of Australian households.

CURRENT RELEASE 1998 This wine rarely wins any prizes for subtlety – big flavour is the main game. The '98 doesn't deviate from the formula. It's a forward peaches-and-cream style with some sweetish butter-toffee character, full body, and a serve of toasty oak, which adds a little astringency to the finish.

Quality	🍷🍷🍷½
Value	★★★
Grapes	chardonnay
Region	Murray Valley, Vic.
Cellar	🍾 1
Alc./Vol.	13.0%
RRP	$12.00

Miranda Golden Botrytis

Nearly all the makers in the Griffith area make a speciality of sweet botrytised wines these days. They've even coined a name for it: Riverina Gold. Miranda is consistently one of the best.

CURRENT RELEASE 1996 Looks like liquid gold. The bouquet is sweet and complex with honey, peach, apricot and marmalade aromas. It tastes very sweet and rich, but zippy acidity keeps it from cloying. The palate has an intense, lush texture and good depth. Serve it with orange syrup cake and cream.

Quality	🍷🍷🍷🍷🍷
Value	★★★★★
Grapes	semillon; riesling
Region	Riverina, NSW
Cellar	🍾 3
Alc./Vol.	10.5%
RRP	$19.00 (375 ml)

Miranda Mirrool Creek Chardonnay

The Miranda enterprise has put on a growth spurt in recent years with expansion to regions as far afield as the Barossa and Victoria's King Valley. Mirrool Creek remains a Riverina product.

CURRENT RELEASE 1998 This is everything an every-day crowd-pleaser should be. It's a bright, gold-coloured chardonnay with ripe peach and cashew on the nose, good depth, and smooth texture in the mouth. Drink it young, as it already shows some development in typical Riverina fashion. Try Chinese chicken-based stirfries.

Quality	🍷🍷🍷½
Value	★★★½
Grapes	chardonnay
Region	Riverina, NSW
Cellar	🍾 1
Alc./Vol.	13.0%
RRP	$9.00 (S)

Miranda Somerton Chardonnay

Quality	♟♟♟⸮
Value	★★★★
Grapes	chardonnay
Region	Riverina, NSW
Cellar	🍶 1
Alc./Vol.	13.0%
RRP	$7.00

If Miranda's Mirrool Creek range of wines seems very reasonably priced, check this out – it's seriously cheap. Riverina wines are a happy hunting ground if you're a Scrooge.

CURRENT RELEASE 1998   This is an uncomplicated white which doesn't skimp on flavour. Okay, so it doesn't have great refinement, but if you're on a tight budget and are after big peachy character of the mouth-filling type with soft acidity, try a bottle. A good match for spicy fried chicken.

Mitchell Growers Semillon

Quality	♟♟♟♟⸮
Value	★★★★★
Grapes	semillon; sauvignon blanc
Region	Clare Valley, SA
Cellar	🍶 5
Alc./Vol.	13.0%
RRP	$15.00

Andrew and Jane Mitchell are riesling experts, and they're also on a mission to lift the profile of Clare Valley semillon with these carefully made wines.

CURRENT RELEASE 1998   Attractive, understated varietal character leads the way on the nose with lemon, lanolin and dry grass aromas. There's also a well-modulated nutty touch of oak from barrel fermentation to add depth and subtle complexity. In the mouth it has clean, dry lemony flavour of medium intensity, again with that quiet whisper of oak. Try it with grilled yellowtail cutlets.

Mitchelton Blackwood Park Botrytis Riesling

Quality	♟♟♟♟⸮
Value	★★★★
Grapes	riesling
Region	Goulburn Valley, Vic.
Cellar	🍶 5
Alc./Vol.	12.0%
RRP	$13.50 (375 ml)

Is Michelton's riesling Victoria's best? Maybe it is, and when conditions are just right that erstwhile vineyard pest, botrytis cinerea, helps produce a very good sweet version.

CURRENT RELEASE 1998   Rarely do a wine label's notes describe a wine as well as this one. It has lime marmalade and ginger-spice on the nose, which is tight and not too luscious. The palate is far less syrupy than a lot of botrytis wines. It has marmalade and citrus riesling flavours of softness and controlled sweetness ahead of a firm, dry finish. If you're adventurous, serve this as a chilled aperitif.

Mitchelton Blackwood Park Riesling

Victoria's Goulburn Valley has had some quiet success with riesling over the years. Mitchelton consistently makes a good each-way bet – it drinks well young, and it ages nicely for a few years.

CURRENT RELEASE 1998   Lively lime, passionfruit and citrus peel aromas, and a dab of spice, make for an aromatic nose. The palate has spice and citrus flavours with a rather pleasant softness in the middle. The finish is crisp and tangy.

Quality	♟♟♟♟?
Value	★★★★†
Grapes	riesling
Region	Goulburn Valley, Vic.
Cellar	▮ 4
Alc./Vol.	12.5%
RRP	$14.80 Ⓢ

Mitchelton Goulburn Valley Marsanne

Mitchelton is the modern face of the Goulburn Valley; its neighbour Chateau Tahbilk is its tradition and its heart. They happily coexist alongside the Goulburn River, making wines of distinctive and individual character.

CURRENT RELEASE 1997   Winemaker Don Lewis has pulled out all stops to build complexity into this marsanne. It has charry, bacon-scented oak, nutty touches, and honeyed fig-like fruit. The palate has fig, stone-fruit and smoky oak flavours, good depth and a creamy–buttery aftertaste. Despite all that character, it's still fresh. Try it with Chinese chicken and almonds.

Quality	♟♟♟♟?
Value	★★★★★
Grapes	marsanne
Region	Goulburn Valley, Vic.
Cellar	▮ 2
Alc./Vol.	13.0%
RRP	$15.60

Mitchelton Victoria Chardonnay

The Mitchelton winemaking team, headed by Don Lewis, employs all the tricks of the trade to build complexity into this wine. In recent times it's been getting some well-deserved recognition, winning the top gold medal at the National Wine Show in Canberra.

CURRENT RELEASE 1997   Compared with the 1996 vintage, this is quite voluptuous. The nose has fig, almond candy and buttery, toasty oak aromas. In the mouth it's rich and densely fruited with deep fig and peach flavours, caramel notes, and good counterbalancing acidity. Roast a chicken to go with this.

Quality	♟♟♟♟?
Value	★★★★†
Grapes	chardonnay
Region	various, Vic.
Cellar	▮ 2
Alc./Vol.	14.0%
RRP	$23.85

Molly Morgan Joe's Block Semillon

Quality	♟♟♟⁊
Value	★★★
Grapes	semillon
Region	Hunter Valley, NSW
Cellar	▮ 5
Alc./Vol.	10.8%
RRP	$19.00

This vineyard recently changed hands. It's now owned by Sydney retailing identities Andrew and Hady Simon (ex-Camperdown Cellars) and John Baker (ex-Grapefellas of Epping).

CURRENT RELEASE 1998 A very delicate, restrained but well-made, young semillon. There are dried herb and straw aromas, and it's fresh and lemony in the mouth with a trace of spice. It's very light and should be served with crab canapés. It will build richness with age.

Moondah Brook Chardonnay

Quality	♟♟♟♟
Value	★★★★⁊
Grapes	chardonnay
Region	various, WA
Cellar	▮ 3
Alc./Vol.	13.5%
RRP	$16.00 Ⓢ

As Moondah Brook has moved from sourcing its grapes from the original vineyard at GinGin, north of Perth, to the cooler vineyards of WA's south, the wines have improved considerably.

CURRENT RELEASE 1998 This is a rather obvious style, which gives plenty of bang for your buck. The colour is rather pale, but the nose is substantial with rich melon, citrus and tropical fruit aromas and some well-integrated creamy lees and oak input. In the mouth it's a middleweight with a fruit-rich palate, some nutty oak and an elegant robe of crisp acidity. Try it alongside pasta with scallops.

Moondah Brook Maritime Dry White

Quality	♟♟♟
Value	★★★
Grapes	chenin blanc; verdelho & others
Region	Swan Valley, other WA
Cellar	▮ 1
Alc./Vol.	12.5%
RRP	$12.00

The smart packaging of this young thing makes you think of balmy breezes, the seaside, the surf, holidays, prawns on the barbie . . . oh well, back to work.

CURRENT RELEASE *non-vintage* A simple nose of juicy tropical aromas with herbaceous touches is typical of modern versions of the traditional Western Australian chenin–verdelho blend. The palate has the same soft fruity character with a green-leafy edge. Drink young with a shellfish salad.

Moorilla Estate Chardonnay

Moorilla's chardonnay is a distinctively different sort of chardonnay. In good years it has pristine fruit character of a purity that isn't common on the mainland.

CURRENT RELEASE 1998 This is a clean, pretty young wine that tingles and tantalises the palate. On the nose there's attractive melon fruit, and the light, lively palate is fruit-dominated despite 100 per cent barrel fermentation. That oak is nicely spicy, but very subdued. It's a deceptively fresh-tasting wine with high acidity, and should be a good keeper. Serve it with grilled flathead fillets with lemon butter.

Quality	🍷🍷🍷🍷
Value	★★★
Grapes	chardonnay
Region	Derwent Valley, Tas.
Cellar	1–5
Alc./Vol.	13.9%
RRP	$28.00

Moorooduc Estate Chardonnay

Richard McIntyre strives to find the secrets of producing the most complex chardonnay possible. To this end he now uses 100 per cent wild vineyard yeasts to ferment his Moorooduc wine in the Burgundian way. Results so far are promising.

CURRENT RELEASE 1997 Very complex chardonnay with a fine cool-climate personality. The nose has appealing grapefruit and nectarine aromas, and buttery oatmeal and cashew complexity against a background of subtle smoky oak. The palate is creamy in texture with a long, succulent aftertaste. Enjoy this with buttery salmon cutlets.

Quality	🍷🍷🍷🍷🍷
Value	★★★★★
Grapes	chardonnay
Region	Mornington Peninsula, Vic.
Cellar	4
Alc./Vol.	13.7%
RRP	$35.00

Mornington Vineyards Estate Chardonnay

Doctors abound among the ranks of the Mornington Peninsula winegrowers. Mornington Vineyards Estate is owned by softly-spoken Scottish-born medical man, Hugh Robinson.

CURRENT RELEASE 1997 In common with a lot of '97 Peninsula chardonnays, this has lots of ripe fruit character. The nose has peach and tropical fruit aromas dressed subtly in understated toasty oak. The palate is soft and harmonious with ripe fruit flavour and a caramelly touch. Good with scallop brochettes.

Quality	🍷🍷🍷🍷
Value	★★★★
Grapes	chardonnay
Region	Mornington Peninsula, Vic.
Cellar	2
Alc./Vol.	13.5%
RRP	$23.00

Mountadam Chardonnay

Quality	??????
Value	★★★
Grapes	chardonnay
Region	Eden Valley, SA
Cellar	2
Alc./Vol.	14.5%
RRP	$32.90

Mountadam have done a lot of pioneering work with chardonnay, including launching the first contemporary unoaked style. This oaked version is always hard to ignore because of its foursquare style.

CURRENT RELEASE 1997 A very 'worked' style again, although the last couple of vintages seem to have had a bit more fruit character than before. The nose has a lot going on with smoky, nutty, mealy and vegetal touches surrounding stone fruit. The palate is big, brawny and dry with oaky firmness and a rather warm finish. Serve with swordfish steaks.

Mount Avoca Rhapsody

Quality	??????
Value	★★★
Grapes	trebbiano; sauvignon blanc
Region	Pyrenees, Vic.
Cellar	2
Alc./Vol.	11.5%
RRP	$12.30

In Victoria's Pyrenees, red wines occupy centre-stage. The whites are a mixed bag, with a handful of very fine wines and some others that are good value, if not quite rhapsodic.

CURRENT RELEASE 1998 This has a rather understated nose with some herbal and herbaceous notes. The palate has green herb and citrus flavours, which are filled out with a soft touch of residual sweetness. The crisp finish keeps things lively. A pleasant young white without any pretensions to greatness. Try it with goat's cheese and prosciutto tarts.

Mount Avoca Sauvignon Blanc

Quality	??????
Value	★★★★
Grapes	sauvignon blanc
Region	Pyrenees, Vic.
Cellar	2
Alc./Vol.	13.0%
RRP	$17.70

The crisp, fresh whites of Mount Avoca provide a pleasant counterpoint in an area where red wines rule. Makers John Barry and son Matthew.

CURRENT RELEASE 1998 This is a very pale lively young thing with a tangy blackcurrant aroma and nettle-like herbaceousness. The palate has the same mouth-watering qualities, and it signs off with a zip of tingling acidity. A good wine for dim sum goodies.

Mount Avoca Trioss

Trioss must refer to the three grape varieties that make up this young white from the Barry family of Mount Avoca.

CURRENT RELEASE 1998 Another well-made, crisp young wine with the typically fresh feel of the Mount Avoca whites. The nose has fragrant lemon-scented aromas with pleasant herbaceousness. In the mouth the lemony flavour is light, tangy and appetising. A good aperitif served with some sushi.

Quality	♟♟♟♟
Value	★★★★
Grapes	sauvignon blanc; chardonnay; semillon
Region	Pyrenees, Vic.
Cellar	▮ 1
Alc./Vol.	12.5%
RRP	$12.30

Mount Horrocks Cordon Cut Riesling

Cordon cutting is a way of making sweet wines by cutting the fruit-bearing cane and leaving the bunches hanging on the vine for some time to shrivel. This concentrates grape sugar and flavouring elements by dehydration.

CURRENT RELEASE 1998 An interesting alternative to the many botrytised sweet whites. Varietal riesling aromas of lime and lemon have essency intensity. In the mouth it's sweet with luscious lime flavour, which is counterpointed by fresh, tingling acidity. A delight with fresh fruit salad and cream.

Quality	♟♟♟♟♟
Value	★★★
Grapes	riesling
Region	Clare Valley, SA
Cellar	▮ 3
Alc./Vol.	12.0%
RRP	$23.00 (375 ml)

Mount Langi Ghiran Pinot Grigio

Pinot gris (aka pinot grigio) is capable of being made into unctuous white wines of non-aromatic richness, which in some ways might offer an alternative to chardonnay. The variety is a recent arrival at Mount Langi Ghiran.

CURRENT RELEASE 1998 Pinot grigio will be an acquired taste for most Australians. When made into a dry wine, it's not driven by fruit-sweetness; rather it has a more savoury, nutty, creamy personality. Mount Langi Ghiran fits the bill with good depth and long flavour, and it's not overly oily like some. Rather like Italian pinot grigio, only better than most.

Quality	♟♟♟♟
Value	★★★★
Grapes	pinot grigio
Region	Grampians, Vic.
Cellar	▮ 2
Alc./Vol.	13.0%
RRP	$21.40

Mount Langi Ghiran Riesling

Quality	♟♟♟♟
Value	★★★★⸀
Grapes	riesling
Region	Grampians, Vic.
Cellar	▬ 5
Alc./Vol.	13.0%
RRP	$18.10

At Langi Ghiran the reds get the kudos, but winemaker Trevor Mast studied in Germany, so he should be pretty able when it comes to making riesling.

CURRENT RELEASE 1998 The colour is pale straw, and the nose has talcum powder, citrus, floral, and spicy aromas. The long palate has delicate dry lime flavour, and an underlying strength of firm acidity suggests good ageing potential. Try it with Vietnamese spring rolls with fresh green herbs.

Mount Riley Sauvignon Blanc

Quality	♟♟♟♟
Value	★★★
Grapes	sauvignon blanc
Region	Marlborough, NZ
Cellar	▬ 2
Alc./Vol.	13.5%
RRP	$16.00

The flood of New Zealand sauvignon blanc shows no sign of abating. Its vivacious personality has plenty of admirers on this side of the Tasman.

CURRENT RELEASE 1998 Piercing varietal aromas meet the nose: there's a grassy, green pea zip and some pine–passionfruit characters. It tastes of green fruit – tangy and wild – with a touch of juicy fruit-sweetness and a crisp finish. Serve it with a lightly dressed salad of green leaves with asparagus and shaved parmigiano.

Mount Tanglefoot King Valley Riesling

Quality	♟♟♟♟
Value	★★★
Grapes	riesling
Region	King Valley, Vic.
Cellar	▬ 3
Alc./Vol.	12.0%
RRP	$16.00

This is a Yarra Ridge brand reserved for little parcels of wine made from special fruit grown outside the Yarra Valley. The wordy back label gives an insight into how Yarra Ridge winemakers while away their time during vintage: 'Sitting on the verandah ... looking towards Mt Tanglefoot at sunset ... the occasional beer ...' You wonder where they got the time to make this wine!

CURRENT RELEASE 1998 Riesling is a magically aromatic grape variety. This is at the floral end of the spectrum with some underlying citrus. The palate is dry and direct with clean acidity. Those Yarra Ridge winemakers suggest drinking this 'with your finest seafood on a balcony with a view'. They ought to know.

Mount Trio Chardonnay

Mount Trio is in the south-west of Western Australia near Albany. Winemaker Gavin Berry makes chardonnay that is very much in the succulent regional style.

CURRENT RELEASE 1998 The nose has juicy passionfruit and melon aromas along with a pleasant leafy freshness. Fruit dominates the palate, which is fresh-tasting and easy to like. Acidity is in nice balance, and oak doesn't intrude on the soft drinkability. It would go nicely with Vietnamese spring rolls with mint, lettuce and nouc cham sauce.

Quality	🍷🍷🍷🍷
Value	★★★★★
Grapes	chardonnay
Region	Great Southern, WA
Cellar	1
Alc./Vol.	13.0%
RRP	$17.00

Murrindindi Chardonnay

Murrindindi chardonnay has a bit of a cult following for its lean-boned, complex personality. Given good vintage conditions, the wines are a bit fuller now than they used to be.

CURRENT RELEASE 1997 A bright straw-yellow wine with a stylish nose that brings together cool-climate finesse and subtle winemaking very nicely. There are aromas of sweet grapefruit and nectarine with butter, cream, nuts and classy oak. The palate is clean and crisp, smoothly textured but not big. Long flavour and a flinty dry finish make a very classy finale. Try it with gravlax of salmon.

Quality	🍷🍷🍷🍷🍷
Value	★★★★★
Grapes	chardonnay
Region	Murrindindi, Vic.
Cellar	5
Alc./Vol.	13.0%
RRP	$24.00

Nepenthe Chardonnay

The exciting newcomer in the Adelaide Hills is a major venture set up by Ed Tweddell, the big medicine man from Faulding's.

CURRENT RELEASE 1997 This has come along nicely since last year's review. It's a full yellow in hue, with a very complex bouquet featuring honey and butterscotch malolactic complexities. There are malty, tea-leafy and slightly sweaty aromas also, which remind us of Western Australia. Some vanilla from oak too. An impressive debut; it just needs more length. Great with barbecued tuna steaks.

Quality	🍷🍷🍷🍷½
Value	★★★★
Grapes	chardonnay
Region	Adelaide Hills, SA
Cellar	3
Alc./Vol.	14.0%
RRP	$26.00

Nepenthe Lenswood Semillon

Quality	TTTTT
Value	★★★★⋆
Grapes	semillon
Region	Adelaide Hills, SA
Cellar	🍾 4
Alc./Vol.	12.5%
RRP	$22.00

Nepenthe received a Penguin award for Best New Producer in last year's *Guide*. It's a very professional outfit, with the technically astute Peter Leske in charge of winemaking.

CURRENT RELEASE 1998 This is a very subtly wooded, beautifully made semillon with delicately nutty oak influence over lemony varietal fruit. In the mouth it's soft and rich, and has excellent texture and weight. The structure is more like chardonnay, but without the viscosity. It's a lovely wine, and drinks well now with pasta alla vongole.

Neudorf Moutere Chardonnay

Quality	TTTTⳆ
Value	★★★
Grapes	chardonnay
Region	Nelson, NZ
Cellar	🍾 5
Alc./Vol.	14.0%
RRP	$52.50

Neudorf means 'new town' in the lingo of the early German migrants who settled the nearby village in 1842. The Nelson district is on the warm end of the South Island.

Previous outstanding vintages: '91, '93, '96

CURRENT RELEASE 1997   This is a special-occasion wine. It's very complex, and has typical New Zealand tight structure and thrilling acidity. The colour is full yellow, and the nose offers butterscotch, oatmeal and toasted almond aromas. It's alive in the mouth, and the aftertaste is long and memorable. Serve it with grilled lobster.

Neudorf Sauvignon Blanc

Quality	TTTT
Value	★★★
Grapes	sauvignon blanc
Region	Nelson, NZ
Cellar	🍾 2
Alc./Vol.	13.5%
RRP	$24.50

The bottle is pretty snappy: it looks expensive and is bound to draw some looks. These days a wine has to look the part: quality-minded winemakers tend to use packaging to make a statement about the quality and care they take with their wine.

CURRENT RELEASE 1998   A deliciously frisky, sassy Kiwi sauvignon. It has excellent varietal fruit to smell and taste. It's a pungent, high-acid style that titillates the tastebuds. We could drink a lot of this: it's very more-ish. Try it with New Zealand mussels.

Ninth Island Chardonnay

This is an unwooded style, and in a good year it's a benchmark for the genre. The acid structure is more like a French chardonnay than an Australian. Maker Andrew Pirie and team.

Previous outstanding vintages: '97

CURRENT RELEASE 1998 Exuberant fruit and tangy acidity are the hallmarks. It's a light yellow shade, and the nose is simple but inviting: lifted passionfruit/tropical fruit. It leads into a light-bodied, refreshing taste with delicacy and mouth-watering acidity. Goes well with grilled Tassie scallops.

Quality	♟♟♟♟
Value	★★★⭑
Grapes	chardonnay
Region	North East Tas.
Cellar	▮ 2
Alc./Vol.	13.0%
RRP	$20.00

Ninth Island Riesling

Very cold-climate vino, here. It's a bracing style that shows off its Tasmanian origins. Maker Andrew Pirie.

CURRENT RELEASE 1998 A green–yellow colour leads into a fragrant, spicy, cool-edged intensity on the nose. There's a hint of sulfur, which will go away in time. It's fairly sweet in the mouth, soft and light-bodied. Chill well and serve with Tassie oysters.

Quality	♟♟♟
Value	★★⭑
Grapes	riesling
Region	Northern Tas.
Cellar	▮ 4+
Alc./Vol.	12.1%
RRP	$18.50

Ninth Island Sauvignon Blanc

Ninth Island is a real island off the coast of northern Tassie. There aren't any vines there, but it's visible from the hills of the Pipers area.

CURRENT RELEASE 1998 This is a pungent one, to polarise drinkers! It smells of composted leaves and tinned asparagus. It's light-bodied and plain, but has just enough varietal sauvignon zestiness to lift it out of the ordinary. It finishes clean and dry and is a satisfying drink with mussel soup.

Quality	♟♟♟?
Value	★★★
Grapes	sauvignon blanc
Region	Northern Tas.
Cellar	▮ 1
Alc./Vol.	12.1%
RRP	$18.50

Ninth Island Straits Dry White

Quality	♥♥♀
Value	★★★
Grapes	sauvignon blanc; semillon; pinot noir
Region	North East Tas.
Cellar	🍷 1
Alc./Vol.	11.5%
RRP	$20.00

This tends to be cold-shouldered in Oxford Street, because of the name. (Check it out, non-Sydneysiders!) **CURRENT RELEASE 1998** An unusual blend which will appeal to those who like acidic wines. The colour is light yellow and it smells of green capsicum, white pepper and salad greens. It's searingly acidic, and the overall impression is of unripe grapes. It has its fans, however, and freshly shucked oysters would suit it well.

Normans Chardonnay

Quality	♥♥♥♥
Value	★★★★ᖉ
Grapes	chardonnay
Region	various, SA
Cellar	🍷 3
Alc./Vol.	13.2%
RRP	$17.00 Ⓢ

The Norman conquest continues: Normans is buying up vineyards and minting new labels with gay abandon as it enters a bullish phase of its long existence. **CURRENT RELEASE 1998** This is a top-quality mid-priced chardonnay which will easily satisfy most drinkers. It's all about fruit, and offers grapefruit and other citrus scents with barely discernible oak. The mouth-feel is especially good: soft and oily. Overall impressions are of subtlety and balance. Goes well with stir-fried tofu and vegetables.

Normans Foundation Chardonnay

Quality	♥♥♥♀
Value	★★★★ᖉ
Grapes	chardonnay
Region	not stated
Cellar	🍷 1
Alc./Vol.	13.0%
RRP	$13.40 Ⓢ

After a somewhat sleepy past, Normans is now a go-ahead public company with a forward-thinking boss in managing director, Rob Byrne. **CURRENT RELEASE 1998** A fruit-style chardonnay, meaning there's little evidence of oak and it relies on straightforward grapey flavour. There's also a trace of residual sweetness. The aromas are of stalky, herbal fruit with perhaps a whisper of wood. The palate has appropriate depth of flavour for the modest price, and the aftertaste is clean and lingers well. Good with fish cakes.

Oakridge Chardonnay

Oakridge is a Yarra showplace these days after a successful 'float' a couple of years ago raised plenty of capital. Ambitious plans for the future should guarantee that we'll hear more of the name.

CURRENT RELEASE 1998   A pale wine with a rich nose full of nutty barrel influences and some banana-like fruit aromas. In the mouth it's soft and medium-bodied, with grapefruit and cashew flavours. Despite the obvious winemaking input it's not particularly complex, and has a rather angular structure ahead of a tangy finish.

Quality	♥♥♥
Value	★★★
Grapes	chardonnay
Region	Yarra Valley, Vic.
Cellar	🍷 2
Alc./Vol.	13.2%
RRP	$18.00

Old Station Vineyard Riesling

The old station in question is Watervale on the abandoned railway line that used to run through the Clare Valley. It's now a walking track that takes you past vineyards like this one.

CURRENT RELEASE 1998   This is a rather broad riesling which shows some development for a wine so young. The nose has regional/varietal lime and mineral aromas, which lack the 'cut' of the best. The palate is dry with good depth, but it lacks delicacy and is a tad short. Chill it well and serve it with a green curry.

Quality	♥♥♥
Value	★★★
Grapes	riesling
Region	Clare Valley, SA
Cellar	🍷 1
Alc./Vol.	12.0%
RRP	$15.45

Orlando Jacob's Creek Chardonnay

A well-known British television wine presenter gave a famous French winemaker a taste of this on her show. He spat it out with a grimace. It was a cheap shot; for the price of one bottle of his white Burgundy you'd get about 15 of Jacob's Creek.

CURRENT RELEASE 1998   Jacob's Creek Chardonnay shows how adept the winemakers at big Australian wineries are at making good wine for the budget buyer. This has attractive melon and peach on the nose and a mellow palate with the merest hint of sweetness to fill it out. The finish is clean and dry.

Quality	♥♥♥
Value	★★★★
Grapes	chardonnay
Region	various
Cellar	🍷 2
Alc./Vol.	13.0%
RRP	$10.00 Ⓢ

Orlando Russet Ridge Chardonnay

Quality 🍷🍷🍷½
Value ★★★
Grapes chardonnay
Region Coonawarra, SA
Cellar 2
Alc./Vol. 13.5%
RRP $17.00

Russet Ridge red came first, and in the manner of these brands a white wasn't far behind.

CURRENT RELEASE 1998 Slightly resinous oak leads the nose here with some tropical fruit aromas underneath. In the mouth it's the same, with oak tipping the balance away from the fruit component. The finish is dry and firm. Overall a reasonable commercial style, which works well with stir-fried vegetables and tofu.

Orlando Steingarten Riesling

Quality 🍷🍷🍷🍷½
Value ★★★½
Grapes riesling
Region Eden Valley, SA
Cellar 2–10
Alc./Vol. 13.0%
RRP $24.00

The Steingarten vineyard was planted on an inhospitable rocky ridge high above the Orlando winery in 1962. This harsh growing environment was an attempt to replicate conditions on the Mosel River in Germany. These days the Steingarten vineyard material is usually boosted with grapes from other high-country vineyards.

CURRENT RELEASE 1998 This is right in the austere style we've come to expect from recent Steingartens. The nose is very restrained with citrus and green apple aromas over a tight minerally core. The palate is sinewy, intense and dry with some spice and tart acidity on the finish. It's still immature and doesn't give much away. Cellaring is a must, then serve it with smoked trout.

Orlando St Helga Riesling

Quality 🍷🍷🍷🍷🍷
Value ★★★★★
Grapes riesling
Region Eden Valley, SA
Cellar 7+
Alc./Vol. 12.0%
RRP $16.00 (S)

The Gramps, original owners of Orlando, made great advances with riesling in the 1950s and '60s. The present regime keeps the torch burning bright.

CURRENT RELEASE 1998 This is a zesty young riesling with a pronounced floral fragrance which adds elegance to the classical spice and lime of Eden Valley grapes. The palate continues the refined feel with delicate flavour, which is dry and tangy. A traditionally steely backbone of acidity will ensure longevity. Riesling goes well with a lot of Asian flavours. Try lemon grass chicken with this one.

Orlando St Hilary Chardonnay

Padthaway chardonnay is one of Australia's success stories, which receives only a fraction of the fanfare of some trendier regions. But wine quality is consistently good and the value exemplary.

CURRENT RELEASE 1998 After a rather less-oaky '97, the wood seems more noticeable in this wine at the moment. Maybe it needs a little time to come together. Certainly under the nutty sweet oak there's fine peach and melon fruit and some complexity. Toasty oak and fine chardonnay fruit perfume the long finish nicely. Keep it for a year, see how it measures up, and open it with a supreme of chicken.

Quality	▼▼▼▼
Value	★★★★ᵏ
Grapes	chardonnay
Region	Padthaway, SA
Cellar	➨ 1–4
Alc./Vol.	13.5%
RRP	$19.50

Palliser Estate Riesling

Older fogeys will recall *The Pallisers* was a pommy TV soap of yesteryear. This Martinborough winery makes more appetising viewing.

CURRENT RELEASE 1998 A very minerally style, which has a pungent aroma of slatey and citrusy fruit that borders on the Germanic. The palate is lean and finishes dry, and the only problem is some harsh phenolics on the finish. It could go well with buttery pan-fried flounder.

Quality	▼▼▼⸮
Value	★★★
Grapes	riesling
Region	Martinborough, NZ
Cellar	▮ 5+
Alc./Vol.	13.0%
RRP	$19.00

Palliser Estate Sauvignon Blanc

Martinborough isn't as famous for this grape as Marlborough, probably because it's a much smaller region. But where in New Zealand does sauvignon blanc *not* do well? Maker Allan Johnson.

CURRENT RELEASE 1998 Mixed feelings about this. There are dusty aromas with exaggerated passionfruit notes, and the buttercup yellow colour shows forward development. The palate is full and round, quite atypical of the variety. It may reflect the warm growing conditions in 1998. There's some hardness on the finish. Try it with grilled snapper.

Quality	▼▼▼
Value	★★ᵏ
Grapes	sauvignon blanc
Region	Martinborough, NZ
Cellar	▮ 1
Alc./Vol.	13.5%
RRP	$23.00

Paracombe Sauvignon Blanc

Quality	♀♀♀♀
Value	★★★☆
Grapes	sauvignon blanc
Region	Adelaide Hills, SA
Cellar	▮ 2
Alc./Vol.	12.5%
RRP	$19.00

Yep, another Adelaide Hills sauvignon blanc, but this is one of the better examples. Paracombe Vineyard was planted in 1983 at Paracombe in the Mount Lofty Ranges.

CURRENT RELEASE 1998   This is an interesting style. It smells of peppermint, cashew nut and coconut, and the more typical tropical fruit flavours come roaring through on the palate. It's rich, and smooth as silk. It probably owes a deal of its flavour to oak, but it's very seductive. Drinks well with Vietnamese wonton rolls.

Paringa Estate Chardonnay

Quality	♀♀♀♀♀
Value	★★★★☆
Grapes	chardonnay
Region	Mornington Peninsula, Vic.
Cellar	▮ 4
Alc./Vol.	14.4%
RRP	$35.00

Lindsay McCall's main claim to fame lies in his ability to make improbably weighty pinot noir on the Mornington Peninsula. When he handles the Peninsula's most successful grape variety, chardonnay, the results can be just as hard to ignore.

CURRENT RELEASE 1998   This is an emphatic young chardonnay which has a nucleus of peachy fruit surrounded by lots of butter, cashew and mealy complexities. The palate is soft and round with supple peachy flavour, nutty interest, and a long clean finish. It's an easy wine to linger over, and it's still a pup; it should be even more interesting with a bit of bottle-age. A good wine to sip with a rich scallop risotto.

Pauletts Riesling

Quality	♀♀♀♀�
Value	★★★★☆
Grapes	riesling
Region	Clare Valley, Vic.
Cellar	⬭ 1–5
Alc./Vol.	11.5%
RRP	$14.00

In common with most other Clare Valley wineries, Pauletts makes good riesling in the classically austere regional style.

CURRENT RELEASE 1998   Very much in style, this has zippy lime aromas, spice and some minerally notes underneath. The palate is medium in intensity with a citrus tang and a long, spiced finish. Slightly closed up at the moment, it should deepen and build complexity with age. Try it with an Alsatian onion tart.

Pegasus Bay Sauvignon Semillon

There's actually a bay named Pegasus in these parts. This wine was oak-aged on lees, but by the taste of it there's also some botrytis involvement.

CURRENT RELEASE 1997 Hey! This is different. It's an attempt to get right away from the usual sem-sav style, and succeeds handsomely. The colour is deep buttercup, and there are scents of toasty French oak, spices, honey and peach. Cinnamon is a strong suit. It's a very complex, full-bodied style, and has much in common with white Bordeaux. Fresh acid cleans up the finish. It could go with chicken.

Quality	▼▼▼▼▽
Value	★★★▸
Grapes	sauvignon blanc; semillon
Region	Canterbury, NZ
Cellar	▮ 2
Alc./Vol.	13.5%
RRP	$24.60

Penfolds Adelaide Hills Chardonnay

This emerged from the Yattarna trials, when Penfolds' winemakers were charged with the task of making an outstanding white wine. It's an awful lot better value for money than Yattarna, the eventual result. Maker Neville Falkenberg.

Previous outstanding vintages: '96, '97

CURRENT RELEASE 1998 A stunning chardonnay in the fruit-driven style that set new parameters for Penfolds whites. The aromas are tropical and herbal, with hints of pineapple and lemons. Those flavours carry onto the palate where it has taut structure, impressive intensity and focus with a somewhat firm finish. This could be cellared too. Try it with leek and scallop gratin.

Quality	▼▼▼▼▼
Value	★★★★
Grapes	chardonnay
Region	Adelaide Hills, SA
Cellar	▮ 5
Alc./Vol.	13.0%
RRP	$33.00 Ⓢ

Penfolds Adelaide Hills Semillon

This was a spin-off from Penfolds' 'White Grange' project, which saw the winemakers attempt to make a flagship white wine to put Penfolds up with the serious players.

CURRENT RELEASE 1997 Clever use of classy oak for fermentation and ageing. A fuller style of semillon with toasty oak-influenced aroma. The palate is rich with plenty of body, yet it avoids broadness. Soft and easy to enjoy now with grilled scampi, but it should cellar into a powerful, rich, full-bodied wine.

Quality	▼▼▼▼▽
Value	★★★▸
Grapes	semillon
Region	Adelaide Hills, SA
Cellar	▮ 6
Alc./Vol.	12.5%
RRP	$27.00

Penfolds Reserve Bin 95A Chardonnay

Quality	♥♥♥♥
Value	★★¼
Grapes	chardonnay
Region	Adelaide Hills, SA
Cellar	▮ 1
Alc./Vol.	13.5%
RRP	$60.00

Penfolds kept this back for a year longer than the '95 Yattarna, and we wonder why. It's starting to lose its attractive freshness. Maker Neville Falkenberg.

Previous outstanding vintages: '94

CURRENT RELEASE 1995 This aged wine is full golden in the shade, and there are toasted-nut and marmalade developed characters aplenty. The flavours are fully mature, but it has plenty of acid and oaky firmness giving it life on the tongue. Drink soon, perhaps with bouillabaisse.

Penfolds Yattarna Chardonnay

Quality	♥♥♥♥♥
Value	★★
Grapes	chardonnay
Region	Adelaide Hills, SA 90%; Tumbarumba, NSW 10%
Cellar	▮ 5+
Alc./Vol.	13.5%
RRP	$90–$150

This is a very fine chardonnay, but we believe the price is outrageous and the link that Penfolds draws between it and Grange is entirely unjustified. Makers John Duval, Neville Falkenberg and team.

Previous outstanding vintages: '95

CURRENT RELEASE 1996 This is an even more refined, subtle wine than the debut '95, but if you're looking for a blockbuster to impress with, look elsewhere. It has a medium–light hue, and a restrained yet complex nose of honey, butter, vanilla, nuts and toast. It showcases a lovely balance between fruit and secondary complexities. It has finesse, good mouth-feel and length, and could be served with scampi. Don't over-chill it!

Penley Estate Chardonnay

Quality	♥♥♥¼
Value	★★★
Grapes	chardonnay
Region	Coonawarra, SA 80%; McLaren Vale, SA 20%
Cellar	▮ 2
Alc./Vol.	13.0%
RRP	$20.50

The Penley whites have never managed to keep up with the brisk standard set by the reds, but hey, Coonawarra is red-winesville.

CURRENT RELEASE 1997 Strange aromas of quince jelly and squash are reflected in a rather thick, heavy palate, which has plenty of flavour but is somewhat dull. There's a hint of peach in the broad flavour which fills the mouth. It's probably best well chilled. Then serve with smoked cod.

Peppertree Chardonnay

This has turned into a highly successful wine for wine-makers Chris Cameron and Chris Archer. The quantity is about 9000 cases, and the grapes are sourced from no less than seven regions.

CURRENT RELEASE 1997 A big, sweet, more-ish crowd-pleaser of a chardonnay. The colour is medium–full yellow, and the bouquet reveals oodles of butterscotch malolactic character and soft, oily fruit. Big, round, peachy softness fills the mouth. Marinate a butterflied chicken and barbecue it.

Quality	♟♟♟♟
Value	★★★✶
Grapes	chardonnay
Region	King Valley, Vic; Padthaway, SA; Hunter Valley, NSW & others
Cellar	▮ 2
Alc./Vol.	12.8%
RRP	$20.35 ⑤

Peppertree Reserve Traminer

This is made from Eden Valley grapes. It's a change from the usual Peppertree traminer, which comes from Oakdale, a Lower Hunter vineyard owned by Peppertree. Maker Chris Cameron.

CURRENT RELEASE 1998 Yup – it's definitely a traminer: the nose has that intensely fragrant lychee aroma. It's a big, rich style with bags of flavour, quite full-bodied with a lot of breadth across the palate. A generous traminer to serve with spring rolls and chilli sauce.

Quality	♟♟♟♟
Value	★★★✶
Grapes	gewürztraminer
Region	Eden Valley, SA
Cellar	▮ 3+
Alc./Vol.	12.0%
RRP	$16.00

Petaluma Chardonnay

The '97 was still current at the time of going to press. It hasn't changed an awful lot since last year's review. It's still a thoroughbred just doing its warm-up laps.
Previous outstanding vintages: '90, '92, '94, '95, '96

CURRENT RELEASE 1997 There's a slight vanilla dominance at this point in its career, although a panoply of other flavours – butterscotch, roasted nuts, poached peach – are there in abundance as well. It retains great finesse and gives the illusion of delicacy on the tongue, when in reality it's intense and has plenty of weight. It's the balance that does it. A good drink with sautéed Balmain bug tails.

Quality	♟♟♟♟♟
Value	★★★★✶
Grapes	chardonnay
Region	Adelaide Hills, SA
Cellar	▮ 6
Alc./Vol.	13.8%
RRP	$40.00

Petaluma Riesling

Quality	YYYYY
Value	★★★★
Grapes	riesling
Region	Clare Valley, SA
Cellar	10
Alc./Vol.	12.7%
RRP	$22.00

The 1998 vintage in Clare didn't suffer the intense heat of '97, and the wines are rated at least as highly. It should turn out beautifully with bottle-age. Maker Brian Croser and team.

Previous outstanding vintages: '80, '85, '86, '88, '90, '92, '93, '94, '95, '96, '97

CURRENT RELEASE 1998   The wine is still a pup, and is somewhat in its kennel. The aromas are shy but clean and attractive, recalling bread-dough and pastry. It shows the more classic citrus theme on palate. It has delicacy, restraint and a real edge of class. Stone-fruit, citrus flavours are sustained, fine and pure. It holds your interest to the last drop. Excellent with Vietnamese salad.

Petaluma Tiers Chardonnay

Quality	YYYYY
Value	★★
Grapes	chardonnay
Region	Adelaide Hills, SA
Cellar	5
Alc./Vol.	14.0%
RRP	$120 – $130+

Petaluma claims the Tiers vineyard, which is the original planting, is on much older and differently structured soils to the rest of the vineyards, and its wine is the best every year. It was a sitting duck for an individual-vineyard bottling. It was all sold as futures: 300 dozen in total, half exported. This partly explains the crazy price, which seemed a deliberate attempt to one-up Penfolds Yattarna.

CURRENT RELEASE 1996   Tasted on release in September '98, this was remarkable for its subtlety and restraint. Four more months in oak than the regular Petaluma Chardonnay, but it's not woody. The aromas are delicate poached pear, cashew, white peach and lightly tropical fruits; the oak beautifully harmonised. Intensely flavoured, tightly structured and concentrated. The key words are harmony, finesse and above all, great length. It should improve with age and peak in 2000–2002.

Peter Lehmann Eden Valley Riesling

Most of Peter Lehmann's grapes come from the Barossa Valley, but Eden Valley is better for riesling. Being higher and cooler, the grapes are more delicate.

CURRENT RELEASE 1998 Subdued but clean aromas of fresh Granny Smith apples and white peaches. Generous palate flavour, excellent weight and length, invigorating acid finish, dry and quite rich. Tremendously good value to drink now with seafood or to cellar for up to five years.

Quality	ΥΥΥΥ̧
Value	★★★★★
Grapes	riesling
Region	Eden Valley, SA
Cellar	🍾 6+
Alc./Vol.	12.0%
RRP	$12.00 Ⓢ

PENGUIN BEST BARGAIN WHITE

Pfitzner Eric's Vineyard Chardonnay

Pfitzner's is one of the vineyards developed by Petaluma in the Piccadilly Valley, and is owned by Dr John Pfitzner. It's made at Petaluma.

CURRENT RELEASE 1996 The colour is showing a glowing yellow, which reflects its age. The rich citrusy nose has an excellent balance of oak and fruit. The palate has vibrant grapefruity flavour and crisp acid. A stylish wine that could still improve. Food: barbecued prawns.

Quality	ΥΥΥΥ
Value	★★★★
Grapes	chardonnay
Region	Adelaide Hills, SA
Cellar	🍾 2
Alc./Vol.	13.7%
RRP	$19.95

CURRENT RELEASE 1997 This really is essence of Adelaide Hills chardonnay. The colour is a light shade of yellow, and the aromas are primarily of fruit in the melon–grapefruit spectrum. It has the delicacy typical of the region, and thrilling tangy harmony in the mouth. Very much a sister to the '96, and could be cellared. Try it with steamed prawns and vegetables with beurre blanc.

Quality	ΥΥΥΥ̧
Value	★★★★˧
Grapes	chardonnay
Region	Adelaide Hills, SA
Cellar	🍾 4
Alc./Vol.	13.5%
RRP	$19.95

Pfitzner Sauvignon Blanc

Quality	♟♟♟𝄽
Value	★★★╵
Grapes	sauvignon blanc
Region	Adelaide Hills, SA
Cellar	▮ 3
Alc./Vol.	13.3%
RRP	$15.00

This is made from first-crop grapes from the 6-hectare Pfitzner vineyard, plus some fruit from another. Both are in the Piccadilly area. Producer Dr John Pfitzner.

CURRENT RELEASE 1998   This has a low-key nose that is neither pungent nor herbaceous, which is not necessarily a negative. The flavours are of tart, crushed leaves and gooseberries, and there's a touch of savouriness on the palate, which could come from subtly handled oak. The oak becomes more apparent the more you sip. Try it with herb braised calamari.

Phillip Island Wines Sauvignon Blanc

Quality	♟♟♟♟♟
Value	★★★★
Grapes	sauvignon blanc
Region	Phillip Island, Vic.
Cellar	▮ 2
Alc./Vol.	12.5%
RRP	$25.00

This vineyard on Phillip Island is an initiative of the Lance family of Diamond Valley Vineyards. The vines are under netting for wind protection, but that alone doesn't explain the quality of this wine. Winemaking is by David Lance and family.

CURRENT RELEASE 1998   A blinder out of left field! It has confectionery and sweet estery aromas from ripe grapes, and no sign of greenness. There's intense tropical fruit flavour on the palate, which has more strength than usually encountered in this grape variety. Vibrant, tangy gooseberry flavour galore. Most impressive. Try it with niçoise salad.

Pierro Chardonnay Unfiltered

Quality	♟♟♟♟♟
Value	★★★╵
Grapes	chardonnay
Region	Margaret River, WA
Cellar	▮ 6
Alc./Vol.	14.5%
RRP	$49.00

To filter or not to filter: zat is zee question. Winemaker Mike Peterkin thinks it does make a subtle difference, so he does an unfiltered bottling for the buffs. It has 'unfiltered' ink-stamped on the back label.

Previous outstanding vintages: '86, '90, '93, '94, '96

CURRENT RELEASE 1997   In its youth this wine is driven by very smart oak. It has aromas of grilled nuts, cedar and bacon bone. The palate is fine and very intense, still restrained in its youth but promising even more if cellared. It has Margaret River concentration. A top wine to serve with barbecued marron.

Pierro Semillon Sauvignon Blanc LTC

Winemaker Mike Peterkin consistently gets more character and complexity into this blend than most makers. LTC, or *Les Trois Cuvées*, signifies a trace of chardonnay in the blend.

CURRENT RELEASE 1998 The colour is a quite-developed medium–full yellow, and the barrel-ferment characters are stronger than in previous vintages. Toasty, smoky secondary aromas entwine with straw, hay-like, dried-herb fruit characters. A flavoursome wine, which is just a little flat on the palate. Good drinking with roast turkey.

Quality	♀♀♀♀
Value	★★★
Grapes	semillon; sauvignon blanc; chardonnay
Region	Margaret River, WA
Cellar	▮ 3
Alc./Vol.	12.5%
RRP	$23.80

Pike's Reserve Riesling

Neil and Andrew Pike own and manage one of the Clare Valley's highest quality wineries. The vineyard is in the Polish Hill River sub-region.

CURRENT RELEASE 1998 An outstanding riesling! It has a lifted floral, almost powder-puff riesling character on the nose. The palate has remarkable intensity. It's a big wine with a dry, quite firm, finish, and fairly prominent acidity. A wine for cellaring. It goes well with pan-fried flounder.

Quality	♀♀♀♀♀
Value	★★★★★
Grapes	riesling
Region	Clare Valley, SA
Cellar	➥ 2–10+
Alc./Vol.	12.0%
RRP	$22.00

Pipers Brook Vineyard Riesling

Pipers Brook now accounts for 35 per cent of the Tasmanian wine grape crush, which makes it a sort of Southcorp of the south. Maker Andrew Pirie.

Previous outstanding vintages: '82, '84, '85, '90, '91, '92, '93, '94, '95

CURRENT RELEASE 1998 A puzzling wine. From an outstandingly successful Tassie vintage, this looks rather light and plain, with some free sulfur lurking on the nose and some sweetness on the tongue. There are earthy aromas and some faint spiciness, and the palate is lean and restrained. It could surprise after some cellaring.

Quality	♀♀♀
Value	★★★
Grapes	riesling
Region	Pipers River, Tas.
Cellar	➥ 2–5+
Alc./Vol.	12.1%
RRP	$23.00

Pipers Brook Vineyard Summit Chardonnay

Quality	ΫΫΫΫℾ
Value	★★ℾ
Grapes	chardonnay
Region	Pipers River, Tas.
Cellar	⬗ 2–10
Alc./Vol.	13.5%
RRP	$78.00

This is Andrew Pirie's big-ticket item, his tilt at fine Burgundy, and it's only produced in the best vintages. There was no '93, '95 or '96.

CURRENT RELEASE 1997 A difficult wine to evaluate young, it's dominated on the nose by heavily toasted oak and on the palate by fierce acidity. Dr Pirie quotes 2010 as the year it will peak, and no doubt the True Believers will pay the $78 and take the plunge. There are scents of burnt coconut with hints of pineapple and straw/hay. It's intense, tightly structured and powerful, with a very long carry. Needs food because of the high acid. Try pheasant in a creamy sauce.

Plantagenet Breakaway Fine White

Quality	ΫΫℾ
Value	★★★
Grapes	semillon; sauvignon blanc; chardonnay; verdelho; riesling
Region	Great Southern, WA
Cellar	▮
Alc./Vol.	12.0%
RRP	$11.90

What is a 'fine' white? There are no laws, so it's open to interpretation. This fruit-salad blend is so fine it's hardly even there.

CURRENT RELEASE 1998 The nose is sweetly lollyish and there's a hint of muscat-like spice. The tropical fruit flavours are very light, bordering on bland. It finishes dry but short, and somewhat watery. Serve with lightly dressed salad.

Plantagenet Chardonnay

Quality	ΫΫΫΫ
Value	★★★ℾ
Grapes	chardonnay
Region	Great Southern, WA
Cellar	▮ 2
Alc./Vol.	14.0%
RRP	$23.00

The winery and its original vineyards are located in the Plantagenet Shire. This is a consistently good producer whose prices are always reasonable. Maker Gavin Berry.

CURRENT RELEASE 1997 Mysteriously, most whites from south-west WA have a tea-leafy/sweaty/passion-fruity aroma, and this is no exception. It has attractive flavour and elegance on the palate, with well-married oak, and drinks well right now. Try it with crab timbale.

Plantagenet Omrah Sauvignon Blanc

The winery was established in 1968 and, apart from its own 58 hectares of vines, it buys in fruit as well. This wine draws on Pemberton and Margaret River.

CURRENT RELEASE 1998 An excellent fruity, general-purpose dry white. It has estery banana and Granny-Smith-apple aromas. The taste is delicate and fresh with sherbety acidity. It doesn't fall into the too-pungent trap. Serve with salads and cold seafood.

Quality	ΨΨΨΨ
Value	★★★★
Grapes	sauvignon blanc
Region	Mount Barker, Pemberton & Margaret River, WA
Cellar	🍾 2
Alc./Vol.	13.0%
RRP	$16.00

Plantagenet Omrah Unoaked Chardonnay

This was one of the first unoaked chardonnays to really fire the public imagination. It probably fires a healthy bank balance nowadays. Maker Gavin Berry.

CURRENT RELEASE 1998 This has spadefuls of the typical passionfruit aroma of the region. The estery nose also has some sweaty aspects. It's a clean, but ultimately simple, flimsily structured wine – but who's going to cellar it anyway? Juicy, light-bodied and undemanding. Drink now, with garfish in beer batter.

Quality	ΨΨΨ
Value	★★★
Grapes	chardonnay
Region	Great Southern, WA
Cellar	🍾 1
Alc./Vol.	13.5%
RRP	$17.00 Ⓢ

Plunkett Chardonnay

The Plunkett winery is in the Strathbogie Ranges, but the cellar-door sales is astutely located beside the Hume Freeway. Maker Sam Plunkett.

CURRENT RELEASE 1997 This is a wine that follows its own star; it doesn't kowtow to conventions. The nose is low-key and the wine is not especially varietal. It has malty aromas and a smooth flow of flavour over the tongue. The fruit and wood are well harmonised and it has length, although it's not especially complex. Try with hokkien noodles.

Quality	ΨΨΨΨ
Value	★★★
Grapes	chardonnay
Region	Strathbogie Ranges, Vic.
Cellar	🍾 2
Alc./Vol.	14.0%
RRP	$22.30

Plunkett Semillon

Quality	♥♥♥♪
Value	★★★
Grapes	semillon
Region	Strathbogie Ranges, Vic.
Cellar	↓ 4
Alc./Vol.	12.5%
RRP	$18.00

Plunkett's is in the Strathbogie Ranges of Central Victoria – not a major wine region, although its establishment in 1991 has drawn fresh interest to the area in recent times. Maker Sam Plunkett.

CURRENT RELEASE 1998   This has a curious aroma of minty, slightly confectionery-like oak. The palate echoes the same theme, with peppermint flavours and a touch of sweetness. It's rich, full and flavoursome, and the finish is slightly broad and lacks a bit of cut. Goes well with crumbed lamb's brains.

Pokolbin Creek Rich Semillon Unwooded

Quality	♥♥♪
Value	★★★
Grapes	semillon
Region	Hunter Valley, NSW
Cellar	↓ 2
Alc./Vol.	11.0%
RRP	$15.00

All of the Pokolbin Creek wines have a little sticker proudly proclaiming them 'oak free'. Could there be such an oak backlash that a winery can hang its entire *raison d'être* on such a slogan? Maker Neil McGuigan (contract).

CURRENT RELEASE 1998   If richness equals residual sugar, then this is rich. Otherwise, it's rather light-on. There are green-herb aromas and some youthful fermentation esters. The sweetness obscures any fruit flavour. Clean and technically well made, but you need to have a sweet tooth.

Poole's Rock Chardonnay

The year 1997 was what winemakers term a difficult vintage in the Broke Fordwich sub-region of the Hunter, where this was grown. The label reveals 10 per cent of it had malolactic fermentation.

CURRENT RELEASE 1997   There are some green fruit characters here, and it seems to lack for sunshine. The aromas are of vanilla and esters with a glue-like overtone, while the palate is lean and narrow. Not especially varietal. Serve with prosciutto melone.

Quality	♟♟♟
Value	★★⋆
Grapes	chardonnay
Region	Hunter Valley, NSW
Cellar	♦ 1
Alc./Vol.	12.5%
RRP	$21.00

CURRENT RELEASE 1998   This was a big scorer at the '98 Hunter Valley Wine Show, but we are less excited. It has green-herb and melon-skin aromas with slightly disjointed coconutty oak. The taste is lean and lemony with nice life and crispness, and it could bloom with moderate ageing. A good, but not too complex, Hunter chardonnay. Try it with lemon chicken.

Quality	♟♟♟♟
Value	★★★
Grapes	chardonnay
Region	Hunter Valley, NSW
Cellar	♦ 4+
Alc./Vol.	13.0%
RRP	$23.60

Port Phillip Estate Chardonnay

The grapes are grown by Diana and Jeffrey Sher. They put a fair bit of effort into their vines, judging by the quality of the fruit in the bottle. Maker is Lindsay McCall, he of Paringa Estate.

CURRENT RELEASE 1997   Marvellously concentrated, rich, power-packed, but fine as well. The dominant aroma is grapefruit, with fine dusty oak and what seems to be a little solids-fermented complexity adding interest. There's a hint of sweetness in balance, and the flavour is long and very satisfying. Try with scallops en brochette.

Quality	♟♟♟♟♟
Value	★★★★⋆
Grapes	chardonnay
Region	Mornington Peninsula, Vic.
Cellar	♦ 5
Alc./Vol.	13.5%
RRP	$26.00

Preece Chardonnay

Quality	▼▼▼⸀
Value	★★★⸀
Grapes	chardonnay
Region	King Valley, Vic.
Cellar	▮ 1
Alc./Vol.	13.0%
RRP	$16.40 ⑤

They should rename this the Lewis chardonnay. Don Lewis has made the wine at Mitchelton for over a quarter of a century, but Colin Preece was scarcely there at all, legendary winemaker though he was (at Seppelt).

CURRENT RELEASE 1998   Don Lewis has settled on a refined, subtle, very lightly wooded style for this easy-drinking wine. It's fruit-driven with a shy, simple, honeydew melon aroma. It's clean, light-bodied and uncomplicated, but it does have intensity and balance. Try it with sashimi.

Queen Adelaide Chardonnay

Quality	▼▼▼⸀
Value	★★★★
Grapes	chardonnay
Region	not stated
Cellar	▮ 1
Alc./Vol.	12.5%
RRP	$6.99 ⑤

This was once a brand of the old Woodleys concern, which until quite recently had a vineyard in the Adelaide suburbs only six kilometres from the city. These days Queen Adelaide is simply a brand of the Southcorp giant without any link to a particular region or winery.

CURRENT RELEASE 1999   This everyday quaffer is an inoffensive young white with a simple grape and melon nose and a light grapey palate. It's very light in body and crisp in acid. Not much character here – but look at the price.

Red Hill Estate Chardonnay

Quality	▼▼▼⸀
Value	★★★
Grapes	chardonnay
Region	Mornington Peninsula, Vic.
Cellar	▮ 4+
Alc./Vol.	12.9%
RRP	$25.00

Red Hill is the name of the town, the region and the vineyard. It gets its name from the rich volcanic soils on the main ridge of the peninsula. Maker Jenny Bright.

CURRENT RELEASE 1998   A restrained, light-bodied, lightly wooded style, which may appear a tad bland in youth but which we suggest you keep till its second birthday. At the moment it's soft, delicate and has melon/cashew nut chardonnay aromas. The palate is soft and has a hint of sweetness. Try it with scallop and lychee salad.

Richmond Grove Barossa Riesling

Riesling master John Vickery's tenure at Richmond Grove has elevated these wines to the ranks of the classics. Theoretically the Barossa version shouldn't be of the same pedigree as the Watervale, but we don't think there's much separating them.

CURRENT RELEASE 1998 The pale, slightly green-tinged appearance is exactly right for a young riesling like this. The nose has lime notes and a hint of cinnamon. In the mouth it has spice and citrus flavours resting on a tight structure of dry acidity. Needs time to evolve. Try it with pan-fried rainbow trout.

Quality	♥♥♥♥♥
Value	★★★★★
Grapes	riesling
Region	Barossa Valley, SA
Cellar	▲ 8+
Alc./Vol.	12.0%
RRP	$15.50

Richmond Grove Marlborough Sauvignon Blanc

This is further evidence that Orlando's intention to make Richmond Grove a 'regional varietal' label knows few boundaries.

Previous outstanding vintages: '97

CURRENT RELEASE 1998 A very exotic style which justifies this international excursion – you simply can't find sauvignon like this in Australia. Pungent tropical fruit aromas recall mango, passionfruit and pineapple. The palate has big flavour – it really is a fruit cocktail. Just off-dry. Drink it with a prawn cocktail.

Quality	♥♥♥♥♥
Value	★★★★★
Grapes	sauvignon blanc
Region	Marlborough, NZ
Cellar	▲ 2
Alc./Vol.	13.0%
RRP	$17.70 Ⓢ

Richmond Grove Watervale Riesling

In the midst of the current debate about the shortcomings of cork closures, Richmond Grove released a portion of this wine through a retail chain with the Stelvin screw-top. It will be interesting to see how these bottles develop alongside their corked brethren.

CURRENT RELEASE 1998 John Vickery weaves his spell again. The nose has lovely floral aromas as well as citrus and talcum powder. The palate is long and tangy with rather austere, essency lime flavour. Acidity is firm. Worth long ageing. When young, serve with grilled fish; when older, it should suit chicken casserole.

Quality	♥♥♥♥♥
Value	★★★★★
Grapes	riesling
Region	Clare Valley, SA
Cellar	➥ 1–8+
Alc./Vol.	12.5%
RRP	$15.50

Riddoch Sauvignon Blanc

Quality	♟♟♟♟♟
Value	★★★★★
Grapes	sauvignon blanc
Region	Coonawarra, SA
Cellar	▮ 3
Alc./Vol.	13.5%
RRP	$18.00 ⑤

PENGUIN BEST SAUVIGNON BLANC

The Wingara Group, formerly the Coonawarra Machinery Company, grows a lot of good sauvignon blanc in its Coonawarra vineyards. Hence in top years like 1998, this second-string wine is as good as the much dearer Katnook Estate. Maker Wayne Stehbens.

CURRENT RELEASE 1998 **This is a benchmark sauvignon blanc. A beautiful unwooded wine, it overflows with a cocktail of gooseberry, capsicum and tropical fruit flavours. The mouth-feel is soft and gentle yet fresh and lively, as this grape should be. The finish is balanced and dry. It deserves pan-fried flathead with red capsicum and plenty of lemon.**

Rimfire Chardonnay Oak Matured

Quality	♟♟♟
Value	★★★⯪
Grapes	chardonnay
Region	Toowoomba, Qld
Cellar	▮ 2
Alc./Vol.	13.0%
RRP	$13.00 (cellar door)

This should get the anti-gun lobby fired up. Actually, the name refers to a racehorse. This vineyard is in the foothills of the Bunya Mountains near Toowoomba, Queensland.

CURRENT RELEASE 1997 This is a good chardonnay, but it relies too much on oak for its character and flavour. The aroma is dominated by toasty, cedary oak and bottle-aged character. The same applies to the palate. It's a good quality wine otherwise, technically A1, with plenty of flavour and drinkability. Will appeal to lovers of oaky chardonnays. Try it with smoked chicken.

Rimfire Estate Chardonnay

Quality	♟♟♟⯪
Value	★★★
Grapes	chardonnay
Region	Toowoomba, Qld
Cellar	▮ 2
Alc./Vol.	12.9%
RRP	$18.00 (cellar door)

Rimfire is at Maclagan near Toowoomba in southern Queensland. There's a cafe and winery at the vineyard.

CURRENT RELEASE 1998 So you didn't think Queensland could produce good wine! Think again. This is a true-to-variety chardonnay with melon and peach aromas, some tropical overtones plus a hint of oak. It has good balance and drinkability. There's a slightly burnt-toast aroma, probably from the wood. The finish lacks a bit of crispness, but it goes well with chicken schnitzel. A surprise package!

Rimfire Estate Pioneer White

The name is a trifle misleading: it gives no indication of the style of wine to come, which is like the old spatleses of yore.

CURRENT RELEASE 1997 The colour is full yellow, showing aged development. The aromas are pungently spicy, of muscat grapes or possibly traminer. It's very sweet in the mouth, and will appeal to lovers of simple, sweet, muscat-flavoured whites. It should drink well with fresh fruit.

Quality	♟♟?
Value	★★★
Grapes	not stated
Region	Toowoomba, Qld
Cellar	♦
Alc./Vol.	11.4%
RRP	$10.50 (cellar door)

Rimfire Estate Settlers Blend

The Connellan family started planting a vineyard in 1991 in an effort to diversify their cattle property. They produce about 5000 cases a year.

CURRENT RELEASE 1998 This is a competently made wine, but it needs airing to get rid of a little excess sulfur on the nose. It has decent, if basic, flavour aided by the merest suggestion of wood. The palate is dry and straightforward. Best with food: try fried chicken.

Quality	♟♟♟
Value	★★★★
Grapes	chardonnay; verdelho; colombard
Region	Toowoomba, Qld
Cellar	♦ 3
Alc./Vol.	13.0%
RRP	$13.00 (cellar door)

Rochford Premier Chardonnay

This vineyard and winery were set up by Bruce Dowding, who was an accountant associated with the Melbourne builder with the serious edifice complex, Bruno Grollo.

CURRENT RELEASE 1996 From a difficult vintage in southern Victoria, this is clearly botrytis-affected, which does not help its cause. The aromas are of apricot and squash (the vegetable), but it lacks chardonnay character. There's a shiver of acid on the palate that startles the tastebuds, and it pulls up short. Needs food: yabby bisque may work.

Quality	♟♟?
Value	★★
Grapes	chardonnay
Region	Macedon, Vic.
Cellar	♦ 2
Alc./Vol.	13.0%
RRP	$29.00

Rosabrook Estate Chardonnay

Quality	ΥΥΥΥ
Value	★★★↾
Grapes	chardonnay
Region	Margaret River, WA
Cellar	▮ 2
Alc./Vol.	13.8%
RRP	$20.00

A creek is a brook in Western Australia, and the Margaret River area is crisscrossed by many of them.
CURRENT RELEASE 1998   This is a ripe, high-alcohol style which tastes a teensy bit sweet, although the high alcohol may be playing tricks in that department (it can give an impression of sugar-sweetness). There are attractive honeysuckle aromas, which are typical of the region. It has good fruit, and the dusty oak is gently handled. Try it with bouillabaisse.

Rosemount Roxburgh Chardonnay

Quality	ΥΥΥΥↂ
Value	★★★↾
Grapes	chardonnay
Region	Hunter Valley, NSW
Cellar	▮ 5+
Alc./Vol.	14.0%
RRP	$51.00

This has always been a big-statement wine, a boots-and-all chardonnay that makes no apology for its style. Big oaky chardonnay is losing in the fashion stakes, but the Americans still lust after it. Maker Philip Shaw.
Previous outstanding vintages: '87, '91, '93, '94
CURRENT RELEASE 1996   The customary Roxburgh style: a big softie, or should that be a *very* big softie? Charred wood characters from heavy-toast oak dominate somewhat, and in the mouth it's very full-bodied and rich, with layer upon layer of complex flavours. A generous mouthful, but some will find it too oaky. Try it with smoked chicken.

Rosemount Show Reserve Chardonnay

Quality	ΥΥΥΥ
Value	★★★
Grapes	chardonnay
Region	Hunter Valley, NSW
Cellar	▮ 3
Alc./Vol.	13.5%
RRP	$24.50 Ⓢ

This is all Hunter Valley fruit, and it also draws heavily on the Roxburgh vineyard near Muswellbrook in the Upper Hunter. Maker Philip Shaw.
Previous outstanding vintages: '87, '93, '94, '96
CURRENT RELEASE 1997   Not really in the same league as the magic '96, but it's a respectable wine from an ordinary year. The aroma has a strong milk-powder malolactic quality, with a touch of flatness, but there are exciting nutty peachy flavours in the mouth with customary Rosemount richness. Good with chicken and pistachio galantine.

Rossetto Promenade Semillon

This is a barrel-fermented style which comes in the special heavy-glass bottle of the 'Semillon of the Riverina' marketing syndicate. It has SR embossed on the bottle shoulder.

CURRENT RELEASE 1998   The colour is golden and very forward in development. There are already a lot of aged toasty, resiny characters in the bouquet, hurried along no doubt by the barrel fermentation. The palate structure is broad, soft and rich, but lacks a little zip. It tastes of peach, nectarine and apricot. Drink now, with lemon-dressed fish and chips.

Quality	▼▼▼⸮
Value	★★★★
Grapes	semillon
Region	Riverina, NSW
Cellar	▮ 1
Alc./Vol.	13.5%
RRP	$12.30

Rothvale Reserve Chardonnay 'F'

Rothvale vineyard is owned by Max Patton and family in Deasy's Road, Pokolbin. The 25-acre vineyard was bought from Tyrrell's in 1997 and doubled in size. There are also cabins to let. 'F' or 'A' denotes French or American oak.

CURRENT RELEASE 1998   The nose has some unusual oak-derived characters, recalling linseed oil, cloves and other spices. It has an elegant structure with lean fig-like flavours and a nice dry aftertaste. Not especially complex, but it may repay short-term cellaring. Food: chicken kebabs.

Quality	▼▼▼▼
Value	★★★
Grapes	chardonnay
Region	Hunter Valley, NSW
Cellar	▮ 3
Alc./Vol.	13.2%
RRP	$28 (cellar door)

Rouge Homme Chardonnay

With the price of land in Coonawarra it's a wonder they can justify selling chardonnay so cheaply. Maybe they won't much longer: don't tell anyone, but the big companies have been ripping out white grapes as fast as they can and planting more red. Maker Paul Gordon.

CURRENT RELEASE 1998   Like the '96, which won our Best Bargain White Award two years ago, this is terrific value. It smells creamy, nutty and melon-like and the fruit–oak balance is masterful. It's anything but simple, and it delights the senses. It's light-bodied and refined, but has richness. Drink it with scallop and leek gratin.

Quality	▼▼▼▼⸮
Value	★★★★★
Grapes	chardonnay
Region	Coonawarra, SA
Cellar	▮ 4
Alc./Vol.	13.5%
RRP	$14.00 ⑤

Rouge Homme Unoaked Chardonnay

Quality	♟♟♟
Value	★★★★
Grapes	chardonnay
Region	Coonawarra, SA
Cellar	▮ 1
Alc./Vol.	13.0%
RRP	$12.00 ⑤

'No wood, no good', quoth one Wolf Blass. In this case, we tend to agree. It's very lightweight, and the question is would it be able to carry any wood?

CURRENT RELEASE 1998 This is a delicate, some might say flimsy, wine. Its aromas are stalky/herbal over melon jam and citron. It lacks intensity and falls away towards the finish. But the price is right, and it could do justice to a caesar salad.

Salisbury Chardonnay

Quality	♟♟♟
Value	★★★⋆
Grapes	chardonnay
Region	Murray Valley, Vic.
Cellar	▮ 1
Alc./Vol.	14.0%
RRP	$10.00 ⑤

The Salisbury people are highly motivated modern producers in the Murray Valley. They use high-tech methods to achieve economies of scale while maintaining good quality. The result is a range of early-drinkers that offer great value.

CURRENT RELEASE 1998 This is a bright, pale gold wine with a typical Riverland nose of ripe peachy fruit, melon and a buttery touch. In the mouth it's direct and fruity. Light to medium intensity of flavour leads to a rather warm alcoholic finish.

Saltram Classic Chardonnay

Quality	♟♟♟
Value	★★★★
Grapes	chardonnay
Region	not stated
Cellar	▮ 1
Alc./Vol.	13.5%
RRP	$12.00 ⑤

Saltram is one of the oldest names in the Barossa, although it hasn't been a totally independent enterprise since 1941. Since then it has been through a series of ownerships, and it's now part of Mildara Blass.

CURRENT RELEASE 1998 A straightforward commercial chardonnay of good quality. It's pale gold in colour, and has a peachy nose with some nuttiness. The palate is soft and mouth-filling with peachy varietal flavour and a fresh finish. Try it with seafood pasta.

Saltram Classic Riesling

Saltram is a Barossa institution and, like most, that reputation was built on tasty reds and only one white – riesling. The Classic edition is a budget-priced example; whether it's a classic is open to question.

CURRENT RELEASE 1998 This is a no-frills riesling which doesn't sing in the way the best Eden Valley wines do. The nose has straightforward lime and lemon aromas, and the palate has soft limey fruit without great intensity. The finish has a lively tang. Serve it with a chicken salad at an informal lunch.

Quality	ΨΨΨ𝟀
Value	★★★ʕ
Grapes	riesling
Region	Barossa Valley, SA
Cellar	🍶 2
Alc./Vol.	11.6%
RRP	$12.00 Ⓢ

Saltram Mamre Brook Chardonnay

With the 1963 vintage Mamre Brook was launched as Saltrams' most prestigious red. Chardonnay was almost unknown then. How times change!

CURRENT RELEASE 1998 There's a real quality feel about this chardonnay, which makes it excellent value. The nose is subtle and complex with stylish melon and peach chardonnay aromas trimmed with well-harmonised nutty oak. The palate has an attractively mellow texture with big peachy fruit flavour, restrained oak and an appealing tang. This is an easy to drink wine, which will go well with stir-fried prawns.

Quality	ΨΨΨΨ𝟀
Value	★★★★★
Grapes	chardonnay
Region	Barossa Valley, SA
Cellar	🍶 3
Alc./Vol.	13.5%
RRP	$16.00

Schinus Chardonnay

Schinus wines are made at Garry Crittenden's Dromana Estate from fruit grown in other areas. The colourful labelling matches the sunny disposition of these easy-drinking young wines.

CURRENT RELEASE 1998 A bright, fruit-driven chardonnay that doesn't require any cerebral exercise to understand it. It's simple; just sweet tropical fruit aromas, the merest hint of barrel influence, a soft, fruit-sweet palate, good persistence, and a tangy finish. Drink it young outdoors with a picnic of cold chicken.

Quality	ΨΨΨΨ
Value	★★★★
Grapes	chardonnay
Region	Goulburn Valley, Vic.; McLaren Vale, SA
Cellar	🍶 2
Alc./Vol.	13.0%
RRP	$15.60

Seaview Chardonnay

Quality	ΨΨΨΨ
Value	★★★★★
Grapes	chardonnay
Region	McLaren Vale, SA
Cellar	🍶 2
Alc./Vol.	13.5%
RRP	$11.00 Ⓢ

In recent years few chardonnays have come close to Seaview in value-for-money terms. It's always a cleverly constructed wine with plenty of character.

CURRENT RELEASE 1998 Right on song in 1998, Seaview offers its usual formula. There's honeydew and cashew on the nose, and the palate is soft and rich with good length. It tastes melony with a hint of butter-caramel in the background, while a whisper of oak adds dimension. Great value. Try it with scallops.

Seaview Edwards and Chaffey Chardonnay

Quality	ΨΨΨΨΨ
Value	★★★★
Grapes	chardonnay
Region	McLaren Vale, SA
Cellar	🍶 3
Alc./Vol.	13.7%
RRP	$26.00

Messrs Edwards and Chaffey founded Seaview long before anybody had thought of growing chardonnay at McLaren Vale. Today it's all over the place.

CURRENT RELEASE 1997 The nose shows a lot of winemaking input as well as good ripe fruit. It's complex, with rich melon and fig, buttery nuances and nutty oak. The multi-layered palate has a creamy texture and dense flavour with a balanced robe of spicy oak. A satisfyingly complete mouthful, which drinks well young. Serve it with rockling fillets.

Selaks Marlborough Ice Wine

Quality	ΨΨΨΨΨ
Value	★★★★
Grapes	riesling;
	gewürztraminer
Region	Marlborough, NZ
Cellar	🍶 3
Alc./Vol.	10.0%
RRP	$20.00 (375 ml)

Made from grapes that are pressed while frozen, thus concentrating the juice by removing the water, which has been crystallised as ice. A painstaking process.

CURRENT RELEASE 1998 Brilliant pale yellow-gold in colour, this has a thrilling nose that is intense, very spicy and aromatic. It smells of lychee and floral perfume. In the mouth it's intensely sweet, but not cloying, with gewürztraminer spice flavours, some white peach and a bracing counterpoint of acidity. Low alcohol makes it fresh and light. A joy to sip with fresh fruit.

Seppelt Botrytis Gewürztraminer

Every so often Seppelt's high country vineyard at Eden Valley has the right conditions for good levels of botrytis infection. The flavours of gewürztraminer suit this sweet style well.

CURRENT RELEASE 1997   The nose has sweet aromas of pear and lychee with a slightly sweaty (though not unpleasant) botrytis touch. The palate has a tropical fruit salad flavour with a citrus edge and relatively soft acid on the finish. This will taste very good alongside a poached fruit dessert.

Quality	▼▼▼▼
Value	★★★★
Grapes	gewürztraminer
Region	Eden Valley, SA
Cellar	2
Alc./Vol.	11.5%
RRP	$12.00 (375 ml)

Seppelt Corella Ridge Chardonnay

You either love the packaging of this Seppelt Victoria range or . . . Oh well, at least the wines can be pretty good.

CURRENT RELEASE 1998   This is a smooth young chardonnay of good intensity. The nose has juicy melon aromas with integrated oak. In the mouth it's peachy, fruit-sweet and clean, with notable oak influence, but the flavour is a little short. Definitely a crowd-pleaser at a good price. Try it with Indonesian fried chicken.

Quality	▼▼▼▼
Value	★★★★
Grapes	chardonnay
Region	various, Vic.
Cellar	1
Alc./Vol.	13.5%
RRP	$13.50 Ⓢ

Seppelt Drumborg Riesling

Drumborg rieslings from Seppelt are usually released young and lively. Pundits always say that they should age well. Mr and Mrs Pundit are absolutely right, here's the proof:

CURRENT RELEASE 1993   Those mysterious aged riesling characters that beguile devotees are all here. The nose has intense lime cordial and buttered toast aromas. The palate is tasty, dry and mouth-filling with excellent balance. Tingly acidity keeps it alive and carries a fragrant aftertaste long after swallowing. Good with stir-fried lobster with ginger and spring onion.

Quality	▼▼▼▼▼
Value	★★★★★
Grapes	riesling
Region	Portland, Vic.
Cellar	3
Alc./Vol.	11.4%
RRP	$22.00

Seppelt Drumborg Sauvignon Blanc

Quality	▼▼▼▼
Value	★★★★
Grapes	sauvignon blanc
Region	Portland, Vic.
Cellar	3
Alc./Vol.	12.5%
RRP	$22.00

The bracing cool climate of the Portland region of Victoria produces white wines with great purity of varietal character. Seppelt were the pioneers down there.

CURRENT RELEASE 1998   A very pale appearance suggests freshness and life. The nose has green leaves, gooseberry, and that pine needles sort of zippy sauvignon aroma that you either love or hate. The tangy, herbaceous palate has a fresh spring-like quality, juicy with succulent acidity. Try it with snappy stir-fried asparagus, snow peas and baby corn.

Sevenhill Semillon

Quality	▼▼▼▼
Value	★★★★
Grapes	semillon
Region	Clare Valley, SA
Cellar	4
Alc./Vol.	13.6%
RRP	$15.80

Sevenhill is the Clare Valley's oldest winery, being founded in 1851 by the Jesuits to make altar wine. Brother John May has been in charge of winemaking for over 25 years.

CURRENT RELEASE 1998   A Clare semillon with more cut and life than some, this has a crisp lemon and herb nose with a hint of semillon 'hair oil' aroma. In the mouth it's dry and tasty with lemon-like flavour and a fine, clean finish. Try it with fried sardines.

Shaw and Smith Reserve Chardonnay

Quality	▼▼▼▼▼
Value	★★★★
Grapes	chardonnay
Region	Adelaide Hills, SA
Cellar	3
Alc./Vol.	13.5%
RRP	$28.30

The Adelaide Hills makes the most aristocratic South Australian chardonnay. The region's winemakers are a who's-who of skilled operators, which doesn't harm the district's reputation at all. Maker Martin Shaw.

CURRENT RELEASE 1997   This has very fine aromas and real complexity. Perfumed ripe melon and creamy, nutty tones give charm and interest on the nose. The palate has finesse rather than power, with soft smooth melon and citrus notes, understated oak and impeccable balance. Very easy to drink, and a good companion to pumpkin–pistachio risotto with crisped prosciutto.

Shaw and Smith Sauvignon Blanc

Michael Hill Smith, one half of the Shaw and Smith partnership, talks of 'capturing the pristine qualities of the fruit' in these wines. He succeeds admirably.

CURRENT RELEASE 1998 As usual this is a squeaky clean wine with an attractive combination of ripeness and leafy tang. The nose is sweet, with tropical fruit aromas balanced by green salad and herbal touches. The palate has the same sorts of flavours, with a varietal character that isn't as piercing as some. Balanced tangy acidity completes the picture. A good match for fresh spring rolls with Vietnamese mint.

Quality	♥♥♥♥
Value	★★★★
Grapes	sauvignon blanc
Region	Adelaide Hills, SA
Cellar	● 1
Alc./Vol.	12.5%
RRP	$20.55

Shottesbrooke Chardonnay

Chardonnay does well in McLaren Vale where it makes rich wines very much in the full-flavoured Australian mould. Maker Nick Holmes.

CURRENT RELEASE 1998 A peachy, complete chardonnay with a lovely balance of fresh fruit and complexity. The nose has peach and melon aromas with a hint of nuttiness and restrained oak. In the mouth it has smooth texture with rich stone-fruit and creamy flavours. A harmonious lick of classy oak is in fine balance. A treat with scallops meunière.

Quality	♥♥♥♥
Value	★★★★ʀ
Grapes	chardonnay
Region	McLaren Vale, SA
Cellar	● 3
Alc./Vol.	14.0%
RRP	$17.30

Skillogalee Gewürztraminer

Sales of gewürztraminer don't exactly set the world on fire here in Australia. Its pungency isn't everybody's cup of tea.

CURRENT RELEASE 1998 This isn't as exotic as gewürz can be; instead it has a light floral nose with orange blossom and spice aromas. The palate has moderate intensity with a hint of residual sweetness to flesh it out. The flavour is rather broad and undistinguished, and acidity is low. Try it with pâté.

Quality	♥♥♥
Value	★★★
Grapes	gewürztraminer
Region	Clare Valley, SA
Cellar	● 1
Alc./Vol.	13.0%
RRP	$18.75

Skillogalee Riesling

Quality	ŶŶŶŶ
Value	★★★★
Grapes	riesling
Region	Clare Valley, Vic.
Cellar	⬤ 1–6
Alc./Vol.	11.5%
RRP	$18.75

Is any Australian white wine more consistently good than Clare Valley riesling? Nearly every Clare maker produces a good one and many are classics.

CURRENT RELEASE 1998   Very Clare. Rather lean and mean at the moment, it needs time to evolve. A succulent lime juice aroma meets the nose. The palate follows suit with a slight hint of sweetness mid-palate and rather severe acidity on the finish. Should age well. Try it with some Thai vegetarian noodles.

Smithbrook Early Release Chardonnay

Quality	ŶŶŶŶŶ
Value	★★★★
Grapes	chardonnay
Region	Pemberton, WA
Cellar	◊ 2
Alc./Vol.	13.5%
RRP	$22.20

This one got an early release for good behaviour. Smithbrook is the Western Australian outpost of Brian Croser's Petaluma empire.

CURRENT RELEASE 1998   The nose of this wine is quite astonishing. Extraordinary tropical fruit aromas leap from the glass, backed by some oak spice. The tropical fruit bowl continues in the mouth with fruit-sweet flavours of melon, pawpaw and pineapple, smooth texture and subtle wood. Crisp acidity emphasises the juicy lusciousness of it all. Serve it with chicken and mango salad.

Smithbrook Sauvignon Blanc

Quality	ŶŶŶŶŶ
Value	★★★★
Grapes	sauvignon blanc
Region	Pemberton, WA
Cellar	◊ 2
Alc./Vol.	13.0%
RRP	$16.45

Smithbrook, the Western Australian outpost of the burgeoning Petaluma empire, is working hard at putting more complexity into sauvignon blanc. They are succeeding.

CURRENT RELEASE 1998   Tune out if you only like the up-front grassy type of sauvignon. Tune in if you're after sauvignon with a bit more. This has floral and herbaceous aromas with some nutty interest from barrel fermentation. The theme continues down the palate, which has good depth, smooth texture, nutty complexity and a clean dry signature. Try with scallops meunière.

Sorrenberg Chardonnay

At Sorrenberg the chardonnays are deliberately made in a minimalist way that's at odds with most Australian practice. The wines have been rather erratic, but they're always interesting.

CURRENT RELEASE 1997 This chardonnay definitely has a French accent. The nose is dominated by secondary winemaking characters that add complex custardy, butter–caramel aromas to very understated citrus fruit. The palate has creamy, buttery malolactic flavour, which gives smoothness and richness, but is the fruit character buried too deep? High acidity gives a firm structure. An intriguing white for the Francophiles. Serve it with pigs' trotters.

Quality	🍷🍷🍷🍷
Value	★★★
Grapes	chardonnay
Region	Beechworth, Vic.
Cellar	4
Alc./Vol.	13.0%
RRP	$32.00

St Hallett Chardonnay

Barossa chardonnay is usually a big mouthful of white wine, more often than not dressed up in an emphatic measure of oak. The St Hallett style is a bit more subdued.

CURRENT RELEASE 1998 This is a cleverly made wine that's pleasantly plump rather than just plain fat. The nose has sweet peachy fruit with nutty, spicy barrel influence. The palate follows suit with richness and good intensity ahead of a dry finish. Good with Hainanese chicken rice.

Quality	🍷🍷🍷🍷
Value	★★★½
Grapes	chardonnay
Region	Barossa Valley, SA
Cellar	3
Alc./Vol.	14.0%
RRP	$19.75

St Hallett Riesling

In the Barossa they're waiting for the day that riesling makes a return to favour with wine consumers. The signs are more encouraging than they were a couple of years ago. Maker Stuart Blackwell.

CURRENT RELEASE 1998 This is a fragrant young white with a spring-like purity of character. The nose has a light aroma of zesty lime, and the palate is tight and lean with brisk lime sherbet-like flavour. A sinewy young wine of potential. A good match for Vietnamese spring rolls.

Quality	🍷🍷🍷🍷
Value	★★★★
Grapes	riesling
Region	Eden Valley, SA
Cellar	1–6+
Alc./Vol.	11.5%
RRP	$19.75

St Huberts Roussanne

Quality	♟♟♟?
Value	★★★
Grapes	roussanne
Region	Yarra Valley, Vic.
Cellar	♦ 2
Alc./Vol.	13.0%
RRP	$20.00

There are many wine lovers who revel in the obscure. This young white wine should be right up their alley. Roussanne originally hails from France's Rhone Valley. CURRENT RELEASE 1998 This wine really glitters in the glass with a pale straw–gold brilliance. The nose has a distinctly 'foreign' aroma of herbs and flowers with a hint of honey. In the mouth it's light and dry with a slightly flowery flavour but not much give. Try it with pan-fried river fish.

St Leonards Semillon

Quality	♟♟♟
Value	★★
Grapes	semillon
Region	Rutherglen, Vic.
Cellar	♦ 3
Alc./Vol.	13.5%
RRP	$15.50

The Rutherglen–Wahgunyah vineyards of Victoria's north-east aren't well known for their white wines. Some makers try very hard to improve them, with mixed success. CURRENT RELEASE 1998 You have to like oak to enjoy this one. The nose has some citrus fruit aroma, but it's well hidden under a timber yard of slightly resinous wood. The palate is oaky and dry with a rather drawing finish. Try with prawns barbecued in the shell.

St Matthias Chardonnay

Quality	♟♟♟?
Value	★★★
Grapes	chardonnay
Region	Tamar Valley, Tas.
Cellar	♦ 2
Alc./Vol.	13.9%
RRP	$17.00

St Matthias is a second string to the Moorilla Estate bow. The chardonnay is in a similar lively style. CURRENT RELEASE 1998 This refreshing style is an understated drop with cool-climate succulence in good measure. The nose has white peach, citrus and restrained nutty nuances. In the mouth it's light and clean with juicy nectarine flavour and a sharp tang of acidity. A good match for a platter of mixed shellfish.

Stonier's Chardonnay

Stonier's Reserve Chardonnay is consistently one of the best on the Mornington Peninsula. This standard label isn't as grand, but it's still a good drink.

CURRENT RELEASE 1998 Attractive pale straw in colour, this has a fruit-driven nose with aromas of melon and a hint of tart pineapple. A dusting of creamy oak is very much in the background. The palate is straightforward with pleasant flavour, light structure and tangy acidity. Easy to like with pan-fried flathead fillets.

Quality	🍷🍷🍷🍷
Value	★★★★
Grapes	chardonnay
Region	Mornington Peninsula, Vic.
Cellar	🍾 2
Alc./Vol.	13.2%
RRP	$21.40

Stonier's Reserve Chardonnay

This could be the Mornington Peninsula's best wine, a testament to the vision of owner Brian Stonier and the skill of winemaker Tod Dexter.

CURRENT RELEASE 1997 Stonier's Reserve Chardonnay tends to disappear very quickly once the bottle is opened. This edition has nectarine, fig and a whisper of pineapple in the complex bouquet, along with subtle oatmeal and vanilla-creamy complexities. The palate has refined stone-fruit flavour with some light butter toffee nuances. Restrained oak backs everything up, and the finish is long and fragrant.

Quality	🍷🍷🍷🍷🍷
Value	★★★★½
Grapes	chardonnay
Region	Mornington Peninsula, Vic.
Cellar	🍾 5
Alc./Vol.	13.5%
RRP	$37.80

Tallara Frog Rock Chardonnay

A new lease of life for an established vineyard in Mudgee. The next generation came along and gave the works a shake-up. Nice, catchy packaging too. Yet another good job from contract winemaker Simon Gilbert. Porters Liquor seems to have snared the retail rights.

CURRENT RELEASE 1998 This is a fine chardonnay that bodes well for this new label. It has a strong sur-lie character to begin, a touch of quince, and some toasty/cedary wood notes. The taste is full and rather chunky, and it airs to show good depth of flavour and style. Nice long finish too. Try it with veal and artichokes.

Quality	🍷🍷🍷🍷
Value	★★★½
Grapes	chardonnay
Region	Mudgee, NSW
Cellar	🍾 3
Alc./Vol.	12.8%
RRP	$20.00

Tallarook Chardonnay

Quality	♥♥♥♥♥
Value	★★★★★
Grapes	chardonnay
Region	Macedon, Vic.
Cellar	🍷 4
Alc./Vol.	13.5%
RRP	$30.00

We're always pleased to see a new name crop up, particularly when there's an obvious commitment to quality. Tallarook has been carefully planned to take best advantage of its vineyard site, and winemaking combines traditional thought with the latest in technique. Good on 'em.

CURRENT RELEASE 1997   This is a classy drop of chardonnay with some French style. The nose and palate show a lot of winemaker-induced overtones, which add nutty, creamy complexity to a subdued core of nectarine and citrus fruit. The palate has a smooth texture and gentle long flavour which finishes nutty and interesting. A first-class effort from a newcomer. Serve it with slow-roasted salmon.

Talunga Chardonnay

Quality	♥♥♥
Value	★★★
Grapes	chardonnay
Region	Adelaide Hills, SA
Cellar	🍷 1
Alc./Vol.	12.5%
RRP	$20.50

They're stretching things up there in the Hills: every marketer wants an Adelaide Hills chardonnay to sell. Trouble is, there's not much to go around and the yields seem to be creeping up . . .

CURRENT RELEASE 1998   This is a light, rather flimsy wine. The nose has a boiled-potato herbaceous note, and the palate has green leafy flavours and a whiff of vanilla. It's rather dilute and pulls up short. It has no faults, and is perfectly palatable with caesar salad.

Talunga Sauvignon Blanc

Quality	♥♥♥
Value	★★★
Grapes	sauvignon blanc
Region	Adelaide Hills, SA
Cellar	🍷 1
Alc./Vol.	12.0%
RRP	$19.70

This is a lowbrow, but high-altitude, sauvignon blanc. The grapes were grown at Gumeracha in the Adelaide Hills.

CURRENT RELEASE 1998   The aroma of this wine shouts of freshly cut green capsicum. It has a light-bodied taste which is soft, but which lacks a bit of intensity and distinction. The herbal flavours are smooth and round and fall away towards the finish. Drink it with a vegetarian terrine.

Talunga Semillon

Yet another boutique producer from the Adelaide Hills doing interesting things. Maker Vince Scaffidi.

CURRENT RELEASE 1998 Fairly light-bodied, this semillon is lean and tart and could improve with a little cellaring. It has a palish colour, and dusty, pepperminty, slightly cosmetic aromas with traces of lemon essence. The palate is frisky with tangy acid and delicate flavour. A vibrant, zesty white to serve with whiting quenelles.

Quality	▼▼▼⸮
Value	★★★
Grapes	semillon
Region	Adelaide Hills SA
Cellar	🍾 4+
Alc./Vol.	12.5%
RRP	$15.00

Tarrawarra Chardonnay

The Besen clothes-matching family ('This goes with that at Sussan . . .') are now into wine and food matching. Maker Clare Halloran.

Previous outstanding vintages: '88, '90, '91, '94, '96

CURRENT RELEASE 1997 A racy, refined style which has abundant lively, cool-climate acidity. The nose is all lemons and other citrus fruits, underlined by subtle spicy oak; the palate is tautly structured and fine, with a hint of apricot among the citrus. A harmonious wine that's starting to build bottle-development. Try abalone.

Quality	▼▼▼▼⸮
Value	★★★★
Grapes	chardonnay
Region	Yarra Valley, Vic.
Cellar	🍾 5
Alc./Vol.	13.5%
RRP	$35.00

Tatachilla Adelaide Hills Sauvignon Blanc

It's a seller's market for sauvignon blanc (and chardonnay!) grapes in the Adelaide Hills. It's a booming region, and all the fruit goes into top-end product.

CURRENT RELEASE 1998 This is a light and somewhat nondescript – but polished – sauvignon, which won't offend anyone. There are grapey aromas that hint at gooseberry and citrus. It's a delicate, lightweight wine all round, and the finish pulls up a trifle short. It's a wine you can sip endlessly, a good quaffer to take to a Vietnamese restaurant.

Quality	▼▼▼⸮
Value	★★★
Grapes	sauvignon blanc
Region	Adelaide Hills, SA
Cellar	🍾 1
Alc./Vol.	12.5%
RRP	$20.00

Tatachilla Chardonnay

Quality	ΨΨΨ𝟁
Value	★★★⸱
Grapes	chardonnay
Region	McLaren Vale, SA
Cellar	▮ 2
Alc./Vol.	13.5%
RRP	$16.50 Ⓢ

The Tatachilla mob are real pros – everything they attempt is at least good, often exceptional. Maker Michael Fragos.

CURRENT RELEASE 1998   This one owes a debt to the almighty oak chip. It's a wood-driven style with a slightly rough, toasted-chip aroma, and this is echoed in a little hardness on the palate. A perfectly reasonable drink-now chardonnay at the right price, and should be a crowd-pleaser. Serve it with barbecued octopus.

Tatachilla Growers Chenin Semillon Sauvignon Blanc

Quality	ΨΨΨ𝟁
Value	★★★★
Grapes	chenin blanc;
	semillon; sauvignon
	blanc
Region	McLaren Vale, SA
Cellar	▮ 2
Alc./Vol.	13.0%
RRP	$12.00 Ⓢ

Tatachilla has 15 hectares of vineyards but takes grapes from a number of growers – hence the title of this wine. There is a red that partners it.

CURRENT RELEASE 1998   This is a wine of some finesse. The semillon shows out at the moment, with lemon and lanolin overtones. The aroma also has a potato-like herbal component, and the acid lends firmness to the finish. A very decent blend at the price. Try it with asparagus gratin.

Te Mata Estate Castle Hill Sauvignon Blanc

Quality	ΨΨΨ𝟁
Value	★★⸱
Grapes	sauvignon blanc
Region	Hawkes Bay, NZ
Cellar	▮ 1
Alc./Vol.	13.0%
RRP	$25.40

Four bottles for 100 bucks seems like a lot to ask for sauvignon blanc, but it's becoming commonplace in Kiwiland.

CURRENT RELEASE 1998   Not a pungent example of this variety, which may appeal to some – indeed, many will see that as an asset. There's plenty of soft, nutty fruit to sniff, and melon-like palate flavour. It's soft, but still has liveliness. It just lacks the intensity of the very best. A good drink with cold meats and salads.

Te Mata Estate Elston Chardonnay

Te Mata Estate makes some of the best chardonnay in New Zealand, some would say THE best. Winemaker since the early eighties is Peter Cowley.

Previous outstanding vintages: '93, '94, '95, '96

CURRENT RELEASE 1997 A tremendously powerful chardonnay, strongly oaked and marked by buttery malolactic characters as well as peachy ripe fruit. Has none of the common New Zealand herbaceous, gooseberry or botrytis flavours. Concentrated fruit gives great depth and finish. A very polished wine. Try roast pheasant.

Quality	♟♟♟♟♟
Value	★★★★★
Grapes	chardonnay
Region	Hawkes Bay, NZ
Cellar	🍾 4+
Alc./Vol.	13.5%
RRP	$40.00

CURRENT RELEASE 1998 A flawless, pristine chardonnay which has signature finesse as well as oodles of personality. Butterscotch, nutty, creamy aromas reflect barrel-fermentation and other winemaking influences, while the mouth flavours suggest butter, peach and tropical fruits, finishing smooth and very long. Enjoy it with truffled egg pasta.

Quality	♟♟♟♟♟
Value	★★★★ⱦ
Grapes	chardonnay
Region	Hawkes Bay, NZ
Cellar	🍾 5+
Alc./Vol.	13.5%
RRP	$40.00

Te Mata Estate Hawkes Bay Chardonnay

This is the junior Te Mata chardonnay. Half of it is fermented in stainless steel, half in oak – in contrast to the Elston, which is all barrel-fermented. Maker Peter Cowley.

CURRENT RELEASE 1997 A delicious chardonnay, showing both the fruity unwooded portion and the more complex portion clearly. There are gooseberry and nectarine flavours from the former, and milk-powder, butterscotch and toasted-nut characters from the latter. It's a softer, lighter wine than the Elston, but it doesn't lack intensity. Drink with New Zealand scampi.

Quality	♟♟♟♟
Value	★★★ⱦ
Grapes	chardonnay
Region	Hawkes Bay, NZ
Cellar	🍾 4
Alc./Vol.	13.5%
RRP	$25.00

Temple Bruer Chenin Blanc

Quality 🍷🍷½
Value ★★★
Grapes chenin blanc
Region Langhorne Creek, SA
Cellar 🍾
Alc./Vol. 12.3%
RRP $12.80

Australian chenin is not usually a variety that improves with age. This one comes from the Angas Delta, near Langhorne Creek.

CURRENT RELEASE 1997 This is showing some age, although the finish doesn't seem to have softened much. The colour is medium–full yellow and it has toasty developed and green herby elements to the bouquet. The palate has a lot of acid and a greenish aspect, which provide some hardness. Best with a meal: try it with spinach quiche.

T'Gallant Pinot Grigio

Quality 🍷🍷🍷
Value ★★½
Grapes pinot gris
Region Mornington Peninsula, Vic.
Cellar 🍾 2
Alc./Vol. 13.6%
RRP $19.75

Pinot Grigio is the Italian way of spelling this grape variety, and fittingly this wine is made more in the Italian style than the Tribute, which more resembles an Alsace version.

CURRENT RELEASE 1998 This is a savoury, non-fruity style with similarly high alcohol to the other wines from this company, and yet the flavour intensity is not particularly high. It has a light yellow colour, a shy nose that is certainly not fruity, and a light-bodied palate with alcohol giving a hot finish. It has some astringency, and could use more fruit weight to balance. A good, rather than great, wine. Serve it with antipasto.

T'Gallant Tribute Pinot Gris

Winemakers Kevin McCarthy and Kathleen Quealy were pioneers with pinot gris on the Mornington Peninsula. They've really started something now . . .
CURRENT RELEASE 1997 This is a no-holds-barred style of pinot gris with enough alcohol to start a party. It has a light yellow colour, and pungent aromas of spices, honey, passionfruit and bracken-like herbs. It has plenty of grapey flavour and is soft, rounded and viscous in the mouth. Some apparent sweetness on the finish may be due more to the alcohol strength than to residual sugar. It's a generous, distinctive unwooded style of dry white, and a good alternative to chardonnay. Serve it with a Thai chicken salad.

Quality	￥￥￥￥
Value	★★★
Grapes	pinot gris
Region	Mornington Peninsula, Vic.
Cellar	◖ 3
Alc./Vol.	14.7%
RRP	$27.00

T'Gallant Triumph Late Harvest Pinot Gris

This is a first effort: a selection of botrytis-affected bunches. Makers Kevin McCarthy and Kathleen Quealy were tempted to label it Selection de Grains Nobles as they do in Alsace, but decided it mightn't be appropriate.
CURRENT RELEASE 1998 This is different! It smells and tastes more like something French, not necessarily Alsatian. Light yellow colour; honey/malt and stony, flinty aromas, which are very complex and which recall some highly sulfured sauternes. There's good intensity, tight structure and a lingering aftertaste. A triumph indeed! Serve it with chicken liver pâté or, even better, pâté de foie gras.

Quality	￥￥￥￥￥
Value	★★★★⋆
Grapes	pinot gris
Region	Mornington Peninsula, Vic.
Cellar	◖ 6+
Alc./Vol.	14.3%
RRP	$19.70 (375 ml)

Tisdall Chardonnay

Quality	♟♟♟
Value	★★★
Grapes	chardonnay
Region	not stated
Cellar	▮ 1
Alc./Vol.	13.0%
RRP	$12.60 Ⓢ

This brand was started by Dr Peter Tisdall in 1979, but has been on the wane for many years. In 1999, owner Mildara Blass sold Tisdall's best vineyard, Mount Helen, which confounded even their own winemakers. Maker Toni Stockhausen.

CURRENT RELEASE 1996 This is now an old wine by today's standards – a sign that sales are slow? It's a full buttercup yellow and has a peachy, resiny bouquet that is rather overblown and broad. There's a rubbery element and the wine has all but lost its fruit-freshness. Drink up. It suits chicken Maryland.

Tollana Adelaide Hills Sauvignon Blanc

Quality	♟♟♟♟
Value	★★★★⊬
Grapes	sauvignon blanc
Region	Adelaide Hills, SA
Cellar	▮ 2
Alc./Vol.	12.5%
RRP	$16.00 Ⓢ

Winemaker Neville Falkenberg was named 1998 Winemaker of the Year by the Barons of the Barossa, for what that's worth.

CURRENT RELEASE 1998 This should be a real crowd-pleaser. It has peppery, capsicum-like aromas, and is quite juicy in the mouth. The finish has a little stalky extractiveness. It's not totally dry, and this heightens its fruitiness. The overall impression is of a soft wine, which fills the mouth. Match it with a seafood cocktail.

Tollana Botrytis Riesling

Quality	♟♟♟♟
Value	★★★★
Grapes	riesling
Region	Coonawarra, SA
Cellar	▮ 4+
Alc./Vol.	11.5%
RRP	$12.00 (375 ml) Ⓢ

Tollana keeps plugging away, consistently turning out some of the best botrytis wine in the country, although its profile is still quite low. Maker Neville Falkenberg.

CURRENT RELEASE 1997 Typically forward in development, this has a golden colour and a bouquet of tea-leaves, apricot jam and vanilla. The same flavours flood the mouth and honey joins in the chorus. It's soft and broad and well balanced, but just lacks the finesse and backbone of the European models. Try it with black-forest cake.

Tollana Eden Valley Riesling

The price this sells for is either criminal or a godsend, depending on your point of view. For punters like you and us, it's unbeatable value for money. Maker Neville Falkenberg.

CURRENT RELEASE 1998 This is always a different style to the others in the Southcorp armoury: it has sweet, almost tropical fruit aromas with juicy citrusy flavours. There are overtones of nettles and dried herbs. The palate has intensity and works well with Alsatian onion tart.

Quality	♟♟♟♟
Value	★★★★★
Grapes	riesling
Region	Eden Valley, SA
Cellar	↓ 4+
Alc./Vol.	12.5%
RRP	$11.80 Ⓢ

Trentham Estate Chardonnay

Tony Murphy's Trentham Estate wines are some of the best value-for-money around, coming as they do from a smart winemaker and good vineyards in an untrendy area.

CURRENT RELEASE 1998 This is a startlingly good wine which stands tall beside much dearer chardonnays. The nose is all honeyed fig and buttery peach; the palate is appropriately viscous and soft, with a roundness enhanced by a hint of sweetness. It has good balance of fruit and winemaker-induced characters. A real crowd-pleaser. Good with Balmain bugs.

Quality	♟♟♟♟
Value	★★★★⋆
Grapes	chardonnay
Region	Murray Valley, NSW
Cellar	↓ 2
Alc./Vol.	13.5%
RRP	$13.50 Ⓢ

Trio Station 3 Steps Chardonnay

Vincorp, which owns this brand, is very ambitious: it plans to be making 80 000 cases of wine in five years. Maker Mark Sheppard.

CURRENT RELEASE 1998 Light peachy aromas introduce a fresh, well-made wine. It's clean as a whistle, and the cashew nut flavours are light- to medium-weight and don't carry much oak. It's soft and very quaffable, and goes well with duck rillette.

Quality	♟♟♟⋆
Value	★★★⋆
Grapes	chardonnay
Region	various, Vic.
Cellar	↓ 2
Alc./Vol.	13.0%
RRP	$14.00 Ⓢ

Turramurra Sauvignon Blanc Fumé Style

Quality	????
Value	★★★
Grapes	sauvignon blanc
Region	Mornington Peninsula, Vic.
Cellar	4
Alc./Vol.	13.5%
RRP	$29.60

The Mornington Peninsula's main claims to fame are its chardonnay and pinot noir. Sauvignon blanc is much less widely planted down there.

CURRENT RELEASE 1998   This is a very complex style of sauvignon, light years away from the fresh fruity style. The nose has complex grass, yeast lees and subtle oak aromas. In the mouth it's well balanced and clean with good depth and a whisper of sweetness in the middle. The texture is rather full and slightly viscous. A serious wine with a touch of the Loire about it. Serve it with some salmon.

Two Churches Barossa Riesling

Quality	????
Value	★★★★
Grapes	riesling
Region	Barossa Valley, SA
Cellar	3
Alc./Vol.	12.0%
RRP	$10.00

There are lots of churches in the Barossa. Indeed, if Adelaide is the city of churches, the Barossa is the Bible Belt of the bibulous. This is a Liquorland own-brand.

CURRENT RELEASE 1997   This is excellent value. It has a slatey, mineral aroma tinged with lemon. The taste is soft, and has good intensity of mineral, lemon flavours, a touch of sweetness and a dry finish. It can take a strong chill, and goes well with John Dory.

Tyrrell's Long Flat Chardonnay

Quality	???
Value	★★★★
Grapes	chardonnay
Region	not stated
Cellar	1
Alc./Vol.	13.5%
RRP	$9.00 $

We note that Murray D. Tyrrell is still signing the label as winemaker, which seems like drawing a long bow. The components of the various Long Flat wines are probably drawn from the four corners of the country these days.

CURRENT RELEASE 1998   It's pretty hard to find a cheap chardonnay that's as well made as this. There are cashew nut, honeydew melon aromas. It has loads of definite chardonnay fruit character, and if you can accept the sweetness level, it's a winner. Otherwise, chill it well and you won't notice so much. Goes well with KFC.

Tyrrell's Long Flat White

While other wines in the Tyrrell's armoury have undergone a facelift, the Long Flat label retains its decidedly homespun look.

CURRENT RELEASE 1998 This will never win any prizes, but when you consider most bottles sell for $5.99, it's a win–win situation for maker and drinker. The aroma is lollyish, with some nondescript ripe fruit aromas; the taste is fairly sweet and bland, but at least it's not labelled DRY white. Low acid for easy quaffability. Try it with a prawn cocktail.

Quality	🍷🍷½
Value	★★★
Grapes	not stated
Region	not stated
Cellar	🍾
Alc./Vol.	10.5%
RRP	$9.00 (S)

Tyrrell's Moon Mountain Chardonnay

This is one of Tyrrell's highly successful Individual Vineyard series. The Moon Mountain vineyard exists – it's in the lower Hunter Valley. Maker Andrew Spinaze.

CURRENT RELEASE 1998 This fine, citrusy, lighter-bodied style of Hunter chardonnay has subtle oak and is a good contrast to Tyrrell's better-known Vat 47. The wine is full yellow in colour, with nutty, toasty aromas showing some development. It's fruit-driven and has some citrusy palate flavours, finishing with fresh, lively acid. Great with oven-baked scampi.

Quality	🍷🍷🍷🍷
Value	★★★½
Grapes	chardonnay
Region	Hunter Valley, NSW
Cellar	🍾 3
Alc./Vol.	13.2%
RRP	$21.30 (S)

Voyager Estate Chardonnay

Funny name for a winery, but the story goes that it's the name of another business interest of owner Michael Wright. He collects voyagers. Maker Stuart Pym.

CURRENT RELEASE 1997 Our bottle seemed a tad disjointed – it could come together given time, but it's already two years old. It has a full yellow shade and the nose is a real treat, offering vanilla, peach, apricot and honey aromas. In the mouth it's very dry and shows lively acid, some alcohol heat, and an oaky firmness. Best with food: try lightly barbecued tuna.

Quality	🍷🍷🍷🍷
Value	★★★½
Grapes	chardonnay
Region	Margaret River, WA
Cellar	🍾 5
Alc./Vol.	13.8%
RRP	$28.00

Voyager Estate Semillon

Quality 🍷🍷½
Value ★★
Grapes semillon
Region Margaret River, WA
Cellar 🍾 2
Alc./Vol. 13.0%
RRP $23.00

Semillon in this region can throw up some challenging flavours. It's a style you can love or hate, but not ignore. Maker Stuart Pym.

CURRENT RELEASE 1997 This is a parody of Margaret River semillon, if you like that sort of thing. The bouquet has dusty, potato, cut-capsicum pungency, and this is all translated onto a dry, slightly dull, palate. An extreme style that lacks in the charm and drinkability departments. Try it with cold seafood and salad.

Wandin Valley Estate Verdelho

Quality 🍷🍷🍷½
Value ★★★
Grapes verdelho
Region Hunter Valley, NSW
Cellar 🍾 2
Alc./Vol. 12.6%
RRP $15.50

Verdelho has a long history in the Hunter Valley. The wine style varies from the very dry to the fruity-sweet, and all points in between.

CURRENT RELEASE 1998 Light tropical fruit betrays the variety on the nose here, but there's also a Hunter regional citrus thing that's almost semillon-like. The palate is pleasant, light, fruity and dry-finishing, but a little short and light-on in flavour intensity. Try it with Thai crab cakes.

Water Wheel Chardonnay

Quality 🍷🍷🍷🍷
Value ★★★★½
Grapes chardonnay
Region Bendigo, Vic.
Cellar 🍾 2
Alc./Vol. 14.0%
RRP $15.00

Water Wheel Chardonnay doesn't finesse around too much. It's always generously proportioned white wine with plenty of flavour at a fair price. What more do you want?

CURRENT RELEASE 1998 Exactly in the Water Wheel mould. The nose has honeyed buttery touches and vanillin oak in harmony with ripe melon fruit aromas. It's mouth-filling and ripe with a dense texture and typical alcoholic sweetness and warmth. Not for long ageing. Serve with shellfish sautéed in white wine.

Water Wheel Sauvignon Blanc

The water wheel is real: it used to power the old flour mill near the winery in slower, gentler times. Maker Peter Cumming.

CURRENT RELEASE 1998   The nose isn't as piercingly herbaceous as many popular sauvignons. Instead it has softly fragrant citrus fruit aromas with some herbal and chalky touches. The palate is ripe and round with good depth. Attractive lemon and tropical fruit flavours lead on to a clean crisp finish.

Quality	♟♟♟♟
Value	★★★★
Grapes	sauvignon blanc
Region	Bendigo, Vic.
Cellar	♟ 1
Alc./Vol.	13.5%
RRP	$15.00

Wellington Iced Riesling

Ex-Charles Sturt University winemaker Andrew Hood specialises in a technique that freezes juice from riesling grapes, concentrating it by removing much of the water component.

CURRENT RELEASE 1998   An interesting style of sweet white wine with an intense nose of lime-cordial-like sweet riesling aromas, and a spicy touch. The palate is sweet and intense with a candied peach flavour, which dovetails nicely into tight, zippy acidity, giving a slight firmness to the finish.

Quality	♟♟♟♟
Value	★★★⯪
Grapes	riesling
Region	Launceston, Tas.
Cellar	♟ 2
Alc./Vol.	10.5%
RRP	$19.75 (375 ml)

Wellington Riesling

Tasmania's climate seems to suit riesling well, giving wines of a more European feel than most mainland vineyards.

CURRENT RELEASE 1997   A highly aromatic yet delicately flavoured wine with a lightly spicy nose of lime-like fruit and minerals. The palate is clean, crisp and Germanic in flavour, not super-intense but very distinctive. The flavour falls away a little towards the end. Works well with bocconcini, tomato and basil bruschetta.

Quality	♟♟♟♟
Value	★★★
Grapes	riesling
Region	Launceston, Tas.
Cellar	♟ 2
Alc./Vol.	12.0%
RRP	$19.75

Westend Richland Chardonnay

Quality	♥♥♥♥
Value	★★★★ย
Grapes	chardonnay
Region	Riverina, NSW
Cellar	▮ 1
Alc./Vol.	13.5%
RRP	$10.95 Ⓢ

Bill Calabria's Westend is an understated winery that's growing in stature among Riverina producers, with an improving range of table wines. The prices remain reasonable – some are amazingly low.

CURRENT RELEASE 1998   This is exactly what honest Riverina chardonnay is all about. There are ripe fig and peach fruit on the nose with a touch of caramelly oak. The palate is smoothly fruited, oak takes a back seat, and it finishes soft and clean. The price makes it a bargain for everyday sipping. Try it with a tropical prawn salad.

Westend Richland Sauvignon Blanc

Quality	♥♥♥♥
Value	★★★★★
Grapes	sauvignon blanc
Region	Riverina, NSW
Cellar	▮ 1
Alc./Vol.	11.5%
RRP	$10.00 Ⓢ

Bill Calabria has rushed this wine – a first release from a new vineyard – onto the market and captured the very essence of the grape. It beats a good many wines double its price.

CURRENT RELEASE 1999   If this was any more alive it would be dangerous. The thing has so much verve and pizzazz. The colour is pale lemon, and it smells of straw, hay, green herbs and a hint of peppermint Lifesavers. There's zesty, sherbety acidity in the mouth balancing intense varietal fruit that's neither green nor flabby. A triumph for the Riverina. But drink it young!

Westend Three Bridges Golden Mist Botrytis Semillon

Quality	♥♥♥♥ย
Value	★★★★ย
Grapes	semillon
Region	Riverina, NSW
Cellar	▮ 2
Alc./Vol.	10.5%
RRP	$22.00 (375 ml)

Bill Calabria's Westend winery is a modest operation near Griffith making another good Riverina sticky.

CURRENT RELEASE 1997   A bright golden wine with the classic sweet citrus, stone-fruit and marmalade aromas of the Riverina Gold style. The flavour is intense with lush apricot-like flavour, smooth texture, good length and a tangy end. There's some finesse here that's missing in some of its competitors. A good companion to crème brûlée.

Will Taylor Clare Valley Riesling

Will Taylor commissions and selects wines for bottling under his label, which are classic regional styles, rather like a traditional European wine merchant. His judgement is very good.

CURRENT RELEASE 1998 This fits the classical mould with an intense nose of spiced apple, some vaguely floral notes and minerally interest. The concentrated slatey palate is dry and austere with a firm backbone. A wine that needs time to realise its potential. Will suit pan-fried prawns with lime and a little zest of chilli.

Quality	?????
Value	★★★★
Grapes	riesling
Region	Clare Valley, SA
Cellar	↦ 1–5+
Alc./Vol.	12.5%
RRP	$19.95

Will Taylor Hunter Valley Semillon

Although Will Taylor's operation is based in South Australia, his intention of bottling Australian classic wine types under his merchant label takes him much further afield.

CURRENT RELEASE 1998 There's no doubt that Hunter semillon is a time-honoured classic and Will Taylor's example is right in archetypal style. The nose has restrained lemon aromas of great varietal purity. The citrus theme follows down the palate, which has a degree of softness in the middle ahead of a clean austere finish. Needs age to show its best. Works well with fritto misto of seafood.

Quality	?????
Value	★★★★
Grapes	semillon
Region	Hunter Valley, NSW
Cellar	↦ 1–6+
Alc./Vol.	11.0%
RRP	$19.95

Willandra Estate Semillon

The Riverina winegrowers are making a bit of a push with their dry white semillon: flash new embossed bottles, gala promotions and an emphasis on cuisine-friendliness. Willandra Estate is a label of Toorak Wines.

CURRENT RELEASE 1998 A rather broad young semillon that doesn't skimp on flavour. The nose has varietal aromas of lemon and herbs with a perfumed intensity. A whiff of oak adds another aspect. In the mouth it has full body, tangy citrus flavour and a sage-like herbal quality. It finishes dry. Try it with baked snapper.

Quality	????
Value	★★★⯪
Grapes	semillon
Region	Riverina, NSW
Cellar	▮ 2
Alc./Vol.	13.0%
RRP	$12.00 Ⓢ

The Willows Riesling

Quality	♥♥♥⏑
Value	★★★★
Grapes	riesling
Region	Barossa Valley, SA
Cellar	➥ 1–6+
Alc./Vol.	12.0%
RRP	$12.50 Ⓢ

Peter Scholz makes this in a traditional, ageworthy style. They tend to go well with delicate foods, such as crab and finer fish, when young, and richer foods when aged. CURRENT RELEASE 1999   A mere stripling, but seems to have a rosy future. The colour is pale lemon; the nose recalls fresh-cut flowers and bread dough. The palate is vibrant, and the crisp acidity lends a degree of firmness which it will grow out of. It needs six months to a year in bottle to show its best. Serve with crab timbale.

Winstead Riesling

Quality	♥♥♥♥⏑
Value	★★★★
Grapes	riesling
Region	Southern Tasmania
Cellar	▮ 5
Alc./Vol.	12.2%
RRP	$22.00

The tiny Winstead vineyard in Tasmania specialises, not surprisingly given the cool climate, in riesling for whites and pinot noir for reds. CURRENT RELEASE 1998   This is a pale, green-tinged riesling which has a very aromatic, Germanic feel about it. The nose has strong, almost traminer-like spice with a touch of lime and blossom. The palate is spicy and rather exotic, clean and dry with a long, fragrantly spicy, aftertaste and tingling acidity.

Wirra Wirra Chardonnay

Quality	♥♥♥♥⏑
Value	★★★★⏐
Grapes	chardonnay
Region	McLaren Vale &
	Adelaide Hills, SA
Cellar	▮ 3
Alc./Vol.	14.0%
RRP	$21.00

Wirra Wirra is often a cut above the pack when it comes to McLaren Vale chardonnay. To the usual attributes of smooth generous flavour it often adds real elegance. Maker Ben Riggs. CURRENT RELEASE 1997   The finesse of some Adelaide Hills material adds refinement to the normal McLaren Vale component here. On the nose there's ripe peach, buttery richness and toasty oak. The palate is smooth and deeply textured with creamy, peachy flavour and a long soft finish.

Wolf Blass Classic Dry White

The oak input has been scaled back in this wine in recent years, in response to changing public taste.

CURRENT RELEASE 1998 This is a pleasant young white with plenty of flavour. The nose is driven by citrus and pear aromas, which are clean and appealing. Some nutty oak and barrel-ferment touches add interest. Similar flavours cross the palate, which is medium-bodied. Oak shows itself again in some firmness at the end. Drink it with seafood pasta.

Quality	▼▼▼▼
Value	★★★★
Grapes	chardonnay; semillon
Region	various
Cellar	♦ 2
Alc./Vol.	13.5%
RRP	$12.00

Wolf Blass Eden Valley Chardonnay

Things are happening in the Wolf Blass camp. Some wines have had a reduction in the oak input, and a new range of good wines labelled simply Blass has arrived to confuse us all.

CURRENT RELEASE 1998 This is still in the Wolf Blass trademark style. The colour is good – a bright pale straw colour. On the nose there's melon fruit, some buttery cashew richness and obvious sweet oak. The palate has some tropical fruit, but oaky flavour dominates. It's medium to full in body with a tasty dry end.

Quality	▼▼▼▼
Value	★★★★
Grapes	chardonnay
Region	various
Cellar	♦ 2
Alc./Vol.	13.0%
RRP	$17.00

Wolf Blass Gold Label Riesling

Quality	♟♟♟♟♟
Value	★★★★★
Grapes	riesling
Region	Eden Valley, Clare Valley, SA
Cellar	▮ 4+
Alc./Vol.	11.5%
RRP	$17.00 ⑤

It's cool in certain circles to bag big name wines like this, while championing the efforts of small producers. The authors love 'em both. This is a classy line made by Wendy Stuckey.

CURRENT RELEASE 1998 These Gold Label rieslings are pretty things which don't have quite the austerity of the traditional style. They may not have the potential longevity either, but they're deliciously put together for drinking in their first few years of life. This has a green tinge to the pale colour, and the nose has intense lime, floral and tropical fruit aromas. The palate is juicy with soft citrus flavour, good length and a clean zip of firm acidity at the end.

Quality	♟♟♟♟♟
Value	★★★★★
Grapes	riesling
Region	Eden Valley & Clare Valley, SA
Cellar	▮ 5+
Alc./Vol.	11.5%
RRP	$17.00 ⑤

PENGUIN WINE OF THE YEAR

CURRENT RELEASE 1999 **How extraordinary that this wine can taste so fantastic just a few weeks after it was bottled! Following a string of great vintages, the '99 is brilliant – and terrific value. If it were chardonnay it would be three times the price. Gold Label is one of Australia's most consistent rieslings, never mind that it's also one of the best buys. The aromas are pungently aromatic with floral, talc, lime and mineral notes that delight the senses. The palate has concentrated lime/citrus and apple flavours inside a framework of lively acidity. It's eminently drinkable, avoiding youthful austerity. The aftertaste is long and aromatic. A sensational riesling to serve with a dressed salad of scallops, lychees and rocket.**

Wolf Blass Riesling

Quality	♟♟♟♟
Value	★★★⯪
Grapes	riesling
Region	Eden Valley & Clare Valley, SA
Cellar	▮ 3
Alc./Vol.	11.0%
RRP	$12.00 ⑤

This is the Wolf Blass riesling with the yellow label. It's found just about everywhere and slots in below the much more distinguished Gold Label in the Blass hierarchy.

CURRENT RELEASE 1999 A correct varietal aroma of spice, florals and lime meets the nose here, but it doesn't sing like the Gold Label. The palate has citrus and spice flavours and it finishes firm and dry. A good white to take to the local Thai BYO restaurant.

Wood Park Meadow Creek Chardonnay

Wood Park is a new name to us, although the Meadow Creek vineyard was planted back in 1972 and has often been used as a source of grapes for other makers. Giaconda's Rick Kinzbrunner is used as a winemaking consultant on this wine, and it shows.

CURRENT RELEASE 1998 Made using some wild yeasts and other non-interventionist methods. The nose has exotic aromas of true complexity – peach, nuts, flint, caramel, burnt matchsticks. Added up they make a Frenchified chardonnay that's worlds away from the Aussie mainstream. The palate is dry and long with measured toasty oak. There's a very slight hollowness in the middle, but all in all this is a marvellous first effort.

Quality	♟♟♟♟♗
Value	★★★★★
Grapes	chardonnay
Region	North East Vic.
Cellar	↓ 5
Alc./Vol.	13.5%
RRP	$24.00

Woodstock Chardonnay

Chardonnay is the most versatile of grapes. With its widespread planting in Australian vineyards over the last couple of decades, it has proven adaptable to most climatic conditions. It's now right at home in the warmth of McLaren Vale.

CURRENT RELEASE 1997 The nose has ripe peach and caramel aromas, and the palate is creamy-textured and mellow in true McLaren Vale style. There's good depth of nutty stone-fruit flavour with a chalky dry finish. It's a straightforward mouthful at a fair price. Try it with veal strips in a creamy sauce.

Quality	♟♟♟♗
Value	★★★★
Grapes	chardonnay
Region	McLaren Vale, SA
Cellar	↓ 2
Alc./Vol.	13.5%
RRP	$17.75

Wyndham Estate Show Reserve Hunter Valley Semillon

Wyndham is one of our most unashamedly commercial operations. Despite being Hunter-Valley-based, the wines can show little regional character. This is an exception.

CURRENT RELEASE 1995 A very Hunter semillon bouquet, with age starting to weave its magic. It's subdued and fine with citrus and honey aromas to the fore. The palate has a smooth feel with good intensity and a flinty, dry end. Serve it with fried sardines.

Quality	♟♟♟♟
Value	★★★★
Grapes	semillon
Region	Hunter Valley, NSW
Cellar	↓ 2
Alc./Vol.	11.5%
RRP	$26.00

Wynns Chardonnay

Quality	♀♀♀♀
Value	★★★★↾
Grapes	chardonnay
Region	Coonawarra, SA
Cellar	▮ 3
Alc./Vol.	13.5%
RRP	$14.50 Ⓢ

Reds get the fanfares at Wynns Coonawarra Estate, but the whites shouldn't be ignored. The chardonnay is always a keenly priced well-made wine.

CURRENT RELEASE 1998   This is more restrained than a lot of its competitors, which is a good thing. It's a straw-coloured drop with melon and nutty/milky aromas. The palate is well balanced and dry. Melon and citrus flavours are of good intensity, and the finish is dry and firm. Grilled prawns would suit.

Wynns Riesling

Quality	♀♀♀♀♀
Value	★★★★★
Grapes	riesling
Region	Coonawarra, SA
Cellar	▮ 5+
Alc./Vol.	12.0%
RRP	$12.00 Ⓢ

Wynns riesling is a perennial bargain. If riesling had been more fashionable in recent years its price would be much higher. Our advice is to make hay while the sun shines!

CURRENT RELEASE 1998   As usual this is a fresh, lively young wine with pure varietal aromas in the classical floral and citrus vein. The palate has dry lime flavour of good depth and intensity. It has a certain severity in youth, which is very appetising. In an ideal world it would get a bit of bottle-age; at this price you can afford to put some away to see what we mean. Try it with salmon sashimi.

Yalumba Oxford Landing Chardonnay

Quality	♀♀♀♀
Value	★★★★
Grapes	chardonnay
Region	Murray Valley, SA
Cellar	▮ 1
Alc./Vol.	13.5%
RRP	$9.00 Ⓢ

Oxford Landing is a place on the Murray River in South Australia. It was established by Yalumba in 1958 and is now the source of the company's volume-selling commercial range.

CURRENT RELEASE 1998   This has all those sunny qualities that make this sort of reasonably priced chardonnay a winner in the popularity stakes. On nose and palate there's juicy tropical and melon fruit of quite voluptuous proportions. It tastes clean and rich, and the finish is soft and clean. Drink with seafood pasta.

Yalumba Oxford Landing Limited Release Semillon

Now we're getting limited-release versions of our volume cellars – what next? Obviously there's a niche market there somewhere. The presentation is very smart and the pricing very keen.

CURRENT RELEASE 1998   Semillon handled like char- donnay has resulted in an interesting alternative. The varietal character is restrained, offering straw-like aromas and herbal flavour, which is dry and tasty. The overlay of nutty oak, yeasty touches and a smooth creamy quality work well. Sharp acidity keeps it all in focus. Good value. Try it with pan-fried blue-eye fillets.

Quality	۲۲۲۲
Value	★★★★★
Grapes	semillon
Region	Murray Valley, SA
Cellar	2
Alc./Vol.	12.5%
RRP	$11.50 Ⓢ

Yalumba Oxford Landing Sauvignon Blanc

Oxford Landing is another of those branded Australian wines that leads the export rush into markets like the UK. Some of them are surprisingly good; others so-so.

CURRENT RELEASE 1998   This offering provides a true sauvignon blanc thrill on a budget. The nose has some of those wild herbaceous notes that polarise drinkers into sauvignon-lovers or -haters. There's also tropical fruiti- ness, which follows down the palate beside that grassy zip. Try it with asparagus.

Quality	۲۲۲۲
Value	★★★★
Grapes	sauvignon blanc
Region	Murray Valley, SA
Cellar	1
Alc./Vol.	12.0%
RRP	$9.00 Ⓢ

Yarra Glen Chardonnay

Another new product from the mercurial Mr Andrew Garrett. The back label is subtitled 'no oak . . . just fruit', which says it all.

CURRENT RELEASE 1998   An attractive modern un- oaked chardonnay with a clean, direct personality. It smells prettily of peach and fruit salad, and it has a soft, simple melony fruitiness in the mouth. The finish is chalky-textured and dry. A straightforward companion to some flashy chicken sandwiches.

Quality	۲۲۲۲
Value	★★★
Grapes	chardonnay
Region	Yarra Valley, Vic.
Cellar	1
Alc./Vol.	13.5%
RRP	$21.00

Yarraman Road Chardonnay

Quality 🍷🍷🍷½
Value ★★★
Grapes chardonnay
Region Upper Hunter Valley, NSW
Cellar 2
Alc./Vol. 12.9%
RRP $21.60

This is the high-quality label from Barrington Estate in the Upper Hunter, which was once Penfolds Wybong Estate, the source of many now-forgotten Penfolds Private Bin wines.

CURRENT RELEASE 1998 On first acquaintance, this seems right in the big Hunter chardonnay tradition, with its pale gold colour and buttery-rich fig syrup and lime nose. Nutty barrel influence adds another aspect to the nose, but in the mouth it's surprisingly simple. Peachy flavour and caramelly oak are there on a shortish palate, which finishes clean and dry. Suits pasta with ham and cheese.

Yarra Valley Hills Kiah Yallambee Chardonnay

Quality 🍷🍷🍷🍷½
Value ★★★★½
Grapes chardonnay
Region Yarra Valley, Vic.
Cellar 1–4
Alc./Vol. 14.0%
RRP $27.00

Yarra Valley Hills sources grapes from a number of vineyards in the region and recently brought the long-established Bianchet vineyard into the fold. Maker Martin Williams.

CURRENT RELEASE 1998 Martin Williams knows his stuff, and he's worked hard on this stylish chardonnay. The nose has grapefruit, malt and mineral qualities with very subdued oak. The citrus-accented palate is silky with good length, crispness and some alcoholic warmth on the finish. Needs time to develop. Try it with oysters.

Yarra Valley Hills Log Creek Sauvignon Blanc Semillon

Quality 🍷🍷🍷🍷
Value ★★★½
Grapes sauvignon blanc; semillon
Region Yarra Valley, Vic.
Cellar 1
Alc./Vol. 13.5%
RRP $24.00

Winemaker Martin Williams has an encyclopaedic wine knowledge, which will be of benefit to Yarra Valley Hills as its vineyards mature. Some of his early efforts there have been excellent.

CURRENT RELEASE 1998 Juicy fruit aromas of succulent ripeness lead the way here. The fruit salad on the nose is repeated in the mouth with some sauvignon herbaceousness taking second place. A whisper of sweetness enhances the effect. The finish is dry. Will go well with charry chicken satays and Indonesian trimmings.

Yarra Valley Hills Warranwood Riesling

The suburban sprawl of Melbourne reaches almost to the gateway of this vineyard, so access to a large market shouldn't be a problem for proprietor Terry Hill.

CURRENT RELEASE 1998 The colour is classically pale and green-tinged. On the nose it's very Germanic, with super-aromatic spice, florals, apple and lime aromas. The palate is pungent with a musk-stick flavour against a fine, spice and citrus background. It finishes firm with a long spicy aftertaste. Distinctly European in style and a good match for smoked trout.

Quality	io io io io
Value	★★★★
Grapes	riesling
Region	Yarra Valley, Vic.
Cellar	▋ 4+
Alc./Vol.	12.0%
RRP	$21.00

Yering Station Chardonnay

In a previous incarnation Yering Station was the first vineyard in Victoria. The original buildings still stand, but these days the wines are made at an impressive new winery nearby.

CURRENT RELEASE 1998 A fruit-driven chardonnay of real freshness that displays its cool-climate origins loud and clear. The nose has crisply inviting melon and citrus aromas. In the mouth it's a light, tangy chardonnay of good intensity with a delicate, lively finish.

Quality	io io io io
Value	★★★★
Grapes	chardonnay
Region	Yarra Valley, Vic.
Cellar	▋ 3
Alc./Vol.	13.5%
RRP	$20.00

Yering Station Reserve Chardonnay

At Yering station they've pulled out all stops on these inaugural Reserve wines. They choose the most outstanding parcels of fruit and vinify them in a traditional French manner. Maker Tom Carson.

CURRENT RELEASE 1997 A gem of a Yarra chardonnay. Sweet fruit aromas, spicy oak, cashew, a herbal touch and buttermilk are all moulded into a complex bouquet which is very subtle. The elegant palate is creamy-textured and seamless, fine and long with a firm structure. Try it with sweetbreads.

Quality	io io io io io
Value	★★★★★
Grapes	chardonnay
Region	Yarra Valley, Vic.
Cellar	▋ 4
Alc./Vol.	13.5%
RRP	$42.00

Sparkling Wines

All Saints St Leonards Cabernet Sauvignon NV

Quality	ŶŶŶ?
Value	★★★
Grapes	cabernet sauvignon
Region	North East Vic.
Cellar	▮ 1
Alc./Vol.	13.5%
RRP	$19.00

Cabernet sauvignon isn't usually the grape of choice for sparkling reds. Shiraz reigns supreme in this area, but Victoria's north-east can produce some very shiraz-like cabernet, so we suppose it doesn't matter.

CURRENT RELEASE *non-vintage* This is a straightforward sparkling red with stewed plum and berries on the nose along with some meaty and earthy notes. The palate is mellow enough but rather one-dimensional, with sweet berry flavour and a fairly tannic grip at the end. Try it with prosciutto.

Andrew Garrett Vintage

Quality	ŶŶŶŶ?
Value	★★★★ˇ
Grapes	chardonnay; pinot noir
Region	not stated
Cellar	▮ 1
Alc./Vol.	11.5%
RRP	$15.00

Mildara Blass fizz-makers aim the Andrew Garrett vintage bubbly at drinkers who like lots of body and flavour.

CURRENT RELEASE 1996 Big on flavour, but not a model of finesse, this is a good sparkler to serve with flavoursome food. It has a bouquet of cracked yeast, vanilla cream and candied peel with a hint of aldehyde. The palate is broad and rich with excellent balance, a dry finish, and a yeasty aftertaste. Great with goujons of fish.

Balnaves Sparkling Cabernet

Quality	ŶŶŶ?
Value	★★★
Grapes	cabernet sauvignon
Region	Coonawarra, SA
Cellar	▮ 3
Alc./Vol.	12.5%
RRP	$24.00

Balnaves is an up-and-coming name. This is a blend of vintages, released in 1997. Maker Peter Bissell.

CURRENT RELEASE *non-vintage* The colour is deep and youthful-looking; the aromas are of rich fruitcake and plum with some toasty character reflecting oak. It's relatively dry on the palate and finishes with some tannin. A decent drier style; try it with turkey.

Banrock Station Sparkling Chardonnay

Banrock Station is a vineyard in the South Australian Riverland. Owners BRL Hardy plough a certain amount of money from each bottle sold into conserving wetlands adjacent to the vineyard. Fifty thousand dollars has been donated so far.

CURRENT RELEASE *non-vintage* The colour is a pale yellow, and there are fresh creamy chardonnay-like aromas, very simple and youthful. It's quite sweet on entry, the palate flavour light but very attractive and true to the grape variety. Good flavour and character at the price. Take it to a party.

Quality	♥♥♥?
Value	★★★★
Grapes	chardonnay
Region	Murray Valley, SA
Cellar	♦
Alc./Vol.	12.0%
RRP	$10.00 ⑤

Barossa Valley Estate E & E Sparkling Shiraz

E & E has become little more than a brand, as the grapes of Elmor Roehr and Elmore Schulz are no longer used. But it's still a hell of a good wine.

CURRENT RELEASE 1994 A big, opulent style that's built to impress. It has rather a lot of coconutty American oak in the bouquet, but also complex undergrowth and earthy characters. It's very full-bodied, powerful and concentrated. Rich, dense and very satisfying to drink, it takes the style to extremes. It should age well. Try it with grilled pork chops and plum sauce.

Quality	♥♥♥♥♥
Value	★★★★
Grapes	shiraz
Region	Barossa Valley, SA
Cellar	♦ 10
Alc./Vol.	14.5%
RRP	$36.80 ⑤

Barossa Valley Estate Ebenezer Sparkling Pinot Noir

Barossa Valley Estate has just gone into a joint venture with BRL Hardy with plans to more than double its output. It's also building a winery in the Marananga area of the Barossa Valley.

CURRENT RELEASE *non-vintage* A deep yellow–gold colour reflects substantial development. The nose is again developed: wet straw, earthy and vanilla characters reveal quite a deal of bottle-age. The palate is mouth-filling, round and soft, finishing quite dry, and again showing forward development considering the wine has only been one year on its lees. Try devils-on-horseback.

Quality	♥♥♥?
Value	★★★
Grapes	pinot noir
Region	Barossa Valley, SA
Cellar	♦
Alc./Vol.	13.0%
RRP	$21.00

Bazzani Saluté Pinot Nero

Quality	ŶŶŶ
Value	★★⊦
Grapes	pinot noir
Region	Pyrenees, Vic.
Cellar	▮ 1
Alc./Vol.	12.0%
RRP	$29.00

Luigi Bazzani is the energetic proprietor of Warrenmang winery and resort in the Pyrenees district of Victoria. Bazzani is his alternative label.

CURRENT RELEASE 1996   A most unusual wine. The colour is slightly bronzed because of pinot noir grapes. The nose has a very gamy aroma, which could be from oak or possibly it's just an unusual expression of pinot noir. The palate lacks a little intensity and has a hard acid finish, which also carries some sweetness. Food: deep-fried crumbed prawns.

Blue Pyrenees Midnight Cuvée

Quality	ŶŶŶŶⱦ
Value	★★★★
Grapes	pinot noir; chardonnay
Region	Pyrenees, Vic.
Cellar	▮ 5
Alc./Vol.	12.5%
RRP	$34.50 Ⓢ

The grapes were harvested after midnight in very cool conditions. How do you hand-snip whole bunches at night for premium fizz without losing fingers? Use high-powered floodlighting!

CURRENT RELEASE *non-vintage*   This is classy fizz! It may not have had a lot of time on lees to achieve great complexity and richness, but it's ultra-fine. The colour is light yellow, and it smells of candied fruits, green apples and bread. Chardonnay seems to dominate. Pear and apple flavours permeate the palate, and it finishes very dry with lively acid, giving a degree of austerity. Beaut stuff with almond bread.

Briar Ridge Pinot Chardonnay Méthode Champenoise

Quality	ŶŶŶŶ
Value	★★★⊦
Grapes	pinot noir; chardonnay
Region	Hunter Valley, NSW
Cellar	▮ 3
Alc./Vol.	11.0%
RRP	$18.00

Winemaker Neil McGuigan is now a 50 per cent owner of this Hunter Valley winery. McGuigan, who worked with Wyndham Estate and his brother Brian for many years, has really found his feet at Briar Ridge.

CURRENT RELEASE 1997   This is a shy little wall-flower. Delicate yellow in shade, it has a light-intensity aroma with freshness and yet some complexity from yeast autolysis, giving hints of smoke, vanilla and cream-iness. The light-bodied palate has delicacy and vibrancy. It could benefit from more age on lees, but that's a wine-maker's issue. A slightly bland wine of very good quality to serve with oysters.

Brands Sparkling Cabernet Sauvignon

Not many sparkling reds come out of Coonawarra. Brands is a good example of the modern sparkling cabernet genre.

CURRENT RELEASE 1997   This has medium depth of dark red colour and a very pure nose of ripe, leafy, berry fruit, unadorned by much oak. Bottle-ferment input is subtle. The palate has smooth, earthy blackcurrant fruit flavour, measured sweetness, and rather firm tannins on the finish. Try it with roast turkey.

Quality	♟♟♟♟
Value	★★★★
Grapes	cabernet sauvignon
Region	Coonawarra, SA
Cellar	▮ 3
Alc./Vol.	12.5%
RRP	$23.00

Broke Estate Cabernets Moussant

Is there such a word as *moussant* in the French wine lexicon? *Mousseux*, yessir, but *moussant*? If it did exist, the EU would probably jump on Broke Estate from a great height.

CURRENT RELEASE 1995   This scored well at the 1998 New South Wales Wine Awards, and deservedly so. It's a very pretty wine. The nose reveals ripe red berries, and there's good intensity of fruit on the palate. It's elegant and balanced and the finish lingers, with well-judged astringency. It would go well with roast guinea fowl.

Quality	♟♟♟♟◗
Value	★★★
Grapes	cabernet sauvignon; cabernet franc
Region	Hunter Valley, NSW
Cellar	▮ 3
Alc./Vol.	13.0%
RRP	$49.00

Brown Brothers Moscato

Why did it take so long for an Australian winery to turn its hand to this traditional Piedmontese sparkling style? It makes for delightfully flirtatious summer quaffing. Maker Terry Barnett.

CURRENT RELEASE 1998   **The clean, fresh, youthful grapey/muscaty aroma is absolutely delicious to smell. Its simple, fresh fruit taste is clean and frisky, and very low in alcohol – so low you could quaff it all day. An uncomplicated, but beautiful, fruit-driven style. Only slightly fizzy, hence it can be sealed with a normal cork, and no champagne wire. Drink it with fresh grapes.**

Quality	♟♟♟♟◗
Value	★★★★★
Grapes	muscat gordo blanco
Region	Murray Valley, Vic.
Cellar	▮
Alc./Vol.	6.0%
RRP	$12.50 Ⓢ

PENGUIN BEST BARGAIN BUBBLY

Brown Brothers Pinot Chardonnay Brut

Quality	♟♟♟♟
Value	★★★t
Grapes	pinot noir; chardonnay
Region	King Valley, Vic.
Cellar	▮ 2
Alc./Vol.	11.5%
RRP	$16.80

This is the common or garden Browns bubbly, and it's anything but common. The grapes come from the King Valley and it competes well against the big boys' bubblies.

CURRENT RELEASE *non-vintage* The nose is shy with some biscuit and bread aromas with vanilla and caramel prominent. It tastes soft and broad on the tongue with some richness but not a lot of finesse, and there's a trace of liqueur sweetness. The flavours recall baked apples with raisins. The finish is all biscuit and vanilla. Good with pistachio nuts.

Brown Brothers Sparkling Shiraz

Quality	♟♟♟
Value	★★★
Grapes	shiraz
Region	King Valley, Vic.
Cellar	▮ 3
Alc./Vol.	13.5%
RRP	$22.50 (cellar door)

Sparkling red is a growth industry, and it would be just like Brown Brothers to have all the bases covered. Maker Terry Barnett and team.

CURRENT RELEASE 1995 This reminds more of cabernet than shiraz: the aromas are of mulberry and currants, and it has a slight dip in the middle palate. The mousse is fluffy, and it's a lighter, non-confrontational style. It has noticeable acid peeking out from under the liqueur. The finish is firm, and it would go with meat pie and tomato sauce.

Brown Brothers Whitlands Pinot Chardonnay Brut

Quality	♟♟♟♟♟
Value	★★★★★
Grapes	pinot noir; chardonnay
Region	Whitfield, Vic.
Cellar	▮ 2
Alc./Vol.	12.0%
RRP	$35.00

We gave this vintage five glasses last year, but it's still current and still one of the great Australian sparkling wines. If anything, another year has enriched it and made it more complex. Maker Terry Barnett and team. *Previous outstanding vintages: '93*

CURRENT RELEASE 1994 This drinks better than many NV (French) Champagnes at much higher prices. There's a hint of pink in the colour, and it smells of rich dried fruits, cooked bread and burnt-toast complexities. It's benefiting from some development. It's a very complex, rich, dry and persistent drop. A masterpiece. Serve it with smoked trout.

Browns of Padthaway Sparkling Shiraz

This large vineyard was established by Donald Brown and family in 1970 to supply other wine companies. There are 210 hectares under vine and the wines are made at Rymill.

CURRENT RELEASE 1995 This is a forward, mature style with lots of undergrowth and vegetal characters. The colour is lightish and developed, and the bouquet has earthy, leathery maturity. The palate is lean and has quite marked sweetness. It should be a good mate for stir-fried beef in hoisin sauce.

Quality	♟♟♟
Value	★★⬧
Grapes	shiraz
Region	Padthaway, SA
Cellar	◊ 1
Alc./Vol.	12.5%
RRP	$26.25

Carrington Brut Reserve NV

Orlando's Carrington range is everywhere, offering reasonable sparkling wines at a good price. The earth may not move when you sip them, but they're unlikely to offend.

CURRENT RELEASE *non-vintage* This has a clear pale appearance with a fair amount of fizz. Despite its low price, the nose offers a touch of complexity with some citrus accents and a measure of biscuity aroma. In the mouth it's right in style, smooth, clean and crisp. A good aperitif on a budget.

Quality	♟♟♟
Value	★★★★
Grapes	not stated
Region	various, SA
Cellar	◊ 1
Alc./Vol.	11.5%
RRP	$10.00 Ⓢ

Carrington Vintage Brut

The Carrington line of sparklers comprises a number of different wines. This has the grandest name and presentation with its black and gold label, but it remains a reasonably priced drop.

CURRENT RELEASE 1997 Appearance is good here: a nice pale straw colour with a fine bead. The nose has soft fruit aromas with hints of biscuit and nutty bottle development. The palate is smooth and easy to drink with a crisp finish. Easy to sip with some canapés.

Quality	♟♟♟⸗
Value	★★★★
Grapes	chardonnay & others
Region	various, SA
Cellar	◊ 1
Alc./Vol.	11.5%
RRP	$10.00 Ⓢ

Charles Melton Sparkling Red

Quality	🍷🍷🍷🍷🍷
Value	★★★
Grapes	shiraz
Region	Barossa Valley, SA
Cellar	🍾 5
Alc./Vol.	13.5%
RRP	$44.00

Charlie Melton is a man who respects tradition and what could be more traditional than a sparkling red? Needless to say it's a copybook example of the genre.

CURRENT RELEASE *non-vintage* Disgorged February 1999. Good depth of clinker-brick colour here. The bouquet is clean and attractive with ripe blackberry, spice and mushroomy aromas. There's also a balanced touch of dusty/sweet oak. A mouthful reveals round blackberry flavour with a hint of licorice, moderate sweetness and some savoury notes. It finishes dry with lovely ripe, fine tannins. More-ish in the extreme. A festive season must-have with roast turkey; at other times try kangaroo.

Clover Hill

Quality	🍷🍷🍷🍷
Value	★★★⯪
Grapes	chardonnay; pinot noir
Region	Pipers River, Tas.
Cellar	🍾 2
Alc./Vol.	12.0%
RRP	$32.90

Clover Hill is Taltarni's Tasmanian outpost. Its speciality is sparkling wine. Quality so far has added more weight to the opinion that Tassie's wine future has bubbles in it.

CURRENT RELEASE 1996 This was a difficult year in Tasmania, but Clover Hill weathered the dismal conditions better than some. This is a pale straw-coloured sparkler with a fine lime/citrus aroma and a very subtle biscuity touch. It's understated and lean-boned with a fragrant citrus flavour. The poor '96 year is reflected in a slightly herbaceous touch mid-palate. It finishes alive and tangy. A very good aperitif.

Cope-Williams Macedon Ranges Brut

Quality	🍷🍷🍷🍷
Value	★★★⯪
Grapes	chardonnay
Region	Macedon, Vic.
Cellar	🍾 1
Alc./Vol.	12.0%
RRP	$32.60

The Cope-Williams operation is a charmingly eccentric place with its own cricket ground and pavilion. It might well be the most visited of the Macedon wineries.

CURRENT RELEASE *non-vintage* An inviting pale straw sparkling wine with a fine, persistent foam. The nose is quite complex, driven by citrus and green apple fruit, but made more elaborate by hints of mushroom, yeast, and an attractive sort of waxy aroma you sometimes see in bubbly from the Loire. The palate is clean and smooth with appley fruit and a long dry finish.

Croser

Just mention the name Brian around the Australian wine industry and everyone knows who you mean. As if Croser wasn't a distinctive enough name. After two vintages that offered less than we expected, this marque is back on song.

Previous outstanding vintages: '90, '92, '94

CURRENT RELEASE 1997 Pour us another glass, please, this'll do nicely. The mousse is so persistent it seems to be on steroids. The bouquet is complex, with candied-fruit, bread and herbal characters, which appeal greatly. Fine citrusy flavour and crisp acid feature in the mouth, where it's delicate, dry and persistent. Lovely bubbly, and an improver. Serve with gravlax.

Quality	♟♟♟♟
Value	★★★★
Grapes	pinot noir 70%; chardonnay 30%
Region	Adelaide Hills, SA
Cellar	🍾 5
Alc./Vol.	12.5%
RRP	$34.00

Cuvée Clare

This is a buyer's own-brand wine sold by Liquorland and produced at Petaluma. Interestingly, the wine is made from riesling, but it doesn't say so anywhere on the package.

CURRENT RELEASE 1996 Very like a German Sekt, with classic floral riesling aroma and no cracked yeast influence. It's all about fruit rather than bottle-aged complexity. It has hi-fi riesling flavour and a touch of liqueur adding a faint sweetness to the finish. This is a very unusual and interesting style of sparkling wine. Use as an aperitif.

Quality	♟♟♟
Value	★★★★
Grapes	riesling
Region	Clare Valley, SA
Cellar	🍾 1
Alc./Vol.	12.5%
RRP	$10.99

D'Arenberg Peppermint Paddock Sparkling Chambourcin

We guess chambourcin lends itself to bubbly because it's naturally high in acid and low in tannin. You need to like ultra-fruity, ultra-young red bubblies to go for this.

CURRENT RELEASE 1997 This tastes somewhat unfinished – like it's barely stopped fermenting! It's raw and estery, and takes simple fruitiness to new levels. The flavours are of berry jams and stalkiness. A useful transitional drink from Berri Dark Grape Juice to adult drinks.

Quality	♟♟♟
Value	★★★
Grapes	chambourcin
Region	McLaren Vale, SA
Cellar	🍾 4
Alc./Vol.	13.5%
RRP	$19.70

Deakin Estate Brut

Quality	♟♟♟⏴
Value	★★★★
Grapes	chardonnay; colombard; chenin blanc
Region	Sunraysia, Vic.
Cellar	▯ 1
Alc./Vol.	12.5%
RRP	$10.00 ⑤

This is a past winner of our Best Bargain Bubbly Award, and it always offers good value. The current model is showing a tad more age than we recalled. Maker Mark Zeppel.

CURRENT RELEASE *non-vintage* This has always been a big peachy fruit style. Generous, but not necessarily a wine of finesse. It reminds us of chardonnay with soft, ripe peach/cashew fruit aromas together with a hint of toasty bottle-age. The palate is soft, broad and open. Chill well and serve with smoked trout pâté.

Delatite Demelza

Quality	♟♟♟♟♟
Value	★★★⏴
Grapes	pinot noir; chardonnay
Region	Mansfield, Vic.
Cellar	▯ 2
Alc./Vol.	13.0%
RRP	$28.50

This is the first commercial release of a sparkling wine from Delatite in Victoria's highlands near the Mount Buller snowfields. Demelza is the name of winemaker Rosie Ritchie's daughter. The wine was made at Delatite and finished at Domaine Chandon.

CURRENT RELEASE 1994/1995 The label says this has 'a pale strawberry hue' – maybe they mean pale straw, since it's definitely white wine rather than pink. No matter – it's an elegant addition to the range of high-quality sparkling wine available from Australia's cooler regions. The nose and palate have delicate hints of wild strawberry and citrus with very subtle touches of vanilla and yeast lees. In the mouth it's elegant, light and fine with a long clean finish. Try it pre-dinner with sushi.

Deutz Marlborough Cuvée

Quality	♟♟♟♟
Value	★★★
Grapes	chardonnay; pinot noir
Region	Marlborough, NZ
Cellar	▯ 3
Alc./Vol.	12.0%
RRP	$24.60

This is a bubbly produced by Montana, New Zealand's biggest wine company, in cahoots with Champagne Deutz of France.

CURRENT RELEASE *non-vintage* A slightly green style of bubbly with fairly hard acid on the palate, but some attractive melon-skin, vaguely sherbety, cool-climate fruit flavours. The wine has good freshness and an excellent frothy sparkle to it, but is a bit austere and herbaceous. Good with bluff oysters.

Domaine Chandon Blanc de Blancs

They skipped the 1994 vintage, so the '95 has been released at a younger age than usual. Blanc de Blancs is rarely as complex as a blend, but this is a pretty fair attempt.
Previous outstanding vintages: '91, '93
CURRENT RELEASE 1995 This is a fine, pure-fruited but essentially simpler wine than the Vintage Brut. The aromas are creamy and citrusy, with hints of melon, marzipan and aniseed. Tightly structured, finessy and dry-finishing, it makes a great partner for crab timbales.

Quality	♟♟♟♟♟
Value	★★★★
Grapes	chardonnay
Region	mainly Yarra Valley, Vic.
Cellar	↓ 3
Alc./Vol.	13.0%
RRP	$32.50 ⑤

Domaine Chandon Blanc de Noirs

The grape sources have been swinging away from the warmer McLaren Vale, Coonawarra, and so on, towards the cooler areas such as Mornington Peninsula. This is the finest Blanc de Noirs we can recall from DC.
Previous outstanding vintages: '90, '92
CURRENT RELEASE 1994 A terrifically fine, trim, restrained yet intense wine with red-grape power and bready/biscuity characters, but also real delicacy. Smoky strawberry and exotic spices can also be found. There's a degree of richness, and the finish is where it sets itself apart from prior releases: it's long, with perfect balance and without excessive grip. Try it with Peking duck.

Quality	♟♟♟♟♟
Value	★★★★↓
Grapes	pinot noir
Region	Mornington Peninsula, Strathbogie Ranges, Whitfield, Yarra Valley & Geelong, Vic.
Cellar	↓ 5
Alc./Vol.	13.0%
RRP	$32.50 ⑤

Domaine Chandon LD Late Disgorged Brut

This is the same wine as the Vintage Brut of that year, but a small proportion was held back and given extra time on lees.
CURRENT RELEASE 1993 It's now a very mature drink, and you have to like the taste of old wine. The toasty, bottle-age characters totally dominate the fruit. There are burnt-bread, honey, butterscotch and dried-herb aromas. The *dosage* is very low, giving a seriously arid finish. Lots of weight and length, too. Best with food, so try salmon roe and sour cream on blinis.

Quality	♟♟♟♟♟
Value	★★★↓
Grapes	pinot noir; chardonnay; pinot meunier
Region	various, Vic, SA & Tas.
Cellar	↓
Alc./Vol.	13.0%
RRP	$40.00

Domaine Chandon Millennium Cuvée

Quality	♟♟♟♟♟
Value	★★★★★
Grapes	chardonnay 55%; pinot noir 45%
Region	various, Vic, SA & Tas.
Cellar	↑ 2
Alc./Vol.	13.0%
RRP	$50.00 (cellar door)

To commemorate the year 2000, 2000 bottles were laid down in 1993 and pre-sold at 2000 cents ($20) each, which has to be one of the best *en-primeur* bargains we've ever seen. It's a great wine, which will be released near the end of 1999, after six and a half years on lees. The last 200 dozen will go on sale at the winery in September/October. Makers Wayne Donaldson, Tony Jordan and team.

CURRENT RELEASE 1993   What a wine! This is Australia's answer to Krug – it's that rich and powerful. The colour is full yellow; the bouquet is terrifically rich and mature with irresistible scents of honey, vanilla, oatmeal and candied fruits. It has unusual viscosity, and while it's the same age as the current LD (late-disgorged), it's finer, softer, richer and smoother. The finish is practically endless. A sensational sparkling wine! Drink it with pride.

Domaine Chandon Rosé Vintage Brut

Quality	♟♟♟♟♟
Value	★★★★
Grapes	pinot noir 55%; chardonnay 45%
Region	various
Cellar	↑ 3
Alc./Vol.	12.5%
RRP	$32.50 Ⓢ

Rosé is often assumed to be a wine for wimps. Not so, at least in this case. This vintage has been a huge success in restaurants.
Previous outstanding vintages: '92, '93, '94
CURRENT RELEASE 1995   The colour is onion-skin pink, and the nose has dusty, vanilla and smoky berry aromas. The palate is very dry and long, and there's a delicate tannin grip on the finish. It's rich and full, with tonnes of flavour, but it doesn't sacrifice finesse. Try it with smoked salmon roulade.

Domaine Chandon Vintage Brut

This lays the strongest claim for the title of best Australian sparkling wine, year after year. It's consistently outstanding and is produced in amazing quantities – something like 70 000 cases. As in Champagne, quality and quantity *can* go hand in hand. Maker Wayne Donaldson and team.

Previous outstanding vintages: '90, '91, '92, '93, '94, '95

CURRENT RELEASE 1996 From a warmer, riper year this has an advanced, mid–full yellow colour. The aromas are dominated by creamy and bready, yeast-dominant notes at present, and the fruit has yet to fully emerge. There are straw and almond hints. It has a big attack on the front palate and finishes very dry and long. Not sure it's as good as the superb '95, but it's a good aperitif. Serve with canapés.

Quality 🍷🍷🍷🍷
Value ★★★½
Grapes pinot noir; chardonnay; pinot meunier
Region various, Vic, SA & Tas.
Cellar 4
Alc./Vol. 13.0%
RRP $32.50 (S)

Elgee Park Cuvée Brut

Baillieu Myer set things in motion on the Mornington Peninsula when he planted vines there in the early seventies. Production at Elgee Park is still small, but the wines are worth seeking.

CURRENT RELEASE 1995 This is a rich sparkler with a citrus, apple and cashew bouquet which has hints of biscuit and yeast. In the mouth it has very fine texture and good length of delicate flavour. High acidity keeps it refreshing, although it does show some bottle development. A good aperitif style with little vol-au-vents.

Quality 🍷🍷🍷🍷
Value ★★★½
Grapes chardonnay; pinot noir
Region Mornington Peninsula, Vic.
Cellar 1
Alc./Vol. 12.4%
RRP $25.50

Eyton on Yarra Pinot Chardonnay

Quality	♛♛♛♛♛
Value	★★★★
Grapes	pinot noir; chardonnay
Region	Yarra Valley, Vic.
Cellar	▮ 2
Alc./Vol.	12.5%
RRP	$30.00

At Eyton they have plenty of reason to open lots of bubbly, what with all the concerts, galas and arty dos that take place there. Just as well they have a good one of their own.

CURRENT RELEASE 1995   This is a stylish sparkling wine with balance and harmony. The bubble is fine and creaming, and the nose has apple and citrus fruit aromas with creamy, biscuity yeast influence. The palate is dry and zippy with delicate fruit in the middle, reasonable depth and a clean, crisp signature. Serve it with sushi.

Fiddlers Creek Cuvée Brut

Quality	♛♛♛
Value	★★★⯪
Grapes	not stated
Region	Pyrenees, Vic.
Cellar	▮ 1
Alc./Vol.	10.5%
RRP	$12.00 Ⓢ

Fiddlers Creek is the second label of Blue Pyrenees Estate at Avoca in the Pyrenees district, Central Victoria. Maker Kim Hart.

CURRENT RELEASE *non-vintage*   Eggy/yeasty, simple, white-grape-driven aromas. The palate is delicate and lacks a bit of intensity and weight, but is quite acceptable, if rather sweet. A decent commercial wine. Drink as an aperitif.

Fleur de Lys Pinot Noir Chardonnay

Quality	♛♛♛♛
Value	★★★★
Grapes	pinot noir; chardonnay
Region	not stated
Cellar	▮ 2
Alc./Vol.	11.5%
RRP	$12.50 Ⓢ

The fleur de lys is a national flower of France, a typical wildflower of the fields. What it's doing on an Aussie wine is anyone's guess.

CURRENT RELEASE *non-vintage*   This is more than a simple, youthful non-vintage. It has some pretence to character and seems to have a little genuine age. The bouquet displays quince, mixed peel and vanilla notes, and there are stone-fruit flavours in the mouth. It has a lot of flavour and some sweetness, so a good chill would not be out of place. Try chat potatoes and chive cream.

Fox Creek Vixen

The folks down at McLaren Vale do a good sparkling red. It's an opulent, ripe style that other regions find hard to match. Makers Sparky and Sarah Marquis.
CURRENT RELEASE *non-vintage* This is serious red bubbly! The colour is dense and youthful; the nose offers fresh cherry, plum and spice fruit and there's some vanilla/charry oak. It's big and rich and fills the mouth. Soft, round and full-bodied, it really gets into every nook and cranny. It would be great with pork spare ribs and plum sauce.

Quality	♆♆♆♆♆
Value	★★★★
Grapes	cabernet franc; shiraz; cabernet sauvignon
Region	McLaren Vale, SA
Cellar	▬ 5
Alc./Vol.	13.5%
RRP	$21.50

Grant Burge Pinot Noir Chardonnay Brut

Barossa sparkling wines usually don't win prizes for delicacy – the Valley is a bit warm for that – but Grant Burge does better than most.
CURRENT RELEASE *non-vintage* This has a fine bead and a crisply tuned nose of peach and citrus with a whisper of biscuity bottle-ferment. The palate is lively and dry with fine sherbetty fruit character balanced refreshingly by crisp acidity. A good aperitif with some little fishy nibbles.

Quality	♆♆♆♆
Value	★★★★
Grapes	pinot noir; chardonnay
Region	Barossa Valley, SA
Cellar	▬
Alc./Vol.	11.5%
RRP	$19.75

Hanging Rock Macedon Cuvée VI

John Ellis makes a distinctively styled bubbly which employs a kind of solero system for its reserve wines, some barrel-ageing and a deliberately high level of aldehyde.
CURRENT RELEASE *non-vintage* Power and complexity are the keywords with this benchmark style of the exciting Macedon district. The colour is full yellow indicating both pinot and age, and it smells of cracked yeast and smoky pinot noir, some biscuity barrel-aged character, and a distinctive nutty aldehyde overtone. It's full-bodied and rich, and the balance is dry. The aftertaste is long and satisfying. Serve with quail-meat canapés.

Quality	♆♆♆♆♆
Value	★★★★
Grapes	pinot noir; chardonnay
Region	Macedon Ranges, Vic.
Cellar	▬ 4
Alc./Vol.	12.5%
RRP	$42.50

Hardys Omni

Quality	♥♥♥
Value	★★★★
Grapes	not stated
Region	various, SA
Cellar	▲
Alc./Vol.	11.5%
RRP	$10.00 ⑤

This wine has blitzed the show system over the last couple of years, and incredibly has won five gold medals! Maker Ed Carr.

CURRENT RELEASE *non-vintage* It's hard to go past this for quality and character at the humble price of around $9. It has a full yellow colour, and very shy, subdued aromas of developed fruit. The emphasis is on bottle development and secondary characters rather than primary fruit. A fairly straightforward, but well-balanced, style with surprising flavour. An anytime aperitif. Good with crab canapés.

Hardys Sir James Brut de Brut

Quality	♥♥♥
Value	★★★
Grapes	pinot noir; chardonnay
Region	not stated
Cellar	▲ 1
Alc./Vol.	12.0%
RRP	$14.00 ⑤

The term 'brut de brut' is used to describe the driest of the dry. The base wine needs to be pretty good to stand on its own without the sweetness to fill it out (and mask imperfections).

CURRENT RELEASE *non-vintage* Delicacy is on hold here, but it does offer a lot of character of the bready, toasty, nutty sort. These elements raise it above the most basic sparklers, but the effect is slightly heavy-handed. The palate is broad and dry-finishing. Serve it with seafood pastries.

Hardys Sir James Sparkling Shiraz

Quality	♥♥♥♥
Value	★★★★
Grapes	shiraz
Region	McLaren Vale & Clare Valley, SA
Cellar	▲ 4+
Alc./Vol.	13.0%
RRP	$25.00 ⑤

Sir James ('Gentleman Jim') Hardy himself is known to be partial to the odd drop of his own brew. He's also known to serve it on the yacht while doing the rounds of Sydney Harbour.

CURRENT RELEASE *non-vintage* A thoroughly seductive style, bursting with rich, ripe juicy flavours of berries and spices. There's a judicious touch of wood lending vanilla notes, and the sweetness is on the high side, which is perfectly okay as it's all in balance. Goes well with Peking duck.

Hunter's Vintage Brut

This baby has had three years on its lees. Only 500 cases were produced so you'll have to get in line. Maker Gary Duke; consultant Dr Tony Jordan.

CURRENT RELEASE 1995   This is a lovely bubbly, and very pinoid. It has a medium yellow colour, and the bouquet is bready and dusty and strongly yeast-influenced. In the mouth it's big and bready and smoky from the pinot, and it finishes long and very dry, with racy acidity. Serve it with fresh caviar.

Quality	♥♥♥♥?
Value	★★★★
Grapes	pinot noir 50%; chardonnay 43%; pinot meunier 7%
Region	Marlborough, NZ
Cellar	4
Alc./Vol.	12.0%
RRP	$30.00

Jacob's Creek Brut Cuvée

Jacob's Creek covers all bases. From starting with a single red wine, the range now encompasses all styles, including a bubbly.

CURRENT RELEASE *non-vintage*   A pleasant undemanding fizz with a light fruity nose of melon and citrus and a whisper of nuttiness. In the mouth it's soft and simple with a trace of sweetness and a mellow finish. An easy-drinking party wine.

Quality	♥♥♥
Value	★★★
Grapes	chardonnay; pinot noir
Region	various, SA
Cellar	1
Alc./Vol.	12.0%
RRP	$13.00 Ⓢ

Jansz Vintage Brut

We keep saying how well Tasmania is suited to sparkling wine production and they keep the good ones coming. Jansz now has a new package, which is reminiscent of some French champagnes right down to the 'serious' metal capsule over the cork.

CURRENT RELEASE 1995   Some past editions of Jansz have been searingly acidic when young, a legacy of progressive disgorgement in the winery and/or a subsequent lack of time on cork. Given the necessary bit of age before and after disgorgement, the wines have been great. This latest is a fine, lean-boned style with a bouquet of citrus, minerals and subtle biscuit. The palate has a herbal touch with citrus and green apple fruit ahead of a long, crisp finish. A great companion to oysters, so get out your knife and start shuckin'.

Quality	♥♥♥♥?
Value	★★★★
Grapes	chardonnay; pinot noir
Region	Pipers River, Tas.
Cellar	3
Alc./Vol.	12.5%
RRP	$29.00

Jenke Kalte Ente

Quality	♙♙♙
Value	★★☆
Grapes	shiraz
Region	Barossa Valley, SA
Cellar	↓ 2
Alc./Vol.	13.5%
RRP	$30.00 (cellar door)

The Jenkes have been Barossa vignerons since 1854. Wanna know what Kalte Ente means? Buy a bottle and read the back label – it's too long to reproduce here. Maker Kym Jenke.

CURRENT RELEASE *non-vintage* The nose and palate are dominated by a stalky character. It's a straightforward, but workmanlike, sparkling red, which has okay depth of flavour and drinks well now. Some vintage port has been included in the expedition liqueur for extra character. Try it with pork spare ribs.

Joseph Sparkling Red

Quality	♙♙♙♙♙
Value	★★★★
Grapes	mainly shiraz
Region	mainly Adelaide Plains, SA
Cellar	↓ 10
Alc./Vol.	13.5%
RRP	$50.00

This is released only in odd years and in small quantities. It always includes about 10 per cent of old Australian reds from the sixties and seventies bought at auction, uncorked, and poured into the blending vat. Maker Joe Grilli.

CURRENT RELEASE *non-vintage* Disgorged 1997. A very individual style of sparkling red. It emphasises secondary, developed characters, with brick-red colour and savoury, walnutty, earthy and fruitcake aromas. There's wonderful aged character, rich and mellow. It's mature, savoury, quite dry on the finish and very long. A food style: try it with venison.

Killawarra 'K' Pinot Noir Chardonnay

Quality	♙♙♙♙
Value	★★★★☆
Grapes	pinot noir; chardonnay
Region	various
Cellar	↓ 1
Alc./Vol.	12.0%
RRP	$14.00 ⑤

This is the top of the successful Killawarra sparkling range from Southcorp. The gold letter K takes prime label position.

CURRENT RELEASE 1997 A wine with an elegance that belies its often heavily discounted price. The nose has finesse with citrus, apple and milk arrowroot aromas of surprising complexity, and the palate follows through in fine style with delicate soft fruit flavour, crispness and a long finish. Serve it with seafood nibbles.

Killawarra 'K' Sparkling Shiraz Cabernet

This used to be the Sparkling Burgundy, but now it's 'K' with a flash new presentation. Like other Killawarra sparklers, it's surprisingly good for the price.
CURRENT RELEASE *non-vintage* A deep purple foam tops this dark bubbly, and it has a fruity plum and blackberry nose. Sweetish berry and plum flavours are quite full, and tannins rather firm. All in all it's quite good. Serve with roast pork and a fruity sauce.

Quality	▼▼▼▼
Value	★★★★
Grapes	shiraz; cabernet sauvignon
Region	various
Cellar	▮ 2
Alc./Vol.	13.0%
RRP	$15.00

Knappstein Chardonnay Pinot Noir Méthode Champenoise

Groovy packaging is the highlight of this low-key introductory sparkler from a leading Clare Valley winery. Maker Andrew Hardy.
CURRENT RELEASE 1993 The nose is fairly subdued but has attractive green apple characters, and these reappear on the palate, where it's fresh and lively with some acid bite, a clean finish and a hint of vanilla. Good flavour and balance. Serve with smoked salmon with sour cream and chives.

Quality	▼▼▼▼
Value	★★★
Grapes	chardonnay; pinot noir
Region	Clare Valley, SA
Cellar	▮ 2
Alc./Vol.	12.5%
RRP	$20.00

Knight Granite Hills Pinot Chardonnay

This new sparkler was awarded Best Sparkling Wine at the 1999 Macedon Ranges Wine Exhibition against tough competition from Cope-Williams, Hanging Rock and Cleveland. Base wine made by Llew Knight; secondary fermentation, disgorging, and so on, was done at Petaluma's Bridgewater Mill.
CURRENT RELEASE 1995 A slightly pink blush colours this fine-beaded sparkling wine. The nose has a delicate strawberry perfume with some citrus and a very restrained pastry-like yeast character. The palate is dry and clean with a pleasant creamy texture and a crisp end.

Quality	▼▼▼▼
Value	★★★
Grapes	pinot noir; chardonnay
Region	Macedon Ranges, Vic.
Cellar	▮ 2
Alc./Vol.	12.5%
RRP	$39.50

Leasingham Classic Clare Sparkling Shiraz

Quality	♟♟♟♟
Value	★★★�½
Grapes	shiraz
Region	Clare Valley, SA
Cellar	▮ 7
Alc./Vol.	13.5%
RRP	$35.00 Ⓢ

This is made from dry-grown grapes off the Schobers vineyard near Auburn, in the southern Clare Valley. It gets three years in wood then 30 months in bottle before release. Maker Ed Carr.

CURRENT RELEASE 1995   This is a classic indeed and shows potential to age in bottle for quite a few years. It has a glowing purple–red hue, a lovely sweet plummy ripe-fruit nose with integrated oak, and a quite sweet, generously flavoured palate. It has elegance and style. Try it with roast turkey and cranberry sauce.

Lindemans Bin 25 Chardonnay Brut

Quality	♟♟♟
Value	★★★★
Grapes	chardonnay
Region	not stated
Cellar	▮ 1
Alc./Vol.	12.0%
RRP	$8.50 Ⓢ

This is a new bubbly from Lindemans. It arrived in a nude bottle with a crown seal. We trust it won't show up in the bottle shops that way.

CURRENT RELEASE 1996   This has some flavour and some aged development, and is good value at the price. The colour is light lemon, and it smells of glacé fruits, vanilla and candy. The taste is fairly broad but flavoursome and carries a kiss of sweetness. There's some genuine aged character. Chill it well and serve with smoked oysters.

McWilliams Hanwood Pinot Chardonnay Brut

Quality	♟♟♟
Value	★★★★
Grapes	pinot noir; chardonnay
Region	South East Australia
Cellar	▮ 1
Alc./Vol.	11.0%
RRP	$10.85 Ⓢ

The label says the grapes were sourced from South Eastern Australia, which is a catch-all under the new Geographic Indications law, and includes all of Victoria, Tasmania, New South Wales, and some of South Australia and Queensland. Just a small area!

CURRENT RELEASE non-vintage   A good wine that just lacks lees-maturation time, hence it's fruit-dominated and lacking in 'Champagne character'. The mousse is vigorous, and it smells of white grapes: peach, yeast, herbs and a touch of grass. There's some fineness to the flavour, and the balance is good. A hint of sweetness is there to close along with reasonable length. Good value and fun with crab mousse.

Moorilla Estate Vintage Brut

Moorilla Estate has occasionally produced a sparkling wine of real style, more proof of Tasmania's suitability for fine fizz, but efforts have been a bit erratic.

CURRENT RELEASE 1996 Pale and lively, the nose is neutral with a clean citrus aroma and a slightly herbaceous touch. Very little yeast autolysis development shows, and the palate follows the understated theme. It's light and simple, but it has good length and firm acidity. A light aperitif style.

Quality	🍷🍷🍷½
Value	★★★
Grapes	chardonnay; pinot noir
Region	Berriedale & Tamar Valley, Tas.
Cellar	2
Alc./Vol.	12.0%
RRP	$28.00

Morris Sparkling Shiraz Durif

Durif is a Rutherglen speciality, and the Morris family knows more about its dark-coloured, formidable wine than most. It's not surprising then that the Morris sparkling red has durif blended in with the more common shiraz.

CURRENT RELEASE *non-vintage* This sparkling red has the sort of emphatic character one expects from Rutherglen material. The colour is deep and the bouquet has earthy ripe berry aromas with a minerally touch. The palate has ripe blackberry flavour of sweetness, weight and power, ahead of very firm, grippy tannins. Those tannins make it a food wine rather than a stand-alone drink. It's well suited to something like Chinese sweet pork spare ribs.

Quality	🍷🍷🍷🍷
Value	★★★½
Grapes	shiraz; durif
Region	Rutherglen, Vic.
Cellar	5+
Alc./Vol.	13.5%
RRP	$19.50

Padthaway Estate Pinot Chardonnay

Padthaway Estate was the first winery in the Padthaway district and boasts the only flat traditional champagne-style wine press in Australia. Maker Nigel Catt; consultant Pam Dunsford.

CURRENT RELEASE 1995 Very bready, toasty, caramelised aromas, complex with a lot of bottle-aged and cracked yeast characters that are also reflected on the palate. It has lots of weight, richness and complexity. Deep powerful, lingering palate flavours. Enjoy it with caviar on blinis.

Quality	🍷🍷🍷🍷½
Value	★★★★
Grapes	pinot noir 85%; chardonnay 12%; pinot meunier 3%
Region	Padthaway, SA
Cellar	2
Alc./Vol.	12.5%
RRP	$20.50

Peter Rumball Sparkling Shiraz

Quality	ҬҬҬҬ¿
Value	★★★★
Grapes	shiraz
Region	Coonawarra & McLaren Vale, SA
Cellar	🍷 5
Alc./Vol.	12.5%
RRP	$21.30

There has been some bottle variation lately, but like the little girl, when it's good it's very, very good. Maker Peter Rumball.

CURRENT RELEASE *non-vintage* A bottle code-numbered SB 11 opened in early 1999 was green, stalky and unimpressive, but usually this wine is the goods. Another bottle (without a batch number) opened at the same time was the customary rich, chocolatey, mellow, complex wine with lovely softness and depth of fruit on the mid-palate. It's a drier style than many, and goes well with Cantonese pork in black bean sauce. (Ratings are for the latter bottle.)

Pirie

Quality	ҬҬҬҬҬ
Value	★★★╁
Grapes	pinot noir 70%; chardonnay 30%
Region	Pipers River, Tas.
Cellar	🍷 4
Alc./Vol.	12.5%
RRP	$44.00

PENGUIN BEST SPARKLING WINE

The release of Pipers Brook's new bubbly was shrouded in more secrecy than Phil Coles' jewellery collection. It was deliberately priced above all competitors and released in March '99 to loud applause. It had two years on lees and one 'on cork' – after disgorgement. Maker Andrew Pirie.

CURRENT RELEASE 1995 **The debut Pirie is a superb wine and a welcome addition to the premium bubbly ranks. It's full-bodied and remarkably soft on the palate, but the most distinctive feature is the bouquet. There are regional honey and hay/straw notes, along with buttery, toasted bread and pastry aromas. Secondary characters, enhanced by malolactic and barrel fermentation, are emphasised – as opposed to primary fruit. Its very rich, almost unctuous, softness gives an illusion of low acidity, but there's acid aplenty. It has good length and the sweetness level is low, giving a dry, but balanced, finish.**

Preece Chardonnay Pinot Noir

This is the second label of Mitchelton, named after the legendary winemaker at Seppelt's Great Western, who helped set Mitchelton up in the early seventies.
CURRENT RELEASE 1996   Quite a big-flavoured bubbly, this. It has attractive fig-like, slightly overripe fruit, and vanilla toffee-apple aromas from the pinot noir in the blend. Caramelly, toasty flavours with some aged development appear on the palate. It's soft, round and generously full in the mouth, with a nice frothy mousse. Could be served as an aperitif.

Quality	♟♟♟
Value	★★★
Grapes	chardonnay; pinot noir
Region	Goulburn Valley, Vic.
Cellar	▮
Alc./Vol.	13.0%
RRP	$19.00 Ⓢ

Richmond Grove Brut NV

This bubbly sits quietly at the bottle shop like a wall-flower at a B&S, while its more glamorously got-up friends dance off to nights of parties and wild abandon.
CURRENT RELEASE *non-vintage*   This has an attractive nose of citrus, stone-fruit and pastry-like ferment aromas. In the mouth it's smooth and lively with good flavour development and a clean, dry finish. Try it with dim sum goodies.

Quality	♟♟♟♟
Value	★★★
Grapes	chardonnay; pinot noir
Region	not stated
Cellar	▮ 1
Alc./Vol.	12.0%
RRP	$13.50

Rockford Black Shiraz

Rockford's Robert O'Callaghan is one of the great characters of the wine industry, a man with as much soul as Aretha Franklin. That's where the comparison ends: this wine is strictly heavy-metal rock'n'roll.
CURRENT RELEASE *non-vintage*   Disgorged September 1998. This is a lovely sweet plummy style with dark chocolate, fruitcake, spices and savoury complexities. The palate has a fine balance of sweetness, fruit and tannin. A 1991 disgorgement tasted at the same time was simply fantastic, so if you have half a D, cellar some! Perfect with aged hard cheeses.

Quality	♟♟♟♟♟
Value	★★★★⊦
Grapes	shiraz
Region	Barossa Valley, SA
Cellar	▮ 15
Alc./Vol.	13.0%
RRP	$50.00

Seaview Brut

Quality	♟♟♟
Value	★★★
Grapes	not stated
Region	various
Cellar	♦
Alc./Vol.	12.0%
RRP	$9.00 ⑤

Gallons of this stuff are gurgled down with great gusto at end-of-year parties everywhere. It's not a wine for cerebral discussion – just drink it while you're dancing on the tables.

CURRENT RELEASE *non-vintage* A simple grapey nose leads on to a soft grape and citrus palate with a whisper of yeasty ferment character. It finishes dry. A clean-tasting sparkler on a budget. Party wine.

Seaview Chardonnay Blanc de Blanc

Quality	♟♟♟♟
Value	★★★★
Grapes	chardonnay
Region	various
Cellar	♦ 2
Alc./Vol.	11.5%
RRP	$18.50 ⑤

Blanc be blanc bubblies, made from chardonnay without the addition of pinot noir, are supposed to be finer-flavoured and lighter in texture than the blends. This Seaview makes a good contrast to the fuller-bodied Pinot Noir Chardonnay Brut.

CURRENT RELEASE 1995 A more delicate version of the Seaview bestseller yet still quite full-flavoured. The bubble is fine and persistent, and the nose has subtle melon and citrus aromas. Yeast input is well controlled and adds a creamy, vanilla bean touch. It finishes clean and crisp.

Seaview Gull Rock

Quality	♟♟♟
Value	★★★★
Grapes	various
Region	various
Cellar	♦ 1
Alc./Vol.	12.0%
RRP	$11.00 ⑤

Seaview cover all bases with their sparkling range, from bargain-basement-everyday to prestigious special occasion.

CURRENT RELEASE *non-vintage* No pretensions here – just a pale, simple fizz at a keen price. The nose is grapey, peachy and pleasant. It's clean-tasting in the mouth, with soft fruit mid-palate and some zippy acidity to finish. A good one for the office party.

Seaview Pinot Noir Chardonnay Brut

Seaview make so many sparkling wines with so many similarities in name and description that it's sometimes hard to differentiate between them. This is the one in the heavy-bottomed bottle with the small rectangular gold label near the base.

CURRENT RELEASE 1996   Value for money is what this wine is all about. It gives plenty of bready yeast character and some stone fruit on the nose. The palate follows suit with good depth and length. The texture is creamy and full with a clean finish. A good all-rounder which would accompany hors d'oeuvres of pâté and seafoods well.

Quality	�♟♟♟
Value	★★★★⯪
Grapes	pinot noir; chardonnay
Region	various
Cellar	↓ 2
Alc./Vol.	12.0%
RRP	$18.50 Ⓢ

Seppelt Original Sparkling Shiraz

Think sparkling red, think Seppelt. No other example of this Aussie icon has the same lineage, and few match it for quality.

CURRENT RELEASE 1994   This is the most friendly of wines, a ripe mix of blackberry, plum and earthy aromas and flavours, smooth and creaming in texture. Well-measured sweetness lifts the mid-palate and, unlike some new-wave sparkling reds, the tannins are mellow and ripe. Serve it with tea-smoked duck.

Quality	♟♟♟♟♟
Value	★★★★★
Grapes	shiraz
Region	not stated
Cellar	↓ 5
Alc./Vol.	13.5%
RRP	$19.00

Seppelt Show Sparkling Shiraz

There may be other sparkling reds, but Seppelt's is the granddaddy of them all.

CURRENT RELEASE 1987   A mellow, velvety sparkling shiraz of seductive style. The bouquet has berry jam, plum, warm sweet spices, earth and mushroomy touches which follow down the palate with smooth, measured sweetness to a long dry signature of soft tannins. Serve with a glazed ham and all the trimmings.

Quality	♟♟♟♟♟
Value	★★★⯪
Grapes	shiraz
Region	Great Western, Vic.
Cellar	↓ 3
Alc./Vol.	13.5%
RRP	$61.00

Skillogalee Sparkling Riesling

Quality	♟♟♟♟
Value	★★★
Grapes	riesling
Region	Clare Valley, SA
Cellar	▮ 1
Alc./Vol.	13.0%
RRP	$22.00

Fizzy riesling is a rare drop. Skillogalee makes one of the few examples we've seen. Use it to trick any smartypants wine know-alls of your acquaintance.

CURRENT RELEASE *non-vintage* A distinct lime cordial note betrays the varietal heritage of this unusual fizz. There's also a hint of stewed apple. The palate has more of the same with a rather firm thread running through it. It finishes dry and slightly toasty. An acquired taste. Serve it with little savoury toasts.

Taltarni Brut Taché

Quality	♟♟♟♟
Value	★★★★
Grapes	chardonnay; pinot noir
Region	Pyrenees, Vic. & Pipers Brook, Tas.
Cellar	▮ 2
Alc./Vol.	12.0%
RRP	$17.25

The name means 'stained', in other words the red pinot grapes have been allowed to leave their mark on the colour. Maker Shane Clohesy.

CURRENT RELEASE *non-vintage* This wine has come on in leaps and bounds since the first releases. It's a commendable rosé style, with generous red-grape flavours, although it's not a wine of finesse. The colour is smoked-salmon pink; the aromas are of caramel and chocolate pudding. It's full-bodied, soft and rich with a dry, lingering aftertaste that satisfies. Try it with smoked salmon.

Tatachilla Pinot Noir Brut

Quality	♟♟♟♟
Value	★★★★
Grapes	pinot noir
Region	McLaren Vale & Adelaide Hills, SA
Cellar	▮ 1
Alc./Vol.	12.0%
RRP	$17.00

Tatachilla is a 're-born' winery in McLaren Vale. Just about every wine they make is an excellent buy. Maker Michael Fragos.

CURRENT RELEASE *non-vintage* Brassy, slightly taché colour. The shy aromas of strawberry and smoky fruit are very typical of pinot noir grapes. It's light-bodied, but has good flavour and quality. The palate is clean and smooth with appealing dryness on the finish. This offers good depth of flavour for the price. A wine of character. Serve with canapés.

Tatachilla Sparkling Malbec

This is barely wine: it tastes and smells like freshly fermented grape juice. Be careful – the colour will stain your shirt.

CURRENT RELEASE *non-vintage* The colour is a vibrant purple–red and it smells of plums, stalks, spices and aniseed – a raw, youthful aroma. The sweet grape-juicy flavour is a tad simplistic and tastes rather unfinished. It's berryish, with a hint of plum jam. Try it with pork spare ribs and black bean sauce.

Quality	♟♟♟♟
Value	★★★
Grapes	malbec
Region	Padthaway, SA
Cellar	🍾 1
Alc./Vol.	14.0%
RRP	$20.00

Thirsty Fish Chardonnay Brut

This is a new release from Southcorp. The pink frosted glass bottle might appeal to someone, but not the authors.

CURRENT RELEASE *non-vintage* This is a puzzling wine: the aromas are of Granny Smith apples, with some brandysnap notes, and the palate is slightly disjointed with a combination of simple white-grape flavour and again that odd brandysnap flavour. There's a fair quota of residual sugar. It should be a crowd-pleaser. Take it to a rave party.

Quality	♟♟♟
Value	★★★
Grapes	chardonnay
Region	not stated
Cellar	🍾
Alc./Vol.	12.0%
RRP	$14.00 ⑤

Tyrrell's Pinot Noir Brut

The Hunter isn't where you'd expect to find fine bubblies, but this is finer than most. The bubbles are put into it at Peterson's.

CURRENT RELEASE 1997 A serious, dry style from one of the Hunter's most serious wineries. It's pale straw in shade, and smells of straw, smoke and nectarine. The bubbles are appropriately frenetic. The palate is creamy, soft but dry, and concludes with appealing balance. Serve it with anchovy-stuffed green olives.

Quality	♟♟♟♟
Value	★★★★
Grapes	pinot noir; chardonnay
Region	Hunter Valley, NSW
Cellar	🍾 3
Alc./Vol.	12.5%
RRP	$18.00

Yalumba Angas Brut Rosé

Quality	♟♟♟♟
Value	★★★★★
Grapes	various
Region	various
Cellar	▮ 1
Alc./Vol.	11.5%
RRP	$9.00 Ⓢ

Angas Brut has been a leader in the low-priced sparkling market for longer than we can remember, and standards have been remarkably consistent.

CURRENT RELEASE *non-vintage* Excellent value again in a festive bright pink sparkler with a fruity nose of cherry and red berries, which is simple and appealing. In the mouth it's fresh and clean with a trace of sweetness in the middle to add a little depth. Serve with smoked salmon sandwiches.

Yarrabank Cuvée

Quality	♟♟♟♟♟
Value	★★★★
Grapes	pinot noir;
	chardonnay
Region	Yarra Valley, Vic.;
	various Vic.
Cellar	▮ 2
Alc./Vol.	12.0%
RRP	$32.90

The much-lauded joint venture between Yering Station and French Champagne house Devaux is resulting in some very good fizz with a distinct French accent.

CURRENT RELEASE 1995 This is more delicate than the '94 at the same stage. It's a pale, fine style with a lovely creamy mousse. The bouquet is light and fragrant with apple, citrus and brioche aromas. It creams across the palate with crisp, subtle, biscuity flavours. The finish is sustained and soft. An aperitif par excellence.

Yellowglen Cuvée Victoria

Quality	♟♟♟♟
Value	★★★
Grapes	pinot noir;
	chardonnay
Region	not stated
Cellar	▮ 3
Alc./Vol.	11.5%
RRP	$31.00

Top-of-the-range from Yellowglen, and it looks the part with a rather flash skittle-shaped bottle and a glittering gold label.

CURRENT RELEASE 1996 A pale wine with a fine bead, the latest Cuvée Victoria is an understated blanc de blanc style (despite a predominance of pinot noir in its make-up), which doesn't have the depth of some of its competitors at the price. The nose has delicate citrus zest and apple fruit with a very restrained nutty biscuity touch. The palate is lean and fine in texture, some would say delicate, but we think it's just a bit light-on in the flavour department. Serve it as an aperitif.

Yellowglen Pinot Noir NV

Rumour has it that this wine was destined for a more expensive Yellowglen label, but somehow it ended up a bit further down the Yellowglen tree.

CURRENT RELEASE *non-vintage* Pale with a good mousse and no pink colour extraction from the red pinot grapes. The nose has strawberry aromas with hints of biscuit and egg custard. Similar characters mark the palate, which is dry with good body and smooth texture. Try it with pâté.

Quality	♆♆♆♆
Value	★★★★
Grapes	pinot noir
Region	various
Cellar	▮ 2
Alc./Vol.	11.5%
RRP	$18.00

Yellowglen Vintage Brut

Yellowglen is now a household name, and owners Mildara Blass haven't been resting on their laurels with it. They seem to have been putting real effort into improving the quality of the mid-range wines in recent years.

CURRENT RELEASE 1996 The nose has lemon and melon aromas with some custard and biscuity notes. It has good intensity, and the palate is pleasantly tasty with medium depth. The flavour is a shade short, but it's nicely balanced. The finish is dry and slightly firm. Goes well with smoked salmon canapés.

Quality	♆♆♆♆
Value	★★★
Grapes	pinot noir; chardonnay; pinot meunier
Region	not stated
Cellar	▮ 1
Alc./Vol.	11.5%
RRP	$22.00

Fortified Wines

All Saints Classic Muscat

Quality	🍷🍷🍷🍷
Value	★★★★★
Grapes	red frontignac
Region	Rutherglen, Vic.
Cellar	🍾
Alc./Vol.	18.0%
RRP	$24.20

This venerable winery was beautifully reconditioned by Brown Brothers, and in early 1999 brother Peter Brown took outright ownership.

CURRENT RELEASE *non-vintage* Like the tokay, this label offers great value. It has a rich, honeyed, muscaty nose with good varietal fruit and complex wood-aged depths. There's a hint of oak together with excellent richness and balance. Wonderful with brandied figs and mascarpone.

All Saints Classic Tokay

Quality	🍷🍷🍷🍷
Value	★★★★★
Grapes	muscadelle
Region	Rutherglen, Vic.
Cellar	🍾
Alc./Vol.	17.0%
RRP	$24.20

This was Best Bargain Fortified two years ago and it could carry off that award any old time. It's great stuff, and so cheap it feels like robbery to buy it.

CURRENT RELEASE *non-vintage* The colour is a promising amber tawny, the bouquet loaded with inviting tea-leafy, malty and golden syrup aromas. In the mouth it has an unctuous texture with great raisiny, pruney concentration, and the flavour isn't tarted up with new oak. A tremendous bargain. Try it with stilton cheese.

Buller Fine Old Muscat

Rutherglen muscats and tokays have a confusing array of names and hierarchies. In future, they'll standardise the wording on their labels so we'll understand them better. This is the basic Buller muscat.

CURRENT RELEASE *non-vintage* It's a skilful blend of young and older material. There are earthy and rose-petal, Turkish delight aromas, indicating very good varietal fruit. It has lovely palate flavour with freshness as well as some aged depth, and a very persistent aftertaste. Try it with dates and figs.

Quality	♟♟♟♟
Value	★★★ʀ
Grapes	red frontignac
Region	Rutherglen, Vic.
Cellar	▮
Alc./Vol.	18.0%
RRP	$21.30

Buller Rare Liqueur Muscat

The Bullers have a winery on the Murray at Swan Hill as well as the Rutherglen base. All the fortifieds are grown and made at Rutherglen.

CURRENT RELEASE *non-vintage* This fits the rare category – it's a truly ancient muscat. If anything, it could benefit from some younger wine to freshen it. The colour is deep and dark; the bouquet suggests resin, oak and molasses, even a hint of Vegemite. It's undeniably rich and concentrated. The finish is a tad austere. A wine for enthusiasts. Good with chocolate-dipped orange zest.

Quality	♟♟♟♟ʀ
Value	★★★ʀ
Grapes	red frontignac
Region	Rutherglen, Vic.
Cellar	▮
Alc./Vol.	19.0%
RRP	$69.00 (375 ml)

Buller Rare Liqueur Tokay

The Rutherglen people have recently discovered packaging. Wines such as this are now marketed in snappy half-bottles with modern labels. Maker Andrew Buller.

CURRENT RELEASE *non-vintage* Here's a fabulous oldie: the colour is amber/brown and the bouquet has developed the complex old tokay character known as 'fish oil'. It's incredibly rich and luscious on the tongue with an unctuous, velvety texture and a seemingly endless aftertaste. Great with stilton cheese.

Quality	♟♟♟♟♟
Value	★★★★
Grapes	muscadelle
Region	Rutherglen, Vic.
Cellar	▮
Alc./Vol.	18.5%
RRP	$69.00 (375 ml)

Campbells Merchant Prince Muscat

Quality	♟♟♟♟♟
Value	★★★★
Grapes	red frontignac
Region	Rutherglen, Vic.
Cellar	▲
Alc./Vol.	18.5%
RRP	$98.00

The Merchant Prince was the name of the ship that brought the first Campbell to Australia. The wine has an average age of 25 years and the oldest material is over 60. It will soon be labelled 'Rare'.

CURRENT RELEASE *non-vintage* This is a great old muscat in a slightly leaner mould and with a drier, less luscious, finish than some. The colour is tawny amber, and there's a lot of rancio in the bouquet together with a slightly burnt or cooked character and a little volatile acidity. It's amazingly powerful and alive in the mouth despite its age, and the finish lingers on and on. Serve with gorgonzola cheese.

Campbells Rutherglen Muscat

Quality	♟♟♟♟
Value	★★★
Grapes	red frontignac
Region	Rutherglen, Vic.
Cellar	▲
Alc./Vol.	17.5%
RRP	$19.00 (375 ml)

Winemaker Colin Campbell has been a prime mover in the promotion of the Rutherglen region, which has recently adopted a hierarchy of muscat wines. This one is the basic level, the first rung on the ladder.

CURRENT RELEASE *non-vintage* The colour is light pinkish-red, and the aroma is of honey, toffee and rose petals. It's lean on the tongue without complexity or a great deal of lusciousness, but it's a decent young muscat and goes well over ice-cream.

Campbells Rutherglen Tokay

Quality	♟♟♟♟
Value	★★★
Grapes	muscadelle
Region	Rutherglen, Vic.
Cellar	▲
Alc./Vol.	17.5%
RRP	$19.00 (375 ml)

The Campbell clan is proud of its Scottish ancestry. You can see it in the names of wines such as Bobbie Burns Shiraz. Maker Colin Campbell.

CURRENT RELEASE *non-vintage* This is a young, simple tokay with a light amber colour, and a straightforward young aroma of sweet floral and confectionery notes. It's lush in the mouth, with a sweeter finish than some, and very good length. A thoroughly delightful youngster. Try it with caramel fudge.

Chambers Rutherglen Tokay

Bill Chambers has been chairman of the Royal Melbourne Wine Show since the year dot. He makes some of the best fortifieds in the country. This is his basic tokay.

CURRENT RELEASE *non-vintage* This has a light amber colour and looks and tastes very young. The nose is youthfully floral with some spirity character. There's a trace of tokay 'fish oil', which is perfectly legit. It has some fire on the palate and good sweetness, drying on the finish. Lively, lean, intense. Drizzle it over ice-cream.

Quality	▼▼▼▼
Value	★★★★
Grapes	muscadelle
Region	Rutherglen, Vic.
Cellar	◑
Alc./Vol.	17.5%
RRP	$20.00

Chambers Special Muscat

They're putting those muscat and tokay prices up in Rutherglen, but then the wines are worth it. If truth be told they've been undervalued for a long time. Blender Bill Chambers.

CURRENT RELEASE *non-vintage* This has a medium brick-red hue with an amber rim, and the bouquet is a thriller. It has malt, raisin and prune aromas with a vanilla bean back-note and some meatiness. There's great intensity and attack on the palate; raisiny flavour with warmth and a little astringency. The complexity reflects considerable age. Goes well with Meredith Blue.

Quality	▼▼▼▼▼
Value	★★★★
Grapes	red frontignac
Region	Rutherglen, Vic.
Cellar	◑
Alc./Vol.	18.0%
RRP	$43.00 (375 ml)

Coolangatta Estate Vintage Port

This vineyard is at Berry, the original Coolangatta – it gave its name to the ship that ran aground at the place that became the new Coolangatta on the New South Wales–Queensland border.

CURRENT RELEASE 1998 This is a good use for chambourcin. It's hardly a classic vintage port but that doesn't matter: it's a lovely drink. Already amazingly smooth, it has a vivid neon-purple colour and a lovely nose of brandy spirit and floral, grapey vanilla nuances. It's spotlessly clean, low in tannin and tails away to a short finish, but is remarkably enjoyable as a baby. Whether it will reward long-cellaring is a moot point. Try with friandises.

Quality	▼▼▼▼
Value	★★★
Grapes	chambourcin
Region	Shoalhaven, NSW
Cellar	◑ 8
Alc./Vol.	18.7%
RRP	$16.00 (375 ml)

D'Arenberg Vintage Fortified

Quality 🍷🍷🍷🍷
Value ★★★½
Grapes shiraz
Region McLaren Vale, SA
Cellar 5–20
Alc./Vol. 18.5%
RRP $21.30

The forgotten vintage port style is still with us in the hands of a dedicated few. D'Arenberg of McLaren Vale is one of them.

CURRENT RELEASE 1997 This is a big solid VP which is built with the cellar in mind. The colour is deep and dense; the nose has syrupy shiraz aromas with some dry spirit and sweet spice. In the mouth it's big and hard, with lush sweet fruit flavour hiding behind an impressive wall of tannins. All that power and tannic grip suggests an ability to age for decades. When it's a bit more mature, drink it with firm ripe blue cheese.

De Bortoli Black Noble

Quality 🍷🍷🍷🍷🍷
Value ★★★★
Grapes semillon
Region Riverina, NSW
Cellar
Alc./Vol. 18.0%
RRP $29.00 (375 ml)

This is made from botrytis-affected semillon with a little pedro ximenez, fortified and wood-matured (for an average eight years) like a port or muscat. It's an interesting new style of fortified and is beautifully packaged. Maker Darren De Bortoli and team.

CURRENT RELEASE *non-vintage* A complex fortified with a difference. It has a blackish-brown colour, and the bouquet has honeyed botrytis nuances as well as toffee, mocha, roasted-nut and raisin aromas. It's sweet and semi-luscious, and the finish carries a kick of acid. It goes very well with mild blue cheeses, such as St Josephs Blue.

Director's Special Tawny Port

Quality 🍷🍷🍷🍷
Value ★★★★★
Grapes not stated
Region not stated
Cellar
Alc./Vol. 17.5%
RRP $13.00 (S)

This is an enduring name for inexpensive port. It used to have the name Yalumba on the label, but since Yalumba sold its fortified brands to Mildara, that's gone west.

CURRENT RELEASE *non-vintage* Great value port! The bouquet offers raisined grapes and assorted dried fruits, with a hint of vanilla. It's sweet on the tongue with just enough aged character to add interest. Serve it with coffee and florentines.

Galway Pipe

Galway Pipe used to be one of those nudge-nudge-wink-wink wines, kept under the counter and rationed out to the lucky few. Times have changed: now it's easy to find. CURRENT RELEASE *non-vintage* This is the archetypal rich, mellow, wood-aged Australian tawny style. Tawny–walnut in colour, the nose has dried fruit, butter toffee and nutty aromas of great charm. In the mouth it has great depth of raisined fruit and the roasted almond touches that come with long wood age. The aftertaste is long and haunting. Enjoy it with a short black coffee after dinner.

Quality	💥💥💥💥💥
Value	★★★★
Grapes	various
Region	Barossa Valley, SA
Cellar	🍷
Alc./Vol.	18.5%
RRP	$28.00

Karl Seppelt Cabernet Vintage Port

Cabernet sauvignon is not a traditional vintage port grape. It tends to make a very pungent wine, which is no great sin – that's half its appeal. CURRENT RELEASE 1994 This is a mixture of good features and bad. The colour is deep and dark; the bouquet shouts 'cabernet!' with intense blackberry jam aromas that are just a little over-the-top. In the mouth it's tight and firm to the point of austerity, with plenty of sweetness but also a hard finish. Will it ever soften? Cellar, then try it with Roaring Forties Blue cheese.

Quality	💥💥💥💥
Value	★★★★
Grapes	cabernet sauvignon
Region	not stated
Cellar	➽ 5–10
Alc./Vol.	18.5%
RRP	$20.00 🍷

Lamonts Vintage Port

Lamonts is where the late Jack Mann plied his trade after he retired from 50 vintages at Houghton. He took his eccentric methods, including his habit of using an industrial meat-mincer on the skins, with him. CURRENT RELEASE 1994 It seems the mincer is alive and well. This is incredibly tannic, with a bitter aggression that must have come from macerated skins. The colour is dusky red/black and there are black-olive developing notes on the nose. The spirit is hot on the palate and the tannin dominates the fruit flavour. Cellar! Then serve with Pyengana cheddar.

Quality	💥💥💥💥
Value	★★★
Grapes	not stated
Region	Swan Valley, WA
Cellar	➽ 6–15
Alc./Vol.	19.5%
RRP	$18.00 (cellar door) 🍷

Lindemans Classic Show Reserve Tawny Port Z186

Quality	🍷🍷🍷🍷🍷
Value	★★★★★
Grapes	not stated
Region	not stated
Cellar	🍷
Alc./Vol.	19.5%
RRP	$50.00

Every two years Lindemans issues a Classic Release, a clutch of artfully matured wines, including the occasional rare old fortified. This is one such wine. Maker Phillip John and team.

CURRENT RELEASE *non-vintage* A classic in the truest sense. It's an extraordinarily complex old wine filled with rancio character. The colour is pale-ish mahogany; the bouquet is exquisitely multi-layered and profound, very mellow and dry on the finish, with a seemingly endless persistence. Serve solo with a fine Havana cigar.

Lindemans Macquarie Tawny Port

Quality	🍷🍷🍷🍷
Value	★★★★★
Grapes	grenache; shiraz
Region	Barossa Valley, SA
Cellar	🍷
Alc./Vol.	19.0%
RRP	$12.50 Ⓢ

Governor Lachlan Macquarie might be amused to see his name on a port. Rum was more likely the daily tipple in his time.

CURRENT RELEASE *non-vintage* **This is terrific value for an inexpensive tawny port and it stacks up well against much dearer wines. A rich, full-tasting tawny, which will please the crowds. It has the right shade of light tawny–amber, and it smells of prunes, raisined grapes and nuts, with a generous undercurrent of complex wood-aged character. Great with chocolates and coffee.**

Matthew Lang Tawny Port

Quality	🍷🍷
Value	★☆
Grapes	not stated
Region	not stated
Cellar	🍷
Alc./Vol.	17.5%
RRP	$6.00 Ⓢ

Matthew Lang is an inexpensive Southcorp brand. This uninspiring style is completely eclipsed by wines that cost as little as $1 more.

CURRENT RELEASE *non-vintage* This is a raw, simple port style with a boiled-sweets character, a washed-out palate and a lean, sweet finish. It's crazy not to spend a couple of bucks more for something much, much better. If you must, serve it with . . . actually we can't think of anything to serve it with.

Morris Old Premium Muscat

Recently repackaged in half-litre bottles, but the price stayed the same – as Mick Morris proudly informed viewers on a recent television program!

CURRENT RELEASE *non-vintage* An extraordinary old wine with a deep, dark hue and a green edge. It has tremendous aged depth and complexity, with some peppery and herbal notes among the toffee and raisined muscat characters. A high level of sweetness and great fruit concentration give it terrific lusciousness. A great benchmark wine. Serve it with gorgonzola cheese.

Quality	♟♟♟♟♟
Value	★★★★★
Grapes	red frontignac
Region	Rutherglen, Vic.
Cellar	▮
Alc./Vol.	18.5%
RRP	$44.50 (500 ml)

Morris Old Premium Tokay

This classic wine has new livery, but the quality is the same. David Morris is in charge today but his father, Mick, and Mick's dad, must also take credit.

CURRENT RELEASE *non-vintage* The colour is a dark nut-brown with green edges, indicating extreme age. The first sniff says malt extract, with rancio and tea-leafy characters chiming in. It's a great wine of tremendous depth, flavour concentration and lusciousness. There's wonderful aged complexity, but also the freshening influence of some younger blending material too. It lingers endlessly. Serve with chocolates and coffee.

Quality	♟♟♟♟♟
Value	★★★★★
Grapes	muscadelle
Region	Rutherglen, Vic.
Cellar	▮
Alc./Vol.	18.0%
RRP	$44.50 (500 ml)

Morris Rutherglen Muscat 'Canister'

This wine comes in a tin canister, hence its nickname. It won the Penguin Best Bargain Fortified Award last year. The same wine can still be bought in half-bottles for $8 – amazing value! Blender David Morris.

CURRENT RELEASE *non-vintage* A superb youngster. Baby muscat doesn't get much better than this. Reddish hue; fruity rose-petal muscat nose with little wood-aged complexity. Excellent fruit, and almost luscious sweetness in the mouth. A charmer. Try with Turkish delight.

Quality	♟♟♟♟
Value	★★★★★
Grapes	red frontignac
Region	Rutherglen, Vic.
Cellar	▮
Alc./Vol.	18.0%
RRP	$16.40 Ⓢ

Penfolds Club Port

Quality	♟♟♟
Value	★★★★
Grapes	shiraz; grenache; mataro
Region	Barossa Valley, SA
Cellar	▮
Alc./Vol.	18.0%
RRP	$9.60 ⑤

The subscript reads 'Old Tawny', which reminds us that there are no laws on the books relating to the use of words like old. Yet.

CURRENT RELEASE *non-vintage* A fruity and quite sweet youngster with simple raisin flavour and aroma. It's clean and well made, but without the sugar there wouldn't be a lot to it. It's simple and falls away fast, leaving a spirity warmth. Serve it with fruitcake.

Penfolds Club Reserve Tawny Port

Quality	♟♟♟♟
Value	★★★★
Grapes	shiraz; grenache; mataro
Region	Barossa Valley, SA
Cellar	▮
Alc./Vol.	18.0%
RRP	$12.90 ⑤

This is the model you're supposed to trade up to from the standard Club. It's certainly a more peppy model.

CURRENT RELEASE *non-vintage* This is a tasty port and very fairly priced. The colour is light–medium tawny–amber and the nose offers malty, raisin and caramel scents with some aged rancio lending extra interest. It's a straightforward, but perfectly agreeable, style with respectable depth of fruit and moderate persistence. It goes well with caramel fudge.

Penfolds Grandfather Port

Quality	♟♟♟♟♟
Value	★★★★
Grapes	shiraz; mataro
Region	Barossa Valley, SA
Cellar	▮
Alc./Vol.	19.0%
RRP	$90.00

This was first released in the sixties, although the solera dates back much further. Penfolds is careful never to release too much in case the aged material is depleted, hence it's always rare. Blender Dean Kraehenbuhl.

CURRENT RELEASE *non-vintage* A tremendously deep, rich, complex old port which smells of malt and walnuts. The palate has great mellow smooth flavour. It's rich, chewy in texture and very long on the aftertaste. Serve with freshly shelled nuts.

Penfolds Magill Bluestone Tawny

The old Magill Cellars in the Adelaide foothills are built from beautiful locally quarried bluestone, hence the name of this port – although we doubt any of the grapes ever came from the Magill vineyard.

CURRENT RELEASE *non-vintage* This is a reasonable port, but it's difficult to see the value-for-money in it when the same company's Club Reserve and Macquarie are so well priced. It has a light tawny–brown colour and a bouquet that leans to malt, with some dusty oak and hints of dried fruits. The flavour is good, but straightforward, with a sweet finish. Goes very well with date slice.

Quality	▼▼▼⟋
Value	★★★
Grapes	shiraz; mataro; muscadelle
Region	Barossa Valley, SA
Cellar	▮
Alc./Vol.	19.0%
RRP	$22.80 Ⓢ

Pfeiffer Old Distillery Muscat

Chris Pfeiffer's winery is in an old brick building that used to be a distillery in Rutherglen's golden past. The address is Distillery Road, Wahgunyah.

CURRENT RELEASE *non-vintage* The colour is light amber and it smells of dusty wood and fresh, raisined muscat grapes. A light, straightforward and probably fairly young, muscat that has pleasant fruit and balance. Good as an ice-cream topping.

Quality	▼▼▼
Value	★★★
Grapes	red frontignac
Region	Rutherglen, Vic.
Cellar	▮
Alc./Vol.	18.0%
RRP	$23.20

Pfeiffer Old Distillery Tokay

If the sign on the cellar-door sales is any guide, Pfeiffers make pfabulous, pfantastic wines. Winemaker is Chris Pfeiffer.

CURRENT RELEASE *non-vintage* This tastes like quite a young tokay: it has a light–medium amber colour and the classic tokay aromas of cold tea-leaves and malt. The palate is very unctuous and sweet and finishes with some heat from the fortifying spirit.

Quality	▼▼▼⟋
Value	★★★
Grapes	muscadelle
Region	Rutherglen, Vic.
Cellar	▮
Alc./Vol.	18.0%
RRP	$23.20

Queen Adelaide Tawny Port

Quality	♟♟♟
Value	★★★★★
Grapes	not stated
Region	not stated
Cellar	▲
Alc./Vol.	18.0%
RRP	$7.40 ⓢ

With fortified wines in the doldrums, bargains abound, and ports are the best buys of the lot. While liqueur muscats and tokays enjoy a certain trendiness, these poor old codgers are yesterday's heroes.

CURRENT RELEASE *non-vintage* Not too complex, but this has everything in the right place, and look at the price. The nose is light, but it has hints of vanilla, grapey aromas of moderate intensity, and a touch of nuttiness. In the mouth it's lightish medium-bodied with pleasant flavour and a toasty, nutty, dry finish. A no-fuss after-dinner sipper.

Rosemount Old Benson Fine Old Liqueur Tawny

Quality	♟♟♟♟
Value	★★★ｒ
Grapes	not stated
Region	not stated
Cellar	▲
Alc./Vol.	18.5%
RRP	$32.00 (500 ml)

A man's best friend is a bottle of good port. This wine commemorates a dog named Benson (1979–94) who used to accompany Sandy Oatley around the Rosemount vineyards.

CURRENT RELEASE *non-vintage* This is a pretty good attempt at a liqueur style. A 10-year-old, it has a deeper tawny hue and richer, more grapey aroma and flavour than usual in a tawny port. It recalls plumcake and vanilla, with a trace of fish oil. It's rich and chunky in the mouth, soft and sweet and generous, with just a trace of rancio. Very drinkable, with stilton cheese.

Seppelt DP 4 Mt Rufus Tawny Port

Quality	♟♟♟
Value	★★★★★
Grapes	not stated
Region	Barossa Valley, SA
Cellar	▲
Alc./Vol.	18.0%
RRP	$8.90 ⓢ

As you go up the tawny port ladder, the value-for-money can get even better. Try this and see.

CURRENT RELEASE *non-vintage* This has good tawny colour and a nose of clean dried fruit aromas, attractive spirit and a touch of grilled nuts. The palate follows suit with smooth flavour, reasonable concentration, and a nutty dry finish. Try it with florentines and coffee.

Seppelt DP 63 Rutherglen Show Muscat

Seppelt used to have a winery in Rutherglen (called
Clydeside, it houses the excellent Tuileries restaurant
these days). Now they take the grapes to the Barossa to
make and age the wines there. Maker James Godfrey.
CURRENT RELEASE *non-vintage* The colour is brick-
red to amber, and it smells dusty, developed and not-
so-fruity. It's a leaner, less luscious, style, which has good
flavour and character but just lacks the big finish of the
greatest muscats. Rancio, spirit and acid dry the finish.
Goes with dried fruits and nuts.

Quality	🍷🍷🍷🍷
Value	★★★★
Grapes	red frontignac
Region	Rutherglen, Vic.
Cellar	🍾
Alc./Vol.	18.0%
RRP	$27.00 (375 ml)

Seppelt DP 116 Show Amontillado

Are we beginning to see a renewal of interest in sherry?
It's early days, but we've noticed people sipping it in the
most fashionable establishments. Maker James Godfrey.
CURRENT RELEASE *non-vintage* Another gem from
Seppeltsfield, this pale amber drop has a bouquet of
vanilla, nutty rancio and tangy flor. The overall impression is dryness, but a little sweet citrus tang adds dimension and complexity. Zippy acidity keeps the palate
fresh. A great experience sipped with oxtail soup on a
cool night.

Quality	🍷🍷🍷🍷🍷
Value	★★★★★
Grapes	palomino
Region	Barossa Valley, SA
Cellar	🍾
Alc./Vol.	21.5%
RRP	$19.70 (375 ml)

Seppelt DP 117 Show Fino

A year or so back the laws were changed to permit local
'sherry' makers to lower their alcohol from 17 per cent
to 15.5 per cent. The difference was astonishing. Maker
James Godfrey.
CURRENT RELEASE *non-vintage* Look at the back label
and make sure you buy a fresh bottle: this style of
wine goes stale fast! When fresh it's the ultimate aperitif:
pale-hued, appley, seabreeze-scented, nutty and almost
aniseed-like. A very clean, refreshing taste that dances on
the tongue. Serve with tapas.

Quality	🍷🍷🍷🍷🍷
Value	★★★★★
Grapes	palomino
Region	Barossa Valley, SA
Cellar	🍾
Alc./Vol.	15.5%
RRP	$19.70 (375 ml)

Seppelt DP 38 Show Oloroso

Quality	♟♟♟♟
Value	★★★★★
Grapes	palomino
Region	Barossa Valley, SA
Cellar	▮
Alc./Vol.	20.5%
RRP	$19.70 (375 ml)

Seppelts are the defenders of the faith when it comes to sherry. The soleras at Seppeltsfield are living treasures. It's a pity more people don't realise the worth of these wines.
CURRENT RELEASE *non-vintage* This is an elaborately flavoured wine of great distinction. It's dark amber in colour, and it has a fascinating interplay between aromas and flavours of wine, wood, spirit, and the controlled oxidation that's such a part of the sherry process. The result is a gorgeous bouquet of sweet candied fruit, roasted almonds and other nuts, spice and vanilla. The palate has a deliciously measured balance between sweetness and dry tangy acidity. The nutty aftertaste lasts for ages. Serve with plain cake and coffee.

Seppelt DP 90 Show Tawny

Quality	♟♟♟♟♟
Value	★★★★
Grapes	mostly shiraz & grenache
Region	Barossa Valley, SA
Cellar	▮
Alc./Vol.	21.5%
RRP	$93.00 (500 ml)

A famous tawny port style blended for show purposes from the old reserve wines held in cask at Seppeltsfield in the Barossa Valley. Average age is over 20 years.
CURRENT RELEASE *non-vintage* This is light years away from those thick, syrupy-sweet ports that were the standard after-dinner drink before breathalysers arrived. It has a pale tawny colour and a penetrating nose of dried fruit, scorched nuts, caramel and dry spirit. The palate is disarmingly light, yet it has great intensity and length. There's sweetness, but it's balanced by a sharp, dry finish. A classic. Great to sip with espresso coffee and good conversation.

Seppelt DP 30 Trafford Tawny

Quality	♟♟♟♟
Value	★★★★★
Grapes	shiraz; grenache
Region	Barossa Valley, SA
Cellar	▮
Alc./Vol.	18.5%
RRP	$12.80 $

At Seppeltsfield they keep vast stocks of maturing fortified wines, some of them positively ancient. James Godfrey oversees these blends with skill and passion.
CURRENT RELEASE *non-vintage* A light, clean, dry nose has some grapey hints along with attractive brandified spirit aromas. In the mouth it's intense, but not heavy, with good acidity and a soft finish. It's light and nutty, very much in the refined liqueur tawny style. Serve it with good coffee and good conversation.

Seppelt Para Liqueur Vintage Tawny Port

Vintage-dated Para Liqueur once gave birth to a wine investment mania that makes the Grange phenomenon look sensible. It disappeared for many years, but returned in 1992 with a 1976 vintage. Remember, it's a tawny port that won't improve with age.

CURRENT RELEASE 1981   This is a delicious drop with a tawny colour and a lovely bouquet of dried fruit and peel, dark toffee, clean spirit and roasted nuts. In the mouth it has penetrating concentrated sweet flavour, vanilla touches and a long roasted almond aftertaste. Great after dinner with coffee and almond brittle.

Quality	♛♛♛♛♛
Value	★★★★★
Grapes	shiraz; grenache
Region	Barossa Valley, SA
Cellar	▮
Alc./Vol.	20.0%
RRP	$35.00

Seppelt Seppeltsfield Show Vintage Shiraz

We're no longer allowed to call these wines 'vintage ports': 'vintage shiraz' seems to be the tag they'll wear from here on in. Only a handful of these wines are produced these days, and the Seppeltsfield line is one of the most illustrious, not to mention the longest-lived. A 1947 tasted this year was superb.

CURRENT RELEASE 1985   Bin GR55/41. A potent nose of blackcurrant, spice and dark chocolate liqueur cherries is allied to good brandy spirit. In the mouth it's dense in flavour and texture with concentrated sweet berry flavour, fragrant spirit, a hint of almond, and underlying ripe tannins on a long finish. Will live a lot longer. A good companion to a cheese selection.

Quality	♛♛♛♛
Value	★★★★
Grapes	shiraz
Region	Barossa Valley, SA
Cellar	▮ 5+
Alc./Vol.	20.5%
RRP	$61.00 ▮

Stanton and Killeen Collectors Muscat

Stanton and Killeen was founded in 1875 and is a fusion of two related families. Chris Killeen is winemaker today.

CURRENT RELEASE *non-vintage*   Concentration is the key word here. Treacly, dusty, raisin/prune characters dominate the bouquet. Rich, luscious flavours of rose water and Turkish delight flood the mouth, the weighty richness enlivened by excellent acid. It has tremendous palate length. Goes well with liqueur-macerated fruits and double cream.

Quality	♛♛♛♛♛
Value	★★★★★
Grapes	red frontignac
Region	Rutherglen, Vic.
Cellar	▮
Alc./Vol.	18.5%
RRP	$47.60

Stanton and Killeen Vintage Port

Quality	🍷🍷🍷🍷🍷
Value	★★★★★
Grapes	shiraz; touriga; durif
Region	Rutherglen, Vic.
Cellar	➡ 3–15+
Alc./Vol.	18.6%
RRP	$28.30

PENGUIN BEST FORTIFIED WINE

Vintage port's market in Australia was always small, but these days it's microscopic.

CURRENT RELEASE 1993 **Along with only a handful of other producers, Stanton and Killeen maintain the faith with an excellent vintage port type. This has very complex character with black cherry, blackberry, licorice and marzipan aromas and flavours. Oak is subdued, and good spirit lifts the wine's aromatic qualities. Fine, ripe tannins underpin everything and should guarantee long life. Be traditional and serve stilton with this. PS: This is a good wine to put down for a long-distant twenty-first birthday.**

Wynns Samuel Port

Quality	🍷🍷🍷
Value	★★★★
Grapes	cabernet sauvignon; touriga
Region	various
Cellar	🍷
Alc./Vol.	18.5%
RRP	$12.00 Ⓢ

When it arrived on the market, Samuel was lauded as a 'new' style: lighter, drier and slightly exotic due to the influence of the Portuguese touriga grape.

CURRENT RELEASE *non-vintage* Series 23. This is lighter in colour and structure than many tawnies. The nose has dried fruit and peel aromas along with a nutty touch. The palate follows in the same vein and it has attractive lightness of body and a dry nutty finish.

Food/Wine Combinations – Reds

Antipasto

Yering Station ED Pinot Noir Rosé

Beef

BRAISED, CASSEROLED, STEWED
Blass Vineyard Selection Shiraz
Cofield Shiraz
Elderton CSM
Grant Burge Holy Trinity
Highwood Shiraz
Leeuwin Prelude Cabernet Merlot
Lenton Brae Margaret River
Lindemans Hunter Valley Shiraz
Maglieri Shiraz
McWilliams Mount Pleasant Phillip Shiraz
Turkey Flat Cabernet Sauvignon
Water Wheel Shiraz
Yalumba Signature Cabernet Shiraz

CARPACCIO
Diamond Valley Vineyards Blue Label Pinot Noir
Hamilton The Hills Pinot Noir

HAMBURGERS
Blass Vineyard Selection Cabernet Sauvignon
Lachlan Ridge Merlot
Lindemans Limestone Coast Shiraz

Passing Clouds Shiraz
Robertson's Well Cabernet Sauvignon
Rosemount Shiraz Cabernet

RIB OF BEEF/ROAST/WELLINGTON
Bannockburn Shiraz
Best's Great Western Cabernet Sauvignon
Brangayne of Orange The Tristan
Campbells Bobbie Burns Shiraz
Cape Mentelle Trinders Cabernet Merlot
Chapel Hill Shiraz
Chateau Tahbilk Cabernet Sauvignon
Clarendon Hills Cabernet Sauvignon
Frankland Estate Olmo's Reward
Knappstein Enterprise Cabernet Sauvignon
Lindemans Pyrus
Maglieri Steve Maglieri Shiraz
Majella Shiraz
Mitchell Peppertree Shiraz
Moss Wood Cabernet Sauvignon
Mount Avoca Shiraz
Saltram Mamre Brook Cabernet Sauvignon
Stonier's Cabernet
Warrenmang Shiraz
Water Wheel Cabernet Sauvignon
Xanadu Cabernet Reserve
Yering Station Reserve Pinot Noir
Zema Estate Family Selection Cabernet Sauvignon

RISSOLES/MEATBALLS
Barossa Valley Estate 'Spires' Shiraz Cabernet
Penfolds Rawson's Retreat
Peter Lehmann Shiraz
Temple Bruer Cornucopia Grenache
Trio Station 3 Steps Shiraz Cabernet

SPARE RIBS
Cape Mentelle Zinfandel
Summerfield Shiraz
Yalumba Reserve Clare Valley Cabernet Sauvignon

STEAK – BARBECUED, GRILLED
Annie's Lane Contour Shiraz
Barossa Valley Estate Ebenezer Cabernet Merlot
Bridgewater Mill Millstone Shiraz
Elderton Cabernet Sauvignon
The Fleurieu Shiraz
Galah Shiraz
Goundrey Reserve Shiraz
Hamilton Hut Block Cabernet
Hardys Tintara Shiraz
Haselgrove Merlot
Katnook Cabernet Sauvignon
Lindemans Padthaway Cabernet Merlot
Maxwell Reserve Merlot
Mount Ida Shiraz
Orlando Jacaranda Ridge Cabernet Sauvignon
Penley Estate Cabernet Sauvignon
Seaview Edwards and Chaffey Cabernet Sauvignon
Seaview Edwards and Chaffey Shiraz
Skillogalee Shiraz

STIRFRIES/KEBABS
Buller Victoria Classic Shiraz Grenache
Darling Park Merlot
Tapestry Cabernet Sauvignon
Woodstock Shiraz

Cheese

AGED HARD (GRUYÈRE, CHEDDAR, PARMESAN, ETC.)
AusVetia Shiraz
Basedow Shiraz
Dalwhinnie Moonambel Cabernet

Dalwhinnie Moonambel Shiraz
Hardys Eileen Hardy Shiraz
Haselgrove H Reserve Shiraz
Henschke Hill of Grace
Highbank Basket Pressed Coonawarra
Moondah Brook Cabernet Sauvignon
Normans Chais Clarendon Shiraz
Penfolds Bin 707 Cabernet Sauvignon
Penfolds Coonawarra Bin 128
Penfolds St Henri Shiraz Cabernet
Petaluma Coonawarra
Pfeiffer Cabernet Sauvignon
Rymill Cabernet Sauvignon

WASHED-RIND
Lindemans Padthaway Cabernet Merlot

Fish

OCEAN TROUT
Moorilla Estate Reserve Pinot Noir

PRAWNS
Nepenthe Lenswood Pinot Noir

SALMON
Fire Gully Pinot Noir
Maritime Estate Pinot Noir
Pipers Brook Vineyard Pellion Pinot Noir

TUNA – CARPACCIO, SEARED
Badger's Brook Pinot Noir
Fox River Pinot Noir
Scotchmans Hill Pinot Noir
Tuck's Ridge Altera Pinot Noir

Game

BUFFALO
Peter Lehmann Cabernet Sauvignon
Temple Bruer Cabernet Merlot

HARE - JUGGED, ROAST SADDLE
Buller Shiraz Mondeuse
Diamond Valley Close Planted Pinot Noir
Hillstowe Buxton's Merlot Cabernet
Passing Clouds Graeme's Blend
Penfolds Old Vine Grenache Mourvèdre Shiraz
Tyrrell's Rufus Stone McLaren Vale Shiraz

KANGAROO - BARBECUED, SEARED
Barossa Valley Estate Ebenezer Shiraz
Henschke Mount Edelstone
Joseph Cabernet Sauvignon Merlot
Leo Buring Clare Valley Shiraz
Port Phillip Estate Reserve Shiraz
Turkey Flat Butchers Block

KID - BRAISED, CASSEROLED
Brand's Stentiford's Reserve Old Vines Shiraz
Charles Melton Nine Popes
Ciavarella Cabernet Sauvignon

RABBIT - CASSEROLED
Lindemans Padthaway Pinot Noir
Pewsey Vale Cabernet Sauvignon

VENISON
Blackjack Shiraz
Clarendon Hills Piggott Range Shiraz
Hungerford Hill Hilltops Cabernet Sauvignon
Lindemans Steven Vineyard Shiraz
Pauletts Andreas Shiraz
Penfolds Bin 407 Cabernet Sauvignon

Te Mata Estate Coleraine Cabernet Merlot
Torbreck Runrig
Wood Park Shiraz Cabernet Sauvignon

Lamb

CASSEROLED, STEWED
Pirramimma Stocks Hill Shiraz
Scarpantoni Block 3 Shiraz

CHOPS/CUTLETS/ROASTED RACKS/STEAKS
Balnaves Cabernet Sauvignon
Bloodwood Cabernet Sauvignon
Chapel Hill Cabernet Sauvignon
Crawford River Cabernet Merlot
Crofters Cabernet Merlot
Giaconda Cabernet
Majella Cabernet
Ryecroft Cabernet Shiraz
Saltram Classic Shiraz
Seppelt Terrain Cabernet Sauvignon
Summerfield Cabernet Sauvignon
Taltarni Shiraz
Yalumba Bush Vine Grenache

ROAST LEG/FILLET
Alkoomi Blackbutt
Bremerton 'YV' Shiraz
Coldstream Hills Reserve Cabernet Sauvignon
Eyton on Yarra NDC Cabernet Sauvignon
Flanagan's Ridge Cabernet Merlot
Geoff Merrill Cabernet Merlot
Henschke Cyril Henschke
Majella The Malleea
McWilliams Barwang Cabernet Sauvignon
Normans Cabernet Sauvignon Cabernet Franc
Orlando St Hugo Cabernet Sauvignon
Plantagenet Cabernet Sauvignon

Rosemount Show Reserve Cabernet Sauvignon
Tatachilla Padthaway Cabernet Sauvignon
Turramurra Estate Cabernet
Wynns Cabernet Sauvignon
Yarra Ridge Reserve Cabernet Sauvignon

SATAYS/KEBABS
Dowie Doole Merlot
James Busby Barossa Valley Shiraz
Wynns Shiraz

SHANKS – BRAISED
Blass Barossa Valley Shiraz
Charles Melton Shiraz
D'Arenberg D'Arry's Original
Flanagan's Ridge Wrattonbully Shiraz
Garry Crittenden 'I' Nebbiolo
Pauletts Cabernet Merlot
Penfolds Kalimna Bin 28
Stanton and Killeen Jack's Block Shiraz
Torbreck The Steading
Turkey Flat Shiraz

Noodles

Yarra Burn Bastard Hill Pinot Noir

Offal

KIDNEYS
Haselgrove Grenache
Stoniers Reserve Pinot Noir

LIVER
Annie's Lane Shiraz
Riddoch Coonawarra Shiraz
Sevenhill Shiraz
Vavasour Pinot Noir

SWEETBREADS
Felton Road Pinot Noir
Port Phillip Estate Reserve Pinot Noir

TONGUE
Hanging Rock Winery 'Rock' Shiraz Grenache Pinot Noir

Oxtail

Balgownie Shiraz
Elderton Command Shiraz

Pasta

Angove's Classic Reserve Cabernet Sauvignon
Element Cabernet Shiraz
Garry Crittenden 'I' Dolcetto
Garry Crittenden 'I' Sangiovese
Lindemans Bin 50 Shiraz
Mitchelton Goulburn Valley Shiraz
Normans Foundation Shiraz Cabernet
Talunga Shiraz
Yalumba Oxford Landing Limited Release Merlot

Pies

LAMB
Pauletts Shiraz
Wynns John Riddoch Cabernet Sauvignon

SHEPHERD'S/MEAT AND SAUCE
Bremerton Old Adam Shiraz
Deakin Estate Cabernet Sauvignon
Deakin Estate Shiraz
The Willows Cabernet Sauvignon

STEAK AND KIDNEY/GAME
Bass Phillip Premium Pinot Noir
Chain of Ponds Ledge Shiraz
D'Arenberg The Footbolt Shiraz
Drayton's Vineyard Reserve Merlot
Garden Gully Grenache
Grant Burge Filsell Shiraz
Happs Merlot
Hardys Tintara Grenache
Heathcote Winery Mail Coach Shiraz
Ivanhoe Wines Shiraz
Lark Hill Cabernet Merlot
Maxwell Ellen Street Shiraz
Preece Cabernet Sauvignon
Seppelt Chalambar Shiraz

Pizza

Krondorf Pioneer's Rest Shiraz Cabernet Sauvignon
Yalumba Oxford Landing Cabernet Shiraz

Pork

CHARCUTERIE
Angove's Classic Reserve Shiraz
Castle Rock Pinot Noir
Yering Station Pinot Noir

CHOPS, ROAST, SPARE RIBS, STIRFRIES
Abercorn Mudgee Shiraz
Jimmy Watsons Cabernet Shiraz
Lenton Brae Cabernet Merlot
Lindemans Bin 45 Cabernet Sauvignon
Montrose Sangiovese
Normans Cabernet Sauvignon

Poultry

CHICKEN – COQ AU VIN
Eyton Pinot Noir
Maglieri Merlot
Whisson Lake Carey Gully Pinot Noir

CHICKEN – GRILLED, ROASTED, SATAYS, SCHNITZEL
Brown Brothers Everton
Crabtree Shiraz Cabernet Sauvignon
Seville Estate Shiraz
Shottesbrooke Cabernet Sauvignon Merlot Malbec
Storm Ridge Pinot Noir

DUCK – BARBECUED, CASSOULET, CONFIT, PEKING,
ROASTED
Ashton Hills Reserve Pinot Noir
Chatsfield Shiraz
Craiglee Shiraz
Dromana Estate Reserve Pinot Noir
Felton Road Block 3 Pinot Noir
Giaconda Pinot Noir
Lark Hill Pinot Noir
Main Ridge Half Acre Pinot Noir
Mount Langi Ghiran Shiraz
Mount Mary Pinot Noir
Mountadam Pinot Noir
Osborns Pinot Noir
Paringa Estate Pinot Noir
Pegasus Bay Pinot Noir
Plunkett Shiraz
Port Phillip Estate Reserve Pinot Noir
Reynolds Orange Merlot
Seppelt Sunday Creek Pinot Noir
Tarrawarra Pinot Noir
The Red Essentials O'Dea's Vineyard Cabernet

GUINEA FOWL – ROASTED
Lenswood Vineyards Pinot Noir
Rochford Premier Pinot Noir
Tatachilla Clarendon Vineyard Merlot

PHEASANT – ROASTED
Hungerford Hill Tumbarumba Pinot Noir

PIGEON/SQUAB – ROASTED
Bannockburn Pinot Noir
Clonakilla Shiraz
Coldstream Hills Reserve Pinot Noir
Darling Park Pinot Noir
Heggies Pinot Noir
Palliser Estate Pinot Noir

QUAIL – BARBECUED, ROASTED
Bindi Block Five Pinot Noir
Bindi Original Vineyard Pinot Noir
Brown Brothers King Valley Barbera
Coldstream Hills Pinot Noir
Green Point Pinot Noir
Hillstowe Udy's Mill Pinot Noir
Moorilla Estate Pinot Noir
Moorooduc Estate Pinot Noir
Rouge Homme Pinot Noir
T'Gallant Juno Pinot Noir

Risotto

Coriole Redstone
Red Hill Estate Pinot Noir
Tunnel Hill Pinot Noir

Sausages

All Saints Cabernet Sauvignon
Cape Mentelle Shiraz

D'Arenberg Twenty-Eight Road Mourvèdre
Galah Cabernet Sauvignon
Jim Barry The Armagh
Lowe Hunter Valley Merlot
McWilliams Hanwood Cabernet Sauvignon
Moondah Brook Shiraz
Rouge Homme Shiraz Cabernet
Tyrrell's Long Flat Red
Woodstock Grenache

Veal

BLANQUETTE
Hanging Rock Heathcote Shiraz
Rosemount Shiraz

CUTLETS
Lillydale Vineyards Cabernet Merlot
Punters Corner Cabernet Sauvignon

OSSO BUCCO
Chain of Ponds Amadeus Cabernet Sauvignon
Drayton's Vineyard Reserve Shiraz
Hewitson l'Oizeau Shiraz
Pike's Premio Sangiovese
Trentham Estate Shiraz

ROAST
Mount Mary Quintet Cabernets
Seaview Shiraz
Stumpy Gully Cabernet Sauvignon

SCALOPPINE, SALTIMBOCCA
Balnaves The Blend
Deakin Estate Merlot
Garry Crittenden Barbera
Jingalla Reserve Shiraz

SCHNITZEL, PAN-FRIED
Blass Adelaide Hills Cabernet Merlot
Orlando Jacob's Creek Shiraz Cabernet Sauvignon
Paracombe Cabernet Franc

VITELLO TONNATO
Tatachilla Partners Cabernet Sauvignon Shiraz

Vegetables

ROASTED
Balgownie Cabernet Sauvignon
Sandhurst Ridge Shiraz

Food/Wine Combinations – Whites

Antipasto

De Bortoli Windy Peak Chardonnay
Fiddlers Creek Semillon
Homes Chardonnay
Leo Buring Clare Valley Semillon
T'Gallant Pinot Grigio

Asian Food

NOODLES
Capel Vale Verdelho
McWilliams Hanwood Chardonnay
Plunkett Chardonnay
Skillogalee Riesling

SALADS/CHICKEN – SPICY THAI, VIETNAMESE
Blass Clare & Eden Valleys Riesling
Chapel Hill Verdelho
Heggies Viognier
Henschke Joseph Hill Gewürztraminer
Hill Smith Estate Airstrip Block Chardonnay
Petaluma Riesling
Tatachilla Adelaide Hills Sauvignon Blanc
T'Gallant Tribute Pinot Gris

SPRING ROLLS/DIM SUM
Ashton Hills Riesling
Hillstowe Buxton Sauvignon Blanc

Mount Avoca Sauvignon Blanc
Mount Langi Ghiran Riesling
Peppertree Reserve Traminer

STIRFRIES
Goldwater Roseland Chardonnay
Miranda Mirrool Creek Chardonnay
Mitchelton Goulburn Valley Marsanne

SUSHI AND SASHIMI
Chateau Leamon Riesling
Henschke Julius Eden Valley Riesling
Kulkunbulla Semillon
Preece Chardonnay
Wolf Blass Gold Label Riesling
Wynns Riesling

WONTONS/PANCAKES
Browns of Padthaway Riesling
Leasingham Bin 7 Riesling
Paracombe Sauvignon Blanc

Calamari/Octopus

Abbey Vale Chardonnay
Angove's Sarnia Farm Chardonnay
Cloudy Bay Chardonnay
Lindemans Padthaway Chardonnay
Maglieri Chardonnay
Pfitzner Sauvignon Blanc
Tatachilla Chardonnay

Cheese

BLUE
Cranswick Estate Autumn Gold Botrytis Semillon

BOCCONCINI AND SALAD
Lenswood Vineyards Semillon
Lenton Brae Semillon Sauvignon Blanc
Wellington Riesling

BRIE/SOFT
Clonakilla Viognier
Highland Heritage Mount Canobolas Chardonnay

GOAT'S
Alkoomi Sauvignon Blanc
Katnook Estate Sauvignon Blanc
Leeuwin Estate Art Series Sauvignon Blanc

Crustaceans

BALMAIN BUG TAILS/MORETON BAY BUGS – SAUTÉED
Fairhall Downs Chardonnay
Geoff Weaver Chardonnay
Petaluma Chardonnay
Trentham Estate Chardonnay

CRAB – CAKES, MOUSSE, OMELETTE, ROULADE, SALAD,
TIMBALE
Cassegrain Verdelho
Chain of Ponds Riesling
The Clare Essentials Polish Hill River Riesling
Cranswick Estate Barrel Fermented Semillon
Heggies Riesling
Hunters Winemakers' Reserve Sauvignon Blanc
Kulkunbulla The Brokenback
Leo Buring Leonay Eden Valley Riesling
Lindemans Hunter Valley Semillon
Martindale Hall Riesling
Molly Morgan Joe's Block Semillon
Plantagenet Chardonnay
The Willows Riesling

LOBSTER/CRAYFISH – BARBECUED, GRILLED
Balnaves Chardonnay
Bindi Chardonnay
Cullen Chardonnay
Devil's Lair Chardonnay
Elgee Park Baillieu Myer Family Reserve Chardonnay
Green Point Chardonnay
Hunters Chardonnay
Leeuwin Estate Art Series Chardonnay
Lenswood Vineyards Chardonnay
Neudorf Moutere Chardonnay
Seppelt Drumborg Riesling

MARRON/YABBIES – COLD, BARBECUED, SAUTÉED
Brown Brothers Verdelho
Castle Rock Chardonnay
Leconfield Chardonnay
Leeuwin Prelude Chardonnay
Lenton Brae Chardonnay
Pierro Chardonnay Unfiltered

PRAWNS – BARBECUED, COCKTAIL, COLD, STIR-FRIED
Abbey Vale Verdelho
Barossa Valley Estate Moculta Semillon
Best's Great Western Riesling
Brokenwood Semillon
Buller Victoria Classic Chenin Blanc Colombard
Geoff Weaver Sauvignon Blanc
Hunter's Riesling
Lindemans Bin 65 Chardonnay
Lindemans Hunter Valley Reserve Chardonnay
Maglieri Semillon
Maritime Estate Pinot Grigio
McWilliams Mount Pleasant Elizabeth
Pfitzner Eric's Vineyard Chardonnay
Plantagenet Omrah Sauvignon Blanc
Richmond Grove Marlborough Sauvignon Blanc

Saltram Mamre Brook Chardonnay
Westend Richland Chardonnay

SCAMPI – BAKED, GRILLED
Chapel Hill Unwooded Chardonnay
Haselgrove 'H' Chardonnay
Penfolds Adelaide Hills Semillon
Penfolds Yattarna Chardonnay
Te Mata Estate Hawkes Bay Chardonnay
Tyrrell's Moon Mountain Chardonnay

Desserts

CAKE
Miranda Golden Botrytis
Tollana Botrytis Riesling

CRÈME BRÛLÉE
De Bortoli Noble One Botrytis Semillon
West End Three Bridges Golden Mist Botrytis Semillon

Fish

BOUILLABAISSE
Penfolds Reserve Bin 95A Chardonnay
Rosabrook Estate Chardonnay

COD/TROUT – SMOKED
Penley Estate Chardonnay
Yarra Valley Hills Warranwood Riesling

FLATHEAD/FLOUNDER/GARFISH/WHITING/ANY WHITE-
FLESHED FISH – FISH AND CHIPS, GRILLED, MEUNIÈRE,
PAN-FRIED
Alkoomi Frankland River Riesling
Annie's Lane Riesling
Annie's Lane Semillon
Brand's Laira Riesling

Briar Ridge Early Harvest Semillon
The Clare Essentials Carlsfield Riesling
Crabtree Watervale Riesling
Craiglee Chardonnay
Cullen Sauvignon Blanc Semillon
Drayton's Vineyard Reserve Semillon
The First Hunter Valley Semillon
Glenguin Chardonnay
Hamilton's Bluff Chairman's Reserve Chardonnay
Hungerford Hill Tumbarumba Chardonnay
Jingalla Wood-aged Verdelho
Leasingham Classic Clare Riesling
Leconfield Old Vines Riesling
McLarens on the Lake Colombard Semillon Chardonnay
Moorilla Estate Chardonnay
Palliser Estate Riesling
Palliser Estate Sauvignon Blanc
Pike's Reserve Riesling
Plantagenet Omrah Unoaked Chardonnay
Riddoch Sauvignon Blanc
Rossetto Promenade Semillon
Stonier's Chardonnay
Two Churches Barossa Riesling

SALMON/OCEAN TROUT/TUNA
The Green Vineyards Chardonnay
Katnook Estate Riesling
Moorooduc Estate Chardonnay
Murrindindi Chardonnay
Nepenthe Chardonnay
Tallarook Chardonnay
Voyager Estate Chardonnay

SNAPPER/WHITING – QUENELLES, STEAMED
Bannockburn Chardonnay
Crawford River Riesling
De Bortoli Windy Peak Rhine Riesling
Fox River Classic White

Hamilton The Hills Chardonnay
Hillstowe Udy's Mill Chardonnay
Talunga Semillon

WHITEBAIT/SNAPPER – FRITTERS
Briar Ridge Hand Picked Chardonnay
Drayton's Vineyard Reserve Chardonnay
Flinders Bay Semillon Sauvignon Blanc
Hamilton Ayliffe's Orchard Sauvignon Blanc

Fruit

All Saints Late Harvest Semillon
Brown Brothers Noble Riesling
Haselgrove 'H' Botrytis Sauvignon Semillon
Heggies Botrytis Riesling
Mount Horrocks Cordon Cut Riesling
Rimfire Estate Pioneer White
Selaks Marlborough Ice Wine

Offal

BRAINS
Jingalla Premium Riesling
Plunkett Semillon

LIVER/PÂTÉ
Ivanhoe Late Picked Gewürztraminer
Skillogalee Gewürztraminer
T'Gallant Triumph Late Harvest Pinot Gris

TONGUE
Fox River Sauvignon Blanc

Pasta

Brangayne of Orange Chardonnay
Cape Mentelle Chardonnay

Heathcote Winery Viognier
Nepenthe Lenswood Semillon
Wolf Blass Classic Dry White
Yalumba Oxford Landing Chardonnay
Yarraman Road Chardonnay

Poultry

CHICKEN – BARBECUED, CASSEROLED, FRIED, GRILLED,
ROASTED, SCHNITZEL, STIR-FRIED
Allandale Chardonnay
Allinda Chardonnay
Angove's Classic Reserve Chardonnay
Ballingal Estate Premium Semillon
Bethany Chardonnay
Briar Ridge Chairman's Selection Chardonnay
Golden Grove Estate Chardonnay
Grant Burge Zerk Semillon
Hesperos Sauvignon Blanc
Ingoldby Chardonnay
Peppertree Chardonnay
Poole's Rock Chardonnay
Rimfire Estate Chardonnay
Rosemount Show Reserve Chardonnay
Rothvale Reserve Chardonnay 'F'
Tyrrell's Long Flat Chardonnay
Tyrrell's Long Flat White

CHICKEN – COLD, SMOKED
Ashwood Grove Chardonnay
Basedow Semillon
Element Chardonnay
Eyton Dalry Road Chardonnay
Fire Gully Semillon Sauvignon Blanc
Hungerford Hill Cowra Chardonnay
Pegasus Bay Sauvignon Semillon
Rimfire Chardonnay Oak Matured

Rosemount Roxburgh Chardonnay
Schinus Chardonnay

DUCK
Hunter's Gewürztraminer

PHEASANT – ROASTED
Pipers Brook Vineyard Summit Chardonnay
Te Mata Elston Chardonnay

Prosciutto

Best's Great Western Chardonnay
Blass Adelaide Hills Chardonnay
Chatsfield Chardonnay
Fox River Chardonnay
Poole's Rock Chardonnay

Quiche/Egg and Bacon Pie

Barossa Valley Estate Spires Semillon Chardonnay
Dalfarras Marsanne
Hay Shed Hill Sauvignon Blanc
Temple Bruer Chenin Blanc

Rice/Risotto

Chatsfield Gewürztraminer
Shaw and Smith Reserve Chardonnay
St Hallett Chardonnay

Salads

ASPARAGUS
Mount Riley Sauvignon Blanc

CAESAR
Brangayne of Orange Sauvignon Blanc
Haselgrove Sauvignon Blanc
Plantagenet Breakaway Fine White
Rouge Homme Unoaked Chardonnay
Talunga Chardonnay

NIÇOISE
Devil's Lair Fifth Leg
Phillip Island Wines Sauvignon Blanc

WALDORF
Best's Victoria Chenin Blanc

Shellfish

MIXED
Amberley Semillon Sauvignon Blanc
Austins Barrabool Chardonnay
Castle Rock Riesling
Cockfighter's Ghost Semillon
Leo Buring Clare Valley Riesling
Peter Lehmann Eden Valley Riesling
St Matthias Chardonnay
Tarrawarra Chardonnay
Tollana Adelaide Hills Sauvignon Blanc
Water Wheel Chardonnay
Will Taylor Hunter Valley Semillon

MUSSELS
Fairhall Downs Sauvignon Blanc
Kim Crawford Marlborough Sauvignon Blanc
Neudorf Sauvignon Blanc

OYSTERS
Barrington Estate Semillon
Bindi Quartz Chardonnay
Forrest Estate Sauvignon Blanc

Hamilton The Slate Quarry Riesling
Hardys Adelaide Hills Sauvignon Blanc
Hungerford Hill Semillon
Ironwood Estate Riesling
Lenswood Vineyards Sauvignon Blanc
Lillydale Vineyards Sauvignon Blanc
Ninth Island Riesling

SCALLOPS – EN BROCHETTE, GRATINÉED, GRILLED,
PAN-FRIED, SAUTÉED
Coldstream Hills Chardonnay
Coolangatta Estate Alexander Berry Chardonnay
Doonkuna Chardonnay
Felton Road Dry Riesling
Forrest Estate Riesling
Harewood Estate Chardonnay
Heggies Chardonnay
Jim Barry Watervale Riesling
Jingalla Late Harvest Riesling
Mornington Vineyards Estate Chardonnay
Ninth Island Chardonnay
Penfolds Adelaide Hills Chardonnay
Port Phillip Estate Chardonnay
Red Hill Estate Chardonnay
Seaview Chardonnay
Shottesbrooke Chardonnay

Veal

Coldstream Hills Reserve Chardonnay
Giaconda Chardonnay

Vegetables

CHARGRILLED, FRIED, GRATINÉED, STUFFED
Deakin Estate Sauvignon Blanc
Fermoy Estate Semillon
Gramp's Chardonnay

Henschke Green's Hill Riesling
Jane Brook Sauvignon Blanc
Knappstein Riesling
Seppelt Drumborg Sauvignon Blanc
Tatachilla Growers Chenin, Semillon, Sauvignon Blanc

CRUDITÉS
Cloudy Bay Sauvignon Blanc
Dromana Estate Reserve Chardonnay

TERRINES
Dalfarras Sauvignon Blanc
Fiddlers Creek Sauvignon Blanc
Henschke Sauvignon Blanc Semillon
Kulkunbulla Nullarbor Chardonnay
Talunga Sauvignon Blanc

Wine Terms

The following are commonly used winemaking terms.

ACID   There are many acids that occur naturally in grapes and it's in the winemaker's interest to retain the favourable ones because these promote freshness and longevity.

AGRAFE   A metal clip used to secure champagne corks during secondary bottle fermentation.

ALCOHOL   Ethyl alcohol (C_2H_5OH) is a by-product of fermentation of sugars. It's the stuff that makes people happy and it adds warmth and texture to wine.

ALCOHOL BY VOLUME (A/V)   The measurement of the amount of alcohol in a wine. It's expressed as a percentage, e.g. 13.0% A/V means there is 13.0% pure alcohol as a percentage of the total volume.

ALDEHYDE   An unwanted and unpleasant organic compound formed between acid and alcohol by oxidation. It's removed by sulfur dioxide.

ALLIER   A type of oak harvested in the French forest of the same name.

APERITIF   A wine that stimulates the appetite.

AROMATIC   A family of grape varieties that have a high terpene content. Riesling and gewürztraminer are examples, and terpenes produce their floral qualities.

AUTOLYSIS   A Vegemite or fresh-baked bread taste and smell imparted by spent yeast cells in sparkling wines.

BACK BLEND   To add unfermented grape juice to wine or to add young wine to old wine in fortifieds.

BARREL FERMENTATION   The process of fermenting a red or white wine in a small barrel, thereby adding a creamy texture and toasty or nutty characters, and better integrating the wood and fruit flavours.

BARRIQUE   A 225-litre barrel.

BAUMÉ The measure of sugar in grape juice used to estimate potential alcohol content. It's usually expressed as a degree, e.g. 12 degrees Baumé juice will produce approximately 12.0% A/V if it's fermented to dryness. The alternative brix scale is approximately double Baumé and must be divided by 1.8 to estimate potential alcohol.

BENTONITE A fine clay (drillers mud) used as a clarifying (fining) agent.

BLEND A combination of two or more grape varieties and/or vintages. *See also* Cuvée

BOTRYTIS CINEREA A fungus that thrives on grapevines in humid conditions and sucks out the water of the grapes thereby concentrating the flavour. Good in white wine but not so good in red. (There is also a loss in quantity.)

BREATHING Uncorking a wine and allowing it to stand for a couple of hours before serving. This introduces oxygen and dissipates bottle odours. Decanting aids breathing.

BRIX *see* Baumé

BRUT The second lowest level of sweetness in sparkling wine; it does not mean there is no added sugar.

BUSH VINE Although pruned the vine is self-supporting in a low-to-the-ground bush. (Still common in the Barossa Valley.)

CARBONIC MACERATION Fermentation in whole (uncrushed) bunches. This is a popular technique in Beaujolais. It produces bright colour and softer tannins.

CHARMAT PROCESS A process for making sparkling wine where the wine is fermented in a tank rather than in a bottle.

CLONE (CLONAL) A recognisable subspecies of vine within a varietal family, e.g. there are numerous clones of pinot noir and these all have subtle character differences.

COLD FERMENTATION (Also Controlled Temperature Fermentation) Usually applied to white wines where the ferment is kept at a low temperature (10–12 degrees Centigrade).

CORDON The arms of the trained grapevine that bear the fruit.

CORDON CUT A technique of cutting the fruit-bearing arms and allowing the berries to dehydrate to concentrate the flavour.

CRUSH Crushing the berries to liberate the free-run juice (*q.v.*). Also used as an expression of a wine company's output: 'This winery has a 1000-tonne crush'.

CUVÉE   A Champagne term meaning a selected blend or batch.

DISGORGE   The process of removing the yeast lees from a sparkling wine. It involves freezing the neck of the bottle and firing out a plug of ice and yeast. The bottle is then topped up and recorked.

DOSAGE   Sweetened wine added to a sparkling wine after disgorgement.

DOWNY MILDEW   A disease that attacks vine leaves and fruit. It's associated with humidity and lack of air circulation.

DRIP IRRIGATION   An accurate way of watering a vineyard. Each vine has its own dripper and a controlled amount of water is applied.

DRYLAND VINEYARD   A vineyard that has no irrigation.

ESTERS   Volatile compounds that can occur during fermentation or maturation. They impart a distinctive chemical taste.

FERMENTATION   The process by which yeast converts sugar to alcohol with a by-product of carbon dioxide.

FINING   The process of removing solids from wine to make it clear. There are several methods used.

FORTIFY   The addition of spirit to increase the amount of alcohol in a wine.

FREE-RUN JUICE   The first juice to come out of the press or drainer (as opposed to pressings).

GENERIC   Wines labelled after their district of origin rather than their grape variety, e.g. Burgundy, Chablis, Champagne etc. These terms can no longer legally be used on Australian labels. *Cf.* Varietal.

GRAFT   Changing the nature/variety of a vine by grafting a different variety on to a root stock.

IMPERIAL   A 6-litre bottle (contains eight 750-ml bottles).

JEROBOAM   A 4.5-litre champagne bottle.

LACCASE   A milky condition on the surface of red wine caused by noble rot. The wine is usually pasteurised.

LACTIC ACID   One of the acids found in grape juice; as the name suggests, it's milky and soft.

LACTOBACILLUS   A micro-organism that ferments carbohydrates (glucose) or malic acid to produce lactic acid.

LEES   The sediment left after fermentation. It consists mainly of dead yeast cells.

MALIC ACID   One of the acids found in grape juice. It has a hard/sharp taste like a Granny Smith apple.

MALOLACTIC FERMENTATION   A secondary process that converts malic acid into lactic acid. It's encouraged in red wines when they are in barrel. If it occurs after bottling, the wine will be fizzy and cloudy.

MERCAPTAN   Ethyl mercaptan is a sulfur compound with a smell like garlic, burnt rubber or asparagus water.

MÉTHODE CHAMPENOISE   The French method for producing effervescence in the bottle; a secondary fermentation process where the carbon dioxide produced is dissolved into the wine.

METHOXYPYRAZINES   Substances that give sauvignon blanc and cabernet sauvignon that added herbaceousness when the grapes aren't fully ripe.

MOUSSE   The froth or head on sparkling wine.

MUST   *see* Free-run juice

NOBLE ROT   *see* Botrytis cinerea

NON-VINTAGE   A wine that is a blend of two or more years.

OAK   The least porous wood, genus *Quercus*, and used for wine storage containers.

OENOLOGY   The science of winemaking.

ORGANIC VITICULTURE   Growing grapes without the use of pesticides, fungicides or chemical fertilisers. Certain chemicals, e.g. copper sulfate, are permitted.

ORGANIC WINES   Wines made from organically grown fruit without the addition of chemicals.

OXIDATION   Browning and dullness of aroma and flavour caused by excessive exposure to air.

pH   The measure of the strength of acidity. The higher the pH the higher the alkalinity and the lower the acidity. Wines with high pH values should not be cellared.

PHENOLICS   A group of chemical compounds which includes the tannins and colour pigments of grapes. A white wine described as 'phenolic' has an excess of tannin, making it taste coarse.

PHYLLOXERA   A louse that attacks the roots of a vine, eventually killing the plant.

PIGEAGE   To foot-press the grapes.

PRESSINGS   The juice extracted by applying pressure to the skins after the free-run juice has been drained.

PRICKED   A wine that is spoilt and smells of vinegar, due to excessive volatile acidity. *Cf.* Volatile.

PUNCHEON   A 500-litre barrel.

RACKING   Draining off wine from the lees or other sediment to clarify it.

SAIGNÉE   French for bleeding: the winemaker has run off part of the juice of a red fermentation to concentrate what's left.

SKIN CONTACT   Allowing the free-run juice to remain in contact with the skins; in the case of white wines, usually for a very short time.

SOLERO SYSTEM   Usually a stack of barrels used for blending maturing wines. The oldest material is at the bottom and is topped up with younger material from the top barrels.

SOLIDS   Minute particles suspended in a wine.

SULFUR DIOXIDE (SO₂)   (Code 220) A chemical added since Roman times to a wine as a preservative and a bactericide.

SUR LIE   Wine that has been kept on lees and not racked or filtered before bottling.

TACHÉ   A French term that means to stain, usually by the addition of a small amount of red wine to sparkling wine to turn it pink.

TANNIN   A complex substance derived from skins, pips and stalks of grapes as well as the oak casks. It has a preservative function and imparts dryness and grip to the finish.

TERROIR   Arcane French expression that describes the complete growing environment of the vine, including climate, aspect, soil, etc., and the direct effect this has on the character of its wine.

VARIETAL   An industry-coined term used to refer to a wine by its grape variety, e.g. 'a shiraz'. *Cf.* Generic.

VÉRAISON   The moment when the grapes change colour and gain sugar.

VERTICAL TASTING   A tasting of consecutive vintages of one wine.

VIGNERON   A grapegrower or vineyard worker.

VINEGAR   Acetic acid produced from fruit.

VINIFY   The process of turning grapes into wine.

VINTAGE   The year of harvest, and the produce of a particular year.

VOLATILE   Excessive volatile acids in a wine.

YEAST   The micro-organism that converts sugar into alcohol.

Tasting Terms

The following terms refer to the sensory evaluation of wine.

AFTERTASTE The taste (sensation) after the wine has been swallowed. It's usually called the finish.

ASTRINGENT (ASTRINGENCY) Applies to the finish of a wine. Astringency is caused by tannins that produce a mouth-puckering sensation and coat the teeth with dryness.

BALANCE 'The state of . . .'; the harmony between components of a wine.

BILGY An unfortunate taste like the bilge of a ship. Usually caused by mouldy old oak.

BITTERNESS A sensation detected at the back of the tongue. It's not correct in wine but is desirable in beer.

BOUQUET The aroma of a finished or mature wine.

BROAD A wine that lacks fruit definition; usually qualified as soft or coarse.

CASSIS A blackcurrant flavour common in cabernet sauvignon. It refers to a liqueur produced in France.

CHALKY An extremely dry sensation on the finish.

CHEESY A dairy character sometimes found in wine, particularly sherries.

CIGAR BOX A smell of tobacco and wood found in cabernet sauvignon.

CLOUDINESS A fault in wine that is caused by suspended solids that make it look dull.

CLOYING Excessive sweetness that clogs the palate.

CORKED Spoiled wine that has reacted with a tainted cork, and smells like wet cardboard. (The taint is caused by trichloroanisole.)

CREAMY The feeling of cream in the mouth, a texture.

CRISP Clean acid on the finish of a white wine.

DEPTH The amount of fruit on the palate.

DRY A wine that does not register sugar in the mouth.

DULL Pertaining to colour; the wine is not bright or shining.

DUMB Lacking nose or flavour on the palate.

DUSTY Applies to a very dry tannic finish; a sensation.

EARTHY Not as bad as it sounds, this is a loamy/mineral character that can add interest to the palate.

FINESSE The state of a wine. It refers to balance and style.

FINISH *see* Aftertaste

FIRM Wine with strong, unyielding tannins.

FLABBY Wine with insufficient acid to balance ripe fruit flavours.

FLESHY Wines of substance with plenty of fruit.

FLINTY A character on the finish that is akin to sucking dry creek pebbles.

GARLIC *see* Mercaptan (in Wine Terms)

GRASSY A cut-grass odour, usually found in semillon and sauvignon blancs.

GRIP The effect on the mouth of tannin on the finish; a puckering sensation.

HARD More tannin or acid than fruit flavour.

HERBACEOUS Herbal smells or flavour in wine.

HOLLOW A wine with a lack of flavour in the middle palate.

HOT Wines high in alcohol that give a feeling of warmth and a slippery texture.

IMPLICIT SWEETNESS A just detectable sweetness from the presence of glycerin (rather than residual sugar).

INKY Tannate of iron present in a wine which imparts a metallic taste.

INTEGRATED (WELL) The component parts of a wine fit together without gaps or disorders.

JAMMY Ripe fruit that takes on the character of stewed jam.

LEATHERY A smell like old leather, not necessarily bad if it's in balance.

LENGTH (LONG) The measure of the registration of flavour in the mouth. (The longer the better.)

LIFTED The wine is given a lift by the presence of either volatile acid or wood tannins, e.g. vanillin oak lift.

LIMPID   A colour term usually applied to star-bright white wine.

MADEIRISED   Wine that has aged to the point where it tastes like a madeira.

MOULDY   Smells like bathroom mould; dank.

MOUTH-FEEL   The sensation the wine causes in the mouth; a textural term.

MUSTY   Stale, flat, out-of-condition wine.

PEPPER   A component in either the nose or the palate that smells or tastes like cracked pepper.

PUNGENT   Wine with a strong nose.

RANCIO   A nutty character found in aged fortifieds that is imparted by time on wood.

RESIDUAL SUGAR   The presence of unfermented grape sugar on the palate; common in sweet wines.

ROUGH   Unpleasant, aggressive wine.

ROUND   A full-bodied wine with plenty of mouth-feel (*q.v.*).

SAPPY   A herbaceous character that resembles sap.

SHORT   A wine lacking in taste and structure. *See also* Length

SPICY   A wine with a high aromatic content; spicy character can also be imparted by wood.

STALKY   Exposure to stalks, e.g. during fermentation. Leaves a bitter character in the wine.

TART   A lively wine with a lot of fresh acid.

TOASTY   A smell of cooked bread.

VANILLIN   The smell and taste of vanilla beans; usually imparted by oak ageing.

VARIETAL   Refers to the distinguishing qualities of the grape variety used in the wine.

Directory of Wineries

AFFLECK VINEYARD
RMB 244
Millynn Rd (off Gundaroo Rd)
Bungendore NSW 2651
(02) 6236 9276

ALAMBIE WINES
Campbell Ave
Irymple Vic. 3498
(03) 5024 6800
fax (03) 5024 6605

ALKOOMI
Wingeballup Rd
Frankland WA 6396
(08) 9855 2229
fax (08) 9855 2284

ALLANDALE
Lovedale Rd
Pokolbin NSW 2320
(02) 4990 4526
fax (02) 4990 1714

ALLANMERE
Lovedale Rd
Pokolbin NSW 2320
(02) 4930 7387

ALL SAINTS ESTATE
All Saints Rd
Wahgunyah Vic. 3687
(02) 6033 1922
fax (02) 6033 3515

AMBERLEY ESTATE
Wildwood & Thornton Rds
Yallingup WA 6282
(08) 9755 2288
fax (08) 9755 2171

ANDERSON WINERY
Lot 13 Chiltern Rd
Rutherglen Vic. 3685
(03) 6032 8111

ANDREW GARRETT
Kangarilla Rd
McLaren Vale SA 5171
(08) 8323 8853
fax (08) 8323 8550

ANGOVE'S
Bookmark Ave
Renmark SA 5341
(08) 8595 1311
fax (08) 8595 1583

ANTCLIFFE'S CHASE
RMB 4510
Caveat
via Seymour Vic. 3660
(03) 5790 4333

ARROWFIELD
Denman Rd
Jerry's Plains NSW 2330
(02) 6576 4041
fax (02) 6576 4144

ASHTON HILLS
Tregarthen Rd
Ashton SA 5137
(08) 8390 1243
fax (08) 8390 1243

ASHWOOD GROVE
(not open to public)
(03) 5030 5291

AVALON
RMB 9556
Whitfield Rd
Wangaratta Vic. 3677
(03) 5729 3629

BABICH WINES
Babich Rd
Henderson NZ
(09) 833 8909

BAILEYS
Taminick Gap Rd
Glenrowan Vic. 3675
(03) 5766 2392
fax (03) 5766 2596

BALDIVIS ESTATE
Lot 165 River Rd
Baldivis WA 6171
(08) 9525 2066
fax (08) 9525 2411

BALGOWNIE
Hermitage Rd
Maiden Gully Vic. 3551
(03) 5449 6222
fax (03) 5449 6506

BALNAVES
Penola–Naracoorte Rd
Coonawarra SA 5263
(08) 8737 2946
fax (08) 8737 2945

BANNOCKBURN
Midland Hwy
Bannockburn Vic. 3331
(03) 5281 1363
fax (03) 5281 1349

BANROCK STATION
(*see* Hardys)

BAROSSA SETTLERS
Trial Hill Rd
Lyndoch SA 5351
(08) 8524 4017

BAROSSA VALLEY ESTATE
Heaslip Rd
Angle Vale SA 5117
(08) 8284 7000
fax (08) 8284 7219

BARRATT
(not open to public)
PO Box 204
Summertown SA 5141
(08) 8390 1788
fax (08) 8390 1788

BARWANG
(*see* McWilliam's)

BASS PHILLIP
Tosch's Rd
Leongatha South Vic. 3953
(03) 5664 3341

BERRI ESTATES
Sturt Hwy
Glossop SA 5344
(08) 8582 0300
fax (08) 8583 2224

BEST'S GREAT WESTERN
Western Hwy
Great Western Vic. 3377
(03) 5356 2250
fax (03) 5356 2430

BETHANY
Bethany Rd
Bethany
via Tanunda SA 5352
(08) 8563 2086
fax (08) 8563 2086

BIANCHET
187 Victoria Rd
Lilydale Vic. 3140
(03) 9739 1779
fax (03) 9739 1277

BINDI
(not open to public)
145 Melton Rd
Gisborne Vic. 3437
(03) 5428 2564
fax (03) 5428 2564

BIRDWOOD ESTATE
PO Box 194
Birdwood SA 5234
(08) 8263 0986

BLACKJACK VINEYARD
Calder Hwy
Harcourt Vic. 3452
(03) 5474 2528
fax (03) 5475 2102

BLEASDALE
Wellington Rd
Langhorne Creek SA 5255
(08) 8537 3001

BLEWITT SPRINGS
Recreational Rd
McLaren Vale SA 5171
(08) 8323 8689

BLOODWOOD ESTATE
4 Griffin Rd
via Orange NSW 2800
(02) 6362 5631

BLUE PYRENEES ESTATE
Vinoca Rd
Avoca Vic. 3467
(03) 5465 3202
fax (03) 5465 3529

BOSTON BAY
Lincoln Hwy
Port Lincoln SA 5605
(08) 8684 3600

BOTOBOLAR
Botobolar La.
PO Box 212
Mudgee NSW 2850
(02) 6373 3840
fax (02) 6373 3789

BOWEN ESTATE
Penola–Naracoorte Rd
Coonawarra SA 5263
(08) 8737 2229
fax (08) 8737 2173

BOYNTONS OF BRIGHT
Ovens Valley Hwy
Porepunkah Vic. 3740
(03) 5756 2356

BRANDS LAIRA
Naracoorte Hwy
Coonawarra SA 5263
(08) 8736 3260
fax (08) 8736 3208

BREMERTON
Strathalbyn Rd
Langhorne Creek SA 5255
(08) 8537 3093
fax (08) 8537 3109

BRIAGOLONG ESTATE
118 Boisdale St
Maffra Vic. 3860
(03) 5147 2322
fax (03) 5147 2400

BRIAR RIDGE
Mount View
Mt View NSW 2321
(02) 4990 3670
fax (02) 4998 7802

BRIDGEWATER MILL
Mount Barker Rd
Bridgewater SA 5155
(08) 8339 3422
fax (08) 8339 5253

BRINDABELLA HILLS
Woodgrove Cl.
via Hall ACT 2618
(06) 230 2583

BROKENWOOD
McDonalds Rd
Pokolbin NSW 2321
(02) 4998 7559
fax (02) 4998 7893

BROOK EDEN
Adams Rd
Lebrina Tas. 7254
(03) 6395 6244

BROOKLAND VALLEY
Caves Rd
Willyabrup WA 6284
(08) 9755 6250
fax (08) 9755 6214

BROWN BROTHERS
Meadow Crk Rd (off the
    Snow Rd)
Milawa Vic. 3678
(03) 5720 5500
fax (03) 5720 5511

BROWNS OF PADTHAWAY
PMB 196
Naracoorte SA 5271
(08) 8765 6063
fax (08) 8765 6083

BULLER & SONS, R L
Calliope
Three Chain Rd
Rutherglen Vic. 3685
(03) 5037 6305

BULLER (RL) & SON
Murray Valley Hwy
Beverford Vic. 3590
(03) 5037 6305
fax (03) 5037 6803
fax (03) 6032 8005

BURGE FAMILY WINEMAKERS
Barossa Hwy
Lyndoch SA 5351
(08) 8524 4644
fax (08) 8524 4444

BURNBRAE
Hargraves Rd
Erudgere
Mudgee NSW 2850
(02) 6373 3504
fax (02) 6373 3601

CALAIS ESTATE
Palmers La.
Pokolbin NSW 2321
(02) 4998 7654
fax (02) 4998 7813

CALLATOOTA ESTATE
Wybong Rd
Wybong NSW 2333
(02) 6547 8149

CAMBEWARRA ESTATE
520 Illaroo Rd
Cambewarra NSW 2541
(02) 4446 0170
fax (02) 4446 0170

CAMPBELLS
Murray Valley Hwy
Rutherglen Vic. 3685
(02) 6032 9458
fax (02) 6032 9870

CANOBOLAS–SMITH
Cargo Rd
Orange NSW 2800
(02) 6365 6113

CAPE CLAIRAULT
via Caves Rd
or Bussell Hwy
CMB Carbunup River
    WA 6280
(08) 9755 6225
fax (08) 9755 6229

CAPELVALE
Lot 5
Capel North West Rd
Capel WA 6271
(08) 9727 2439
fax (08) 9727 2164

CAPE MENTELLE
Wallcliffe Rd
Margaret River WA 6285
(08) 9757 3266
fax (08) 9757 3233

CAPERCAILLIE
Londons Rd
Lovedale NSW 2325
(02) 4990 2904
fax (02) 4991 1886

CASSEGRAIN
Fern Bank Ck Rd
Port Macquarie NSW 2444
(02) 6583 7777
fax (02) 6584 0353

CASTLE ROCK ESTATE
Porongurup Rd
Porongurup WA 6324
(08) 9853 1035
fax (08) 9853 1010

CHAIN OF PONDS
Gumeracha Cellars
PO Box 365
Main Rd
Gumeracha SA 5233
(08) 8389 1415
fax (08) 8336 2462

CHAMBERS ROSEWOOD
Corowa–Rutherglen Rd
Rutherglen Vic. 3685
(02) 6032 8641
fax (02) 6032 8101

CHAPEL HILL
Chapel Hill Rd
McLaren Vale SA 5171
(08) 8323 8429
fax (08) 8323 9245

CHARLES CIMICKY
Gomersal Rd
Lyndoch SA 5351
(08) 8524 4025
fax (08) 8524 4772

CHARLES MELTON
Krondorf Rd
Tanunda SA 5352
(08) 8563 3606
fax (08) 8563 3422

**CHARLES STURT
UNIVERSITY**
Boorooma St
North Wagga Wagga
    NSW 2678
(02) 6933 2435
fax (02) 6933 2107

CHATEAU LEAMON
Calder Hwy
Bendigo Vic. 3550
(03) 5447 7995

CHATEAU REYNELLA
Reynella Rd
Reynella SA 5161
(08) 8392 2222
fax (08) 8392 2202

CHATEAU TAHBILK
Tabilk Vic. 3607
via Nagambie
(03) 5794 2555
fax (03) 5794 2360

CHATEAU YALDARA
Gomersal Rd
Lyndoch SA 5351
(08) 8524 4200
fax (08) 8524 4678

CHATSFIELD
O'Neill Rd
Mount Barker WA 6324
(08) 9851 1704
fax (08) 9841 6811

CLARENDON HILLS
(not open to public)
(08) 8364 1484

CLEVELAND
Shannons Rd
Lancefield Vic. 3435
(03) 5429 1449
fax (03) 5429 2017

CLONAKILLA
Crisps La.
Murrumbateman
   NSW 2582
(02) 6251 1938 (A.H.)

CLOUDY BAY
(see Cape Mentelle)

CLOVER HILL
(see Taltarni)

COBAW RIDGE
Perc Boyer's La.
East Pastoria
via Kyneton Vic. 3444
(03) 5423 5227

COLDSTREAM HILLS
31 Maddens La.
Coldstream Vic. 3770
(03) 5964 9388
fax (03) 5964 9389

CONSTABLE HERSHON
1 Gillards Road
Pokolbin NSW 2320
(02) 4998 7887
fax (02) 4998 7887

COOLANGATTA ESTATE
Coolangatta Resort
via Berry NSW 2535
(02) 4448 7131
fax (02) 4448 7997

COOMBEND
Swansea Tas. 7190
(03) 6257 8256
fax (03) 6257 8484

COOPERS CREEK WINERY
Highway 16
Haupai
Auckland NZ
(09) 412 8560

COPE WILLIAMS WINERY
Glenfern Rd
Romsey Vic. 3434
(03) 5429 5428
fax (03) 5429 2655

CORIOLE
Chaffeys Rd
McLaren Vale SA 5171
(08) 8323 8305
fax (08) 8323 9136

COWRA ESTATE
Boorowa Rd
Cowra NSW 2794
(02) 6342 3650

CRABTREE WATERVALE CELLARS
North Tce
Watervale SA 5452
(08) 8843 0069
fax (08) 8843 0144

CRAIG AVON
Craig Avon La.
Merricks North Vic. 3926
(03) 5989 7465

CRAIGIE KNOWE
Cranbrook Tas. 7190
(03) 6223 5620

CRAIGLEE
Sunbury Rd
Sunbury Vic. 3429
(03) 9744 1160

CRAIGMOOR
Craigmoor Rd
Mudgee NSW 2850
(02) 6372 2208

CRAIGOW
Richmond Rd
Cambridge Tas. 7170
(03) 6248 5482

CRANEFORD
Main St
Springton SA 5235
(08) 8568 2220
fax (08) 8568 2538

CRAWFORD RIVER
Condah Vic. 3303
(03) 5578 2267

CULLENS
Caves Rd
Willyabrup
via Cowaramup WA 6284
(08) 9755 5277

CURRENCY CREEK
Winery Rd
Currency Creek SA 5214
(08) 8555 4069

DALFARRAS
(see Chateau Tahbilk)

DALRYMPLE
Pipers Brook Rd
Pipers Brook Tas. 7254
(03) 6382 7222

DALRY ROAD
(see Eyton on Yarra)

DALWHINNIE
Taltarni Rd
Moonambel Vic. 3478
(03) 5467 2388

D'ARENBERG
Osborn Rd
McLaren Vale SA 5171
(08) 8323 8206

DARLING ESTATE
(by appointment only)
Whitfield Rd
Cheshunt Vic. 3678
(03) 5729 8396
fax (03) 5729 8396

DARLING PARK
Lot 1 Browne La.
Red Hill 3937
(03) 5989 2732
fax (03) 5989 2254

DAVID TRAEGER
399 High St
Nagambie Vic. 3608
(03) 5794 2514

DAVID WYNN
(see Mountadam)

DEAKIN ESTATE
(see Katnook)

De BORTOLI
De Bortoli Rd
Bibul NSW 2680
(02) 6964 9444
fax (02) 6964 9400

De BORTOLI
Pinnacle La.
Dixons Creek Vic. 3775
(03) 5965 2271

DELAMERE
4238 Bridport Rd
Pipers Brook Tas. 7254
(03) 6382 7190

DELATITE
Stoney's Rd
Mansfield Vic. 3722
(03) 5775 2922
fax (03) 5775 2911

DEMONDRILLE
RMB 97 Prunevale Rd
Prunevale
via Harden NSW 2587
(02) 6384 4272
fax (02) 6384 4292

DENNIS'S OF McLAREN VALE
Kangarilla Rd
McLaren Vale SA 5171
(08) 8323 8665
fax (08) 8323 9121

DEVIL'S LAIR
(not open to public)
PO Box 212
Margaret River WA 6285
(08) 9757 7573
fax (08) 9757 7533

**DIAMOND VALLEY
VINEYARDS**
Kinglake Rd
St Andrews Vic. 3761
(03) 9710 1484
fax (03) 9710 1369

DOMAINE CHANDON
Maroondah Hwy
Coldstream Vic. 3770
(03) 9739 1110
fax (03) 9739 1095

DOONKUNA ESTATE
Barton Hwy
Murrumbateman
   NSW 2582
(02) 6227 5811
fax (02) 6227 5085

DRAYTON'S BELLEVUE
Oakey Creek Rd
Pokolbin NSW 2320
(02) 4998 7513
fax (02) 4998 7743

DROMANA ESTATE
Bittern–Dromana Rd
Dromana Vic. 3936
(03) 5987 3275
fax (03) 5981 0714

DUNCAN ESTATE
Spring Gully Rd
Clare SA 5453
(08) 8843 4335

EDEN RIDGE
(*see* Mountadam)

ELAN VINEYARD
17 Turners Rd
Bittern Vic. 3918
(03) 5983 1858

ELDERTON
3 Tanunda Rd
Nuriootpa SA 5355
(08) 8862 1058 or
1800 88 8500
fax (08) 8862 2844

ELGEE PARK
(no cellar door)
Junction Rd
Merricks Nth
PO Box 211
Red Hill South Vic. 3926
(03) 5989 7338
fax (03) 5989 7553

EPPALOCK RIDGE
Metcalfe Pool Rd
Redesdale Vic. 3444
(03) 5425 3135

EVANS & TATE
38 Swan St
Henley Brook WA 6055
(09) 296 4666

EVANS FAMILY
Palmers La.
Pokolbin NSW 2320
(02) 4998 7333

EYTON ON YARRA
Cnr Maroondah Hwy
   & Hill Rd
Coldstream Vic. 3770
(03) 5962 2119
fax (03) 5962 5319

FERGUSSON'S
Wills Rd
Yarra Glen Vic. 3775
(03) 5965 2237

FERMOY ESTATE
Metricup Rd
Willyabrup WA 6284
(08) 9755 6285
fax (08) 9755 6251

FERN HILL ESTATE
Ingoldby Rd
McLaren Flat SA 5171
(08) 8383 0167
fax (08) 8383 0107

FIDDLER'S CREEK
(*see* Blue Pyrenees Estate)

FIRE GULLY
(*see* Pierro)

FORREST ESTATE
Blicks Rd
Renwick
Blenheim NZ
(03) 572 9084
fax (03) 572 9084

FOX CREEK
Malpas Rd
Willunga SA 5172
(08) 8556 2403
fax (08) 8556 2104

FRANKLAND ESTATE
Frankland Rd
Frankland WA 6396
(08) 9855 1555
fax (08) 9855 1549

FREYCINET VINEYARD
Tasman Hwy
Bicheno Tas. 7215
(03) 6257 8587

GALAFREY
114 York St
Albany WA 6330
(08) 9841 6533

GALAH WINES
Box 231
Ashton SA 5137
(08) 8390 1243

GARDEN GULLY
Western Hwy
Great Western Vic. 3377
(03) 5356 2400

GEOFF MERRILL
(*see* Mount Hurtle)

GEOFF WEAVER
(not open to public)
2 Gilpin La.
Mitcham SA 5062
(08) 8272 2105
fax (08) 8271 0177

GIACONDA
(not open to public)
(03) 5727 0246

GILBERT'S
Albany Hwy
Kendenup WA 6323
(08) 9851 4028
(08) 9851 4021

GLENARA
126 Range Rd Nth
Upper Hermitage SA 5131
(08) 8380 5277
fax (08) 8380 5056

GLENGUIN
Lot 8 Milbrodale Rd
Broke NSW 2330
(02) 6579 1011
fax (02) 6579 1009

GOONA WARRA
Sunbury Rd
Sunbury Vic. 3429
(03) 9744 7211
fax (03) 9744 7648

GOUNDREY
Muir Hwy
Mount Barker WA 6324
(08) 9851 1777
fax (08) 9848 1018

GRAMP'S
(*see* Orlando)

GRAND CRU ESTATE
Ross Dewell's Rd
Springton SA 5235
(08) 8568 2378

GRANT BURGE
Jacobs Creek
Barossa Valley Hwy
Tanunda SA 5352
(08) 8563 3666

GREENOCK CREEK
Radford Rd
Seppeltsfield SA 5360
(08) 8562 8103
fax (08) 8562 8259

GREEN POINT
(*see* Domaine Chandon)

GROSSET
King St
Auburn SA 5451
(08) 8849 2175

HAINAULT
255 Walnut Road
Bickley WA 6076
(08) 9293 8339
fax (08) 9293 8339

HAMILTON
Willunga Vineyards
Main South Rd
Willunga SA 5172
(08) 8556 2288
fax (08) 8556 2868

HANGING ROCK
Jim Rd
Newham Vic. 3442
(03) 5427 0542
fax (03) 5427 0310

HANSON WINES
'Oolorong'
49 Cleveland Ave
Lower Plenty Vic. 3093
(03) 9439 7425

HAPP'S
Commonage Rd
Dunsborough WA 6281
(08) 9755 3300
fax (08) 9755 3846

**HARCOURT VALLEY
VINEYARD**
Calder Hwy
Harcourt Vic. 3453
(03) 5474 2223

HARDYS
(*see* Chateau Reynella)

HASELGROVE WINES
Foggo Rd
McLaren Vale SA 5171
(08) 8323 8706
fax (08) 8323 8049

HAY SHED HILL
Harmans Mill Rd
Willyabrup WA 6285
(08) 9755 6234
fax (08) 9755 6305

HEATHCOTE WINERY
183 High St
Heathcote Vic. 3523
(03) 5433 2595
fax (03) 5433 3081

HEEMSKERK
Pipers Brook Tas. 7254
(03) 6382 7133
fax (03) 6382 7242

HEGGIES
(*see* Yalumba)

HELM'S
Yass River Rd
Murrumbateman
   NSW 2582
(02) 6227 5536 (A.H.)
(02) 6227 5953

HENSCHKE
Moculta Rd
Keyneton SA 5353
(08) 8564 8223
fax (08) 8564 8294

HERITAGE WINES
Seppeltsfield Rd
Marananga
via Tununda SA 5352
(08) 8562 2880

HICKINBOTHAM
Nepean Hwy
Dromana Vic. 3936
(03) 5981 0355
fax (03) 5981 0355

HIGHBANK
Penola–Naracoorte Rd
Coonawarra SA 5263
(08) 8737 2020

HIGHFIELD
Brookby Rd
RD 2 Blenheim NZ
(03) 572 8592
fax (03) 572 9257

HILL SMITH ESTATE
(*see* Yalumba)

HILLSTOWE WINES
104 Main Rd
Hahndorf SA 5245
(08) 8388 1400
fax (08) 8388 1411

HOLLICK
Racecourse Rd
Coonawarra SA 5263
(08) 8737 2318
fax (08) 8737 2952

HORSESHOE VINEYARD
Horseshoe Road
Horses Valley
Denman NSW 2328
(02) 6547 3528

HOTHAM VALLEY
(by appointment only)
South Wandering Rd
Wandering WA 6308
(08) 9884 1525
fax (08) 9884 1079

HOUGHTON
Dale Rd
Middle Swan WA 6056
(08) 9274 5100

HOWARD PARK
Scotsdale Rd
Denmark WA 6333
(08) 9848 2345
fax (08) 9848 2064

HUGH HAMILTON WINES
PO Box 615
McLaren Vale SA 5171
(08) 8323 8689
fax (08) 8323 9488

HUGO
Elliott Rd
McLaren Flat SA 5171
(08) 8383 0098
fax (08) 8383 0446

HUNGERFORD HILL
(*see* Tulloch or Lindemans)

HUNTER'S WINES
Rapaura Rd
Blenheim NZ
(03) 572 8489
fax (03) 572 8457

HUNTINGTON ESTATE
Cassilis Rd
Mudgee NSW 2850
(02) 6373 3825
fax (02) 6373 3730

IDYLL
Ballan Rd
Moorabool Vic. 3221
(03) 5276 1280
fax (03) 5276 1537

INGLEWOOD
18 Craig Street
Artarmon NSW 2064
(02) 9436 3022
fax (02) 9439 7930

INGOLDBY
Kangarilla Rd
McLaren Vale SA 5171
(08) 8383 0005

INNISFAIL
(not open to public)
(03) 5276 1258

JAMES IRVINE
Roeslers Rd
Eden Valley SA 5235
PO Box 308
Angaston SA 5353
(08) 8564 1046
fax (08) 8564 1046

JASPER HILL
Drummonds La
Heathcote Vic. 3523
(03) 5433 2528

JEIR CREEK WINES
Gooda Creek Rd
Murrumbateman
  NSW 2582
(02) 6227 5999

JENKE VINEYARDS
Jenke Rd
Rowland Flat SA 5352
(08) 8524 4154
fax (08) 8524 4154

JIM BARRY
Main North Rd
Clare SA 5453
(08) 8842 2261

JINDALEE
(not open to public)
13 Shepherd Court
North Geelong Vic. 3251

JINGALLA
Bolganup Dam Rd
Porongurup WA 6324
(08) 9853 1023
fax (08) 9853 1023

JOHN GEHRIG
Oxley Vic. 3678
(03) 5727 3395

JOSEPH
(*see* Primo Estate)

KARINA VINEYARDS
RMB 4055
Harrisons Rd
Dromana Vic. 3936
(03) 5981 0137

KARRIVALE
Woodlands Rd
Porongurup WA 6324
(08) 9853 1009
fax (08) 9853 1129

KARRIVIEW
RMB 913
Roberts Rd
Denmark WA 6333
(08) 9840 9381

KATNOOK ESTATE
Riddoch Hwy
Coonawarra SA 5263
(08) 8737 2394
fax (08) 8737 2397

KAYS
Kays Rd
McLaren Vale SA 5171
(08) 8323 8211
fax (08) 8323 9199

KIES ESTATE
Hoffnungsthal Rd
Lyndoch SA 5351
(08) 8524 4511

KILLAWARRA
(*see* Southcorp Wines)

KILLERBY
Minnimup Rd
Gelorup WA 6230
(08) 9795 7222
fax (08) 9795 7835

KINGS CREEK
237 Myers Rd
Bittern Vic. 3918
(03) 5983 2102
fax (03) 5983 5153

KINGSTON ESTATE
Sturt Hwy
Kingston-on-Murray
  SA 5331
(08) 8583 0244
fax (08) 8583 0304

KNAPPSTEIN WINES
2 Pioneer Ave
Clare SA 5453
(08) 8842 2600
fax (08) 8842 3831

KNIGHTS
Burke and Wills Track
Baynton
via Kyneton Vic. 3444
(03) 5423 7264
mobile 015 843 676
fax (03) 5423 7288

KOPPAMURRA
(no cellar door)
PO Box 110
Blackwood SA 5051
(08) 8271 4127
fax (08) 8271 0726

KRONDORF
Krondorf Rd
Tanunda SA 5352
(08) 8563 2145
fax (08) 8562 3055

KYEEMA
(not open to public)
PO Box 282
Belconnen ACT 2616
(02) 6254 7557

LAANECOORIE
(cellar door by
  arrangement)
RMB 1330
Dunolly Vic. 3472
(03) 5468 7260
mobile 018 518 887

LAKE'S FOLLY
Broke Rd
Pokolbin NSW 2320
(02) 4998 7507
fax (02) 4998 7322

LALLA GULLY
(not open to public)
(03) 6331 2325
fax (03) 6331 7948

LAMONT'S
Bisdee Rd
Millendon WA 6056
(08) 9296 4485
fax (08) 9296 1663

LANCEFIELD WINERY
Woodend Rd
Lancefield Vic. 3435
(03) 5433 5292

LARK HILL
RMB 281
Gundaroo Rd
Bungendore NSW 2621
(02) 6238 1393

LAUREL BANK
(by appointment only)
130 Black Snake La.
Granton Tas. 7030
(03) 6263 5977
fax (03) 6263 3117

LEASINGHAM
7 Dominic St
Clare SA 5453
(08) 8842 2555
fax (08) 8842 3293

LECONFIELD
Riddoch Hwy
Coonawarra SA 5263
(08) 8737 2326
fax (08) 8737 2285

LEEUWIN ESTATE
Stevens Rd
Margaret River WA 6285
(08) 9757 6253
fax (08) 9757 6364

LELAND ESTATE
PO Lenswood SA 5240
(08) 8389 6928

LENGS & COOTER
24 Lindsay Tce
Belair SA 5052
(08) 8278 3998

LENSWOOD VINEYARDS
3 Cyril John Crt
Athelstone SA 5076
(08) 8365 3766
fax (08) 8365 3766

LENTON BRAE
Caves Rd
Willyabrup WA 6280
(08) 9755 6255
fax (08) 9755 6268

LEO BURING
Sturt Hwy
Tanunda SA 5352
(08) 8563 2184
fax (08) 8563 2804

LEYDENS VALE
(*see* Blue Pyrenees Estate)

LILLYDALE VINEYARDS
Davross Crt
Seville Vic. 3139
(03) 5964 2016

LILLYPILLY ESTATE
Farm 16
Lilly Pilly Rd
Leeton NSW 2705
(02) 6953 4069
fax (02) 6953 4980

LINDEMANS
McDonalds Rd
Pokolbin NSW 2320
(02) 4998 7501
fax (02) 4998 7682

LONG GULLY
Long Gully Rd
Healesville Vic. 3777
(03) 5962 3663
fax (03) 59807 2213

LONGLEAT
Old Weir Rd
Murchison Vic. 3610
(03) 5826 2294
fax (03) 5826 2510

LOVEGROVE OF COTTLES BRIDGE
Heidelberg Kinglake Road
Cottlesbridge Vic. 3099
(03) 9718 1569
fax (03) 9718 1028

MADEW
(by appointment only)
Westering Vineyard
Federal Hwy
Lake George NSW 2581
(02) 4848 0026
fax (02) 4848 0026

MADFISH
(*see* Howard Park)

MAGLIERI
Douglas Gully Rd
McLaren Flat SA 5171
(08) 8323 8648

MAIN RIDGE
Lot 48 Williams Rd
Red Hill Vic. 3937
(03) 5989 2686

MALCOLM CREEK
(not open to public)
(08) 8264 2255

MARIENBERG
2 Chalk Hill Rd
McClaren Vale SA 5171
(08) 8323 9666
fax (08) 8323 9600

MASSONI HOME PTY LTD
(by appointment only)
Mornington–Flinders Rd
Red Hill Vic. 3937
(03) 5989 2352

MAXWELL
Cnr Olivers & Chalkhill
   Rds
McLaren Vale SA 5171
(08) 8323 8200

McALISTER
(not open to public)
(03) 5149 7229

McGUIGAN BROTHERS
Cnr Broke & McDonalds
   Rds
Pokolbin NSW 2320
(02) 4998 7400
fax (02) 4998 7401

McWILLIAM'S
Hanwood NSW 2680
(02) 6963 0001
fax (02) 6963 0002

MEADOWBANK
Glenora Tas. 7140
(03) 6286 1234
fax (03) 6286 1133

MERRICKS ESTATE
Cnr Thompsons La.
   & Frankston–Flinders Rd
Merricks Vic. 3916
(03) 5989 8416
fax (03) 9629 4035

MIDDLETON ESTATE
Flagstaff Hill Rd
Middleton SA 5213
(08) 8555 4136
fax (08) 8555 4108

MILBURN PARK
(*see* Salisbury Estate)

MILDARA
(various locations)
(03) 9690 9966
(head office)

MILDURA VINEYARDS
Campbell Ave
Irymple Vic. 3498

MINTARO CELLARS
Leasingham Rd
Mintaro SA 5415
(08) 8843 9046

MIRAMAR
Henry Lawson Dr.
Mudgee NSW 2850
(02) 6373 3874

MIRANDA WINES
57 Jordaryan Ave
Griffith NSW 2680
(02) 6962 4033
fax (02) 6962 6944

MIRROOL CREEK
(*see* Miranda)

MITCHELL
Hughes Park Rd
Sevenhill via Clare
   SA 5453
(08) 8843 4258

MITCHELTON WINES
Mitcheltstown
Nagambie 3608
(03) 5794 2710
fax (03) 5794 2615

MONTANA
PO Box 18-293
Glen Innis
Auckland NZ
(09) 570 5549

MONTARA
Chalambar Rd
Ararat Vic. 3377
(03) 5352 3868
fax (03) 5352 4968

MONTROSE
Henry Lawson Dr.
Mudgee NSW 2850
(02) 6373 3853

MOONDAH BROOK
(*see* Houghton)

MOORILLA ESTATE
655 Main Rd
Berridale Tas. 7011
(03) 6249 2949

MOOROODUC ESTATE
Derril Rd
Moorooduc Vic. 3933
(03) 5978 8585

MORNING CLOUD
(cellar door by
   appointment)
15 Ocean View Ave
Red Hill South Vic. 3937
(03) 5989 2762
fax (03) 5989 2700

**MORNINGTON
VINEYARDS ESTATE**
(by appointment only)
Moorooduc Rd
Mornington Vic. 3931
(03) 5974 2097

MORRIS
off Murray Valley Hwy
Mia Mia Vineyards
Rutherglen Vic. 3685
(02) 6026 7303
fax (02) 6026 7445

MOSS BROTHERS
Caves Rd
Willyabrup WA 6280
(08) 9755 6270
fax (08) 9755 6298

MOSS WOOD
Metricup Rd
Willyabrup WA 6280
(08) 9755 6266
fax (08) 9755 6303

MOUNTADAM
High Eden Ridge
Eden Valley SA 5235
(08) 8564 1101

MOUNT AVOCA
Moates La.
Avoca Vic. 3467
(03) 5465 3282

MOUNT HORROCKS
PO Box 72
Watervale SA 5452
(08) 8849 2243
fax (08) 8849 2243

MOUNT HURTLE
291 Pimpala Rd
Woodcroft SA 5162
(08) 8381 6877
fax (08) 8322 2244

MOUNT LANGI GHIRAN
Warrak Rd
Buangor Vic. 3375
(03) 5354 3207
fax (03) 5354 3277

MOUNT MARY
(not open to public)
(03) 9739 1761
fax (03) 9739 0137

MOUNT PRIOR VINEYARD
Cnr River Rd & Popes La.
Rutherglen Vic. 3685
(02) 6026 5591
fax (02) 6026 5590

MT PLEASANT
Marrowbone Rd
Pokolbin NSW 2321
(02) 4998 7505

MT WILLIAM WINERY
Mount William Rd
Tantaraboo Vic. 3764
(03) 5429 1595
fax (03) 5429 1998

MURRINDINDI
(not open to public)
(03) 5797 8217

NAUTILUS
(*see* Yalumba)

NEPENTHE VINEYARDS
(not open to public)
(08) 8389 8218

NGATARAWA
305 Ngatarawa Rd
Bridge Pa
Hastings NZ
(06) 879 7603

NICHOLSON RIVER
Liddells Rd
Nicholson Vic. 3882
(03) 5156 8241

NORMANS
Grants Gully Rd
Clarendon SA 5157
(08) 8383 6138
fax (08) 8383 6089

NOTLEY GORGE
(vineyard only)
Loop Road
Glengarry Tas. 7275
(03) 6396 1166
fax (03) 6396 1200

OAKRIDGE ESTATE
864 Maroondah Hwy
Coldstream Vic. 3770
(03) 5964 3379
fax (03) 5964 2061

OAKVALE WINERY
Broke Rd
Pokolbin NSW 2320
(02) 4998 7520

OLD KENT RIVER
Turpin Rd
Rocky Gully WA 6397
(08) 9855 1589
fax (08) 9855 1589

ORLANDO
Barossa Valley Way
Rowland Flat SA 5352
(08) 8521 3111
fax (08) 8521 3102

PALMER WINES
Caves Rd
Willyabrup WA 6280
(08) 9797 1881
fax (08) 9797 0534

PANKHURST WINES
Woodgrove Rd
Hall ACT 2618
(02) 6230 2592

PARADISE ENOUGH
(weekends & holidays only)
Stewarts Rd
Kongwak Vic. 3951
(03) 5657 4241

PARINGA ESTATE
44 Paringa Rd
Red Hill South Vic. 3937
(03) 5989 2669

PARKER COONAWARRA ESTATE
(cellar-door sales at
    Bushmans Inn, Penola)
Office:
110B Elizabeth Bay Rd
Elizabeth Bay NSW 2011
(02) 9357 3376
fax (02) 9358 1517

PASSING CLOUDS
Powlett Rd
via Inglewood
Kingower Vic. 3517
(03) 5438 8257

PATTERSONS
St Werburghs Rd
Mount Barker WA 6324
(08) 9851 2063
fax (08) 9851 2063

PAULETT'S
Polish Hill River Rd
Sevenhill SA 5453
(08) 8843 4328
fax (08) 8843 4202

PEEL ESTATE
Fletcher Rd
Baldivis WA 6210
(08) 9524 1221

PEGASUS BAY
Stockgrove Rd
Waipara
Amberley RD 2
North Canterbury NZ
(03) 314 6869
fax (03) 355 5937

PENDARVES ESTATE
Lot 12 Old North Rd
Belford NSW 2335
(02) 6574 7222

PENFOLDS
(*see* Southcorp Wines)

PENLEY ESTATE
McLean's Rd
Coonawarra 5263
(08) 8736 3211
fax (08) 8736 3124

PEPPERS CREEK
Cnr Ekerts & Broke Rds
Pokolbin NSW 2321
(02) 4998 7532

PEPPER TREE WINES
Halls Rd
Pokolbin NSW 2320
(02) 4998 7539
fax (02) 4998 7746

PETALUMA
(not open to public)
(08) 8339 4122
fax (08) 8339 5253

PETER LEHMANN
Para Rd
Tanunda SA 5352
(08) 8563 2500
fax (08) 8563 3402

PETER RUMBALL
(no cellar door)
(08) 8332 2761
fax (08) 8364 0188

PETERSONS
PO Box 182
Mount View Rd
Mount View NSW 2325
(02) 4990 1704

PFEIFFER
Distillery Rd
Wahgunyah Vic. 3687
(02) 6033 3889

PHILLIP ISLAND WINES
Lot 1 Berrys Beach Rd
Phillip Island Vic. 3922
(03) 5956 8465

PIBBIN FARM
Greenhill Rd
Balhannah SA 5242
(08) 8388 4794

PICARDY
(not open to public)
(08) 9776 0036
fax (08) 9776 0036

PICCADILLY FIELDS
(not open to public)
(08) 8390 1997

PIERRO
Caves Rd
Willyabrup WA 6280
(08) 9755 6220
fax (08) 9755 6308

PIKES POLISH HILL ESTATE
Polish Hill River Rd
Seven Hill SA 5453
(08) 8843 4370
fax (08) 8843 4353

PIPERS BROOK
3959 Bridport Hwy
Pipers Brook Tas. 7254
(03) 6382 7197
fax (03) 6382 7226

PIRRAMIMMA
Johnston Rd
McLaren Vale SA 5171
(08) 8323 8205
fax (08) 8323 9224

PLANTAGENET
Albany Hwy
Mount Barker WA 6324
(08) 9851 2150
fax (08) 9851 1839

PLUNKETT'S
Cnr Lambing Gully Rd &
   Hume Fwy
Avenel Vic. 3664
(03) 5796 2150
fax (03) 5796 2147

POOLE'S ROCK
(not open to public)
Lot 41 Wollombi Road
Broke NSW 2330
(02) 6579 1251
fax (02) 6579 1277

PORT PHILLIP ESTATE
261 Red Hill Rd
Red Hill Vic. 3937
(03) 5989 2708
fax (03) 5989 2891

PORTREE VINEYARD
RMB 700
Lancefield Vic. 3435
(03) 5429 1422
fax (03) 5429 2205

PREECE
(*see* Mitchelton)

PRIMO ESTATE
Cnr Old Port Wakefield
   & Angle Vale Rds
Virginia SA 5120
(08) 8380 9442

PRINCE ALBERT
Lemins Rd
Waurn Ponds Vic. 3221
(03) 5243 5091
fax (03) 5241 8091

QUEEN ADELAIDE
(*see* Seppelt)

QUELLTALER ESTATE
Main North Rd
Watervale SA 5452
(08) 8843 0003
fax (08) 8843 0096

REDBANK
Sunraysia Hwy
Redbank Vic. 3478
(03) 5467 7255

RED HILL ESTATE
53 Red Hill–Shoreham Rd
Red Hill South Vic. 3937
(03) 5989 2838

REDMAN
Riddoch Hwy
Coonawarra SA 5263
(08) 8736 3331
fax (08) 8736 3013

RENMANO
Renmark Ave
Renmark SA 5341
(08) 8586 6771
fax (08) 8586 5939

REYNOLDS YARRAMAN
Yarraman Rd
Wybong NSW 2333
(02) 6547 8127
fax (02) 6547 8013

RIBBON VALE ESTATE
Lot 5 Caves Rd
via Cowaramup
Willyabrup WA 6284
(08) 9755 6272

RICHMOND GROVE
(*see* Orlando)

RIDDOCH
(*see* Katnook)

ROBINVALE WINES
Sealake Rd
Robinvale Vic. 3549
(03) 5026 3955
fax (03) 5026 1123

ROCHECOMBE
(*see* Heemskerk)

ROCHFORD
Romsey Park
via Woodend Rd
Rochford Vic. 3442
(08) 5429 1428

ROCKFORD
Krondorf Rd
Tanunda SA 5352
(08) 8563 2720

ROMSEY PARK
(*see* Rochford)

ROMSEY VINEYARDS
(*see* Cope Williams)

ROSABROOK ESTATE
Rosa Brook Rd
Margaret River WA 6285
(08) 9757 2286
fax (08) 9757 3634

ROSEMOUNT
Rosemount Rd
Denman NSW 2328
(02) 6547 2467
fax (02) 6547 2742

ROTHBURY ESTATE
Broke Rd
Pokolbin NSW 2321
(02) 4998 7555
fax (02) 4998 7553

ROUGE HOMME
(*see* Lindemans)

RUFUS STONE
(*see* Tyrrell's)

RYECROFT
Ingoldby Rd
McLaren Flat SA 5171
(08) 8383 0001

RYMILL
The Riddoch Run
    Vineyards (off Main Rd)
Coonawarra SA 5263
(08) 8736 5001
fax (08) 8736 5040

SADDLERS CREEK WINERY
Marrowbone Rd
Pokolbin NSW 2321
(02) 4991 1770
fax (02) 4991 1778

SALISBURY ESTATE
(*see* Alambie)

SALITAGE
Vasse Hwy
Pemberton WA 6260
(08) 9776 1599
fax (08) 9776 1504

SALTRAM
Angaston Rd
Angaston SA 5353
(08) 8564 3355

SANDALFORD
West Swan Rd
Caversham WA 6055
(08) 9274 5922
fax (08) 9274 2154

SANDSTONE VINEYARD
(cellar door by
    appointment)
Caves & Johnson Rds
Willyabrup WA 6280
(08) 9755 6271
fax (08) 9755 6292

SCARBOROUGH WINES
Gillards Rd
Pokolbin NSW 2321
(02) 4998 7563

SCARPANTONI
Kangarilla Rd
McLaren Flat SA 5171
(08) 8383 0186
fax (08) 8383 0490

SCHINUS
(*see* Dromana Estate)

SCOTCHMAN'S HILL
Scotchmans Rd
Drysdale Vic. 3222
(03) 5251 3176
fax (03) 5253 1743

SEAVIEW
Chaffeys Rd
McLaren Vale SA 5171
(08) 8323 8250

SEPPELT
Seppeltsfield
via Tanunda SA 5352
(08) 8562 8028
fax (08) 8562 8333

SEVENHILL
College Rd
Sevenhill
via Clare SA 5453
(08) 8843 4222
fax (08) 8843 4382

SEVILLE ESTATE
Linwood Rd
Seville Vic. 3139
(03) 5964 4556
fax (03) 5943 4222

SHANTELL
Melba Hwy
Dixons Creek Vic. 3775
(03) 5965 2264
fax (03) 9819 5311

SHAREFARMERS
(*see* Petaluma)

SHAW & SMITH
(not open to public)
(08) 8370 9725

SHOTTESBROOKE
1 Bagshaws Rd
McLaren Flat SA 5171
(08) 8383 0002
fax (08) 8383 0222

SIMON HACKETT
(not open to public)
(08) 8331 7348

SIMON WHITLAM
(*see* Arrowfield)

SKILLOGALEE
Skillogalee Rd
via Sevenhill SA 5453
(08) 8843 4311
fax (08) 8843 4343

SMITHBROOK
(not open to public)
(08) 9772 3557
fax (08) 9772 3579

SOUTHCORP WINES
Tanunda Rd
Nuriootpa SA 5355
(08) 8560 9389
fax (08) 8560 9669

STANTON & KILLEEN
Murray Valley Hwy
Rutherglen Vic. 3685
(02) 6032 9457

STEPHEN JOHN WINES
Government Rd
Watervale SA 5452
(08) 8843 0105
fax (08) 8843 0105

STEVENS CAMBRAI
Hamiltons Rd
McLaren Flat SA 5171
(08) 8323 0251

ST FRANCIS
Bridge St
Old Reynella SA 5161
(08) 8381 1925
fax (08) 8322 0921

ST HALLETT
St Halletts Rd
Tanunda SA 5352
(08) 8563 2319
fax (08) 8563 2901

ST HUBERTS
Maroondah Hwy
Coldstream Vic. 3770
(03) 9739 1118
fax (03) 9739 1015

ST LEONARDS
St Leonard Rd
Wahgunyah Vic. 3687
(02) 6033 1004
fax (02) 6033 3636

ST MARY'S VINEYARD
V and A La.
via Coonawarra SA 5263
(08) 8736 6070
fax (08) 8736 6045

STONELEIGH
Corbans Wines
Great Northern Rd
Henderson NZ
(09) 836 6189

**STONEY VINEYARD/
DOMAINE A**
Teatree Rd
Campania Tas. 7026
(03) 6260 4174
fax (03) 6260 4390

STONIER'S WINERY
362 Frankston–Flinders Rd
Merricks Vic. 3916
(03) 5989 8300
fax (03) 5989 8709

SUMMERFIELD
Main Rd
Moonambel Vic. 3478
(03) 5467 2264
fax (03) 5467 2380

SUTHERLAND
Deasey's Rd
Pokolbin NSW 2321
(02) 4998 7650

TALTARNI VINEYARDS
off Moonambel–Stawell Rd
Moonambel Vic. 3478
(03) 5467 2218
fax (03) 5467 2306

TAMBURLAINE WINES
McDonalds Rd
Pokolbin NSW 2321
(02) 4998 7570
fax (02) 4998 7763

TANGLEWOOD DOWNS
Bulldog Creek Rd
Merricks North
(03) 5974 3325

TAPESTRY
Merrivale Wines
Olivers Rd
McLaren Vale SA 5171
(08) 8323 9196
fax (08) 8323 9746

TARRAWARRA
Healesville Rd
Yarra Glen Vic. 3775
(03) 5962 3311
fax (03) 5962 3311

TATACHILLA WINERY
151 Main Rd
McLaren Vale SA 5171
(08) 8323 8656
fax (08) 8323 9096

TAYLORS
Mintaro Rd
Auburn SA 5451
(08) 8849 2008

TEMPLE BRUER
Angas River Delta
via Strathalbyn SA 5255
(08) 8537 0203
fax (08) 8537 0131

T'GALLANT
Lot 2 Mornington–Flinders
  Rd
Main Ridge Vic. 3937
(03) 5989 6565
fax (03) 5989 6577

THALGARA ESTATE
De Beyers Rd
Pokolbin NSW 2321
(02) 4998 7717

TIM ADAMS
Wendouree Rd
Clare SA 5453
(08) 8842 2429
fax (08) 8842 2429

TIM GRAMP
PO Box 810
Unley SA 5061
(08) 8379 3658
fax (08) 8338 2160

TISDALL
Cornelia Creek Rd
Echuca Vic. 3564
(03) 5482 1911
fax (03) 5482 2516

TOLLANA
(*see* Southcorp Wines)

TORRESAN ESTATE
Manning Rd
Flagstaff Hill SA 5159
(08) 8270 2500

TRENTHAM ESTATE
Sturt Hwy
Trentham Cliffs
via Gol Gol NSW 2738
(03) 5024 8888
fax (03) 5024 8800

TULLOCH
De Beyers Rd
Pokolbin NSW 2321
(02) 4998 7503
fax (02) 4998 7682

TUNNEL HILL
(*see* Tarrawarra)

TURKEY FLAT
James Rd
Tanunda SA 5352
(08) 8563 2851
fax (08) 8563 3610

TYRRELL'S
Broke Rd
Pokolbin NSW 2321
(02) 4993 7000
fax (02) 4998 7723

VASSE FELIX
Cnr Caves & Harmans Rds
Cowaramup WA 6284
(08) 9755 5242
fax (08) 9755 5425

VERITAS
94 Langmeil Rd
Tanunda SA 5352
(08) 8563 2330

VIRGIN HILLS
(not open to public)
(03) 5423 9169

VOYAGER ESTATE
Stevens Rd
Margaret River WA 6285
(08) 9757 6358
fax (08) 9757 6405

WANDIN VALLEY ESTATE
Wilderness Rd
Rothbury NSW 2321
(02) 4930 7317
fax (02) 4930 7814

WANINGA
Hughes Park Rd
Sevenhill
via Clare SA 5453
(08) 8843 4395
fax (08) 8843 4395

WANTIRNA ESTATE
(not open to public)
(03) 9801 2367

**WARDS GATEWAY
CELLARS**
Barossa Valley Hwy
Lyndoch SA 5351
(08) 8524 4138

WARRAMATE
27 Maddens La.
Gruyere Vic. 3770
(03) 5964 9219

WARRENMANG
Mountain Ck Rd
Moonambel Vic. 3478
(03) 5467 2233
fax (03) 5467 2309

**WATERWHEEL
VINEYARDS**
Lyndhurst St
Bridgewater-on-Loddon
Bridgewater Vic. 3516
(03) 5437 3060
fax (03) 5437 3082

WELLINGTON WINES
34 Cornwall St
Rose Bay Tas. 7015
(03) 6248 5844

WENDOUREE
Wendouree Rd
Clare SA 5453
(08) 8842 2896

WESTFIELD
Memorial Ave
Baskerville WA 6056
(08) 9296 4356

WIGNALLS KING RIVER
Chester Pass Rd
Albany WA 6330
(08) 9841 2848

WILD DUCK CREEK
Springflat Rd
Heathcote Vic. 3523
(03) 5433 3133

WILDWOOD
St Johns La.
via Wildwood Vic. 3428
(03) 9307 1118

WILLESPIE
Harmans Mill Rd
Willyabrup WA 6280
(08) 9755 6248
fax (08) 9755 6210

WILLOWS VINEYARD, THE
Light Pass Rd
Barossa Valley SA 5355
(08) 8562 1080

WILSON VINEYARD, THE
Polish Hill River
via Clare SA 5453
(08) 8843 4310

WILTON ESTATE
Whitton Stock Route
Yenda NSW 2681
(02) 6968 1303
fax (02) 6968 1328

WINCHELSEA ESTATE
C/- Nicks
   Wine Merchants
(03) 9639 0696

WING FIELDS
(*see* Water Wheel)

WIRILDA CREEK
Lot 32 McMurtrie Rd
McLaren Vale SA 5171
(08) 8323 9688

WIRRA WIRRA
McMurtrie Rd
McLaren Vale SA 5171
(08) 8323 8414
fax (08) 8323 8596

WOLF BLASS
Sturt Hwy
Nuriootpa SA 5355
(08) 8562 1955
fax (08) 8562 2156

WOODSTOCK
Douglas Gully Rd
McLaren Flat SA 5171
(08) 8383 0156
fax (08) 8383 0437

WOODY NOOK
Metricup Rd
Metricup WA 6280
(08) 9755 7547
fax (08) 9755 7547

WYANGAN ESTATE
(*see* Miranda)

WYANGA PARK
Baades Rd
Lakes Entrance Vic. 3909
(03) 5155 1508
fax (03) 5155 1443

WYNDHAM ESTATE
Dalwood Rd
Dalwood NSW 2321
(02) 4938 3444
fax (02) 4938 3422

WYNNS
Memorial Dr.
Coonawarra SA 5263
(08) 8736 3266

XANADU
Terry Rd (off
   Railway Tce)
Margaret River WA 6285
(08) 9757 2581
fax (08) 9757 3389

YALUMBA
Eden Valley Rd
Angaston SA 5353
(08) 8561 3200
fax (08) 8561 3392

YARRA BURN
Settlement Rd
Yarra Junction Vic. 3797
(03) 5967 1428
fax (03) 5967 1146

YARRA RIDGE
Glenview Rd
Yarra Glen Vic. 3775
(03) 9730 1022
fax (03) 9730 1131

YARRA VALLEY HILLS
Old Don Rd
Healesville Vic. 3777
(03) 5962 4173
fax (03) 5762 4059

YARRA YERING
Briarty Rd
Gruyere Vic. 3770
(03) 5964 9267

YELLOWGLEN
White's Rd
Smythesdale Vic. 3351
(03) 5342 8617

YERINGBERG
(not open to public)
(03) 9739 1453
fax (03) 9739 0048

YERING STATION
Melba Hwy
Yering Vic. 3775
(03) 9730 1107
fax (03) 9739 0135

ZEMA ESTATE
Penola–Naracoorte Rd
Coonawarra SA 5263
(08) 8736 3219
fax (08) 8736 3280

The Penguin Wine Cellar Book
Huon Hooke

The Penguin Wine Cellar Book is a must-have for wine lovers. It is designed to help you catalogue your wine collection, and in so doing entices you to keep a personal journal of your wines and of your experiences of drinking and sharing them.

Huon Hooke, co-author of *The Penguin Good Australian Wine Guide*, has written a lively, highly informative introduction to cellaring wine in Australian conditions, including his recommendations for selecting the best cellarable Australian wines. This splendid hardback volume will be the perfect gift for anyone who loves wine - a lot or even just a little! It is designed, like good red wine, for long-keeping.

The Champagne Companion
Michael Edwards

The Champagne Companion is a full-colour guide to this most exuberant of wines. It features information and notes on more than 100 international brands, including all of the *grandes marques* as well as many of the smaller growers.

The *Companion* also tells you how to decode champagne labels, and explains the process by which champagne is made. Discover why this wine is regarded as a superb handmade creation – from the hand-picked grapes to the skill in blending the wines.

Champagne is for rejoicing, and this guide is designed to enhance your enjoyment.

The Port Companion
Godfrey Spence

From the sunny vineyards of Portugal's Douro Valley, to the red brick lodges in the Vila Nova de Gaia, *The Port Companion* escorts you to the world of exclusive ports.

Beautifully illustrated and meticulously researched, this is an A to Z reference containing everything you need to know – history and information on port and the port-making process; tips on storing, decanting and serving; food matching; and an extensive directory listing ports from all the major houses.

A book for those who are new to the delights of port and for discerning aficionados.